CHEVROLET *by the numbers*™

The Essential Chevrolet Parts Reference

1955–1959

By Alan L. Colvin

BentleyPublishers®
.com

BENTLEY PUBLISHERS® | Automotive Reference™

Bentley Publishers, a division of Robert Bentley, Inc.
1734 Massachusetts Avenue
Cambridge, MA 02138 USA
800-423-4595 / 617-547-4170

Information that makes the difference®

BentleyPublishers®.com

Technical contact information

We welcome your feedback. Please submit corrections and additions to our technical discussion forum at:

`http://www.BentleyPublishers.com`

Updates and corrections

We will evaluate submissions and post appropriate editorial changes online as updates or tech discussion. Appropriate updates and corrections will be added to the book in future printings. Check for updates and corrections for this book before beginning work on your vehicle. See the following web address for additional information:

`http://www.BentleyPublishers.com/updates/`

This book was published by Bentley Publishers, 1734 Massachusetts Avenue, Cambridge, Massachusetts 02138 USA. Bentley Publishers is a trademark of Robert Bentley, Inc. Chevrolet has not reviewed and does not warrant the accuracy or completeness of the technical specifications and information described in this book.

ISBN 978-0-8376-0875-4
Bentley Stock No. GC59
GM Part Number 12366584
Mfg. code: GC59-06-D-1504

Library of Congress Cataloging-in-Publication Data
Colvin, Alan, 1959–
Chevrolet by the numbers : the essential Chevrolet parts reference, 1955-1959 / by Alan Colvin.
p. cm.
Includes index.
ISBN 978-0-8376-0875-4 (pbk. : acid-free)
1. Chevrolet automobile--Parts--Catalogs. 2. Chevrolet automobile--Parts--Code Numbers. I. Title.
TL215.C5C623 1996
629.28'72--dc20 96-14612
CIP

On the Front Cover: 1959 Fuelie convertible owned by Rich Miller, photo by Mike Mueller.
On the Back Cover: From the top: 1) 1956 Bel Air owned by Fred Gaugh, Jerome Cain, Terry Schaefer; 1957 Nomad owned by Erol and Susan Turcu; 1957 Airbox Corvette owned by Milton Robson; 1958 Impala owned by Walter Cutlip; 1959 Impala owned by Dick Hubbard; 1959 El Camino owned by Doug Stapleton; all photos by Mike Mueller.

The paper used in this publication is acid free and meets the requirements of the National Standard for Information Sciences-Permanence of Paper for Printed Library Materials. ∞

Manufactured in the United States of America.

CHEVROLET *by the numbers*™

1955–1959

Table Of Contents

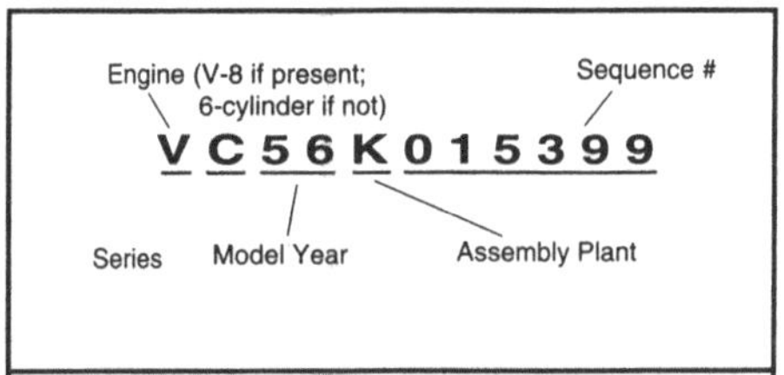

1955–1957 Chevrolet VIN Style

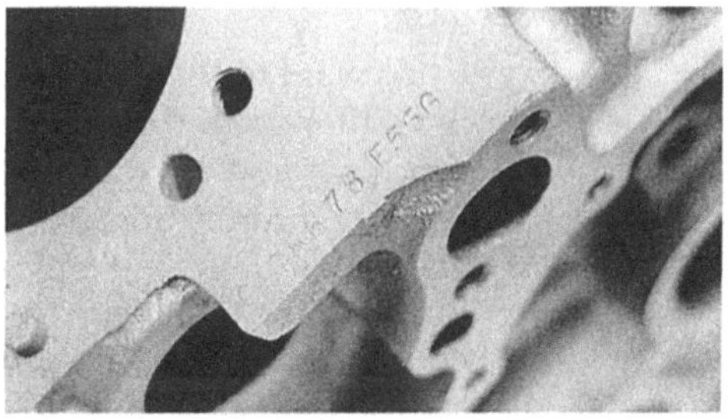

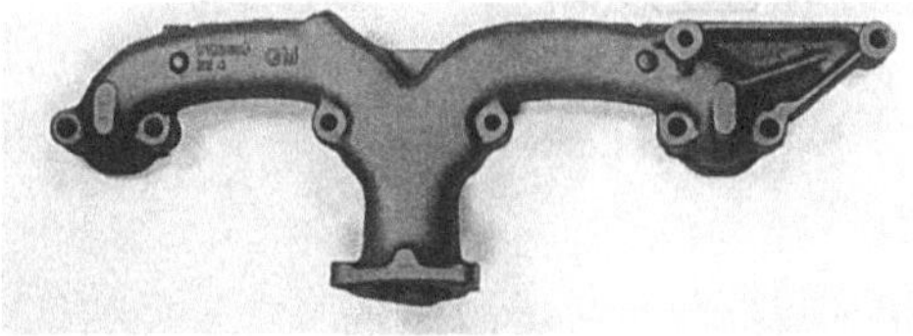

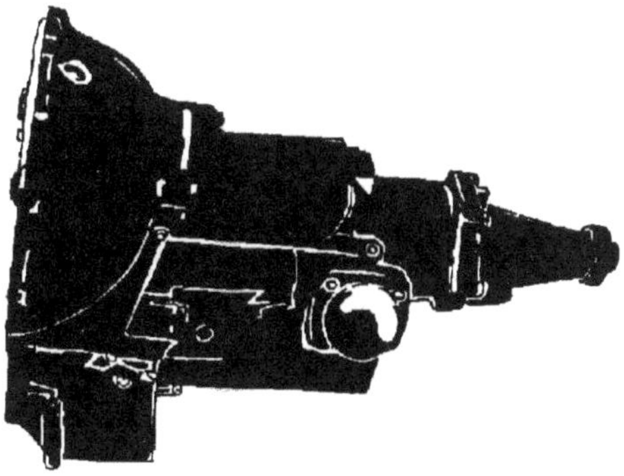

Dedication

I want to dedicate this book to my Lord and Savior, Jesus Christ. Only He could give me the strength, courage and endurance to complete such a task. It is my prayer that everyone who reads this book will come to have an understanding and faith in Him as I have.

I want to thank my wife, Julé, for enduring the many hardships necessary to complete this book series. We have grown stronger, wiser and more considerate through this process more than any other time in our marriage. Julé, I love you.

I also want to thank my publisher, Robert Bentley Publishers, Inc. To Michael Bentley, and my editor, John Kittredge, thank you for your professionalism, your courage when I missed deadlines and your understanding heart in the face of sometimes seemingly insurmountable odds. I sincerely appreciate you for making me look like the author I wished I could be.

Finally, I want to thank the many people who shared their time and expertise to make this book project complete. Someone once said that "nobody knows everything" and I can truly testify to that statement. This project would not have been completed if not for all of my friends and acquaintances helping in their own special way. I hope all of you feel as much a part of this book project as I do. It wouldn't have happened without all of you.

Take Care.

Introduction

The author at his desk.

THE ORIGINAL IDEA FOR THIS BOOK was conceived almost twenty years ago, when I first got into the car restoration hobby. As I began to search for parts to restore a 1957 Chevrolet (my first car), I quickly realized that there was no single, comprehensive source of casting information to which I could turn to determine the authenticity of the parts I needed. (By casting information, I mean the series of identification numbers Chevrolet cast into each part. These "casting numbers" are used as the basis for all parts identification in this book.) I have always been a "pack-rat" and had saved thousands of car magazines. From these I gleaned some information, but by and large, I still could not identify most of the parts I needed. I realized I had to create my own parts reference source book.

After years of research, hundreds of phone calls and thousands of conversations with various fellow club members, I developed what came to be known as my "little black book of numbers." This book enabled me to quickly identify parts and their application by their casting numbers. I took this little book wherever I went, many times to the spring and fall swap meets in Carlisle, Pennsylvania. Practically every time I would be looking in my book to identify a part, someone would tap on my shoulder and offer to buy the book; one fellow offered me several hundred dollars.

I couldn't sell the book as I had no copies and the information was irreplaceable, but it did make me think that if these people were that interested, others would be also. I didn't realize, however, that it would be another ten years before the project would start to take shape. In the meantime, I was continually on the lookout to buy any factory information that would help further my quest for casting numbers.

In the beginning of this research process, I located several sets of old documents written by the Automotive Engine Rebuilders Association. From them I began to compile a basic list of casting numbers. I also used years and years of Hemmings Motor News.

Once I had a master parts list, I began to cross-reference this with other engine rebuilder catalogs. As I progressed, I realized that there were potential problems. First, there was the possibility of wrong information and printing typos in my resource material. Also, several of my source lists were geared to making a part applicable for as many years as possible for interchange purposes. Thus, a part could be listed as applicable from 1960 through 1964, when in fact it was *originally* used only in 1960.

Alan's "little black book."

Introduction

In the spring of 1991, I came to a crossroads. I realized that my methods were not going to give me the accuracy I wanted. I could either give up, or press on to the next level. Because I have a great love for the car hobby, I decided that, above all, I wanted to create a series of books readers would want, need, and enjoy reading while at the same time learning about the identification of drivetrain components. To be able to accomplish this task, I knew that verifiable, documented parts and their history were paramount to the book's goals. To secure this legitimate "paper trail," traceable back to the original sources, it was clear that I had to take the next step and contact General Motors for their records.

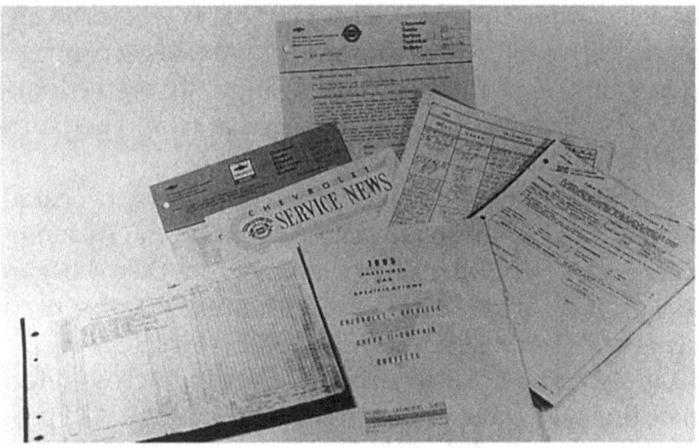

A small sampling of the various reference materials.

There followed several months of letters and phone calls to many of my General Motors contacts, after which I was granted clearance to conduct extensive research in numerous GM divisions. (The GM of today is not the same corporation that existed from 1955 through 1975. GM has been split up several times over the years, creating a giant quagmire of old records in various locations and separate legal departments.) These clearances allowed me to gain invaluable information in the form of original parts blueprints, twenty years of Chevrolet Engineering Specifications, twenty years of Automobile Manufacturer's Association (AMA) Specifications, and numerous original parts lists. I spent months poring over information from several different General Motors divisions, including AC Rochester in Rochester, New York, the GM Powertrain Division in Warren, Michigan, the Tonawanda Engine Plant in Buffalo, New York, the Flint Engine Plant in Flint, Michigan, Delco-Remy in Anderson, Indiana, the Saginaw Final Drive and Forge Division in Saginaw, Michigan, and also the Chevrolet-Pontiac-Canada Group in Sterling Heights, Michigan. I also collected a great deal of information from the Chevrolet Archives in Warren, Michigan, and from the National Automotive History Collection in the Detroit Public Library. Original documents pertaining to Saginaw and Muncie transmissions were obtained directly from the Muncie Transmission plant in Muncie, Indiana.

I spent several weeks in Chevrolet's Central Office Records Retention Area: hundreds of file drawers full of original photos, specifications and engineering data, sitting in a sub-basement, surrounded by a twenty-foot-high woven wire fence and padlocked gates. *Very Restricted.* This area is sealed off to everyone except specific Chevrolet employees or special VIPs. Unfortunately, much of the engineering data from the 1950s that was stored on microfilm in this facility has been destroyed due to Chevrolet's ten-year records retention policy. While this was a major disappointment to me, most of the other records were fortunately still available—thousands of Chevrolet documents which have never left that room. I was allowed to photocopy many of these records, in the process disabling one *HUGE* photocopying machine. Some of these records were so old and brittle that it was necessary to copy them over in longhand to keep from damaging them. Many times I felt as if I were holding Chevrolet's Dead Sea Scrolls in my hands, in my own time-warp, looking down a long corridor of rich Chevrolet history.

In another building several miles from the Chevrolet Tech Center I reviewed hundreds of original parts blueprints, many copies of which are used to illustrate this book. There are no actual blueprints stored at this facility. All original blueprints have been photographed, reduced and placed in aperture card files. I should note that the aperture card files were arranged in such a way that if I had no prior knowledge of the Chevrolet parts system and a listing of casting numbers, it could have taken me years to extrapolate any useful information.

By this time I had numerous questions about original General Motors parts that could only be answered by the Chevrolet engineers who created those parts, but most of the engineers have now retired. My next step was to try to locate these men. Once I did, they graciously spent hours of their own time researching old documents and contributing from their own archives.

I also spent hours talking to experts in the field. These ranged from business owners, to auto shop teachers, to various club, organization and society members. Some of these experts specialized in certain models, while others specialized in certain years. I also used years and years of information that I had collected in the form of Chevrolet Service News Bulletins, original parts books, and Chevrolet Technical Service Bulletins.

My research brought me in to contact with many original equipment manufacturers (OEMs). Many of these OEMs had retained their early parts lists and blueprint material. Once I had fulfilled their clearance requirements, I was able to obtain their documents as well. Among these manufacturers were the Carter Carburetor Division of Federal-Mogul and Kelsey-Hayes Wheel Corp, Romulus, Michigan.

As I pulled all of this information together, I had to do a tremendous amount of cross-referencing and double checking. As I built upon the lists, all of the casting numbers were then verified by at least three or four different sources. The various original blueprints that I obtained serve to identify and verify specific parts and numbers as no other method can. Also, after the individual chapters were completed, they were sent out to various experts to check for accuracy.

The Chevrolet Parts System

To fully understand how I have set this book up, you first must have a basic concept of the Chevrolet Parts System. Although I do not include every step in my explanation, it should familiarize you with the process.

All early Chevrolet parts have a seven-digit part number, for example 3700000. Chevrolet Central Office in Warren, Michigan, controlled the Parts Numbering System and created a large numerical "bank" that each Engineering Group in Chevrolet had access to. All Chief Engineers could "pull" a group of numbers in blocks to assign to a specific assembly under design. If a cylinder head assembly required 40 part numbers, a group of 40 numbers was pulled out of the system and assigned to that engineer for that cylinder head.

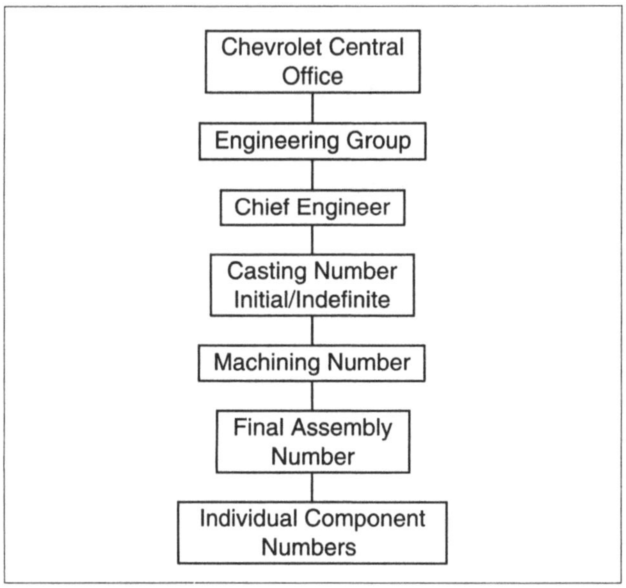

Chevrolet parts numbering system.

In most cases, the first number of that group was the *casting* number (or *identification* number) for that part. This number would stay with the part indefinitely, until the part was superseded by a design change. The next number in the sequence was usually the machine number. This number was assigned to the part of the complete assembly that required a machining process, such as a raw cylinder head casting. The next number in the total sequence would usually be the final assembly number, which contained all of the component parts of the complete assembly. The final numbers that composed the complete assembly would be each individual component, such as valves, guides, springs, etc. Please see the following diagram to understand the sequence of component parts numbering.

This system was not infallible. There are several documented cases where the system was changed slightly or numbers were switched around in the sequence. After all, Chevrolet Motor Division was in the business to sell cars, not classics. GM had specific policies to keep assembly plant lines in motion. They routinely substituted an originally designed part with another part that would serve the same correct function until the original part was again delivered to the plant and reinstated on the assembly line. This is typically how many odd parts end up on totally unrestored vehicles.

Although no complete casting number list has been found in Chevrolet's Archives, casting numbers were tracked by Chevrolet Service and Engineering for changes in design and model usage in both service and production. Both the Chevrolet Technical Service Bulletins (TSBs) and the Chevrolet Service News show these changes. Many times these changes were tied to a specific change-over date and Vehicle Identification Number (VIN). However, Chevrolet Service Parts created a separate set of problems.

Chevrolet Service constantly changed the part numbers offered over their dealership service counters. Example: A new part number 3700001 is issued by the engineering group for a cylinder head in model year 1955. The casting number on this head is 3700000. This cylinder head is used for three model years, and in the process has ten different part numbers assigned to it because it is used for ten different applications with different valve sizes, springs, etc. In model year 1959, Chevrolet Service decides that they can manufacture one *new* cylinder head that will fit all of these applications. They assign it a new part number 3800001. Now, in the 1959 Parts Catalog only one head is shown to cover ten applications, whereas in the 1958 Parts Catalog each application and head had its own number. Since this is a completely new cylinder head it now has a new casting number, too: 3800000.

See the problem here? Chevrolet Service was in business to supply correct parts for repairing Chevrolet vehicles, not to create archives for restoring these cars back to originality. Much information can be taken from old parts books, but keep in mind why they exist. If Chevrolet Service could replace ten parts (and part numbers) with one new part, that's exactly what they did.

Matching Numbers

One of the most misused and misunderstood phrases in the restoration hobby is "numbers matching." Everyone, from those who have large collections of cars to people who have only a vague interest in the hobby, has their own interpretation of what constitutes a numbers matching car. Many hobbyists use the term loosely with no clue to what it actually means.

"Numbers matching" simply means a car which not only appears in original factory condition, but in which all pertinent identification numbers, as well as all casting numbers and dates, are correct for that specific model and pre-date the final assembly date of the car. (The term probably originated in the Corvette restoration hobby. It seems these cars were the first to be restored back to true originality.) It is important to also make the distinction that a car is only original once, period.

There are more and more "manufactured" cars turning up in collectors' hands, cleverly documented to be original numbers matching vehicles. What I mean by "manufactured" is that the car has been rebuilt with correct casting numbers to appear original and to match the documentation to be included in the sale of the car.

To say that this situation is creating a major problem in the hobby is a vast understatement. Thousands of dollars are being invested into many matching number cars which in fact are complete forgeries, built for the primary purpose of selling an incorrect car as a documented original. Many enthusiasts are unsure as to what composes a correct car. Much of the information that has been published to date in this area has been incorrect in several aspects.

Checking A Car

Knowledge is the ultimate weapon in the fight against counterfeit Chevrolet muscle cars. Before you ever set out to acquire or restore any Chevrolet vehicle, become as informed as you can about the specific model you are interested in. This is your best defense to keep from being ripped off. Next, check *all* pertinent identification numbers. The total amount of numbers will vary from year to year, but there are some basic ones.

The first and most important number is the Vehicle Identification Number (VIN). Depending upon what year of Chevrolet you are interested in, the VIN and its plate can tell you many things. The VIN will typically specify the designated engine type, model series, model year, assembly plant and sequence number. When looking at a VIN, also check the rivets or the tackweld attaching it to the body. Are they similar to other unrestored models like this car? Do the rivets show signs of age or do they look new? Does the tag itself look new? VIN styles sometimes changed drastically from year to year, so do your research. Also remember that many secondary VINs were stamped in various body locations through the years. This was done to help law enforcement agencies identify stolen parts and/or cars. Once you start learning these secondary VIN locations, you can feel confident you are becoming more knowledgeable about your specific model.

After you validate the VIN, the next detail you should check is the vehicle trim tag. Trim tags are usually found on the firewall or cowl area of all Chevrolet vehicles. The trim tag contains information concerning the specific model, trim, assembly plant, paint code, and some option information. The *body* build date is also stamped as well. The body build date is very important in that all casting and stamping numbers on the car should *precede* the body build date. There are a few documented cases in which the drivetrain has been installed after a body build date, but this scenario is rare.

One fallacy concerning matching numbers is that if the engine stamping numbers correspond to the VIN, then the car is a matching numbers car and the remainder of the cars identification numbers would be correct and original as well. This is not correct. In today's car restoration hobby, you cannot trust the car's total originality on only the engine block stamping alone.

Get to know what sort of codes and stampings to look for on parts. For example, there are two stampings on an engine block. The first stamping is the engine assembly build date code. The second code was the VIN designation stamping. Check all casting and stamping numbers as well on the block, cylinder heads, intake manifold, exhaust manifolds, distributor, carburetor, and so on. Learn what size typeface and specific coding is correct for your model year. Not all parts were stamped in the same area.

Finally, there is paperwork. Broadcast sheets, build sheets, original invoices, window stickers, bills of sale, and protect-o-plates used to be what the hobby regarded as irrefutable proof that a car was original and was being represented as correct. This is no longer the case. All of these documents can and are being reproduced today. There are even people advertising that they can make the documents look old to replicate original documents. Due to this fact, all documents are now being regarded as false until proven otherwise. This is very unfortunate for the hobby.

How To Use This Book

This brings me to the primary purpose of this book: to acquaint you with the direct correlation of *casting numbers* to the identification of drivetrain parts for the purpose of validating and restoring early Chevrolet vehicles. In a book of this type, the accuracy of each casting number and model-usage listing is very important. There are so many numbers on any given Chevrolet vehicle, it can overwhelm the average enthusiast. I have tried to make this book as easy to use as possible, while maintaining the accuracy needed to set this book apart from other so-called "restoration guides."

Casting Number Charts

This book is arranged for two primary purposes. The first is to be able to quickly find a specific casting number or application, whichever is applicable to a reader's needs at the time. All casting number information is in numerical order so you can quickly find a casting number if you only have the part. The casting number is critical because it does not change across model applications. (If there are deviations in the casting number usage, they are noted in the book.) For example, the same engine or transmission used in 1955 on a Corvette and a Passenger car in many cases has the same casting number. Part numbers will only help if the part you are looking for is in the original box. Any part can be put into a box with a rare part number on it, but the casting number will always be on the part. You won't find many 30-year-old drivetrain parts still in the original box. The casting number is always the number you want to refer to when checking parts at a swap meet or on a car you intend to buy.

The second purpose is to allow you to quickly find a model year application heading and efficiently find whatever model year and car type you have, while cross referencing back to the casting number lists. Included in the back of this book is a page on which you can fill in all pertinent information about your car so you can turn to that one page for quick reference while searching for parts.

Model Identification

The table below is a breakdown of Chevrolet passenger car model lines and body styles in those model lines.

Model Year

It is very important to understand the difference between the calendar year and the model year for a given car. A calendar year is just that, from January 1 through December 31. The model year is the period of time a Chevrolet model was produced and available to the general public. This is also sometimes called the production year. This period usually ran from August through June of the following calendar year. For example, production for 1964 models actually started in August 1963. Mid-year changes usually occurred around January or February.

All charts in this book reflect dating by the model year, not the calendar year. Also note that for a car built early in a model year, many parts correct for that car would be dated from the previous calendar year.

Date Coding

Almost all Chevrolet parts have some kind of date coding cast or stamped into the part. Date codes, contrary to current popular belief, were not used to make today's restorations easier. Chevrolet needed a way to track engineering and production changes, relative to model usage. Date codes on parts allowed changes to be documented and recorded. Many of the references in Chevrolet Technical Service Bulletins (TSBs) and *Chevrolet Service News* to document parts changes were made by build date or casting date.

There are two types of date coding. The first is referred to as the casting date code, and is the most common. On most parts such as blocks, cylinder heads, intakes and exhaust manifolds, this date code represents the *calendar* date of part *manufacture*.

1955 Through 1959 Model Identification

1955		1956		1957		1958		1959	
Model	**Series**	**Model**	**Series**	**Model**	**Series**	**Model**	**Body Style**	**Model**	**Body Style**
Passenger	150	*Passenger*	150	*Passenger*	150	*Passenger*	Delray	*Passenger*	Biscayne
	210		210		210		Yeoman		Brookwood
	Bel Air		Bel Air		Bel Air		Biscayne		Parkwood
Corvette		*Corvette*		*Corvette*			Bel Air		Kingswood
							Impala		Bel Air
							Nomad		Impala
						Corvette			El Camino
								Corvette	

The second type of date code is found on distributors and alternators. This code is stamped into the part and represents the *calendar* date of final *assembly,* since the entire part is made of many small parts which are not dated.

Many date codes do not use the letter "I" because it is easily confused with the number "1." As a result, the December code would be "M" instead of "L."

Date Code Chart

Part	Code Type	Month Code Range	Location
Block*	Casting	A to L	Rear/side of block
Heads	Casting	A to L	Top of head, between rocker studs
Carburetor			
Carter	Stamped	A to M	Tag or base
Holley	Stamped	1 to 0, A, B	Air horn
Rochester	Stamped	A to M	Tag or body
Intake Manifold	Casting	A to L	Top/bottom
Exhaust Manifold	Casting	A to L	Front/back
Water pump	Casting	A to L	Front face
Distributor	Stamped	A to M, less I	Tag or base
Alternator	Stamped	A to M, less I	Riveted tag, or housing
Transmission			Maincase, extension housing, or sidecover
Saginaw/Muncie	Casting	A to L	
Muncie 4-speed	See text	A to L	
Borg Warner	Casting	A to L	
Rear Axle	Casting	A to L	Center sec.
Wheels	Stamped	01 to 12	Rim at valve stem

*Some documented blocks have been found with a December "M" month code.

Conclusion

As you can see, this book is quite different from any other ever offered to the Chevrolet restoration hobby. What makes this book different from similar books, parts books, and interchange manuals is that all of these books fall short in incorporating the correct, verifiable information that is paramount to this project. A generic *interchange* manual can rely only on what the manufacturer originally supplied to them for information. The interchange manuals have no hands-on experience, no access to original parts blueprints, and no references who are experts in their respective automotive field. Many other books have not done the proper research to tie all of these factors together. Many have been rushed to the market to capitalize on a market that needs this information, without regard to authenticity and factory produced proof to back their efforts. All of the research that was done to produce this book relates directly back to Chevrolet's original records.

You will find this book to be very beneficial for a number of reasons. First of all, it provides the Chevrolet restorer with one comprehensive source to turn to in order to restore a car with the correct original drivetrain parts. Second, this book will help clarify the application of parts you may already have on hand. With this book you can discover parts that are correct for your car, but were manufactured for other Chevrolet models as well. For example, the owner of a Chevrolet Impala, which is possibly not as "collectible" in many cases as a Corvette, will find that he can use many Corvette parts to correctly restore his car. A Corvette owner, by using this book, now has a new parts "avenue" that could save time and money over normal Corvette restoration circles. Finally, I hope this book helps put a stop to misrepresentation in the sale of parts.

I want to express my sincere thanks to all of those GM employees who assisted me in gaining access to all Chevrolet restricted facilities. The actual worth of the original documentation obtained from these facilities will be immeasurable to the Chevrolet restoration hobby for decades to come.

I hope this series of books will help preserve the rich history of Chevrolet, by forever documenting the chronological and numerical history of drivetrain parts of these great cars for generations of car enthusiasts to come.

Chapter 1
Vehicle Identification

1. Introduction

Just as there are numbers that identify each component installed on a vehicle, there are numbers that relate to the whole vehicle to identify such things as model, engine, accessories, and trim. These numbers are the Vehicle Identification Number (VIN), Trim Tag numbers, and Model Identification number. See Fig. 1-1.

2. Vehicle Identification Number (VIN)

The Vehicle Identification Number (VIN) is probably the most important number on a car. If you do not know how to decode a VIN on a particular Chevrolet, you will be unable to verify other components or numbers.

1955–1959 VIN Location

Model	Year	Location
Passenger	1955–59	Left front door hinge pillar
Corvette	1955	Left front door hinge pillar just below the courtesy lamp door switch.
Corvette	1956–59	Left front door hinge pillar just below the upper door hinge

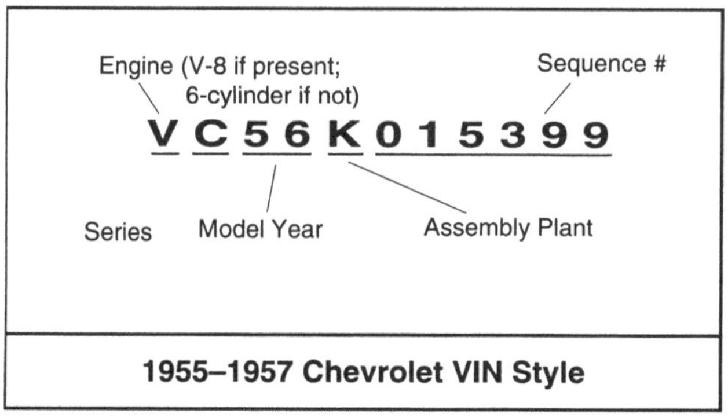

Fig. 1-1. Typical VIN for 1955 through 1957 Chevrolet models. See text for explanation of decoding digits.

*Fig. 1-2. **Top:** Location of Vehicle Identification Number (VIN) varies with model and year. Typical Passenger car shown. **Bottom:** Trim tag location for 1955 Passenger car with air conditioning, on driver's side of cowl.*

2.1 1955 Through 1957 VIN Decoding

The 1955 and 1956 VIN sequence is the same for both years. The VIN begins with one or two letters. If it begins with two letters, the first letter will always be the letter "V," which designates a V-8 engine equipped car. The absence of the letter "V" designates that the car originally had a 6-cylinder engine.

The next letter designates the series of the car. The letter "A" is a 1500 series, "B" is 2100 series, "C" is 2400 series,

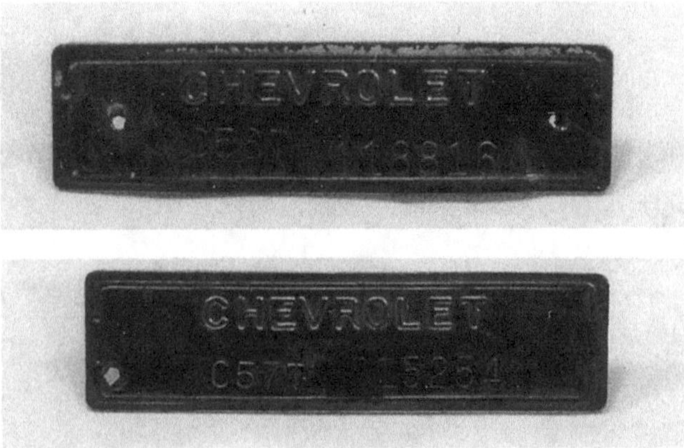

0023801/0023800

Fig. 1-3. *Top: 1956 VIN plate VC56T 118816 indicates V-8 equipped 1956 Chevrolet Passenger car Bel Air Series, 18,816th car built at Tarrytown, NY Final Assembly Plant. Bottom: 1957 VIN plate.*

"D" is 1508 series, and "E" is the 2900 series or Corvette. The VIN code charts give a complete breakdown of these letter series designations. In order to tell exactly what model the car is inside the series, you must refer to the Fisher Body number off the firewall trim tag. For more information, see **Model Identification** in this chapter.

1955–1959 Model Year Code

Number Code	Model Year
55	1955
56	1956
57	1957
58	1958
59	1959

The next two digits designate the model year of the car. After the model year designation, the next digit is a single letter plant code. Every final assembly plant had a letter assigned to the plant and this was stamped on each VIN in this sequence order.

The last six digits following the assembly plant letter code represent the sequential number of that car from that assembly plant. Serial numbers for all passenger cars will be continuous at each plant regardless of series. All Corvettes are serial numbered separately. The 1955–56 starting unit number is 001001.

The 1957 VIN sequence is the same as the 1955–56 VIN sequence with only one difference. The VIN starting unit number is 100001 instead of the 001001 starting unit number for 1955/6. Please see the examples below for a clear explanation of all 1955–57 VIN sequences.

Vehicle Identification and Accessory Codes

I would like to take the opportunity here to express some of my thoughts concerning the history and future of the restoration hobby. For as long as I can remember I have had an infatuation with the automobile. I started drawing and playing with cars at a very early age. My love for the automobile continued throughout my adolescence and into my adulthood. I bought my first car at the age of 15. After several nice cars, including a 1970 SS Monte Carlo and a couple of 1969 Camaros, I began to go to swap meets and car shows. I took my extra parts to sell or trade. Finally, after several years of buying and selling, I decided to start my own full-time business and began traveling the country, mostly in the Super Chevy Show circuit.

One conclusion that I have reached over the years is that the hobby that existed when I began is no longer. In the beginning it was primarily a used parts business. If your car needed a new interior, you searched junk yards and *Hemming's Motor News* until you found a good used interior. Soon, however, the hobby began to turn into a "restoration" market as more and more entrepreneurs saw the opportunity to make money. Don't get me wrong, all of us have benefitted from the restoration market in some way, myself included. However, the restoration market has now grown so strong that many restorers believe any part can be regarded as a reproduction part. This is where I beg to differ.

While working on this book over the last few years, I often pondered how I would discuss the trim tags and the accessory codes on them. I spent hundreds of hours researching accessory codes and almost as many hours talking to members of most of the major car clubs about their own trim tag projects. As I compiled all of this information and came up with new and exciting revelations on the accessory codes, one thought kept coming to me: I was creating the most comprehensive Chevrolet restoration book available but, if I included the accessory codes, it could become, as Verne Frantz of Jersey Late Greats termed it, "The Complete Guide to How to Build a Bogus Car."

With the deadline for publication of this series drawing nearer, I knew I had to make a decision. I could publish all of the accessory codes and be known for how smart I was, or I could keep the information and devise a way to verify cars at a later date. I have decided to keep the information private. Let me explain further.

There are people out there who will supply anyone with a product, no matter what the cost. In the past, if a car still had its original protect-o-plate, it was worth more. Now, however, since reproductions are available, any car can have a protect-o-plate. Does this make the car with an original protect-o-plate worth more or less? I believe that it makes it worth less because it brings in an element of doubt as to the car's originality. A correct original car should be able to stand on its own merit, without a protect-o-plate or window sticker.

I did not want that to happen with trim tags. In my discussions with other enthusiasts I kept coming back to one fact: The trim tag is, to paraphrase a letter Verne Frantz wrote to me,

continued

2.2 1958 Through 1959 VIN Decoding

The 1958–59 VIN sequence is basically identical to the 1955–57 VIN with one exception. The V-8 designation has been eliminated and the model series have been re-aligned to identify 6- and 8-cylinder cars from the actual series designations.

The first digit in the VIN is a series prefix letter. This letter will tell you the series the car is from, and that will consequently tell you if the car originally had a 6- or 8-cylinder engine. To know the actual model number of the car, you will need to read the firewall trim tag. In 1958, the Fisher Body Company began using the Chevrolet series number as their own Fisher Body number. To fully understand this system, please see **8. Trim Tag Information** for more discussion.

The next two numbers in the VIN sequence designate the model year of the car. The next letter designates the final assembly plant.

The last six digits following the assembly plant letter code are the sequential numbers or serial number of that car from that specific assembly plant. Serial numbers for all passenger cars will be continuous at each assembly plant regardless of series. All Corvettes are serial numbered separately. The 1958–59 starting unit number is 100001.

2.3 Canadian VIN System

There were thousands of Chevrolet passenger cars built in Canada at Oshawa from 1955 through 1959, and many of these cars were imported into the United States over the years. Although the Chevrolet model lines were virtually identical, the VIN systems were not. I have decided to show the Canadian VIN system here.

U. S.-built cars were not generally exported to Canada prior to the 1965 model year. 1964 and prior Canadian built Chevrolet vehicles were built primarily for Canadian consumption.

1955–58

First digit is always model year designator (5-8). The next four or five digits designate the model identification number, with the 5th digit always being a letter if there are five digits. The last six digits of the VIN are the sequential number of that particular car. Final assembly plant code is not shown in 1955–58 Canadian VIN.

Example:
51037D600001 = 1955 Bel Air 2-door hardtop

1959–63

This VIN style is identical to 1955–58 with the exception that the sequence number is five digits instead of six digits.

Example:
9183700001 = 1959 Impala 2-door hardtop

Accessory Codes (cont'd)

the last positive identifier of the originality of any car and should *not* be regarded as a reproduction part. A proper restoration is one which has been done to match the codes on the plate, not one in which the plate has been altered to match the restored car. Other pieces of documentation, such as protect-o-plates, build sheets, order forms, or window stickers, do not disclose the unknown codes that the trim tag contains. If the trim tag had basic information like valve tappet adjustment instructions, rather than model, paint, trim and option codes, it would be reproduced and sold for probably $20.00. What makes the same plate with different information worth $250.00 to $300.00? Simple. The increased value that the information on the tag adds to the car. When you look at a car that has air conditioning, you can clearly see that it has air conditioning; the same holds true for a car that is painted red, you can see it is a red car.

Echoing my own thoughts, Verne pointed out that extra original equipment adds value to a car; so does original paint color. When the codes on the trim tag show that the car should be red and have air conditioning, the result is added value to the car. Not only because the numbers and letters on the trim tag happen to match the options on the car, but also because of what the presence of those codes implies: that the car was originally ordered with those options. As long as the tag is the original to that car, those codes can and should be used to document and verify the originality of the car. In this case, they also verify increased value. But in the case of a reproduction trim tag, that increased value is false.

The trim tag accessory codes are not known to the general public. In my research I have found that some codes were specific to certain assembly plants. Many assembly plants used several types of plates over a period of several years while other plants used just one. If the correct codes and specific details were furnished in this book, all of the cars out there would become suspect—are they true restorations or faked ones? Are you confident enough to trust the trim tag? I have run across several "restored" cars with reproduction trim tags that have codes so wrong they stand out like a sore thumb to a knowledgeable person. Until the hobby decides that this is wrong and learns to police itself, I cannot in good faith publish the accessory codes.

(I would like to thank Verne Frantz, Jr., President of the Jersey Late Greats, Inc., for his help in this area. This club is currently offering a decoding service for 1958–64 full-size Chevrolets and can be contacted at the address in the back of this book. I would like to establish a similar national trim tag validation service for all 1955–75 Chevrolet cars. If you have an interest in this type of service, please contact me through the P.O. box listed at the back of this book.)

3. 1955 VIN CODE CHARTS

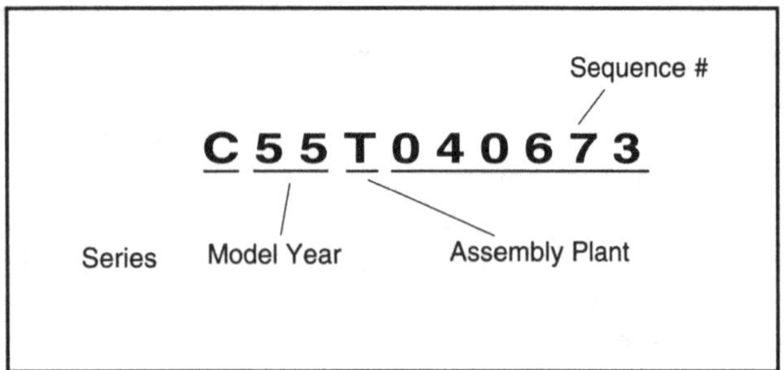

Sample 1955 Chevrolet VIN Style

0023014

0023802

Fig. 1-4. Original 1955 VIN tag from 6-cylinder model (series prefix is "C").

Example: 1955 VIN C 55 T 040673

- C = Series: 2400 Series
- 55 = Model Year: 1955
- F = Final Assembly Plant: Tarrytown, NY
- 040673 = Sequence Number: 39,672nd Passenger car built at Tarrytown in that model year

1955 VIN Model Designation Codes*

Engine	Series Code	Series
6-Cylinder	A	1500 (except 1508)
	B	2100
	C	2400
	D	1508
	E	2900 (Corvette)
8-Cylinder	VA	1500 (except 1508)
	VB	2100
	VC	2400
	VD	1508
	VE	2900 (Corvette)

*Please refer to Section **9. Model Identification** for a complete breakdown of these model designations.

0023016

Fig. 1-5. 1955 Bel Air two-door hardtop.

1955 VIN Charts

1955 VIN Assembly Plant Codes

Letter Code	Assembly Plant	Body Type*
A	Atlanta, Georgia	1
B	Baltimore, Maryland	1
F	Flint, Michigan	1
J	Janesville, Wisconsin	1
K	Kansas City, Missouri	1
L	Los Angeles, California	1
N	Norwood, Ohio	1
O	Oakland, California	1
S	St. Louis, Missouri	1, 2
T	Tarrytown, New York	1
*1: Passenger car; 2: Corvette		

1955 VIN Begin Sequence Numbers

Model	Begin Sequence Number	Plant
Passenger	001001	All
Corvette	001001	St. Louis

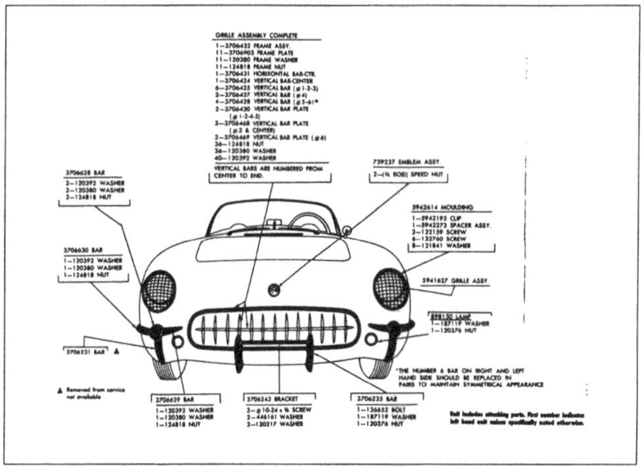

0023018

Fig. 1-7. Front view of 1955 Corvette.

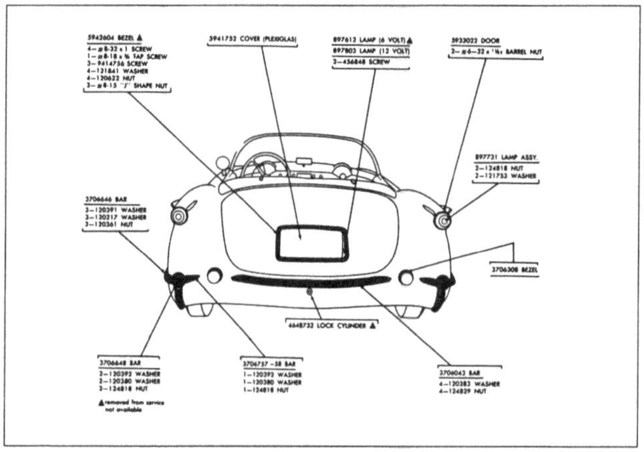

0023019

Fig. 1-8. Rear view of 1955 Corvette.

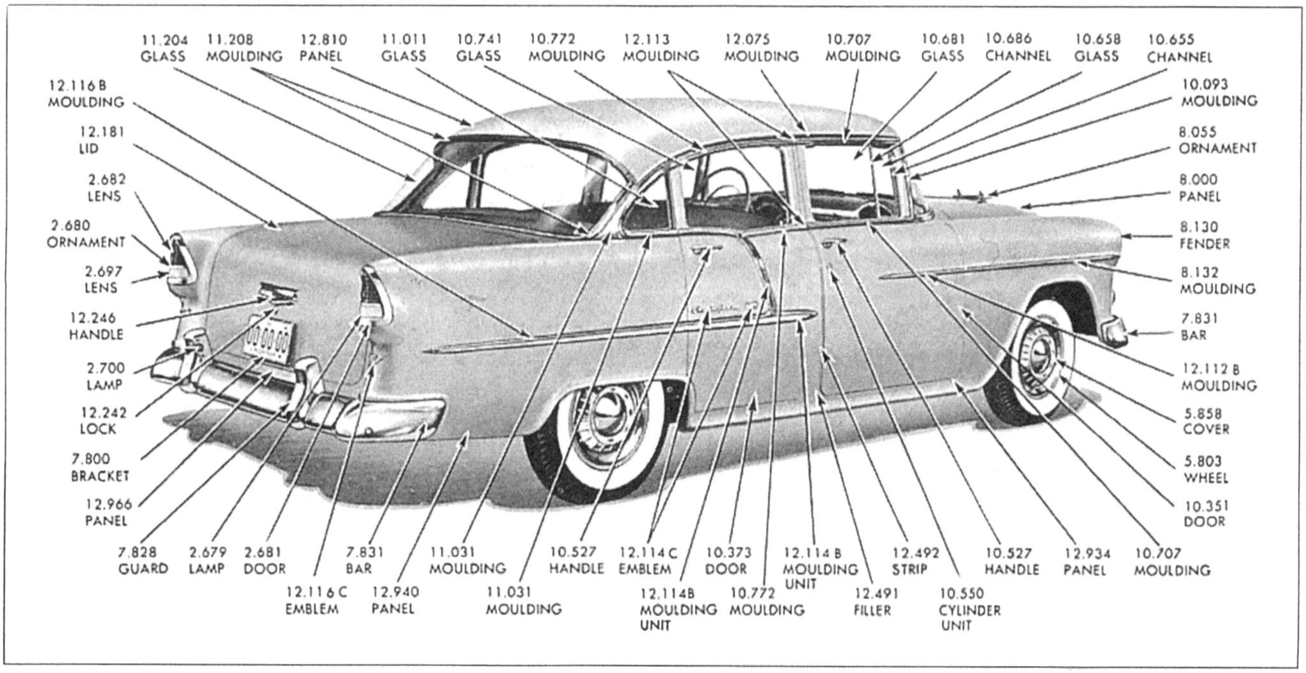

0023017

Fig. 1-6. 1955 Bel Air four-door sedan.

4. 1956 VIN CODE CHARTS

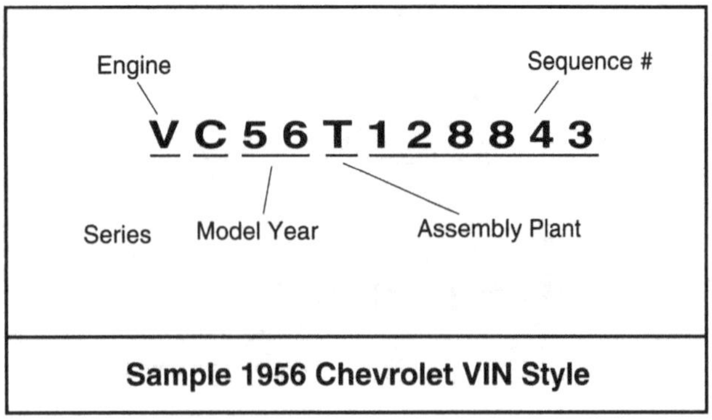

0023020

Example: 1956 VIN V C 56 T 128843

- V = Engine: V8
- C = Series: 2400 Series
- 56 = Model Year: 1956
- T = Final Assembly Plant: Tarrytown, NY
- 128843 = Sequence Number: 127,842nd Passenger car built at Tarrytown in that model year

0023803

Fig. 1-9. 1956 VIN for V-8 model built at Tarrytown, New York.

1956 VIN Model Designation Codes*

Engine	Series Code	Series
6-Cylinder	A	1500 (except 1508)
	B	2100
	C	2400
	D	1508
8-Cylinder	VA	1500 (except 1508)
	VB	2100
	VC	2400
	VD	1508
	VE	2900 (Corvette)

*Please refer to Section **9. Model Identification** for a complete breakdown of these model designations.

0023021

Fig. 1-10. 1956 Model line-up in Chevrolet Engineering Executive Garage for employees show.

1956 VIN CHARTS

1956 VIN Assembly Plant Codes

Letter Code	Assembly Plant	Body Type*
A	Atlanta, Georgia	1
B	Baltimore, Maryland	1
F	Flint, Michigan	1
J	Janesville, Wisconsin	1
K	Kansas City, Missouri	1
L	Los Angeles, California	1
N	Norwood, Ohio	1
O	Oakland, California	1
S	St. Louis, Missouri	1, 2
T	Tarrytown, New York	1
*1: Passenger car; 2: Corvette		

0023022

Fig. 1-11. 1956 Bel Air Convertible.

1956 VIN Begin Sequence Numbers

Model	Begin Sequence Number	Plant
Passenger	001001	All
Corvette	001001	St. Louis

0023023

Fig. 1-12. 1956 Bel Air Convertible interior.

0023024

Fig. 1-13. 1956 Bel Air Nomad Wagon.

5. 1957 VIN CODE CHARTS

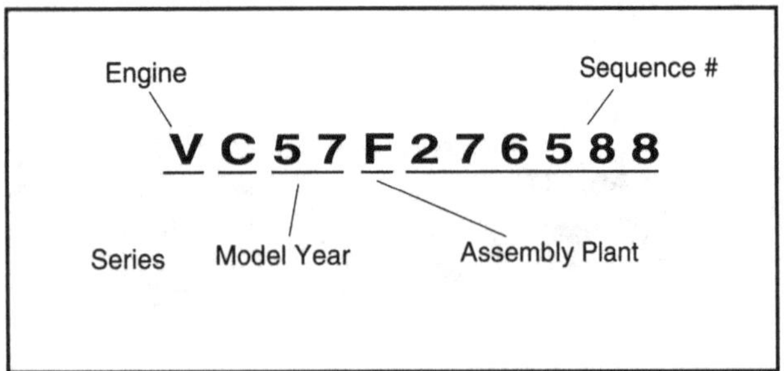

Sample 1957 Chevrolet VIN Style

0023026

Example: 1957 VIN V C 57 F 276588

- V = Engine:V8
- C = Series: 2400 Series
- 57= Model year:1957
- F = Final Assembly Plant: Flint, Michigan
- 276588 = Sequence Number: 176,587th Passenger car built at Flint in that model year

0023804

Fig. 1-14. 1957 VIN from V-8 equipped Bel Air model.

1957 VIN Model Designation Codes*

Engine	Series Code	Series
6-Cylinder	A	1500 (except 1508)
	B	2100
	C	2400
	D	1508
8-Cylinder	VA	1500 (except 1508)
	VB	2100
	VC	2400
	VD	1508
	VE	2900 (Corvette)
*Please refer to Section 9. **Model Identification** for a complete breakdown of these model designations.		

0023025

Fig. 1-15. 1957 Bel Air Convertible.

1957 VIN Charts

1957 VIN Assembly Plant Codes

Letter Code	Assembly Plant	Body Type*
A	Atlanta, Georgia	1
B	Baltimore, Maryland	1
F	Flint, Michigan	1
J	Janesville, Wisconsin	1
K	Kansas City, Missouri	1
L	Los Angeles, California	1
N	Norwood, Ohio	1
O	Oakland, California	1
S	St. Louis, Missouri	1, 2
T	Tarrytown, New York	1
*1: Passenger car; 2: Corvette		

1957 VIN Begin Sequence Numbers

Model	Begin Sequence Number	Plant
Passenger	100001	All
Corvette	100001	St. Louis

0023028

Fig. 1-17. 1957 150 two-door Sedan.

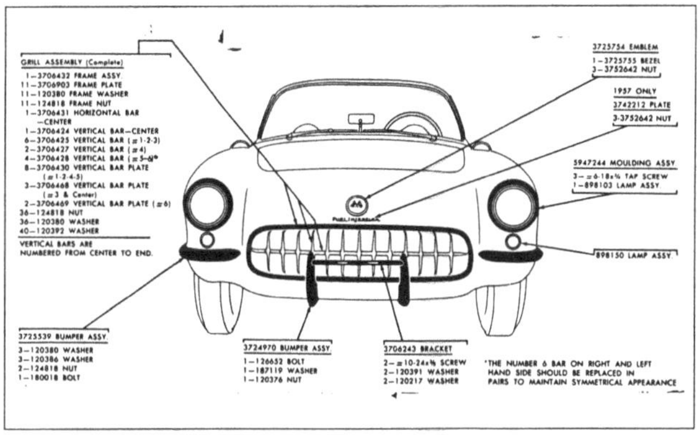

0023029

Fig. 1-18. 1957 Corvette.

0023027

Fig. 1-16. 1957 210 four-door Wagon used as army vehicle.

1958 VIN CHARTS

6. 1958 VIN CODE CHARTS

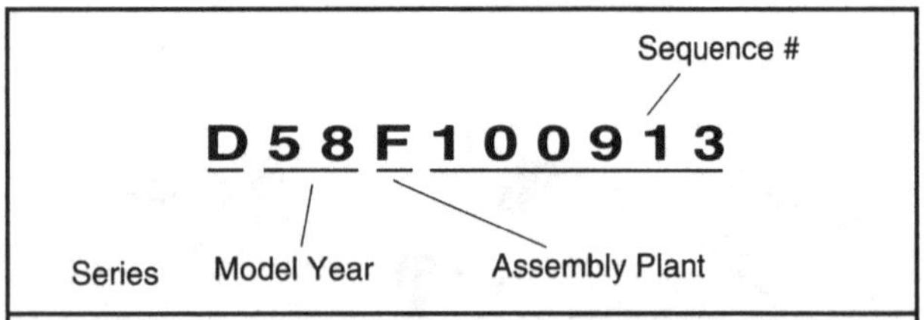

Sample 1958 Chevrolet VIN Style

0023030

0023805/0023806

Fig. 1-19. Two 1958 VIN tags, the top from a Flint-built car, the bottom from a Baltimore-built car. Note that Flint tag has all characters stamped into tag, while Baltimore tag has embossed "A". Also note different font sizes and use of gang stamp on Baltimore tag.

Example: 1958 VIN D 58 F 100913

- D = Series: 1600 Series
- 58= Model year: 1958
- F = Final Assembly Plant: Flint, Michigan
- 100913 = Sequence Number: 912th Passenger car built at Flint in that model year

1958 VIN Model Series Codes*

Series Code	Series	Engine
A	1100	6-Cylinder
B	1200	8-Cylinder
C	1500	6-Cylinder
D	1600	8-Cylinder
E	1700	6-Cylinder
F	1800	8-Cylinder
G	1100 (Sedan Delivery)	6-Cylinder
H	1200 (Sedan Delivery)	8-Cylinder
J	800 (Corvette)	8-Cylinder

*Please refer to Section **9. Model Identification** for a complete breakdown of these model designations. The actual model of the car will be found on the firewall trim tag.

0023032

Fig. 1-21. 1958 Corvette. While 1959 model is similar, hood louvers are 1958-only.

0023031

Fig. 1-20. 1958 Bel Air two-door Sedan.

1958 VIN Charts

1958 VIN Assembly Plant Codes

Letter Code	Assembly Plant	Body Type*
A	Atlanta, Georgia	1
B	Baltimore, Maryland	1
F	Flint, Michigan	1
J	Janesville, Wisconsin	1
K	Kansas City, Missouri	1
L	Los Angeles, California	1
N	Norwood, Ohio	1
O	Oakland, California	1
S	St. Louis, Missouri	1, 2
T	Tarrytown, New York	1
W	Willow Run, Michigan	1
*1: Passenger car; 2: Corvette		

1958 VIN Begin Sequence Numbers

Model	Begin Sequence Number	Plant
Passenger	100001	All
Corvette	100001	St. Louis

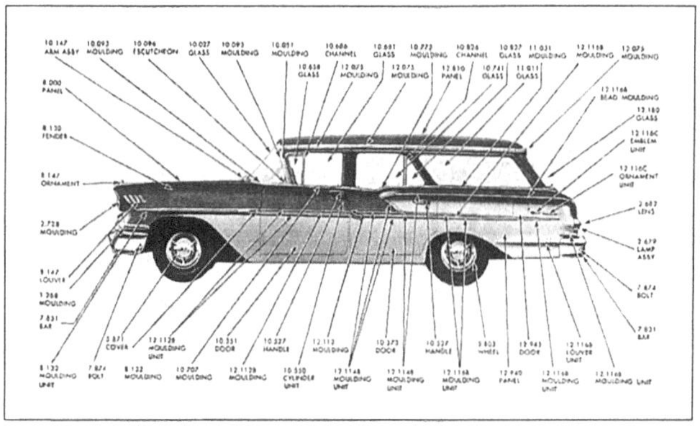

0023034

Fig. 1-22. 1958 Nomad Wagon.

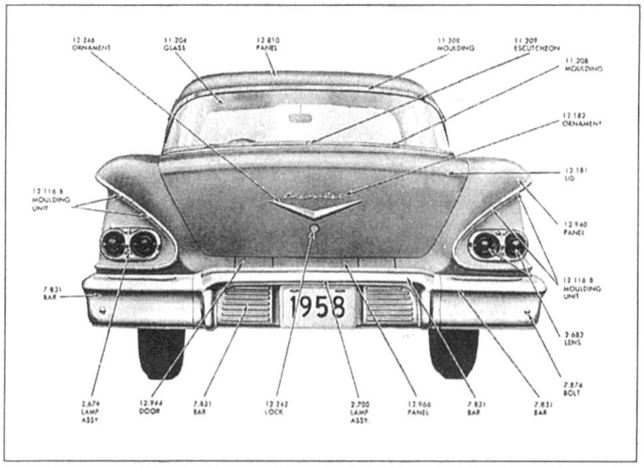

0023033

Fig. 1-23. 1958 Passenger rear end.

0023035

Fig. 1-24. 1958 Bel Air Impala Sport Coupe.

7. 1959 VIN CODE CHARTS

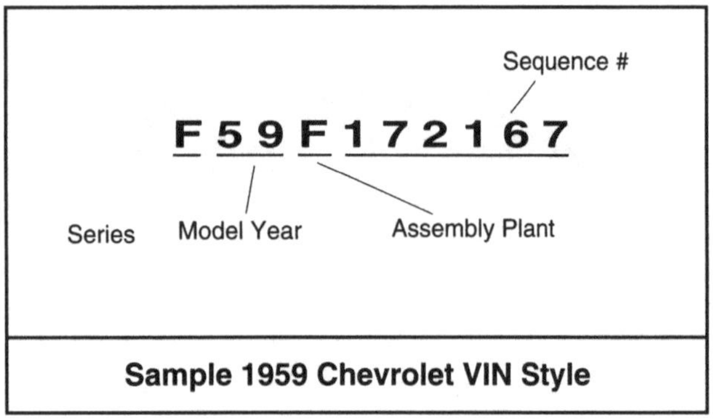

0023036

Example: 1959 VIN F 59 F 172167

- F = Series: 1800 Series
- 59= Model year:1959
- F = Final Assembly Plant: Flint, Michigan
- 172167 = Sequence Number: 72167th Passenger car built at Flint in that model year.

0023807

Fig. 1-25. Original VIN plate shows that two separate gang stampings were used at Flint plant in 1959.

1959 VIN Model Series Codes

Series Code	Series	Engine
A	1100	6-Cylinder
B	1200	8-Cylinder
C	1500	6-Cylinder
D	1600	8-Cylinder
E	1700	6-Cylinder
F	1800	8-Cylinder
G	1100 (Sedan Delivery)	6-Cylinder
H	1200 (Sedan Delivery)	8-Cylinder
J	800 (Corvette)	8-Cylinder
*Please refer to Section **9. Model Identification** for a complete breakdown of these model designations. The actual model of the car will be found on the firewall trim tag.		

0023037

Fig. 1-27. 1959 Corvette Convertible.

0023038

Fig. 1-26. 1959 Impala Convertible. Note badge on right rear, just above bumper, noting "LevelAir" air suspension package.

1959 VIN CHARTS

1959 VIN Assembly Plant Codes

Letter Code	Assembly Plant	Body Type*
A	Atlanta, Georgia	1
B	Baltimore, Maryland	1
F	Flint, Michigan	1
G	Framingham, Massachusetts**	1
J	Janesville, Wisconsin	1
K	Kansas City, Missouri	1
L	Los Angeles, California	1
N	Norwood, Ohio	1
O	Oakland, California	1
S	St. Louis, Missouri	1, 2
T	Tarrytown, New York	1
W	Willow Run, Michigan	1

*1: Passenger car; 2: Corvette

**Some Chevrolet documentation states that the Framingham Assembly Plant began production in 1959. This plant was regarded as a General Motors Pontiac plant at this time. This is yet to be documented.

1959 VIN Begin Sequence Numbers

Model	Begin Sequence Number	Plant
Passenger	100001	All
Corvette	100001	St. Louis

0023039

Fig. 1-29. *1959 Impala Coupe.*

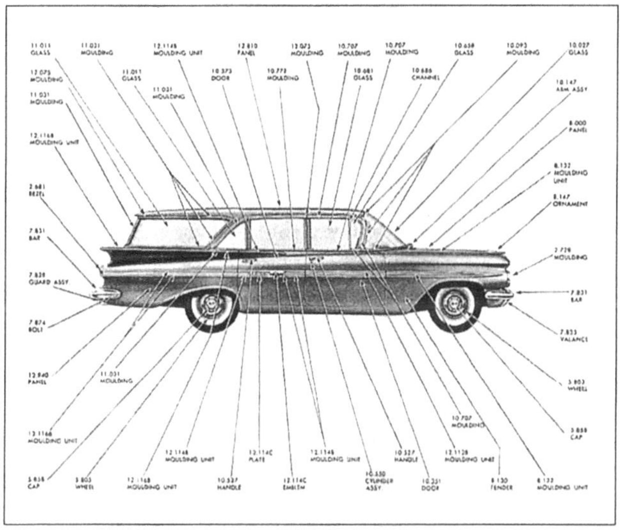

0023041

Fig. 1-30. *1959 Nomad Station Wagon.*

0023040

Fig. 1-28. *1959 Impala Sport Sedan. Note difference in C-pillar design compared to Coupe.*

8. Trim Tag Information

In this section I will explain the information found on 1955 through 1959 Chevrolet firewall trim tags. It is imperative to know how to interpret this information on your own car or a car you intend to purchase, because it allows you to verify the model and the original paint and trim combinations for the car.

There were two basic trim tag designs used from 1955 through 1959. The first was used for 1955–58 cars excluding Corvette. The second was for 1959 cars excluding Corvette. All trim tags were attached by special rivets. The position of the trim tag changed from year to year. See the headings below by year and model for individual trim tag locations and decoding of trim tag information.

NOTE—
Although theoretically there was one style of trim tag used for each model year, there were a number of different trim tag designs, and many final assembly plants used more than one style of trim tag. The exact breakdown is not being disclosed. A full explanation of why is given on page 2 of this chapter.

1955–58 Trim Tag Location

Model	Year	Location
Passenger Cars	1955–56 Standard Cars	Right side of cowl area below the windshield, riveted in place.
	1955–56 with A/C	Left side of cowl below the windshield, riveted in place. In some cases the location on the right side may have rivets in the cowl.
	1957 (1st design)	On the cowl panel, just to the driver's side of center
	1957 (2nd design)	On the cowl just below the heater control valve*
	1958	In the middle of the firewall behind the distributor

*Some assembly plants may have used the 1958 trim tag position on late 1957 models. This has not been verified.

Notes on Early Trim Tags

In my research on these cars I had several conversations with Marty Heim, who has done much of his own research on early Chevrolet trim tags. In one of those conversations Marty noted, "The 1955–56 trim tag format had been in use since at least 1947, possibly all post-war cars included. Because of the uniformity and consistency of the Style and Body information on the tags, I have concluded that the tags were supplied to the Fisher Body plants, pre-numbered with the style numbers and sequential body numbers, by a single source. The Trim, Paint, and Accessory codes, which lack consistency, were then added at the body plant.

"Obviously, Trim and Paint codes were common, but paint code suffix letters (necessary for determining two-tone masking) were often omitted. Accessory code designations varied widely, were used inconsistently, and when used were often added to the Trim or Paint lines instead of the designated Accessory line. (See Fig. 1-33.)

"Because of the incomplete and inconsistent nature of the trim tags, I question whether the tag could have served as the 'build document.' It seems that a more complete and accurate document would have been needed to produce a body assembly."

0023044

Fig. 1-31. Trim tag for 1956 Passenger car without air conditioning. Location is on passenger side of cowl.

8.1 1955 Through 1958 Trim Tags

The 1955–58 trim tag is considered the "first design" trim tag. All 1955–56 Standard Chevrolet passenger cars without A/C have a 2 1/2" x 4" trim tag affixed to the right side of the cowl area below the windshield. See Fig. 1-31. 1955–56 cars with A/C have the tag affixed to the driver's side of the cowl. See earlier Fig. 1-2.

Most of the trim tags on 1955–56 factory air conditioned cars were attached by standard General Motors rivets. Other cars used special rivet-head bolts and nuts to attach the tag. See Fig. 1-32. Also note that some cars with air conditioning had holes on the passenger side of the cowl with standard rivets in place. The reason for this is unknown.

Another anomaly for 1955 cars is the trim tag for Passenger cars with the special metallic Anniversary Gold paint that commemorated the 50 millionth GM vehicle built. As documented in a GM publication, five thousand gold Chevrolets were prepared for display in dealership showrooms. All were 4-door sedans. The actual celebration vehicle was a 2-door hardtop, and it had 716 trim pieces removed and gold plated. Fig. 1-33 shows the special paint code (689) used on the 5,000 commemorative cars. Most paint charts do not mention this paint combination at all.

1957 cars used two different trim tag positions. The 1957 first design trim tag was located on the cowl panel,

0023810/0023811

Fig. 1-32. *Front and rear views of trim tag for 1956 car with factory A/C built at Janesville. Note distinctive look of rivet head bolt and nut arrangement to secure tag to cowl.*

0023813

Fig. 1-33. *Trim tag from a 1955 Anniversary Gold 4-door sedan, showing unique paint code. Note that the accessory codes are on the Trim and Paint lines, not on the ACC. line.*

just to the driver's side of center. Due to the positioning of this tag, it sometimes was drilled to attach hardware for certain options. Fig. 1-34 shows the trim tag for a Kansas City built car with factory A/C that had holes drilled to attach and route the fast idle cable. Due to the damaging of trim tags, Chevrolet decided to move the

0023809

Fig. 1-34. *Early 1957 trim tag from Kansas City built car with factory A/C has holes drilled to attach fast idle cable.*

tag location, but it is unknown when and if all assembly plants went to the second tag position. The June, 1957 issue of *Chevrolet Service News* states that "The 1957 passenger car body identification plate which was formerly centered on the front of the dash panel will in future production be installed in the area immediately below the heater water control valve (Ranco Valve)".

The second trim tag position on 1957 Passenger cars is on the cowl just below the heater control valve. The 1958 trim tag is found in the middle of the firewall behind the distributor.

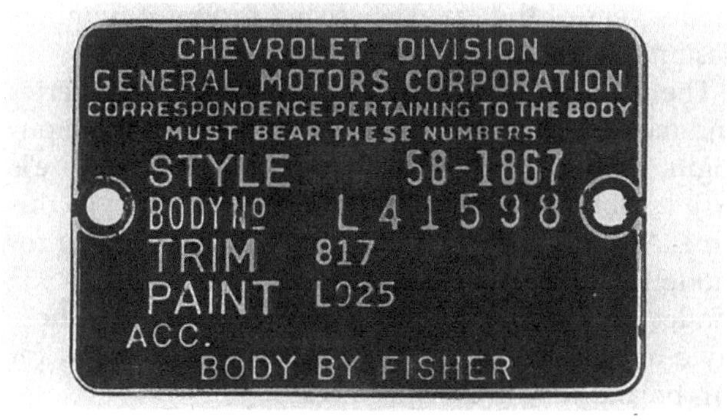

0023043

Fig. 1-35. *1958 trim tag.*

As you can see in the accompanying photos, the 1956 firewall tag is shown and is identical to the 1955 trim tag. In this chapter we will decode the trim tag by position number. This will enable us to show the differences from 1955 to 1958 at the position rather than in text form.

Trim Tag Position Designations

There are eleven basic positions on the 1955 through 1958 Chevrolet trim tag where information is listed. See Fig. 1-36. At each position there is either a word describing the type of data to be listed, or a group of numbers

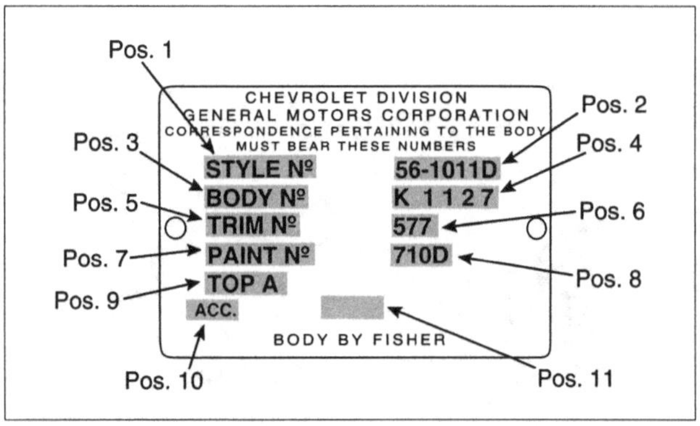

0023045

Fig. 1-36. Example of typical 1955–58 trim tag, showing positions where model and trim information is listed.

or letters—the data itself. I will decode the trim tag information by position. Since there are some changes to tag design over this five year period, I will point out the differences at each position.

Position #1: The words "Style No." spelled out. This spelling stays the same for the 1955 and 1956 model years. Style No. refers to the actual year and body style code immediately following in position #2.

In 1957 and 1958, only the word Style is used in this position. The word No. is eliminated.

Position #2: Model year and model number code. This consists of two sets of numbers separated by a dash or hyphen. The first two letters designate the model year of the car. The second group of numbers designates the style number of the car.

The style number corresponds to the model series and model of the car. This style number is always four digits, sometimes followed by a letter or letters. There is no available documentation to decode the letters at this time. All 1955–57 cars use the style on the trim tag for model identification. Please see the following 1955 model identification breakdown chart to decode these style numbers or refer to **9. Model Identification** for this breakdown on 1956–64 models.

Beginning in 1958, the Fisher Body Company began using the Chevrolet series number as their own Fisher Body number. From 1958–64 the complete model number in its entirety was stamped on the firewall tag. *All* 1958–64 firewall tags are stamped with a V-8 model number. No tags were ever stamped with a 6- cylinder model number. You must refer to the VIN to correctly identify a 6- or 8-cylinder car.

Position #3: The words "Body No." refer to the information in Position #4. The spelling stays the same for the 1955–58 model years.

Position #4: The manufacturing plant and the sequential body number. This position consists of one or two letters followed by a number.

The first letter or letters designate the plant which produced the car. There were 12 separate Fisher Body plants that produced 1955 Chevrolet cars.

The numbers following the plant letter code represents the sequential number that car represented in that manufacturing plant. This number has no correlation to the VIN. All plants started with number 1 and went up sequentially for each body style. In the photo in Fig. 1-27 you can see that the coding in Position #4 reads "K 1127." This decodes as the Kansas City, Missouri, Fisher Body plant and the 1127th car of that particular *1011D* body style (Bel Air 2-Door Sedan) off of that manufacturing line.

1955 Chevrolet/Fisher Body Plant Codes

Letter Code	Plant Location
A or AG	Atlanta, Georgia
CL (Station Wagon, Sedan Delivery)	Cleveland, Ohio
F	Flint, Michigan
J (Also Hardtop Coupe)	Janesville, Wisconsin
K	Kansas City, Missouri
L (Cabriolet, Hardtop Coupe)	Lansing, Michigan
M	Baltimore, Maryland
N	Norwood, Ohio
O	Oakland, California
S (Also Hardtop Coupe, Station Wagon)	St. Louis, Missouri
T	Tarrytown, New York
VN	Van Nuys, California

1956 Chevrolet/Fisher Body Plant Codes

Letter Code	Plant Location
A or AG	Atlanta, Georgia
CL (Station Wagon, Sedan Delivery)	Cleveland, Ohio
F	Flint, Michigan
J (Also Station Wagon)	Janesville, Wisconsin
K	Kansas City, Missouri
L (Cabriolet, Hardtop Coupe)	Lansing, Michigan
M	Baltimore, Maryland
N	Norwood, Ohio
O	Oakland, California*
S (Also Station Wagon)	St. Louis, Missouri
T	Tarrytown, New York
VN	Van Nuys, California
*All plants made Hardtop Coupes. All plants except Oakland made four-door Hardtop Sedans.	

1957–58 Chevrolet/Fisher Body Plant Codes

Letter Code	Plant Location
AG	Atlanta, Georgia
CL (Station Wagon, Sedan Delivery)	Cleveland, Ohio

1957–58 Chevrolet/Fisher Body Plant Codes (cont'd)

Letter Code	Plant Location
F	Flint, Michigan
J	Janesville, Wisconsin
K	Kansas City, Missouri
L (Cabriolet, Hardtop Coupe)	Lansing, Michigan
M	Baltimore, Maryland
N	Norwood, Ohio
O	Oakland, California*
S	St. Louis, Missouri
T	Tarrytown, New York
VN	Van Nuys, California
*All plants made Hardtop Coupes. All plants except Oakland made four-door Hardtop Sedans.	

Position #5: The words "Trim No." refer to the interior trim information listed in Position #6. The spelling of Trim No. is the same for the 1955–56 model years.

In the 1957 and 1958 model years the word No. is eliminated. Only the word Trim is used.

Position #6: The interior trim code assigned to this car. The trim codes are specific to the model code of the car so look closely to be sure they match up. Please refer to the Trim Combination Charts at the end of this chapter for a complete listing.

Position #7: The words "Paint No." This refers to the exterior paint codes in Position #8. This spelling remained the same for the 1955–56 model years.

In the 1957 and 1958 model years the word No is dropped. Only the word Paint is used.

Effective approximately March 15, 1958, Chevrolet began using acrylic paint at the Janesville plant. By April 1, 1958 almost all cars at Janesville were painted with acrylic finishes, with the exception of two-door station wagons, Impala convertibles and Sedan Delivery models. With this paint change, the letter "L" prefix was added to the color combination code on the trim tag. Please see the Technical Service Bulletin in Fig. 1-37 for a complete explanation.

Position #8: The exterior paint code of the car. This number will always have three digits, but occasionally a letter suffix will be added. The suffix indicates the paint specification or paint configuration to which the car would be painted: A = Solid Body Color, C = 210 Model, D = Bel Air Model, E = 150 Model. Please see the Trim Combination charts at the end of this chapter for detailed listings.

Position #9: The word "Top," only on 1955–56 Model #2434 convertibles. It is followed by a number or letter that depicts the color of the top. It is usually the letter "A" or "B," or the number "1" or "2." This position is still being researched at this time as to what plants used which coding system.

On 1957–58 models the word "Top" was dropped and the letters "ACC" were substituted in its place.

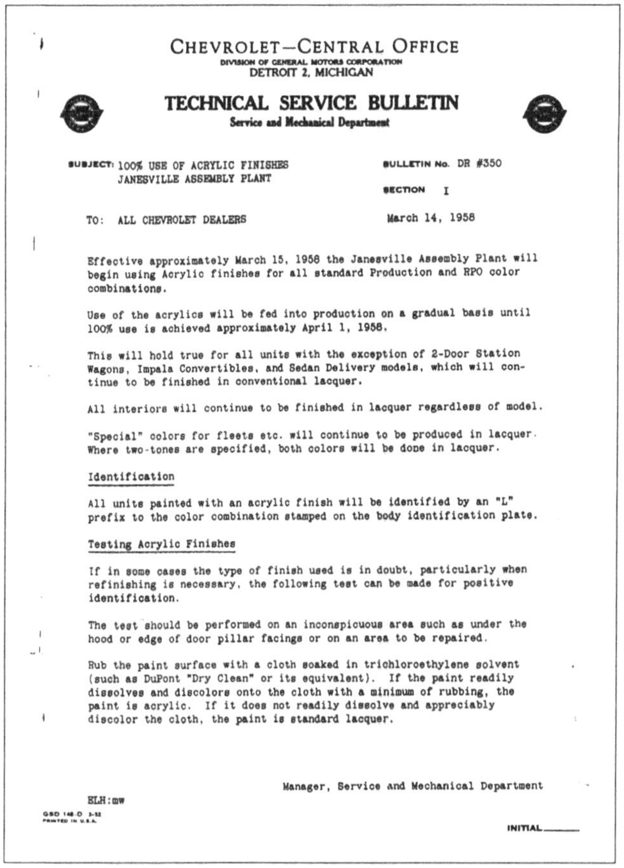

CHEVROLET—CENTRAL OFFICE
DIVISION OF GENERAL MOTORS CORPORATION
DETROIT 2, MICHIGAN

TECHNICAL SERVICE BULLETIN
Service and Mechanical Department

SUBJECT: 100% USE OF ACRYLIC FINISHES
JANESVILLE ASSEMBLY PLANT

BULLETIN No. DR #350

SECTION I

TO: ALL CHEVROLET DEALERS

March 14, 1958

Effective approximately March 15, 1958 the Janesville Assembly Plant will begin using Acrylic finishes for all standard Production and RPO color combinations.

Use of the acrylics will be fed into production on a gradual basis until 100% use is achieved approximately April 1, 1958.

This will hold true for all units with the exception of 2-Door Station Wagons, Impala Convertibles, and Sedan Delivery models, which will continue to be finished in conventional lacquer.

All interiors will continue to be finished in lacquer regardless of model.

"Special" colors for fleets etc. will continue to be produced in lacquer. Where two-tones are specified, both colors will be done in lacquer.

Identification

All units painted with an acrylic finish will be identified by an "L" prefix to the color combination stamped on the body identification plate.

Testing Acrylic Finishes

If in some cases the type of finish used is in doubt, particularly when refinishing is necessary, the following test can be made for positive identification.

The test should be performed on an inconspicuous area such as under the hood or edge of door pillar facings or on an area to be repaired.

Rub the paint surface with a cloth soaked in trichloroethylene solvent (such as DuPont "Dry Clean" or its equivalent). If the paint readily dissolves and discolors onto the cloth with a minimum of rubbing, the paint is acrylic. If it does not readily dissolve and appreciably discolor the cloth, the paint is standard lacquer.

Manager, Service and Mechanical Department

ELH:mw

GSD 148-D 3-52
PRINTED IN U.S.A.

INITIAL______

0023046

Fig. 1-37. TSB details changeover to acrylic finishes at Janesville Assembly Plant.

Position #10: The letters "ACC" represent the word accessory and refer to the accessories that are listed in position #11. The spelling remained unchanged throughout the 1955 and 1956 model years. The position of the ACC changed for the 1957–58 model years.

Position #11: The accessory code options. These codes were added to the trim tag while the car was in the Fisher Body section of the final assembly plant, prior to moving on to the Chevrolet final drive line assembly section. The codes defined the specific changes that were to be made to the body by the Fisher Body assembly line workers in order for it to accept particular Chevrolet drive line options. Not all options were coded on the trim tag and these codes varied from plant to plant and model to model. For more information on accessory codes, see page 2 of this chapter.

8.2 1959 Trim Tags

There were three basic styles of firewall trim tags from 1959 through the 1964 model year. All 1959 cars used what is considered the "second design" trim tag. This trim tag was a completely new design as compared to the

0022035

0022035/0022036

Fig. 1-38. Two 1960 Impala "second design" trim tags.

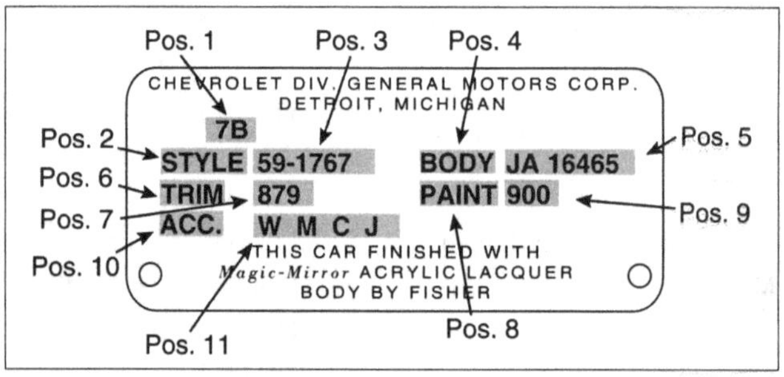

0023900

Fig. 1-39. Example of typical 1959 trim tag, showing positions where model and trim information is listed.

1955–58 first design trim tag. This tag was 1-3/4" high x 4" long. The corners of this tag were rounded and there was now different General Motors information stamped above and below the model, paint and trim information. Also, notice that the assembly plant codes have changed with the new second design trim tag.

This particular tag was used on some Chevrolet cars produced by B-O-P (Buick-Oldsmobile-Pontiac) assembly plants through the 1966 model year.

1959 Trim Tag Location

Model	Year	Location
Passenger Cars	1959	On the driver's side on the upper portion of the cowl.

Trim Tag Position Designations

There are eleven basic positions on the 1959 Chevrolet trim tag. At each position there is a word describing the type of data to be listed. This is usually followed by a group of numbers that designate the data. Since there are significant changes to the design of the tag over this six year period, we will point out the specific differences at that time. We will decode the trim tag by position number. This will enable us to discuss the differences from 1959 through 1964 model years at the position rather than in text form.

Position #1: The body build date. The body build date represents the date of the final body assembly only. Many restorers believe that this date represents the final assembly date of the complete vehicle, but this is incorrect.

This position denotes a month and week code. The month and week code remain the same for all years. The earliest documented build date is 02D, 1960 (February, fourth week). From this information we can conclude that no 1959 or early 1960 cars that were built prior to late February should have a build date code.

1959 Month Codes

01 = January	07 = July
02 = February	08 = August
03 = March	09 = September
04 = April	10 = October
05 = May	11 = November
06 = June	12 = December

1959 Week Codes

A = First Week	D = Fourth Week
B = Second Week	E = Fifth Week
C = Third Week	

Example: 7B = July/Second Week

Position #2: The word "Style" spelled out. This spelling stays the same from 1959 through the 1964 model year, though some late 1964 tags may say "ST." Style refers to the actual year and body style number immediately following in position #3.

Position #3: Model year and model number code. This code consists of two sets of numbers usually separated by a hyphen or blank space. The first two numbers designate the model year of the car. The second group of numbers designate the actual model number of the car. This model number consists of four numbers. A full description of the model number breakdown can be found later in this chapter.

NOTE—
The model number always indicates a *V-8 equipped car.* The firewall trim tags were only stamped with a V-8 designation even if a six-cylinder was installed from the factory. Engine verification must be made by checking the VIN.

Position #4: The word "Body," referring to the information in position #5. The position of this word remained the same from 1959 until the changeover to the 1964 third design trim tag.

Position #5: The assembly plant letter code and the sequential production number of the body.

There were two Fisher Body plants producing car bodies with no final assembly plant. These plants were Euclid, Ohio, and Lansing, Michigan. The Euclid plant produced and supplied car bodies to the Atlanta, Tarrytown, Baltimore and Flint Final Assembly Plants. If a car body was produced by the Euclid or Lansing Assembly plant, it will undoubtedly have a different VIN final assembly plant code letter. Please see earlier for a complete breakdown of VIN applications.

The body sequence number is the number of that body that was produced in that plant of a particular body style. All car bodies came down the final assembly line a random style order. This order would be adjusted depending upon the actual sale demand of a particular style.

1959 Chevrolet/Fisher Body Plant Codes*

Letter Code	Plant Location
AT	Atlanta, Georgia
BA	Baltimore, Maryland
EP (Station Wagon, Sedan Delivery)	Cleveland, Ohio
FC	Flint, Michigan
JA	Janesville, Wisconsin
KC	Kansas City, Missouri
LA (Cabriolet, Hardtop Coupe)	Lansing, Michigan
NW	Norwood, Ohio
OA	Oakland, California
SL	St. Louis, Missouri
TA	Tarrytown, New York
VN	Van Nuys, California
*Some Chevrolet documentation states that the Framingham Assembly Plant began production in 1959. This is yet to be documented.	

Position #6: The word "Trim" refers to the information in position #7. The spelling and position remain the same through the 1964 model year, though some late 1964 tags may say "TR."

Position #7: The interior trim code. The trim codes can vary greatly from year to year and are sometimes specific to a particular model. Please see the end of this chapter for a complete breakdown of all interior trim codes.

All trim codes consist of a three-digit number that is specific to each car model. Sometimes there is a single number or letter following the three-digit trim code which designated a specific interior color to the assembly line worker in that particular plant. A few plants included an additional number after the three-digit code on convertibles to designate a top color.

Position #8: The word "Paint" refers to the exterior paint codes in position #9. As discussed earlier, the position of the word "Paint" remained in this position until the third design trim tag was released.

Position #9: The exterior paint code of the car. This code will always consist of three numbers, but is sometimes followed by a letter, which designates a specific color combination. These letters were used in many plants in the 1958 through 1961 model years. There were three plants, however, that did not use this system. The meaning of the letters changed from one plant to another. The letter "A" represents a single color, while the letters "B" through "F" represent two-tone color combinations on a specific body style. The following is a breakdown of the 1958/59 letter code suffixes.

- A: Single Color
- B: Two Tone/1100–1200 Series
- C: Two Tone/1500–1600 Series
- D: Two Tone/1700–1800 Series (Except 1747/1847/1867)
- E: Two Tone/Convertible - 1747/1847/1867, Special 1847 Sport Coupe

There were also many cars shipped from the Euclid Assembly Plant that had an extra letter "A" after the paint code. These cars were shipped to the Atlanta Final Assembly Plant. All other cars that did not have an "A" were shipped to other final assembly plants. Some Euclid cars that were shipped to the other plants contained the letter code, but this did not hold true for all plants. In 1964, there were double and triple paint codes used on the trim tag. The first letter would indicate the lower body color. The second letter would indicate the upper body color. If a third letter is present, it will designate the wheel color for that particular car.

Position #10: The letters "ACC." represent the word accessory and refer to the accessories that are listed in position #11. The spelling and position remained unchanged throughout the 1959–64 model years until the introduction of the fourth design 1964 trim tag. This trim tag eliminates the ACC and only the accessory codes are listed in position #11.

Position #11: The accessory code options. These codes were added to the trim tag while the car was in the Fisher Body section of the final assembly plant, prior to moving on to the Chevrolet final drive line assembly section. The codes defined the specific changes that were to be made to the body by the Fisher Body assembly line workers in order for it to accept particular

Chevrolet driveline options. Not all options were coded on the trim tag and these codes varied from plant to plant and model to model. For more information on accessory codes, see page 2 of this chapter.

8.3 Corvette Trim Tags

1955–59 Corvettes did not have a trim tag. The only way that you can positively verify the original paint and/or interior is to acquire the original dealer invoice or other original paperwork. Not all dealer invoices show the original paint but most do show the interior code and color. Also, if the car still has the original interior, there may be an assembly line sheet in between the seat springs that would indicate the interior color. On 1955–62 Corvettes there is also the possibility that the paint code was written in white chalk under the spare tire cover. On 1956–57 Corvettes a chalk mark was written on the front crossmember indicating the paint code. Finally, if the car has not been restored some factory paint overspray may still be visible on the floorpan or on the inside of the car behind the interior door panels.

8.4 Canadian Trim Tags

As discussed in section 2.3, there were many 1955–59 cars built at the Oshawa plant in Canada. Just as the VIN style differed on these cars, so did the trim tag information. In general, compared to U.S. trim tags Canadian tags were more descriptive and had more pertinent information specific to the car.

Trim Tag Position Designations

There are six basic positions on the Canadian trim tag. At each position there is a word describing the type of data to be listed. This is usually followed by a group of numbers that designate the data. Since there are significant changes to the design of the tag over this six

0023814

Fig. 1-40. 1955 Canadian trim tag.

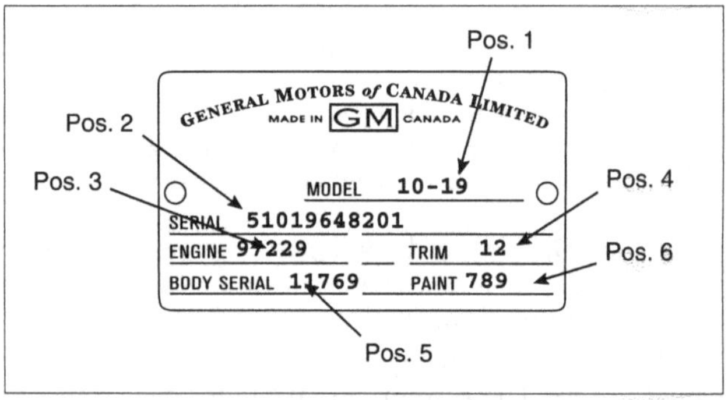

0023815

Fig. 1-41. Example of 1955 Canadian trim tag, showing positions where model and trim information is listed.

year period, we will point out the specific differences at that time. We will decode the trim tag by position number.

Position #1: Usually indicates the Model Number, which on Canadian cars was the same as the U.S. number with a hyphen between the first two and last two digits.

Position #2: The car serial number. Unlike U.S. cars, the VIN was tied to the actual body of the car.

Position #3: The sequential number of the engine, which was also stamped on the engine. In 1955, the sequential number for 235 engines started with number 52501; for 265 engines the number was 2001. If the number 9 preceded the sequential number on 235 or 265 engines, the application used an automatic transmission for that body.

Position #4: The Canadian trim combination. GM of Canada made their own decisions regarding trim and paint combinations. While some descriptions may be the same as U.S. cars, some may not be. The numbering system was also different, even if the trim was the same as used in the U.S.

Position #5: The sequential number of a particular body style (position #1). All Canadian body numbers started at 001 for each model year. For example, the serial number for the first body type for a model #1211 or for #1269 will start with 001.

Position #6: The paint code. While some descriptions may be the same as U.S. cars, some may not be. The numbering system was also different, even if the paint combinations were the same as used in the U.S.

9. MODEL IDENTIFICATION NUMBER

In this section I will explain the use and decoding of the Chevrolet Model Identification numbers. Model identification is just as important to the hobbyist as the Vehicle Identification Number (VIN) because almost all specific information about a car depends on the model number. The options that are allowed on certain cars relate back to the model, along with interior trim and paint combinations.

Decoding the Model Identification number can be a little tricky, primarily because of VIN changes across the range of years and because its location changes.

9.1 1955–57 Model Identification

The 1955–57 model identification coding is the same for all three years of production. However, not all models were available each of the three years. You must look under the year of usage to be sure of the model number.

The model number consists of four digits. The first two digits represent the model series. For example in the model number "1502," the digits 15 represent the 150 model series. The digits 02 always represent a two-door sedan in all of the model series. The model is designated in the VIN plate on the driver side door jam and in the firewall trim tag. We will concentrate on the firewall trim tag here to explain the model usage.

From 1955 through 1957 the model number was stamped only in the VIN. It was *not* stamped on the firewall tag. A "Style" number was used on the trim tag, and this was sometimes called the Fisher Body Number. (Fisher Body Company was actually a separate company owned by General Motors that prepared the car bodies, while Chevrolet prepared the drivetrain chassis.) During 1955–57 Fisher Body Company assigned body "style" numbers that represented the Chevrolet model numbers, but this is not the same as the Model number. You may cross-reference this style number to the interior trim and exterior paint combinations in this chapter as well. All coding should match up to each other and cross-reference with the style number that is represented on the firewall tag. Note that many of the Fisher Body style numbers have a letter or letters following the style number. The significance of these letters is now being researched.

9.2 1958–59 Model Identification

In 1958, the Fisher Body Company began using the Chevrolet series number as their own Fisher Body number. This greatly simplifies the decoding process. As in 1955–57, the 1958–59 model designations consisted of a four-digit number. The first two digits designated the model series. This model series number indicated whether the car was originally equipped with a 6- or 8-cylinder engine. The second set of numbers represented the type of model inside the car series.

For example, in 1958, in the model number "1121," 11 represents the 1100 series (6-cylinder only), while 21 represents a two-door utility sedan. Note that 21 also represents a two-door utility sedan in the 1200 series (V-8 only). The third and fourth digit descriptions do not change regardless of the series usage.

The result of this is that you do not have a style number that then refers to an actual Chevrolet model number. This type of model identification continued through the 1964 model year. As in 1955–57 the model designation can be cross checked with the interior trim and paint combination chart numbers, which usually refer to model number availability.

From 1958–64 the complete model number in its entirety was stamped on the firewall trim tag. All firewall tags are stamped with a V-8 model number. This procedure continued until 1973, when all firewall tag formats changed and engine designations were shown in the car's VIN only.

1955 Model Designations

Model	Series	Model#	Description	Style #
Passenger	150	1502	2-Door Sedan	1211
		1503	4-Door Sedan	1219
		1508	2-Door Sedan Delivery	1271
		1512	2-Door Utility Sedan	1211B
		1529	2-Door Station Wagon Handyman	1263F
	210	2102	2-Door Sedan	1011
		2103	4-Door Sedan	1019
		2109	4-Door Station Wagon Townsman	1062F
		2124	2-Door Club Coupe Delray	1011A
		2129	2-Door Station Wagon Handyman	1063F
		2154	2-Door Hardtop Coupe	1037

continued on next page

1955 Model Designations (cont'd)

Model	Series	Model#	Description	Style #
Passenger (cont'd)	Bel Air	2402	2-Door Sedan	1011D
		2403	4-Door Sedan	1019D
		2409	4-Door Station Wagon Beauville	1062DF
		2429	2-Door Station Wagon Nomad	1064DF
		2434	2-Door Convertible	1067D/DTX ONLY
		2454	2-Door Hardtop Sport Coupe	1037D
Corvette		2934	2-Door Convertible	Corvette

1956 Model Designations

Model	Series	Model#	Description	Style #
Passenger	150	1502	2-Door Sedan	1211
		1503	4-Door Sedan	1219
		1508	2-Door Sedan Delivery	1271
		1512	2-Door Utility Sedan	1211B
		1529	2-Door Station Wagon Handyman	1263F
	210	2102	2-Door Sedan	1011
		2103	4-Door Sedan	1019
		2109	4-Door Station Wagon Townsman	1062F
		2113	4-Door Hardtop Sport Sedan	1039
		2119	4-Door Station Wagon Beauville	1062FC
		2124	2-Door Club Coupe Delray	1011A
		2129	2-Door Station Wagon Handyman	1063F
		2154	2-Door Hardtop Coupe	1037
	Bel Air	2402	2-Door Sedan	1011D
		2403	4-Door Sedan	1019D
		2413	4-Door Hardtop Sport Sedan	1039D
		2419	4-Door Station Wagon Beauville	1062DFC
		2429	2-Door Station Wagon Nomad	1064DF
		2434	2-Door Convertible	1067DTX only
		2454	2-Door Hardtop Sport Coupe	1037D
Corvette		2934	2-Door Convertible	Corvette

1957 Model Designations

Model	Series	Model#	Description	Style #
Passenger	150	1502	2-Door Sedan	1211
		1503	4-Door Sedan	1219
		1508	2-Door Sedan Delivery	1271
		1512	2-Door Utility Sedan	1211B
		1529	2-Door Station Wagon Handyman	1263F
	210	2102	2-Door Sedan	1011
		2103	4-Door Sedan	1019
		2109	4-Door Station Wagon Townsman	1062F
		2113	4-Door Hardtop Sport Sedan	1039
		2119	4-Door Station Wagon Beauville	1062FC
		2124	2-Door Club Coupe Delray	1011A
		2129	2-Door Station Wagon Handyman	1063F
		2154	2-Door Hardtop Coupe	1037

1957 Model Designations (cont'd)

Model	Series	Model#	Description	Style #
Passenger (cont'd)	Bel Air	2402	2-Door Sedan	1011D
		2403	4-Door Sedan	1019D
		2409	4-Door Station Wagon Beauville	1062DF
		2413	4-Door Hardtop Sport Sedan	1039D
		2429	2-Door Station Wagon Nomad	1064DF
		2434	2-Door Convertible	1067DTX Only
		2454	2-Door Hardtop Sport Coupe	1037D
Corvette		2934	2-Door Convertible	Corvette

1958 Model Designations

Model	Series	Model#	Description	Style
Passenger	1100 (6-cyl.)(exc. SDL)	1121	2-Door Utility Sedan	Delray
		1141	2-Door Sedan	Delray
		1149	4-Door Sedan	Delray
		1191	2-Door Station Wagon, 6 Pass.	Yeoman
		1193	4-Door Station Wagon, 6 Pass.	Yeoman
	1200 (8-cyl.)(exc. SDL)	1221	2-Door Utility Sedan	Delray
		1241	2-Door Sedan	Delray
		1249	4 Door Sedan	Delray
		1291	2-Door Station Wagon, 6 Pass.	Yeoman
		1293	4-Door Station Wagon, 6 Pass.	Yeoman
	1500 (6 cyl.)	1541	2-Door Sedan	Biscayne
		1549	4-Door Sedan	Biscayne
		1593	4-Door Station Wagon, 6 Pass.	Brookwood
		1594	4-Door Station Wagon, 9 Pass.	Brookwood
	1600 (8 cyl.)	1641	2-Door Sedan	Biscayne
		1649	4-Door Sedan	Biscayne
		1693	4-Door Station Wagon, 6 Pass.	Brookwood
		1694	4-Door Station Wagon, 9 Pass.	Brookwood
	1700 (6 cyl.)	1731	2-Door Hardtop Sport Coupe	Bel Air
		1739	4-Door Hardtop Sport Sedan	Bel Air
		1741	2-Door Sedan	Bel Air
		1747	2-Door Hardtop Sport Coupe	Impala
		1749	4-Door Sedan	Bel Air
		1767	2-Door Convertible	Impala
		1793	4-Door Station Wagon, 6 Pass.	Nomad
	1800 (8 cyl.)	1831	2-Door Hardtop Sport Coupe	Bel Air
		1839	4-Door Hardtop Sport Sedan	Bel Air
		1841	2-Door Sedan	Bel Air
		1847	2-Door Hardtop Sport Coupe	Impala
		1849	4-Door Sedan	Bel Air
		1867	2-Door Convertible	Impala
		1893	4-Door Wagon, 6 Pass.	Nomad
	1100 (6 cyl.)	1171	2-Door Sedan Delivery	Delray
	1200 (8 cyl.)	1271	2-Door Sedan Delivery	Delray
Corvette	800 (8-cyl.)	867	2-Door Convertible	Corvette

1959 Model Designations

Model	Series	Model#	Description	Style
Passenger	1100 (6-cyl.)(exc. SDL, PDL)	1111	2-Door Sedan	Biscayne
		1115	2-Door Station Wagon, 6 Pass.	Brookwood
		1119	4-Door Sedan	Biscayne
		1121	2-Door Utility Sedan	Biscayne
		1135	4-Door Station Wagon, 6 Pass.	Brookwood
	1200 (8 cyl.)	1211	2-Door Sedan	Biscayne
		1215	2-Door Station Wagon, 6 Pass.	Brookwood
		1219	4-Door Sedan	Biscayne
		1221	2-Door Utility Sedan	Biscayne
		1235	4-Door Station Wagon, 6 Pass.	Brookwood
	1500 (6 cyl.)	1511	2 Door Sedan	Bel Air
		1519	4-Door Sedan	Bel Air
		1535	4-Door Station Wagon, 6 Pass.	Parkwood
		1539	4-Door Hardtop Sport Sedan	Bel Air
		1545	4-Door Station Wagon, 9 Pass.	Kingswood
	1600 (8 cyl.)	1611	2-Door Sedan	Bel Air
		1619	4-Door Sedan	Bel Air
		1635	4-Door Station Wagon, 6 Pass.	Parkwood
		1639	4-Door Hardtop Sport Sedan	Bel Air
		1645	4-Door Station Wagon, 9 Pass.	Kingswood
	1700 (6 cyl.)	1719	4-Door Sedan	Impala
		1735	4-Door Station Wagon, 6 Pass.	Nomad
		1737	2-Door Hardtop Sport Coupe	Impala
		1739	4-Door Hardtop Sport Sedan	Impala
		1767	2-Door Convertible	Impala
	1800 (8 cyl.)	1819	4-Door Sedan	Impala
		1835	4-Door Station Wagon, 6 Pass.	Nomad
		1837	2-Door Hardtop Sport Coupe	Impala
		1839	4-Door Hardtop Sport Sedan	Impala
		1867	2-Door Convertible	Impala
	1100 (6-cyl.)	1170	2-Door Sedan Delivery	Biscayne
		1180	2-Door Sedan Pick-Up	El Camino
	1200 (8-cyl.)	1270	2-Door Sedan Delivery	Biscayne
		1280	2-Door Sedan Pick-Up	El Camino
Corvette	Series 800 (8-cyl.)	867	2-Door Convertible	Corvette

10. INTERIOR/EXTERIOR TRIM CHARTS

The following charts are reproduced from the original Chevrolet Engineering Specifications for each model year. In some cases, the interior and/or exterior options could have changed during the production year.

1955 Trim Combinations

EXTERIOR-INTERIOR COLOR COMBINATIONS ONE-COLOR EXTERIORS

Upper Body	Lower Body, Sheet Metal, Wheels	Wheel Stripe (No Stripe on Series 2400)	Trim Combinations	Instrument Panel Center, Radio Cover Plate	Upper and Lower Instrument Panel, Steering Wheel, Steering Column, Steering Wheel Hub, Garnish Moldings, Dir. Signal Housing, Ash Tray Cover Panel, Door Locking Knob, Heater Cover Panel	Series 1500: 1502 1503 1512	Series 1500: 1529	Series 1500: 1508	Series 2100: 2102 2103	Series 2100: 2124	Series 2100: 2109 2129	Series 2400: 2402 2403	Series 2400: 2434	Series 2400: 2454	Series 2400: 2409	Series 2400: 2434 Top Color	Series 2400: Rear Fender Molding Insert Series 2400
Onyx Black	Onyx Black	Argent	Gray & Black	India Ivory	Shadow Gray ó	●											
			Beige & Brown	Shoreline Beige	Autumn Bronze fl			●									
			Blue	Skyline Blue $	Glacier Blue				●			●					Winter White
			Beige & Red	Bright Metal	Gypsy Red								●			White	Winter White
			Red	Bright Metal	Gypsy Red									●			Winter White
			Black & Ivory	India Ivory	Onyx Black					●							
Sea-Mist Green	Sea-Mist Green	Black	Gray & Black	India Ivory	Shadow Gray ó	●											
			Green	Sea-Mist Green $	Neptune Green fi		●		●			●					Winter White
			Beige & Brown	Shoreline Beige	Autumn Bronze fl			●									
			Green & Beige	Shoreline Beige	Neptune Green					●							
Neptune Green *	Neptune Green	Argent	Gray & Black	India Ivory	Shadow Gray ó	●											
			Green	Sea-Mist Green $	Neptune Green fi		●		●		●	●		●			Winter White
			Beige & Brown	Shoreline Beige	Autumn Bronze fl			●									
			Green & Beige	Shoreline Beige	Neptune Green					●							
			Beige	Bright Metal	Neptune Green										●		Winter White
Skyline Blue *	Skyline Blue	Black	Gray & Black	India Ivory	Shadow Gray ó	●											
			Beige & Brown	Shoreline Beige	Autumn Bronze fl			●									
			Blue	Skyline Blue $	Glacier Blue				●			●					Winter White
			Blue & Beige	Shoreline Beige	Glacier Blue					●							
Glacier Blue	Glacier Blue	Argent	Gray & Black	India Ivory	Shadow Gray ó	●											
			Beige & Brown	Shoreline Beige	Autumn Bronze fl			●									
			Blue	Skyline Blue $	Glacier Blue				●			●		●			Winter White
			Blue & Beige	Shoreline Beige $	Glacier Blue					●					●		Winter White
			Blue	Shoreline Beige	Glacier Blue						●						
Copper Maroon *	Copper Maroon	Argent	Gray & Black	India Ivory	Shadow Gray ó	●											
			Brown	Shoreline Beige	Copper Maroon				●								
			Beige & Brown	Bright Metal	Copper Maroon							●					Winter White
Shoreline Beige	Shoreline Beige	Black	Gray & Black	India Ivory	Shadow Gray ó	●											
			Brown	Shoreline Beige	Autumn Bronze				●		●						
			Beige & Brown	Bright Metal	Autumn Bronze							●					Winter White
			Red	Bright Metal	Gypsy Red									●			Winter White
			Blue & Beige	Bright Metal	Glacier Blue										●		Winter White
Autumn Bronze	Autumn Bronze	Argent	Gray & Black	India Ivory	Shadow Gray ó	●											
			Brown	Shoreline Beige	Autumn Bronze fl		●		●		●						
India Ivory	India Ivory	Black	Gray & Black	India Ivory	Shadow Gray ó	●											
			Beige & Brown	Shoreline Beige	Autumn Bronze fl			●									
			Blue	Skyline Blue $	Glacier Blue				●			●					Winter White
			Black & Ivory	India Ivory	Onyx Black					●							
Shadow Gray *	Shadow Gray	Argent	Gray & Black	India Ivory	Shadow Gray ó	●											
			Beige & Brown	Shoreline Beige	Autumn Bronze fl			●									
			Blue	Skyline Blue $	Glacier Blue				●			●					Winter White
Gypsy Red *	Gypsy Red	Argent	Beige & Red	Bright Metal	Gypsy Red								●			Beige	Winter White
			Beige & Brown	Shoreline Beige	Autumn Bronze fl			●									
Regal Turquoise	Regal Turquoise		Beige	Bright Metal	Regal Turquoise										●		Winter White
Coral	Coral		Coral & Gray	Bright Metal	Coral								●			White	Winter White
Harvest Gold	Harvest Gold		Green	Bright Metal	Neptune Green									●			Winter White

* - Available on special order on 1508. ó - Black steering wheel and hub. $ - Bright metal on 2400.
fl - Shoreline Beige steering wheel rim and spokes. fi - Sea-Mist Green steering wheel rim and spokes.

0023901

CORVETTE

EXTERIOR-INTERIOR COLORS

EXTERIOR		TOP COLOR	WHEELS	INTERIOR
Polo White	567	White	Red	Red
Harvest Gold**	632	Dark Green	Yellow	Yellow
Gypsy Red**	596	Beige	Red	Light Beige
Corvette Copper**	573	White	Bronze	Dark Beige
Pennant Blue*	570	Beige	Red	Dark Beige

*Pennant blue exterior color discontinued April 1, 1955
**New exterior colors introduced during April, 1955

INTERIOR COLORS

ITEM	Red	Yellow	Light Beige	Dark Beige
Upper Inst. Panel	Red	Green	Red	Bronze
Steering Column Steering Whl Hub & Spokes Dir. Sig. Housing	Red	Green	Beige	White
Lower Inst. Panel Door Trim Molding	White	Yellow	Beige	White
Steering Wheel Rim	White	Yellow	Red	Bronze
Seats Door Panels Cowl Side Kick Panels	Red	Yellow	Light Beige	Dark Beige

10-29-54. Revised: 6-10-55, • - Data revised.

0023051

1955 Trim Combinations (continued)

EXTERIOR-INTERIOR COLOR COMBINATIONS TWO-COLOR EXTERIORS

Upper Body	Lower Body, Sheet Metal, Wheels	Wheel Stripe (No Stripe on Series 2400)	Trim Combinations	Instrument Panel Center, Radio Cover Plate	Upper and Lower Instrument Panel, Steering Wheel, Steering Column, Steering Wheel Hub, Garnish Moldings, Dir. Signal Housing, Ash Tray Cover Panel, Door Locking Knob, Heater Cover Panel	Series 1500: 1502 1503 1512	Series 1500: 1508	Series 1500: 1529	Series 2100: 2102 2103	Series 2100: 2124	Series 2100: 2109 2129	Series 2400: 2402 2403	Series 2400: 2454 •	Series 2400: 2434	Series 2400: 2409	Series 2400: 2434 Top Color	Series 2400: Rear Fender Molding Insert Series 2400
Sea-Mist Green	Neptune Green	Argent	Gray & Black	India Ivory	Shadow Gray ó	●											
			Green	Sea-Mist Green $	Neptune Green ñ			●	●		●	●					Winter White
Skyline Blue	Glacier Blue	Argent	Gray & Black	India Ivory	Shadow Gray ó	●											
			Blue	Skyline Blue $	Glacier Blue				●			●					Winter White
Neptune Green	Shoreline Beige		Green	Bright Metal	Neptune Green								●				Winter White
India Ivory	Skyline Blue	Black	Gray & Black	India Ivory	Shadow Gray ó	●											
			Blue	Skyline Blue $	Glacier Blue				●			●	●				Winter White
			Beige & Blue	Shoreline Beige	Glacier Glue					●							
India Ivory	Shadow Gray	Argent	Gray & Black	India Ivory	Shadow Gray ó	●											
			Blue	Skyline Blue $	Glacier Blue				●			●					Winter White
Autumn Bronze	Shoreline Beige	Black	Brown	Shoreline Beige	Autumn Bronze						●						
India Ivory	Sea-Mist Green	Black	Green	Sea-Mist Green	Neptune Green				●								
			Beige & Green	Shoreline Beige	Neptune Green					●							
Shoreline Beige	Autumn Bronze	Argent	Brown	Shoreline Beige	Autumn Bronze			●	●								
			Beige & Brown	Bright Metal	Autumn Bronze ñ							●		●		Beige	Winter White
			Beige	Bright Metal	Autumn Bronze										●		Winter White
Glacier Blue	Shoreline Beige	Black	Blue	Skyline Blue	Glacier Blue				●								
			Beige & Blue	Shoreline Beige	Glacier Blue					●							
India Ivory	Onyx Black	Argent	Ivory & Black	India Ivory	Onyx Black					●							
India Ivory	Gypsy Red	Argent	Ivory & Black	India Ivory	Onyx Black					●							
Glacier Blue	Skyline Blue	Black	Blue	Shoreline Beige $	Glacier Blue						●			●		Blue	Winter White
India Ivory	Regal Turquoise		Ivory & Turquoise	Bright Metal	Regal Turquoise							●		●		White	Winter White
			Turquoise	Bright Metal	Regal Turquoise								●				Winter White
Shoreline Beige	Neptune Green	Argent	Gray & Black	India Ivory	Shadow Gray ó	●											
			Green	Sea-Mist Green $	Neptune Green				●			●	●				Winter White
Shoreline Beige	Glacier Blue	Argent	Blue	Shoreline Beige $	Glacier Blue						●		●				Winter White
			Blue & Beige	Bright Metal	Glacier Blue										●		Winter White
Shoreline Beige	Gypsy Red		Red	Bright Metal	Gypsy Red								●				Winter White
			Beige & Red	Bright Metal	Gypsy Red									●		Beige	Winter White
			Beige	Bright Metal	Gypsy Red										●		Winter White
Onyx Black	India Ivory	Black	Ivory & Black	India Ivory	Onyx Black					●							
Shadow Gray	Coral		Coral & Gray	Bright Metal	Coral							●	●				Winter White
Neptune Green	Sea-Mist Green		Green	Bright Metal	Neptune Green									●		Green	Winter White
			Beige	Bright Metal	Neptune Green										●		Winter White
India Ivory	Coral		Coral & Gray	Bright Metal	Coral									●		White	Winter White
India Ivory	Harvest Gold	Black	Beige & Green	Shoreline Beige	Neptune Green					●							
			Green	Bright Metal	Neptune Green							●	●	●		White	Winter White

ó - Black steering wheel hub.
$ - Bright metal on 2400.
ñ - Shoreline Beige steering wheel rim and spokes.
• - Both styles of two-tone exteriors are available in the same colors and interior trim.

0023902

1955 EXTERIOR-INTERIOR COLOR COMBINATIONS ONE COLOR EXTERIORS

SERIES 1500

Body and Wheel Color	Paint Comb. No.	1502 1503 1512: Trim	Trim Comb. No.	Instrument Panel Center, Radio cover plate	Inst. Panel upper and lower, Steering Wheel, Column and Hub, Garnish Mouldings, Dir. Sig. Hsg., Ash Tray, Cover Panel Locking Knobs, Heater Cover Panel⊕
Onyx Black•	585	Gray and Black	500	India Ivory	Shadow Gray
Sea Mist Green*	586	Gray and Black	500	India Ivory	Shadow Gray
Neptune Green•	587	Gray and Black	500	India Ivory	Shadow Gray
Skyline Blue*	588	Gray and Black	500	India Ivory	Shadow Gray
Cashmere Blue•	683	Gray and Black	500	India Ivory	Shadow Gray
Glacier Blue•	589	Gray and Black	500	India Ivory	Shadow Gray
Copper Maroon•	590	Gray and Black	500	India Ivory	Shadow Gray
Shoreline Beige*	591	Gray and Black	500	India Ivory	Shadow Gray
Autumn Bronze•	592	Gray and Black	500	India Ivory	Shadow Gray
India Ivory*	593	Gray and Black	500	India Ivory	Shadow Gray
Shadow Gray•	594	Gray and Black	500	India Ivory	Shadow Gray

•Wheel stripes are Argent Silver. *Wheel stripes are Onyx Black.
⊕Black steering wheel and hub.

Body and Wheel Color	Paint comb. No.	1508: Trim	Trim comb. No.	Instrument Panel Center, Radio Cover Plate	Inst. Panel upr. & lwr., Strg. Wheel, Column, Hub, Garnish, Moulding, Dir. Sig. Hsg., Ashtray Cover Panel, Locking Knobs, Heater Cover Panel	1529: Trim	Trim comb. No.	Instrument Panel Center, Radio Cover Plate	Inst. Panel upr. & lwr., Strg. Wheel, Column & Hub, Garnish Mouldings, Dir. Sig. Hsg., Ashtray Cover Panel, Locking Knobs, Heater Cover Panel
Onyx Black•	585	Beige & Brown	501	Shoreline Beige	Autumn Bronze† Navajo Tan▲				
Sea Mist Green*	586	Beige & Brown	501	Shoreline Beige	Autumn Bronze† Navajo Tan▲	Green	524	Sea Mist Green	Neptune Green♯
Neptune Green•	587	Beige & Brown	501	Shoreline Beige	Autumn Bronze† Navajo Tan▲	Green	524	Sea Mist Green	Neptune Green♯
Skyline Blue*	588	Beige & Brown	501	Shoreline Beige	Autumn Bronze†				
Cashmere Blue•	683	Beige & Brown	501	Shoreline Beige	Navajo Tan▲				
Glacier Blue•	589	Beige & Brown	501	Shoreline Beige	Autumn Bronze† Navajo Tan▲				
Copper Maroon•	590	Beige & Brown	501	Shoreline Beige	Autumn Bronze†				
Autumn Bronze•	592					Brown	502	Shoreline Beige	Autumn Bronze†
India Ivory*	593	Beige & Brown	501	Shoreline Beige	Autumn Bronze† Navajo Tan▲				
Shadow Gray•	594	Beige & Brown	501	Shoreline Beige	Autumn Bronze† Navajo Tan▲				
Gypsy Red•	596	Beige & Brown	501	Shoreline Beige	Autumn Bronze† Navajo Tan▲				

•Wheel stripes are Argent Silver. *Wheel stripes are Onyx Black. ▲Spring Color.
†Shoreline Beige steering wheel rim and spokes. ♯May have Sea Mist Green Steering wheel rim and spokes.

1955 ONE COLOR EXTERIORS (Cont.)

SERIES 2100

Body and Wheel Color	Paint Comb. No.	2102 2103 2154: Trim	Trim Comb. No.	Instrument Panel—Center, Radio Cover Plate	Inst. Panel—Upr. & Lwr., Steering Wheel, Column and Hub, Garnish Mouldings, Dir. Signal Housing, Ash Tray Cover Panel, Door Locking Knobs, Heater Cover Panel	2124: Trim	Trim Comb. No.	Instrument Panel—Center, Radio Cover Plate	Inst. Panel—Upr. & Lwr., Steering Wheel, Column and Hub, Garnish Mouldings, Dir. Signal Housing, Ash Tray Cover Panel, Door Locking Knobs, Heater Cover Panel
Onyx Black•	585	Blue	503	India Ivory	Glacier Blue	Black & Ivory	508	India Ivory	Onyx Black
Sea Mist Green*	586	Green	504	Sea Mist Green	Neptune Green♯	Green & Beige	507	Shoreline Beige	Neptune Green
Neptune Green•	587	Green	504	Sea Mist Green	Neptune Green♯	Green & Beige	507	Shoreline Beige	Neptune Green
Skyline Blue*	588	Blue	503	Skyline Blue	Glacier Blue	Blue & Beige	506	Shoreline Beige	Glacier Blue
Cashmere Blue•	683	Blue	503	India Ivory	Glacier Blue	Blue & Beige	506	India Ivory	Glacier Blue
Glacier Blue•	589	Blue	503	Skyline Blue India Ivory▲	Glacier Blue	Blue & Beige	506	Shoreline Beige India Ivory▲	Glacier Blue
Copper Maroon•	590	Brown	505	Shoreline Beige	Copper Maroon				
Shoreline Beige*	591	Brown	505	Shoreline Beige	Autumn Bronze Navajo Tan▲				
Autumn Bronze•	592	Brown	505	Shoreline Beige	Autumn Bronze♯				
India Ivory*	593	Blue	503	Skyline Blue India Ivory▲	Glacier Blue	Black & Ivory	508	India Ivory	Onyx Black
Shadow Gray•	594	Blue	503	Skyline Blue India Ivory▲	Glacier Blue				

•Wheel stripes are Argent Silver. *Wheel stripes are Onyx Black.
♯May have Sea Mist Green steering wheel rim and spokes. ▲Spring color.

Body and Wheel Color	Paint Comb. No.	2109 2129: Trim	Trim Comb. No.	Instrument Panel center, Radio Cover Plate	Inst. Panel-upr. and lwr., Steering Wheel, Column Hub, Garnish mouldings, Dir. Signal Housing, Ash Tray Cover Panel, Door Locking Knobs, Heater Cover Panel
Neptune Green•	587	Green	515	Sea Mist Green	Neptune Green♯
Glacier Blue•	589	Blue	514	Shoreline Beige, India Ivory▲	Glacier Blue
Shoreline Beige*	591	Brown	516	Shoreline Beige	Autumn Bronze, Navajo Tan▲
Autumn Bronze•	592	Brown	516	Shoreline Beige	Autumn Bronze†

•Wheel stripes are Argent Silver. *Wheel stripes are Onyx Black. ♯May have Sea Mist Green steering wheel rim and spokes.
▲Spring Color. †Shoreline Beige steering wheel rim and spokes.

0023903

1955 Trim Combinations (continued)

1955 ONE COLOR EXTERIORS (Cont.)
SERIES 2400

Body* and Wheel Color	Paint Comb. No.	2402 2403 Trim	Trim Comb. No.	Inst. Panel—Center, Radio Cover Plate	Inst. Panel—Upr. & Lwr., Steering Wheel, Column and Hub, Garnish Mouldings, Dir. Signal Housing, Ash Tray Cover Panel, Door Locking Knobs, Heater Cover Panel	2454 Trim	Trim Comb. No.	Inst. Panel—Center, Radio Cover Plate	Inst. Panel—Upr. & Lwr., Steering Wheel, Column and Hub, Garnish Mouldings, Dir. Signal Housing, Ash Tray Cover Panel, Door Locking Parts, Heater Cover Panel
Onyx Black	585	Blue	509	Bright Metal	Glacier Blue	Red	521	Bright Metal	Gypsy Red
Sea Mist Green	586	Green	510	Bright Metal	Neptune Green•				
Neptune Green	587	Green	510	Bright Metal	Neptune Green•	Green	520	Bright Metal	Neptune Green•
Skyline Blue	588	Blue	509	Bright Metal	Glacier Blue				
Cashmere Blue	683	Blue	509	Bright Metal	Glacier Blue				
Glacier Blue	589	Blue	509	Bright Metal	Glacier Blue	Blue	519	Bright Metal	Glacier Blue
Copper Maroon	590	Beige&Brn.	511	Bright Metal	Copper Maroon				
Shoreline Beige	591	Beige&Brn.	511	Bright Metal	Autumn Bronze Navajo Tan▲	Red	521	Bright Metal	Gypsy Red
India Ivory	593	Blue	509	Bright Metal	Glacier Blue				
Shadow Gray	594	Blue	509	Bright Metal	Glacier Blue				
Harvest Gold	630					Green	520	Bright Metal	Neptune Green

*Rear Fender Moulding Insert—Winter White.

•May have Sea Mist Green steering wheel rim and spokes.

▲Spring Color.

Body* and Wheel Color	Paint Comb. No.	Trim 2409	Trim Comb. No.	Trim 2434	Trim Comb. No.	Inst. Panel—Center, Radio Cover Plate	Inst. Panel—Upr. & Lwr., Steering Wheel, Column & Hub, Garnish Mouldings, Dir. Signal Housing, Ash Tray Cover Panel, Door Locking Parts, Heater Cover Panel	Top Color 2434
Onyx Black	585			Beige & Red	525	Bright Metal	Gypsy Red	White
Neptune Green	587	Beige	517			Bright Metal	Neptune Green	
Glacier Blue	589	Blue & Beige	518			Bright Metal	Glacier Blue	
Shoreline Beige	591	Blue & Beige	518			Bright Metal	Glacier Blue	
Gypsy Red	596			Beige & Red	525	Bright Metal	Gypsy Red	Beige
Regal Turquoise	598	Beige	517			Bright Metal	Regal Turquoise	
Coral	626			Coral & Gray	533	Bright Metal	Coral, Shadow Gray▲	White

*Rear Fender Moulding Insert—Winter White.

▲Spring Color.

1955 EXTERIOR-INTERIOR COLOR COMBINATIONS
TWO-COLOR EXTERIORS
SERIES 1500

Color Combination: Upper Body	Lower Body, Sheet Metal, Wheels	Paint Comb. No.	1502 1503 1512 Trim	Trim Comb. No.	Inst. Panel-Center, Radio Cover Plate	Inst. Panel—upr. & lwr., Steering Wheel, Steering Column, Steering Wheel Hub, Garnish Mouldings, Dir. Signal Hsg., Ash Tray Cover Panel, Door Locking Knob, Heater Cover Panel	1629 Trim	Trim Comb. No.	Inst. Panel-Center, Radio Cover Plate	Inst. Panel—lwr. & upr., Steering Wheel, Steering Column, Steering Wheel Hub, Garnish Mouldings, Dir. Signal Hsg., Ash Tray Cover Panel, Door Locking Knob, Heater Cover Panel
Sea Mist Green	Neptune Green•	599	Gray & Black	500	India Ivory	Shadow Gray	Green	524	Sea Mist Green	Neptune Green≠
India Ivory	Cashmere Blue*	682	Gray & Black	500	India Ivory	Shadow Gray				
Skyline Blue	Glacier Blue•	600	Gray & Black	500	India Ivory	Shadow Gray				
India Ivory	Skyline Blue*	602	Gray & Black	500	India Ivory	Shadow Gray				
India Ivory	Shadow Gray•	624	Gray & Black	500	India Ivory	Shadow Gray				
Shoreline Beige	Autumn Bronze•	606					Straw & Brown	502	Shoreline Beige	Autumn Bronze
Shoreline Beige	Neptune Green•	613	Gray & Black	500	India Ivory	Shadow Gray				
Shoreline Beige	Glacier Blue•	614	Gray & Black	500	India Ivory	Shadow Gray				
India Ivory	Navajo Tan•	684					Straw & Brown	502	Shoreline Beige	Navajo Tan

•Wheel stripes are Argent Silver. *Wheel stripes are Onyx Black.
•Black steering wheel hub. ≠May have Sea Mist Green steering wheel rim and spokes.

SERIES 2100

Upper Body (exc. 2154) Roof, Deck, Pillars, & Partial Quarters (2154)	Lower Body, Sheet Metal, Wheels	Paint Comb. No.	Trim 2102 2103 2154	Trim Comb. No.	Trim 2124	Trim Comb. No.	Trim 2109 2129	Trim Comb. No.	Inst. Panel-Center, Radio Cover Plate	Inst. Panel—upr. & lwr., Steering Wheel, Steering Column, Steering Wheel Hub, Garnish Mouldings, Dir. Signal Housing, Ash Tray Cover Panel, Door Locking Knob, Heater Cover Panel
Sea Mist Green	Neptune Green•	599	Green	504			Green	515	Sea Mist Green	Neptune Green
Skyline Blue	Glacier Blue•	600	Blue	503					Skyline Blue	Glacier Blue
India Ivory	Cashmere Blue*	682	Blue	503	Beige & Blue	506	Beige & Blue	514	India Ivory	Glacier Blue
India Ivory	Skyline Blue*	602	Blue	503	Beige & Blue	506			Skyline Blue[1] Shoreline Beige[2]	Glacier Blue
India Ivory	Shadow Gray•	624	Blue	503					Skyline Blue India Ivory▲	Glacier Blue
India Ivory	Sea Mist Green*	605	Green	504	Beige & Green	507			Sea Mist Green[1] Shoreline Beige[3]	Neptune Green
Autumn Bronze	Shoreline Beige*	603					Beige&Brown	516	Shoreline Beige	Autumn Bronze
Shoreline Beige	Autumn Bronze•	606	Brown	505					Shoreline Beige	Autumn Bronze
Glacier Blue	Shoreline Beige*	607	Blue	503	Beige & Blue	506			Skyline Blue[1] Shoreline Beige[2]	Glacier Blue

•Wheel stripes are Argent Silver. *Wheel stripes are Onyx Black. ▲Spring color.
[1]2102-2103-2154. [2]2124. [3]2109-2129 before spring colors.

0023904

1955 TWO COLOR EXTERIORS (Cont.)
SERIES 2100

Upper Body (exc. 2154) Roof, Deck, Pillars, & Partial Quarters (2154)	Lower Body, Sheet Metal, Wheels	Paint Comb. No.	Trim 2102 2103 2154	Trim Comb. No.	Trim 2124	Trim Comb. No.	Trim 2109 2129	Trim Comb. No.	Inst. Panel-Center, Radio Cover Plate	Inst. Panel—upr. & lwr., Steering Wheel, Steering Column, Steering Wheel Hub, Garnish Mouldings, Dir. Signal Housing, Ash Tray Cover Panel, Door Locking Knob, Heater Cover Panel
India Ivory	Onyx Black•	608			Ivory & Black	508			India Ivory	Onyx Black
India Ivory	Gypsy Red•	617			Ivory & Black	508			India Ivory	Onyx Black
Glacier Blue	Skyline Blue*	610					Blue & Beige	514	Shoreline Beige	Glacier Blue
Shoreline Beige	Neptune Green•	613	Green	504					Sea Mist Green	Neptune Green
Shoreline Beige	Glacier Blue•	614	Blue	503	Beige & Blue	506	Beige & Blue	514	Shoreline Beige[3] Indian Ivory▲	Glacier Blue
Onyx Black	India Ivory*	628			Ivory & Black	508			India Ivory	Onyx Black
India Ivory	Harvest Gold*	631			Beige & Green	507			Shoreline Beige	Neptune Green
India Ivory	Navajo Tan•	684	Brown	505			Beige&Brown	516	Shoreline Beige	Navajo Tan

•Wheel stripes are Argent Silver. *Wheel stripes are Onyx Black. ▲Spring color. [3]2109-2129 before spring colors.

2400 SERIES

Color Combination*: Roof, Deck, Pillars, Partial Quarters	Lower Body, Sheet Metal, Wheels	Paint Comb. No.	Trim 2402 2403	Trim Comb. No.	Trim 2454	Trim Comb. No.	Inst. Panel—Center, Radio Cover Plate	Inst. Panel—Upr. & Lwr., Steering Wheel, Column and Hub, Garnish Mouldings, Dir. Signal Hsg., Ash Tray Cover Panel, Door Locking Knob, Heater Cover Panel
Sea Mist Green	Neptune Green	599	Green	510			Bright Metal	Neptune Green≠
India Ivory	Cashmere Blue	682	Blue	509	Blue	519	Bright Metal	Glacier Blue
Skyline Blue	Glacier Blue	600	Blue	509			Bright Metal	Glacier Blue
Neptune Green	Shoreline Beige	601			Green	520	Bright Metal	Neptune Green
India Ivory	Skyline Blue	602	Blue	509	Blue	519	Bright Metal	Glacier Blue
India Ivory	Shadow Gray	624	Blue	509			Bright Metal	Glacier Blue
Shoreline Beige	Autumn Bronze	606	Beige & Brown	511			Bright Metal	Autumn Bronze•
India Ivory	Onyx Black	608	Ivory & Gray	549	Ivory & Gray	550	Bright Metal	Shadow Gray
India Ivory	Regal Turquoise	612	Ivory & Turquoise	513	Turquoise	522	Bright Metal	Regal Turquoise
Shoreline Beige	Neptune Green	613	Green	510	Green	520	Bright Metal	Neptune Green
Shoreline Beige	Glacier Blue	614	Blue	509	Blue	519	Bright Metal	Glacier Blue
Shoreline Beige	Gypsy Red	615			Red	521	Bright Metal	Gypsy Red
Onyx Black	India Ivory	628	Ivory & Gray	549	Ivory & Gray	550	Bright Metal	Shadow Gray
Shadow Gray	Coral	627	Coral & Gray	531	Coral & Gray	532	Bright Metal	Coral, Shadow Gray▲
India Ivory	Harvest Gold	631	Green	510	Green	520	Bright Metal	Neptune Green
India Ivory	Navajo Tan	684	Beige & Brown	511	Green	520	Bright Metal	Navajo Tan (2402-3) Neptune Green (2454)
India Ivory	Dusk Rose	685	Ivory & Gray	549	Ivory & Gray	550	Bright Metal	Dusk Rose

*Rear Fender Molding Insert—Winter White
≠May have Sea Mist Green steering wheel rim and spokes
•Shoreline Beige steering wheel rim and spokes
▲Spring color

1955 TWO COLOR EXTERIORS (Cont.)
2400 SERIES

Color Combination: Roof, Deck, Pillars, Partial Quarters	Lower Body, Sheet Metal, Wheels	Paint Comb. No.	Trim 2409	Trim Comb. No.	Trim 2429	Trim Comb. No.	Inst. Panel—Center, Radio Cover Plate	Inst. Panel—Upr. & Lwr., Steering Wheel, Column & Hub, Garnish Moldings, Dir. Signal Housing, Ash Tray Cover Panel, Door Locking Knob, Heater Cover Panel
Shoreline Beige	Glacier Blue	614	Blue & Beige	518	Blue & Beige	542	Bright Metal	Glacier Blue
Sea Mist Green	Neptune Green	599			Green & Beige	541	Bright Metal	Neptune Green
India Ivory	Cashmere Blue	682	Blue & Beige	518	Blue & Beige	542	Bright Metal	Glacier Blue
India Ivory	Regal Turquoise	612			Ivory & Turquoise	545	Bright Metal	Regal Turquoise
Shoreline Beige	Gypsy Red	615	Beige	517	Red & Beige	544	Bright Metal	Gypsy Red
Shoreline Beige	Autumn Bronze	606	Beige	517			Bright Metal	Autumn Bronze
Shadow Gray	Coral	627			Coral & Gray	546	Bright Metal	Shadow Gray
Neptune Green	Sea Mist Green	604	Beige	517			Bright Metal	Neptune Green
India Ivory	Harvest Gold	631			Green & Beige	541	Bright Metal	Neptune Green
India Ivory	Navajo Tan	684	Beige	517	Brown & Beige	543	Bright Metal	Navajo Tan
India Ivory	Dusk Rose	685			Ivory & Gray	552	Bright Metal	Dusk Rose

Color Combination: Deck, Partial Quarters	Lower Body, Sheet Metal, Wheels	Paint Comb. No.	2434 Trim	Trim Comb. No.	Inst. Panel—Center, Radio Cover Plate	Inst. Panel—Upr. & Lwr., Steering Wheel, Column and Hub, Garnish Mouldings, Dir. Signal Hsg., Ash Tray Cover Panel, Door Locking Knob, Heater Cover Panel	Top Color
India Ivory	Cashmere Blue	682	Blue	527	Bright Metal	Glacier Blue	White
India Ivory	Onyx Black	608	Ivory & Gray	551	Bright Metal	Shadow Gray	White
India Ivory	Regal Turquoise	612	Ivory & Turquoise	537	Bright Metal	Regal Turquoise	White
Shoreline Beige	Autumn Bronze	606	Beige & Brown	528	Bright Metal	Autumn Bronze•	Beige
Glacier Blue	Skyline Blue	610	Blue	527	Bright Metal	Glacier Blue	Blue
Shoreline Beige	Gypsy Red	615	Beige & Red	525	Bright Metal	Gypsy Red	Beige
Shadow Gray	Coral	627	Coral & Gray	533	Bright Metal	Shadow Gray	Gray
Neptune Green	Sea Mist Green	604	Green	526	Bright Metal	Neptune Green	Green
India Ivory	Coral	629	Coral & Gray	533	Bright Metal	Coral	White
India Ivory	Harvest Gold	631	Green	526	Bright Metal	Neptune Green	White
India Ivory	Navajo Tan	684	Beige & Brown	528	Bright Metal	Navajo Tan	White
India Ivory	Dusk Rose	685	Ivory & Gray	551	Bright Metal	Dusk Rose	White

•Shoreline Beige steering wheel rim and spokes

0023905

1956 Trim Combinations

EXTERIOR-INTERIOR COLOR COMBINATIONS
ONE-COLOR EXTERIORS

Upper and Lower Body, Sheet Metal Wheels	Wheel Stripe (No Stripe on 2400 Series)	Trim Combinations (Standard Trim only on Series 1500 Sedans): Standard Trim	Trim Combinations: Optional Trim	Series 21-2400: Instrument Panel Center, Radio Cover Panel. On 2429 only - Upper Garnish Mldg., Windshield Pillar Molding, Windshield Lower Garnish Molding, Quarter Window Molding	Series 1500: Instrument Panel Center and Lower, Cigarette Lighter Button, Radio Cover Panel, Steering Wheel Column and Hub, Ash Tray Cover Panel, Heater Cover Panel, Directional Signal Housing	Upper and Lower Instrument Panel 21-2400, Upper Instrument Panel 1500, Steering Wheel, Column and Hub 21-2400, Garnish Molding 15-21-2400 except 2429, Directional Signal Housing 21-2400, Ash Tray Cover Panel 21-2400, Heater Cover Panel 21-2400, Door Lock Rod Knobs 15-21-2400: With Standard Trim	With Optional Trim	Series 2400: 2402 2403	Series 2400: 2413 2454	Series 2400: 2434	Series 2400: 2429	Series 2400: 2419	Series 2100: 2102 2103 2113 2154	Series 2100: 2124	Series 2100: 2109 2119 2129	Series 1500: 1502 1503 1512	Series 1500: 1529	Series 1500: 1508	Convertible Top Color 2434
Onyx Black	Argent	Black & Gold	None	None	Dune Beige	Onyx Black	None									●			
		Gold & Charcoal	None	None	Dune Beige	Onyx Black	None										●		
		Ivory & Charcoal	None	Indie Ivory	None	Onyx Black	None						●		●				
		Ivory & Black	None	Indie Ivory	None	Onyx Black	None							●					
		Ivory & Charcoal	Yellow & Charcoal	Bright	None	Onyx Black	Onyx Black	●	●	●	●	●							Ivory or Black
Pinecrest Green	Black	Black & Gold	None	None	Dune Beige	Onyx Black	None									●			
		Gold & Charcoal	None	None	Dune Beige	Onyx Black	None											●	
		Gold & Dk. Green	None	None	Dune Beige	Sherwood Green	None										●		
		Ivory & Charcoal	Ivory & Dk. Green	Indie Ivory	None	Onyx Black	Sherwood Green						●		●				
		Ivory & Black	Ivory & Dk. Green	Indie Ivory	None	Onyx Black	Sherwood Green							●					
		Ivory & Charcoal	Lt. & Dk. Green	Bright	None	Onyx Black	Sherwood Green	●	●	●									Ivory, Black or Tan
		Ivory & Charcoal	None	Bright	None	Onyx Black	None					●							
Sherwood Green	Argent	Black & Gold	None	None	Dune Beige	Onyx Black	None									●			
		Gold & Dk. Green	None	None	Dune Beige	Dark Green	None										●		
		Ivory & Charcoal	Ivory & Dk. Green	Indie Ivory	None	Onyx Black	Sherwood Green						●		●				
		Ivory & Black	Ivory & Dk. Green	Indie Ivory	None	Onyx Black	Sherwood Green							●					
		Ivory & Charcoal	Lt. & Dk. Green	Bright	None	Onyx Black	Sherwood Green	●	●	●									Ivory or Tan
Nassau Blue	Black	Black & Gold	None	None	Dune Beige	Onyx Black	None									●			
		Gold & Charcoal	None	None	Dune Beige	Onyx Black	None										●	●	
		Ivory & Charcoal	Ivory & Dk. Blue	Indie Ivory	None	Onyx Black	Harbor Blue						●						
		Ivory & Charcoal	None	Indie Ivory	None	Onyx Black	None								●				
		Ivory & Black	None	Indie Ivory	None	Onyx Black	None							●					
		Ivory & Charcoal	Lt. & Dk. Blue	Bright	None	Onyx Black	Harbor Blue	●	●	●									Blue, Ivory or Tan
		Ivory & Charcoal	None	Bright	None	Onyx Black	None					●							
Matador Red	Black	Black & Gold	None	None	Dune Beige	Onyx Black	None									●			
		Gold & Charcoal	None	None	Dune Beige	Onyx Black	None											●	
		Ivory & Charcoal	None	Indie Ivory	None	Onyx Black	None						●		●				
		Ivory & Black	None	Indie Ivory	None	Onyx Black	None							●					
		Ivory & Charcoal	None	Bright	None	Onyx Black	None	●											
		Ivory & Charcoal	Red & Beige	Bright	None	Onyx Black	Matador Red		●			●							
		Ivory & Charcoal	Ivory & Red	Bright	None	Onyx Black	Matador Red			●									Ivory or Black
Twilight Turquoise	Black	Black & Gold	None	None	Dune Beige	Onyx Black	None									●			
		Ivory & Charcoal	None	Onyx Black	None	Onyx Black	None						●						
		Ivory & Charcoal	Ivory & Dk. Turq.	Onyx Black	None	Onyx Black	Twilight Turquoise								●				
		Ivory & Black	Ivory & Dk. Turq.	Ivory	None	Onyx Black	Twilight Turquoise							●					
		Ivory & Charcoal	Lt. & Dk. Turq.	Bright	None	Onyx Black	Twilight Turquoise	●	●				●						
		Ivory & Charcoal	Ivory & Dk. Turq.	Bright	None	Onyx Black	Twilight Turquoise			●									Ivory, Black or Tan
Indie Ivory	Black	Black & Gold	None	None	Dune Beige	Onyx Black	None									●			
		Gold & Charcoal	None	None	Dune Beige	Onyx Black	None										●	●	
		Ivory & Charcoal	None	Indie Ivory	None	Onyx Black	None						●		●				Ivory or Black
		Ivory & Black	None	Indie Ivory	None	Onyx Black	None							●					
		Ivory & Charcoal	None	Bright	None	Onyx Black	None	●	●	●		●							
Crocus Yellow	Black	Black & Gold	None	None	Dune Beige	Onyx Black	None									●			
		Gold & Charcoal	None	None	Dune Beige	Onyx Black	None										●		
		Ivory & Charcoal	None	Indie Ivory	None	Onyx Black	None						●		●				
		Ivory & Black	None	Indie Ivory	None	Onyx Black	None							●					
		Ivory & Charcoal	Yellow & Charcoal	Bright	None	Onyx Black	Onyx Black	●	●	●		●							Ivory or Black
Harbor Blue	Argent	Gold & Charcoal	None	None	Dune Beige	Onyx Black	None											●	
		Ivory & Charcoal	Ivory & Dk. Blue	Indie Ivory	None	Onyx Black	Harbor Blue						●						
		Ivory & Charcoal	Lt. & Dk. Blue	Bright	None	Onyx Black	Harbor Blue	●	●	●									Blue, Ivory or Tan
Dusk Plum	Argent	Ivory & Charcoal	None	Indie Ivory	None	Onyx Black	None						●						
		Ivory & Black	None	Indie Ivory	None	Onyx Black	None							●					
		Ivory & Charcoal	None	Bright ·	None	Onyx Black	None	●		●		●							Ivory or Tan

0023906

EXTERIOR-INTERIOR COLOR COMBINATIONS
TWO-COLOR EXTERIORS

Exterior Colors: First Color §	Exterior Colors: Second Color §	Wheel Stripes (Series 15-2100)	Trim Combinations (Standard Trim only on Series 1500 Sedans): Standard Trim	Trim Combinations: Optional Trim	Series 21-2400: Inst. Panel Center, Radio Cover Panel. On 2429 only - Upper Garnish Mldg. Windshield Pillar Molding, Windshield Lower Garnish Molding, Quarter Window Molding	Series 1500: Inst. Panel Center and Lower, Cig. Lighter Button, Radio Cover Panel, Steering Wheel, Column and Hub, Ash Tray Cover Panel, Heater Cover Panel, Directional Signal Housing	Upper and Lower Instrument Panel 21-2400, Upper Instrument Panel 1500, Steering Wheel, Column and Hub 21-2400, Garnish Molding 15-21-2400 except 2429, Directional Signal Housing 21-2400, Ash Tray Cover Panel 21-2400, Heater Cover Panel 21-2400, Door Lock Rod Knob 15-21-2400: With Standard Trim	With Optional Trim	Series 2400: 2402 2403	Series 2400: 2413 2454	Series 2400: 2434	Series 2400: 2429	Series 2400: 2419	Series 2100: 2102 2103 2113 2154	Series 2100: 2124	Series 2100: 2109 2119 2129	Series 1500: 1502 1503 1512	Series 1500: 1529	Series 1500: 1508	Model 2434 Top Color
Indie Ivory	Onyx Black	Argent	Ivory & Charcoal	None	Bright *	None	Onyx Black	None	●	●	●	●	●	●		●				Ivory or Black
			Ivory & Black	None	Indie Ivory	None	Onyx Black	None							●					
			Black & Gold	None	None	Dune Beige	Onyx Black	None									●			
			Charcoal & Gold	None	None	Dune Beige	Onyx Black	None										●		
Sherwood Green	Pinecrest Green	Black	Ivory & Charcoal	Lt. & Dk. Green	Bright	None	Onyx Black	Sherwood Green	●	●		●								
			Ivory & Charcoal	Ivory & Dk. Green	Indie Ivory	None	Onyx Black	Sherwood Green						●		●				
			Ivory & Black	Ivory & Dk. Green	Indie Ivory	None	Onyx Black	Sherwood Green							●					
			Black & Gold	None	None	Dune Beige	Onyx Black	None									●			
			Charcoal & Gold	Green & Bold	None	Dune Beige	Onyx Black	Sherwood Green										●		
Indie Ivory	Sherwood Green	Argent	Ivory & Charcoal	Lt. & Dk. Green	Bright	None	Onyx Black	Sherwood Green	●	●	●	●								Ivory or Black ¢
			Ivory & Charcoal	Ivory & Dk. Green	Indie Ivory	None	Onyx Black	Sherwood Green						●		●				
			Ivory & Black	Ivory & Dk. Green	Indie Ivory	None	Onyx Black	Sherwood Green							●					
			Charcoal & Gold	Green & Gold	None	Dune Beige	Onyx Black	Sherwood Green										●		
Indie Ivory	Pinecrest Green	Black	Ivory & Charcoal	Lt. & Dk. Green	Bright	None	Onyx Black	Sherwood Green	●	●	●	●								Ivory or Black
			Ivory & Charcoal	None	Bright	None	Onyx Black	None					●							
			Ivory & Charcoal	Ivory & Dk. Green	Indie Ivory	None	Onyx Black	Sherwood Green						●		●				
			Ivory & Black	Ivory & Dk. Green	Indie Ivory	None	Onyx Black	Sherwood Green							●					
			Black & Gold	None	None	Dune Beige	Onyx Black	None									●			
			Charcoal & Gold	Green & Gold	None	Dune Beige	Onyx Black	Sherwood Green										●		
Crocus Yellow	Laurel Green	Argent	Ivory & Charcoal	Yellow & Charcoal	Bright	None	Onyx Black	Onyx Black	●	●	●	●	●							Ivory or Black
			Ivory & Charcoal	None	Indie Ivory	None	Onyx Black	None						●		●				
			Ivory & Black	None	Indie Ivory	None	Onyx Black	None							●					
Nassau Blue	Harbor Blue	Argent	Ivory & Charcoal	Lt. & Dk. Blue	Bright	None	Onyx Black	Harbor Blue	●	●	●	●								Ivory or Blue
			Ivory & Charcoal	Ivory & Dk. Blue	Indie Ivory	None	Onyx Black	Harbor Blue						●						
Indie Ivory	Nassau Blue	Black	Ivory & Charcoal	Lt. & Dk. Blue	Bright	None	Onyx Black	Harbor Blue	●	●	●	●								Ivory or Blue
			Ivory & Charcoal	None	Bright	None	Onyx Black	None					●							
			Ivory & Charcoal	Ivory & Dk. Blue	Indie Ivory	None	Onyx Black	Harbor Blue						●						
			Ivory & Charcoal	None	Indie Ivory	None	Onyx Black	None								●				
			Ivory & Black	None	Indie Ivory	None	Onyx Black	None							●					
			Black & Gold	None	None	Dune Beige	Onyx Black	None									●			
			Charcoal & Gold	None	None	Dune Beige	Onyx Black	None										●		
Indie Ivory	Dusk Plum	Argent	Ivory & Charcoal	None	Bright *	None	Onyx Black	None	●	●	●	●	●	●		●				Ivory or Black ¢
			Ivory & Black	None	Indie Ivory	None	Onyx Black	None							●					
Adobe Beige	Sierra Gold	None	None	Tan & Copper	Bright	None	None	Sierra Gold	●	●	●	●	●							Tan or Black ¢
Indie Ivory	Dawn Gray	Black	Ivory & Charcoal	None	Bright *	None	Onyx Black	None	●	●	●	●	●	●		●				Ivory or Black
Onyx Black	Crocus Yellow	Black	Ivory & Charcoal	Yellow & Charcoal	Bright	None	Onyx Black	Onyx Black	●	●	●	●	●							Ivory ¢ or Black
			Ivory & Charcoal	None	Indie Ivory	None	Onyx Black	None						●		●				
			Ivory & Black	None	Indie Ivory	None	Onyx Black	None							●					
			Black & Gold	None	None	Dune Beige	Onyx Black	None									●			
			Charcoal & Gold	None	None	Dune Beige	Onyx Black	None										●		
Indie Ivory	Matador Red	Black	Ivory & Charcoal	None	Bright *	None	Onyx Black	None	●					●		●				
			Ivory & Charcoal	Ivory & Red	Bright	None	Onyx Black	Matador Red			●									Ivory or Black
			Ivory & Black	None	Indie Ivory	None	Onyx Black	None							●					
			Black & Gold	None	None	None	Onyx Black	None									●			
Dune Beige	Matador Red	None	Ivory & Charcoal	Red & Beige	Bright	None	Onyx Black	Matador Red		●		●	●							
Indie Ivory	Twilight Turquoise	Argent	Ivory & Charcoal	Lt. & Dk. Turquoise	Bright	None	Onyx Black	Twilight Turquoise	●	●		●	●							
			Ivory & Charcoal	Ivory & Dk. Turquoise	Bright *	None	Onyx Black	Twilight Turquoise			●					●				Ivory or Black
			Ivory & Charcoal	None	Indie Ivory	None	Onyx Black	None						●						
			Ivory & Black	Ivory & Turquoise	Indie Ivory	None	Onyx Black	Twilight Turquoise							●					

§ - On Series 2400 models, the first color is used on the roof, pillars, rear deck, upper quarter panels and the area between the two body side moldings. The second color is used on the hood, front fenders, lower body and wheels. However on model 2429, the first color is used for the tail gate, upper quarter panels and area between the two body side moldings. The second color is used on the roof pillars, lift gate, hood, front fenders, lower body and wheels. On model 2419 the first color is used on the tail gate, upper quarter panels, pillars, lift gate and the area between the two body side moldings. The second color is used for the roof, front fenders, lower body and wheels. No conventional two-toning is available on any model in the 2400 Series.

§ - On Series 2100 models conventional two-toning is available where the first color is used on the roof panel only. The second color is used for the remaining areas. In addition a second method of two-toning uses the first color on the hood, upper side and rear deck or tail gate. The second color is used for the roof, pillars, lower body and wheels and lift gate.

§ - On Series 1500 models conventional two-toning is also available with the first color used on the roof panel only. The second color is used on the remaining areas, including pillars and wheels. Special two-toning uses the first color on the hood and body upper side. The second color is used on the roof, pillars, deck and body side lower, lift and tail gate.

* - Indie Ivory on Series 2100.

¢ - This color held to minimum in this exterior combination because of poor color harmony.

0023907

1956 Trim Combinations (continued)

1956 EXTERIOR-INTERIOR COLOR COMBINATIONS ONE COLOR EXTERIORS

SERIES 1500

Body and Wheel Color	Paint Comb. No.	Trim (1502 1503 1512)	Trim Comb. No.	Instrument Panel—Center and lower, Cigarette Lighter Button, Radio Cover Panel, Steering Wheel, Column & Hub, Ash Tray Cover Panel, Heater Cover Panel, Directional Signal Housing	Upper Instrument Panel, Garnish Mouldings, Door Lock Rod Knobs
Onxy Black•	687	Black & Gold	560	Dune Beige, Adobe Beige♦	Onyx Black
Pinecrest Green*	688	Black & Gold	560	Dune Beige, Adobe Beige♦	Onyx Black
Sherwood Green•	690	Black & Gold	560	Dune Beige, Adobe Beige♦	Onyx Black
Nassau Blue*	691	Black & Gold	560	Dune Beige, Adobe Beige♦	Onyx Black
Matador Red*	697	Black & Gold	560	Dune Beige, Adobe Beige♦	Onyx Black
Twilight Turquoise*	698	Black & Gold	560	Dune Be.ge	Onyx Black
Tropical Turquoise•	749	Black & Gold	560	Adobe Beige	Onyx Black
India Ivory*	694	Black & Gold	560	Dune Beige, Adobe Beige♦	Onyx Black
Crocus Yellow*	695	Black & Gold	560	Dune Beige	Onyx Black
Calypso Cream*	750	Black & Gold	560	Adobe Beige	Onyx Black

•Wheel stripes are Argent Silver

*Wheel stripes are Onyx Black

♦Spring color

Body and Wheel Color	Paint Comb. No.	Trim 1508	Trim Comb. No.	Trim 1529	Trim Comb. No.	Instrument Panel—Center & lower, Cigarette Lighter Button, Radio Cover Panel, Steering Wheel, Column & Hub, Ash Tray Cover Panel, Heater Cover Panel, Directional Signal Housing	Upper Instrument Panel, Garnish Mouldings, Door Lock Rod Knobs
Onyx Black•	687			Gold & Charcoal	616	Dune Beige, Adobe Beige♦	Onxy Black
Pinecrest Green*	688	Gold & Charcoal	615	Gold & Charcoal	616	Dune Beige (1508), Adobe Beige♦ (1508-29)	Onyx Black
Pinecrest Green*	688			Gold & Dk. Green	562	Dune Beige, Adobe Beige♦	Sherwood Green
Sherwood Green•	690			Gold & Dk. Green	562	Dune Beige, Adobe Beige♦	Sherwood Green
Sherwood Green•	690			Gold & Charcoal	616	Adobe Beige	Onyx Black
Nassau Blue*	691	Gold & Charcoal	615	Gold & Charcoal	616	Dune Beige, Adobe Beige♦	Onyx Black
Matador Red*	697	Gold & Charcoal	615			Dune Beige, Adobe Beige♦	Onyx Black
India Ivory*	694	Gold & Charcoal	615	Gold & Charcoal	616	Dune Beige, Adobe Beige♦	Onyx Black
Crocus Yellow*	695			Gold & Charcoal	616	Dune Beige	Onyx Black
Harbor Blue•	692	Gold & Charcoal	615			Dune Beige, Adobe Beige♦	Onyx Black
Calypso Cream*	750			Gold & Charcoal	616	Adobe Beige	Onyx Black

•Wheel stripes are Argent Silver

*Wheel stripes are Onyx Black

♦Spring color

1956 ONE COLOR EXTERIORS (Cont.)

SERIES 2100

Body and Wheel Color	Paint Comb. No.	Trim 2102 2103 2113 2154	Trim Comb. No.	Trim 2109 2119 2129	Trim Comb. No.	Inst. Panel—Center, Radio Cover Panel	Instrument Panel—upper & lower, Steering Wheel, Column & Hub, Garnish Mouldings, Dir. Signal Hsg., Heater Cover Panel, Ash Tray Cover Panel, Door Lock Rod Knobs
Onyx Black•	687	Ivory & Charcoal	564	Ivory & Charcoal	609	India Ivory	Onyx Black
Pinecrest Green*	688	Ivory & Charcoal Opt. Ivory & Green	564 565	Ivory & Charcoal Opt. Ivory & Green	609 570	India Ivory India Ivory	Onyx Black Opt. Sherwood Green
Sherwood Green•	690	Ivory & Charcoal Opt. Ivory & Green	564 565	Ivory & Charcoal Opt. Ivory & Green	609 570	India Ivory India Ivory	Onyx Black Opt. Sherwood Green
Nassau Blue*	691	Ivory & Charcoal Opt. Ivory & Blue	564 566	Ivory & Charcoal	609	India Ivory India Ivory	Onyx Black Opt. Harbor Blue
Matador Red*	697	Ivory & Charcoal	564	Ivory & Charcoal	609	India Ivory	Onyx Black
Twilight Turquoise*	698	Ivory & Charcoal	564	Ivory & Charcoal Opt. Ivory & Turquoise	609 572	Onyx Black Onyx Black	Onyx Black Opt. Twilight Turquoise
Tropical Turquoise•	749	Ivory & Charcoal	564	Ivory & Charcoal Opt. Ivory & Turquoise	609 572	India Ivory India Ivory	Onyx Black Opt. Tropical Turquoise
India Ivory*	694	Ivory & Charcoal	564	Ivory & Charcoal	609	India Ivory	Onyx Black
Crocus Yellow*	695	Ivory & Charcoal	564	Ivory & Charcoal	609	India Ivory	Onyx Black
Harbor Blue•	692	Ivory & Charcoal Opt. Ivory & Blue	564 566			India Ivory India Ivory	Onyx Black Opt. Harbor Blue
Dusk Plum•	693	Ivory & Charcoal	564			India Ivory	Onyx Black
Inca Silver*	752	Ivory & Charcoal	564	Ivory & Charcoal	609	India Ivory	Onyx Black

•Wheel stripes are Argent Silver *Wheel stripes are Onyx Black

Opt.—Optional trim combination

NOTE: Ivory trim also known as Starfrost

Body and Wheel Color	Paint Comb. No.	Trim (2124)	Trim Comb. No.	Instrument Panel—Center, Radio Cover Panel	Inst. Panel—Upper & lower, Steering Wheel, Column & Hub, Garnish Mouldings, Dir. Signal Housing, Ash Tray Cover Panel, Heater Cover Panel, Door Lock Rod Knobs
Onyx Black•	687	Ivory & Black	567	India Ivory	Onyx Black
Pinecrest Green*	688	Ivory & Black Opt. Ivory & Green	567 568	India Ivory India Ivory	Onyx Black Opt. Sherwood Green
Sherwood Green•	690	Ivory & Black Opt. Ivory & Green	567 568	India Ivory India Ivory	Onyx Black Opt. Sherwood Green
Nassau Blue*	691	Ivory & Black	567	India Ivory	Onyx Black
Matador Red*	697	Ivory & Black	567	India Ivory	Onyx Black
Twilight Turquoise*	698	Ivory & Black Opt. Ivory & Turquoise	567 569	India Ivory India Ivory	Onyx Black Opt. Twilight Turquoise
Tropical Turquoise•	749	Ivory & Black Opt. Ivory & Turquoise	567 569	India Ivory India Ivory	Onyx Black Opt. Tropical Turquoise
India Ivory*	694	Ivory & Black	567	India Ivory	Onyx Black
Crocus Yellow*	695	Ivory & Black	567	India Ivory	Onyx Black
Dusk Plum•	693	Ivory & Black	567	India Ivory	Onyx Black
Inca Silver*	752	Ivory & Black	567	India Ivory	Onyx Black

•Wheel stripes are Argent Silver *Wheel stripes are Onyx Black

Opt.—Optional trim combinations

0023908

1956 ONE COLOR EXTERIORS (Cont.)

SERIES 2400

Body and Wheel Color	Paint Comb. No.	Trim (2402 2403 2413 2434 2454)	Trim Comb. No.	Inst. Panel—center, Radio Cover Panel	Inst. Panel—upr. and lwr., Steering Wheel, Column, Hub, Garnish Mouldings, Dir. Signal Housing, Ash Tray Cover Panel, Heater Cover Panel, Door Lock Rod Knobs	Top Color 2434
Onyx Black	687	Ivory and Charcoal Opt. Yellow and Charcoal	573-579-602 578-585-604	Bright Metal Bright Metal	Onyx Black Onyx Black	Ivory or Black Ivory or Black
Pinecrest Green	688	Ivory and Charcoal Opt. Lt. and Dk. Green	573-579-602 574-580-606	Bright Mefal Bright Metal	Onyx Black Opt. Sherwood Green	Ivory, Black or Tan Ivory, Black or Tan
Sherwood Green	690	Ivory and Charcoal Opt. Lt. and Dk. Green	573-579-602 574-580-606	Bright Metal Bright Metal	Onyx Black Opt. Sherwood Green	Ivory or Tan Ivory or Tan
Nassau Blue	691	Ivory and Charcoal Opt. Lt. and Dk. Blue	573-579-602 575-581-607	Bright Metal Bright Metal	Onyx Black Opt. Harbor Blue	Blue, Ivory or Tan Blue, Ivory or Tan
Matador Red	697	Ivory and Charcoal	573-579-602	Bright Metal	Onyx Black	Ivory or Black
Matador Red (2413-2454)	697	Opt. Red and Beige	583▲	Bright Metal	Opt. Matador Red	
Matador Red (2434)	697	Opt. Ivory and Red	605	Bright Metal	Opt. Matador Red	Ivory or Black
Twilight Turquoise	698	Ivory and Charcoal	573-579-602	Bright Metal	Onyx Black	Ivory, Black or Tan
Twi. Turq. (2402-03-13-54)	698	Opt. Lt. and Dk. Turq.	577-584	Bright Metal	Opt. Twilight Turquoise	
Twi. Turq. (2434)	698	Opt. Ivory and Turquoise	603	Bright Metal	Opt. Twilight Turquoise	Ivory, Black or Tan
Tropical Turquoise	749	Ivory and Charcoal	573-579-602	Bright Metal	Onyx Black	Ivory, Black or Tan
Trop. Turq. (2402-03-13-54)	749	Opt. Lt. & Dk. Turquoise	577-584	Bright Metal	Opt. Tropical Turquoise	
Trop. Turq. (2434)	749	Opt. Ivory and Turquoise	603	Bright Metal	Opt. Tropical Turquoise	Ivory, Black or Tan
India Ivory	694	Ivory and Charcoal	573-579-602	Bright Metal	Onyx Black	Ivory or Black
Crocus Yellow	695	Ivory and Charcoal Opt. Yellow and Charcoal	573-579-602 578-585-604	Bright Metal Bright Metal	Onyx Black Onyx Black	Ivory or Black Ivory or Black
Harbor Blue	692	Ivory and Charcoal Opt. Lt. and Dk. Blue	573-579-602 575-581-607	Bright Metal Bright Metal	Onyx Black Opt. Harbor Blue	Blue, Ivory or Tan Blue, Ivory or Tan
Dusk Plum	693	Ivory and Charcoal	573-579-602	Bright Metal	Onyx Black	Ivory or Tan
Inca Silver	752	Ivory and Charcoal	573-579-602	Bright Metal	Onyx Black	Ivory or Black

▲Superseded by Combination #628 (Red Taupe pattern cloth and Red imitation leather).
Opt.—Optional Trim Combination.

Body and Wheel Color	Paint Comb. No.	Trim (2419 2429)	Trim Comb. No.	Model	Inst. Panel—center, Radio Cover Panel 2429 ONLY Upper garnish moulding, w/shield pillar mldg., w/shield lower garnish mldg., qtr. window moulding	Inst. Panel—upr. & lwr., Steering Wheel, Hub & Column, Garnish Mouldings (exc. 2429), Dir. Signal Housing, Ash Tray Cover Panel, Heater Cover Panel, Door Lock Rod Knobs
Onyx Black	687	Ivory and Charcoal Opt. Yellow and Charcoal	610-611 588-595	2419-2429 2419-2429	Bright Metal Bright Metal	Onyx Black Onyx Black
Pinecrest Green	688	Ivory and Charcoal	610	2419	Bright Metal	Onyx Black
Nassau Blue	691	Ivory and Charcoal	610	2419	Bright Metal	Onyx Black
Matador Red	697	Ivory and Charcoal Opt. Red and Beige	610 586▲	2419 2419	Bright Metal Bright Metal	Onyx Black Opt. Matador Red
India Ivory	694	Ivory and Charcoal	610	2419	Bright Metal	Onyx Black
Crocus Yellow	695	Ivory and Charcoal Opt. Yellow and Charcoal	610 588	2419 2419	Bright Metal Bright Metal	Onyx Black Onyx Black
Dusk Plum	693	Ivory and Charcoal	610	2419	Bright Metal	Onyx Black
Inca Silver	752	Ivory and Charcoal	610-611	2419-2429	Bright Metal	Onyx Black

▲Superseded by Combination #629 (Red Taupe pattern cloth and Red imitation leather).
Opt.—Optional Trim Combination.

1956 EXTERIOR-INTERIOR COLOR COMBINATIONS TWO-COLOR EXTERIORS

SERIES 1500

First Body Color (See Note)	Second Body Color (See Note)	Paint Comb. No.	Trim 1502 1503 1512	Trim Comb. No.	Trim 1529	Trim Comb. No.	Inst. Panel—ctr. and lwr., Cig. Lighter Button, Radio Cover Panel, Steering Wheel, Column and Hub, Ash Tray, Cover Panel, Heater Cover Panel, Dir. Signal Housing	Inst. Panel—upper, Garnish Mouldings, Door Lock Rod Knob
India Ivory	Onyx Black•	701	Black and Gold	560	Charcoal and Gold	616	Dune Beige, Adobe Beige▲	Onyx Black
Sherwood Green	Pinecrest Green*	702	Black and Gold	560	Charcoal and Gold Opt. Green and Gold	616 562	Dune Beige, Adobe Beige▲ Dune Beige, Adobe Beige▲	Onyx Black Opt. Sherwood Green
India Ivory	Sherwood Green•	706			Charcoal and Gold Opt. Green and Gold	616 562	Dune Beige, Adobe Beige▲ Dune Beige, Adobe Beige▲	Onyx Black Opt. Sherwood Green
India Ivory	Pinecrest Green*	705	Black and Gold	560	Charcoal and Gold Opt. Green & Gold	616 562	Dune Beige, Adobe Beige▲ Dune Beige, Adobe Beige▲	Onyx Black Opt. Sherwood Green
India Ivory	Nassau Blue*	707	Black and Gold	560	Charcoal and Gold	616	Dune Beige, Adobe Beige▲	Onyx Black
Adobe Beige	Sierra Gold*	700			Gold and Charcoal	616	Adobe Beige	Onyx Black
Calypso Cream	Grecian Gold*	756	Gold and Black	560	Gold and Charcoal	616	Adobe Beige	Onyx Black
Onyx Black	Calypso Cream*	755	Gold and Black	560	Gold and Charcoal	616	Adobe Beige	Onyx Black
Onyx Black	Crocus Yellow*	696	Black and Gold	560	Charcoal and Gold	616	Dune Beige	Onyx Black
India Ivory	Matador Red*	711	Black and Gold	560			Dune Beige, Adobe Beige▲	Onyx Black

•Wheel stripes are Argent Silver. *Wheel Stripes are Onyx Black. ▲Spring Color.

NOTE: On Series 1500 models conventional two-toning is also available with the first color used on the roof panel only. The second color is used on the remaining areas, including pillars and wheels. Special two-toning uses the first color on the hood and body upper side. The second color is used on the roof, pillars, deck and body side lower, lift and tail gate.

SERIES 2100

First Body Color (See Note)	Second Body Color (See Note)	Paint Comb. No.	Trim* 2102 2103 2113 2154	Trim Comb. No.	Trim* 2109 2119 2129	Trim Comb. No.	Inst. Panel—Center, Radio Cover Panel	Inst. Panel—Upr. and Lwr., Steering Wheel, Column and Hub, Garnish Mouldings, Dir. Signal Housing, Ash Tray Cover Panel, Heater Cover Panel, Door Lock Rod Knob
India Ivory	Onyx Black•	701	Ivory & Charcoal	564	Ivory & Charcoal	609	India Ivory	Onyx Black
Sherwood Green	Pinecrest Green*	702	Ivory & Charcoal Opt. Ivory & Green	564 565	Ivory & Charcoal Opt. Ivory & Green	609 570	India Ivory India Ivory	Onyx Black Opt. Sherwood Green
India Ivory	Sherwood Green•	706	Ivory & Charcoal Opt. Ivory & Green	564 565	Ivory & Charcoal Opt. Ivory & Green	609 570	India Ivory India Ivory	Onyx Black Opt. Sherwood Green
India Ivory	Pinecrest Green*	705	Ivory & Charcoal Opt. Ivory & Green	564 565	Ivory & Charcoal Opt. Ivory & Green	609 570	India Ivory India Ivory	Onyx Black Opt. Sherwood Green
Crocus Yellow	Laurel Green•	717	Ivory & Charcoal	564	Ivory & Charcoal	609	India Ivory	Onyx Black
Nassau Blue	Harbor Blue•	703	Ivory & Charcoal Opt. Ivory & Blue	564 566			India Ivory India Ivory	Onyx Black Opt. Harbor Blue
India Ivory	Nassau Blue*	707	Ivory & Charcoal Opt. Ivory & Blue	564 566	Ivory & Charcoal	609	India Ivory India Ivory	Onyx Black Opt. Harbor Blue
India Ivory	Dusk Plum•	708	Ivory & Charcoal	564	Ivory & Charcoal	609	India Ivory	Onyx Black
India Ivory	Dawn Gray*	721	Ivory & Charcoal	564	Ivory & Charcoal	609	India Ivory	Onyx Black
Adobe Beige	Sierra Gold*	700			Ivory & Charcoal	609	India Ivory	Onyx Black

0023900

1956 Trim Combinations (continued)

1956 TWO COLOR EXTERIORS (Cont.)
SERIES 2100 (Cont.)

First Body Color (See Note)	Second Body Color (See Note)	Paint Comb. No.	2102 2103 2109 2113 2119 2129 2154 Trim* 2102 2103 2113 2154	Trim Comb. No.	Trim* 2109 2119 2129	Trim Comb. No.	Inst. Panel—Center Radio Cover Panel	Inst. Panel—Upr. and Lwr., Steering Wheel, Column and Hub, Garnish Mouldings, Dir. Signal Housing, Ash Tray Cover Panel, Heater Cover Panel, Door Lock Rod Knob
Imperial Ivory	Inca Silver*	757	Ivory & Charcoal	564	Ivory & Charcoal	609	India Ivory	Onyx Black
Calypso Cream	Grecian Gold*	756			Ivory & Charcoal	609	India Ivory	Onyx Black
Onyx Black	Crocus Yellow*	696	Ivory & Charcoal	564	Ivory & Charcoal	609	India Ivory	Onyx Black
India Ivory	Matador Red*	711	Ivory & Charcoal	564	Ivory & Charcoal	609	India Ivory	Onyx Black
India Ivory	Twilight Turquoise•	710	Ivory & Charcoal	564	Ivory & Charcoal Opt. Ivory & Turquoise	609 572	India Ivory India Ivory	Onyx Black Opt. Twilight Turquoise
India Ivory	Tropical Turquoise•	754	Ivory & Charcoal	564	Ivory & Charcoal Opt. Ivory & Turquoise	609 572	India Ivory India Ivory	Onyx Black Opt. Tropical Turquoise

•Wheel Stripes are Argent Silver. *Wheel Stripes are Onyx Black.

Opt.—Optional Trim Combination. ▴Ivory Trim also known as Starfrost.

NOTE: On Series 2100 models conventional two-toning is available where the first color is used on the roof panel only. The second color is used for the remaining areas. In addition a second method of two-toning uses the first color on the hood, upper side and rear deck or tail gate. The second color is used for the roof, pillars, lower body and wheels and lift gate.

First Body Color (See Note)	Second Body Color (See Note)	Paint Comb. No.	2124 Trim	Trim Comb. No.	Inst. Panel—Center, Radio Cover Panel	Inst. Panel—Upr. and Lwr., Steering Wheel, Column and Hub, Garnish Mouldings, Dir. Signal Housing, Ash Tray Cover Panel, Heater Cover Panel, Door Lock Rod Knob
India Ivory	Onyx Black•	701	Ivory & Black	567	India Ivory	Onyx Black
Sherwood Green	Pinecrest Green*	702	Ivory & Black Opt. Ivory & Green	567 568	India Ivory India Ivory	Onyx Black Opt. Sherwood Green
India Ivory	Sherwood Green•	706	Ivory & Black Opt. Ivory & Green	567 568	India Ivory India Ivory	Onyx Black Opt. Sherwood Green
India Ivory	Pinecrest Green*	705	Ivory & Black Opt. Ivory & Green	567 568	India Ivory India Ivory	Onyx Black Opt. Sherwood Green
Crocus Yellow	Laurel Green•	717	Ivory & Black	567	India Ivory	Onyx Black
India Ivory	Nassau Blue*	707	Ivory & Black	567	India Ivory	Onyx Black
India Ivory	Dusk Plum•	708	Ivory & Black	567	India Ivory	Onyx Black
Imperial Ivory	Inca Silver*	757	Ivory & Black	567	India Ivory	Onyx Black
Calypso Cream	Grecian Gold*	756	Ivory & Black	567	India Ivory	Onyx Black
Onyx Black	Crocus Yellow*	696	Ivory & Black	567	India Ivory	Onyx Black
India Ivory	Matador Red*	711	Ivory & Black	567	India Ivory	Onyx Black
India Ivory	Twilight Turquoise•	710	Ivory & Black Opt. Ivory & Turquoise	567 569	India Ivory India Ivory	Onyx Black Opt. Twilight Turquoise
India Ivory	Tropical Turquoise•	754	Ivory & Black Opt. Ivory & Turquoise	567 569	India Ivory India Ivory	Onyx Black Opt. Tropical Turquoise

•Wheel Stripes are Argent Silver. *Wheel Stripes are Onyx Black.

Opt.—Optional Trim Combination.

NOTE: On Series 2100 models conventional two-toning is available where the first color is used on the roof panel only. The second color is used for the remaining areas. In addition a second method of two-toning uses the first color on the hood, upper side and rear deck or tail gate. The second color is used for the roof, pillars, lower body and wheels and lift gate.

1956 TWO COLOR EXTERIORS (Cont.)
SERIES 2400

First Body Color (See Note)	Second Body Color (See Note)	Paint Comb. No.	2400 Trim	Trim Comb. No.	Models	Inst. Panel—Center, Radio Cover Panel 2429 ONLY Upr. Garnish Moulding, W/shield Pillar Moulding, Qtr. Window Moulding, W/shield lwr. Gar. Mould.	Inst. Panel—Upr. & lwr., Steer. Wheel, Col. & Hub, Garn. Moulds. (exc. 2429) Dir. Signal Housing, Ash Tray Cover Panel, Heater Cover Panel, Door Lock Rod Knob	Top Color 2434
India Ivory	Onyx Black	701	Ivory & Charcoal	573-579 602-610-611	All	Bright Metal	Onyx Black	Ivory or Black
Sherwood Green	Pinecrest Green	702	Ivory & Charcoal Opt. Lt. & Dk. Green	573-579 611 574-580 590	All (exc. 2419-34) All (exc. 2419-34)	Bright Metal Bright Metal	Onyx Black Opt. Sherwood Green	
India Ivory	Sherwood Green	706	Ivory & Charcoal Opt. Lt. & Dk. Green	573-579 602-611 574-580 590-606	All (exc. 2419) All (exc. 2419)	Bright Metal Bright Metal	Onyx Black Opt. Sherwood Green	Ivory or Black Ivory or Black
India Ivory	Pinecrest Green	705	Ivory & Charcoal Opt. Lt. & Dk. Green	573-579 602-610-611 574-580 590-606	All All (exc. 2419)	Bright Metal Bright Metal	Onyx Black Opt. Sherwood Green	Ivory or Black Ivory or Black
Crocus Yellow	Laurel Green	717	Ivory & Charcoal Opt. Yellow & Charcoal	573-579 602-610-611 578-585 588-595-604	All All	Bright Metal Bright Metal	Onyx Black Onyx Black	Ivory or Black Ivory or Black
Nassau Blue	Harbor Blue	703	Ivory & Charcoal Opt. Lt. & Dk. Blue	573-579 602-611 575-581 591-607	All (exc. 2419) All (exc. 2419)	Bright Metal Bright Metal	Onyx Black Opt. Harbor Blue	Ivory or Blue Ivory or Blue
India Ivory	Nassau Blue	707	Ivory & Charcoal Opt. Lt. & Dk. Blue	573-579 602-610-611 575-581 591-607	All All (exc. 2419)	Bright Metal Bright Metal	Onyx Black Opt. Harbor Blue	Ivory or Blue Ivory or Blue
India Ivory	Dusk Plum	708	Ivory & Charcoal	573-579 602-610-611	All	Bright Metal	Onyx Black	Ivory or Black
Adobe Beige	Sierra Gold	700	Tan & Copper	617-618 619-620-621	All	Bright Metal	Sierra Gold	Tan or Black
India Ivory	Dawn Gray	721	Ivory & Charcoal	573-579 602-610-611	All	Bright Metal	Onyx Black	Ivory or Black
Imperial Ivory	Inca Silver	757	Ivory & Charcoal	573-579 602-610-611	All	Bright Metal	Onyx Black	Ivory or Black

Opt.—Optional Trim Combination.

NOTE: On Series 2400 models, the first color is used on the roof, pillars, rear deck, upper quarter panels and the area between the two body side moldings. The second color is used on the hood, front fenders, lower body and wheels. However on model 2429, the first color is used for the tail gate, upper quarter panels and area between the two body side moldings. The second color is used on the roof pillars, lift gate, hood, front fenders, lower body and wheels. On model 2419 the first color is used on the tail gate, upper quarter panels, pillars, lift gate and the area between the two body side moldings. The second color is used for the roof, front fenders, lower body and wheels. No conventional two-toning is available on any model in the 2400 Series

0023910

1956 TWO COLOR EXTERIORS (Cont.)
SERIES 2400 (Cont.)

First Body Color (See Note)	Second Body Color (See Note)	Paint Comb. No.	2400 Trim	Trim Comb. No.	Models	Inst. Panel—Center, Radio Cover Panel 2429 ONLY Upr. Garnish Moulding, W/shield Pillar Moulding, Qtr. Window Moulding, W/shield lwr. Gar. Mould.	Inst. Panel—Upr. & lwr., Steer. Wheel, Col. & Hub, Garn. Moulds. (exc. 2429) Dir. Signal Housing, Ash Tray Cover Panel, Heater Cover Panel, Door Lock Rod Knob	Top Color 2434
Calypso Cream	Grecian Gold	756	Ivory & Charcoal Opt. Cream & Charcoal	573-579 602-610-611 626-627 630-631-632	All All	Bright Metal Bright Metal	Onyx Black Onyx Black	Ivory or Black Ivory or Black
Onyx Black	Crocus Yellow	696	Ivory & Charcoal Opt. Yellow & Charcoal	573-579 602-610-611 578-585 588-595-604	All All	Bright Metal Bright Metal	Onyx Black Onyx Black	Ivory or Black Ivory or Black
India Ivory	Matador Red	711	Ivory & Charcoal Opt. Ivory & Red	573 602 605	2402 2403 2434	Bright Metal Bright Metal	Onyx Black Opt. Matador Red	Ivory or Black Ivory or Black
Dune Beige	Matador Red	715	Ivory & Charcoal Opt. Red & Beige▴	579-610 611 583-586 593	2413-2429 2419-2454 2413-2429 2419-2554	Bright Metal Bright Metal	Onyx Black Opt. Matador Red	
Adobe Beige	Matador Red	763	Ivory & Charcoal Opt. Red & Beige▴	579-610 611 583-586 593	2413-2429 2419-2454 2413-2429 2419-2454	Bright Metal Bright Metal	Onyx Black Opt. Matador Red	
India Ivory	Twilight Turquoise	710	Ivory & Charcoal Opt. Lt. & Dk. Turquoise Opt. Ivory & Turquoise	573-579 602-610-611 577-584 587-594 603	All All (exc. 2434) 2434	Bright Metal Bright Metal Bright Metal	Onyx Black Opt. Twilight Turquoise Opt. Twilight Turquoise	Ivory or Black Ivory or Black
India Ivory	Tropical Turquoise	754	Ivory & Charcoal Opt. Lt. & Dk. Turquoise Opt. Ivory & Turquoise	573-579 602-610-611 577-584 587-594 603	All All (exc. 2434) 2434	Bright Metal Bright Metal Bright Metal	Onyx Black Opt. Tropical Turquoise Opt. Tropical Turquoise	Ivory or Black Ivory or Black

Opt.—Optional Trim Combination.

▴Superceded by combinations 628-629-633 (Red Taupe Pattern Cloth & Red Imitation Leather).

NOTE: On Series 2400 models, the first color is used on the roof, pillars, rear deck, upper quarter panels and the area between the two body side moldings. The second color is used on the hood, front fenders, lower body and wheels. However on model 2429, the first color is used for the tail gate, upper quarter panels and area between the two body side moldings. The second color is used on the roof pillars, lift gate, hood, front fenders, lower body and wheels On model 2419 the first color is used on the tail gate, upper quarter panels, pillars, lift gate and the area between the two body side moldings. The second color is used for the roof, front fenders, lower body and wheels. No conventional two-toning is available on any model in the 2400 Series.

0023911

Corvette
EXTERIOR - INTERIOR COLOR COMBINATIONS

BODY COLOR	DOOR & FRONT FENDER DEPRESSION*	CONVERTIBLE TOP	WHEELS	INTERIOR TRIM	UPPER INSTRUMENT PANEL	LOWER INSTRUMENT PANEL, STEERING COLUMN, DIRECTION SIGNAL HOUSING, STEERING WHEEL HUB AND PLASTIC SIDEWALL PANEL	STEER WHEEL
Onyx Black	Silver	Black or White or Beige	Black	Red	Black	Red	Red
Aztec Copper	Beige	Beige or White	Copper	Beige	Copper	Beige	Beige
Cascade Green	Beige	Black or White or Beige	Green	Beige	Green	Beige	Beige
Arctic Blue	Silver	Black or White or Beige	Blue	Red	Blue	Beige	Red
				Beige	Blue	Beige	Beige
Venetian Red	Beige	Black or White or Beige	Red	Red	Red	Beige	Red
Polo White	Silver	Black or White or Beige	Red	Red	Red 1st des White 2nd des	White 1st des Beige 2nd des	Red
Inca Silver	Imperial Ivory	Black or White	Silver	Red Beige	Silver Silver	Beige Beige	Red Beige

* - Front fender depression is also available painted body color.

INTERIOR COLORS AND FABRICS

AREA		MATERIAL	TRIM COMBINATION RED	TRIM COMBINATION BEIGE
Seats	Cushion	Waffle Pattern Vinyl	Red	Beige
	Backrest			
	Cushion Bolster	Leather Grain Vinyl		
	Backrest Bolster			
Sidewalls	Top Roll			
	Upper Panel	Waffle Pattern Vinyl		
	Decorative Molding	Metal	Bright	
	Lower Panel & Armrest	Leather Grain Vinyl	Red	Beige
	Scuff Pad	Textured Metal	Bright	
Cowl Side Kick Panels		Waffle Pattern Vinyl	Red	Beige
Windlace		Leather Grain Vinyl		
Floor Covering		Carpet	Red	Copper
Top Storage Well		Paint	Red	Beige
Rear Compartment	Mat	Rubber	Red	Black
	Trim Board	Composition Board	Red	Beige

1957 Trim Combinations

EXTERIOR - INTERIOR COLOR COMBINATIONS ONE COLOR EXTERIORS SERIES 2400

OUTSIDE COLOR	ALL SERIES 2400 EXCEPT 2434: Instrument panel upper and lower; garnish moldings; door lock rod knobs; heater cover panel; ash tray face plate.	ALL SERIES 2400 EXCEPT 2434: Turn signal housing; steering wheel; instrument cluster; gearshift control housing.	ALL SERIES 2400 EXCEPT 2434: Trim	2434 ONLY: Instrument panel upper and lower; garnish moldings; door lock rod knobs; heater cover panel; ash tray face plate.	2434 ONLY: Turn signal housing; steering wheel; instrument cluster; gearshift control housing.	2434 ONLY: Trim	FOLDING TOP Std.	FOLDING TOP Opt.
Onyx Black	Onyx Black	Silver †	Silver and Black	Matador Red	Red	Red and Silver	Ivory	Black
Inco Silver	Matador Red	Matador Red	Red and Black	Matador Red	Red	Red and Silver	Ivory	Black
Imperial Ivory	Matador Red	Matador Red	Red and Black	Matador Red	Red	Red and Silver	Ivory	Black
Matador Red	Matador Red	Matador Red	Red and Black	Matador Red	Red	Red and Silver	Ivory	Black
Harbor Blue	Harbor Blue	Harbor Blue	Medium and Dark Blue	Harbor Blue	Harbor Blue	Medium and Light Blue	Ivory	Light Blue
Larkspur Blue	Harbor Blue	Harbor Blue	Medium and Dark Blue	Harbor Blue	Harbor Blue	Medium and Light Blue	Ivory	Light Blue
Tropical Turquoise	Tropical Turquoise	Tropical Turquoise	Medium and Dark Turquoise	Tropical Turquoise	Tropical Turquoise	Medium Turquoise	Ivory	Black
Surf Green	Highland Green	Highland Green	Medium and Dark Green	Highland Green	Highland Green	Medium and Light Green	Ivory	Medium Green
Highland Green	Highland Green	Highland Green	Medium and Dark Green	Highland Green	Highland Green	Medium and Light Green	Ivory	Medium Green
Colonial Cream	Onyx Black	Silver	Yellow and Black	Onyx Black	Silver	Yellow and Silver	Ivory	Black
Sierra Gold	Sierra Gold	Sierra Gold	Beige and Copper	Sierra Gold	Sierra Gold	Beige and Copper	Ivory	Tan Beige
Adobe Beige	Sierra Gold	Sierra Gold	Beige and Copper	Sierra Gold	Sierra Gold	Beige and Copper	Ivory	Tan Beige
Coronado Yellow (2434 only)	—	—	—	Onyx Black	Silver	Ivory and Silver	Ivory	Black
Canyon Coral (2434 only)	—	—	—	Onyx Black	Silver	Ivory and Silver	Ivory	Black
Dusk Pearl (2434 only)	—	—	—	Onyx Black	Silver	Ivory and Silver	Ivory	Black
Laurel Green (2434 only)	—	—	—	Onyx Black	Silver	Ivory and Silver	Ivory	Black

Instrument panel center and radio cover panel are bright metal in all Series 2400 cars.

†Also available in red and black trim (669, 676, 690, 697); except Convertibles (2434). If car has red and black trim; instrument cluster, steering wheel, etc. is red. If car has silver and black trim; instrument cluster, steering wheel, etc. is silver.

EXTERIOR - INTERIOR COLOR COMBINATIONS ONE COLOR EXTERIORS SERIES 2100

OUTSIDE COLOR	2102 2103 2113 2154: Trim	2102 2103 2113 2154: Instrument panel upper and lower; garnish moldings; door locking rod knobs; ash tray face plate; heater cover panel	2102 2103 2113 2154: Turn signal housing; steering wheel; instrument cluster; gearshift control housing.	2109 2119 2129 2124: Trim	2109 2119 2129 2124: Instrument panel upper and lower; garnish moldings; door locking rod knobs; ash tray face plate; heater cover panel	2109 2119 2129 2124: Turn signal housing; steering wheel; instrument cluster; gearshift control housing.
Onyx Black	Ivory and Charcoal	Onyx Black	Silver	Ivory and Charcoal	Onyx Black	Silver
Inco Silver	Ivory and Charcoal	Onyx Black	Silver	Ivory and Charcoal	Onyx Black	Silver
Imperial Ivory	Ivory and Charcoal	Onyx Black	Silver	Ivory and Charcoal	Onyx Black	Silver
Harbor Blue	Light and Medium Blue	Harbor Blue	Larkspur Blue	Ivory and Charcoal	Onyx Black	Silver
Larkspur Blue	Light and Medium Blue	Harbor Blue	Larkspur Blue	Ivory and Charcoal	Onyx Black	Silver
Tropical Turquoise	Ivory and Charcoal	Onyx Black	Silver	Ivory and Charcoal	Onyx Black	Silver
Surf Green	Light and Medium Green	Highland Green	Surf Green	Light and Medium Green	Highland Green	Surf Green
Highland Green	Light and Medium Green	Highland Green	Surf Green	Light and Medium Green	Highland Green	Surf Green
Colonial Cream	Ivory and Charcoal	Onyx Black	Silver	Ivory and Charcoal	Onyx Black	Silver
Sierra Gold	N.A.	—	—	Copper and Beige	Sierra Gold	Sierra Gold*
Adobe Beige	Ivory and Charcoal	Onyx Black	Silver	Copper and Beige	Sierra Gold	Sierra Gold*
Matador Red	Ivory and Charcoal	Onyx Black	Silver	Ivory and Charcoal	Onyx Black	Silver

* - Beige in 2124 Instrument panel center, radio cover panel, and clock cover panel are silver on all Series 2100 cars.

SERIES 1500

OUTSIDE COLOR	1502 1503 1512 1508: Trim	1502 1503 1512 1508: Instrument panel upper; garnish moldings; door locking rod knobs.	1502 1503 1512 1508: Instrument panel center and lower; turn signal housing; steering wheel; horn button cap; instrument cluster; gearshift control housing.	1529 ONLY: Trim	1529 ONLY: Instrument panel upper; garnish moldings; door locking rod knobs.	1529 ONLY: Instrument panel center and lower; turn signal housing; steering wheel; horn button cap; instrument cluster; gearshift control housing.
Onyx Black	Black and Gray	Onyx Black	Silver	Black and Gray	Onyx Black	Silver
Imperial Ivory	Black and Gray	Onyx Black	Silver	Black and Gray	Onyx Black	Silver
Harbor Blue	Black and Gray	Onyx Black	Silver	Black and Gray	Onyx Black	Silver
Larkspur Blue	Black and Gray	Onyx Black	Silver	Black and Gray	Onyx Black	Silver
Tropical Turquoise (N.A. in 1508)	Black and Gray	Onyx Black	Silver	Black and Gray	Onyx Black	Silver
Surf Green	Black and Gray	Onyx Black	Silver	Light and Dark Green	Highland Green	Silver
Highland Green	Black and Gray	Onyx Black	Silver	Light and Dark Green	Highland Green	Silver
Colonial Cream (N.A. in 1508)	Black and Gray	Onyx Black	Silver	Black and Gray	Onyx Black	Silver
Adobe Beige (N.A. in 1508)	Black and Gray	Onyx Black	Silver	Light and Dark Green	Highland Green	Silver
Matador Red	Black and Gray	Onyx Black	Silver	Black and Gray	Onyx Black	Silver

0023912

EXTERIOR - INTERIOR COLOR COMBINATIONS TWO COLOR EXTERIORS SERIES 2400

OUTSIDE COLORS: FIRST COLOR*	OUTSIDE COLORS: SECOND COLOR*	Trim	Instrument panel upper and lower; garnish moldings; door lock rod knobs; heat cover panel; ash tray face plate.	Turn signal housing; steering wheel; instrument cluster; gearshift control housing.
India Ivory	Onyx Black	Red and Black	Matador Red	Matador Red
Imperial Ivory	Inco Silver	Red and Black	Matador Red	Matador Red
Larkspur Blue	Harbor Blue	Medium and Dark Blue	Harbor Blue	Larkspur Blue
India Ivory	Larkspur Blue	Medium and Dark Blue	Harbor Blue	Larkspur Blue
India Ivory	Tropical Turquoise	Medium and Dark Turquoise	Tropical Turquoise	Tropical Turquoise
Surf Green	Highland Green	Medium and Dark Green	Highland Green	Surf Green
India Ivory	Surf Green	Medium and Dark Green	Highland Green	Surf Green
India Ivory	Coronado Yellow	Silver and Black	Onyx Black	Silver
Onyx Black	Colonial Cream	Yellow and Black	Onyx Black	Silver
India Ivory	Colonial Cream	Yellow and Black	Onyx Black	Silver
India Ivory	Canyon Coral	Silver and Black	Onyx Black	Silver
Adobe Beige	Sierra Gold	Beige and Copper	Sierra Gold	Adobe Beige
India Ivory	Matador Red	Red and Black	Matador Red	Matador Red
Imperial Ivory	Dusk Pearl	Silver and Black	Onyx Black	Silver
Colonial Cream	Laurel Green	Silver and Black	Onyx Black	Silver

* - First color covers roof and pillars; second color covers remainder of exterior. Instrument panel center and radio cover panel are bright metal in all Series 2400 cars.

EXTERIOR - INTERIOR COLOR COMBINATIONS TWO COLOR EXTERIORS SERIES 2100

OUTSIDE COLORS: FIRST* COLOR	OUTSIDE COLORS: SECOND* COLOR	2102 2103 2113 2154: Trim	2102 2103 2113 2154: Instrument panel upper and lower; garnish moldings; door locking rod knobs; ash tray face plate; heater cover panel.	2102 2103 2113 2154: Turn signal housing; steering wheel; instrument panel cluster; gearshift control housing.	2109 2119 2129 2124: Trim	2109 2119 2129 2124: Instrument panel upper and lower; garnish moldings; door locking rod knobs; ash tray face plate; heater cover panel.	2109 2119 2129 2124: Turn signal housing; steering wheel; instrument panel cluster; gearshift control housing.
India Ivory	Onyx Black	Ivory and Charcoal	Onyx Black	Silver	Ivory and Charcoal	Onyx Black	Silver
Imperial Ivory	Inca Silver	Ivory and Charcoal	Onyx Black	Silver	Ivory and Charcoal	Onyx Black	Silver
Larkspur Blue	Harbor Blue	Light and Medium Blue	Harbor Blue	Larkspur Blue	Ivory and Charcoal	Onyx Black	Silver
India Ivory	Larkspur Blue	Light and Medium Blue	Harbor Blue	Larkspur Blue	Ivory and Charcoal	Onyx Black	Silver
India Ivory	Tropical Turquoise	Ivory and Charcoal	Onyx Black	Silver	Ivory and Charcoal	Onyx Black	Silver
Surf Green	Highland Green	Light and Medium Green	Highland Green	Surf Green	Light and Medium Green	Highland Green	Surf Green
India Ivory	Surf Green	Light and Medium Green	Highland Green	Surf Green	Light and Medium Green	Highland Green	Surf Green
India Ivory	Coronado Yellow	Ivory and Charcoal	Onyx Black	Silver	Ivory and Charcoal	Onyx Black	Silver
Colonial Cream	Onyx Black	Ivory and Charcoal	Onyx Black	Silver	Ivory and Charcoal	Onyx Black	Silver
India Ivory	Colonial Cream	Ivory and Charcoal	Onyx Black	Silver	Ivory and Charcoal	Onyx Black	Silver
India Ivory	Canyon Coral	Ivory and Charcoal	Onyx Black	Silver	Ivory and Charcoal	Onyx Black	Silver
India Ivory	Matador Red	Ivory and Charcoal	Onyx Black	Silver	Ivory and Charcoal	Onyx Black	Silver
Imperial Ivory	Dusk Pearl	Ivory and Charcoal	Onyx Black	Silver	Ivory and Charcoal	Onyx Black	Silver
Colonial Cream	Laurel Green	Ivory and Charcoal	Onyx Black	Silver	Ivory and Charcoal	Onyx Black	Silver
Adobe Beige	Sierra Gold	N.A.	—	—	Copper and Beige	Sierra Gold	Adobe Beige

* - First color covers roof, pillars, and insert area; second color covers remaining exterior areas.
Instrument panel center, radio cover panel, and clock cover panel are silver on all Series 2100 cars.

SERIES 1500

OUTSIDE COLORS: FIRST* COLOR	OUTSIDE COLORS: SECOND* COLOR	1502 1503 1512: Trim	1502 1503 1512: Instrument panel upper; garnish moldings; door locking rod knobs.	1502 1503 1512: Instrument panel center and lower; turn signal housing; steering wheel; horn button cap; instrument cluster; gearshift control housing.	1529 ONLY: Trim	1529 ONLY: Instrument panel upper; garnish moldings; door locking rod knobs.	1529 ONLY: Instrument panel center and lower; turn signal housing; steering wheel; horn button cap; instrument cluster; gearshift control housing.
India Ivory	Onyx Black	Black and Gray	Onyx Black	Silver	Black and Gray	Onyx Black	Silver
Larkspur Blue	Harbor Blue	Black and Gray	Onyx Black	Silver	Black and Gray	Onyx Black	Silver
India Ivory	Larkspur Blue	Black and Gray	Onyx Black	Silver	Black and Gray	Onyx Black	Silver
India Ivory	Tropical Turquoise	Black and Gray	Onyx Black	Silver	Black and Gray	Onyx Black	Silver
Highland Green	Surf Green	Black and Gray	Onyx Black	Silver	Light and Dark Green	Highland Green	Silver
India Ivory	Surf Green	Black and Gray	Onyx Black	Silver	Light and Dark Green	Highland Green	Silver
Onyx Black	Colonial Cream	Black and Gray	Onyx Black	Silver	Black and Gray	Onyx Black	Silver
India Ivory	Colonial Cream	Black and Gray	Onyx Black	Silver	Light and Dark Green	Highland Green	Silver
India Ivory	Matador Red	Black and Gray	Onyx Black	Silver	Black and Gray	Onyx Black	Silver
Imperial Ivory	Inca Silver	Black and Gray	Onyx Black	Silver	Black and Gray	Onyx Black	Silver

* - First color covers upper quarters and deck or tailgate; second color covers remaining exterior areas.

0023913

1957 Trim Combinations (continued)

1957 CHEVROLET PASSENGER CAR PAINT CHART

PAINT COMBINATIONS

Color Combination Number	BODY SHEET METAL		2100 AND 2400 SERIES								1500 SERIES		
			Instrument Panel Upper and Lower, Garnish Moldings, Door Lock Rod Knobs, Heater Cover Panel, Ash Tray Face Plate				Turn Signal Housing, Steering Wheel, Instrument Cluster, Gearshift Control Housing				Instrument Panel Upper, Garnish Moldings, Door Lock Rod Knobs		Instrument Panel Center and Lower, Turn Signal Housing, Horn Button Cap, Instrument Cluster, Gearshift Control Housing
			2400 Series		2100 Series		2400 Series		2100 Series				
	Upper Color	Lower Color	2434	All Others	2102-03-13-54	2109-19-24-29	2434	All Others	2102-03-13-54	2109-19-24-29	1502-03-08-12	1529	All Models
793	Onyx Black		Matador Red	Onyx Black	Onyx Black		Matador Red	†	Silver		Onyx Black		Silver
794	Imperial Ivory		Matador Red		Onyx Black		Matador Red		Silver		Onyx Black		Silver
795	Larkspur Blue		Larkspur Blue	Harbor Blue	Harbor Blue	Onyx Black	Harbor Blue		Larkspur Blue	Silver	Onyx Black		Silver
796	Harbor Blue		Larkspur Blue	Harbor Blue	Harbor Blue	Onyx Black	Harbor Blue		Larkspur Blue	Silver	Onyx Black		Silver
797	Surf Green		Highland Green		Highland Green		Highland Green		Surf Green		Onyx Black	Highland Green	Silver
798	Highland Green		Highland Green		Highland Green		Highland Green		Surf Green		Onyx Black	Highland Green	Silver
799 ◇	Tropical Turquoise		Tropical Turquoise		Onyx Black		Tropical Turquoise		Silver		Onyx Black		Silver
800 ◇	Colonial Cream		Onyx Black		Onyx Black		Silver		Silver		Onyx Black		Silver
801	Canyon Coral		Onyx Black	--	--		Silver	--	--		--		--
802	Matador Red		Matador Red		Onyx Black		Matador Red		Silver		Onyx Black		Silver
803	Coronado Yellow		Onyx Black	--	--		Silver	--	--		--		--
804	Inca Silver		Matador Red		Onyx Black		Matador Red		Silver		--		--
805	Sierra Gold		Adobe Beige	Sierra Gold	--	Sierra Gold	Sierra Gold		--	Sierra Gold*	--		--
806 ◇	Adobe Beige		Sierra Gold		Onyx Black	Sierra Gold	Sierra Gold		Silver	Sierra Gold*	Onyx Black	Highland Green	Silver
807	India Ivory	Onyx Black	Matador Red		Onyx Black		Matador Red		Silver		Onyx Black		Silver
808	Imperial Ivory	Inca Silver	Matador Red		Onyx Black		Matador Red		Silver		Onyx Black		Silver
809	Larkspur Blue	Harbor Blue	Harbor Blue		Harbor Blue	Onyx Black	Larkspur Blue		Larkspur Blue	Silver	Onyx Black		Silver
810	India Ivory	Larkspur Blue	Harbor Blue		Harbor Blue	Onyx Black	Larkspur Blue		Larkspur Blue	Silver	Onyx Black		Silver
811	India Ivory	Tropical Turquoise	Tropical Turquoise		Onyx Black		Tropical Turquoise		Silver		Onyx Black		Silver
812	Surf Green ▲	Highland Green ▲	Highland Green		Highland Green		Surf Green		Surf Green		Onyx Black	Highland Green	Silver
813	India Ivory	Surf Green	Highland Green		Highland Green		Surf Green		Surf Green		Onyx Black	Highland Green	Silver
814	India Ivory	Coronado Yellow	Onyx Black		Onyx Black		Silver		Silver		--		--
815	Onyx Black ●	Colonial Cream ●	Onyx Black		Onyx Black		Silver		Silver		Onyx Black		Silver
816	India Ivory	Colonial Cream	Onyx Black		Onyx Black		Silver		Silver		Onyx Black	Highland Green	Silver
817	India Ivory	Canyon Coral	Onyx Black		Onyx Black		Silver		Silver		--		--
818	Adobe Beige	Sierra Gold	Sierra Gold		--	Sierra Gold	Adobe Beige		--	Adobe Beige	--		--
819	India Ivory	Matador Red	Matador Red		Onyx Black		Matador Red		Silver		Onyx Black		Silver
820	Colonial Cream	Laurel Green	Onyx Black		Onyx Black		Silver		Silver		--		--
821	Dusk Pearl		Onyx Black	--	--		Silver	--	--		--		--
822	Imperial Ivory	Dusk Pearl	Onyx Black		Onyx Black		Silver		Silver		--		--
823	Laurel Green		Onyx Black	--	--		Silver	--	--		--		--

* This color changed to Beige in 2124.
▲ These colors reversed on 1500 models.
● These colors reversed on 2100 models.
◇ Not available in 1508 model.

†Also available in red and black trim (669, 676, 690, 697); except Convertibles (2434). If car has red and black trim; instrument cluster, steering wheel, etc. is red. If car has silver and black trim; instrument cluster, steering wheel, etc. is silver.

0023914

1957 EXTERIOR-INTERIOR COLOR COMBINATIONS ONE COLOR EXTERIORS

SERIES 1500

OUTSIDE COLOR	Paint Comb. No.	1502 1503 1508 1512				1529 ONLY			
		Trim	Trim Comb. No.	Instrument panel upper; garnish moldings; door locking rod knobs	Instrument panel center and lower; turn signal housing; steering wheel; horn button cap; instrument cluster; gearshift control housing	Trim	Trim Comb. No.	Instrument panel upper; garnish moldings; door locking rod knobs	Instrument panel center and lower; turn signal housing; steering wheel; horn button cap; instrument cluster; gearshift control housing
Onyx Black	793	Black and Gray	650 651	Onyx Black	Silver	Black and Gray	652	Onyx Black	Silver
Imperial Ivory	794	Black and Gray	650 651	Onyx Black	Silver	Black and Gray	652	Onyx Black	Silver
Harbor Blue	796	Black and Gray	650 651	Onyx Black	Silver	Black and Gray	652	Onyx Black	Silver
Larkspur Blue	795	Black and Gray	650 651	Onyx Black	Silver	Black and Gray	652	Onyx Black	Silver
Tropical Turquoise (N.A. in 1508)	799	Black and Gray	650	Onyx Black	Silver	Black and Gray	652	Onyx Black	Silver
Surf Green	797	Black and Gray	650 651	Onyx Black	Silver	Light and Dark Green	653	Highland Green	Silver
Highland Green	798	Black and Gray	650 651	Onyx Black	Silver	Light and Dark Green	653	Highland Green	Silver
Colonial Cream (N.A. in 1508)	800	Black and Gray	650	Onyx Black	Silver	Black and Gray	652	Onyx Black	Silver
Adobe Beige (N.A. in 1508)	806	Black and Gray	650	Onyx Black	Silver	Light and Dark Green	653	Highland Green	Silver
Matador Red	802	Black and Gray	650 651	Onyx Black	Silver	Black and Gray	652	Onyx Black	Silver

1957 ONE COLOR EXTERIORS (Cont.)

SERIES 2100

OUTSIDE COLOR	Paint Comb. No.	2102 2103 2113 2154				2109 2119 2129 2124			
		Trim	Trim Comb. No.	Instrument panel upper and lower; garnish moldings; door locking rod knobs; ash tray face plate; heater cover panel	Turn signal housing; steering wheel; instrument cluster; gearshift control housing	Trim	Trim Comb. No.	Instrument panel upper and lower; garnish moldings; door locking rod knobs; ash tray face plate; heater cover panel	Turn signal housing; steering wheel; instrument cluster; gearshift control housing
Onyx Black	793	Ivory and Charcoal	654	Onyx Black	Silver	Ivory and Charcoal	657-660	Onyx Black	Silver
Inca Silver	804	Ivory and Charcoal	654	Onyx Black	Silver	Ivory and Charcoal	657-660	Onyx Black	Silver
Imperial Ivory	794	Ivory and Charcoal	654	Onyx Black	Silver	Ivory and Charcoal	657-660	Onyx Black	Silver
Harbor Blue	796	Light and Med. Blue		Harbor Blue	Larkspur Blue	Ivory and Charcoal	657-660	Onyx Black	Silver
Larkspur Blue	795	Light and Med. Blue	656	Harbor Blue	Larkspur Blue	Ivory and Charcoal	657-660	Onyx Black	Silver
Tropical Turquoise	799	Ivory and Charcoal	654	Onyx Black	Silver	Ivory and Charcoal	657-660	Onyx Black	Silver
Surf Green	797	Light and Med. Green	655	Highland Green	Surf Green	Light and Med. Green	658-661	Highland Green	Surf Green
Highland Green	798	Light and Med. Green	655	Highland Green	Surf Green	Light and Med. Green	658-661	Highland Green	Surf Green
Colonial Cream	800	Ivory and Charcoal	654	Onyx Black	Silver	Ivory and Charcoal	657-660	Onyx Black	Silver
Sierra Gold	805					Copper and Beige	659-662	Sierra Gold	Sierra Gold*
Adobe Beige	806	Ivory and Charcoal	654	Onyx Black	Silver	Copper and Beige	659-662	Sierra Gold	Sierra Gold*
Matador Red	802	Ivory and Charcoal	654	Onyx Black	Silver	Ivory and Charcoal	657-660	Onyx Black	Silver

Instrument panel center, radio cover panel, and clock cover panel are silver on all Series 2100 cars. *Beige in 2124.

0023915

1957 Trim Combinations (continued)

1957 ONE COLOR EXTERIORS (Cont.)
SERIES 2400

Outside Color	Paint Comb. No.	ALL SERIES 2400 EXCEPT 2434: Instrument panel upper and lower; garnish moldings; door lock rod knobs; heater cover panel; ash tray face plate	Turn signal housing steering wheel instrument cluster; gearshift control housing	Trim	Trim Comb. No.	2434 ONLY: Instrument panel upper and lower; garnish moldings; door lock rod knobs; heater cover panel; ash tray face plate.	Turn signal housing; steering wheel, instrument cluster; gearshift control housing.	Trim	Trim Comb. No.	Folding Top Std.	Folding Top Opt.
Onyx Black	793	Onyx Black	Silver †	Silver and Black	663, 670, 684, 691	Matador Red	Red	Red and Silver	683	Ivory	Black
Inca Silver	804	Matador Red	Matador Red	Red and Black	669, 676, 690, 697	Matador Red	Red	Red and Silver	683	Ivory	Black
Imperial Ivory	794	Matador Red	Matador Red	Red and Black	669, 676, 690, 697	Matador Red	Red	Red and Silver	683	Ivory	Black
Matador Red	802	Matador Red	Matador Red	Red and Black	669, 676, 690, 697	Matador Red	Red	Red and Silver	683	Ivory	Black
Harbor Blue	796	Harbor Blue	Harbor Blue	Medium and Dark Blue	665, 672, 686, 693	Harbor Blue	Larkspur Blue	Medium and Light Blue	679	Ivory	Light Blue
Larkspur Blue	795	Harbor Blue	Harbor Blue	Medium Dark Blue	665, 672, 686, 693	Harbor Blue	Larkspur Blue	Medium and Light Blue	679	Ivory	Light Blue
Tropical Turquoise	799	Tropical Turquoise	Tropical Turquoise	Medium and Dark Turquoise	666, 673, 687, 694	Tropical Turquoise	Tropical Turquoise	Medium Turquoise	680	Ivory	Black
Surf Green	797	Highland Green	Highland Green	Medium and Dark Green	664, 671, 685, 692	Highland Green	Highland Green	Medium and Light Green	678	Ivory	Medium Green
Highland Green	798	Highland Green	Highland Green	Medium and Dark Green	664, 671, 685, 692	Highland Green	Highland Green	Medium and Light Green	678	Ivory	Medium Green
Colonial Cream	800	Onyx Black	Silver	Yellow and Black	668, 675, 689, 696	Onyx Black	Silver	Yellow and Silver	682	Ivory	Black
Sierra Gold	805	Sierra Gold	Sierra Gold	Beige and Copper	667, 674, 688, 695	Sierra Gold	Adobe Beige	Beige and Copper	681	Ivory	Tan or Beige
Adobe Beige	806	Sierra Gold	Sierra Gold	Beige and Copper	667, 674, 688, 695	Sierra Gold	Sierra Gold	Beige and Copper	681	Ivory	Tan or Beige
Coronado Yellow	803					Onyx Black	Silver	Ivory and Silver	677	Ivory	Black
Canyon Coral	801					Onyx Black	Silver	Ivory and Silver	677	Ivory	Black
Dusk Pearl	821					Onyx Black	Silver	Ivory and Silver	677	Ivory	Black
Laurel Green	823					Onyx Black	Silver	Ivory and Silver	677	Ivory	Black

Instrument panel center and radio cover panel are bright metal in all Series 2400 cars.

†Also available in red and black trim (669, 676, 690, 697); except Convertibles (2434). If car has red and black trim; instrument cluster, steering wheel, etc. is red. If car has silver and black trim; instrument cluster, steering wheel, etc. is silver.

1957 EXTERIOR-INTERIOR COLOR COMBINATIONS TWO COLOR EXTERIORS
SERIES 1500

First* Color	Second* Color	Paint Comb. No.	1502, 1503, 1612: Trim	Trim Comb. No.	Instrument panel upper; garnish moldings; door locking rod knobs.	Instrument panel center and lower; turn signal housing; steering wheel; horn button cap; instrument cluster; gearshift control housing	1529 ONLY: Trim	Trim Comb. No.	Instrument panel upper; garnish moldings; door locking rod knobs.	Instrument panel center and lower; turn signal housing; steering wheel; horn button cap; instrument cluster; gearshift control housing.
India Ivory	Onyx Black	807	Black and Gray	650	Onyx Black	Silver	Black and Gray	652	Onyx Black	Silver
Larkspur Blue	Harbor Blue	809	Black and Gray	650	Onyx Black	Silver	Black and Gray	652	Onyx Black	Silver
India Ivory	Larkspur Blue	810	Black and Gray	650	Onyx Black	Silver	Black and Gray	652	Onyx Black	Silver
India Ivory	Tropical Turquoise	811	Black and Gray	650	Onyx Black	Silver	Black and Gray	652	Onyx Black	Silver
Highland Green	Surf Green	812	Black and Gray	650	Onyx Black	Silver	Light and Dark Green	653	Highland Green	Silver
India Ivory	Surf Green	813	Black and Gray	650	Onyx Black	Silver	Light and Dark Green	653	Highland Green	Silver
Onyx Black	Colonial Cream	815	Black and Gray	650	Onyx Black	Silver	Black and Gray	652	Onyx Black	Silver
India Ivory	Colonial Cream	816	Black and Gray	650	Onyx Black	Silver	Light and Dark Green	653	Highland Green	Silver
India Ivory	Matador Red	819	Black and Gray	650	Onyx Black	Silver	Black and Gray	652	Onyx Black	Silver
Imperial Ivory	Inca Silver	808	Black and Gray	650	Onyx Black	Silver	Black and Gray	652	Onyx Black	Silver

*First color covers upper quarters and deck or tailgate; second color covers remaining exterior areas.

0023916

1957 TWO COLOR EXTERIORS (Cont.)
SERIES 2100

First* Color	Second* Color	Paint Comb. No.	2102, 2103, 2113, 2154: Trim	Trim Comb. No.	Instrument panel upper and lower; garnish moldings; door locking rod knobs; ash tray face plate; heater cover panel.	Turn signal housing; steering wheel; instrument panel cluster; gearshift control housing.	2109, 2119, 2129, 2124: Trim	Trim Comb. No.	Instrument panel upper and lower; garnish moldings; door locking rod knobs; ash tray face plate; heater cover panel.	Turn signal housing steering wheel; instrument panel cluster, gearshift control housing.
India Ivory	Onyx Black	807	Ivory and Charcoal	654	Onyx Black	Silver	Ivory and Charcoal	657 660	Onyx Black	Silver
Imperial Ivory	Inca Silver	808	Ivory and Charcoal	654	Onyx Black	Silver	Ivory and Charcoal	657 660	Onyx Black	Silver
Larkspur Blue	Harbor Blue	809	Light and Medium Blue	656	Harbor Blue	Larkspur Blue	Ivory and Charcoal	657 660	Onyx Black	Silver
India Ivory	Larkspur Blue	810	Light and Medium Blue	656	Harbor Blue	Larkspur Blue	Ivory and Charcoal	657 660	Onyx Black	Silver
India Ivory	Tropical Turquoise	811	Ivory and Charcoal	654	Onyx Black	Silver	Ivory and Charcoal	657 660	Onyx Black	Silver
Surf Green	Highland Green	812	Light and Medium Green	655	Highland Green	Surf Green	Light and Medium Green	658 661	Highland Green	Surf Green
India Ivory	Surf Green	813	Light and Medium Green	655	Highland Green	Surf Green	Light and Medium Green	658 661	Highland Green	Surf Green
India Ivory	Coronado Yellow	814	Ivory and Charcoal	654	Onyx Black	Silver	Ivory and Charcoal	657 660	Onyx Black	Silver
Colonial Cream	Onyx Black	815	Ivory and Charcoal	654	Onyx Black	Silver	Ivory and Charcoal	657 660	Onyx Black	Silver
India Ivory	Colonial Cream	816	Ivory and Charcoal	654	Onyx Black	Silver	Ivory and Charcoal	657 660	Onyx Black	Silver
India Ivory	Canyon Coral	817	Ivory and Charcoal	654	Onyx Black	Silver	Ivory and Charcoal	657 660	Onyx Black	Silver
India Ivory	Matador Red	819	Ivory and Charcoal	654	Onyx Black	Silver	Ivory and Charcoal	657 660	Onyx Black	Silver
Imperial Ivory	Dusk Pearl	822	Ivory and Charcoal	654	Onyx Black	Silver	Ivory and Charcoal	657 660	Onyx Black	Silver
Colonial Cream	Laurel Green	820	Ivory and Charcoal	654	Onyx Black	Silver	Ivory and Charcoal	657 660	Onyx Black	Silver
Adobe Beige	Sierra Gold	818					Copper and Beige	659 662	Sierra Gold	Adobe Beige

*First color covers roof, pillars, and insert area; second covers remaining exterior areas.

Instrument panel center, radio cover panel, and clock cover panel are silver on all Series 2100 cars.

1957 TWO COLOR EXTERIORS (Cont.)
SERIES 2400

First Color*	Second Color*	Paint Comb. No.	Trim	Trim Comb. No.	Instrument panel upper and lower; garnish moldings; door lock rod knobs; heater cover panel; ash tray face plate	Turn signal housing steering wheel; instrument cluster gearshift control housing
India Ivory	Onyx Black	807	Red and Black	669-676 690-697	Matador Red	Matador Red
Imperial Ivory	Inca Silver	808	Red and Black	669-676 690-697	Matador Red	Matador Red
Larkspur Blue	Harbor Blue	809	Medium and Dark Blue	665-672 686-693	Harbor Blue	Larkspur Blue
India Ivory	Larkspur Blue	810	Medium and Dark Blue	665-672 686-693	Harbor Blue	Larkspur Blue
India Ivory	Tropical Turquoise	811	Medium and Dark Turquoise	666-673 587-694	Tropical Turquoise	Tropical Turquoise
Surf Green	Highland Green	812	Medium and Dark Green	664-671 685-692	Highland Green	Surf Green
India Ivory	Surf Green	813	Medium and Dark Green	664-671 685-692	Highland Green	Surf Green
India Ivory	Coronado Yellow	814	Silver and Black	663-670 684-691	Onyx Black	Silver
Onyx Black	Colonial Cream	815	Yellow and Black	668-675 689-696	Onyx Black	Silver
India Ivory	Colonial Cream	816	Yellow and Black	668-675 689-696	Onyx Black	Silver
India Ivory	Canyon Coral	817	Silver and Black	663-670 684-691	Onyx Black	Silver
Adobe Beige	Sierra Gold	818	Beige and Copper	667-674 688-695	Sierra Gold	Adobe Beige
India Ivory	Matador Red	819	Red and Black	669-676 690-697	Matador Red	Matador Red
Imperial Ivory	Dusk Pearl	822	Silver and Black	663-670 684-691	Onyx Black	Silver
Colonial Cream	Laurel Green	820	Silver and Black	663-670 684-691	Onyx Black	Silver

*First color covers roof and pillars; second color covers remainder of exterior.
Instrument panel center and radio cover panel are bright metal in all Series 2400 cars.

0023917

1957 Trim Combinations (continued)

Corvette

EXTERIOR - INTERIOR COLOR COMBINATIONS

BODY COLOR	DOOR & FRONT FENDER DEPRESSION*	CONVERTIBLE TOP	WHEELS	INTERIOR TRIM	UPPER INSTRUMENT PANEL	LOWER INSTRUMENT PANEL, STEERING COLUMN, DIRECTION SIGNAL HOUSING, STEERING WHEEL HUB AND PLASTIC SIDEWALL PANEL	STEER WHEEL
Onyx Black	Silver	Black or White or Beige	Black	Red	Black	Red	Red
Aztec Copper	Beige	Beige or White	Copper	Beige	Copper	Beige	Beige
Cascade Green	Beige	Black or White or Beige	Green	Beige	Green	Beige	Beige
Arctic Blue	Silver	Black or White or Beige	Blue	Red	Blue	Beige	Red
				Beige	Blue	Beige	Beige
Venetian Red	Beige	Black or White or Beige	Red	Red	Red	Beige	Red
Polo White	Silver	Black or White or Beige	Red	Red	Red 1st des White 2nd des	White 1st des Beige 2nd des	Red
Inca Silver	Imperial Ivory	Black or White	Silver	Red Beige	Silver Silver	Beige Beige	Red Beige

* - Front fender depression is also available painted body color.

INTERIOR COLORS AND FABRICS

AREA		MATERIAL	TRIM COMBINATION	
			RED	BEIGE
Seats	Cushion	Waffle Pattern Vinyl	Red	Beige
	Backrest			
	Cushion Bolster	Leather Grain Vinyl		
	Backrest Bolster			
Sidewalls	Top Roll			
	Upper Panel	Waffle Pattern Vinyl		
	Decorative Molding	Metal	Bright	
	Lower Panel & Armrest	Leather Grain Vinyl	Red	Beige
	Scuff Pad	Textured Metal	Bright	
Cowl Side Kick Panels		Waffle Pattern Vinyl	Red	Beige
Windlace		Leather Grain Vinyl		
Floor Covering		Carpet	Red	Copper
Top Storage Well		Paint	Red	Beige
Rear Compartment	Mat	Rubber	Red	Black
	Trim Board	Composition Board	Red	Beige

1958 Trim Combinations

EXTERIOR - INTERIOR COLOR COMBINATIONS
BEL AIR SERIES
IMPALA MODELS

EXTERIOR COLORS &			Instrument panel upper and lower; garnish moldings; door lock knobs; glove box door lower; radio grille screen; package shelf *; direction signal and shift lever housing; steering wheel sides ʀ; steering jacket insert and cover; heater cover plate; ash tray face plate	Instrument panel center; glove box door upper; seat end panels; radio cover plate.	Interior trim combinations
SINGLE	TWO-COLOR *				
	Roof Color	Body Color			
Onyx Black 900	Arctic White	Onyx Black	Onyx Black	Bright Metal	Black, Silver and Turquoise
Glen Green 903	Arctic White	Glen Green	Forest Green	Bright Metal	3-Tone Green
Forest Green 905	Glen Green	Forest Green			
Colonial Cream 925	Arctic White	Colonial Cream			
Cashmere Blue 910	Arctic White	Cashmere Blue	Fathom Blue	Bright Metal	3-Tone Blue
Fathom Blue 912	Cashmere Blue	Fathom Blue			
Silver Blue (A) 930	Snowcrest White (A)	Silver Blue (A)			
Aegean Turquoise 916	Arctic White	Aegean Turquoise	Aegean Turquoise	Bright Metal	3-Tone Turquoise
Tropic Turquoise 914	Tropic Turquoise	Aegean Turquoise			
	Arctic White	Tropic Turquoise			
Snowcrest White (A)* 936					
Snowcrest White (A)‡ 936			Rio Red	Bright Metal	Red, Silver and Black
Anniversary Gold 918	Anniversary Gold	Honey Beige	Anniversary Gold	Bright Metal	Beige, Gold and Copper
Sierra Gold 920	Arctic White	Sierra Gold			
Honey Beige 938					
Rio Red 923	Arctic White	Rio Red	Rio Red	Bright Metal	Red, Silver and Black
Cay Coral 932	Arctic White	Cay Coral	Dark Coral	Bright Metal	3-Tone Coral

(A) - Acrylic
* - Impala Sport Coupe only
‡ - Impala Convertible only
ʀ - Upper and lower areas of steering wheel painted Silver
& - All wheels painted Silver

0023064

1958 Trim Combinations

EXTERIOR - INTERIOR COLOR COMBINATIONS
BISCAYNE SERIES
(Models 15-1641, 15-1649)

EXTERIOR COLORS				Instrument panel upper and lower; garnish moldings; door lock knobs; glove box door lower; radio grille screen; direction signal and shift lever housing; steering wheel; steering jacket insert and cover.	Instrument panel center; glove box door upper; radio and clock cover plates.	Interior trim combinations
SINGLE ʀ	TWO-COLOR					
	Roof and Lower Body	Pillars and Upper Body	Wheels			
Onyx Black 900	Arctic White	Onyx Black	Onyx Black	Gunmetal	Silver	Gunmetal, Silver and White
Rio Red 923	Arctic White	Rio Red	Rio Red			
Cay Coral 932	Arctic White	Cay Coral	Cay Coral			
Forest Green 905	Glen Green	Forest Green	Glen Green	Forest Green	Glen Green	3-Tone Green
Glen Green 903	Glen Green	Arctic White	Glen Green			
Colonial Cream 925	Arctic White	Colonial Cream	Colonial Cream			
Cashmere Blue 910	Cashmere Blue	Arctic White	Cashmere Blue	Fathom Blue	Silver Blue	3-Tone Blue
Fathom Blue 912	Cashmere Blue	Fathom Blue	Cashmere Blue			
Silver Blue (A) 930	Snowcrest White (A)	Silver Blue (A)	Silver Blue (A)			
Tropic Turquoise 914	Arctic White	Aegean Turq.	Aegean Turq.	Aegean Turquoise	Tropic Turquoise	3-Tone Turquoise
Aegean Turquoise 916	Tropic Turquoise	Arctic White	Tropic Turq.			
Snowcrest White (A) 936	Tropic Turquoise	Aegean Turq.	Tropic Turq.			
Anniversary Gold 918				Anniversary Gold	Honey Beige	Beige and Gold
Sierra Gold 920	Sierra Gold	Arctic White	Sierra Gold			
Honey Beige 938	Honey Beige	Anniversary Gold	Anniversary Gold			

(A) - Acrylic
ʀ - Wheels painted body color

0023062

EXTERIOR - INTERIOR COLOR COMBINATIONS
BEL AIR SERIES AND NOMAD STATION WAGON
(Except Impala Models)

EXTERIOR COLORS &			Instrument panel upper and lower; garnish moldings; door lock knobs; glove box door lower; radio grille screen; heater and ash tray face plate; direction signal and shift lever housing; steering jacket insert and cover; steering wheel.	Instrument panel center; glove box door upper; radio cover plates.	Interior trim combination
SINGLE	TWO-COLORS				
	Roof and Upper Body	Lower Body Color			
Onyx Black 900	Onyx Black	Arctic White	Gunmetal	Bright Metal	Gunmetal, Silver and White
Rio Red 923	Rio Red	Arctic White			
Snowcrest White (A) 936					
Glen Green 903	Arctic White	Glen Green	Forest Green	Bright Metal	3-Tone Green
Forest Green 905	Forest Green	Glen Green			
Colonial Cream 925	Colonial Cream	Arctic White			
Cashmere Blue 910	Arctic White	Cashmere Blue	Fathom Blue	Bright Metal	3-Tone Blue
Fathom Blue 912	Fathom Blue	Cashmere Blue			
Silver Blue (A) 930	Silver Blue (A)	Snowcrest White (A)			
Tropic Turquoise 914	Aegean Turquoise	Arctic White	Aegean Turquoise	Bright Metal	3-Tone Turquoise
Aegean Turquoise 916	Aegean Turquoise	Tropic Turquoise			
	Arctic White	Tropic Turquoise			
Sierra Gold 920	Arctic White	Sierra Gold	Anniversary Gold	Bright Metal	Beige and Gold
Honey Beige 938	Anniversary Gold	Honey Beige			
Anniversary Gold 918					
Cay Coral 932	Cay Coral	Arctic White	Dark Coral	Bright Metal	3-Tone Coral

(A) - Acrylic
& - All wheels painted Silver

0023063

1958 Trim Combinations (continued)

EXTERIOR - INTERIOR COLOR COMBINATIONS
STATION WAGON SERIES
(Models 15-1693, 15-1694)*

EXTERIOR COLORS				Instrument panel upper and lower; garnish moldings; door lock knobs; glove box door lower; radio grille screen; direction signal and shift lever housing; steering wheel; steering jacket insert and cover.	Instrument panel center; glove box door upper; radio and clock cover plates.	Interior trim combinations
SINGLE ª	TWO-COLOR					
	Roof and Lower Body	Pillars and Upper Body	Wheels			
Onyx Black 900	Arctic White	Onyx Black	Onyx Black	Gunmetal	Silver	Gunmetal, Silver and White
Glen Green 903	Glen Green	Arctic White	Glen Green			
Cashmere Blue 910	Cashmere Blue	Arctic White	Cashmere Blue			
Rio Red 923	Arctic White	Rio Red	Rio Red			
Colonial Cream 925	Arctic White	Colonial-Cream	Colonial Cream			
Silver Blue (A) 930	Snowcrest White (A)	Silver Blue (A)	Silver Blue (A)			
Cay Coral 932	Arctic White	Cay Coral	Cay Coral			
Tropic Turquoise 914	Tropic Turquoise	Aegean Turq.	Tropic Turq.	Aegean Turquoise	Tropic Turquoise	3-Tone Turquoise
Snowcrest White (A) 936	Tropic Turquoise	Arctic White	Tropic Turq.			
Aegean Turquoise 916	Arctic White	Aegean Turq.	Aegean Turq.			
Forest Green 905	Glen Green	Forest Green	Glen Green	Anniversary Gold	Honey Beige	Beige and Gold
Fathom Blue 912	Cashmere Blue	Fathom Blue	Cashmere Blue			
Anniversary Gold 918						
Sierra Gold 920	Sierra Gold	Arctic White	Sierra Gold			
Honey Beige 938	Honey Beige	Anniversary Gold	Anniversary Gold			

(A) - Acrylic ª - Wheels painted body color
* - See Bel Air Series for Models 17-1893

0023066

CORVETTE
INTERIOR COLORS AND FABRICS

Item		Material	Trim Combination		
			Charcoal	Blue-Gray	Red
Seats	Cushion	Chatham Grain Vinyl	Charcoal	Blue-Gray	Red
	Backrest				
	Cushion Bolster				
	Backrest Bolster				
Headlining **					
Sidewalls	Upper Panel				
	Lower Panel	Textured Metal	Bright		
	Divider Molding and Armrest End Insert	Metal			
	Armrest	Chatham Grain Vinyl	Charcoal	Blue-Gray	Red
	Scuff Pad	Paint			
Cowl Side Kick Panels		Chatham Grain Vinyl			
Step Plate		Metal	Bright		
Floor Covering		Carpet	Charcoal	Blue-Gray	Red
Top Storage Well		Paint			
Reflectors		Plastic	Red		
Rear Compartment	Mat	Rubber	Charcoal	Blue-Gray	Red
	Trim Board	Composition Board			

** - Hardtop only

0023055

EXTERIOR-INTERIOR COLOR COMBINATIONS

Body Color and Wheels*	Body Cove Area (Optional)	Folding Top	Interior Trim Instrument panel and cluster, steering wheel and hub, direction signal housing, heater cover panel, radio grille screen, defroster escutcheon, cockpit housing divider.		
			Charcoal	Blue Gray	Red
Charcoal 512**	Inca Silver	Black or White	Charcoal	Blue-Gray	Red
Snowcrest White 510**		Black White or Blue-Gray	Charcoal	Blue-Gray	Red
Silver Blue 502**		White or Blue-Gray	Charcoal	Blue-Gray	
Regal Turquoise 504**	Snowcrest White	Black or White	Charcoal		
Panama Yellow 508**		Black or White	Charcoal		
Signet Red 506**		Black or White	Charcoal		Red

* - Includes hardtop when used.
** - Color code changed when body olor was same as body cove area. Color codes are as follows: Charcoal - 500; Silver blue - 502; Regal tourquoise - 540; Signet red - 506; Panama yellow - 508; Snowcrest white - 510

0023067

EXTERIOR - INTERIOR COLOR COMBINATIONS
STATION WAGON SERIES
(Models 11-1291, 11-1293)*

EXTERIOR COLORS				Instrument panel upper and lower; garnish moldings; door lock knobs; glove box door lower; radio grille screen; direction signal and shift lever housing; steering jacket insert and cover.	Instrument panel center; glove box door upper; radio and clock cover plates.	Interior trim combinations
SINGLE ª	TWO-COLOR					
	Roof and Upper Body	Lower Body	Wheels			
Onyx Black 900	Onyx Black	Arctic White	Onyx Black	Gunmetal	Silver	Gunmetal and Silver
Glen Green 903	Arctic White	Glen Green	Glen Green			
Cashmere Blue 910	Arctic White	Cashmere Blue	Cashmere Blue			
Tropic Turquoise 914	Arctic White	Tropic Turquoise	Tropic Turq.			
Aegean Turquoise 916	Aegean Turq.	Arctic White	Aegean Turq.			
Rio Red 923	Rio Red	Arctic White	Rio Red			
Colonial Cream 925	Colonial Cream	Arctic White	Colonial Cream			
Silver Blue (A) 930	Silver Blue (A)	Snowcrest White (A)	Silver Blue (A)			
Cay Coral 932	Cay Coral	Arctic White	Cay Coral			
Forest Green 905	Forest Green	Glen Green	Glen Green	Gold	Beige	Gold and Beige
Fathom Blue 912	Fathom Blue	Cashmere Blue	Fathom Blue			
Anniversary Gold 918	Anniversary Gold	Honey Beige	Anniversary Gold			
Sierra Gold 920	Arctic White	Sierra Gold	Sierra Gold			
Snowcrest White (A) 936						
Honey Beige 938						
	Aegean Turq.	Tropic Turquoise	Aegean Turq.			

(A) - Acrylic
ª - Wheels painted body color
* - See Bel Air Series for Models 17-1893

0023065

EXTERIOR - INTERIOR COLOR COMBINATIONS
DELRAY SERIES
(Models 11-1221, 11-1241, 11-1249)

EXTERIOR COLORS				Instrument panel upper and lower; garnish moldings; door lock knobs; glove box door lower; radio grille screen; direction signal and shift lever housing; steering wheel, steering jacket insert and cover.	Instrument panel center; glove box door upper; radio and clock cover plates.	Interior trim combinations
SINGLE ª	TWO-COLOR					
	Roof and Upper Body	Lower Body	Wheels			
Onyx Black 900	Onyx Black	Arctic White	Onyx Black	Gunmetal	Silver	Gunmetal and Silver
Glen Green 903	Arctic White	Glen Green	Glen Green			
Forest Green 905	Forest Green	Glen Green	Glen Green			
Cashmere Blue 910	Arctic White	Cashmere Blue	Cashmere Blue			
Fathom Blue 912	Fathom Blue	Cashmere Blue	Fathom Blue			
Rio Red 923	Rio Red	Arctic White	Rio Red			
Colonial Cream 925	Colonial Cream	Arctic White	Colonial Cream			
Tropic Turquoise 914	Aegean Turq.	Tropic Turquoise	Tropic Turq.			
Aegean Turquoise 916	Aegean Turq.	Arctic White	Aegean Turq.			
Silver Blue (A) 930	Arctic White	Tropic Turquoise	Aegean Turq.			
Honey Beige 938						
Anniversary Gold 918	Anniversary Gold	Honey Beige	Anniversary Gold			
Sierra Gold 920	Arctic White	Sierra Gold	Sierra Gold			
Cay Coral 932	Cay Coral	Arctic White	Cay Coral			
Snowcrest White (A) 936	Silver Blue (A)	Snowcrest White (A)	Silver Blue (A)			

(A) - Acrylic ª - Wheels painted body color

0023068

1959 Trim Combinations

EXTERIOR - INTERIOR COLOR COMBINATIONS
BISCAYNE SERIES, EL CAMINO, SEDAN DELIVERY, AND BROOKWOOD STATION WAGONS

EXTERIOR			INTERIOR	
SOLID COLORS	TWO-TONE COLORS **		FABRICS	PAINT
	Roof & Upper Deck (or Tailgate)	Lower Body & Wheels		
Tuxedo Black ¢ 900	Snowcrest White	Tuxedo Black	Light and Medium Gray	Medium Gray
Crown Sapphire 914	Snowcrest White	Crown Sapphire		
Gothic Gold 920	Satin Beige	Gothic Gold		
Roman Red ¢ 923	Snowcrest White	Roman Red		
Snowcrest White ¢ 936	Snowcrest White	Grecian Gray		
Cameo Coral 942	Satin Beige	Cameo Coral		
Grecian Gray 940				
Satin Beige 938				
Highland Green ¢ 905	Snowcrest White	Highland Green	Light and Medium Green *	Medium Green *
Aspen Green ¢ 903	Aspen Green	Classic Cream		
Classic Cream 925				
Frost Blue ¢ 910	Frost Blue	Harbor Blue	Light and Medium Blue *	Dark Blue *
Harbor Blue 912	Harbor Blue	Frost Blue		

* - Gray is substituted for models 11-1221, 11-1270 ¢ - Only colors available on models 11-1270
** - Two-Tone not available for models 11-1270

0023069

EXTERIOR - INTERIOR COLOR COMBINATIONS
IMPALA SERIES AND NOMAD STATION WAGON

EXTERIOR			INTERIOR	
SOLID COLORS	TWO-TONE COLORS *		FABRICS	PAINT
	Roof & Upper Deck (or Tailgate)	Lower Body & Wheels		
Tuxedo Black 900	Snowcrest White	Tuxedo Black	Light and Medium Gray	Medium Gray **
Roman Red 923	Snowcrest White	Roman Red		
Snowcrest White 936	Snowcrest White	Grecian Gray		
Cameo Coral 942	Satin Beige	Cameo Coral		
Grecian Gray 940				
Highland Green 905	Snowcrest White	Highland Green	Light and Medium	Medium Green **
Aspen Green 903	Aspen Green	Classic Cream		
Classic Cream 925				
Frost Blue 910	Frost Blue	Harbor Blue	Light and Medium Blue	Dark Blue **
Harbor Blue 912	Harbor Blue	Frost Blue		
Crown Sapphire 914	Snowcrest White	Crown Sapphire	Light and Medium Turquoise	Medium Turquoise **
Snowcrest White 936				
Gothic Gold 920	Satin Beige	Gothic Gold	Light and Medium Copper	Medium Copper **
Satin Beige 938				
Tuxedo Black 900	Snowcrest White	Tuxedo Black	Red ¢	Red ¢
Roman Red 923	Snowcrest White	Roman Red		
Snowcrest White 936	Snowcrest White	Grecian Gray		
Grecian Gray 940				

* - Not available for Convertible. ¢ - Not available for 4-Door Sedan or Nor [illegible]
** - Upper and lower portions of steering wheel painted a light tone.

0023071

EXTERIOR - INTERIOR COLOR COMBINATIONS
BEL AIR SERIES; KINGSWOOD AND PARKWOOD STATION WAGONS

EXTERIOR			INTERIOR	
SOLID COLORS	TWO-TONE COLORS		FABRICS	PAINT
	Roof & Upper Deck (or Tailgate)	Lower Body & Wheels		
Tuxedo Black 900	Snowcrest White	Tuxedo Black	Light and Medium Gray	Medium Gray
Roman Red 923	Snowcrest White	Roman Red		
Snowcrest White 936	Snowcrest White	Grecian Gray		
Cameo Coral 942	Satin Beige	Cameo Coral		
Grecian Gray 940				
Highland Green 905	Snowcrest White	Highland Green	Light and Medium Green	Medium Green
Aspen Green 903	Aspen Green	Classic Cream		
Classic Cream 925				
Frost Blue 910	Frost Blue	Harbor Blue	Light and Medium Blue	Dark Blue
Harbor Blue 912	Harbor Blue	Frost Blue		
Crown Sapphire 914	Snowcrest White	Crown Sapphire	Light and Medium Turquoise	Medium Turquoise
Gothic Gold 920	Satin Beige	Gothic Gold	Light and Medium Copper	Medium Copper
Satin Beige 938				

0023070

1959 CORVETTE EXTERIOR-INTERIOR COLOR COMBINATIONS

EXTERIOR*						INTERIOR			
Body ¢	Cove Area (optional)	Folding Top				Black	Blue	Tur-quoise	Red
		Black	White	Tur-quoise	Light Blue				
Tuxedo Black	Inca Silver	X	X			X	X		X
Classic Cream	Snowcrest White	X	X			X			
Frost Blue			X		X		X		X
Crown Sapphire			X	X				X	
Roman Red		X	X			X			X
Snowcrest White	Inca Silver	X	X	X	X	X	X	X	X
Inca Silver	Snowcrest White	X	X			X			X

* - Wheels painted black.
¢ - Includes hardtop, when used.

0023073

IMPALA CONVERTIBLE TOP COLORS

EXTERIOR COLOR		TOP COLOR			
		Ivory	Black	Green	Blue
Tuxedo Black	900	X	X		
Aspen Green	903	X	X	X	
Highland Green	905	X		X	
Crown Sapphire	914	X	X		
Frost Blue	910	X	X		X
Harbor Blue	912	X			X
Gothic Gold	920	X	X		
Roman Red	923	X	X		
Snowcrest White	936	X	X		
Grecian Gray	940	X	X		
Classic Cream	925	X	X	X	
Cameo Coral	942	X	X		
Satin Beige	938	X	X		

0023072

Chapter 2

Engine Code Identification

1. Introduction

In this chapter I will describe the specific types of engine codes and how they were originally stamped on a particular engine. I will begin by discussing engine code location and format, and end with a listing of the engine code suffixes, which indicated which engine/transmission combination was used in a particular body style in a specific year.

In addition to the engine code, many later model Chevrolet engines had part of the Vehicle Identification Number (VIN) stamped on them to identify the unit with the vehicle in which they were installed. Through Chevrolet Technical Service Bulletins, Chevrolet indicated which engines were to receive the VIN stamp; however, it is possible that other engines could also have been stamped. It is known that all Corvettes had the VIN code stamped beginning in January 1960. The Corvette is the only verifiable Chevrolet vehicle to date that received a VIN stamp on the engine pad for the 1960 model year. For passenger cars, all indications point to the 1962 327/300HP and 409 engines as being the first to have the VIN stamp.

1.1 Code Location

The engine assembly code and portion of the VIN code were stamped on a block pad, located immediately forward of the right hand cylinder head. See Fig. 2-1.

The engine assembly code was stamped on the engine assembly line prior to the installation of the cylinder head, while the VIN code was stamped much later, at the final assembly plant when the engine was mated with the drivetrain.

The position of the engine assembly codes on the block pad changed over the years. The position of the 1955–56 V-8 engine assembly codes varied and many times took up the complete stamping pad. Almost all V-8 engine stampings during the 1957–59 model years

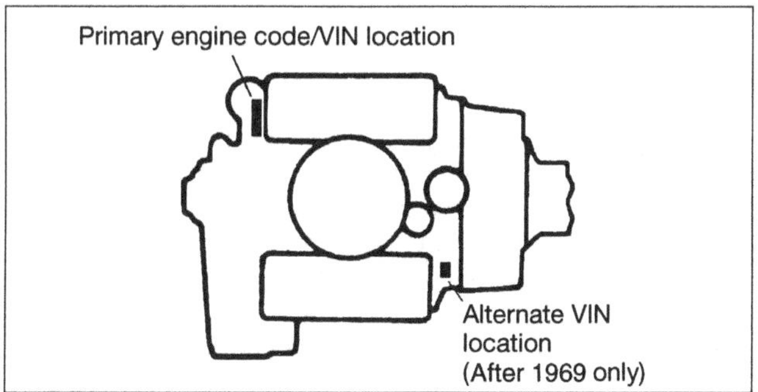

Fig. 2-1. Eight-cylinder engine code location.

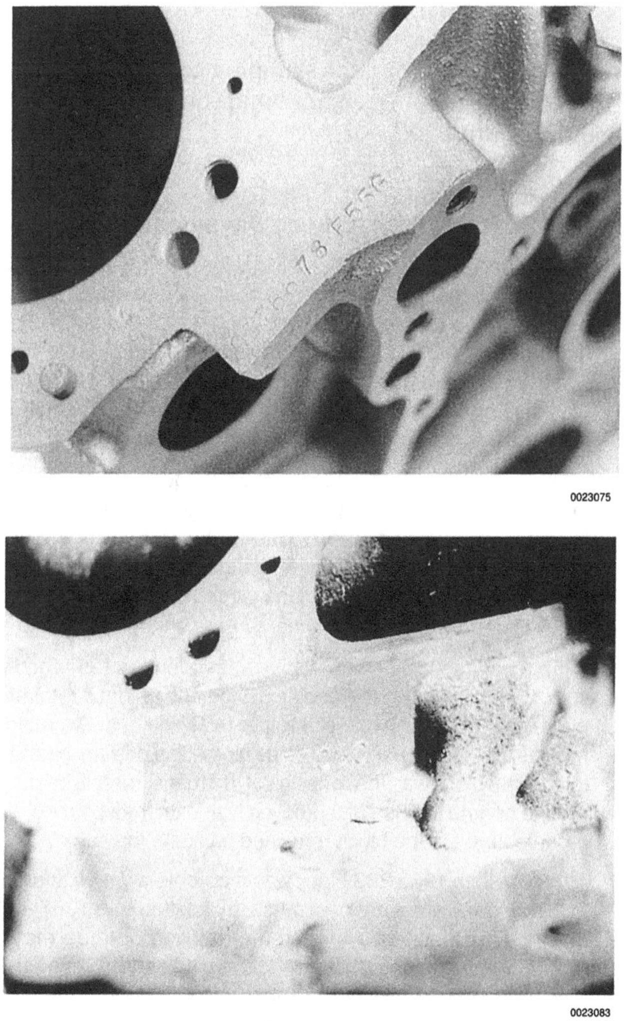

Fig. 2-2. ***Top:*** *Typical 1955–56 engine code stamping—here for 1955 265/162 HP engine).* ***Bottom:*** *Typical 1957–59 engine code stamping—here FI08C (January 8, 1957) for 1957 265/162 HP engine.*

were located on the left hand side of the engine stamp pad, although some have been found on the right, such as the stamping in figure 2-2 bottom. Beginning in the 1960 model year and lasting through the 1964 model year, the engine assembly plant code was moved to the right hand side of the pad and any vehicle identification number would be stamped on the left. As a result, many VIN codes had to be stamped in a skewed manner to fit on the pad.

On 1965 and later blocks the position of the codes was reversed. The engine assembly code was moved to the left side of the block pad, while the VIN was stamped on the right side of the pad. Exactly when this changeover took place for all engines is unclear. To further deter theft, on some later model engines the VIN code was also stamped near the transmission flange of the block.

1.2 1955 Through 1956 Engine Code Identification

The 1955–56 engine code stamping consists of an engine sequence number, engine build source, production year, and suffix code.

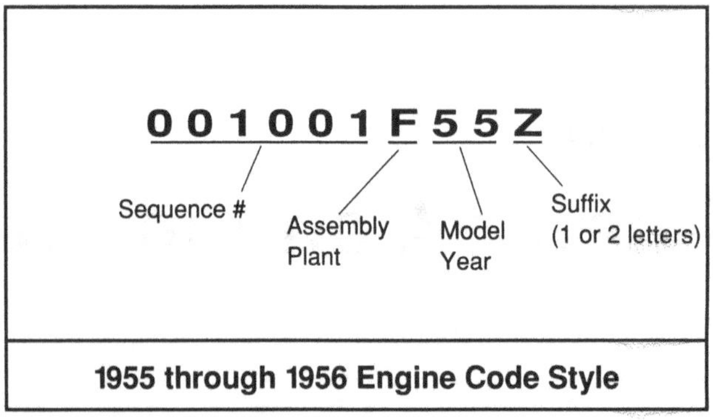

Fig. 2-3. Example of 1955–56 engine code.

Note that the V-8 stamping pad is 3-1/8" long and is considered the "short pad." This pad was used up until January of 1965, when it changed to a length of 3-9/16" to 3-5/8" long.

The first seven digits of the engine code represent the engine unit number that was produced in that engine plant. The first five of these numbers were stamped in a group by a gang stamp. The next two numbers were

1955 Through 1959 Engine Development

1955: The first Chevrolet small block engine was released for the 1955 model year. This first block utilized an oil bypass breather tube that was cast into the rear of the block. The block did not have an oil filter provision and there were only two motor mount holes on each side of the block. This block was also characterized by very thin cylinder walls, which in many cases did not allow for a standard overbore.

1956: The 1956-57 265 block was changed in two specific areas. First, the bypass breather tube now proceeds down the passenger side of the engine to the oil pan. This block was also the first small block to feature an oil filter boss that was cast into the underside of the block. All 265 engines from 1955-57 featured a grooved rear journal on the camshaft.

1957: The first 283 engine was released for the 1957 model year. It was similar to the earlier 265 engine in that it retained the passenger side bypass breather tube and only two motor mounting holes on each side of the block. The primary change for the 283 block was the redesign of the rear camshaft bearing area to negate the use of a grooved rear camshaft bearing. All other features of the block remained basically the same.

1958-59: The 1958 283 block was a completely new design. The cylinder walls were cast much thicker than the 1957 283 blocks. This block also utilized the addition of three motor mount holes cast into the side of the block surrounding the forward freeze plug. This change was necessary due to a completely new body for the 1958 Chevrolet and a frame design where the engine was mounted lower in the chassis of the car. This block had some minor casting changes and subsequent casting number changes through the 1964 model year, but a major change has not been found.

All 1958-59 Chevrolet small blocks had a 2.30 inch main journal diameter and a 2.0 inch rod journal diameter. This remained constant in all small block engines until 1968 when both diameters were increased. All 1955-59 Chevrolet small block engines have a 2-bolt main configuration.

The 348 W-block was first released for production for the 1958 model year. The 348 engine was the first W-block and was used extensively in both cars and trucks from 1958 through 1961. The W-block engines were originally developed because of the rising demand for automatic transmissions and the apparent need for a powerplant which could provide optimum low- and mid- range performance. The 283 engine would not provide this criteria for the larger, heavier models planned for the 1958 model year.

The first design 348 block had no provisions for spark plug cooling holes to supply water to the cylinder heads. This block design dictates the use of the corresponding heads to complete the engine assembly. Chevrolet must have realized very early that this design was deficient because late in the model year they released a new block and cylinder head design which featured provisions for spark plug cooling. This design was used for all 1959-61 348 engine applications. All 348 blocks have a 2-bolt main configuration. After several high performance 348 engines that were successful in racing circles, the engineers began developing a replacement that turned out to be the now famous 409.

stamped individually into the block so that the gang stamp holder would only necessitate a new number change every 100 engines. The final four or five characters were also stamped into the block in a gang stamp holder.

Only two engine plants were producing engines at that time, Flint, Michigan, and Tonawanda, New York. All engines, including 6-cylinder, were numbered as they were produced at the engine assembly plant. All engine unit numbers started with 0001001. All 6- and 8-cylinder engines were numbered separately. After the engine unit number, a letter "F" or "T" will appear. This designates either the Flint, Michigan (F) or Tonawanda, New York (T) plant.

1955–56 Engine Assembly Plant Codes

Year	Engine Plant	Notes
1955–56	F - Flint, Michigan T - Tonawanda, New York	Both engine assembly plants stamped the continuous engine sequence number starting with 0001001, followed by the source plant letter (F or T), the model year ('55 or '56) and the engine code suffix on all 265 cubic inch engines.

The next two numbers will represent the model year of that engine. In this case, it will either be 55 (1955) or 56 (1956).

The last letter or letters represent the engine suffix code that was assigned that assembly. This code usually specifies the transmission option or other pertinent information vital to that engine application.

1955–56 stamped characters are somewhat different than 1957–59 characters. The most prominent difference is that the '55–56 zeroes are square in shape, while '57–59 zeroes are more oval in shape.

1.3 1957 Through 1959 Engine Code Identification

The 1957–59 engine production code consists of an engine build source, production date, and an engine suffix code. The engine sequential number is not used in the block stamp code. Also, depending on the month in which the engine was produced, the code can consist of up to seven characters. Please see the example below.

The first letter always designates the engine plant. All engines built from 1957–59 were built at one of two plants, either Flint, Michigan, or Tonawanda, New York.

The first letter in the engine stamping code will always be the letter "F" for the Flint plant, or the letter "T" for the Tonawanda plant. Any engine stamped that is different from the above example should be *closely* scrutinized.

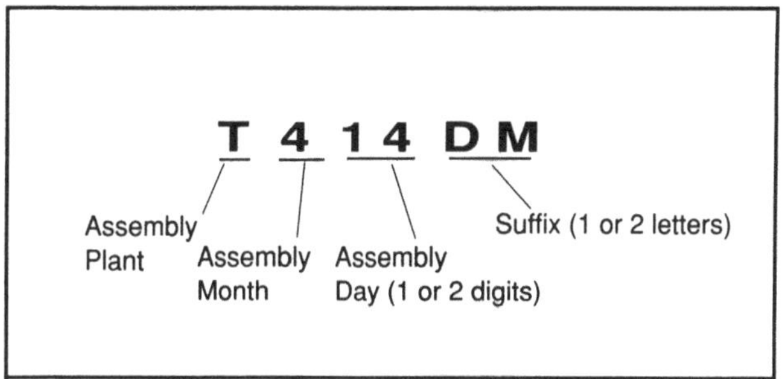

1957 through 1959 Engine Code Style

0023077

Fig. 2-4. Example of 1957–59 engine code.

1957–59 Engine Assembly Plant Codes

Year	Engine Plant	Notes
1957–59	C - Canadian engines F - Flint, Michigan T - Tonawanda, New York	All final assembly plants stamped the source plant letter designation (F or T), followed by the engine production date and the engine code suffix on all 265, 283, and 348 cubic inch engines.

The second digit represents the month build code. On 1957–59 model year engines, the month designation will either be one or two digits. For example: January = 1, December = 12. Starting in 1960 and continuing through the 1964 model year, the month code designation changed to two digits for all months. For example, January = 01, etc.

It should be noted that both engine plants used the letter "I" to signify the number "1" in all engine stampings. This was done to reduce the possibility of reading the code wrong. Sometimes, when this code was being stamped by hand, the code would be stamped too lightly on the engine block, which made it difficult to read.

The next number sequence in the engine code stamping represents the day of engine assembly. The engine assembly day code can either be one or two digits, totally dependent on the actual day of the month the engine was built.

The final group of letters or letter at the end of the engine code simply represent the actual engine suffix letter code of that particular block when it was originally manufactured.

It should also be noted that all 348 and 409 engine stamp codes are positioned on the block stamp pad the same as on a small block engine. The engine plant stamp code is positioned on the right, while the VIN stamp is located on the left. Although no 348 engines have been verified with a VIN stamp, there are many verified cases of 1962 and later 409 engines with the VIN code on the left side of the pad.

PARTS FOR 1955 ENGINE ASSEMBLIES

DATE 11-4-54

MOTOR NUMBER	SUFFIX	PASS. MODELS	CYLINDER & CASE	CRANKSHAFT	CAMSHAFT	HOUSING	PLATE CLUTCH	FLYWHEEL	HARMONIC BALANCER	CYLINDER HEAD	HEAD GASKET	INLET MANIFOLD	RIGHT BANK EXHAUST MANIFOLD	RIGHT BANK ROCKER ARM COVER BOLT
3704509	F55G	CONVENTIONAL	3702794	3704840 BUSHING	3713453	3703872	3836097	3703868	3836220	3704883	3836498	3704934	3705178	
3704511	F55F	POWERGLIDE		3704841 NO BUSHING	3704212 2 DOTS WHITE FRONT	3836173 P.G.		3701681 P.G.						
3836533	F55GC	OVERDRIVE					3836534 BLUE							
3718105	F55GD	CONVENTIONAL 4-B-C										3711347 SHORT STUDS		
3718109	F55FB	POWERGLIDE 4-B-C		3704841 NO BUSHING	3704212 2 DOTS WHITE FRONT	3836173 P.G.		3701681 PG				3711347 SHORT STUDS		
3718107	F55GE	OVERDRIVE 4-B-C					3836534 BLUE					3711347 SHORT STUDS		
3718603	F55GF	CONVENTIONAL AIR-C							3714501 DOUBLE PULLEY				3718602 BRACKET	3718916 2 OUTSIDE FLANGE
3718613	F55FC	POWERGLIDE AIR-C		3704841 NO BUSHING	3704212 2 DOTS WHITE FRONT	3836173 P.G.		3701681 PG	3714501 DOUBLE PULLEY				3718602 BRACKET	3718916 2 OUTSIDE FLANGE
3718617	F55GA	CONVENTIONAL 4-B-C AIR-C							3714501 DOUBLE PULLEY			3711347 SHORT STUDS	3718602 BRACKET	3718916 2 OUTSIDE FLANGE
3718619	F55FD	POWERGLIDE 4-B-C AIR-C		3704841 NO BUSHING	3704212 2 DOTS WHITE FRONT	3836173 P.G.		3701881 PG	3714501 DOUBLE PULLEY			3711347 SHORT STUDS	3718602 BRACKET	3718916 2 OUTSIDE FLANGE
3836613	F55GB	CONVENTIONAL LOW COMPRESSION								3713528	4			
3836615	F55FA	POWERGLIDE LOW COMPRESSION		3704841 NO BUSHING	3704212 2 DOTS WHITE FRONT	3836173 P.G.		3701681 P.G.		3713528	4			
3836673	F55GH	CONVENTIONAL LOW COMP. H.D. CLUTCH					3836011			3713528	4			
3719489	F55GJ	CONVENTIONAL H.D. CLUTCH					3836011							
3719491	F55GK	CONVENTIONAL AIR-C H.D. CLUTCH					3836011		3714501 DOUBLE PULLEY				3718602 BRACKET	3718916 2 OUTSIDE FLANGE
3719493	F55GL	CONVENTIONAL 4-B-C H.D. CLUTCH					3836011					3711347 SHORT STUDS		
3719495	F55GM	CONVENTIONAL AIR-C 4-B-C H.D. CLUTCH					3836011		3714501 DOUBLE PULLEY			3711347 SHORT STUDS	3718602 BRACKET	3718916 2 OUTSIDE FLANGE

0023078

Fig. 2-5. 1955 model year engine parts identifier for the Flint Assembly Plant. The chart was posted on the line for parts identification by engine assembly line workers.

1.4 Engine Code Character Sizes

There were several character sizes that were used from 1955–59. We will first discuss the engine assembly build date stamping. All 1955–59 characters in this stamping are 3/16" high. The engine assembly plant stamped the engine assembly date and usage code on the block by hand. In most cases, the characters were fitted into a metal holder and locked in place by an Allen key. The holder was placed over the number pad and struck with a dead blow hammer on the assembly line prior to the installation of the cylinder head. As mentioned above, no vehicle identification number (VIN) was stamped on a block prior to January of 1960. These VIN letters were 5/32" high and remained this height through the 1967 model year.

2. Engine Suffix Codes

The following tables list all engine suffix codes for 1955 through 1959. The tables are designed for access either by suffix code or by application.

When trying to identify an engine block, the engine code suffix should be the last part of the stamping you check. Often, when trying to match numbers, the suffix is the first part of the engine code you look at because it contains much information about engine specifications. Unfortunately, when you look at the suffix code first you tend to overlook other vital aspects that should be checked on the engine, such as cross- referencing casting dates on the block, cylinder head, intake and so on. Many engines over the years used the same suffix codes for totally different applications. Unless you check the casting dates, you could be easily duped into buying an incorrect part for your application.

Abbreviations used in the following tables:

A/C	Air Conditioning
Alum.	Aluminum
BBL	Barrel
H.D.	Heavy Duty
Hyd.	Hydraulic
L.C.	Low Compression
Mech.	Mechanical
O.D.	Overdrive
Perf.	Performance
P/S	Power Steering
RHD	Right Hand Drive
Spec.	Special

1955 Engine Code Suffix Identification

Model	Model No.	Engine	Horsepower	Transmission, Options	Suffix
Passenger	15-21-2400	265	162	Powerglide	F
			180	Dual Exhaust, 4BBL	FB
			162	Powerglide, A/C	FC
			180	Powerglide, Dual Exhaust, 4BBL, A/C	FD
			162	3-Speed	G
			162	Overdrive	GC
			180	3-Speed, Dual Exhaust, 4BBL	GD
			180	Overdrive, Dual Exhaust, 4BBL	GE
			162	3-Speed, A/C	GF
			180	3-Speed, 4BBL, A/C	GG
			162	H.D. Clutch	GJ
			162	H.D. Clutch, A/C	GK
			180	3-Speed, Dual Exhaust, 4BBL, H.D. Clutch	GL
			180	3-Speed, Dual Exhaust, 4BBL, A/C, H.D. Clutch	GM
			180	Overdrive, Dual Exhaust,4 BBL, A/C, H.D.Clutch	GN
			162	Overdrive, A/C	GQ
Corvette	2934	265	195	4BBL, Powerglide	FG
			195	4BBL, 3-Speed	GR

1956 Engine Code Suffix Identification

Model	Model No.	Engine	Horsepower	Transmission, Options	Suffix
Passenger	15-21-2400	265	170	Powerglide	F
			205	Powerglide, 4BBL	FB
			162	Powerglide, A/C	FC
			205	Powerglide, A/C, 4BBL	FD
			205	Powerglide, 4BBL	FH
			162	3-Speed	G
			162	Overdrive	GC
			205	Overdrive, 4BBL	GE
			162	3-Speed, A/C	GF
			162	H.D. Clutch	GJ
			162	H.D. Clutch, A/C	GK
			205	4BBL	GL
			205	4BBL, A/C	GM
			205	Overdrive, A/C, 4BBL	GN
			162	Overdrive, A/C	GQ
			225	Dual 4BBL	GS
			240	Dual 4BBL, Hi-lift Camshaft	GT
Corvette	2934	265	225	Powerglide, Dual 4BBL	FG
			210	Powerglide, 4BBL	FK
			225	3-Speed, Dual 4BBL	GR
			240	3-Speed, Dual 4BBL, Hi-lift Camshaft	GU
			210	3-Speed, 4BBL	GV

1957 Engine Code Suffix Identification

<table>
<tr><th>Model</th><th>Model No.</th><th>Engine</th><th>Horsepower</th><th>Transmission, Options</th><th>Suffix</th></tr>
<tr><td rowspan="21">Passenger</td><td rowspan="3">15-21-2400</td><td rowspan="3">265</td><td rowspan="3">162</td><td>3-Speed</td><td>C</td></tr>
<tr><td>Overdrive</td><td>CD</td></tr>
<tr><td>3-Speed</td><td>CE</td></tr>
<tr><td rowspan="18">15-21-2400</td><td rowspan="18">283</td><td>220</td><td>4BBL</td><td>E</td></tr>
<tr><td>245</td><td>3-Speed, Dual 4BBL</td><td>EA</td></tr>
<tr><td>270</td><td>Dual 4BBL, Hi-lift Camshaft</td><td>EB</td></tr>
<tr><td>220</td><td>Overdrive, 4BBL</td><td>EC</td></tr>
<tr><td>250</td><td>Fuel Injection</td><td>EJ</td></tr>
<tr><td>283</td><td>Fuel Injection, Hi-lift Camshaft</td><td>EK</td></tr>
<tr><td>185</td><td>Powerglide</td><td>F</td></tr>
<tr><td>185</td><td>Powerglide, A/C</td><td>FA</td></tr>
<tr><td>220</td><td>Powerglide, 4BBL</td><td>FC</td></tr>
<tr><td>245</td><td>Powerglide, Dual 4BBL</td><td>FD</td></tr>
<tr><td>220</td><td>Powerglide, 4BBL, A/C</td><td>FE</td></tr>
<tr><td>250</td><td>Powerglide, Fuel Injection</td><td>FJ</td></tr>
<tr><td>185</td><td>Turboglide</td><td>G</td></tr>
<tr><td>220</td><td>Turboglide, 4BBL</td><td>GC</td></tr>
<tr><td>245</td><td>Turboglide, Dual 4BBL</td><td>GD</td></tr>
<tr><td>250</td><td>Turboglide, Fuel Injection</td><td>GF</td></tr>
<tr><td rowspan="9">Corvette</td><td rowspan="9">2934</td><td rowspan="9">283</td><td>220</td><td>3-Speed, 4BBL</td><td>EF</td></tr>
<tr><td>270</td><td>Man. Trans, Dual 4BBL, Hi-lift Camshaft</td><td>EG</td></tr>
<tr><td>245</td><td>Man. Trans, Dual 4BBL</td><td>EH</td></tr>
<tr><td>283</td><td>Man. Trans, Fuel Injection, Hi-lift Camshaft</td><td>EL</td></tr>
<tr><td>250</td><td>Man. Trans, Fuel Injection</td><td>EM</td></tr>
<tr><td>283</td><td>Fuel Injection, Hi-lift Camshaft, Air Intake</td><td>EN*</td></tr>
<tr><td>245</td><td>Powerglide, Dual 4BBL</td><td>FG</td></tr>
<tr><td>220</td><td>Powerglide, 4BBL</td><td>FH</td></tr>
<tr><td>250</td><td>Powerglide, Fuel Injection</td><td>FK</td></tr>
<tr><td colspan="6">*Existence of EN block is unverified; 579E equipped Corvette may have been supplied with EL coded engines.</td></tr>
</table>

1958 Engine Code Suffix Identification

Model	Model No.	Engine	Horsepower	Transmission, Options	Suffix
Passenger	12-16-1800	283	185	3-Speed Transmission	C
			185	H.D. Clutch	CB
			185	Overdrive	CD
			230	4BBL, 3-Speed	CF
			230	Overdrive, 4BBL	CG
			250	Fuel Injection, 3-Speed	CH
			290	Fuel Injection, Hi-lift Camshaft	CJ
			250	Fuel Injection, 4-Speed	CY
			290	Fuel Injection, Hi-lift Camshaft, 4-Speed	CZ
			185	Powerglide	D
			230	Powerglide, 4BBL	DB
			185	Powerglide, Air Suspension	DE
			230	Powerglide, 4BBL, Air Suspension	DF
			185	Turboglide	E
			230	Turboglide, 4BBL	EB
			250	Turboglide, Fuel Injection	EC
			185	Turboglide, Air Suspension	ED
			230	Turboglide, 4BBL, Air Suspension	EF
	12-16-1800	348	250*	3-Speed Transmission	F
			280	3-Speed, 3 x 2BBL	FA
			315	3-Speed, 3 x 2BBL, Hi-lift Camshaft	FB
			315	Hi-lift Camshaft, 4BBL	FD
			250	Powerglide	G
			250	Turboglide	H
			280	Turboglide, 3 x 2BBL	HA
Corvette	867	283	230	Man. Trans., 4BBL	CQ
			250	Man. Trans, Fuel Injection	CR
			290	Man. Trans, Fuel Injection, Hi-lift Camshaft	CS
			245	Man. Trans, Dual 4BBL	CT
			270**	Man. Trans, Dual 4BBL, Hi-lift Camshaft	CU
			230	Powerglide, 4BBL	DG
			250	Powerglide, Fuel Injection	DH
			245	Powerglide, Dual 4BBL	DJ

*To date, there has not been a Chevrolet suffix code found for the 348/265HP or the 348/300HP engines.
**Engine not available until approximately 1/20/58.

CHAPTER 2

1959 Engine Code Suffix Identification

Model	Model No.	Engine	Horsepower	Transmission, Options	Suffix
Passenger	12-16-1800	283	185	3-Speed	C
			185	Overdrive	CD
			230	3-Speed, 4BBL	CF
			230	Overdrive, 4BBL	CG
			250	3-Speed, Fuel Injection	CH
			290	3-Speed, Fuel Injection, Hi-lift Camshaft	CJ
			185	Powerglide	D
			230	Powerglide, 4BBL	DB
			185	Powerglide, Air Suspension	DE
			230	Powerglide, 4BBL, Air Suspension	DF
			185	Powerglide, A/C	DK
			185	Powerglide, A/C, Air Suspension	DL
			230	Powerglide, A/C, 4BBL	DM
			230	Powerglide, A/C, 4BBL, Air Suspension	DN
			250	Powerglide, Fuel Injection	DP
			185	Turboglide	E
			230	Turboglide, 4BBL	EB
			250	Turboglide, Fuel Injection	EC
			185	Turboglide, Air Suspension	ED
			230	Turboglide, 4BBL, Air Suspension	EF
			185	Turboglide, A/C	EG
			185	Turboglide, A/C, Air Suspension	EH
			230	Turboglide, A/C, 4BBL	EJ
			230	Turboglide, A/C, 4BBL, Air Suspension	EK
	12-16-1800	348	250	3-Speed	F
			280	3-Speed, 3 x 2BBL	FA
			315	3-Speed, 3 x 2BBL, Hi-lift Camshaft	FB
			305	Hi-lift Camshaft	FD
			335	3 x 2BBL, Special High Performance	FE
			320	4BBL, Special High Performance	FG
			250	Powerglide	G
			280	Powerglide, 3 x 2BBL	GB
			305	Powerglide, Hi-lift Camshaft	GD
			250	Turboglide	H
			280	Turboglide, 3 x 2BBL	HA
Corvette	867	283	230	Man. Trans, 4BBL	CQ
			250	Man. Trans, Fuel Injection	CR
			290	Man. Trans, Fuel Injection, Hi-lift Camshaft	CS
			245	Man. Trans, Dual 4BBL	CT
			270	Man. Trans, Dual 4BBL, Hi-lift Camshaft	CU
			230	Powerglide	DG
			250	Powerglide, Fuel Injection	DH
			245	Powerglide, Dual 4BBL	DJ

Chapter 3

Engine Block Identification

1. Introduction

There were only seven different engine blocks installed on cars from 1955 through 1959. At the same time, there were only three basic engine displacements, so in many cases there are a limited number of blocks that can appear correct for a specific engine application.

There are a number of ways to identify an engine block. The main ones are the block casting number, the block casting date, and the engine code stamping.

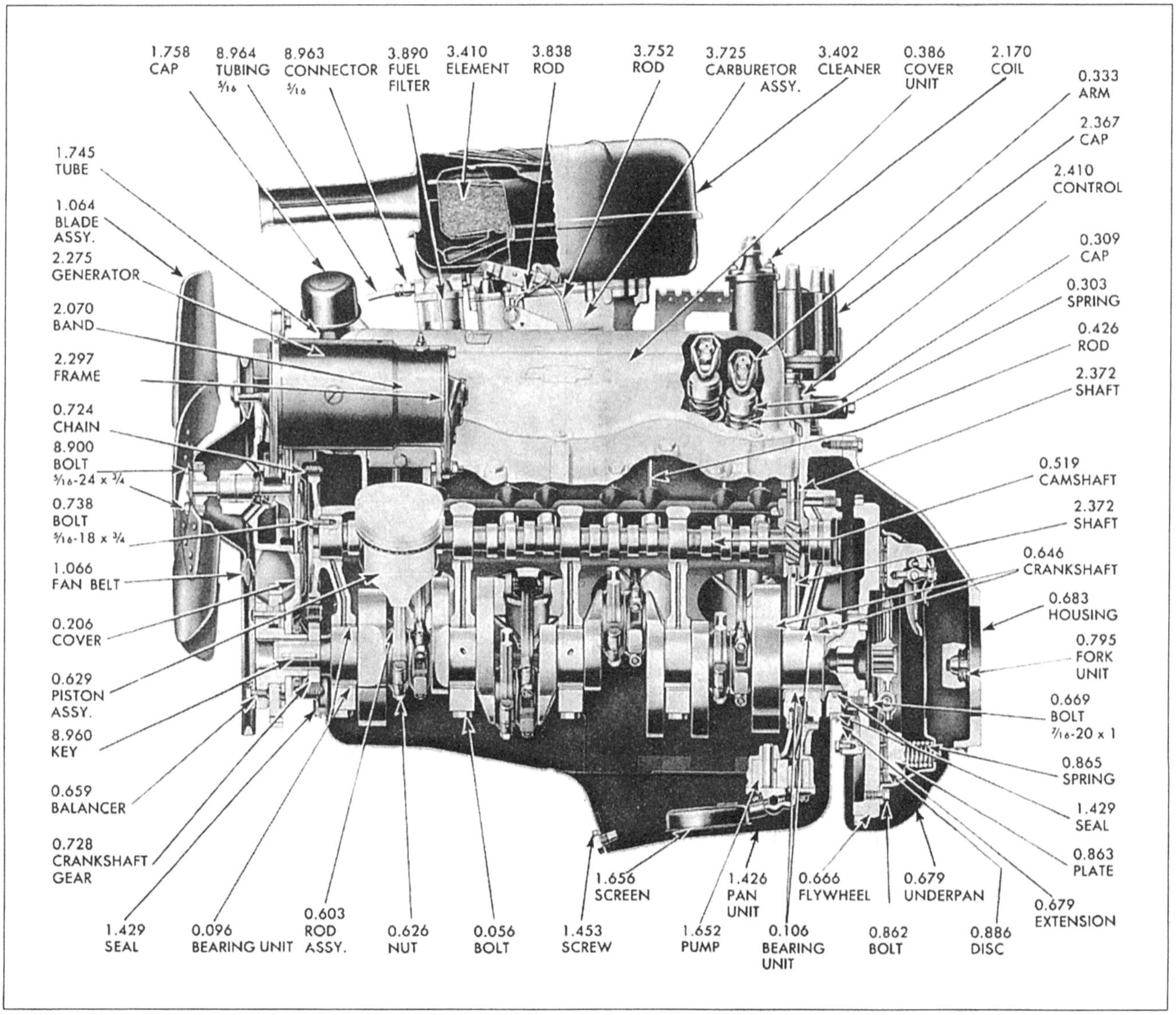

Fig. 3-1. Cross-section of typical 1958–61 348 V-8 engine.

All original blocks have a special grain which was machined into the surface of the block deck. The grain pattern is a series of very fine straight lines, called "broach" marks, running from front to back along the top of the block. The original equipment that left these marks is no longer in use, although there are rumors that the service can be bought in certain engine circles. Most modern milling machines use a rotary cutter which leaves a swirl broach pattern. Still, there are several ways in which to try to duplicate the original grain pattern. Also be aware that there are many people who are providing original GM stamping equipment to restorers for the sole purpose of restamping blocks.

1.1 Block Casting Number and Casting Date

The block casting number is the most important identification because it will probably be the last number on a block to be altered or changed to counterfeit or misrepresent a block. The casting number is usually found at the rear left side of the block, on top of the bellhousing flange. See Fig. 3-2. In some cases, during a production changeover, blocks had the original casting number ground off and a new casting number hand stamped into the block.

The casting date can usually be found at the rear of the block to the right of the casting number. Some blocks have the casting date on the long side of the block, near the freeze plug. These blocks are identified in the *Notes* under each casting number listing. On some Saginaw Foundry 409 blocks built after 1962 the casting date is above the oil filter.

The casting date code is in alphanumeric sequence. The first digit will usually be a letter code, which specifies the month the block was cast. The remaining digits in the date code refer to the day of the month and year of the block casting. Some casting dates have been found with all three digits represented as numbers such as "345." These types of dates are not common in restoration circles.

There were two main plants casting parts for Chevrolet engines during this time period: Flint, Michigan, and Tonawanda, New York. Tonawanda cast all components for engines assembled there. Most Tonawanda engine component castings, including most W-block components, will have a "T" cast into the surface of the part to designate it as a Tonawanda casting. In addition, almost all Tonawanda cast parts will have a two-digit year date code (55, 56, 57, etc.) to indicate the year the part was cast. Some parts for the Flint plant (engine blocks, cylinder heads and intake manifolds) were cast in Saginaw, Michigan. These parts would have the single-digit year date code (5, 6, 7, etc.). Engines assembled in Flint with the single- digit year code were used in both passenger and Corvette applications. Flint blocks

0023084

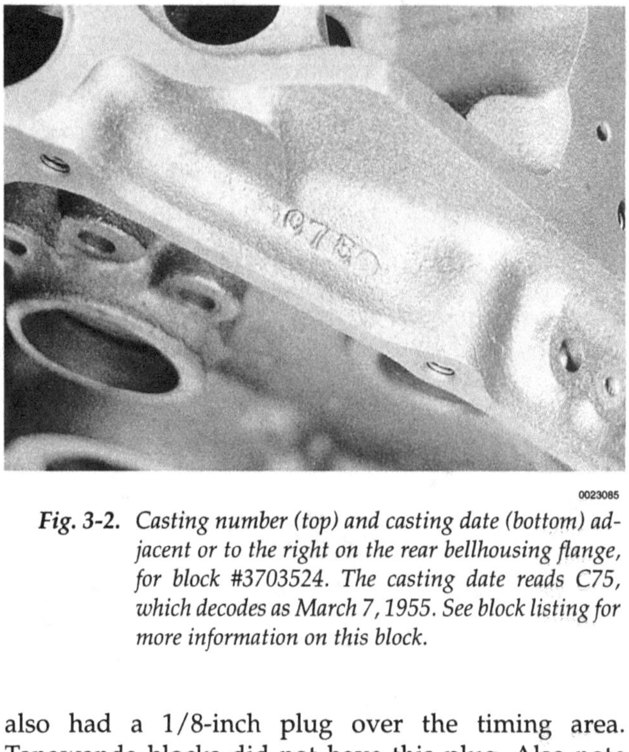

0023085

Fig. 3-2. Casting number (top) and casting date (bottom) adjacent or to the right on the rear bellhousing flange, for block #3703524. The casting date reads C75, which decodes as March 7, 1955. See block listing for more information on this block.

also had a 1/8-inch plug over the timing area. Tonawanda blocks did not have this plug. Also note that there were some W-block parts cast with the letters "CFD" which represented the Central Foundry Division located in Saginaw, Michigan. These parts would have the single-digit year date code the same as all other Saginaw produced parts.

Flint Example: A 8 5

- A = Month: January
- 8 = Day: 8th day
- 5 = Year: 1955

Tonawanda Example: A 8 55

- A = Month: January
- 8 = Day: 8th day
- 55 = Calendar Year: 1955

Engine Block Month Codes (1st Letter)

A - January	E - May	I - September
B - February	F - June	J - October
C - March	G - July	K - November
D - April	H - August	L - December

NOTE—
When checking date codes of specific engine parts, always remember the following. First verify the build date of your car. (Refer to Chapter 1 for more information on build dates.) The date codes of the various engine components should generally be dated one to three months prior to the car build date. This time lapse allows for assembly of that engine, transport to the car assembly plant and installation in the car.

NOTE—
It has been documented that in the period leading up to a possible strike, engines were built and stockpiled up to a six-month supply. The one- to three-month rule would not apply to these engines.

1.2 Casting Clock Code

Although the casting clock is not applicable to 1955–59 engines, I believe that Chevrolet engine restorers should be made aware of it here. Sometime during the 1964 model year, a casting clock code was added to some Saginaw blocks, intake manifolds, and exhaust manifolds to indicate the hour of the shift in which the part was made. This clock code is approximately two inches in diameter, and it is usually found at the rear face of the block, near the casting number.

The clock circle is made up of ten dots, each representing one hour of a specific shift. There is a second dot outside of the circle, which represents the beginning of a ten-hour shift. The Saginaw foundry usually operated in two shifts, the first from 7:00 AM to 4:00 PM, the second from 4:00 PM until midnight. Parts cast at the start of a shift would have the single clock hand pointing toward the double-dot hour position. Parts cast four hours into a shift would have the hand pointing to the fourth dot clockwise from the double dot. The screw head in the center of the clock designated the shift. A flat-head screw meant first shift, and a round-head screw the second shift.

1.3 Engine Code Stamping Number

Many restorers believe that the engine code stamping number is more important than the casting date because the engine code number contains more information pertaining to the "original" use of the block. It is also very easy to locate and verify. However, for these same two reasons, many original blocks are restamped with a non-original code to represent a rare or desirable block for resale. There are several locations in which a restorer/buyer can look on the stamp pad that may clue that person in to an altered or misrepresented block.

See Chapter 2 for a thorough discussion of identifying engine codes.

1955 Through 1959 Engine Applications

Size	Year	Bore (in.)	Stroke (in.)	Main Journal (in.)	Rod Journal (in.)	Intake Valve Size	Exhaust Valve Size	Bearing Cap	Notes
Small Block Engines									
265	1955–57	3.75	3.00	2.3	2.0	1.72	1.50	2-bolt	First Chevrolet V-8 Engine
283	1957-67	3.875	3.0	2.3	2.0	1.72	1.50	2-bolt	Revised 265 Bore
W-Block Engines									
348	1958–61	4.125	3.25	2.50	2.20	1.94/2.06	1.66/1.72	2-bolt	Engine designated Mark I, built at Tonawanda Engine Plant exclusively, predecessor to the 409 and Mark IV engines.

Engine Assembly Order

The following is the assembly order for engines at the Flint and Tonawanda assembly plants. This order of assembly is general in scope. Small variations were usually made from model year to model year.

Flint Order	Tonawanda Order
Raw castings enter plant	Raw castings received (all major engine parts cast at Tonawanda)
Block machining (broaching) in 1 to 2 days:	Block washed
Block starts down line, upside down. Bore sizes on oil pan rail broadcast ahead to piston area	Oil gallery plugs
Galley plugs	Transmission alignment pins
Camshaft	Camshaft
Crankshaft installed	Crankshaft installed
Flywheel and pressure plate	Flywheel and pressure plate
Cam and crank sprockets, timing chain	Cam and crank sprockets, timing chain
Piston hook-up and installation	Piston hook-up and installation
Front engine cover and seal	Front engine cover and seal
Harmonic balancer	Harmonic balancer
Oil pump shaft and oil pump	Oil pump shaft and oil pump
Windage tray bolts (if applic.)	Windage tray bolts (if applic.)
Oil pan and hardware	Oil pan and hardware
Clutch housing	TDC determined, timing pointer
Engine turned upright	Engine turned upright
TDC determined, timing pointer	Cam lifters
Cam lifters	Cylinder heads
Cylinder heads	Rocker arms, balls (studs already in head)
Rocker arms, balls, studs	Valves adjusted
Intake manifold	Intake manifold
Valves adjusted	Water outlet
Rocker covers	Water pump
Misc. brackets and switches	Build date/suffix code stamped
Build date/suffix code stamped	Spark plugs
Water test with vacuum gauge	Distributor
Oil cavity test	Misc. brackets
Painted	Exhaust manifolds
Distributor	Bench check (vacuum test)
Coil and plug wires	Rocker covers
Spark plugs	Paint
Temperature switches	Hot test
Hot test	Water and oil drained
Water and oil drained	Racked & readied for shipping
Exhaust manifolds	
Spark plug wire supports, heat shields, other misc. brackets	
Component verification	
Racked & readied for shipping	

2. ENGINE BLOCK CASTING NUMBERS

The following information is in a table format, arranged by casting number in numerical order for quick and easy reference. The *Year* column specifies the model year in which the block was used. The *Model* column specifies the model in which the casting number was available. The *Engine* and *Horsepower* columns dictate which engine and what horsepower the block was used for. The final column tells whether the crankshaft was retained in the block by a 2-bolt or 4-bolt main bearing cap configuration. All blocks shown in this book will have 2-bolt mains.

> NOTE—
> The letter "N" on crankshaft bearing caps indicates a cast nodular iron main bearing cap. The lack of an N indicates a standard forged crankshaft bearing cap. Most high performance blocks after 1962 used nodular iron main bearing caps.

> NOTE—
> Main bearing configurations are derived from original Flint and Tonawanda build records.

Block #3703524

Year	Model	Engine	Horsepower	Main	Notes
1955	Passenger	265	162, 180	2-bolt	This block was used for the complete 1955 model year for all applications including trucks. The bypass breather tube was cast into the back of the block above bellhousing on the driver's side and exits below the oil pan. This block had no oil filter provision in the block. It also had only two motor mountings on each side. Thin wall 265 design.
	Corvette	265	195	2-bolt	

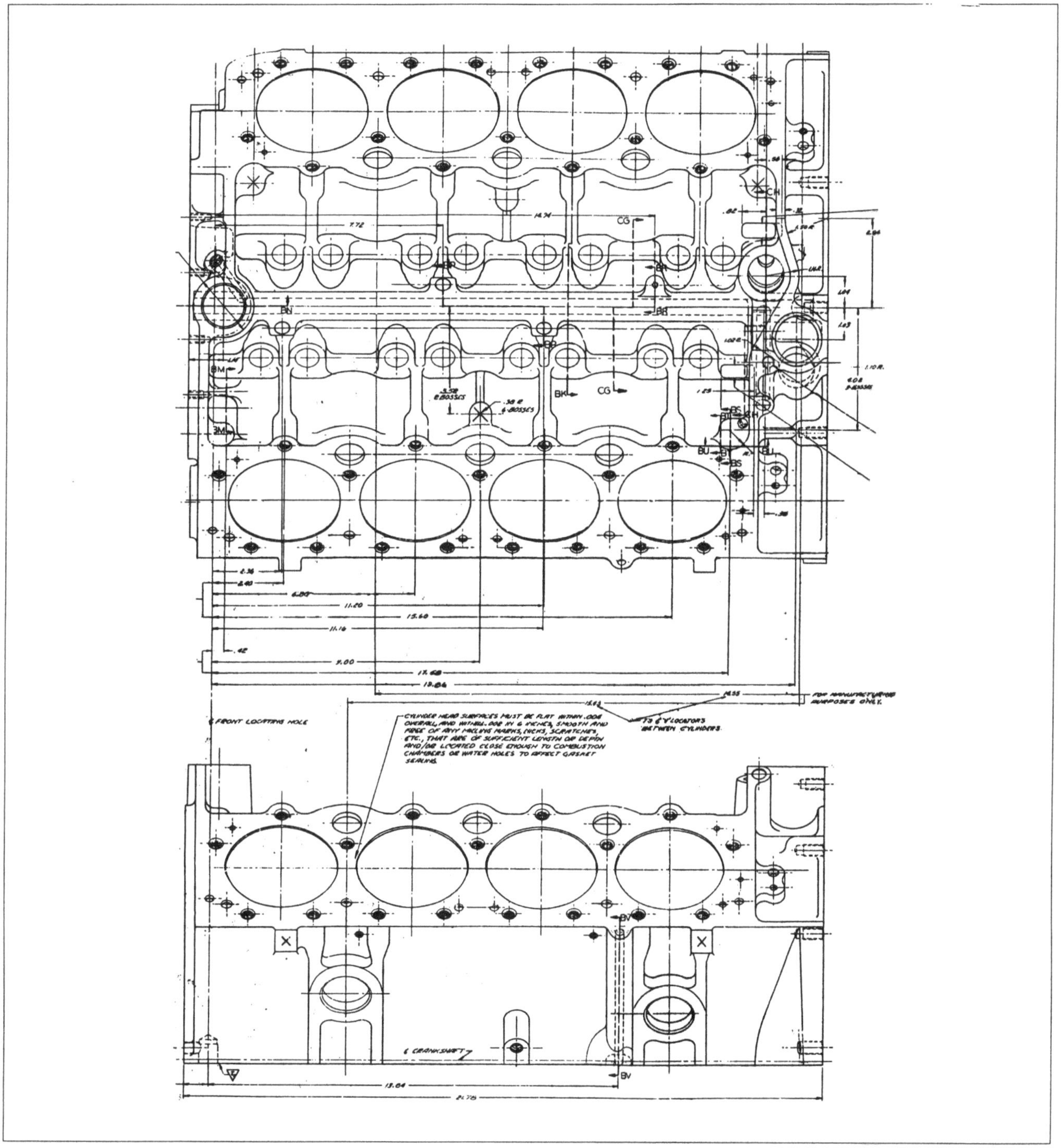

0023087

Fig. 3-3. Top and side view of #3703524.

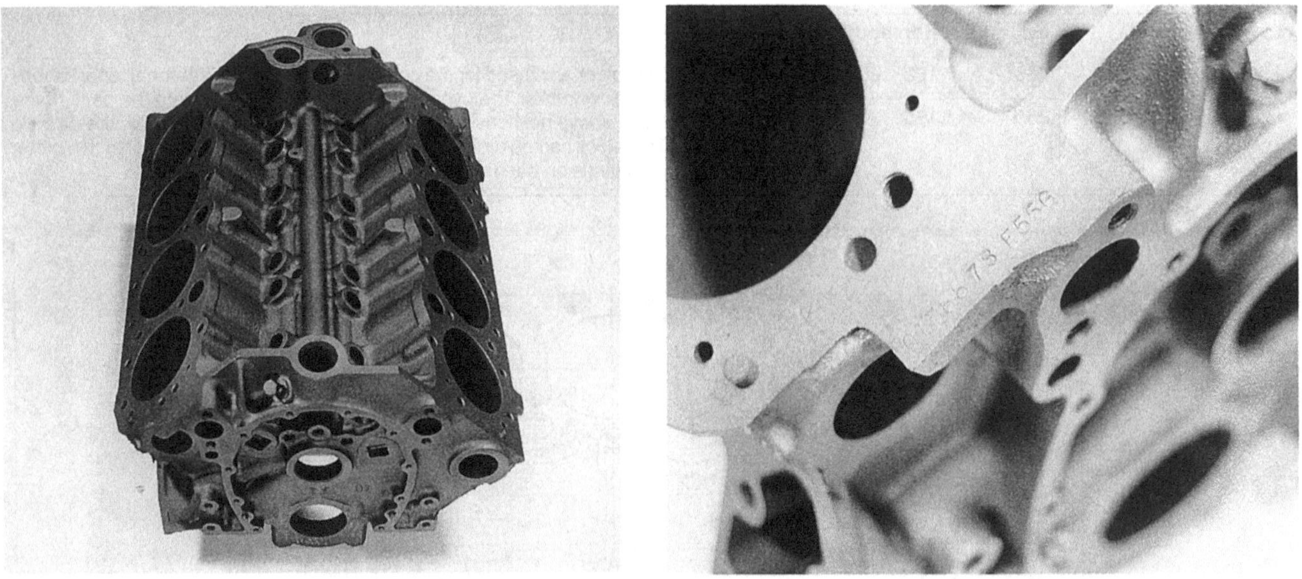

0023086 0023075

Fig. 3-4. ***Left:*** *Overall view of #3703524.* ***Right:*** *Close-up of build date stamp.*

0023088 0023089

Fig. 3-5. ***Left:*** *Rear of #3703524 block with pointer showing 1955 crankcase vent hole.* ***Right:*** *#3703524 recessed oil draft tube hole.*

Block #3720991

Year	Model	Engine	Horsepower	Main	Notes
1956	Passenger	265	162, 170, 205, 225	2-Bolt	This block was used for the complete 1956 and 1957 model years for all applications including trucks. The bypass breather tube now went down the passenger side of the engine to the oil pan. This block was the first design that featured an oil filter boss cast to the underside of the block.
	Corvette	265	210, 225, 240	2-Bolt	

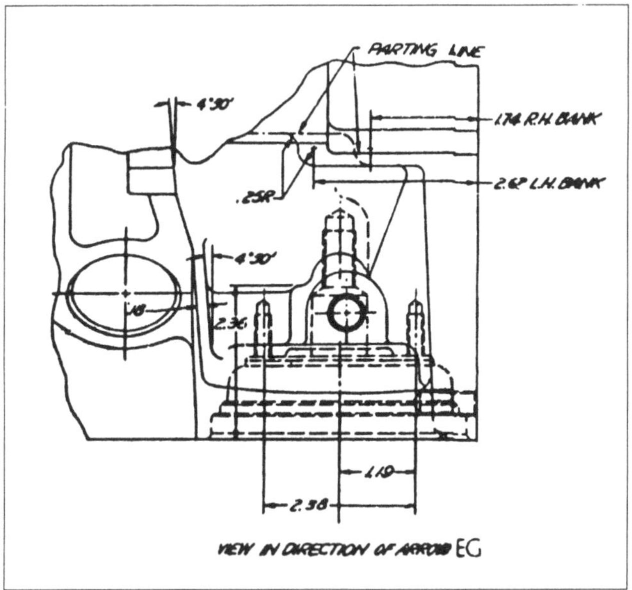

0023090

0023091

Fig. 3-6. Blueprint (left) shows cut view of oil filter boss, while photo (right) shows actual #3720991 revised oil filter area.

0023092

0023093

Fig. 3-7. ***Left:*** *Oil filter area side of block.* ***Right:*** *#3720991 distributor hole at rear of block.*

Block #3731548

Year	Model	Engine	Horsepower	Main	Notes
1957	Passenger	283	185, 220, 245, 250, 270, 283	2-Bolt	This block was a similar design to the 1956 265 #3720991 block. It was used in all applications including trucks (265 engine only) for the complete 1957 model year. This block's rear camshaft bearing area was redesigned so a grooved rear cam journal would not be necessary. This block has only one motor mounting on each side, at the front of the block.
	Corvette	283	220, 245, 250, 270, 283	2-Bolt	

Block #3737739

Year	Model	Engine	Horsepower	Main	Notes
1958	Passenger	283	185, 230, 250, 290	2-Bolt	This block was a completely new design 283 block. The cylinder walls were cast much thicker than the 1957 block. This block was the first small block to have three motor mount holes cast into the side, surrounding the forward freeze plug. This block is predominantly a 1958 block, but some very early 1959 cars could have been equipped to use up existing stock.
	Corvette	283	230, 245, 250, 270, 290	2-Bolt	

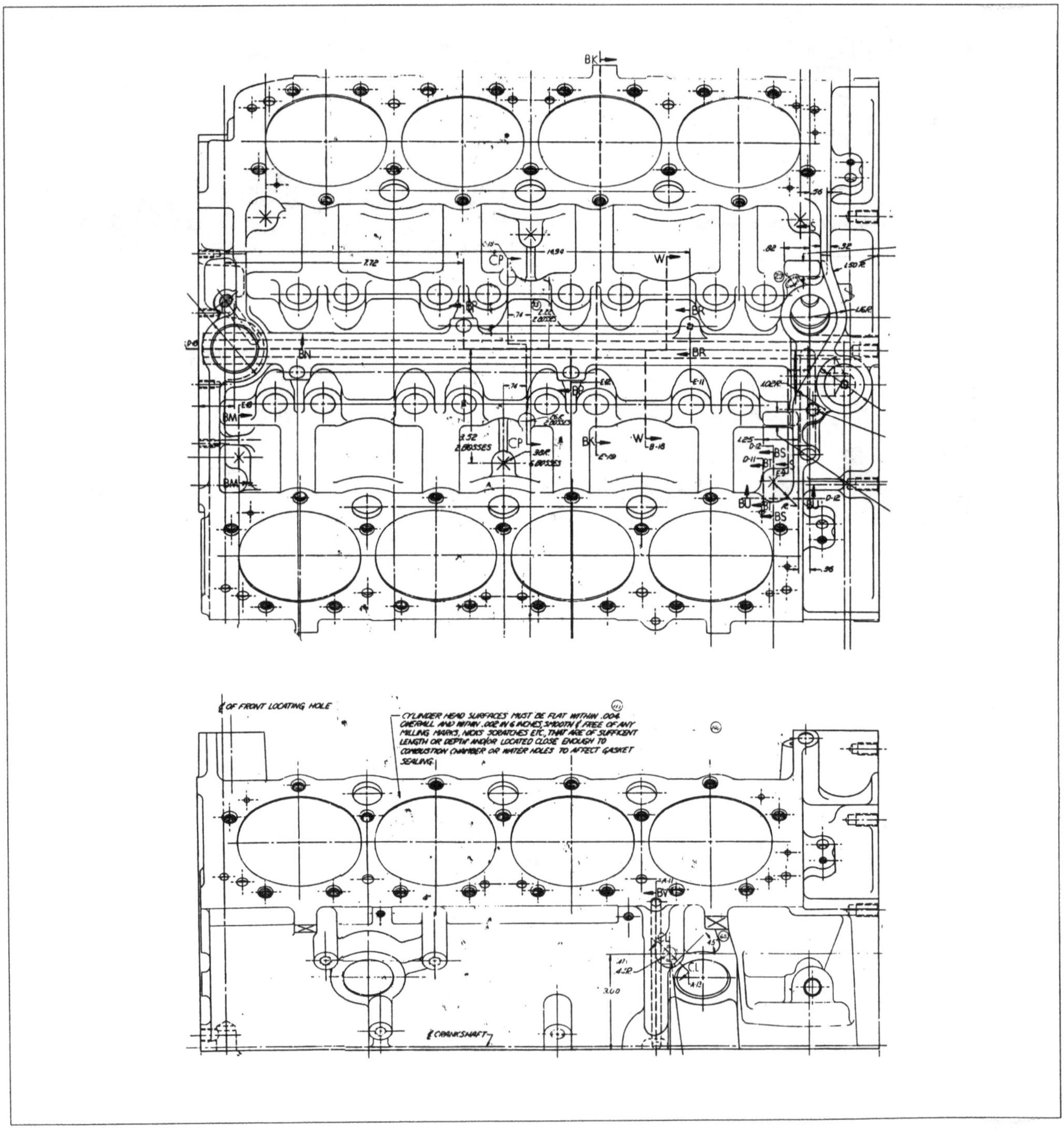

0023094

Fig. 3-8. Top and side view of #3737739 block, with arrow pointing to motor mounting bosses around front freeze plug.

0023095

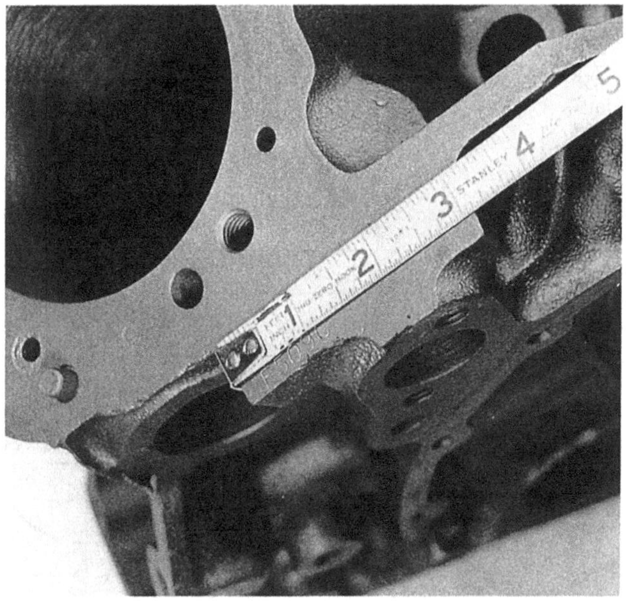

0023096

Fig. 3-9. ***Left:*** *Overall frontal view of block #3737739.* ***Right:*** *Stamping pad length of all blocks remained constant until 1965 #3782870 block.*

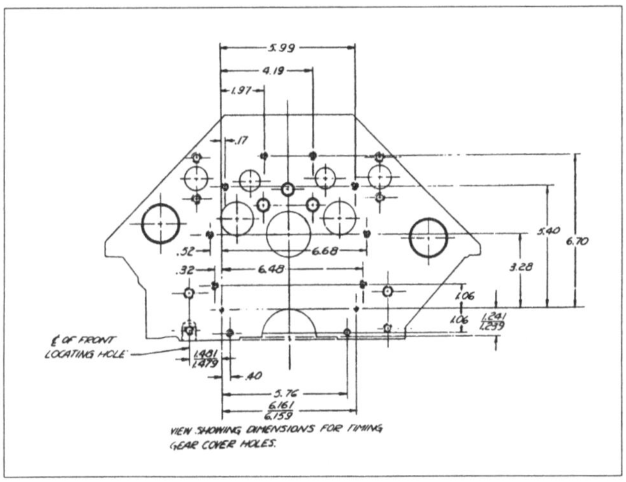

0023097

Fig. 3-10. Dimensions of timing gear cover holes for #3737739.

0023098

Fig. 3-11. Side view of #3737739, with pointer showing new three-hole motor mount position.

Block #3751872

Year	Model	Engine	Horsepower	Main	Notes
1958 (Early)	Passenger	348	250, 280, 315	2-Bolt	This was the first 348 block ever cast. It can only be used for 1958 engine applications and only uses 1958 cylinder heads. This block has no provisions for spark plug cooling holes to the 1958 cylinder heads. This block was superseded by the #3755011 block on specific engines later in the 1958 model year. The correct cylinder head for this block is #3732791.

Block #3755011[Δ]

Year	Model	Engine	Horsepower	Main	Notes
1958 (late), 1959	Passenger	348	250, 280, 315	2-Bolt	This was the second design 348 block released for the 1959 model year. This block was designed to provide water cooling to the new cylinder heads. It was used for 1958 348 truck applications after 3/37/58 and 348/315HP applications after 5/21/58. This is verified through Chevrolet Technical Service Bulletin DR #369. ΔThis block was used for all 1959–61 348 engines including service replacement blocks.

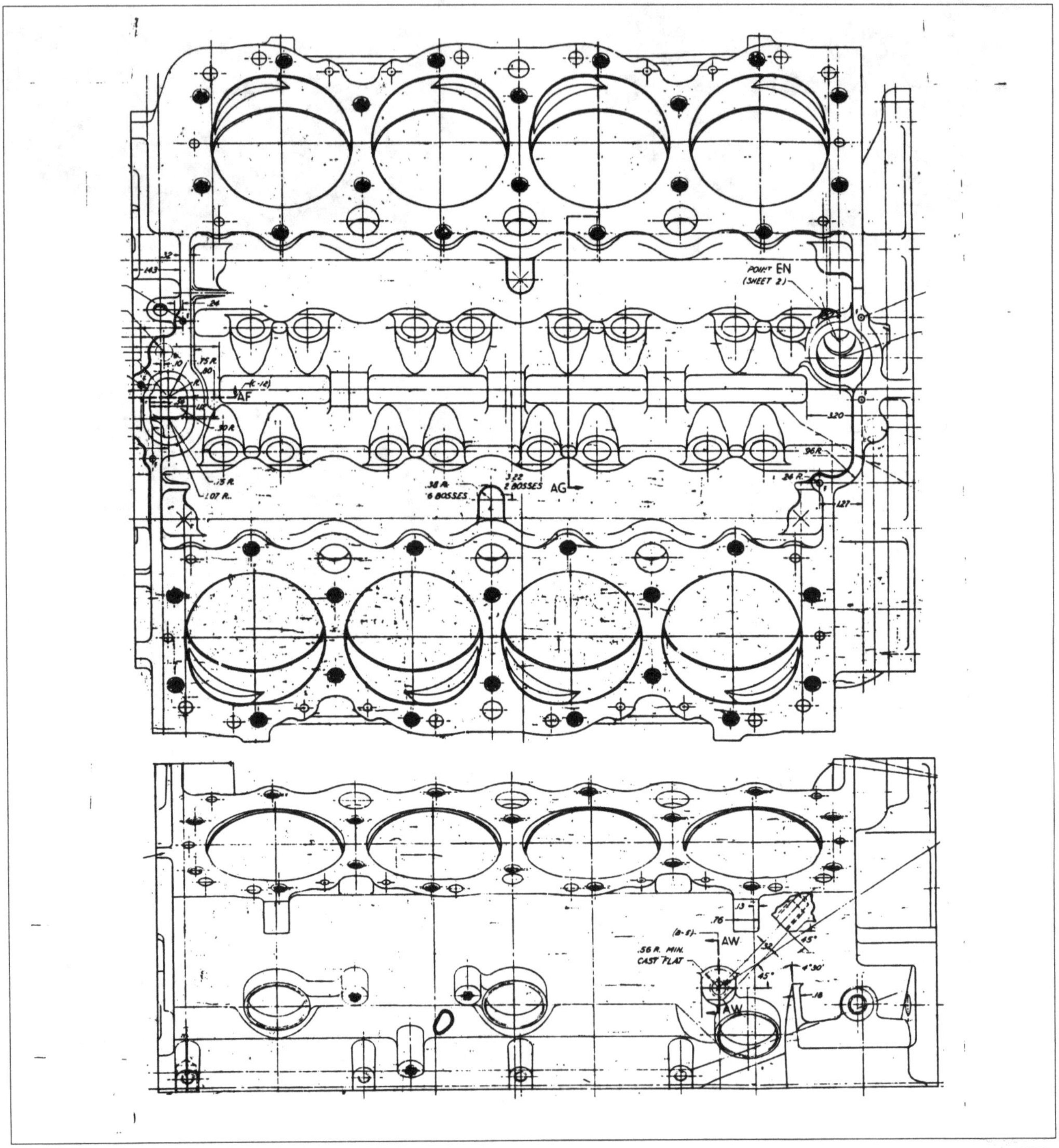

0022053

Fig. 3-12. Top and side view of #3755011.

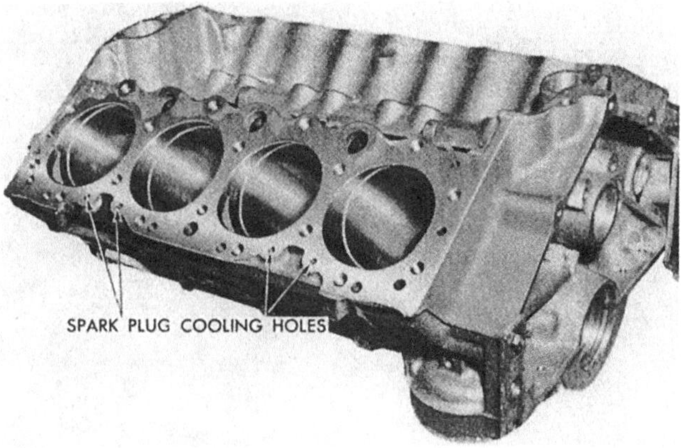

0023102

Fig. 3-13. This photo illustrates the late 1958–59 348 cylinder block spark plug cooling holes.

Block #3756519^Δ^

Year	Model	Engine	Horsepower	Main	Notes
1959	Passenger	283	185, 230, 250, 290	2-Bolt	This block was used from 1959 through the 1961 model year. There is a possibility that there could be late 1958 usage for this block, but it is unverified at this time. Please refer to cylinder heads #3748770 and #3755550 in Chapter 5 for information concerning heads used on this block. ΔThis block was used in the 1960 and 1961 model years.
	Corvette	283	230, 245, 250, 270, 290	2-Bolt	

0023103

Fig. 3-14. 1959 283 cylinder block spark plug cooling holes.

0023099

Fig. 3-15. Overall frontal view of block #3756519.

0023100

Fig. 3-16. Overall side view of block #3756519.

0023101

Fig. 3-17. Overall rear view of block #3756519.

Chapter 4

Crankshaft Identification

1. Introduction

In this chapter I will identify all crankshafts and matching engine combinations installed in Chevrolet cars from 1955 through 1959. During this period, only one type of crankshaft was manufactured by Chevrolet: forged steel. The forged steel crank was initially introduced in 1955 in the 265 engine. As production figures rose and manufacturing costs began to increase, Chevrolet decided to install a less expensive cast nodular iron crankshaft in many later model low and intermediate performance passenger cars. The forged steel crankshaft was then reserved for all high performance applications, including Corvette.

You can identify each of these crankshafts, without having to fully disassemble the engine, by checking the parting line (or manufacturing seam) of the crankshaft. The seam was produced by the two halves of the crankshaft mold that came together to produce the part. The seam extends down the entire length of the crank. When the engine is assembled this parting line is visible on the crankshaft flywheel flange.

In a cast nodular crank, the parting line is very thin, usually 1/32" wide, and it stands up above the surface of the crankshaft. The forged steel parting line is much wider, usually 1/4" to 1/2". There is no visible ridge on the forged crank. The texture of the forged crank is also much smoother than the cast iron.

Another distinguishing feature between crankshafts is the result of a special treatment called Tuftriding. From all indications, this treatment began in the 1964 model year on Corvette 327/365 and 375HP crankshafts. The treatment involved a chemical heat-treating process that hardened the rod and main bearing journal surfaces of most forged steel crankshafts to be used in high performance applications. Tuftrided crankshafts have a dull gray finish.

Many small block crankshafts, including truck and all high performance applications, also have cross-drilled main bearing journals. This cross-drilling process was used to insure that all bearings and bearing journals are supplied with oil during the complete rotation of the crankshaft. All Tuftrided cranks have been cross-drilled, but not all cross-drilled cranks have been Tuftrided.

Finally, all crankshafts were manufactured with a casting number. This casting number is located on the rough surface of one of the counterweights or between the bearing journals. The chart at the end of this chapter lists casting numbers in numerical order.

Any further information that is specific to a particular crankshaft will be explained under each individual heading.

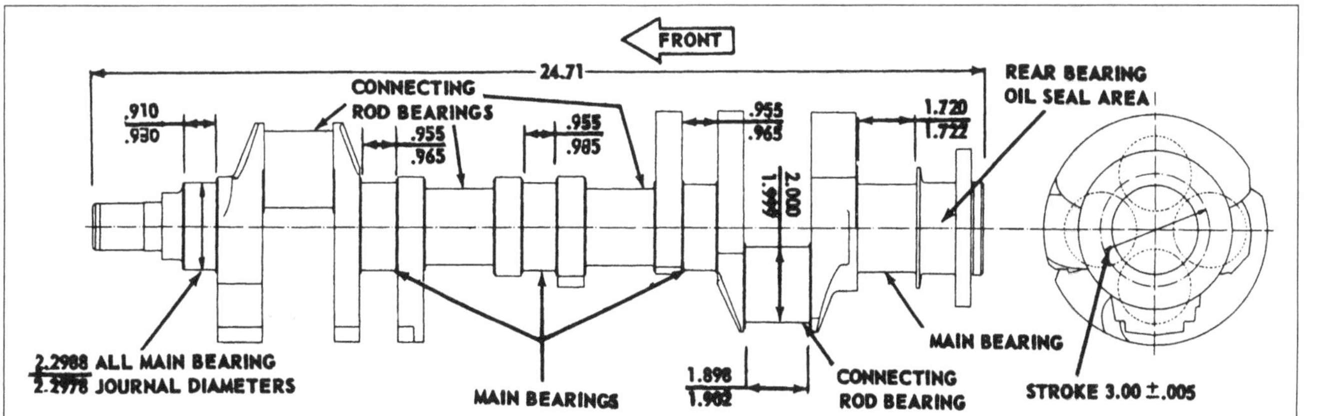

Fig. 4-1. Typical 8-cylinder crankshaft.

NOTE—
Many of the crankshaft dimensions (rod and main journals) in this chapter are given in rounded numbers (i.e. 2.10, 3.00) since that is the way the dimensions are commonly described. The crankshaft illustrations give the factory dimensions, often to four decimal places, which is necessary for accurate machining.

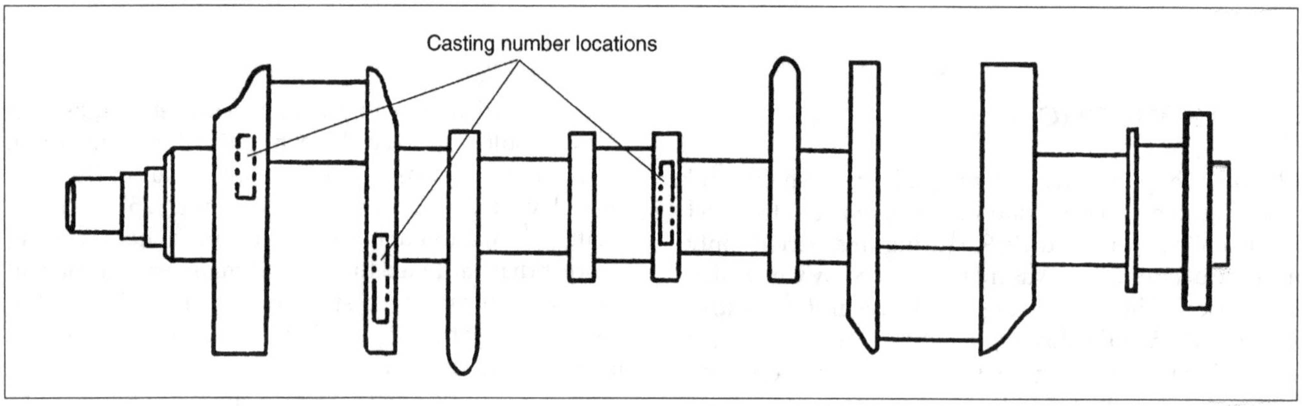

0022069

Fig. 4-2. Typical locations of crankshaft casting numbers.

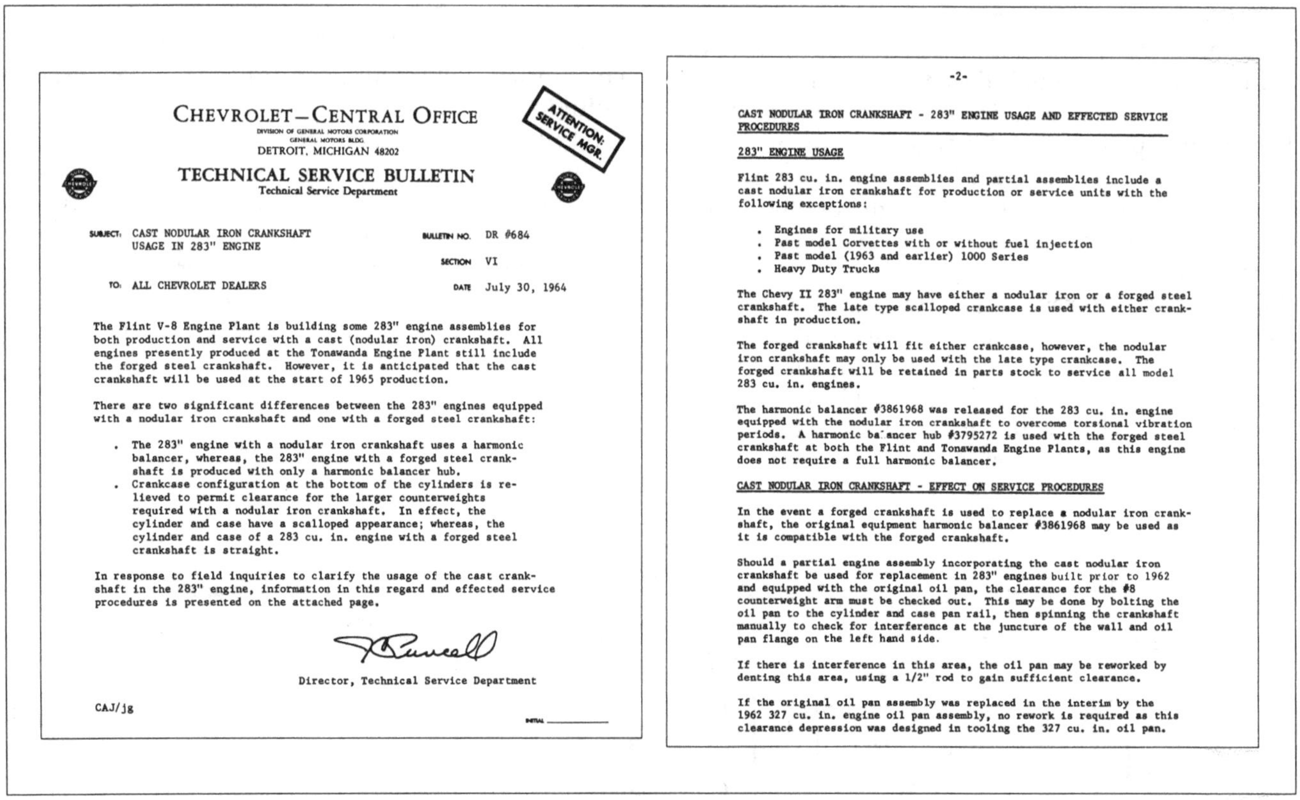

CHEVROLET—CENTRAL OFFICE
DIVISION OF GENERAL MOTORS CORPORATION
GENERAL MOTORS BLDG.
DETROIT, MICHIGAN 48202

ATTENTION: SERVICE MGR.

TECHNICAL SERVICE BULLETIN
Technical Service Department

SUBJECT: CAST NODULAR IRON CRANKSHAFT USAGE IN 283" ENGINE

BULLETIN NO. DR #684

SECTION VI

TO: ALL CHEVROLET DEALERS

DATE July 30, 1964

The Flint V-8 Engine Plant is building some 283" engine assemblies for both production and service with a cast (nodular iron) crankshaft. All engines presently produced at the Tonawanda Engine Plant still include the forged steel crankshaft. However, it is anticipated that the cast crankshaft will be used at the start of 1965 production.

There are two significant differences between the 283" engines equipped with a nodular iron crankshaft and one with a forged steel crankshaft:

- The 283" engine with a nodular iron crankshaft uses a harmonic balancer, whereas, the 283" engine with a forged steel crankshaft is produced with only a harmonic balancer hub.
- Crankcase configuration at the bottom of the cylinders is relieved to permit clearance for the larger counterweights required with a nodular iron crankshaft. In effect, the cylinder and case have a scalloped appearance; whereas, the cylinder and case of a 283 cu. in. engine with a forged steel crankshaft is straight.

In response to field inquiries to clarify the usage of the cast crankshaft in the 283" engine, information in this regard and effected service procedures is presented on the attached page.

Director, Technical Service Department

CAJ/jg

INITIAL ________

-2-

CAST NODULAR IRON CRANKSHAFT - 283" ENGINE USAGE AND EFFECTED SERVICE PROCEDURES

283" ENGINE USAGE

Flint 283 cu. in. engine assemblies and partial assemblies include a cast nodular iron crankshaft for production or service units with the following exceptions:

- Engines for military use
- Past model Corvettes with or without fuel injection
- Past model (1963 and earlier) 1000 Series
- Heavy Duty Trucks

The Chevy II 283" engine may have either a nodular iron or a forged steel crankshaft. The late type scalloped crankcase is used with either crankshaft in production.

The forged crankshaft will fit either crankcase, however, the nodular iron crankshaft may only be used with the late type crankcase. The forged crankshaft will be retained in parts stock to service all model 283 cu. in. engines.

The harmonic balancer #3861968 was released for the 283 cu. in. engine equipped with the nodular iron crankshaft to overcome torsional vibration periods. A harmonic balancer hub #3795272 is used with the forged steel crankshaft at both the Flint and Tonawanda Engine Plants, as this engine does not require a full harmonic balancer.

CAST NODULAR IRON CRANKSHAFT - EFFECT ON SERVICE PROCEDURES

In the event a forged crankshaft is used to replace a nodular iron crankshaft, the original equipment harmonic balancer #3861968 may be used as it is compatible with the forged crankshaft.

Should a partial engine assembly incorporating the cast nodular iron crankshaft be used for replacement in 283" engines built prior to 1962 and equipped with the original oil pan, the clearance for the #8 counterweight arm must be checked out. This may be done by bolting the oil pan to the cylinder and case pan rail, then spinning the crankshaft manually to check for interference at the juncture of the wall and oil pan flange on the left hand side.

If there is interference in this area, the oil pan may be reworked by denting this area, using a 1/2" rod to gain sufficient clearance.

If the original oil pan assembly was replaced in the interim by the 1962 327 cu. in. engine oil pan assembly, no rework is required as this clearance depression was designed in tooling the 327 cu. in. oil pan.

0022070

Fig. 4-3. Chevrolet TSB shows changes to 1965 283 crankshafts, which indicates that all prior (1957–64) 283 crankshafts were forged steel.

2. Chevrolet Small Block Crankshafts

265 Crankshaft, 1955–1957

Engine	Year(s)	Stroke	Rod Journal	Main Journal
265	1955–57	3.00 in.	2.00 in.	2.30 in.
The 265 crankshaft was produced in only one style, forged steel. The crankshaft flange is identical to the 283 crank.				

Crankshaft Flange

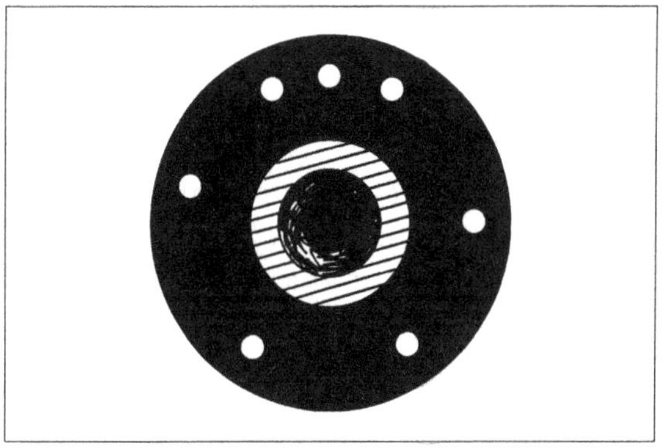

Crankshaft Dimensions

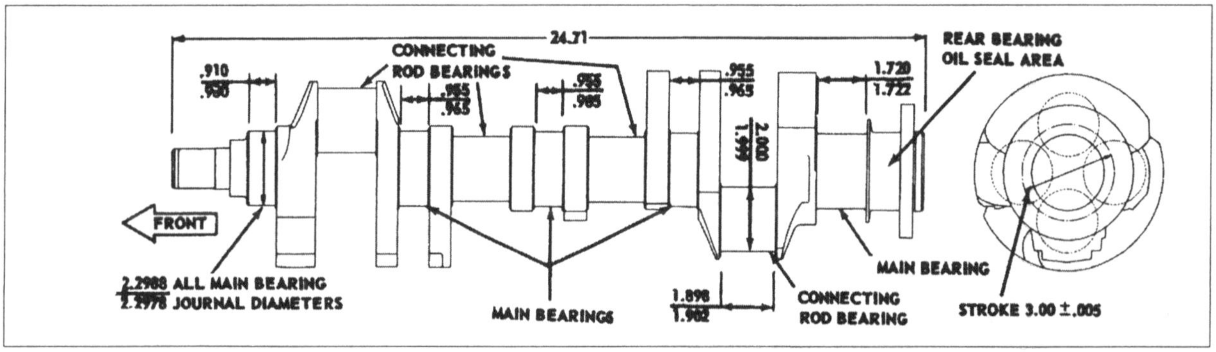

283 Crankshaft, 1957 Through 1959△

Engine	Year(s)	Stroke	Rod Journal	Main Journal
283	1957–59	3.00 in.	2.00 in.	2.30 in.
The 283 crankshaft was produced in both styles, forged steel and cast nodular iron. The Flint engine plant began producing 283 engines with cast cranks some time before July 30, 1964 (end of 1964 production). The Tonawanda plant began using the cast crank after the 1965 model start-up. See the TSB on the previous page for more information. Many 283 high performance car and truck crankshafts had a threaded pulley bolt hole on the front of the crank for attachment of the pulley. There was a special 283 HP crankshaft with the same casting number but with different counterweights; this crankshaft was also used in truck applications. △This crankshaft was also used on 1960 through 1967 283 models.				

Crankshaft Flange

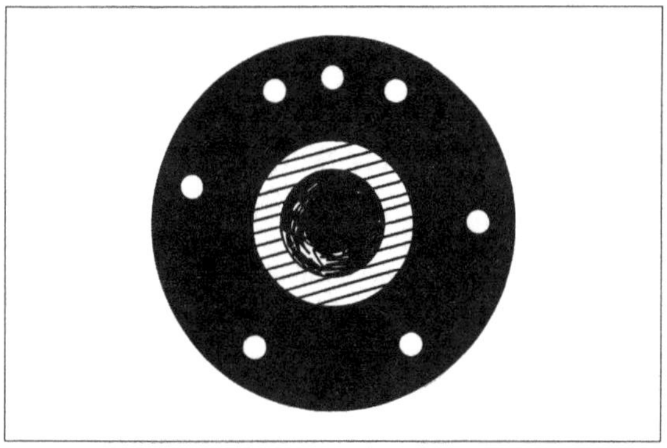

Crankshaft Dimensions

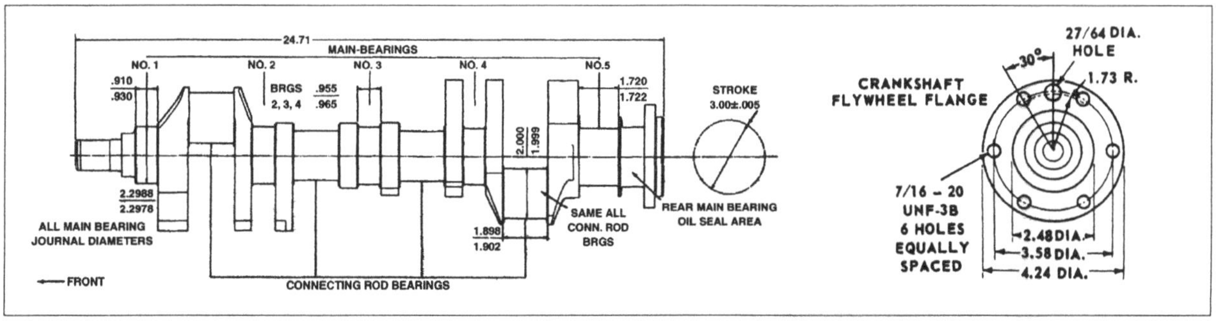

3. CHEVROLET W-BLOCK CRANKSHAFTS

348 Crankshaft

Engine	Year(s)	Stroke	Rod Journal	Main Journal
348	1958–61*	3.25 in.	2.10 in.	2.50 in.

*The 348 engine officially stopped production in 1961, however, many parts continued to be produced in Tonawanda for service installation. All 348 crankshafts are forged steel. Some sources indicate that 348 truck crankshafts have a threaded pulley bolt hole for attachment of the crank pulley.

Crankshaft Flange

0022078

Crankshaft Dimensions

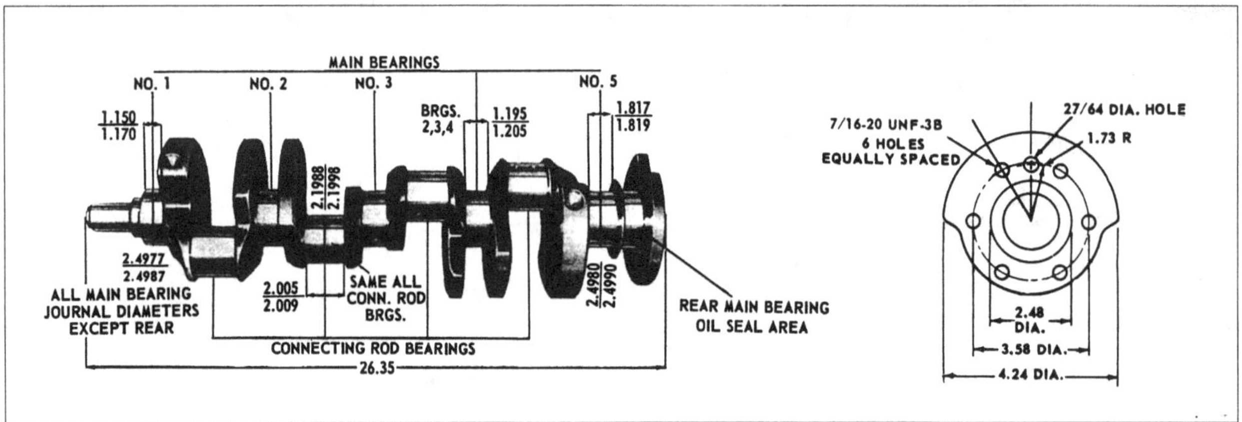

0022287

4. CRANKSHAFT CASTING NUMBERS

NOTE—
Crankshaft stock was normally depleted in engine production during the same model year, however, there may be some crankshaft carry-over very earlier in the following model year.

Crankshaft Specifications, 1955–1959

Casting #	Year	Engine/HP	Construction	Main Journ.	Rod Journ.	Stroke	Notes
3732692	1958–59	348 all	Forged Steel	2.50	2.20	3.25	Except Turboglide
3733223	1958–59	348 all	Forged Steel	2.50	2.20	3.25	Except Turboglide
3735236	1955–59	265/283 all	Forged Steel	2.30	2.00	3.00	Except Turboglide
3815822	1955–59	265/283 all	Forged Steel	2.30	2.00	3.00	
3834627	1955–59	265/283	Forged Steel	2.30	2.00	3.00	
3836266	1955–59	265/283	Forged Steel	2.30	2.00	3.00	
3876764	1957–59	265/283 all	Forged Steel	2.30	2.00	3.00	

Chapter 5

Cylinder Head Identification

1. INTRODUCTION

There are a number of ways to identify cylinder heads. The primary one is the head casting number and date, but there are also other identifying features, including combustion chamber design, and external casting marks on the end of the head.

Cylinder Head Casting Number

The cylinder head casting number is the single most important identifying feature on a head because it will probably be the last feature that could be altered or changed. The casting number is usually found on the top of the head, in between two valves and the rocker arm studs. See Fig. 5-2.

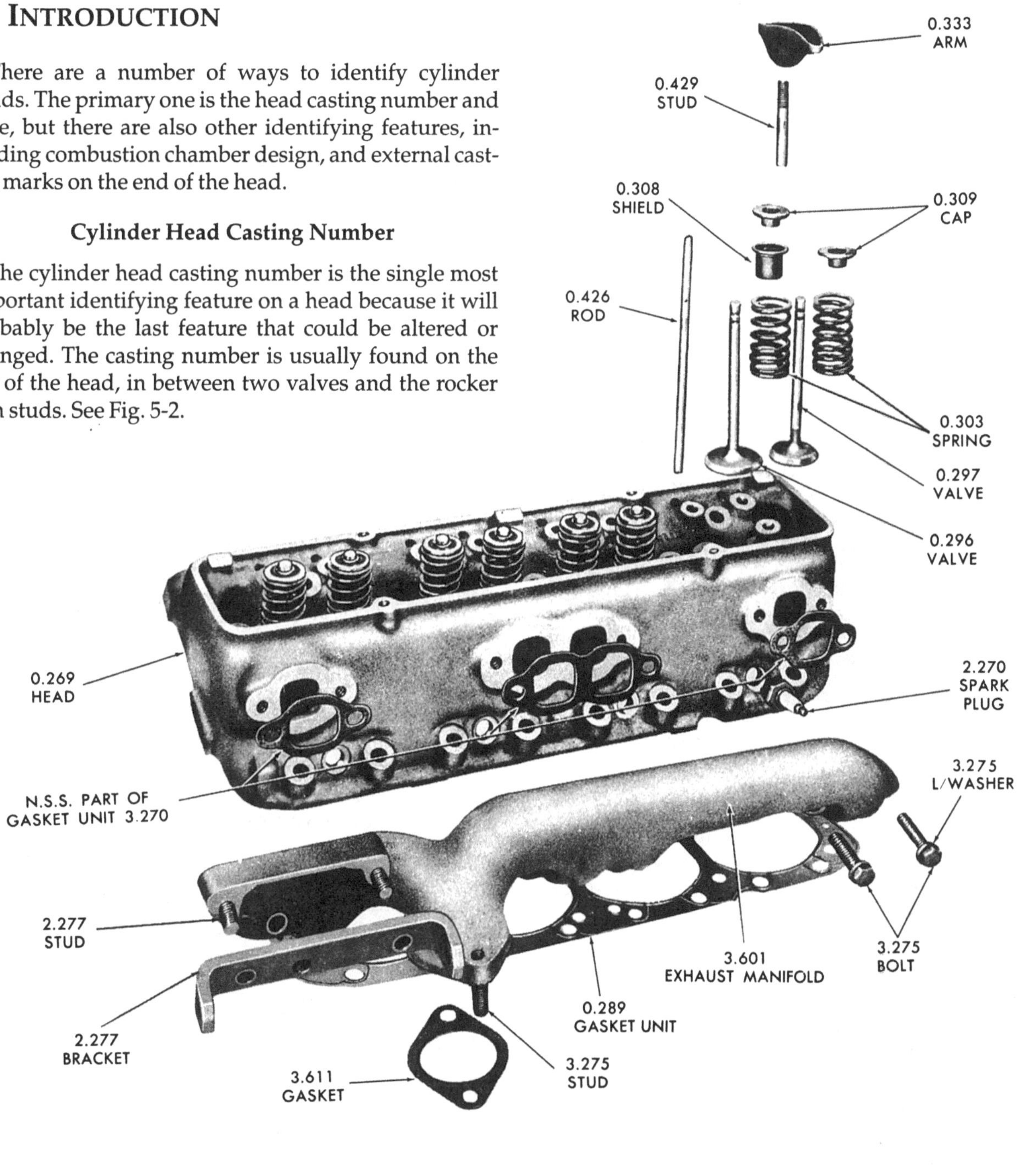

Fig. 5-1. Typical V-8 cylinder head exploded view.

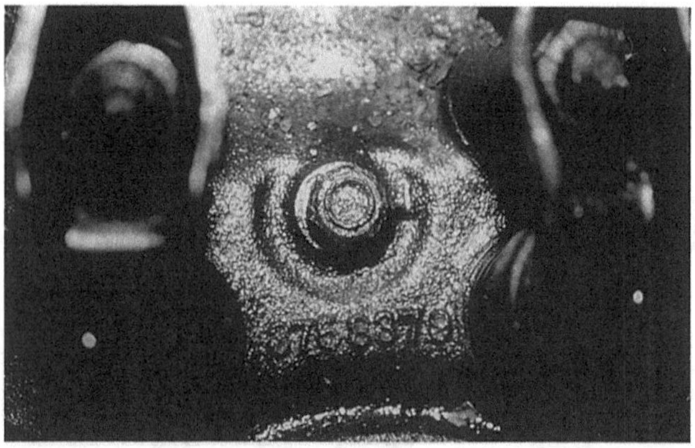

0023106

Fig. 5-2. Casting number for cylinder head #3758379.

Cylinder Head Casting Date

The casting date is usually found adjacent to the casting number. You should look closely at a cylinder head's casting date because many heads have been found that have been altered to represent an earlier or more expensive cylinder head.

0023107

Fig. 5-3. Casting date J1359 (October 13, 1959) for cylinder head #3758379.

The casting date code is in alphanumeric sequence. The first digit will usually be a letter code, which specifies the month the head was cast. Some casting dates have been found with all three digits represented as numbers such as "349," which decodes as March 4, 1959. These types of dates are not common in restoration circles. The table below gives month code letter designations. The remaining digits in the date refer to the day of the month and year of the casting.

Flint Example: Date code B 18 9

- B = Month: February
- 18 = Casting date: 18th
- 9 = Calendar Year: 1959

Tonawanda Example: Date code B 18 59

- B = Month: February
- 18 = Casting date: 18th
- 59 = Calendar Year: 1959

Cylinder Head Month Codes (1st Letter)

A - January	E - May	I - September
B - February	F - June	J - October
C - March	G - July	K - November
D - April	H - August	L - December

Note that there were two main plants casting Chevrolet engine parts during this time period: Flint, Michigan, and Tonawanda, New York. Tonawanda cast all components for engines assembled there. Most Tonawanda engine component castings, including most W-block components, will have a "T" cast into the surface of the part to designate it as a Tonawanda casting. In addition, all Tonawanda cast heads will have a two-digit code to indicate the year the part was cast.

Some parts for the Flint plant (engine blocks, cylinder heads and intake manifolds) were cast in Saginaw, Michigan. These parts would have the single-digit year date code. Engines assembled in Flint with the single-digit year code were used in both passenger and Corvette applications. Also note that there were some W-block parts cast with the letters "CFD," which represented the Central Foundry Division located in Saginaw, Michigan. These parts would have the single-digit year date code the same as all other Saginaw produced parts. Small block head changeover dates vary from year to year.

Combustion Chamber Design

There were several basic combustion chamber styles used on small block heads from 1955 through 1959. The styles were commonly known by their combustion chamber size. Although each combustion chamber had a specific shape, most 1955–59 heads used the same basic design. In 1960, the first true high performance head (62cc/new design) was introduced on the Corvette 283/315HP engine. Generally speaking, the smaller the size of the combustion chamber, the higher the compression ratio and increased performance.

Cylinder Head Bosses

Depending on the model year, one or more bosses may be present on the head.

Some heads have additional bosses for the mounting of accessory brackets, such as for air conditioning. All heads installed from 1955 through 1959 do not have a temperature sending unit boss. The temperature sending unit is located in the intake manifold until the 1968 model year.

Spark Plug Seat Design

All 1955 through 1959 model year cars were produced with an "N" series, or flat gasket spark plug seat. Spark plug seat design did not change to a "peanut" or tapered spark plug seat until the 1970 model year.

External Casting Marks

All small block heads had various symbols cast into the end of the head. These symbols are mentioned under each casting number. These symbols make small block identification easy without removing a valve cover, although valve sizes should also be checked. Note that Flint and Tonawanda casting symbols were somewhat different when compared to each other. The Flint casting symbol was taller and sharper, while the Tonawanda casting symbol was shorter. Many 348/409 heads are identical externally and have no external casting marks.

The 1958 348 head is distinguishable from later years in that it did not have water cooling cavities around the spark plug recesses. 1959 and later 348/409 head design is distinctive in that there are cored cooling slots that are visible at the spark plug relief area. See Fig. 5-4.

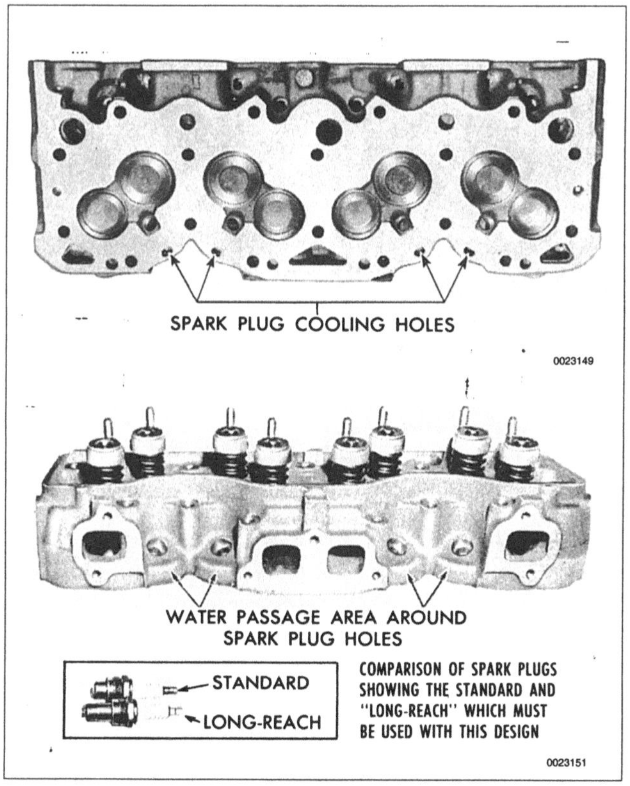

Fig. 5-4. *Late 1958 348 cylinder head spark plug cooling holes and new spark plugs required with design.*

The scalloped type valve covers are the only common denominator of a 348/409 head. These heads should be identified by referring to the casting number.

2. Cylinder Head Casting Numbers

The charts on the following pages list in order of casting number the cylinder heads installed on 1955 through 1959 cars. The casting number is always found on the top, or rocker side, of the head.

Under each listing additional information pertaining to the cylinder head is broken down into several headings to give information necessary to correctly identify the cylinder head.

The *Year* heading is the model year in which the casting number was used. Please note that many casting numbers were used over many model years.

In the *Valve Size* column the first number refers to the intake valve size, while the second number refers to the exhaust valve size. This information is very important because some engines will use the same casting number but with a different valve size. Unfortunately, the only way to validate a correct valve size is to remove the cylinder heads from the engine to measure the valves.

The *Combustion Chamber* volume heading is included for several reasons. It is primarily an additional check to prove the originality of a cylinder head. This figure was listed on every cylinder head blueprint from Chevrolet and shows the original manufacturing specifications for the cylinder head. Second, it gives a figure of comparison between cylinder heads that are similar to one another in other aspects. Finally, no other publication has been able to procure these original combustion chamber volumes, so this should be useful reference material. These figures can be easily checked on a head at a local machine shop.

Please note that all 348/409 engines (W-block) do not have a combustion chamber volume in the cylinder head like other Chevrolet V-8 engines. The combustion chamber on W-block engines was designed to be in the block. Those figures are not included here due to the possibility of confusion.

Head #3703523

Year	Model	Engine	Horsepower	Valve Size (in.) Intake/Exhaust	Combustion Chamber (cc.)	Notes
1955	Passenger	265	162, 180	1.72/1.50	67.4242	This is the first small block cylinder head. It is the only head which was available in the 1955 model year. The first high performance head was not offered until 1956. This cylinder head has staggered valve cover mounting bolt holes. Casting symbol:  0023145
	Corvette	265	195			

0023108

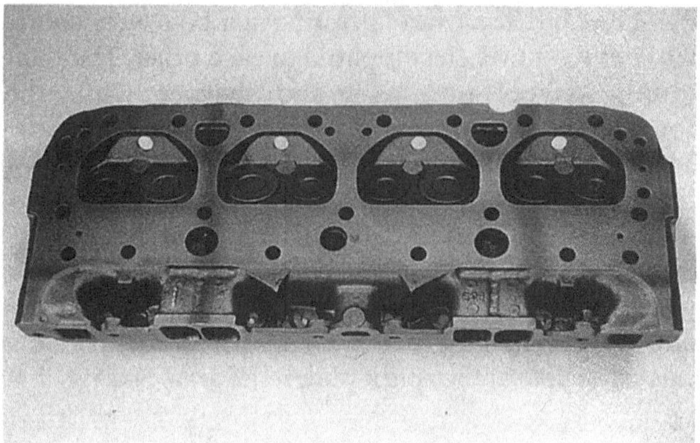

0023109

0023111

Fig. 5-5. ***Top, left and right:*** *Rocker and valve side of #3703523 head.*
Bottom: *Combustion chamber detail.*

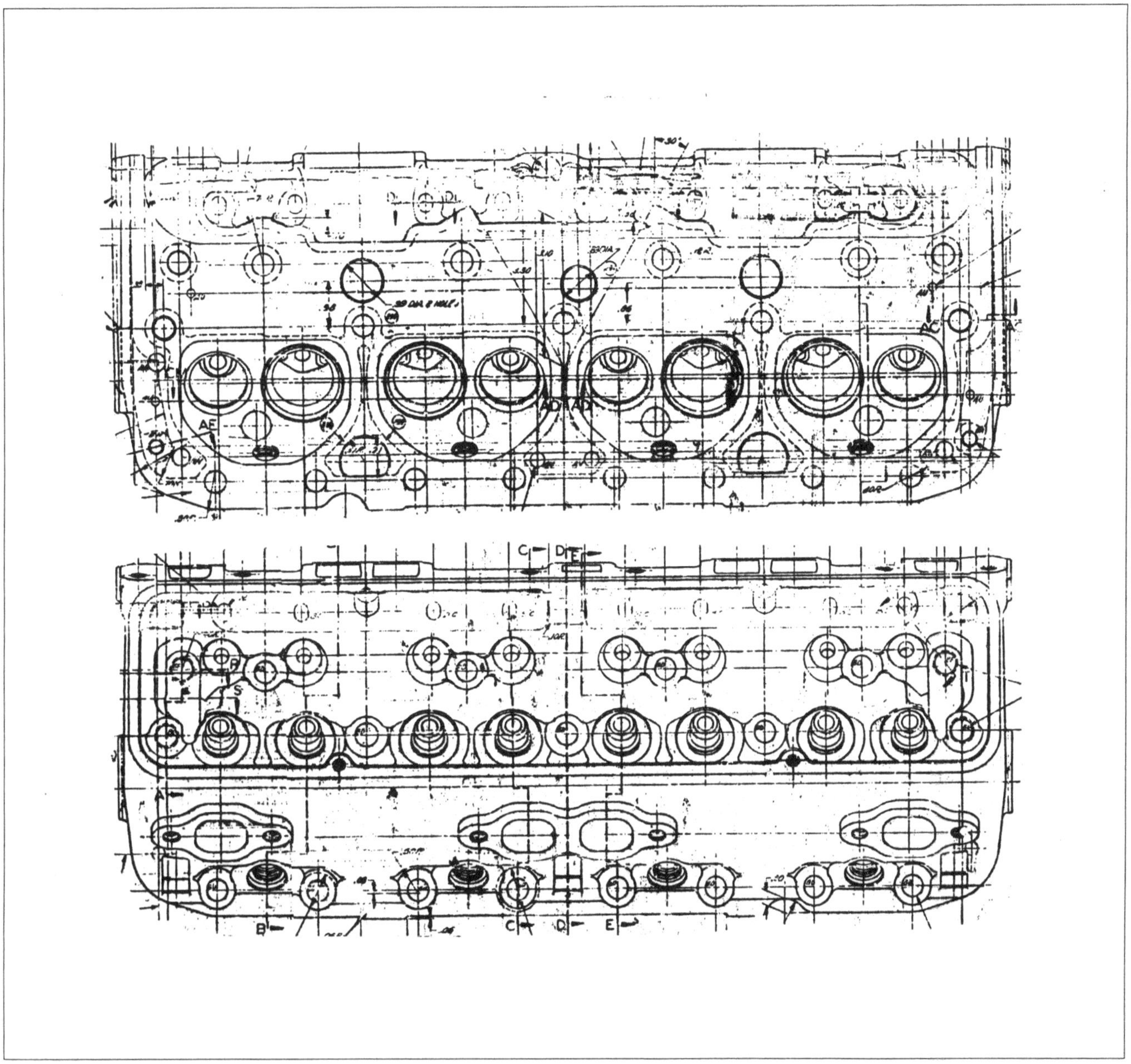

0023110

Fig. 5-6. Blueprint of #3703523.

Head #3725306

Year	Model	Engine	Horsepower	Valve Size (in.) Intake/Exhaust	Combustion Chamber (cc.)	Notes
1956	Passenger	265	205	1.72/1.50	55.6685	This cylinder head was the first high performance head Chevrolet manufactured. It had a very small combustion chamber like the #3740997 head. It was identical to the #3837064 head except for combustion chamber size and the external identification symbol. This cylinder head also uses the two-stud exhaust manifolds on the early 225HP applications. This head has staggered valve cover bolt holes. Casting symbol:  0023142
	Corvette	265	210, 225HP (Early)			

0023112

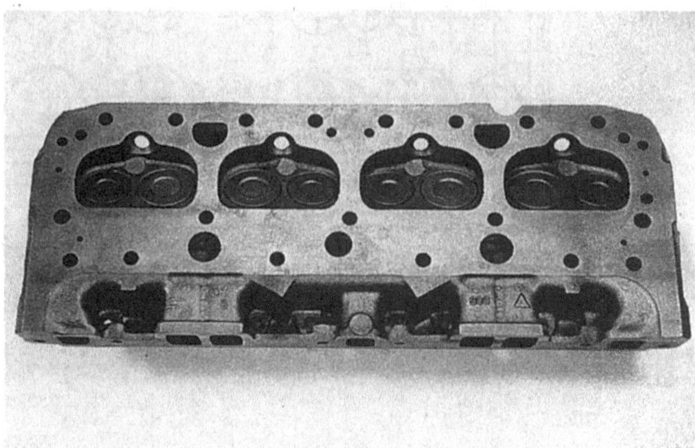

0023113

0023114

Fig. 5-7. ***Top, left and right:*** *Rocker and valve side of #3725306 head.*
Bottom: *Combustion chamber detail.*

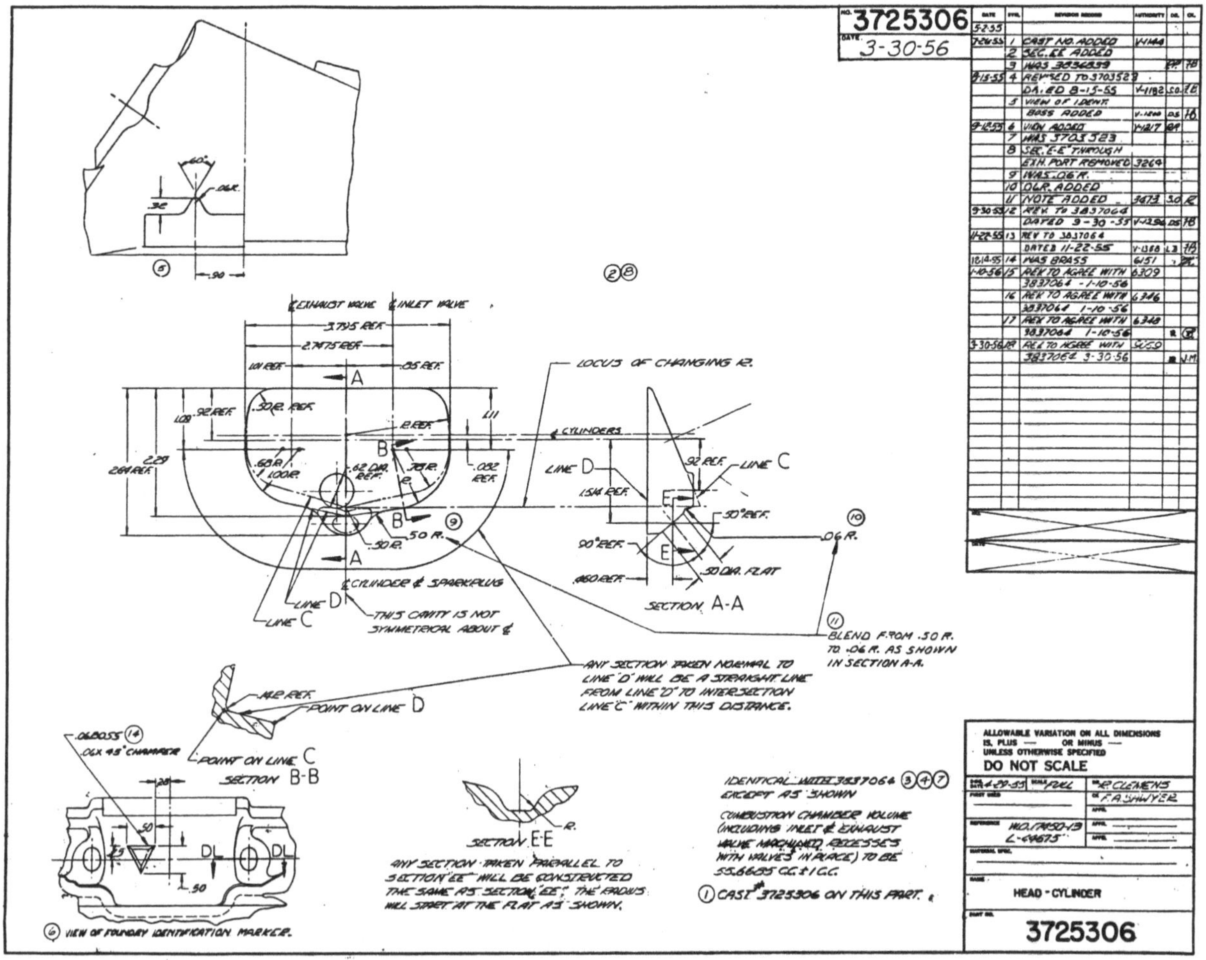

0023115

Fig. 5-8. Blueprint of #3725306 indicates that it is identical with #3837064 except as shown.

Head #3731539

Year	Model	Engine	Horsepower	Valve Size (in.) Intake/Exhaust	Combustion Chamber (cc.)	Notes
1957	Passenger	283	220, 283	1.72/1.50	60.1122	This cylinder head was used only in the 220HP 283 engines in passenger cars and the 283/283HP engines in both passenger cars and Corvettes. It was identical to the #3731554 head except for changes in the combustion chamber and an increase in the valve guide boss diameter. It has staggered valve cover bolt holes. Casting symbol:  0023142
	Corvette	283	283			

0023116

0023117

00023118

Fig. 5-9. ***Top, left and right:*** *Rocker and valve side of #3731539 head.*
Bottom: *Combustion chamber detail.*

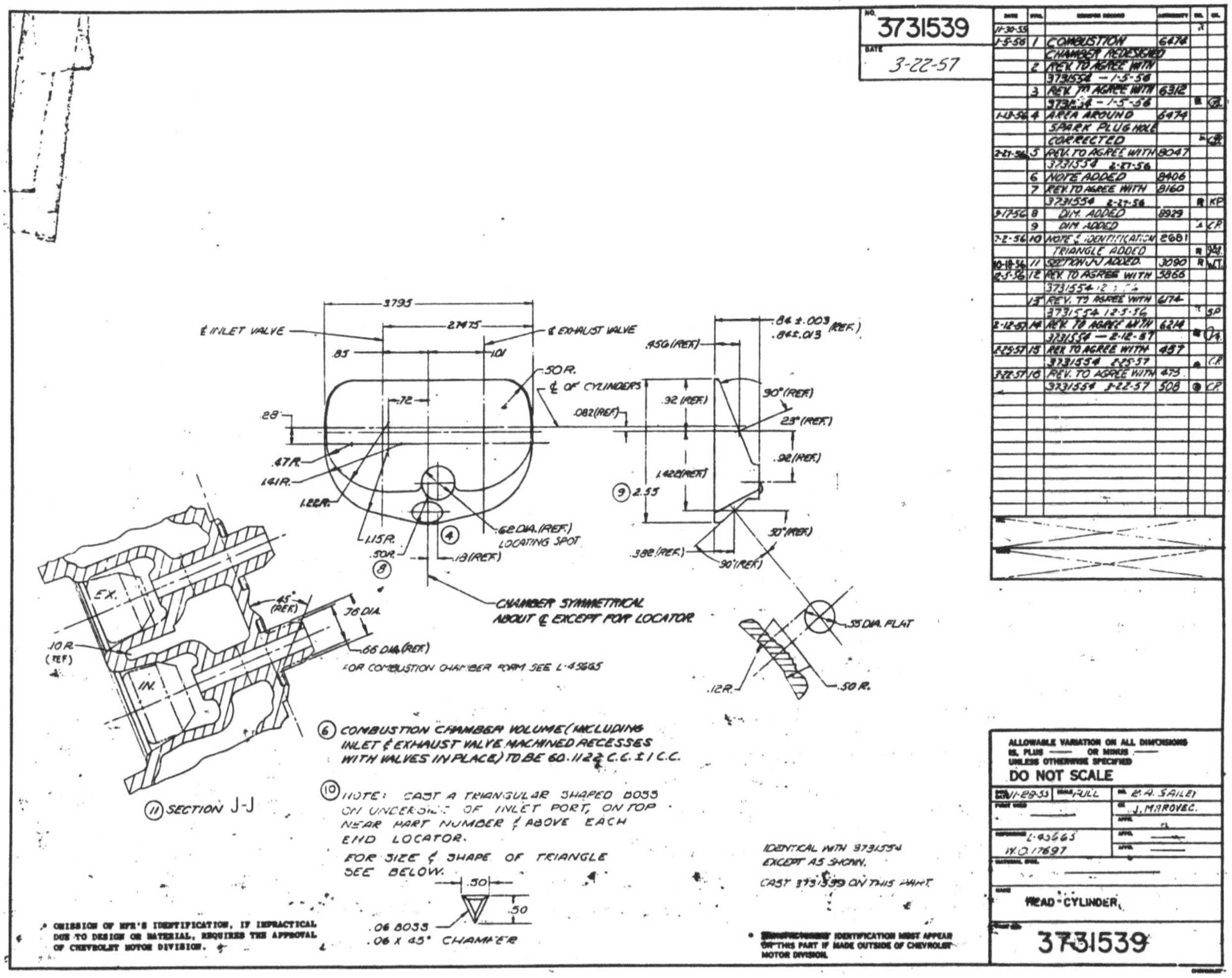

0023119

Fig. 5-10. Blueprint of #3731539 indicates that it is identical with #3731554 except as shown. Note direction to cast triangular boss on underside of inlet port, which can be seen in Figure 5-9.

Head #3731554

Year	Model	Engine	Horsepower	Valve Size (in.) Intake/Exhaust	Combustion Chamber (cc.)	Notes
1957	Passenger	265	162	1.72/1.50	69.8119	This was the only low/standard cylinder head used in 1957. It was only installed in passenger cars. This cylinder head has staggered valve cover bolt holes. Casting symbol:  0023145
		283	185			

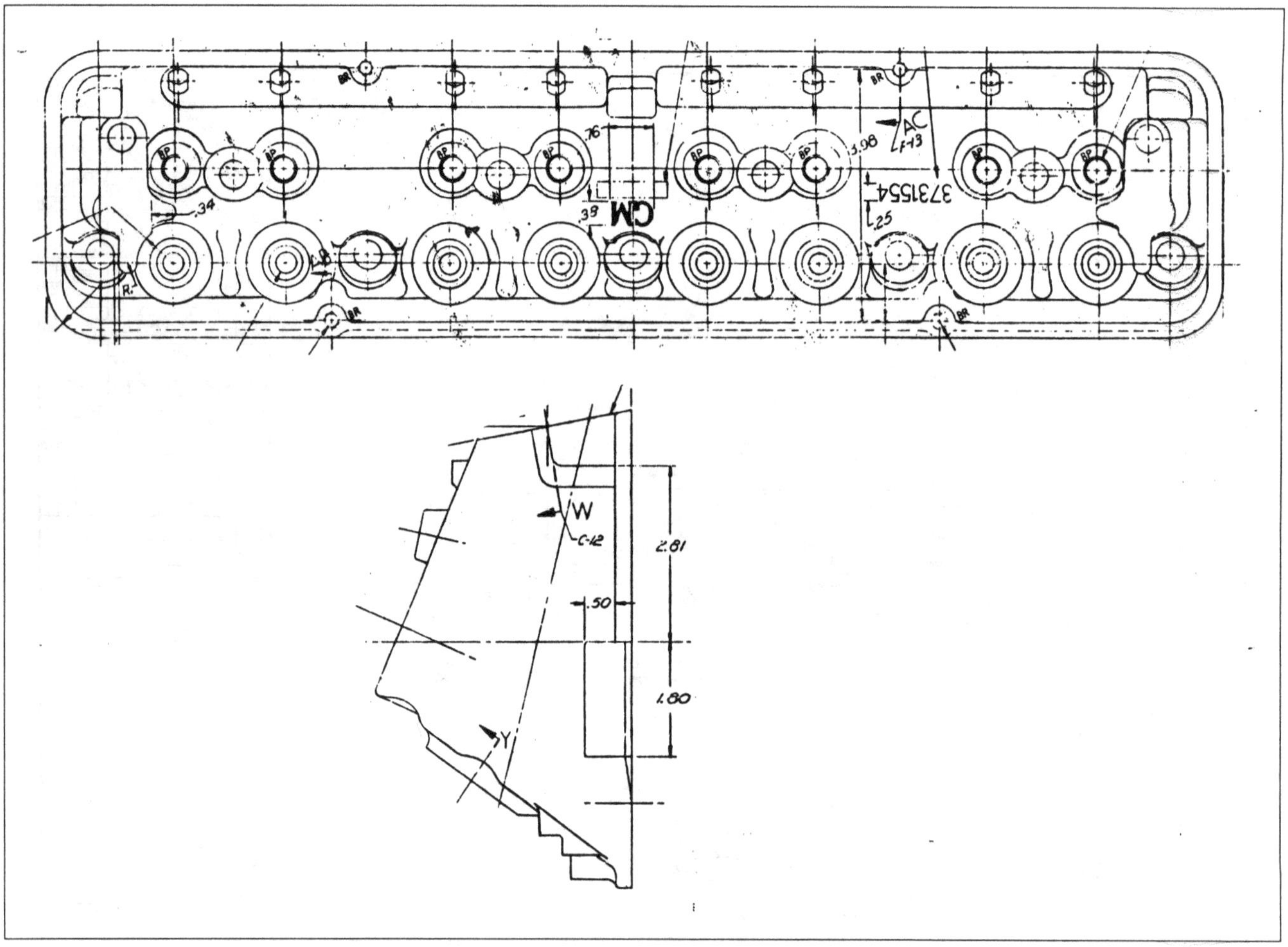

0023120

Fig. 5-11. *Rocker side of #3731554 head, and detail of external identification symbol.*

Head #3731762

Year	Model	Engine	Horsepower	Valve Size (in.) Intake/Exhaust	Combustion Chamber (cc.)	Notes
1956	Passenger	265	225 (Late)	1.72/1.50	55.6685	This cylinder head was released late in the 1956 model year. It had the same small combustion chamber as the #3725306 head. It was identical with #3703523 except that the valve guide boss diameter has been increased. There was also a truck version of this cylinder head released, but it has a much larger combustion chamber and a large "T" in the middle of the rocker arm area. The truck #3731762 cylinder head "twin tower" external head marking is also slightly different from the passenger car cylinder head. The towers are taller and closer together (1959). This cylinder head was also used in early 1957 production. This cylinder head has staggered valve cover bolt holes. (Note: following photo is of 056 head and is used for general identification purposes only.) Casting symbol:  0022247
	Corvette	265	225 (Late), 240			

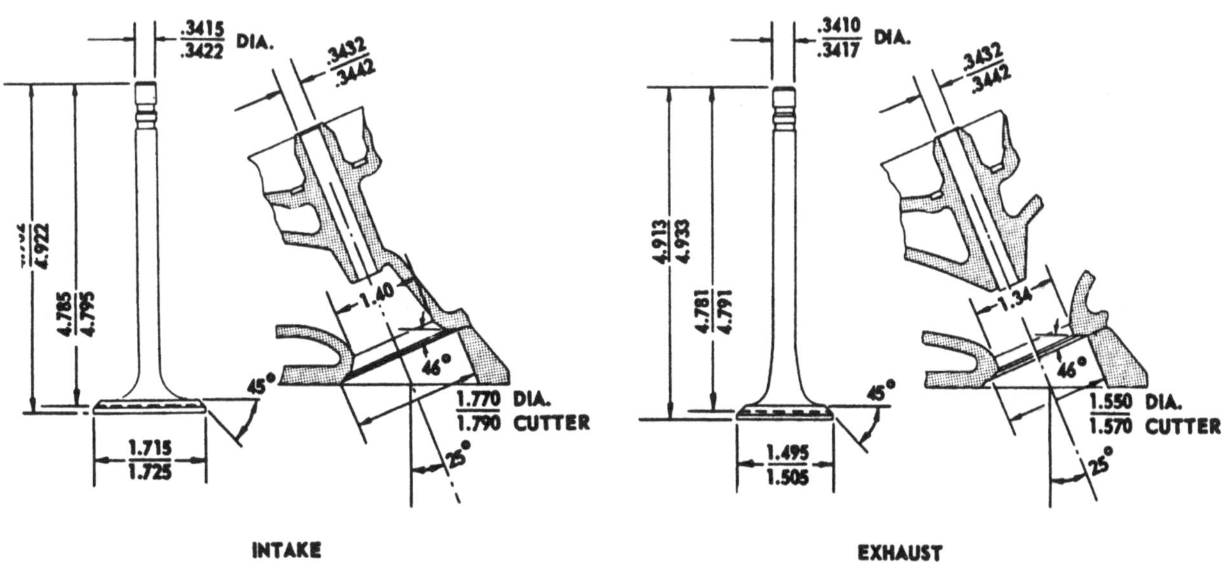

0023121

Fig. 5-12. Diagram of valve and cut through view of cylinder head from 1956 Specifications shows valve guide diameters.

Head #3732791

Year	Model	Engine	Horsepower	Valve Size (in.) Intake/Exhaust	Combustion Chamber (cc.)	Notes
1958	Passenger	348	250, 280, 315	1.94/1.66	N/A	This cylinder head is the first design of the 1958 model year. It was used on all engines and did not have water cooling cavities around the spark plug recesses. This head used only one valve size. This design is totally different from later designs. This is an early 1958 cylinder head only.

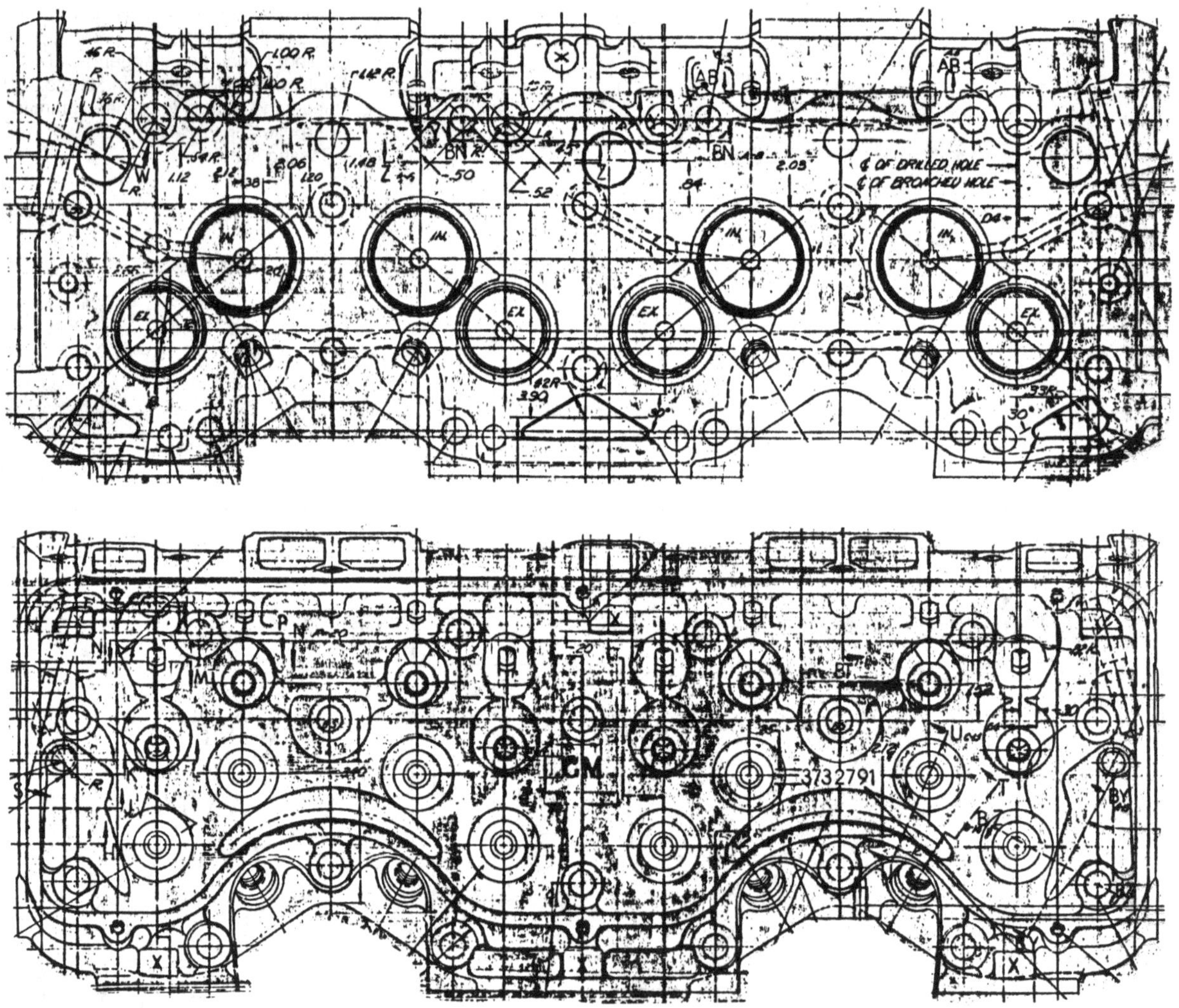

0023122

Fig. 5-13. Valve and rocker view of head #3732791.

Head #3740997

Year	Model	Engine	Horsepower	Valve Size (in.) Intake/Exhaust	Combustion Chamber (cc.)	Notes
1957	Passenger	283	245, 250, 270	1.72/1.50	55.6685	This cylinder head is identical with #3731554 except that the combustion chamber has been changed and the valve guide boss diameter has been increased. On high performance applications the head was supplied with swirl polished valves with lightweight stems. This head has staggered valve cover bolt holes and the same style combustion chamber as #3731762. Casting symbol:  0023143
	Corvette	283	220, 245, 250, 270			

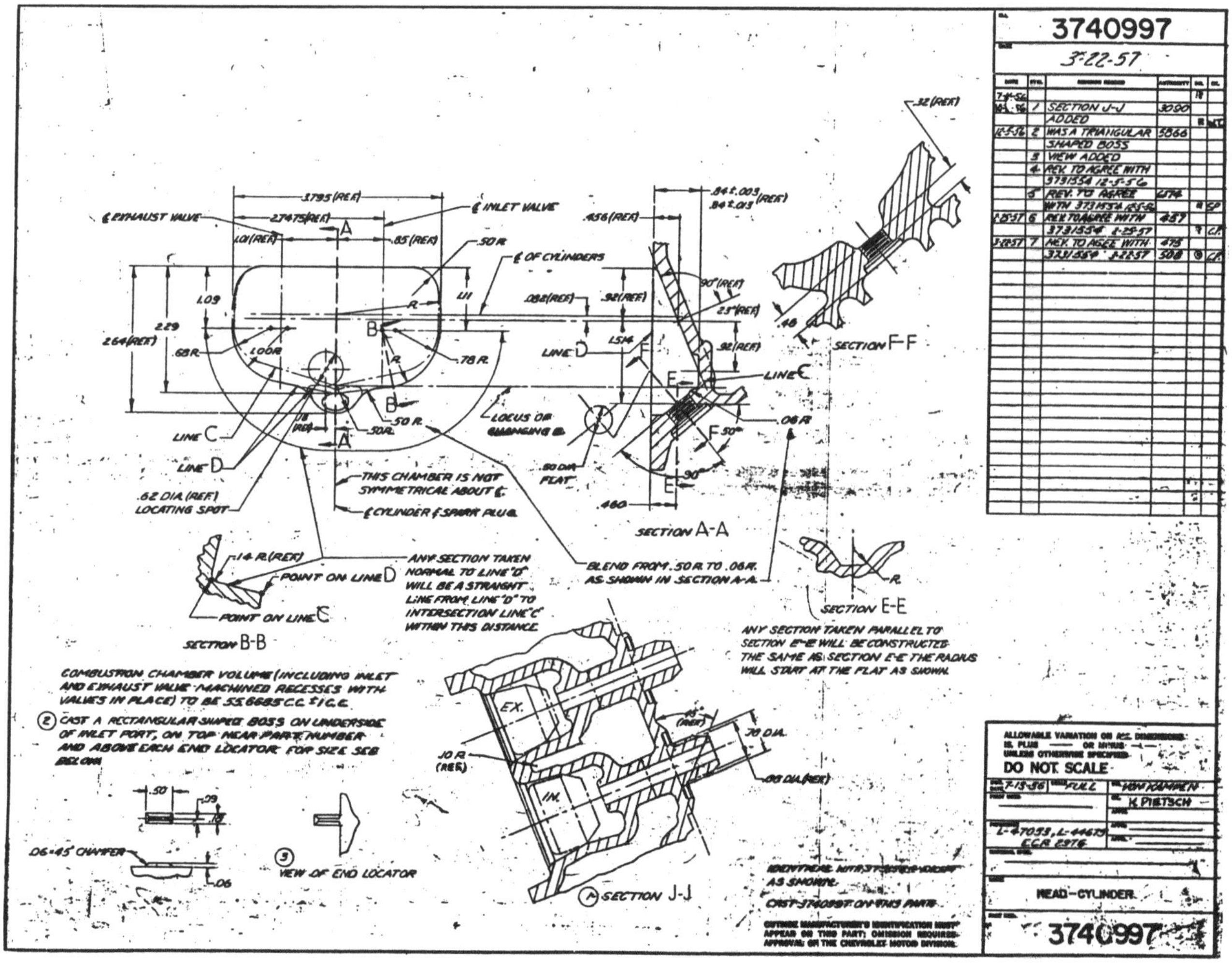

0023123

Fig. 5-14. Blueprint of #3740997 show it is identical with #3731554 except as shown.

Head #3743056

Year	Model	Engine	Horsepower	Valve Size (in.) Intake/Exhaust	Combustion Chamber (cc.)	Notes
1958	Passenger	283	230, 250, 290 (all unverified)	1.72/1.50	55.6685	This cylinder head is identical with #3740997, with the same combustion chamber design as well. This head has staggered valve cover bolt holes. This unverified cylinder head is considered a mystery head in that it could possibly have been used in all of the above applications. Some reliable sources in the past have listed this head as a verified 1957 Corvette fuel injection head and then later retracted the validity of the application. It is unknown at this time why. Also, the appearance of the "twin tower" casting symbol is slightly different from the "997" head. Casting symbol:  0022247
	Corvette	283	230, 245, 250, 270, 290 (all unverified)			

0023124

0023125

0023126

Fig. 5-15. ***Top, left and right:*** *Rocker and valve side of #3743056 head. Pointer indicates "twin tower" casting mark, which matches mark on end of head.* ***Bottom:*** *Combustion chamber detail.*

Head #3748770

Year	Model	Engine	Horsepower	Valve Size (in.) Intake/Exhaust	Combustion Chamber (cc.)	Notes
1958	Passenger	283	230, 250, 290	1.72/1.50	59.669	This cylinder head can be identified by an external cast pyramid on one end of head and a machined boss on the opposite end. "X58" is cast on the outside of the cylinder head next to the exhaust manifold. This was the only "powerpack" cylinder head available in the 1958 model year. Possible usage could have included *very* early 1959 engines (unverified). This head has staggered valve cover bolt holes. Some "770" heads have three holes drilled in the end of head. These heads are not correct for Corvette applications, but were used for passenger car level air applications and trucks. All "770" heads have steam hole recesses opposite the spark plug. Please refer to Chapter 3, block #3756519 for more information. Also refer to cylinder head #3755550 as these heads also have steam holes opposite the spark plug. Casting symbol:  0023144
	Corvette	283	230, 245, 250, 270, 290			

0023131

Fig. 5-16. This small "pyramid" casting symbol appears on end of head opposite standard "powerpack" symbol cast on other end (shown above).

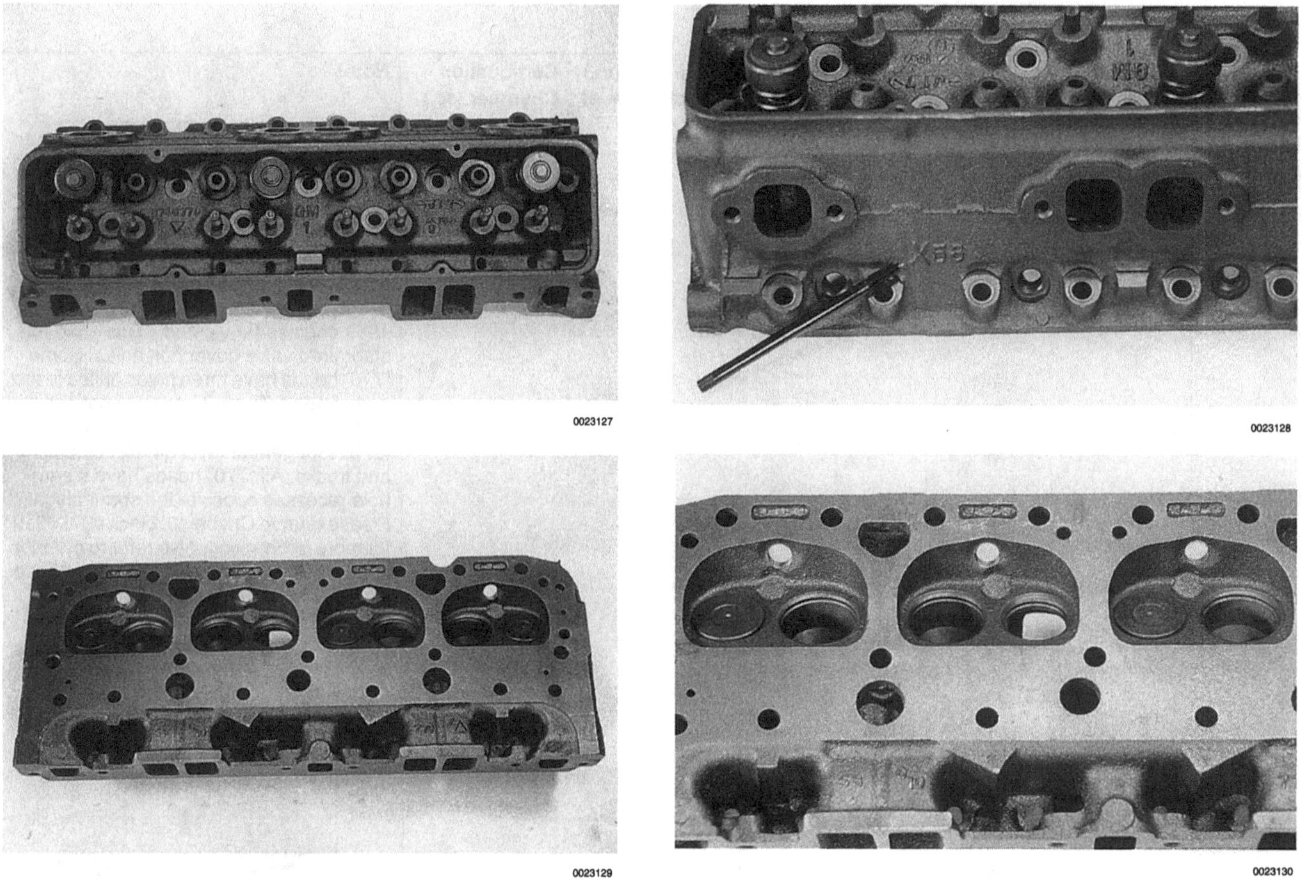

Fig. 5-17. ***Top, left and right:*** *Rocker side of #3748770 head. Note cast "X58" as discussed in text above.* ***Bottom, left and right:*** *Valve side and combustion chamber detail.*

Head #3748772

Year	Model	Engine	Horsepower	Valve Size (in.) Intake/Exhaust	Combustion Chamber (cc.)	Notes
1958	Passenger	283	185	1.72/1.50	69.369	This head was used on 1958 2-barrel engines only. It was similar to cylinder head #3731554. The combustion chamber was changed slightly. This cylinder head has staggered valve cover bolt holes. Casting symbol:  0023145

Head #3755537

Year	Model	Engine	Horsepower	Valve Size (in.) Intake/Exhaust	Combustion Chamber (cc.)	Notes
1959	Passenger	283	185	1.72/1.50	69.369	This cylinder head was the first design 1959 cylinder head for 2-barrel 283 engines. It was similar to the #3748772 head in that it has the same combustion chamber volume. It features staggered valve cover mounting bolt holes. Casting symbol:  0023145

Head #3755549

Year	Model	Engine	Horsepower	Valve Size (in.) Intake/Exhaust	Combustion Chamber (cc.)	Notes
1959	Passenger	283	185	1.72/1.50	69.369	This cylinder head was the second design in 1959 for 2-barrel engines. It was similar to the #3748772 head. It featured the same combustion chamber volume. It has staggered valve cover bolt holes. Casting symbol:  0023145

Head #3755550

Year	Model	Engine	Horsepower	Valve Size (in.) Intake/Exhaust	Combustion Chamber (cc.)	Notes
1959	Passenger	283	230, 250, 290	1.72/1.50	59.669	This cylinder head can be identified by an external cast pyramid on one end of head and a machined boss on the opposite end identical to the "770" cylinder head. This was a "powerpack" design head with the small combustion chamber. It was considered the early 1959 Corvette head. This cylinder head features staggered valve cover mounting holes. Some "550" heads have three holes drilled in the end of head. These heads are not correct for Corvette applications. These heads were used for passenger car level air applications and trucks. There were some early "550" heads that have "X58" cast on them that were apparently for late 1958 production. The "X58" was dropped for all 1959 production. The "550" head has spark plug steam recesses on all heads. From all indications, all "550" heads used on Corvette 290HP applications also had drilled cooling holes opposite the steam recesses which lined up with the cylinder block cooling holes. Please refer to Chapter 3 block #3756519 and cylinder head #3748770. Casting symbol (Note: Small pyramid design appears on both ends of head and is almost identical except for drilled and tapped hole used in cars and trucks only, not Corvette):  0023146
	Corvette	283	230, 245, 250, 270, 290			

0023150

Fig. 5-18. *1959 283/290 HP cylinder head cooling holes.*

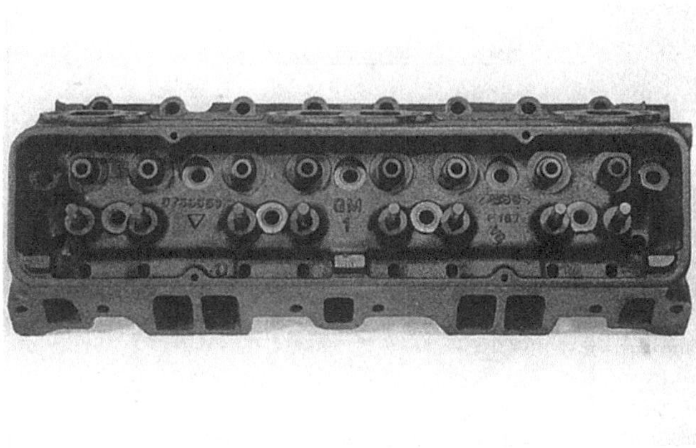

0023132

0023133

0023134

Fig. 5-19. ***Top, left and right:*** *Rocker and valve side of #3755550 head.*
Bottom: *Combustion chamber detail.*

Head #3758379

Year	Model	Engine	Horsepower	Valve Size (in.) Intake/Exhaust	Combustion Chamber (cc.)	Notes
1958 (Late)	Passenger	348	250, 280, 315	1.94/1.66	N/A	This cylinder head was the second design of the 1958 model year. There are major differences in the internal design of this head as compared to the #3732791 cylinder head. The area around the spark plugs has been redesigned to allow for water cooling passages. This cylinder head is distinctive in that there are cored cooling slots that are visible at the spark plug relief area.

CHEVROLET—CENTRAL OFFICE
DIVISION OF GENERAL MOTORS CORPORATION
DETROIT 2, MICHIGAN

TECHNICAL SERVICE BULLETIN
Service and Mechanical Department

REVISED

SUBJECT: SPARK PLUG COOLING
"348" ENGINE
TRUCK - POLICE CRUISER

BULLETIN No. DR #369

SECTION VI

TO: ALL CHEVROLET DEALERS

September 23, 1958

An improved means of spark plug cooling has been incorporated into the "348" Truck and special turnpike police cruiser engines. The new design provides for coolant flow completely around the spark plug jacket to reduce operating temperatures and provide greater spark plug and piston durability in heavy duty operations. This change entered production on truck engine #T-327 and police cruiser engine (RPO 573) #T-521.

Changes were required in the following items to provide the new coolant flow -

- Cylinder Block - additional cored water passages (See Figure #1).
- Cylinder Head - additional cored water passages (See Figure #2).
- Cylinder Head Gasket - beaded area and hole added (See Figure #4).
- Spark Plug - longer reach base required by thicker cylinder head boss. Identified by "N" following heat range - example: AC-42-N.
- Oil Level Gauge attachment - attaching bracket relocated (See Fig. #3).

SERVICE

Only the water cooled spark plug type cylinder block will be provided for all "348" engine service replacement.

Where it becomes necessary to make a cylinder block replacement and special service heads are required, (early cylinder heads cannot be re-used with water cooled spark plug type block), contact your Zone Service Manager for handling procedure.

SPECIAL SERVICE HEAD

To eliminate the necessity of providing a separate head for both early and water cooled spark plug type units, a single head with the water passages blocked will be serviced for both uses. When the head is to be used on a late block with the spark plug cooling provision, it will be necessary to drill four (4) 9/32" diameter holes in each head as shown in figure #2.

FIGURE #1 - VIEW OF CYLINDER BLOCK

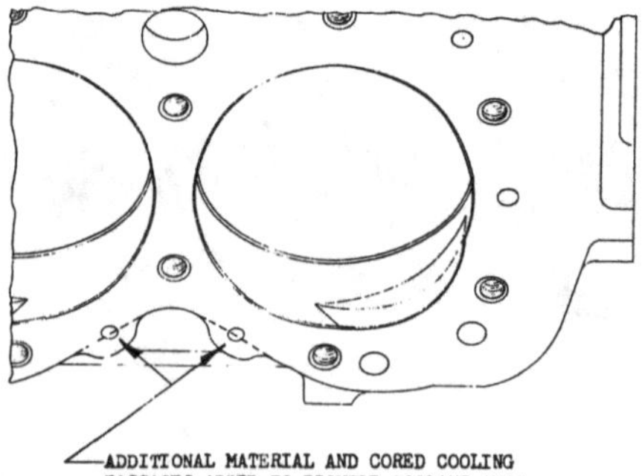

ADDITIONAL MATERIAL AND CORED COOLING PASSAGES ADDED TO PROVIDE COOLANT FLOW AROUND SPARK PLUG JACKET

FIGURE #2 - VIEW OF CYLINDER HEAD

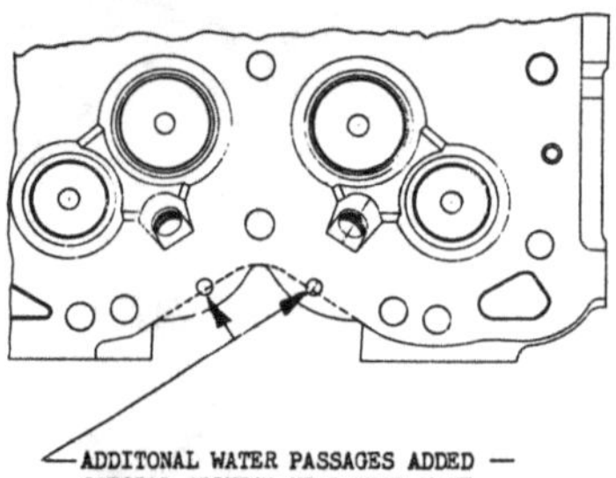

ADDITONAL WATER PASSAGES ADDED — SPECIAL SERVICE HEAD WILL HAVE PASSAGES BLOCKED FOR USE WITH EARLY DESIGN BLOCKS. NECESSARY TO DRILL FOUR (4) 9/32" DIAMETER HOLES (LOCATIONS MARKED ON HEAD WHEN USED WITH SPARK PLUG COOLING TYPE BLOCK)

0023135

Fig. 5-20. Technical Service Bulletin DR #369 shows date of spark plug cooling changeover for truck and police cruiser 348 head.

Head #3759256

Year	Model	Engine	Horsepower	Valve Size (in.) Intake/Exhaust	Combustion Chamber (cc.)	Notes
1959	Passenger	348	250, 280, 305, 320, 335	1.94/1.66	N/A	This head is identical with the #3758379 cylinder head except that the spark plug cooling holes have been omitted and the exhaust port has been redesigned.

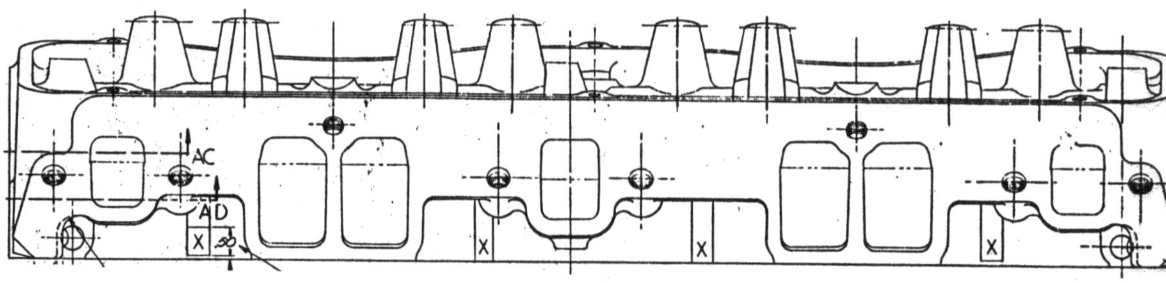

0023825

Fig. 5-21. Side view of #3758379.

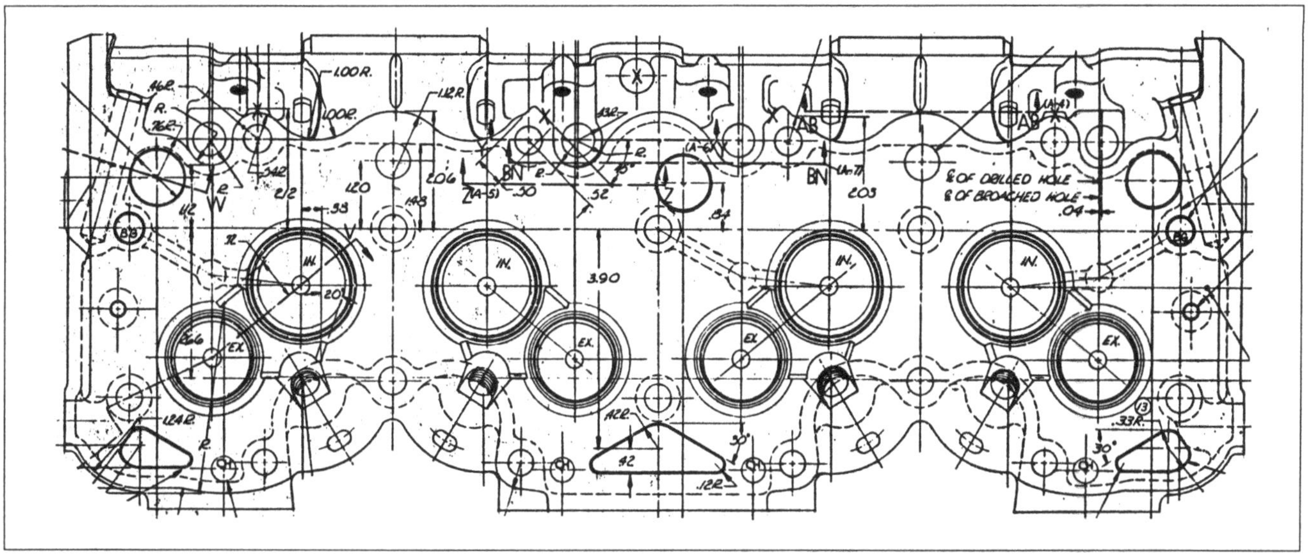

0023152

Fig. 5-22. Valve view of #3758379.

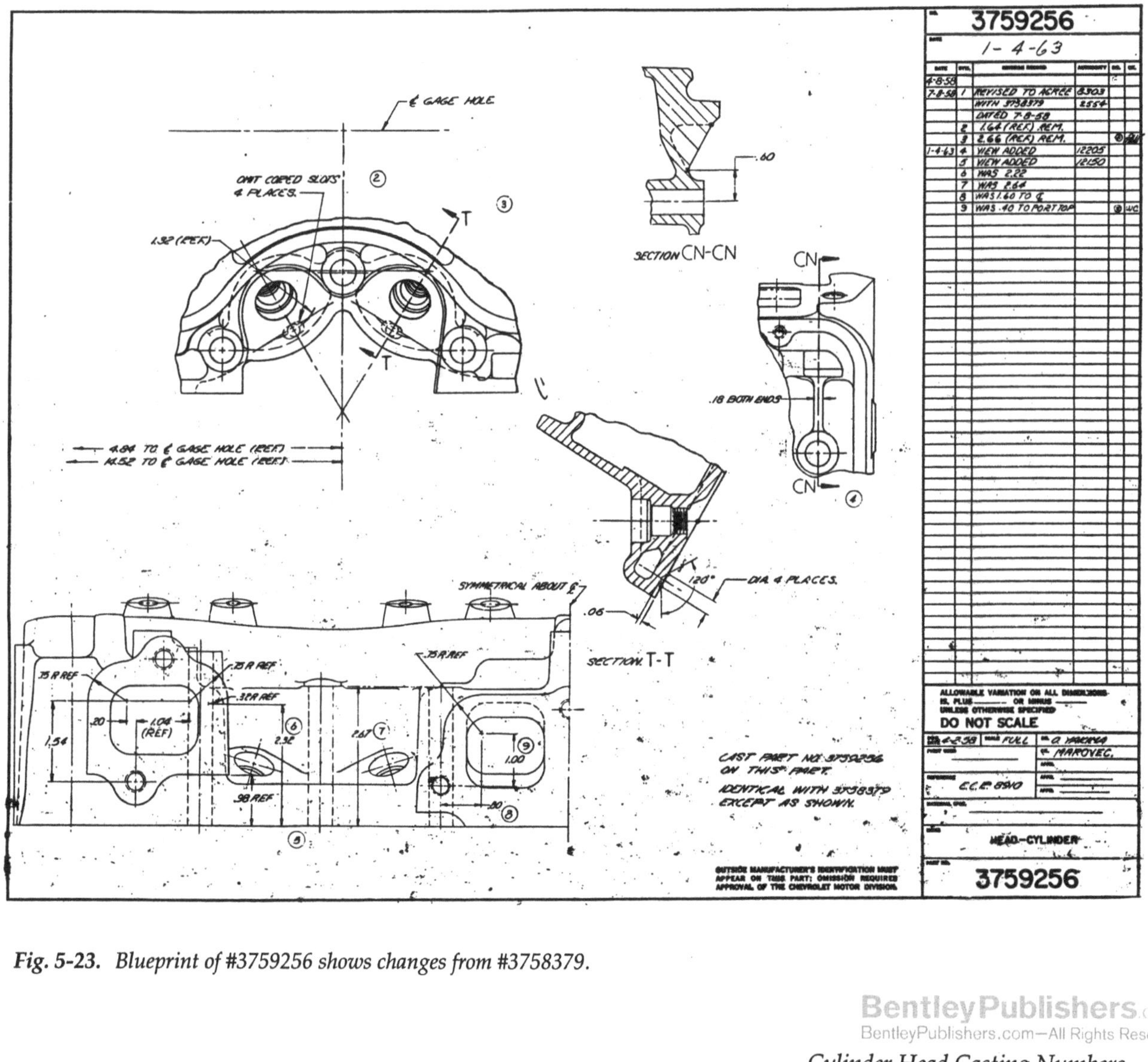

Fig. 5-23. Blueprint of #3759256 shows changes from #3758379.

Head #3760116

Year	Model	Engine	Horsepower	Valve Size (in.) Intake/Exhaust	Combustion Chamber (cc.)	Notes
1959 (Early)	Passenger	283	230, 250, 290	1.72/1.50	59.669	This was another early 1959 head. It was used on all high horsepower 283 passenger cars. No Corvette engines were supposedly built with this head. This head has the same small combustion chamber as all powerpack heads. Casting symbol:  0023142
	Corvette (unverified)	283	230, 250, 290			

Head #3767460

Year	Model	Engine	Horsepower	Valve Size (in.) Intake/Exhaust	Combustion Chamber (cc.)	Notes
1959 (Late)	Passenger	283	185	1.72/1.60	69.369	This head is the 2-barrel counterpart to the #3767465 4-barrel head. This head features revised oil drain back troughs, thus requiring the new straight valve cover mounting bolt holes. It is identical to the #3767465 head except for a change to the combustion chamber. This head was brought into production in May of 1959 and all cars were slated to receive them by July 1, 1959. (TSB DR #410)

CHEVROLET—CENTRAL OFFICE
DIVISION OF GENERAL MOTORS CORPORATION
DETROIT 2, MICHIGAN

TECHNICAL SERVICE BULLETIN
Service and Mechanical Department

SUBJECT: REDESIGNED CYLINDER HEADS 283 CU. IN. ENGINES - 1959 PASSENGER CAR - EXCEPT CORVETTE

BULLETIN No. DR #410
SECTION VI

TO: ALL CHEVROLET DEALERS

May 22, 1959

Cylinder heads having revised oil drain back troughs in the casting are now in partial production in 283" passenger car engines with 2 and 4-barrel carburetion. The new heads do not have oil seals on the intake valve guides.

Currently, approximately 25% of the subject engines are being produced with the new heads. 100% production will be reached about July 1, 1959.

A new Rocker Arm Cover Gasket, Part #3770632 is available for service use with the redesigned cylinder heads.

Manager, Service and Mechanical Department

0023137

Fig. 5-24. Technical Service Bulletin DR #410 details start of production of 283 heads with oil drain back troughs.

Head #3767465

Year	Model	Engine	Horsepower	Valve Size (in.) Intake/Exhaust	Combustion Chamber (cc.)	Notes
1959 (Late)	Passenger	283	230, 250, 290*	1.72/1.50	59.669	This cylinder head was used on passenger cars and Corvettes. It was identical to #3767460 except for a changed combustion chamber. Also, four steam pockets have been added to the underside of the cylinder head. The external identification symbol changed to a "powerpack" design, and a cast triangular boss was added to the underside of the #7 inlet port for foundry identification purposes. This cylinder head features revised oil drain back troughs, thus requiring the new straight valve cover mounting bolt holes. This head was brought into production in May 1959, and all cars were slated to receive them by July 1, 1959. (TSB DR #410) Casting symbol:  0023142
	Corvette	283	230, 245, 250, 270, 290 (Unverified)			

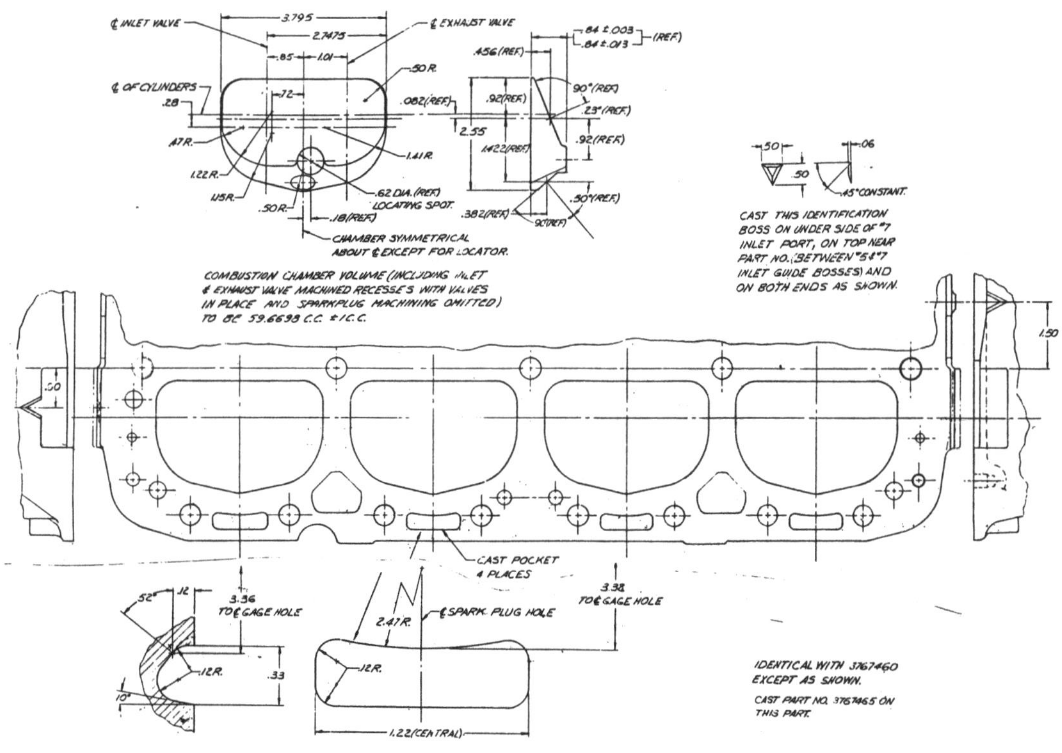

0023138

Fig. 5-25. Blueprint of #3767465 shows changes from #3767460.

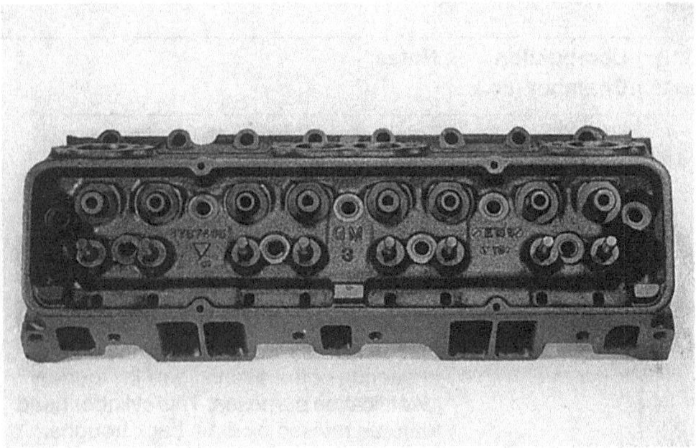

0023139

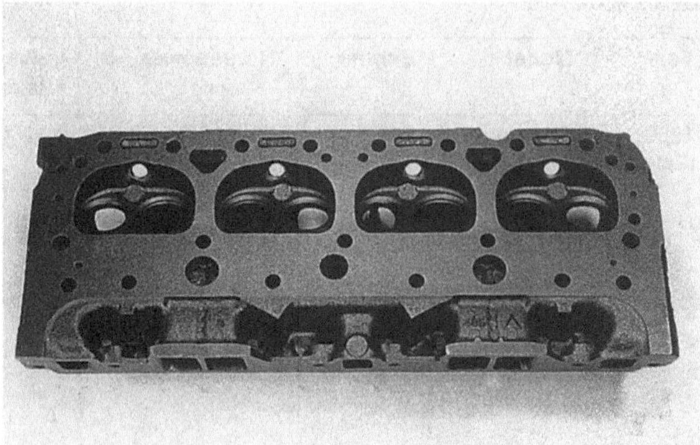

0023140

0023141

Fig. 5-26. ***Top, left and right:*** *Rocker and valve side of #3767465 head.*
Bottom: *Combustion chamber detail.*

Head #3767754[Δ]

Year	Model	Engine	Horsepower	Valve Size (in.) Intake/Exhaust	Combustion Chamber (cc.)	Notes
1959 (Late)	Passenger	283	230, 250, 290	1.72/1.50	59.669	There is very little known about this cylinder head. Its usage seems very limited and only on passenger cars. It is possible that this was a transitional cylinder head. This was the typical powerpack cylinder head. Casting symbol:  0023142 ΔThis head was also used in 1960–61

Head #3837064

Year	Model	Engine	Horsepower	Valve Size (in.) Intake/Exhaust	Combustion Chamber (cc.)	Notes
1956	Passenger	265	162, 170	1.72/1.50	67.424	This was the standard 2-barrel head used on all passenger cars in 1956. It is identical with the #3703523 cylinder head except that the combustion chamber shape has changed. The valve guide diameters have also been increased. This cylinder head has staggered valve cover mounting bolt holes. Casting symbol:  0023145

Chapter 6

Connecting Rod Identification

1. Introduction

The connecting rod in an internal combustion engine is probably the most critical part. The rod transfers all the explosive power created in the combustion chamber to the crankshaft. Most catastrophic engine failures result from a connecting rod failure of some sort. In an effort to reduce rod failures and warranty claims, Chevrolet produced many variations of the original design 265 connecting rod over the years. The changes were mostly in the type of metal and/or manufacturing processes used.

The most common additional manufacturing steps used by the factory were shot-peening, magnafluxing, and heat-treating. In shot-peening the connecting rod is bombarded by cast iron shot or pellets. This increases the surface hardness of the rod and makes it more resistant to failure. In magnafluxing the rod is magnetized and fine iron dust is sprinkled over it. The iron dust is attracted by any imperfections or cracks, making them visible to the naked eye. In heat- treating the rod is heated to approximately 500° for ten or more hours. This allows the connecting rod to relax any torsional stress or twisting that occurred during manufacturing. Almost all of Chevrolet's high performance connecting rods were subjected to all three of these procedures.

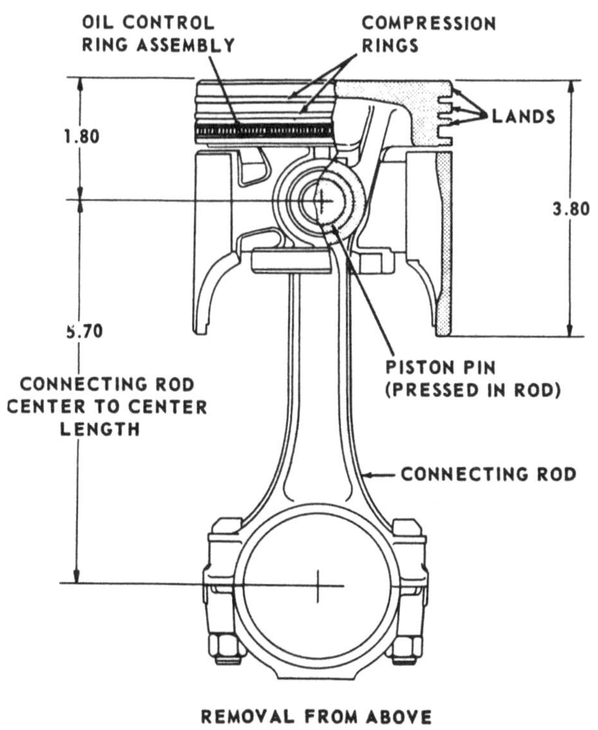

Fig. 6-1. Typical 8-cylinder connecting rod, with piston installed.

There were only a couple of rod bolts used from 1955 through 1959. These bolts varied in length, type of thread, and torque settings. All of the small block engines from used an 11/32 24 x 1 7/8" rod bolt. The 1958–59 348 engines used a 3/8 24 x 2" rod bolt. It is difficult to specify all the exact rod bolt usages.

Because of the vast amount of small block engine combinations, rods are listed by release or design. Please note that the terms "First design," "Second design," etc. do not refer to the order in which the rods were released, but are only a way to categorize the rods. Also, due to the millions of small block connecting rods that were manufactured, for identification purposes I have listed all the small block rods that were produced by Chevrolet through 1975.

2. Small Block Connecting Rods

All small block connecting rods, excluding those for the 1970 and later 400 engine, have a 5.70" center-to-center distance (the distance from the center of the piston pin hole to the center of the rod bearing hole).

All connecting rods produced prior to 1968, excluding those for the 1967 Camaro 350 engine, have a 2.0" rod journal diameter. All connecting rods produced after 1968, including those for the 1967 Camaro 350 engine, have a larger 2.10" rod journal diameter.

Connecting rods built until May of 1967 have V-groove holes in the rod cap, which were designed to shoot oil into the bore of the block. This feature was discontinued because it was found to be unnecessary. This has been verified through Chevrolet Service News.

First Design

- All 265 and 283 engines through 1967
- All small rod journal
- Standard forged steel composition
- Pressed-pin piston design
- No heat-treatment, magnafluxing, or shot-peening
- Small rod beam
- All had 11/32" diameter rod bolts
- A common rod

Second Design

- All 327 engines, excluding high performance applications
- Forged steel construction
- Pressed-pin piston design
- Rods produced from 1962 through 1967 had small journal diameter and 11/32" diameter rod bolts
- Rods produced in 1968 and 1969 had large journal diameter and 3/8" rod bolts
- Small rod beam

> **NOTE—**
> Approximately 6,000 327/275HP engines coupled with the Powerglide transmission, and built in early 1968 production, used the 1967 rod with a 11/32" rod bolt.

Third Design

- All 327 high performance applications (truck also)
- Forged steel construction (much stronger than the standard 327 rod)
- Pressed-pin piston design
- Heavier beam
- Journal sizes are the same as the standard size
- The standard rod for Corvettes

Fourth Design

- All 302 engines
- Forged steel construction
- Shot-peened, heat treated, and magnafluxed
- Babbitt dipped (a very expensive rod to manufacture)
- 1967 302 rod used the small 2.0" journal diameter and an 11/32" diameter rod bolt
- 1968 and 1969 302 used the large 2.10" journal diameter and a 3/8" diameter rod bolt
- All 302 rod bolt P.S.I. (pounds per square inch) ratings were increased
- 1967 and early 1968 302 used a pressed-pin piston design
- Mid-year 1968, the design changed to a floating-pin piston design
- All fourth design rods are commonly called "pink rods." The name comes from the pink or purple paint used on them to identify the rods at the assembly plant

Fifth Design

- All 350 engines
- All 307 engines from 1968 through 1973
- Forged steel construction
- This rod used the standard 3/8" rod bolt in all cases except the 1967 Camaro 350 engine.
- Large rod journal diameter
- Pressed-pin piston design

Sixth Design

- All high-performance 350 engines (LT1)
- Forged steel construction
- Heat-treated, shot-peened, and magnafluxed
- Originally introduced in 1970 as a pressed-pin
- Large rod diameter journal and the high-rpm rod bolts used in the 302
- Expensive connecting rod

3. W-Block Connecting Rods

348 Connecting Rods

- Forged steel construction
- Rod journal diameter 2.20"
- Rod center-to-center length 6.125"
- 3/8" rod bolts
- Basically a beefed- up version of the small block rod. Chevrolet lists a different rod for 1960–61 high performance applications but the differences are unknown at this time

409 Connecting Rods

- Forged steel construction
- Rod journal diameter 2.20"
- Rod center-to-center length 6.0"
- 3/8" rod bolts
- Locknut has only one end chamfered
- There were no high performance connecting rods specifically manufactured for these engines by Chevrolet, but there were forged aluminum connecting rods made by Mickey Thompson and other manufacturers

427 Z11/Mystery Engine Connecting Rods

- Drop forged steel construction
- Rod journal diameter 2.20"
- Rod center-to-center length 6.135"
- 3/8" 24 x 2-25/64" rod bolt
- Uses .150" stroker crankshaft
- Weight 28.8 oz.

Chapter 7

Piston Identification

1. Introduction

This chapter covers the specific piston usage in all Chevrolet engines from 1955 through 1959. I have shown all popular piston shapes, but please note that piston designs changed slightly from model year to model year. The drawings indicate the general design of the piston, not the final design. However, with the description and pertinent information regarding each piston, you should be able to make a judgement call as to the originality of the piston and/or engine.

This information should be useful at the beginning of the engine restoration process. There has never been one source to which a restorer can turn to verify what piston was used to build a particular engine. Many engine rebuilders usually refer to aftermarket catalogs to supply pistons. This is fine, except that many of the pistons necessary to correctly rebuild an engine are no longer available. Although the final decision is up to the owner of the car, the information in this chapter will allow the restorer a choice in piston selection.

The piston charts are arranged in chronological order by model year. Under each year are the specific piston applications. The charts begin with each car *Model* in which that piston was used. Next is the *Engine/Horsepower* application. Many pistons were used in a variety of engines. All engines that use the piston will be listed together, beginning with the smallest V-8 engine.

The next listings are general *Piston Characteristics*, to further aid identification, the type of *Material* that was used to manufacture the piston, and the *Skirt Type*, which is the design of the piston skirt. Most pistons will be of the "slipper" design.

The *Compression Ring Groove Depth* and *Oil Ring Groove Depth* are listed next. These depths were kept to a very close tolerance during manufacturing and should provide an accurate way of measuring and correctly identifying a piston.

The *Piston Pin Type* refers to the design of the piston pin. Almost all piston pins used a pressed fit. *Piston Pin Offset* refers to the offset of the piston pin relative to the center of piston casting. Most cast pistons will show some type of offset, while high performance forged aluminum pistons will not.

The final listing, piston *Weight*, will allow you to correctly identify a specific piston by weight alone if you have access to a scale. This weight figure will also give you a good idea as to the original reciprocating weight of the engine assembly as it was originally built by Chevrolet.

2. 1955 Pistons

Model	Passenger car Corvette
Engine	265/162, 180 HP (Passenger) 265/195 HP (Corvette)
Piston Characteristics	Flat head design with no valve reliefs in piston. Piston is tin plated, oval sized with controlled thermo expansion. Piston is cam ground, no piston pin bushings.
Material	Cast alloy aluminum w/steel struts
Skirt Type	Slipper
Compression Ring Groove Depth (in.)	0.2116–0.2180
Oil Ring Groove Depth (in.)	0.2041–0.2105
Oil Ring Holes	Number & Size: 8, .156 Drill
Piston Pin Type	Pressed fit
Piston Pin Offset	Major thrust side
Weight (oz.)	18.77

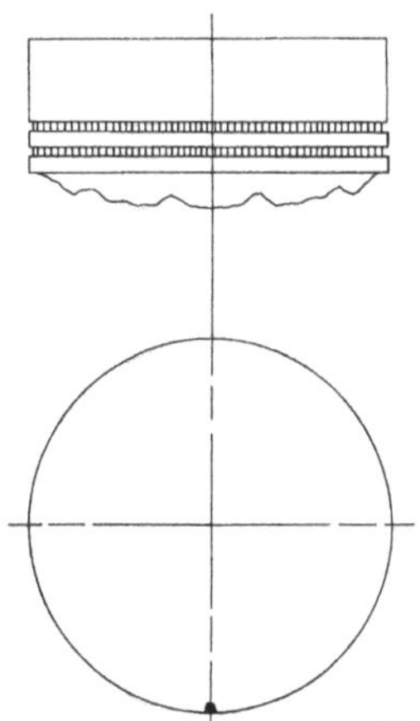

0023918

3. 1956 PISTONS

Model	Passenger car Corvette
Engine	265/162, 170, 205 HP (Passenger) 265/210 HP (Corvette)
Piston Characteristics	Flat head design with no valve reliefs in piston. Piston is tin plated, oval sized with controlled thermo expansion. Piston is cam ground, no piston pin bushings.
Material	Cast alloy aluminum with steel struts
Skirt Type	Slipper
Compression Ring Groove Depth (in.)	0.2118–0.2183
Oil Ring Groove Depth (in.)	0.2043–0.2108
Oil Ring Holes	Number & Size: 8, .156 Drill
Piston Pin Type	Pressed fit
Piston Pin Offset	Major thrust side
Weight (oz.)	18.77

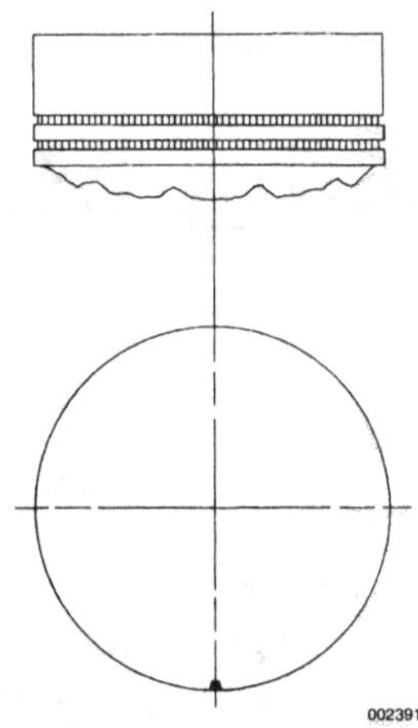

0023918

Model	Passenger Corvette
Engine	265/225 HP (Passenger) 265/240 HP (Corvette)
Piston Characteristics*	Flat head design with valve reliefs in piston head to insure adequate valve clearance at high RPM
Material	Cast alloy aluminum with steel struts
Skirt Type	Slipper
Compression Ring Groove Depth (in.)	0.2118–0.2183
Oil Ring Groove Depth (in.)	0.2043–0.2108
Oil Ring Holes	Number & Size: 8, .156 Drill
Piston Pin Type	Pressed fit
Piston Pin Offset	Major thrust side
Weight (oz.)	18.77

*This piston used a different number #1 compression piston ring from the standard engine. The standard engines used a cast alloy iron ring, which was treated with a heat resistant coating. These pistons used a cast alloy iron ring with a chrome plated outside diameter.

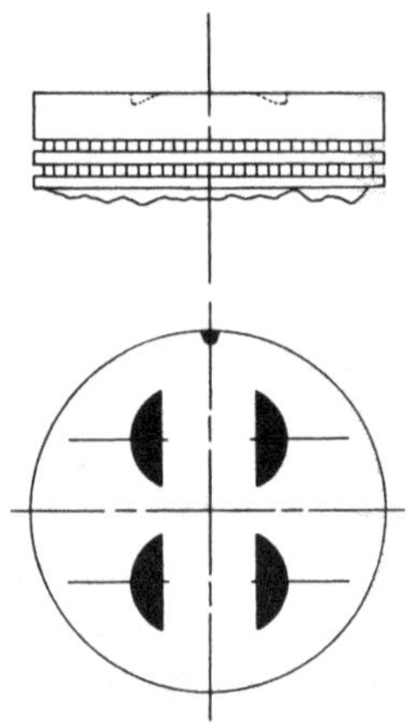

0022227

4. 1957 PISTONS

Model	Passenger
Engine	283/185, 220 HP
Piston Characteristics	Flat head design with no valve reliefs in piston. Piston is tin plated, oval sized with controlled thermo expansion. Piston is cam ground, no piston pin bushings.
Material	Cast alloy aluminum with steel struts
Skirt Type	Slipper
Compression Ring Groove Depth (in.)	0.2153–0.2218
Oil Ring Groove Depth (in.)	0.2093–0.2158
Piston Pin Type	Pressed fit
Piston Pin Offset	Major thrust side
Weight (oz.)	20.96

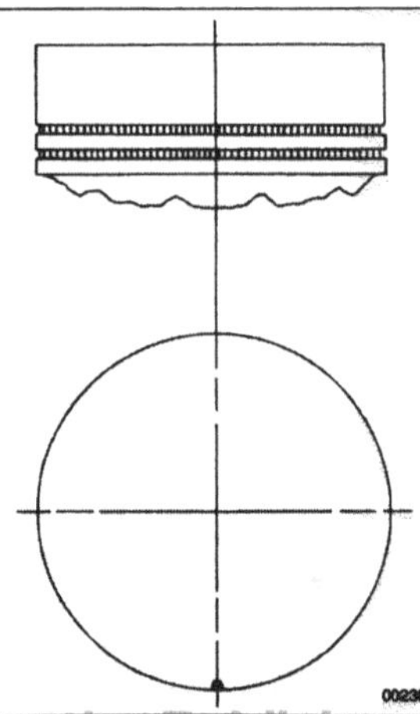

0023918

Model	Passenger car	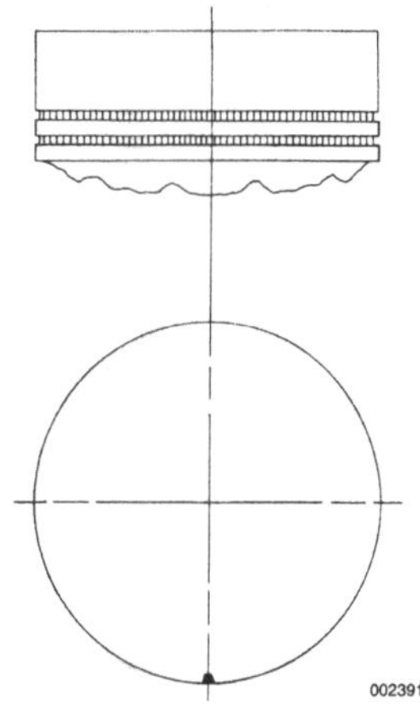
Engine	265/162 HP	
Piston Characteristics	Flat head design with no valve reliefs in piston. Piston is tin plated, oval sized with controlled thermo expansion. Piston is cam ground, no piston pin bushings.	
Material	Cast alloy aluminum with steel struts	
Skirt Type	Slipper	
Compression Ring Groove Depth (in.)	0.2117–0.2183	
Oil Ring Groove Depth (in.)	0.2043–0.2107	
Piston Pin Type	Pressed fit	
Piston Pin Offset	Major thrust side	
Weight (oz.)	21.44	0023918

Model	Passenger Corvette	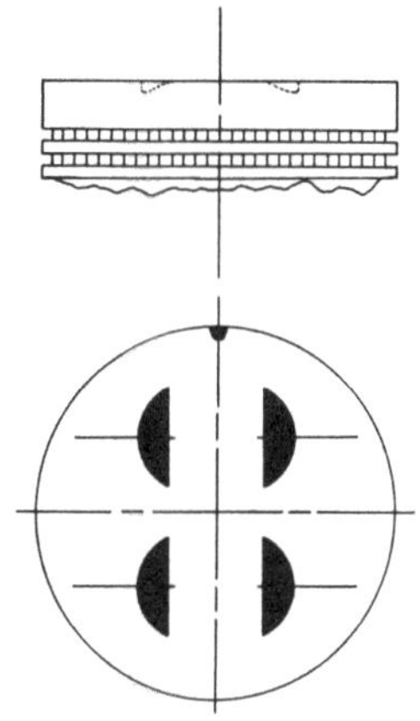
Engine	283/220 HP (Corvette) 283/245, 250, 270 HP (Passenger & Corvette)	
Piston Characteristics	Flat head design with valve reliefs in piston head to insure adequate valve clearance	
Material	Cast alloy aluminum with steel struts	
Skirt Type	Slipper	
Compression Ring Groove Depth (in.)	0.2153–0.2218	
Oil Ring Groove Depth (in.)	0.2093–0.2158	
Piston Pin Type	Pressed fit	
Piston Pin Offset	Major thrust side	
Weight (oz.)	21.12	0022227

Model	Passenger Corvette	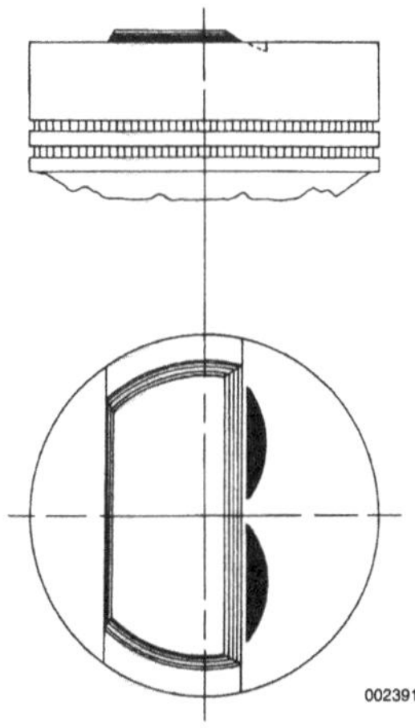
Engine	283/283 HP (Passenger & Corvette)	
Piston Characteristics	Domed head design only used on 283 HP engines in 1957. Piston has machined reliefs to insure adequate clearance at high RPM	
Material	Cast alloy aluminum with steel struts	
Skirt Type	Slipper	
Compression Ring Groove Depth (in.)	0.2153–0.2218	
Oil Ring Groove Depth (in.)	0.2093–0.2158	
Piston Pin Type	Pressed fit	
Weight (oz.)	21.12	0023919

5. 1958 Pistons

Model	Passenger car Corvette
Engine	283/185 HP (Passenger) 283/230, 250HP (Passenger & Corvette) 283/245, 270 HP (Corvette)
Piston Characteristics	Flat head design with valve reliefs to insure adequate valve clearance. Controlled expansion.
Material	Cast alloy aluminum with steel struts
Skirt Type	Slipper
Compression Ring Groove Depth (in.)	0.2153–0.2218
Oil Ring Groove Depth (in.)	0.2093–0.2158
Piston Pin Type	Pressed fit
Piston Pin Offset	Major thrust side .060
Weight (oz.)	20.48

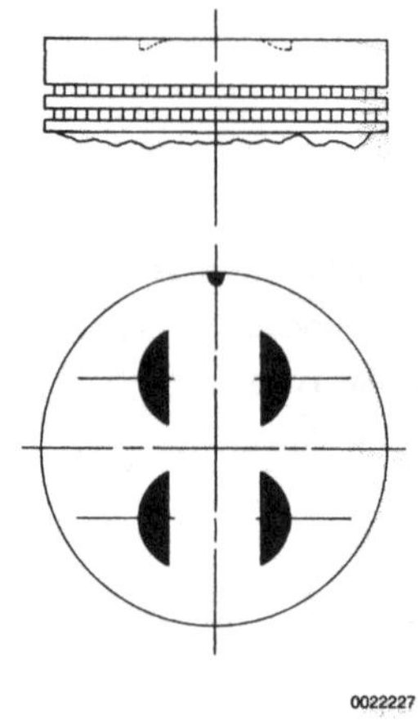

Model	Passenger Corvette
Engine	283/290 HP (Passenger (unverified) & Corvette)
Piston Characteristics	Domed head design only used on 290 HP engines in 1958. Piston has machined reliefs to insure adequate clearance at high RPM. Increased compression ratio.
Material	Cast alloy aluminum with steel struts
Skirt Type	Slipper
Compression Ring Groove Depth (in.)	0.2153–0.2218
Oil Ring Groove Depth (in.)	0.2093–0.2158
Piston Pin Type	Pressed fit
Piston Pin Offset	Major thrust side .060
Weight (oz.)	21.12

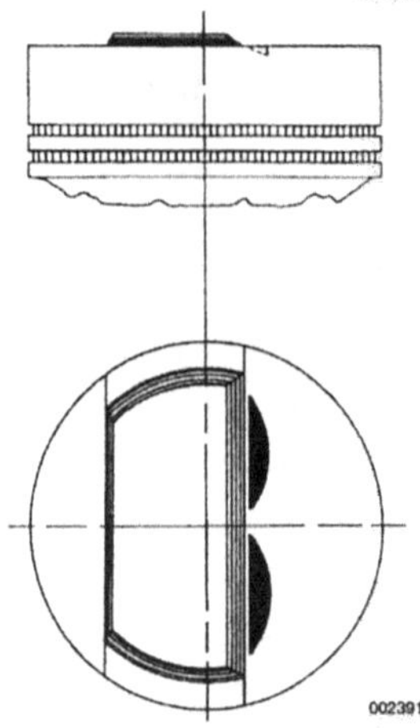

Model	Passenger
Engine	348/250, 280, 315 HP
Piston Characteristics	Peak roof design with no valve reliefs in piston. Autothermic.
Material	Cast alloy aluminum with steel struts
Skirt Type	Slipper
Compression Ring Groove Depth (in.)	0.2282–0.2348
Oil Ring Groove Depth (in.)	0.2182–0.2247
Piston Pin Type	Pressed fit
Piston Pin Offset	Major thrust side .060
Weight (oz.)	28.08

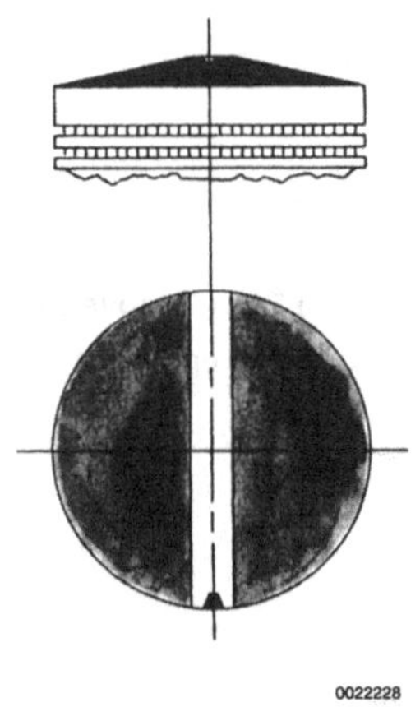

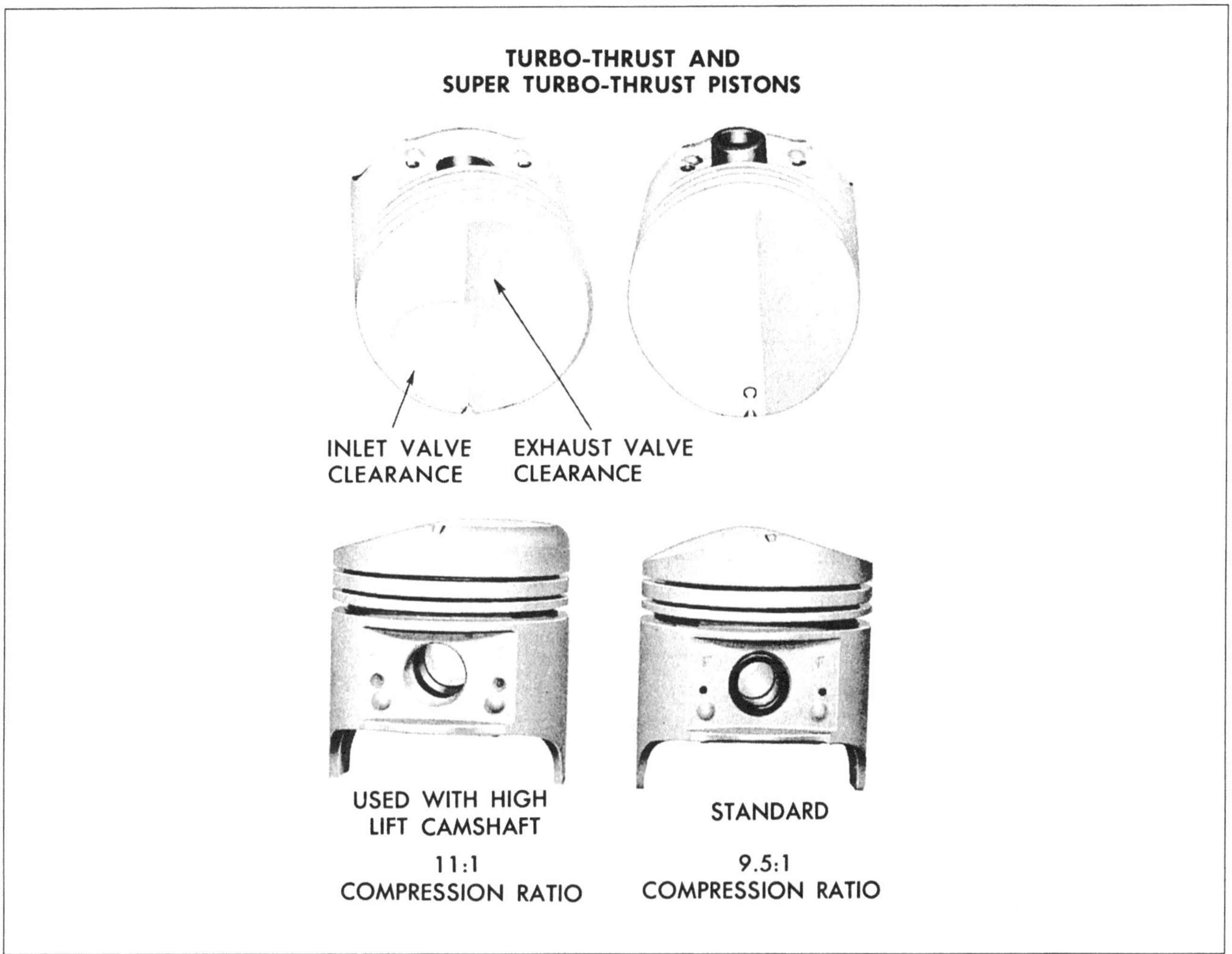

0023153

Fig. 7-1. This photo depicts the standard 348 piston compared with the high lift camshaft 348 piston.

6. 1959 PISTONS

Model	Passenger Corvette	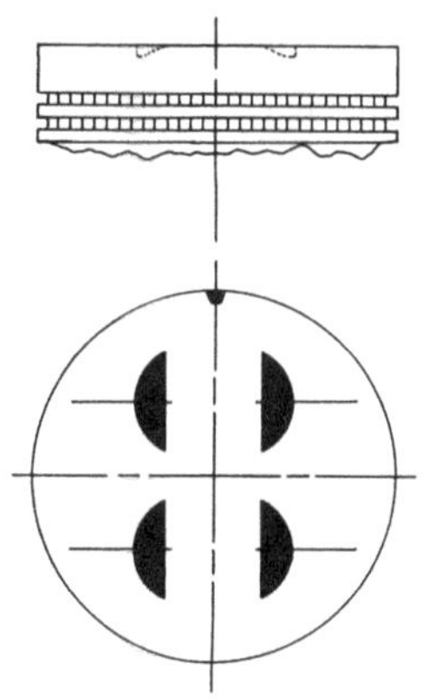 0022227
Engine	283/185 HP (Passenger) 283/230, 250 HP (Passenger & Corvette) 283/245, 270 HP (Corvette)	
Piston Characteristics	Flat head design with valve reliefs to insure adequate valve clearance.	
Material	Cast alloy aluminum with steel struts	
Skirt Type	Slipper	
Compression Ring Groove Depth (in.)	0.2153–0.2218	
Oil Ring Groove Depth (in.)	0.2093–0.2158	
Piston Pin Type	Pressed fit	
Piston Pin Offset	Major thrust side .060	
Weight (oz.)	20.96	

Model	Passenger Corvette
Engine	283/290 HP (Passenger & Corvette)
Piston Characteristics	Domed head design only used on 290 HP engines in 1959. Piston has machined reliefs to insure adequate clearance at high RPM.
Material	Cast alloy aluminum with steel struts
Skirt Type	Slipper
Compression Ring Groove Depth (in.)	0.2153–0.2218
Oil Ring Groove Depth (in.)	0.2093–0.2158
Piston Pin Type	Pressed fit
Piston Pin Offset	Major thrust side .060
Weight (oz.)	25.60

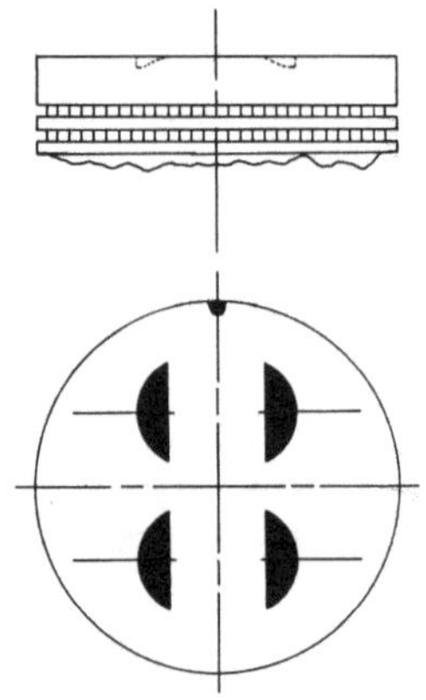

0022227

Model	Passenger
Engine	348/250, 280 HP
Piston Characteristics	Peak roof design with no valve reliefs in piston. Autothermic.
Material	Cast alloy aluminum with steel struts
Skirt Type	Slipper
Compression Ring Groove Depth (in.)	0.2283–0.2334
Oil Ring Groove Depth (in.)	0.2183–0.2234
Piston Pin Type	Pressed fit
Piston Pin Offset	Major thrust side .060
Weight (oz.)	26.72

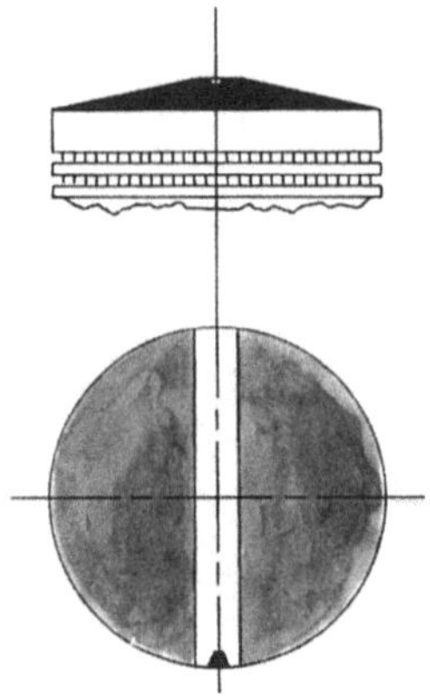

0022228

Model	Passenger
Engine	348/305, 320, 335 HP
Piston Characteristics	Piston has a half-flat design with machined reliefs for valve clearance and half slanted downward 16 degrees. Autothermic.
Material	Cast alloy aluminum with steel struts
Skirt Type	Slipper
Compression Ring Groove Depth (in.)	0.2283–0.2334
Oil Ring Groove Depth (in.)	0.2183–0.2234
Piston Pin Type	Pressed fit
Piston Pin Offset	Major thrust side .060
Weight (oz.)	29.20

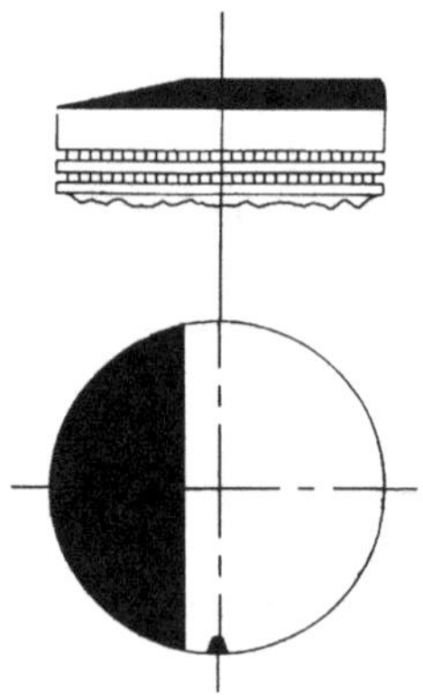

0023154

Chapter 8

Carburetor Identification

1. Introduction

This chapter will cover the identification of Carter and Rochester carburetors used from 1955 through 1959. The carburetors will be discussed and identified by manufacturer. All models will be discussed and specific applications (if known) listed.

2. Carter Carburetors

Carter WCFB Carburetor

The Carter WCFB (Wrought Cast Four Barrel) carburetor was used in a variety of applications on Chevrolet products from 1955 through 1965. These uses included single and dual four barrel applications for both Passenger car and Corvette. The WCFB was a small four-

0022249

Fig. 8-1. *Typical 1957–61 WCFB 2x4 carburetor setup (245HP).*

0023155

Fig. 8-2. Overall view of typical Carter WCFB carb.

0023156

Fig. 8-3. 1955 Carter WCFB #2218S, right hand side.

barrel with a CFM rating of approximately 400. WCFBs have a squarish body and an air horn which protrudes above the air cleaner flange. This air horn is somewhat rectangular in shape. In all dual four-barrel applications these carburetors used mechanical linkage.

0023157

Fig. 8-4. 1955 Carter WCFB #2218S, left hand side. Note linkage type.

Carter AFB Carburetor

The first design Carter AFB (Aluminum Four Barrel) was introduced in 1957. It was 1959 before Chevrolet used this AFB on the 348 engine. This AFB can be distinguished by the very noticeable round air horn at the top of the carburetor body. This first design is easy to identify because it has a 4.5-inch diameter air cleaner base. This design was used up until the 1961 409 was released. The CFM (cubic feet per minute) rating of this carburetor was 500.

0022515

Fig. 8-5. Overall view of typical Carter AFB carburetor. This is a #3461S carb for 1962–65 Passenger/Corvette.

The second design AFB carburetor was larger overall than the previous AFB. The air horn is more pronounced and extends down on one side into the carburetor body itself. This is considered the "modern" AFB and was used on high performance 327 and 409 engines up through 1965. This second design can be easily identified by a 5.5-inch diameter air cleaner base. Please note that both AFB designs were used intermittently on various cars and by many car manufacturers, so be very careful to check the stamping numbers when looking for a specific Chevrolet carburetor. The rating for this carburetor was approximately 600 CFM.

2.1 Carter Carburetor Identification

All Carter AFB, AVS and WCFB carburetors were originally produced with a triangular metal identification tag with a seven-digit Chevrolet part number stamped on it. The tag was attached to the carburetor air horn screw. In most models, the attaching screw was located on the driver side of the carburetor toward the rear of the engine, just left of center.

The actual carburetor ID number was stamped below the Chevrolet part number. This was a four-digit number followed by an S. Although the meaning of the "S" is unknown, it always follows every Carter model number. Sometimes the suffix is "SA," or "SB." The A designates the first level of engineering revision, i.e. the first time the model was revised. The letter B designates the second level of revision, while also incorporating the first level.

The build date of the carburetor is usually stamped below the ID number. This is signified by a letter, followed by a number. The letter designates the month the carburetor was built and the number represents the year.

0023158

Fig. 8-6. 1955 Carter WCFB #2218S Identification tag. Date: D-5.

0022251

Fig. 8-7. WCFB identification tag 2613S with K-8 Date = October, 1958 carburetor for a 1959 car. The 2613 S carb was used through 1961.

Example: A6 = January 1956

A - January	G - July
B- February	H - August
C - March	J - September
D - April	K - October
E - May	L - November
F - June	M - December

All AFB and AVS models had additional carburetor identification numbers roll stamped into the base of the carburetor. The roll stamp identification displayed the month and year code first. This was then followed by a change symbol. The actual carburetor ID number is either below or after the change symbol.

3461S
CG3

Fig. 8-8. Typical Carter roll stamp.

Carter WCFB Carburetors

Carb	Years	Model	Engine/Trans.	Chevy Part #	Air Horn Casting #	Main Body Casting #
2218 S*	1955 (1st Design)	Passenger	265/180HP	3717637	6-889 (Early), 6-1020 (Late),	0-900 (Early), 0-953 (Late)
		Corvette	265/195HP	3717637	6-889 (Early), 6-1020 (Late),	0-900 (Early), 0-953 (Late)
2351 S**	1955 (2nd Design)	Passenger	265/180HP	3724158	6-1020	0-953
		Corvette	265/195HP	3724158	6-1020	0-953
2362 S (Rear)	1956 (1st Design)	Passenger, Corvette	265/225HP	3720953	6-1114, 6-1122, 6-1151, 6-1156 (Progressively); 6-1203 (Poss. Very Late)	0-049
	1957	Passenger (Early) Corvette (Early)	283/245HP	3720953	6-1151, 6-1156, 6-1203 (Progressively)	0-049
2366 S,SA	1956 (1st Design)	Passenger	265/205HP	3726255	6-1098 (Early), 6-1151 (Late)	0-953
		Corvette	265/210HP	3726255	6-1098 (Early), 6-1151 (Late)	0-953

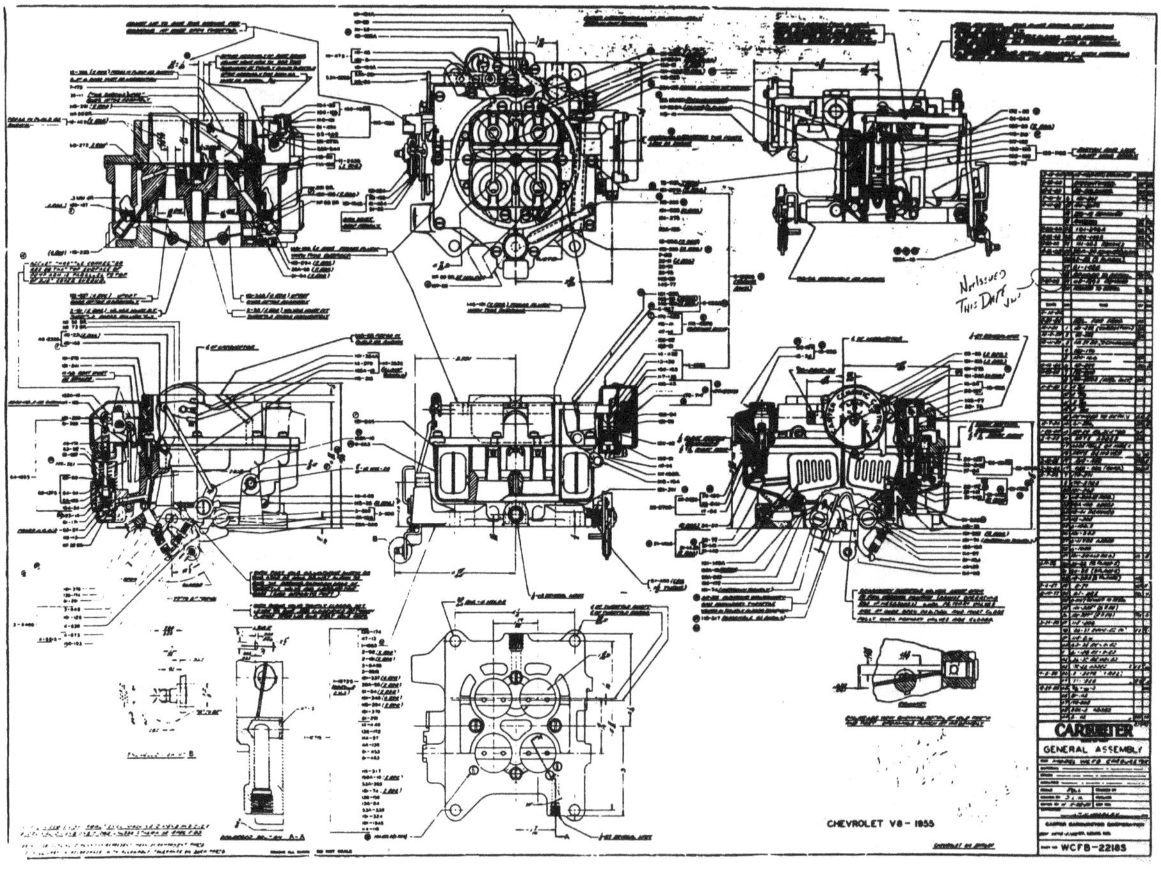

0023159

Fig. 8-9. Carter WCFB carburetor WCFB #2218S

*Early production. Used first type accelerator linkage. Casting #1063 on face of flange.
**Late production. Used later design accelerator linkage

continued on next page

Carter WCFB Carburetors

Carb	Years	Model	Engine/Trans.	Chevy Part #	Air Horn Casting #	Main Body Casting #
2419 S (Front)	1956 (1st Design)	Passenger, Corvette	265/225HP	3730599	6-1114, 6-1122, 6-1151, 6-1156 (Progressively); 6-1203 (Poss. Very Late)	0-049
	1957	Passenger, Corvette	283/245HP (Early, until October 1956)	3730599	6-1151, 6-1156, 6-1203 (Progressively)	0-049
2505 S, SA	1957 (1st design)	Passenger, Corvette (early)	283/220HP A/T	3748134	6-1271 (6-1299 Possible, Unverified)	0-108, 0-1108
2555 S	1957	Passenger	283/220HP S/T	3733246	6-1271 (6-1299 Possible, Unverified)	0-108, 0-1108
2613 S (Front)	1957	Chevrolet factory race cars, Prototypes	283/270HP	3741089	6-1299	0-049, 0-1049
	1958–61 (1961 1st Design)	Corvette	283/270HP	3741089	6-1299	0-049, 0-1049
2614 S (Rear)	1957	Chevrolet factory race cars, Prototypes	283/270HP	3741090	6-1299	0-049, 0-1049
	1958–61	Corvette	283/270HP	3741090	6-1299	0-049, 0-1049
2626 S (Front)	1957 (2nd Design)	Passenger, Corvette	283/245HP (Late, Used after October 1956)	3744002	6-1203 (Poss.Very Early), 6-1299 (Most)	0-049, 0-1049 (Possible)
	1958–61 (1961 1st Design, used until September 1961)	Corvette	283/245HP	3744002	6-1299	0-049, 0-1049
2627 S (Rear)	1957 (2nd Design)	Passenger, Corvette	283/245HP (Late, Used after October 1956)	3744004	6-1203 (Poss.Very Early), 6-1299 (Most)	0-049, 0-1049 (Possible)
	1958–61	Corvette	283/245HP	3744004	1958–61: 6-1299	1958–61:0-049, 0-1049
2655 S	1957 (2nd Design)	Passenger, Corvette (Late)	283/220HP	3744925	6-1271 (6-1299 Possible, Unverified)	0-108, 0-1108
2656 S	1958	Passenger	348/250HP A/T	3744081	6-1354	0-207, 0-1207
2657 S	1958	Passenger	348/250HP S/T	3744082	6-1354	0-207, 0-1207
2669 S	1958	Passenger, Corvette	283/230HP	3766384	6-1354	0-208, 0-1208
2816 S	1959	Passenger	348/250HP A/T	3756678	6-1396	0-207, 0-1207
2817 S	1959–60 (Early, used until January 1960)	Passenger	348/250HP S/T	3756677	6-1396	0-207, 0-1207
2818 S	1959	Passenger, Corvette	283/230HP	3756676	6-1396	0-208, 0-1208
	1960	Passenger, Corvette	283/230HP S/T (1st Design, used through January 1960)	3756676	6-1396	0-208, 0-1208

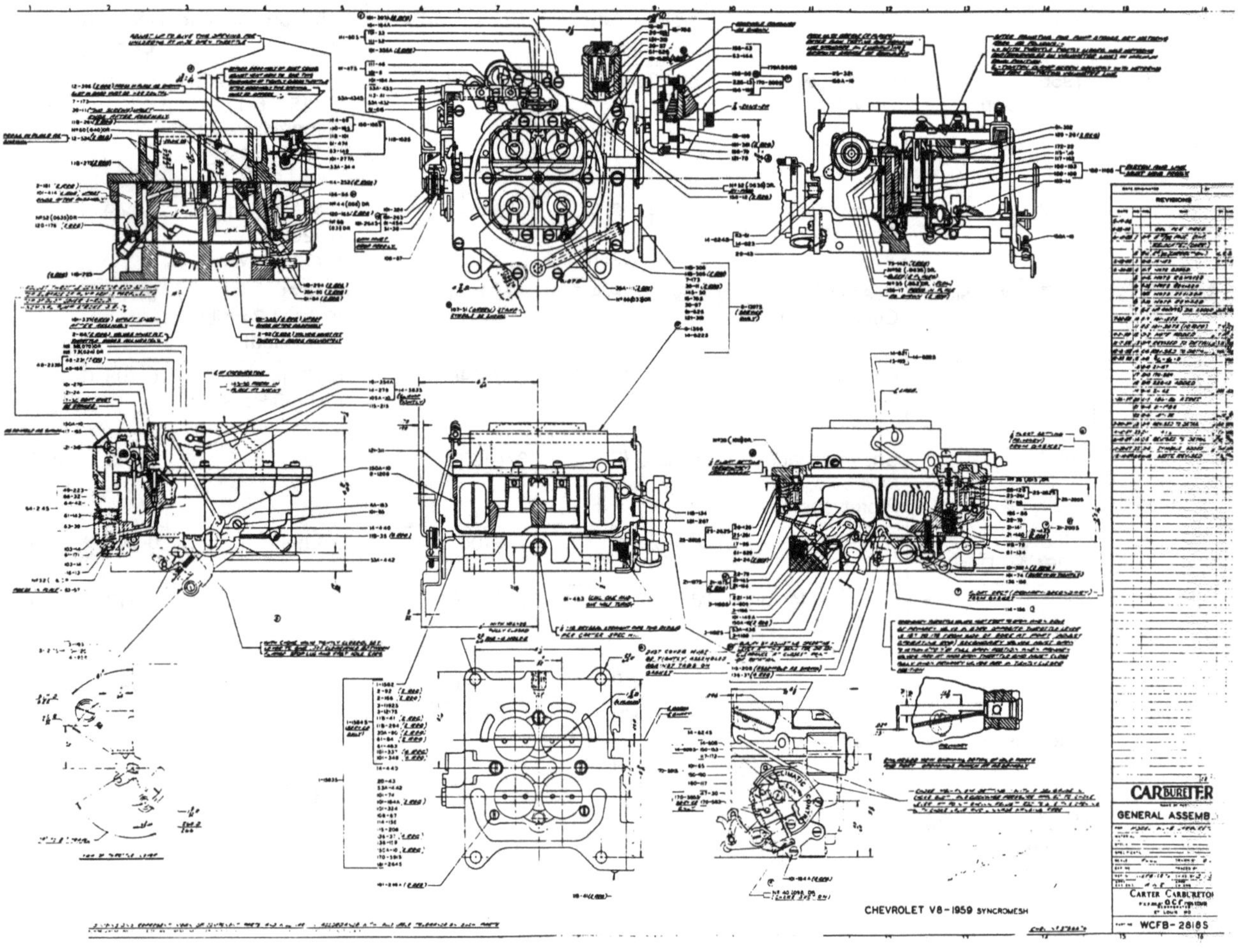

0022253

Fig. 8-10. *Carter WCFB carburetor #2818S.*

Carter AFB Carburetors

Carb	Years	Model	Engine/Trans.	Chevy Part #	Air Horn Casting #	Main Body Casting #
2859 S (4.5)	1958	Passenger	348 (Unverified)	3760264	Unknown	Unknown
2897 S (4.5)	1959, 1960 (Early, Unverified)	Passenger	348/305, 320HP	3764593	Unknown	Unknown
3012 S (4.5)	1960	Passenger	348/305, 320, 340HP (Late Introduction)	3772600	6-1518	0-1376
	1961	Passenger	348/305, 340HP 409/360HP	3772600	6-1518	0-1376

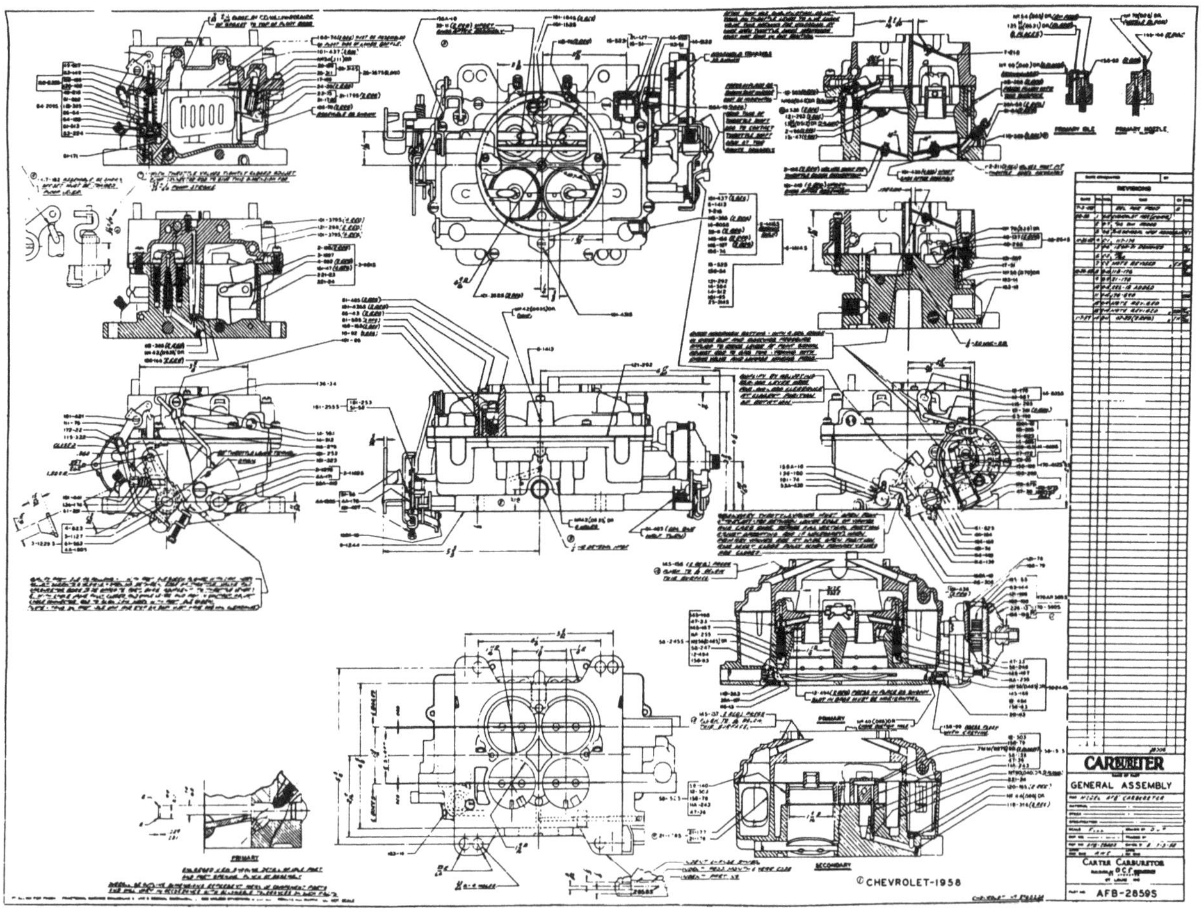

0023160

Fig. 8-11. Carter AFB carburetor #2859S.

3. ROCHESTER CARBURETORS

The Rochester 4GC carburetor was the first Rochester 4BBL to be installed on a passenger car. It was first released in 1956 on the 265/205HP engine. This carburetor was commonly interchanged with the Carter WCFB on certain engines. This carburetor was very square in design and had a round air horn. Most usage occurred on low and medium performance 4BBL engines from 1956 through 1966. The CFM rating of this carburetor ranged from 400 to 450, depending on application.

There were several design changes instituted for the 1959 model year on Rochester triple two-barrel carburetors. The Venturi cluster in the center carburetor incorporates a trumpet type boost Venturi for better fuel flow and fuel distribution. The accelerator pump fuel inlet channel and inlet check ball have been removed from the front and rear carburetors. All fuel is supplied to the pump well through a slot in the side of the pump chamber, the same as in the model 2GC carburetor. A new fuel inlet filter, also the same as on the 2GC, is incorporated in each carburetor air horn. Air conditioned models use a "idle compensator" in the center carburetor.

Rochester Carburetor Designation Breakdown

2G	Rochester 2BBL (Manual Choke)
2GC	Rochester 2BBL (Automatic choke on carb)
2GV	Rochester 2BBL (Auto: Choke-Remote)
4G	Early Rochester 4BBL (Manual Choke)
4GC	Early Rochester 4BBL (Auto Choke on Carb)

NOTE—
During the production of Rochester carburetors, a number of Rochester designs were produced by Carter under license for Chevrolet.

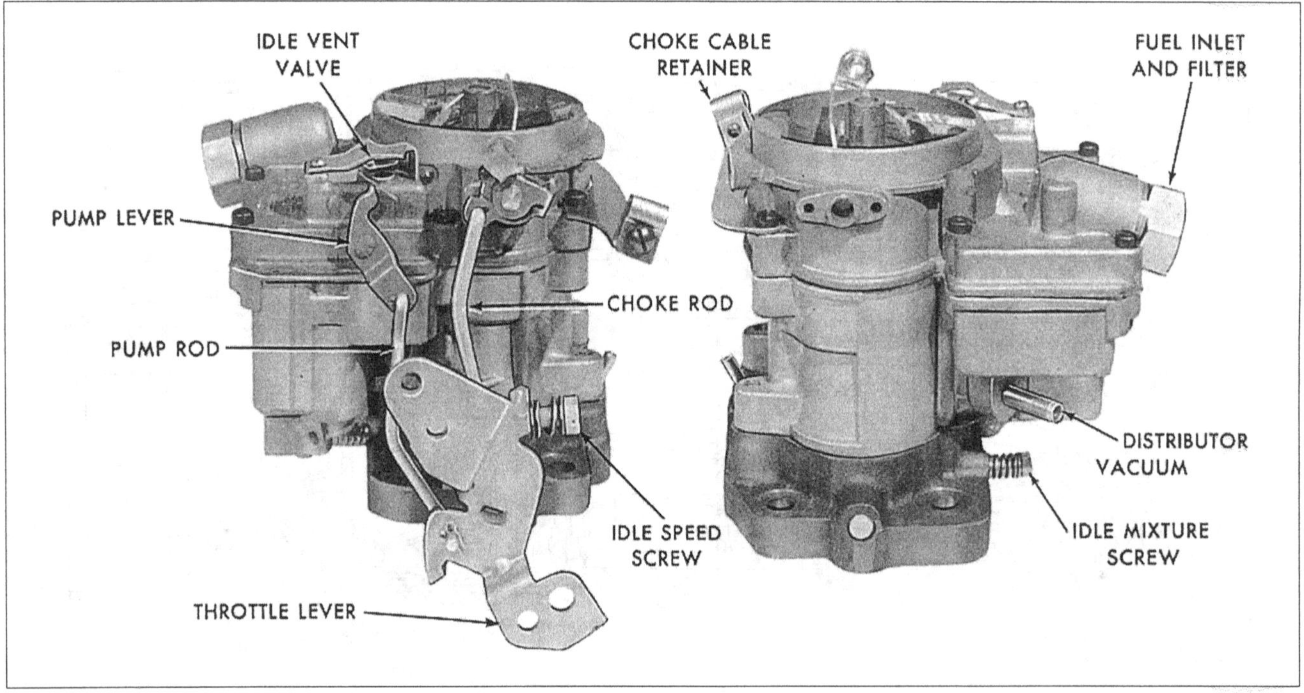

Fig. 8-12. Rochester 2G carburetor.

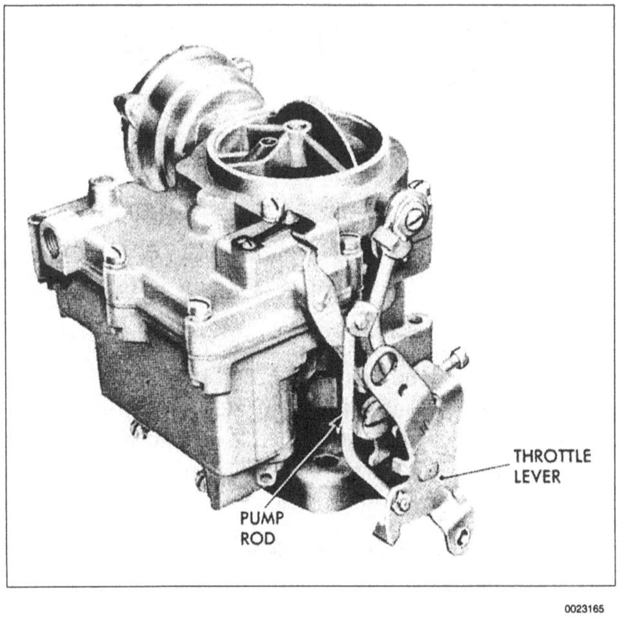

Fig. 8-13. Overall view of Rochester 2GC carburetor.

NOTE—
Throttle valves in later production carburetors are coated with a soft plastic material to prevent air intake at idle. On carburetor overhaul use kerosene for cleaning these throttle body assemblies.

3.1 Rochester Carburetor Identification

There are two types of identifications for earlier Rochester Carburetors. One is a triangular stamped metal tag, which is installed beneath the air horn screw. This tag was used on Models B, 2G, and 4G. The second type of tag used was a circular tag, which was recessed in a cavity in the side of the float bowl. This tag was used on the early model M (Monojet) and 4M Quadrajet carburetors.

The metal tags have several features that should be noted here. The seven-digit number is the carburetor model number. Below the model number are several other letters and numbers that denote manufacturing information. The digit that appears alone is a change letter. This letter signifies an engineering or production change. The change letter starts with "A" and goes up through the alphabet, as subsequent changes were made through the model year to that carburetor.

The letter and number that appear together indicate the month and year the carburetor was built. For example, "C8" indicates that the carburetor was built in March (C) of 1968 (8). Each month is assigned a consecutive letter except that the letter "I" is skipped because it can be confused with the number "1."

The two-digit number (or letters) on the triangular tag designates a factory inspector number on the production line. On the circular tag, these numbers (letters) indicate the actual assembly plant code.

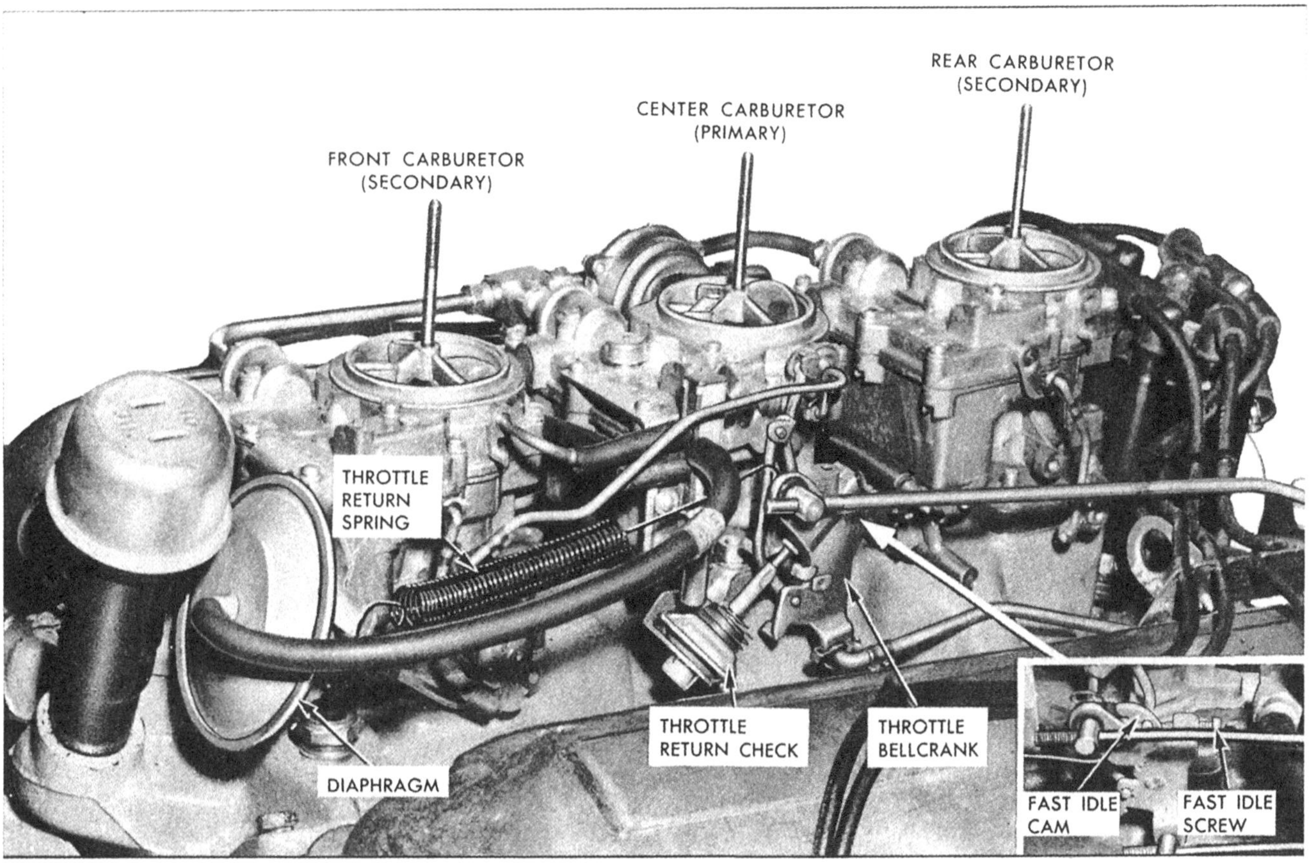

Fig. 8-14. *3 x 2BBL carburetor system, driver's side.*

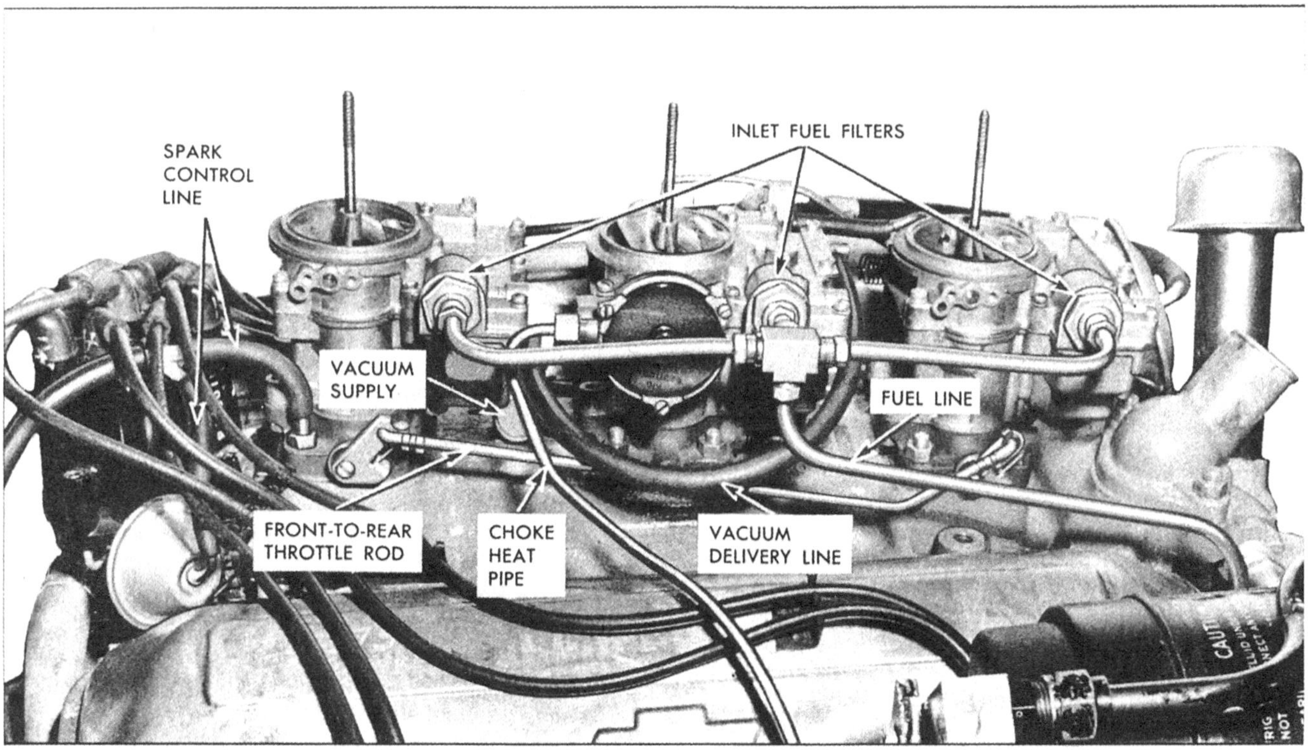

Fig. 8-15. *3 x 2BBL carburetor system, passenger side.*

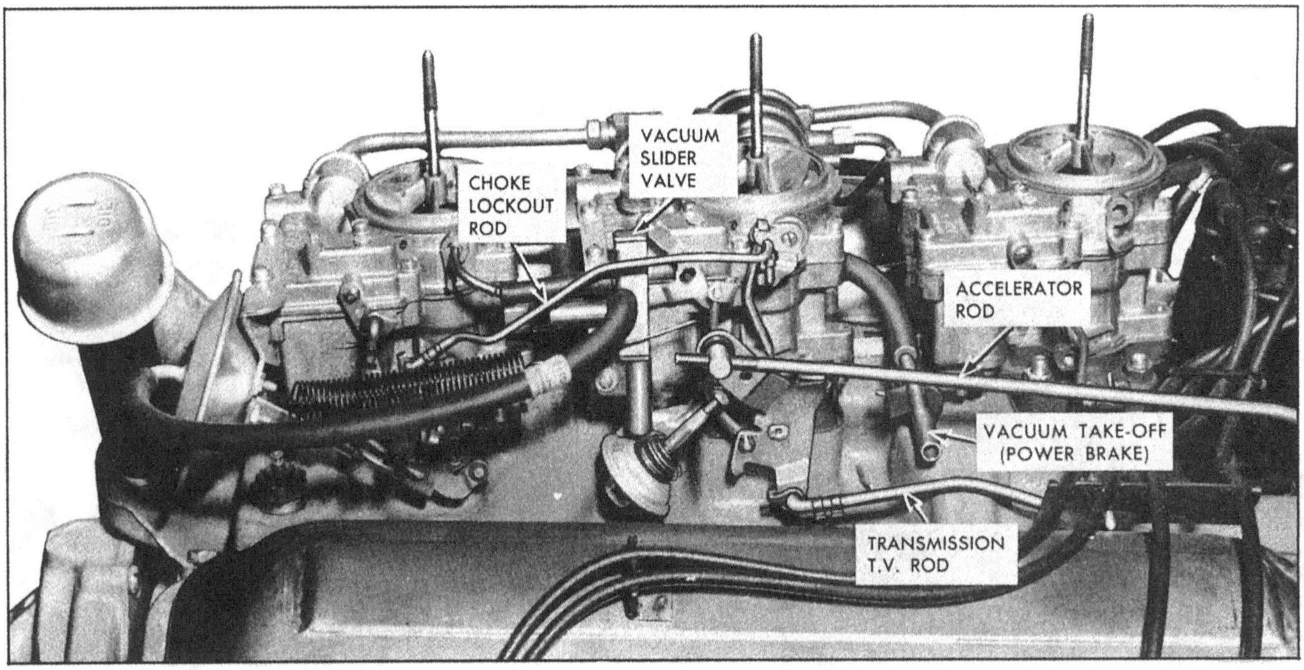

0023164

Fig. 8-16. 3 x 2BBL carburetor system detailing passenger side.

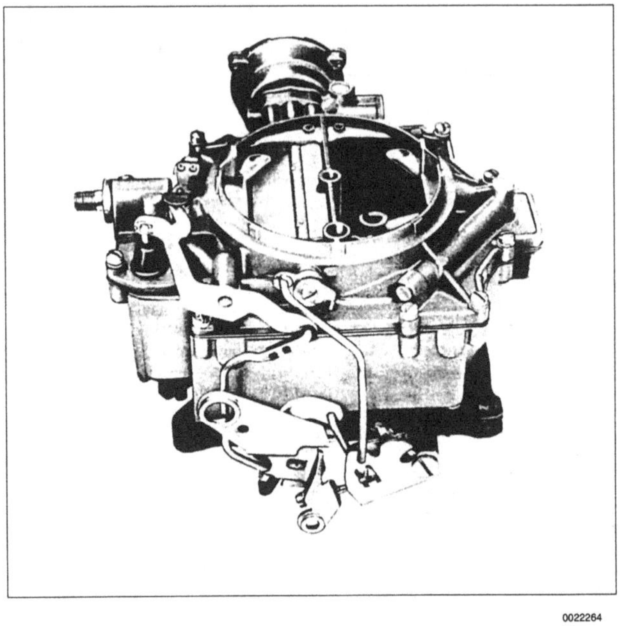

0022264

Fig. 8-17. Rochester 4GC 4BBL carburetor.

Decoding Stamping Numbers

The decoding of the stamping number or part number of Rochester Carburetors can be difficult to understand. From all indications, all stamping numbers followed a numerical sequence that basically ran with the release of each model year production. As the model years progressed, so did the seven-digit numerical stamping number. Although this fact has remained true up through present day Rochester products, a pattern emerged starting in the 1964 model year that could further identify any Rochester carburetor. The following is a breakdown of 1964 and later Rochester carburetor stampings, what each number inside the complete stamping number means, and how that correlates to the carburetor and its original use. The decoding will be done by position number. This will enable all identification to be shown at the position rather than in text form.

> NOTE—
> Some carburetors may be incorrectly stamped. This operation was performed manually and was prone to human error. Also, many carburetors were used over a two-year period, which could cause problems in the date coding. The actual carburetor numbers for identifying specific applications were taken from General Motors documents and verified. Those actual application numbers should be used over the decoding process.

- **Example: Rochester Stamping Numbers # 70 2 4 1 0 0**
- **70 = Prefix Code**: All Rochester Carburetors built from 1955 through 1959 should have a "70" prefix for the carburetor stamping number, though it may be missing on some carburetors. The coding is the same for 2- and 4-barrel carburetors. In 1976 the prefix changed to "170." 170 carburetors are not covered in this book.

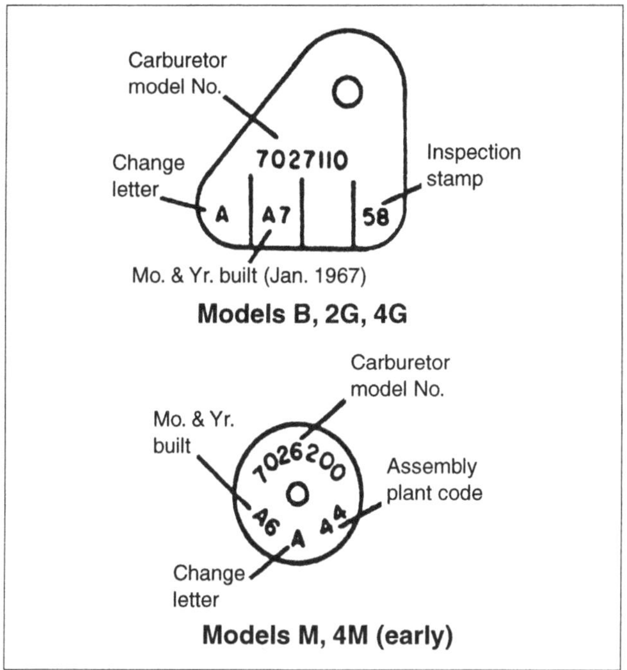

0022252

Fig. 8-18. Two styles of carburetor identification tags used on early Rochester carburetors.

- **2 = Decade Produced**: 2 represents the decade that the carburetor was produced. This holds true with the exception of the number "3" in this position. The number "3" designates a specific A.I.R. (Air Injection Reactor) carburetor. Most of these carburetors were installed on factory engines in 1966 and 1967. It is possible that some could have been produced for service after 1967, but this has not been verified. The decade designations are as follows:
  1 = 1950s Production
  2 = 1960s Production
  3 = 1960s Production w/A.I.R.
  4 = 1970–1975 Production
  5 = 1976–1979 Production
- **4 = Year Produced**: This position represents the actual year of production within the preceding decade. This position number can range from 0 through 9.
- **1 = Model**: This position shows the actual model of the carburetor. It also designates whether the carburetor was assembled for the 49 State Federal Emissions Standards or for the California Emissions Standards. The following chart is basically self-explanatory.
  0 = Monojet Carburetor (1BBL), Federal Standards
  1 = Two Jet Carburetor (2BBL), Federal Standards
  2 = Quadrajet Carburetor (4BBL), Federal Standards
  3 = Monojet Carburetor (1BBL), California Standards
  4 = Two Jet Carburetor (2BBL), California Standards
  5 = Quadrajet Carburetor (4BBL), California Standards (including high altitude)
- **0 = Division**: This position designates the actual General Motors Division in which the carburetor was made. Due to the variety and complications involved in giving all the General Motor codes, I only list the Chevrolet codes. The numbers 0, 1, and 2 are all used by AC-Rochester to designate Chevrolet carburetors.
- **0 = Transmission**: This position usually designates whether the carburetor was to be installed on a manual or automatic transmission engine. The identification breakdown is as follows:
  Even Numbers = Automatic Transmissions
  Odd Numbers = Manual Transmissions

Rochester 2BBL Carburetors

Number	Carb	Year	Model	Engine/App.
7005810	2GC	1955	Passenger	265/162HP A/T
7006825	2GC	1955	Passenger	265/162HP S/T
7008004	2GC	1955 (Late)	Passenger	265/162HP A/T
7008005	2GC	1955 (Late)	Passenger	265/162HP S/T
7008387	2GC	1956	Passenger	265/162HP S/T
7008388	2GC	1956	Passenger	265/170HP A/T
7009345	2GC	1956	Passenger	265/162HP S/T
7010647	2GC	1957 (Early)	Passenger	265/162HP S/T, 283/185HP S/T
7010648	2GC	1957 (Early)	Passenger	265/162HP A/T, 283/185HP A/T
7011131	2GC	1957 (Late)	Passenger	265/162HP S/T, 283/185HP S/T
7011224	2GC	1957 (Late)	Passenger	265/162HP A/T, 283/185HP S/T
7011951	2G (Front)	1958	Passenger	348/280, 315HP S/T (Early)
7011952	2G (Front)	1958	Passenger	348/280, 315HP A/T
7011953	2G (Rear)	1958	Passenger	348/280, 315HP S/T (Early)
7012133	2GC	1958	Passenger	283/185HP S/T
7012451	2GC	1958	Passenger	283/185HP S/T
7012452	2GC	1958	Passenger	283/185HP A/T
7012500	2GC	1958	Passenger	283/185HP A/T
7012503	2GC (Center)	1958	Passenger	348/280, 315HP All
7012851	2G (Front)	1958	Passenger	348/280, 315HP S/T (Late)
7012853	2G (Rear)	1958	Passenger	348/280, 315HP S/T (Late), All A/T
7013007	2GC	1959	Passenger	283/185HP S/T
		1960		283/170HP S/T
7013008	2GC	1959	Passenger	283/185HP A/T
		1960		283/170HP A/T
7013015	2G (Front)	1959	Passenger	348/280, 315HP All
		1960–61		348/280HP All

continued on next page

Rochester 2BBL Carburetors

Number	Carb	Year	Model	Engine/App.
7013016	2GC (Center)	1959	Passenger	348/280, 315HP A/T
		1960–61		348/280HP A/T
7013017	2G (Rear)	1959	Passenger	348/280, 315HP All
		1960–61		348/280HP All
7013018	2GC	1959	Passenger	283/185HP A/T
		1960		283/170HP A/T (Possible early)
7013020	2GC (Center)	1959	Passenger	348/280, 315HP S/T
		1960–61		348/280HP S/T
7013026	2GC (Center)	1959–60	Passenger	348/280, 315HP A/T
7013082	2GC	1959	Passenger	283/185HP A/T
		1960		283/170HP A/T (Possible early)
7013973	2G (Front)	1959	Passenger	348/335HP S/T
		1960		348/335HP S/T
		1961		348/350HP All
7013974	2GC (Center)	1959	Passenger	348/335HP S/T
		1960		348/335HP S/T
		1961		348/350HP All
7013975	2GC (Rear)	1959	Passenger	348/335HP S/T
		1960		348/335HP S/T
		1961		348/350HP All

The venturi cluster was changed from part No. 7009493 to 7011497 on synchromesh carburetors. Change is not warranted on earlier units. To improve part throttle performance, main metering jets were changed on all three 2GC model carburetors. On synchromesh and governor equipped carburetors the main metering jets were changed from 7002952 (52) to 7002953 (53). On automatic transmission carburetors the main metering jets were changed from 7002952 (52) to 7002951 (51).

Rochester 4BBL Carburetors

Number	Carb	Year	Model	Engine/App.
7008737	4GC	1956	Passenger	265/205, 210HP All
7009846*	4GC	1957 (Early)	Passenger	283/220HP All
7011108	4GC	1958	Passenger	348/250HP A/T
7012126**	4GC	1957 (Late)	Passenger	283/220HP All
7012128	4GC	1958	Passenger	283/230HP A/T
7013004	4GC	1959	Passenger	283/230HP All
		1960		283/230HP A/T
7013006	4GC	1959–60	Passenger	348/250HP A/T
7013010	4GC	1959	Passenger	283/230HP All
		1960		283/230HP A/T
7013012	4GC	1959–60	Passenger	348/25OHP A/T

*On carburetor No. 7009846, a primary main metering jet change from No. 7002645 (45) to 7002647 (47) was indicated by an "A" stamped on the identification tag. The later "B" marking on the metal tag indicates primary main metering jets changed from No. 7002647 (47) to 7002648 (48) and first idle discharge hole relocated with size reduced from .038" to .030". Both "B" changes are incorporated in carburetor No. 7012126.

**This carburetor assembly incorporates a new pump jet design. There are four (.024") pump jets instead of the customary two. The reason for the new design is to give more complete atomization of the pump discharge fuel. The new cluster No. 7011576, replaces cluster No. 7009697 and can be used on the earlier production carburetors.

Chapter 9

Intake Manifold Identification

1. Introduction

All intake manifolds on Chevrolet engines in these years listed rest on top of the cylinder heads and underneath the carburetor. Two types of intake manifolds were installed on Chevrolet vehicles covered in this book: aluminum and cast iron. Cast iron manifolds were generally used on low performance engines. Aluminum intake manifolds, almost without exception, are found on high performance engines. Almost all Chevrolet aluminum intakes were cast by Winters Industries in Canton, Ohio and will usually carry the Winters "snowflake" logo on the intake.

Most intake manifolds have a casting number on top of the intake near the carburetor. This number is raised above the actual casting of the manifold. Although relatively easy to read and find on aluminum manifolds, on cast iron manifolds the numbers may be somewhat corroded, so have a stiff wire brush handy. The numbers "6," "8," "5," and "3" are easily confused or mistaken for each other and should be looked at very closely.

In some cases, casting numbers may have been ground off at the factory and new numbers hand stamped. This was occasionally done to use stock on-hand after a major design change.

Most aluminum intake manifolds have dates cast into the underside of the intake, usually under the oil splash shield. Most cast iron intakes have dates cast into the top of the intake, usually near the casting number. Some intakes have complete dates (2-2-65) and some have dates cast in an alpha code i.e. Jan = A, Feb = B, March = C, etc. Date codes usually follow the same pattern as engine blocks and cylinder heads. The following is a breakdown of the casting date month codes:

The number or numbers following the month code letter represent the day of the month that the manifold was cast. The last number indicates the calendar year. Never count on identifying an intake manifold by its date. Only use this as a method of narrowing down the age of the manifold. Always use the casting number for identification.

Flint Example: A 13 9

- A = Month: January
- 13 = Day: 13th day of month
- 9 = Year: 1959

Tonawanda Example: B 18 59

- B = Month: February
- 18 = Day: 18th day of month
- 59 = Year: 1959

Intake Manifold Month Codes (1st Letter)

A - January	E - May	I - September
B - February	F - June	J - October
C - March	G - July	K - November
D - April	H - August	L - December

Experimental Intakes

Many experimental intakes were either installed on pre-production vehicles, given to factory-backed race teams, or stolen from the General Motors Proving Grounds. It is highly possible that you may run across one of these intakes. Almost all of Chevrolet's experimental parts were cast with an "0-" or an "L-" casting number prefix, usually followed by a six-digit casting number. These intakes will also carry a date code, but usually one to three years prior to the model year the manifold was designed for. Nothing is impossible, but it's fairly safe to say that no experimental intakes were intended to be released and final assembled on a factory production engine. Sometimes these intakes will have two casting dates. No particular "higher value" can be assigned to a part, just because it is experimental.

> **NOTE —**
> When checking date codes of specific engine parts, always remember the following. First verify the build date of your car. (Refer to Chapter 1 for more information.) The date codes of engine components should generally be dated one to three months prior to the car build date. This time lapse allows for assembly of that engine, transport to the car assembly plant and installation in your car.

2. ALUMINUM INTAKE MANIFOLDS

Manifold #3728725

Carb Type	Year	Model	Engine	Horsepower
2 x 4 Carter WCFB	1956	Corvette	265	225 1st Design
This manifold was the first aluminum high performance intake Chevrolet produced. It was only used in production Corvettes during the early part of the 1956 model year. It is considered the "early" or first design 2 x 4 manifold. This manifold is known as the *only* early four-hole plenum intake, but reliable sources have discovered early #3731394 intakes with this same plenum. The date of this change indicated on the Chevrolet blueprint appears to be 3/26/56. This intake has an oil splash shield riveted to the bottom.				

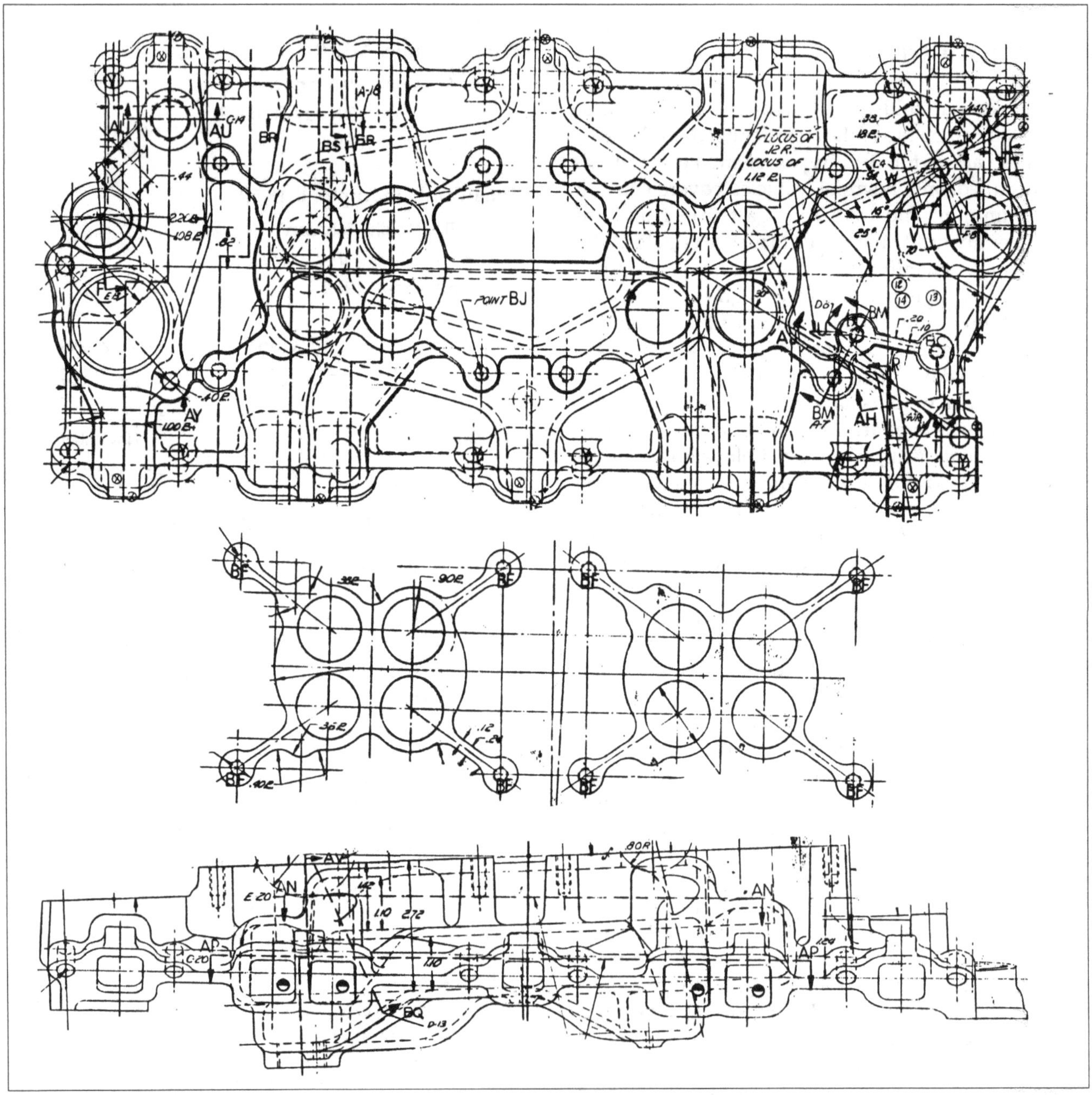

0023173

Fig. 9-1. Overall top view, carburetor mounting pads and side view of #3728725 intake manifolds.

Manifold #3731394

Carb Type	Year	Model	Engine	Horsepower
2 x 4 Carter WCFB	1956	Passenger	265	225 2nd Design
		Corvette	265	225, 240 2nd Design
This intake was the second design 2 x 4 intake in the 1956 model year. Indications from Chevrolet blueprints show that this intake came in to production after 2/27/56. Early #3731394 intakes have been found with the four-hole plenum like the #3728725 intake. The primary difference between #3728725 and #3731394 is the plenum, and that the intake runners are a bit larger on the 394 intake. Later #3731394 intakes have a different three-hole plenum. This intake also has an oil splash shield riveted to the bottom. Note that the 1956 passenger car 2 x 4 option became available on or about February 14, 1956.				

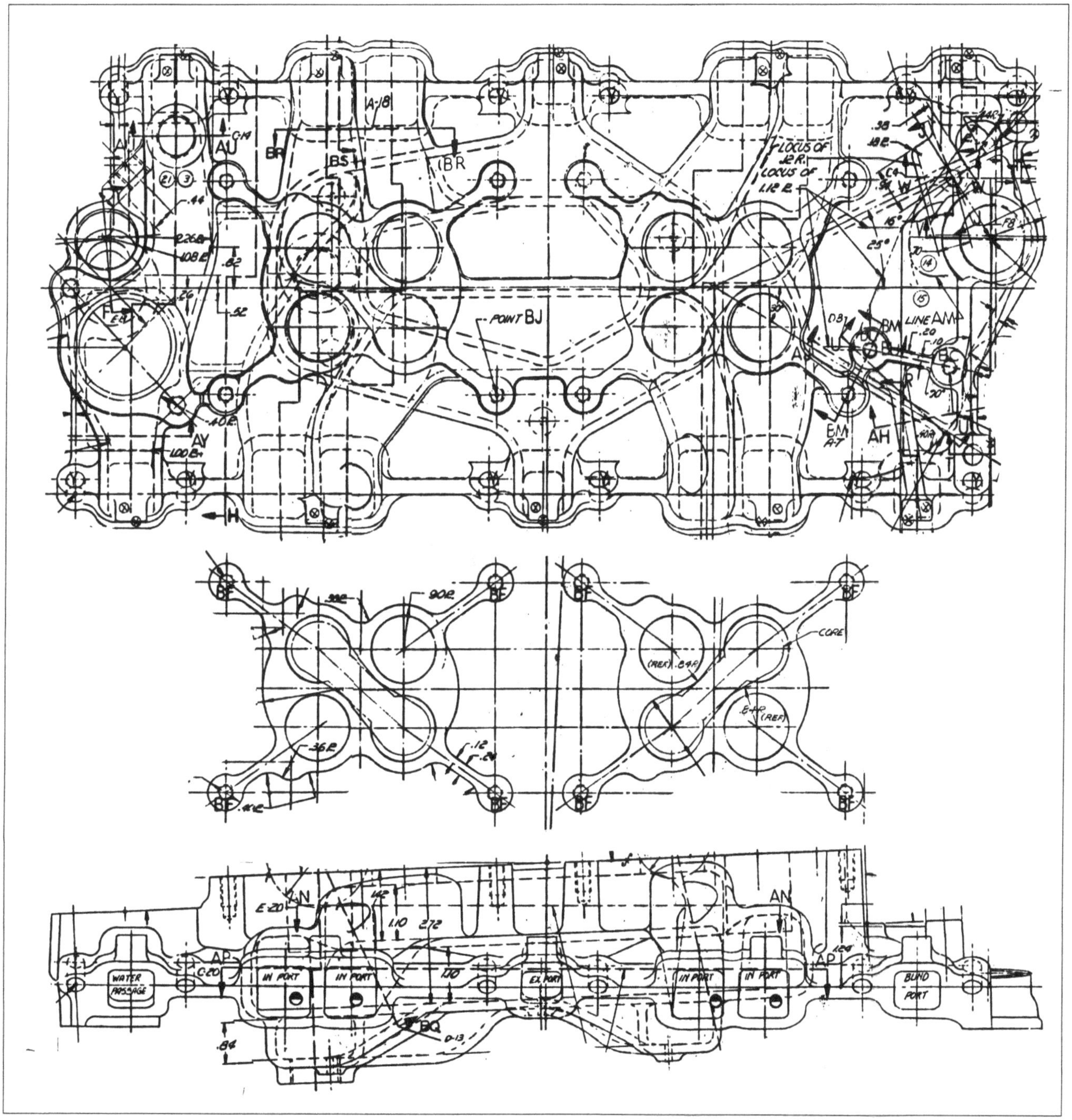

0023174

Fig. 9-2. Overall top view, carburetor pads, and side view of intake manifold. Note new design of carburetor pads.

0023177

Fig. 9-3. *Casting number for #3731394 is peculiar in that it is between and below the carburetor mounting bosses.*

0023175

Fig. 9-4. *Overall frontal view of #3731394 manifold.*

0023176

Fig. 9-5. *Temperature sending unit on #3731394 manifold.*

Manifold #3739653$^{\Delta}$

Carb Type	Year	Model	Engine	Horsepower
2 x 4 Carter WCFB	1957	Passenger, Corvette	283	245, 270
	1958–59	Corvette	283	245, 270
This manifold was used for 1957 and later production only. It was installed on all 1957 Passenger cars with the 283/245 and 270HP applications. It was also used on all 2 x 4 Corvette applications from 1957–61. This intake has a three-hole plenum like the 1956 second design #3731394. The primary difference between #3731394 and #3739653 is a change in the distributor boss diameter. This intake was used extensively as a service replacement manifold. It has an oil splash shield riveted to the bottom. $^{\Delta}$This manifold was used in later model years.				

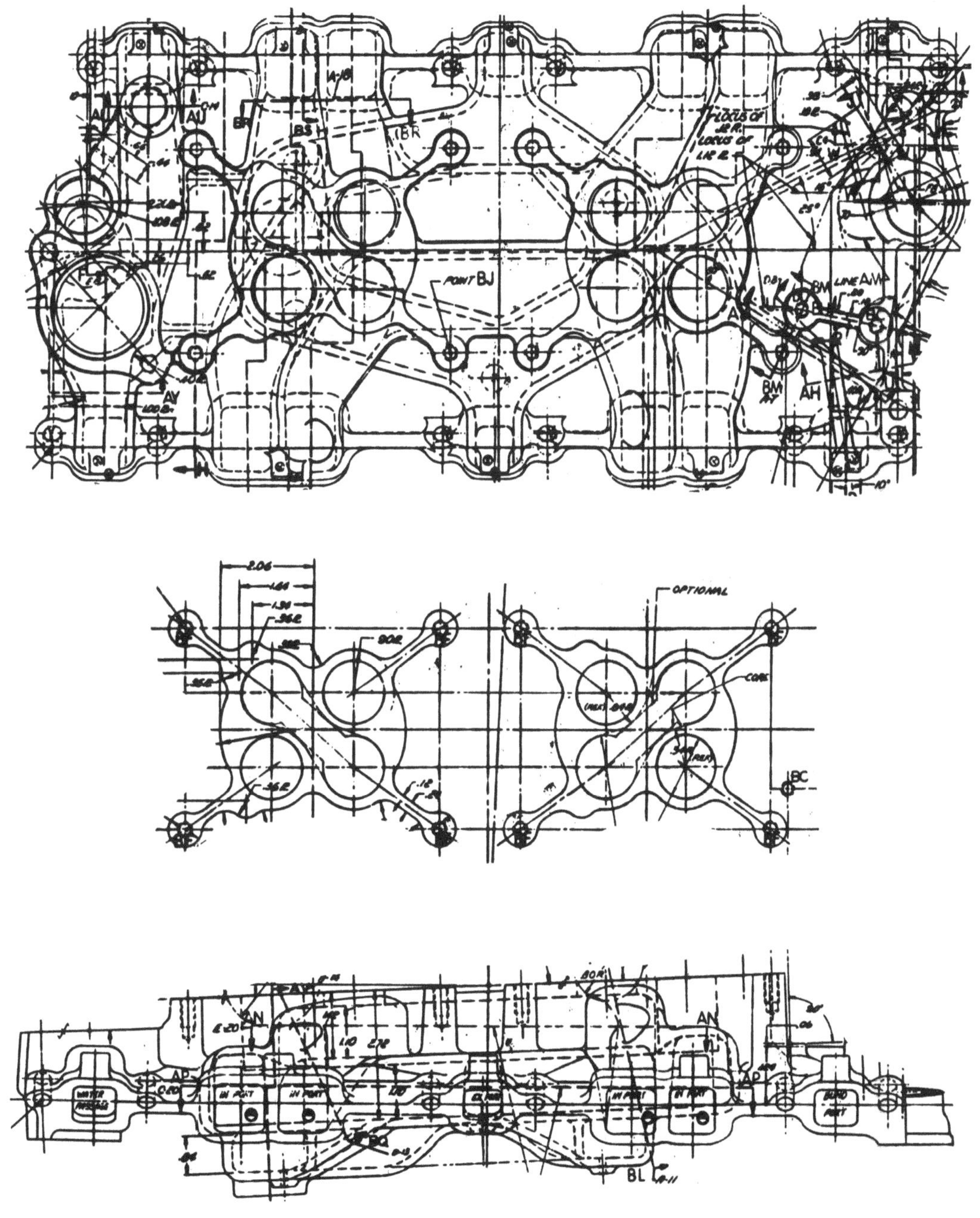

0022116

Fig. 9-6. Blueprint shows overall top view, carburetor pads, and side view of #3739653.

Manifold #3780540

Carb Type	Year	Model	Engine	Horsepower
4BBL Carter AFB	1959	Passenger	348	305 (manual only), 320
This intake manifold was only used on the these engine applications. This intake is identical with #3767579 except for some minor changes. The intake runners and all plenum chambers have been redesigned. This intake is substantially a higher profile intake than #3767579. This intake has an oil splash shield riveted to the bottom.				

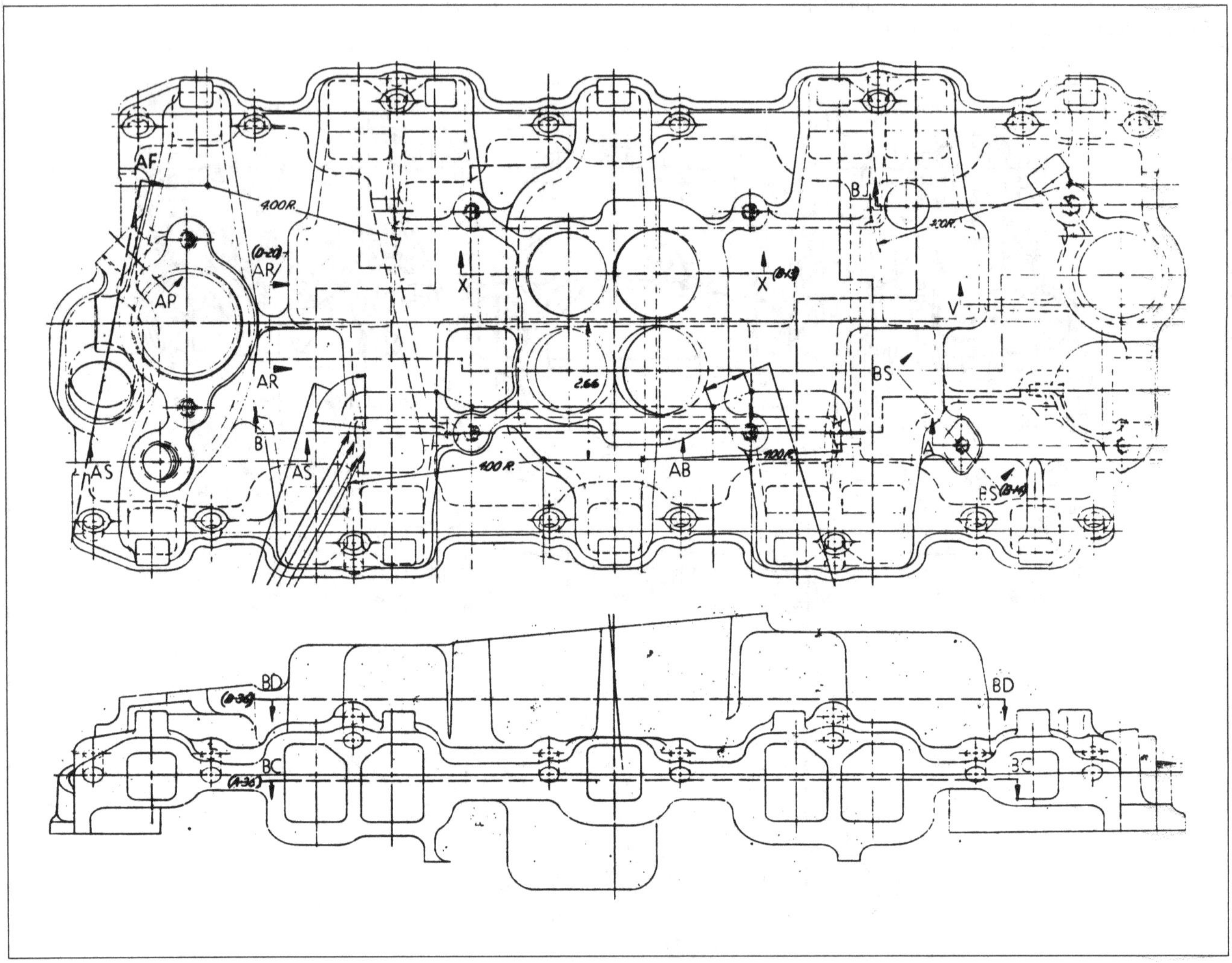

0023172

Fig. 9-7. Overall top and side view of #3780540.

3. Cast Iron Intake Manifolds

Manifold #3704790

Carb Type	Year	Model	Engine	Horsepower
2BBL Rochester	1955	Passenger	265	162
First V-8 design 265 2-barrel manifold, used only in 1955 model production. This intake has a 2-1/2" x 2-1/2" oil splash shield riveted to the bottom.				

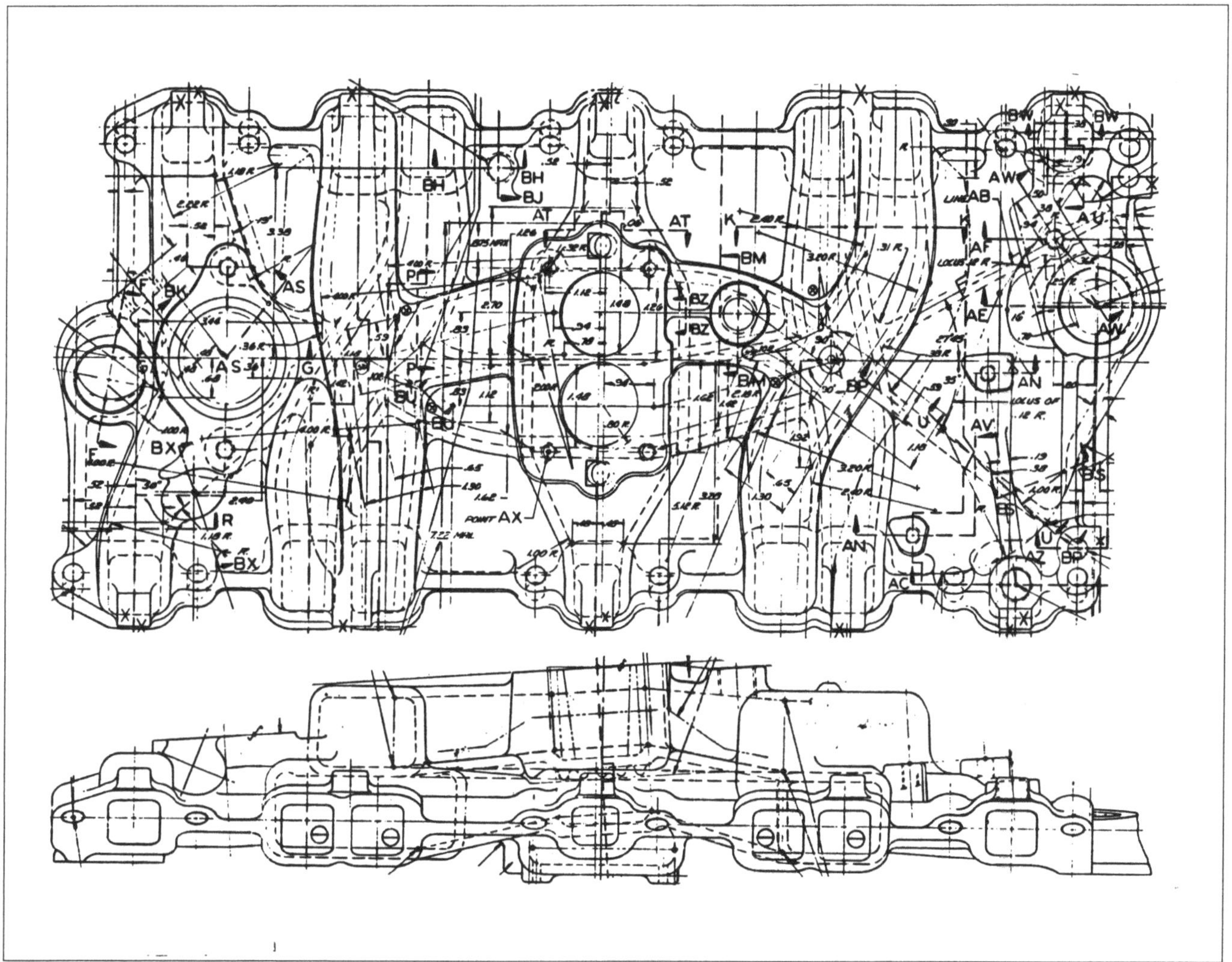

0023166

Fig. 9-8. Top and side view of #3704790.

Manifold #3711348

Carb Type	Year	Model	Engine	Horsepower
4BBL Carter WCFB	1955	Passenger	265	180
		Corvette	265	195
First V-8 design 265 4-barrel manifold. There were 133 revisions made to this manifold between the dates of 4/22/54 and 3/9/57. This manifold has a 1955-only carburetor base plate. This manifold was used as a service replacement until 1967 under part #3717211. This manifold has an oil splash shield.				

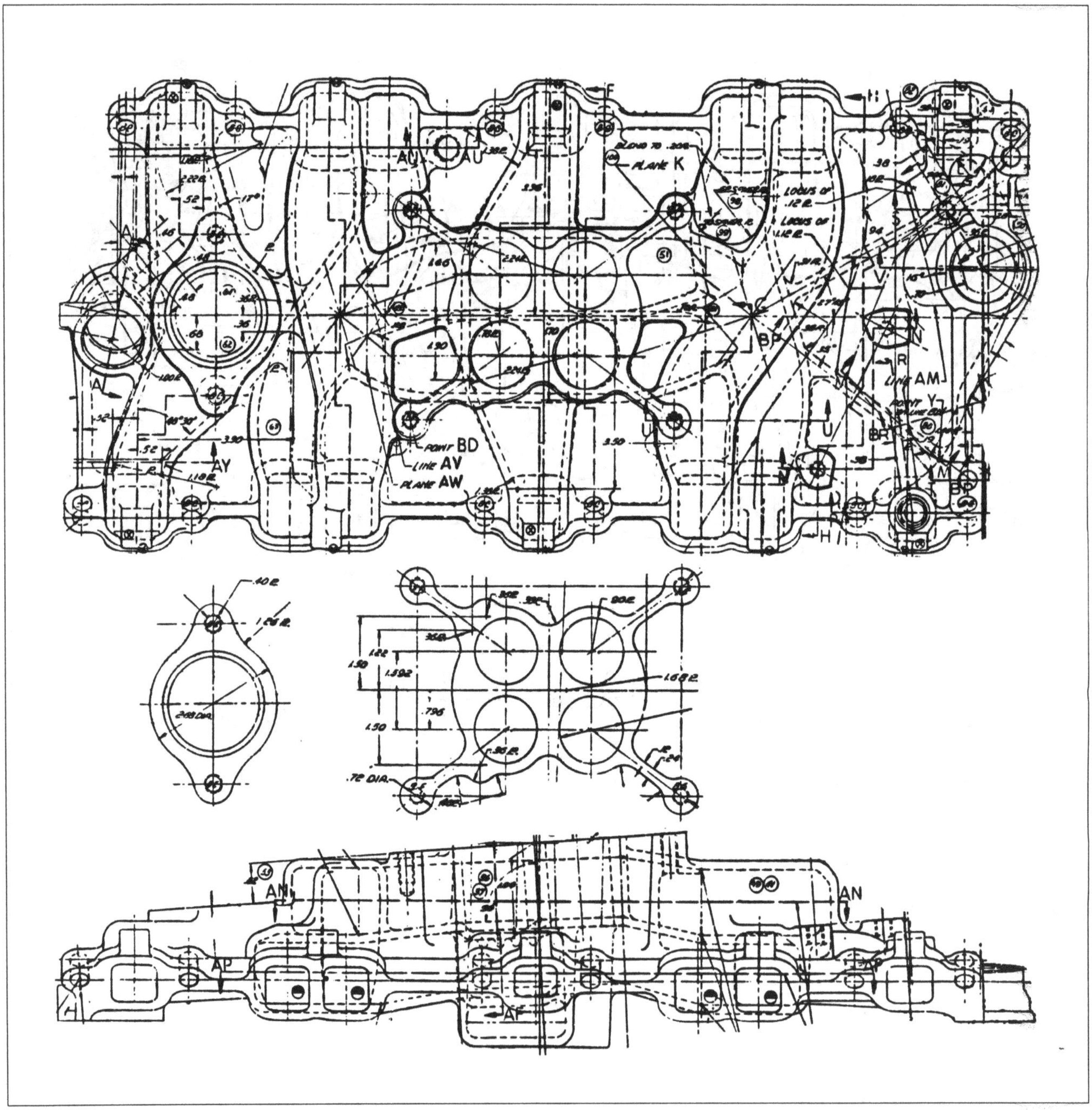

0023167

Fig. 9-9. Top, side view and carburetor mounting flange for #3711348.

Manifold #3731398

Carb Type	Year	Model	Engine	Horsepower
4BBL Carter WCFB/ Roch.	1957	Passenger	283	210
4BBL Carter WCFB (only)	1957	Corvette	283	220
This manifold was used only in production during the 1957 model year. It has a new-design carburetor base plate and a new large heater hose inlet boss to the left of the thermostat housing. This intake has an oil splash shield.				

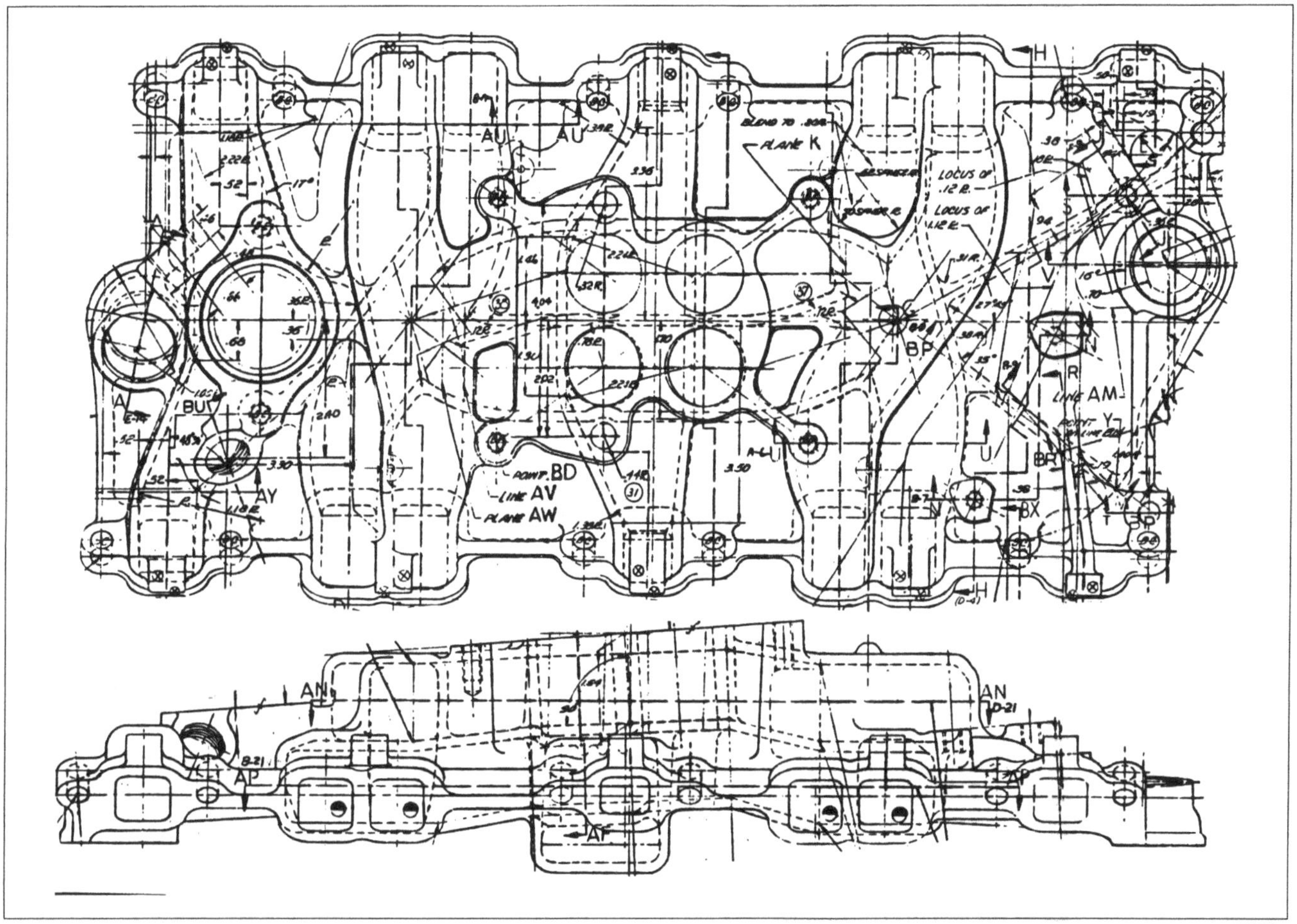

0023168

Fig. 9-10. Top and side view for #3731398.

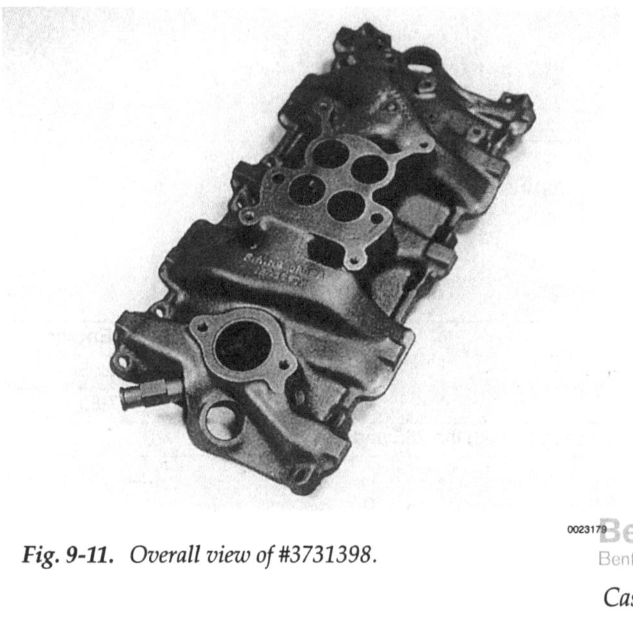

0023179

Fig. 9-11. Overall view of #3731398.

Manifold #3732757$^{\Delta}$

Carb Type	Year	Model	Engine	Horsepower
4BBL Carter WCFB/ Rochester	1958–59	Passenger	348	250
This manifold was used for all 1958–61 348/250HP applications. This intake has an oil splash shield riveted to the bottom. $^{\Delta}$This manifold was used in later model years				

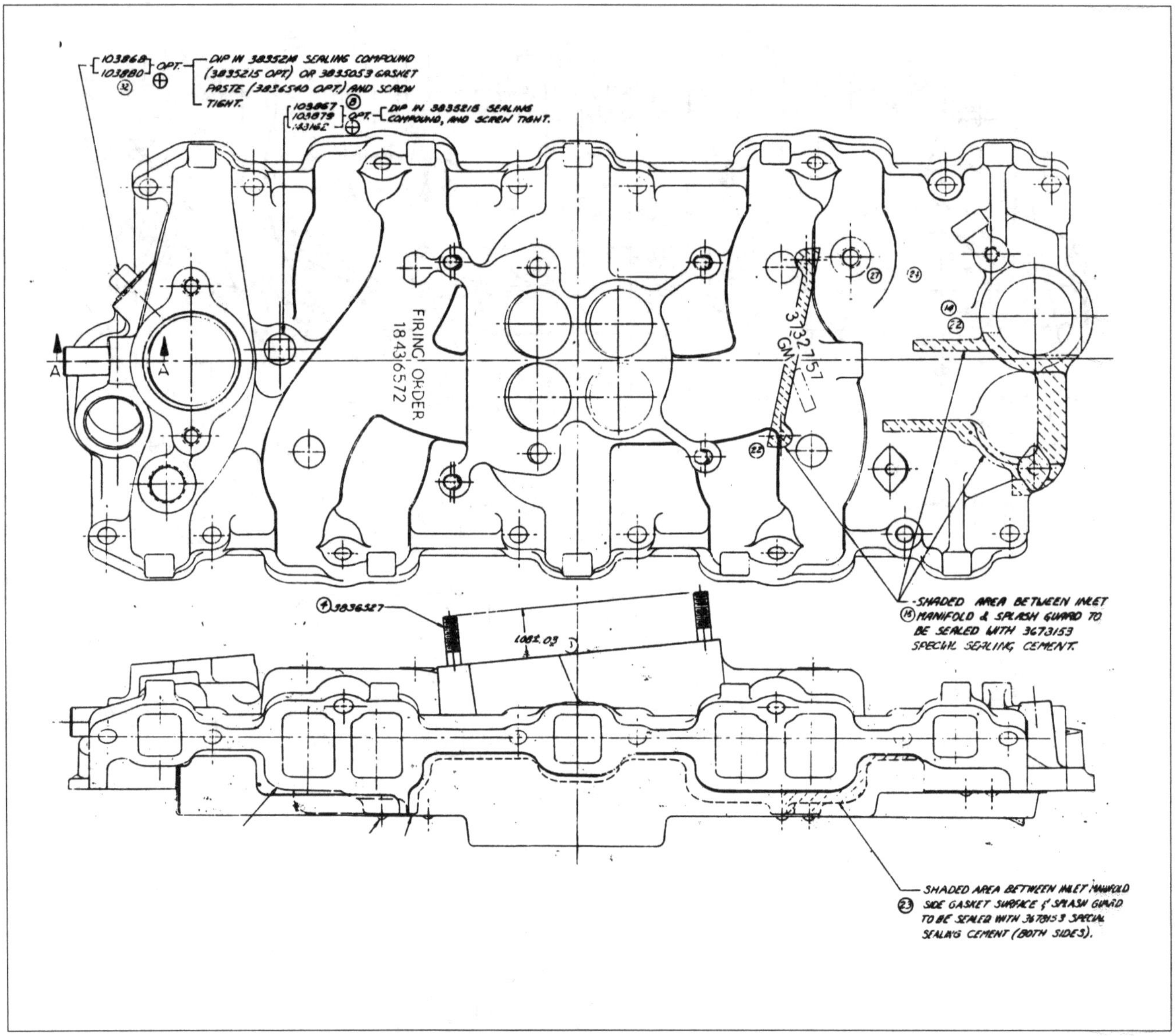

0022150

Fig. 9-12. Blueprint shows #3732757 top and side view.

Manifold #3732880

Carb Type	Year	Model	Engine	Horsepower
2BBL Rochester	1957	Passenger	265	162
			283	185
This was a 1957-only 2-barrel manifold used on both the 265 and 283 engines.				

Manifold #3735444

Carb Type	Year	Model	Engine	Horsepower
2BBLRochester	1956	Passenger	265	162,170
This manifold is identical with #3837107 except that four round locating bosses on the bottom of the manifold have been omitted. This manifold was released after 2/6/56 only on 1956 production vehicles. This intake does not have oil splash shield.				

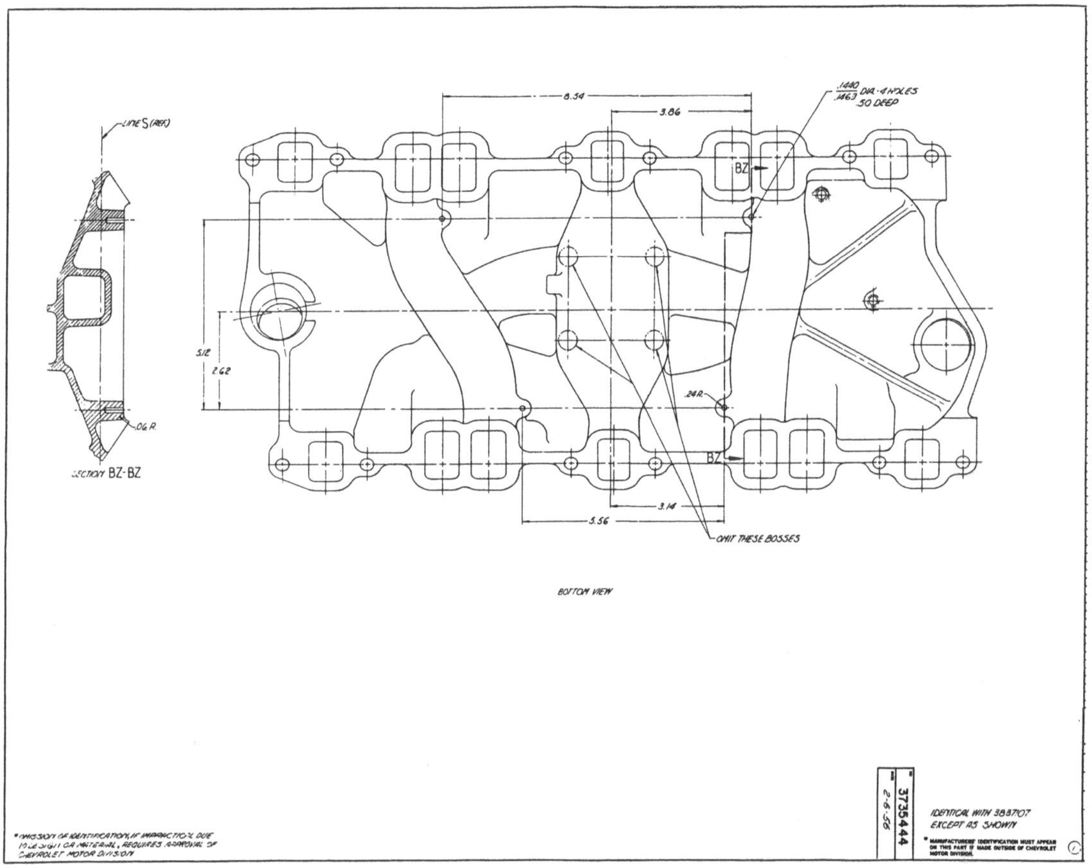

0023169

Fig. 9-13. Blueprint indicates changes made to #3735444, and that it is identical with #3837107 except as shown.

CHEVROLET—CENTRAL OFFICE

DIVISION OF GENERAL MOTORS CORPORATION

DETROIT 2, MICHIGAN

TECHNICAL SERVICE BULLETIN

Service and Mechanical Department

REFER DR #244

SUBJECT:	INLET MANIFOLD HEAT REQUIREMENT 265 V-8 TRUCK AND PASSENGER ENGINES - 1955-1956	BULLETIN No.	DR #253
		SECTION	VI
TO:	ALL CHEVROLET DEALERS	June 29, 1956	

In heavy-duty truck operations where ring plugging, inlet manifold crossover filling and malfunctioning of tappets is experienced due to localized hot spots, as covered in TSB #391 - DR #244, dated March 30, 1956, an Inlet Manifold Oil Guard is in production and available in service to further minimize this condition.

The oil guard entered production on engines, both truck and passenger at the Flint Engine plant on June 15, 1956.

PARTS DATA

PART NO.	DESCRIPTION	QUANTITY
3735442	Inlet Manifold Oil Splash Guard	1
456819	Drive Stud	6 (2 spares)

SERVICE INSTALLATION PROCEDURE

Remove old guard by cutting off the heads of four drive studs which hold the guard in place. This may be accomplished by using a cold chisel. The remaining part of the stud is to be left in to seal up the hole.

NOTE: A careful inspection should be made to determine that the remaining shank of the drive rivet is tight in the manifold. Should one of the drive rivets fall out, a leak would occur which would permit exhaust gasses to enter the tappet deck and exit through the oil separator at a rate which might cause oil pull-over.

Place the new #3735442 guard in place on the underside of the manifold. Since the new guard will locate itself when laid in place, it may be used as a template for locating the four holes to be drilled for attachment. Outer four (4) holes are for service attachment - one located at each corner.

On early engines having long ventilator (oil separator) it will be necessary to cut a relief in the guard. When short ventilators are available in Parts Stock the ventilator may be changed.

0023180

Fig. 9-14. Technical Service Bulletin details oil splash shield entering production at the Flint Engine Plant on June 15, 1956.

Manifold #3735448

Carb Type	Year	Model	Engine	Horsepower
4BBL Carter WCFB/Rochester	1956	Passenger	265	205
4BBL Carter WCFB	1956	Corvette	265	210
This manifold was initially used in 1956 production only, but was later used as a service replacement. It is identical with #3837109 except that four locating bosses on the underside of the manifold have been omitted. Also, four holes have been drilled into the bottom to attach an oil splash shield.				

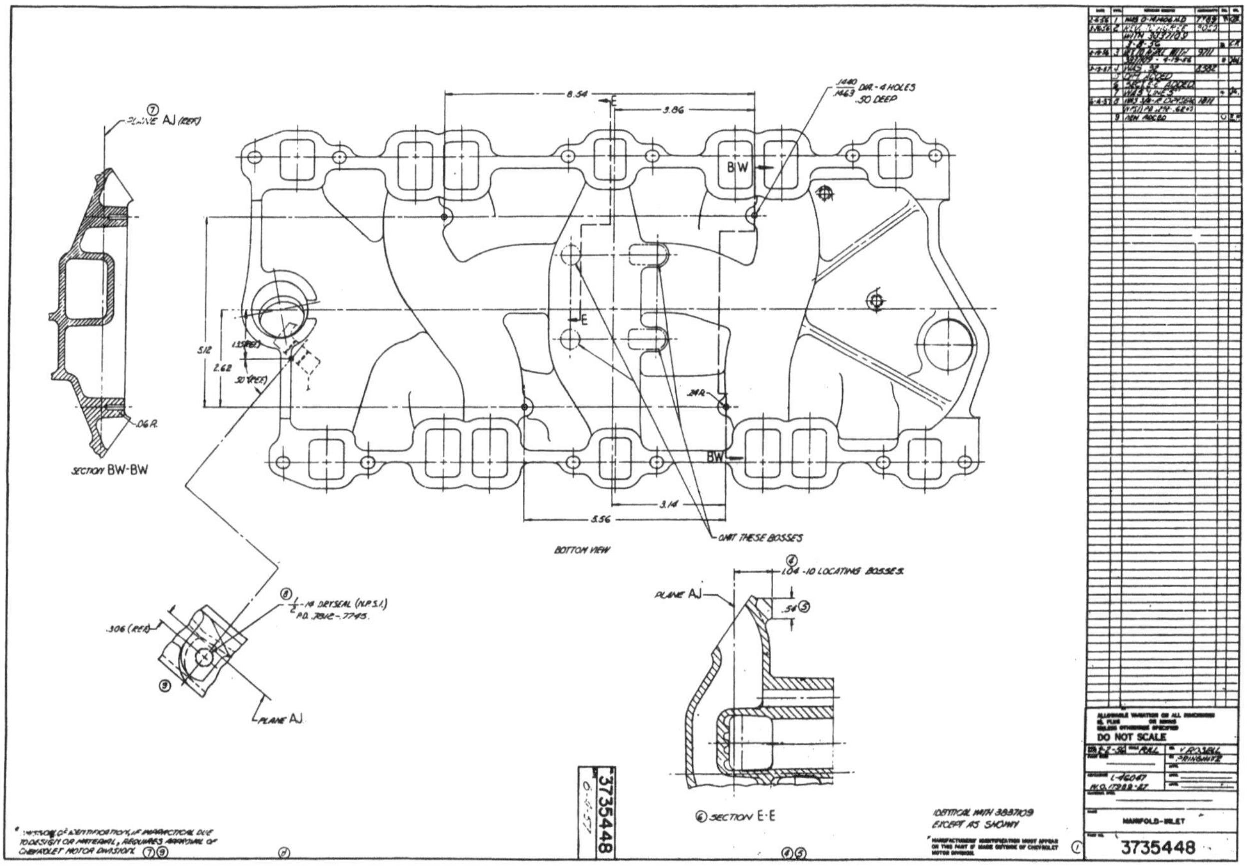

0023170

Fig. 9-15. Blueprint indicates #3735448 is identical with #3837109 except as shown. Print indicates the addition of a heat shield added to this manifold.

Manifold #3746826$^{\Delta}$

Carb Type	Year	Model	Engine	Horsepower
2BBL Rochester	1958–59	Passenger	283	185
This manifold was used on all 1958–63 283 2-barrel engines. This intake was also used on all 1962–63 Chevy II 283 service conversion engine applications. This intake is identical to #3840905 intake except that this manifold lacks a power brake boss (behind the carburetor mounting flange and on top of the #8 intake runner). This manifold used hollow carburetor studs from 1958 through 1962. In 1963 it used a regular carburetor stud. This intake has an oil splash shield riveted to the bottom. $^{\Delta}$This manifold was used in later model years.				

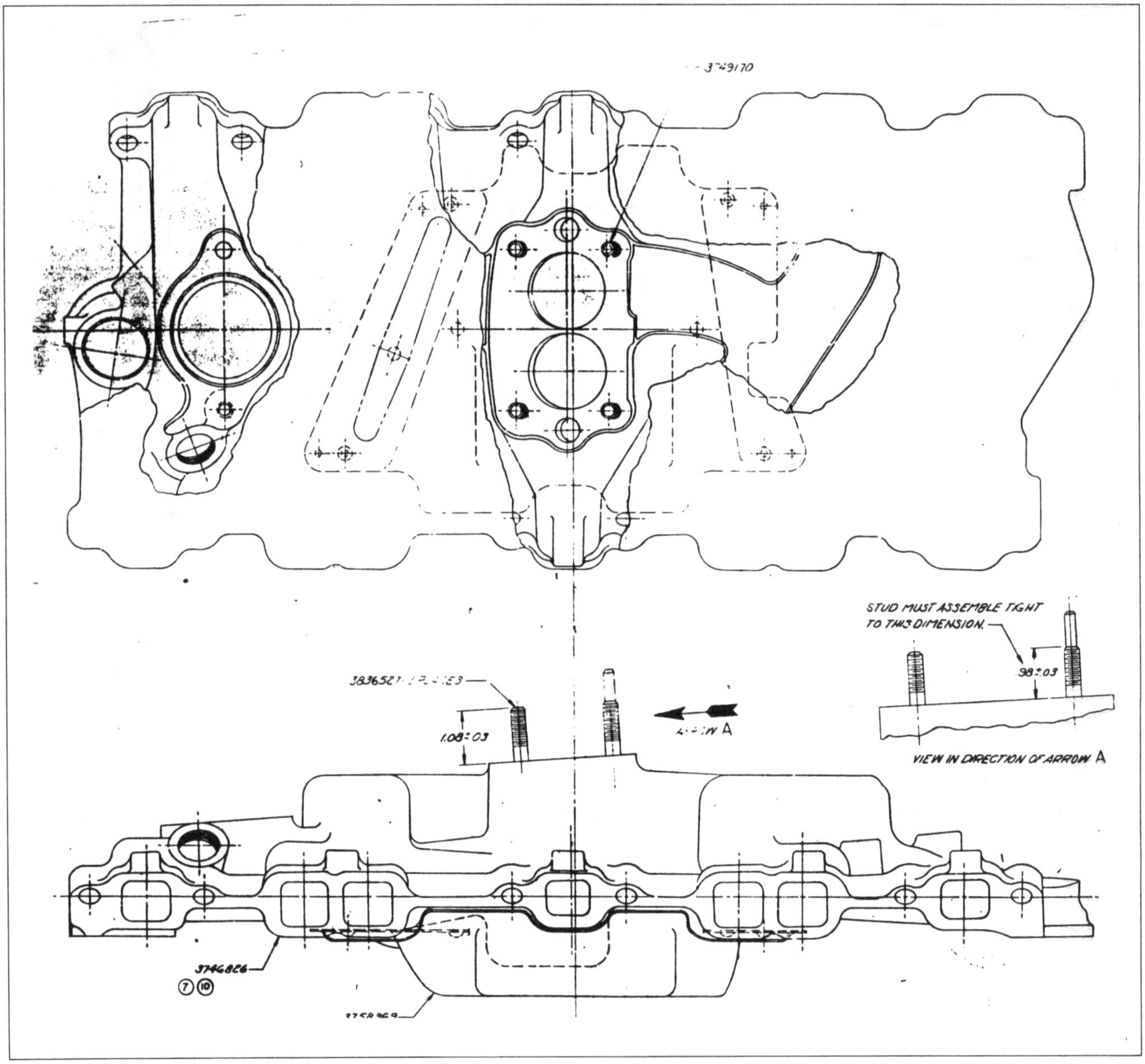

0022151

Fig. 9-16. Blueprint shows #3746826 top and side view.

Manifold #3746829$^{\Delta}$

Carb Type	Year	Model	Engine	Horsepower
4BBL Carter WCFB/Rochester	1958–59	Passenger	283	230
4BBL Carter WCFB (only)	1958–59	Corvette	283	230
This manifold was used on all Passenger and Corvette 283 4-barrel applications from 1958 through 1961. This intake has a large oil splash shield riveted to the bottom. $^{\Delta}$This manifold was used in later model years.				

0023178

Fig. 9-17. Overall view of #3746829.

Manifold #3749948$^{\Delta}$

Carb Type	Year	Model	Engine	Horsepower
3 x 2 Rochester	1958	Passenger	348	280, 315 1st Design w/o Bypass (Early)
	1958	Passenger	348	280, 315 2nd Design with Bypass (Late)
	1959	Passenger	348	280, 315, 335
This intake was used on all 1958–61 348 3 x 2 engines. It was originally designed to be an aluminum intake, but for unknown reasons Chevrolet switched the material to cast iron before it reached production. There are two versions of this manifold. The 1958 version does not have a bypass at the front of the intake, due to the fact that early 1958 cylinder heads did not have water-cooled provisions. Late 1958 through 1961 intakes will have the bypass provision. This intake has an oil splash shield riveted to the bottom. $^{\Delta}$This manifold was used in later model years.				

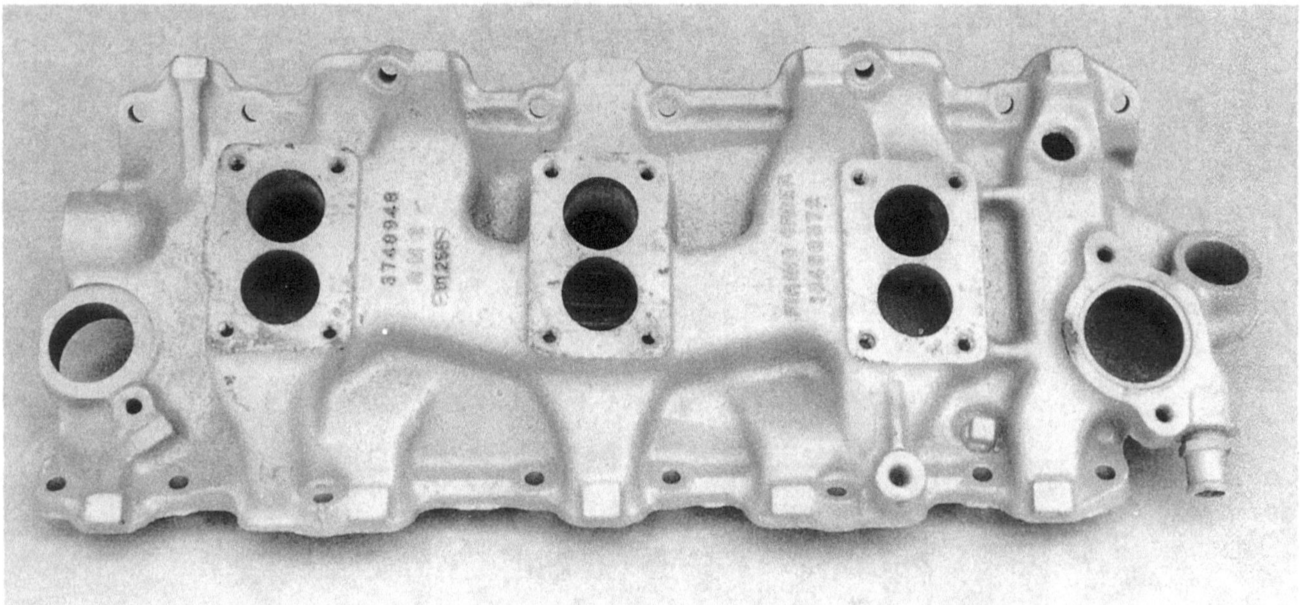

0022487

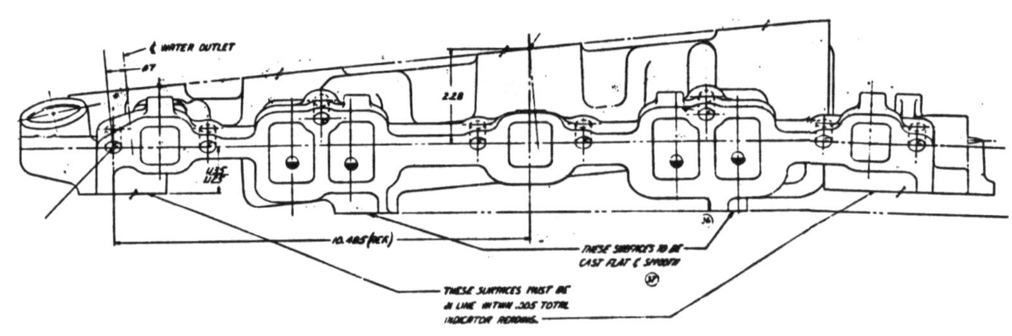

0022152

Fig. 9-18. Top and side view of #3749948. Note that last two digits of casting date (58) indicate that this was a Tonawanda casting. Most 348/409 parts were Tonawanda cast (not all).

Manifold #3770083$^{\Delta}$

Carb Type	Year	Model	Engine	Horsepower
4BBL Carter	1959	Passenger	348	305 (Powerglide only)
This intake manifold was used exclusively on all 1959–61 348/305HP Powerglide transmission applications only. It was also used until 1964 as a service replacement manifold. This intake could be considered a medium-rise manifold. It has an oil splash shield riveted to the bottom. It is possible that this intake casting number could have changed to #3770084 during the 1959 model year. $^{\Delta}$This manifold was used in later model years.				

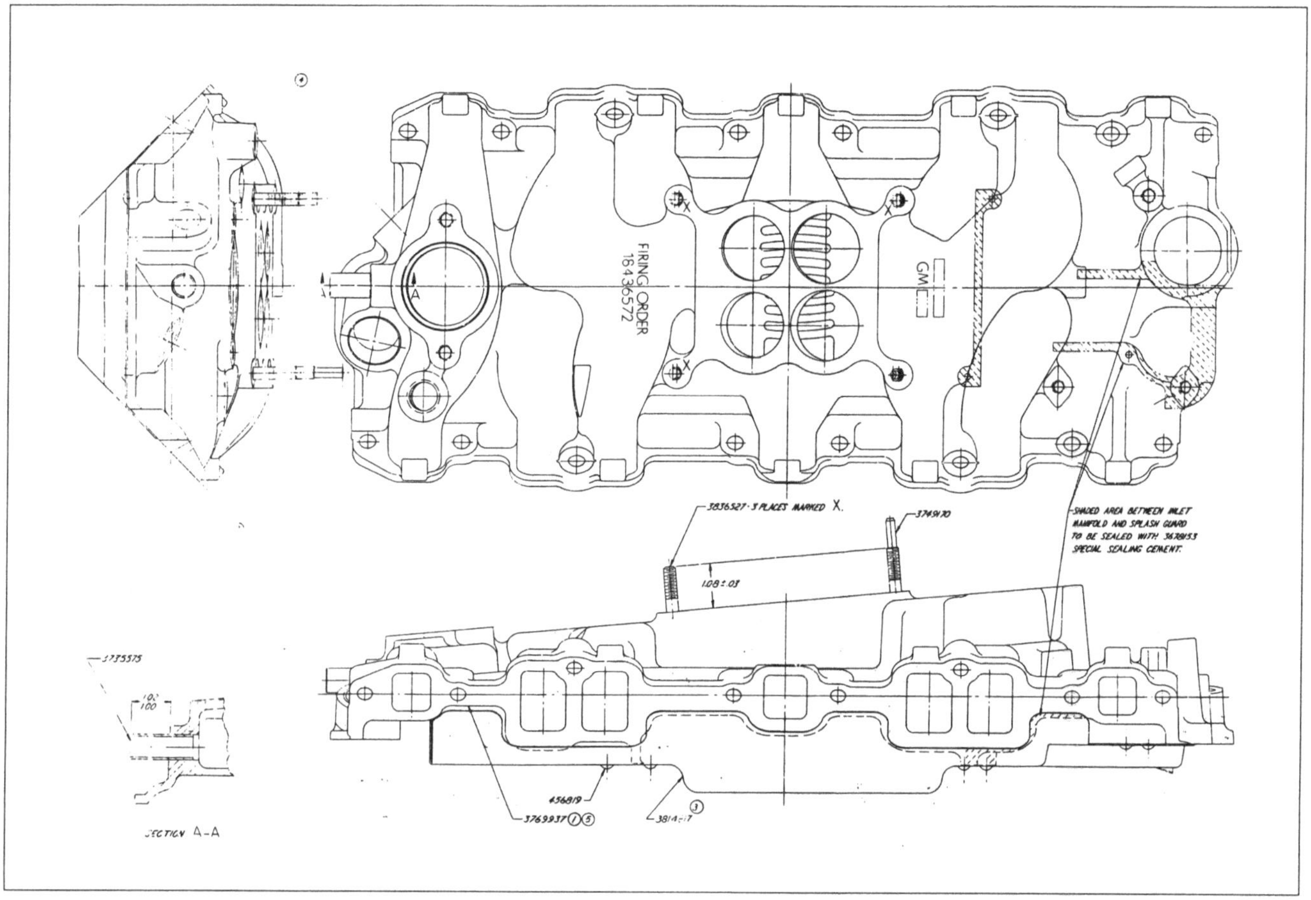

Fig. 9-19. Top, side, and front view of #3770083.

Manifold #3837109

Carb Type	Year	Model	Engine	Horsepower
4BBL Carter WCFB/ Rochester	1956	Passenger	265	205
4BBL Carter WCFB (only)	1956	Corvette	265	210 (Unverified)
This intake was used in 1956 production only. It was also used as a service replacement intake until after 1965. This intake is almost identical with #3731398 intake, except that the raised vacuum fitting boss on the rear manifold runner omitted on #3837109. This intake has a small oil splash shield riveted to the bottom.				

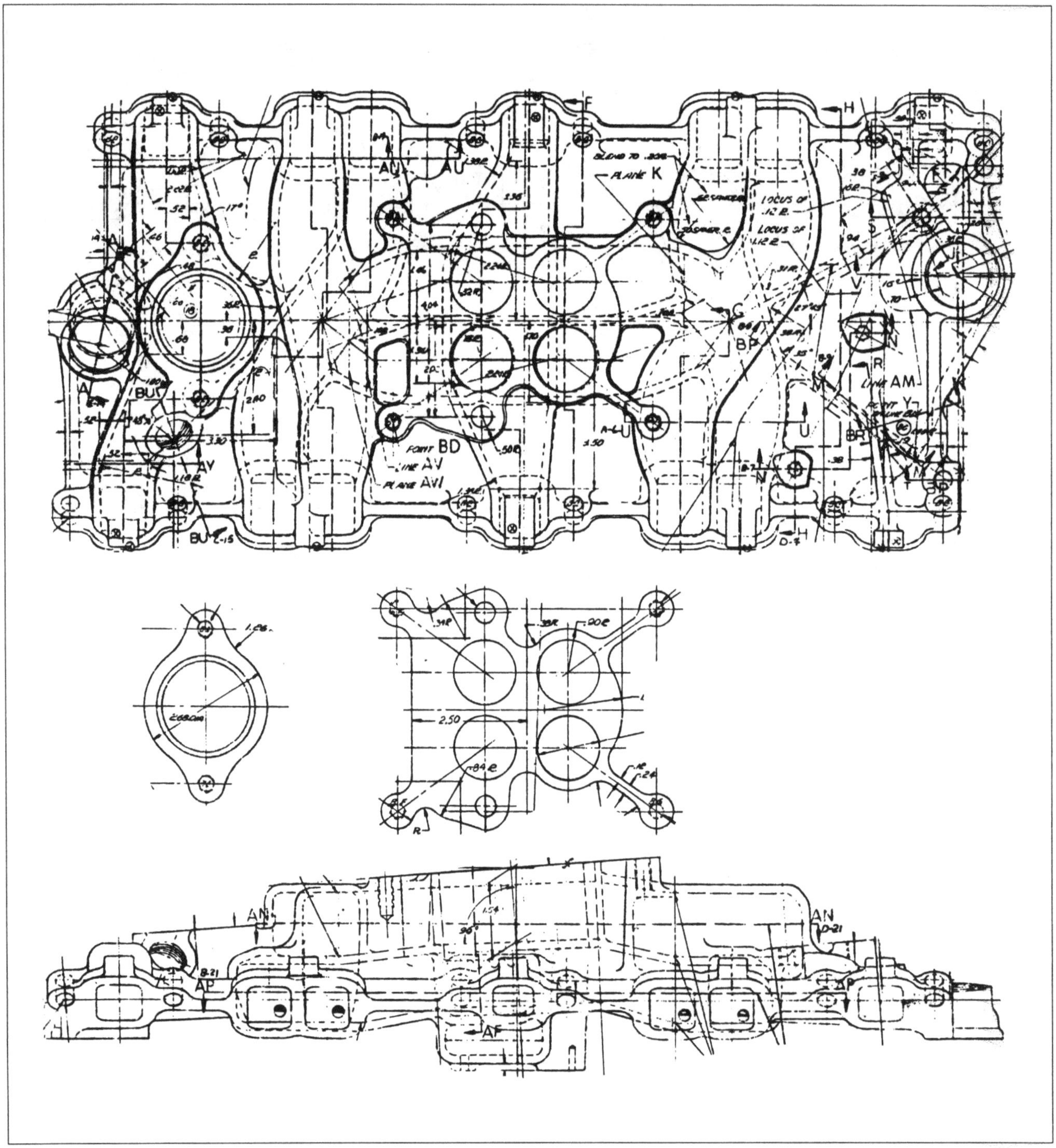

0023171

Fig. 9-20. Top and side view, and carburetor mounting flange for #3837109.

Chapter 10

Exhaust Manifold Identification

1. Introduction

All Chevrolet factory exhaust manifolds are cast iron. Since the manifolds are cast, the actual casting number and date are raised above the surface of the part. Most casting numbers are visible when the manifold is installed on the engine. The casting number location and casting date location will vary from year to year and sometimes manifold to manifold. Some manifolds will not carry a casting date at all. Small block exhaust manifolds usually do not carry a year designation. 2" outlet small block manifolds will have a casting date; most 2-1/2" manifolds do not have a casting date.

There were two types of manifold designs being cast, the first the Flint, Michigan design, and the second the Tonawanda, New York design. Although usually very similar in appearance, there are usually subtle differences between the designs. See Fig. 10-1. It is very important to realize from a restoration point of view that a Flint engine would only have a Flint built exhaust manifold, and vice versa. These differences are usually easy to spot and can be a quick tip-off to an incorrectly restored engine.

Casting date codes follow the same pattern as engine blocks. The number or numbers following the month

0023816

Fig. 10-2. *Close-up of casting number and casting date for #3704791 Tonawanda manifold. Note cast "T".*

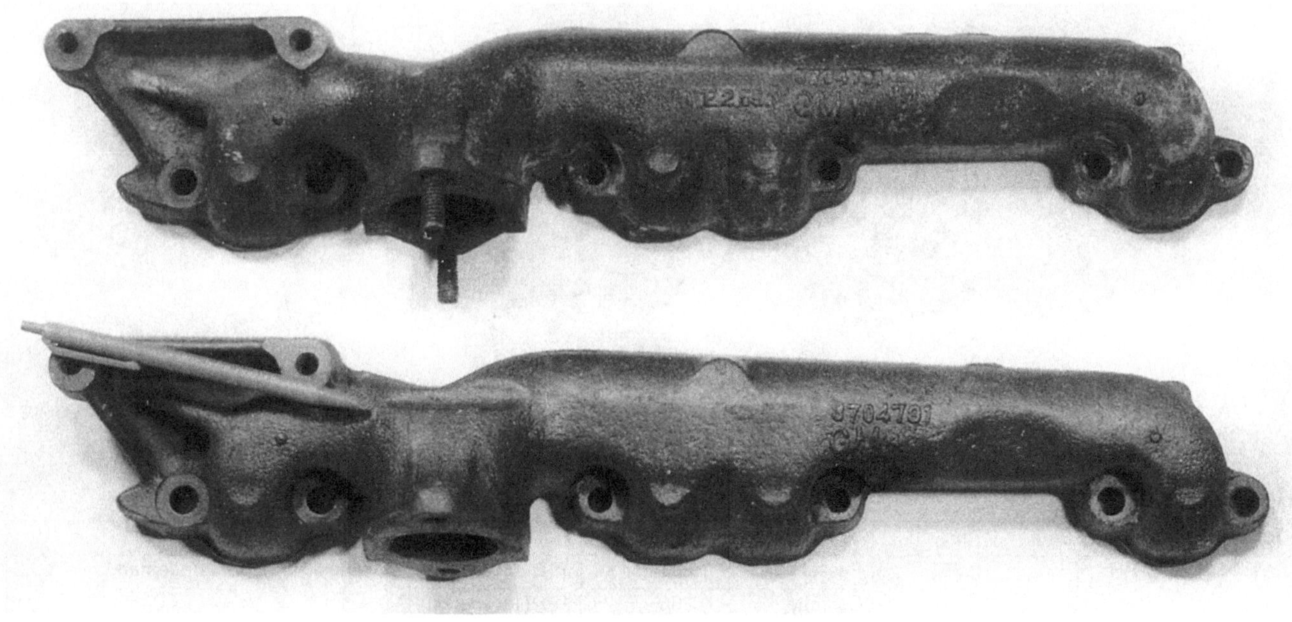

0023815

Fig. 10-1. *Two # 3704791 exhaust manifolds, the top cast in Tonawanda, the bottom cast in Flint. Note reinforcement rib on the Flint manifold (pointer).*

code letter represent the day of the month that the manifold was cast. A last number is sometimes present to indicate the year. The following is a breakdown of the casting date month codes:

Exhaust Manifold Month Codes (1st Letter)

A - January	E - May	I - September
B - February	F - June	J - October
C - March	G - July	K - November
D - April	H - August	L - December

> **NOTE—**
> When checking date codes of specific engine parts, always remember the following. First verify the build date of your car. (Refer to Chapter 1 for more information on build dates.) The date codes of the various engine components should generally be dated one to three months prior to the car build date. This time lapse allows for assembly of that engine, transport to the car assembly plant and installation in the car.

0023197

Fig. 10-3. Close-up of casting number and casting date for #3837069 manifold Date "H1356" decodes as August 13, 1956.

2. Exhaust Manifold Casting Numbers

Manifold #3704791

Outlet Size	Outlet Side	Year	Model	Engine	Horsepower	Notes
1.74	LH	1955	Passenger	265	162, 180	Casting # above GM trademark
			Corvette	265	195 (1st Design)	

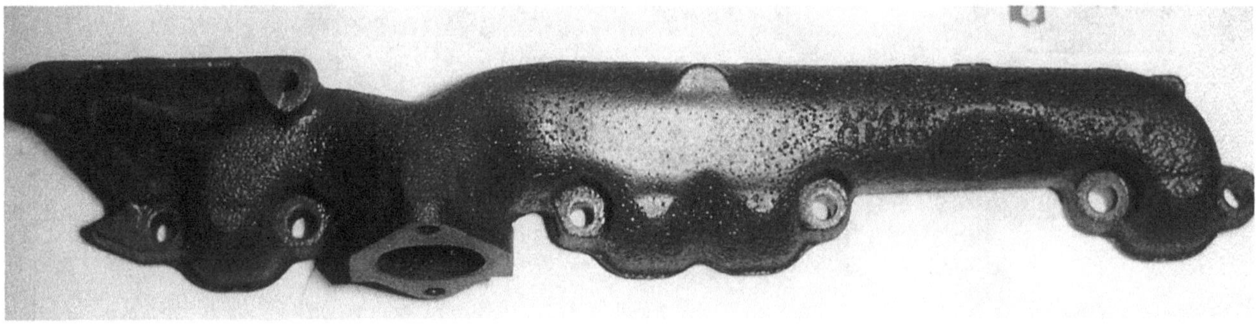

0023199

Fig. 10-4. Frontal view of # 3704791.

Manifold #3704792

Outlet Size	Outlet Side	Year	Model	Engine	Horsepower	Notes
1.81	RH	1955	Passenger	265	162, 180	Casting # above GM trademark
			Corvette	265	195 (1st Design)	

0023198

0023196

Fig. 10-5. Front and rear view of #3704792.

Manifold #3718604

Outlet Size	Outlet Side	Year	Model	Engine	Horsepower	Notes
1.81	RH	1955	Passenger	265	162, 180	This manifold was used on all factory air conditioned passenger cars in 1955 and possibly early 1956.
		1956 (early, unverified)	Passenger	265	162, 205	

0023817/0023818

Fig. 10-6. #3718604 manifold used on factory A/C cars. Note cast holes at end of manifold for mounting compressor bracketing.

Manifold #3725563

Outlet Size	Outlet Side	Year	Model	Engine	Horsepower	Notes
1.74	LH	1956	Corvette	265	225 (1st Design)	Casting # above GM trademark, first "Rams Horn" design released, 2-bolt exhaust flange
	RH	1956	Corvette	265	225 (1st Design)	

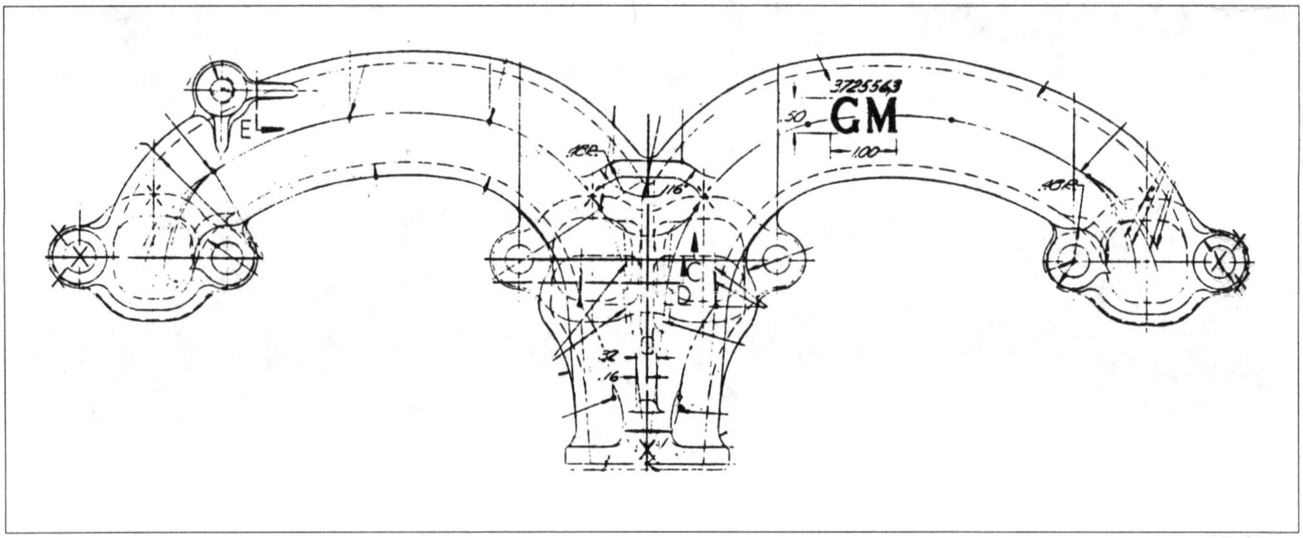

Fig. 10-7. Front view of #3725563.

Manifold #3731557

Outlet Size	Outlet Side	Year	Model	Engine	Horsepower	Notes
1.88	LH	1956	Passenger	265	225, 240 (aft. Feb. 1956)	Casting # in middle of "Rams Horn." Has generator bracket on front of manifold, 3-bolt exhaust flange
			Corvette	265	210, 225, 240 (2nd Design)	

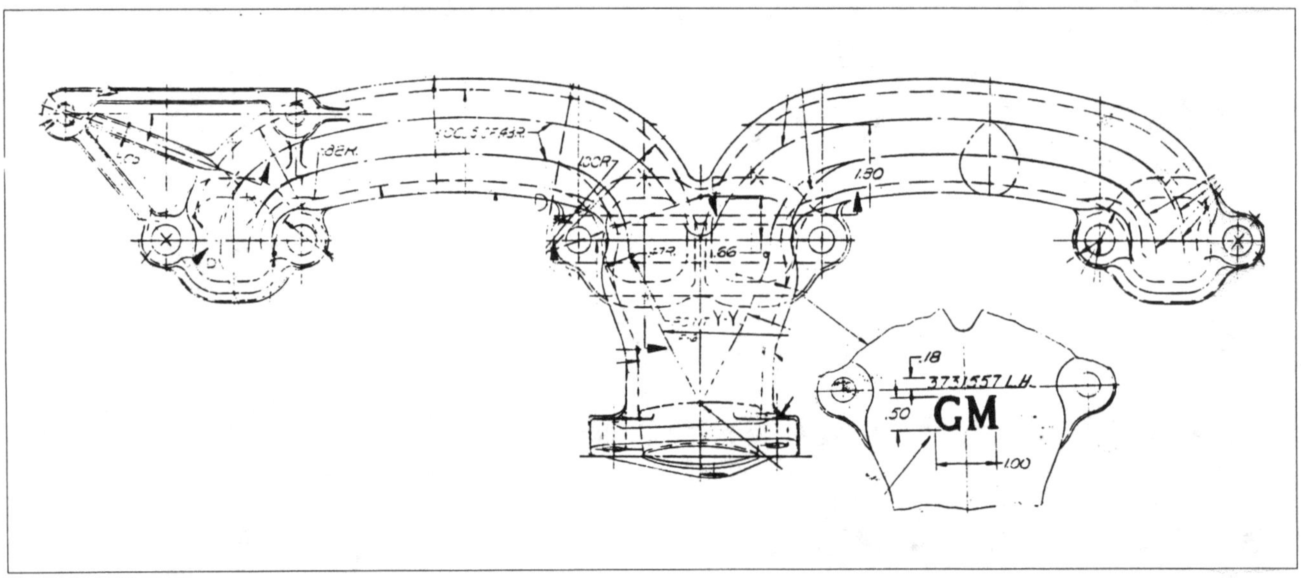

Fig. 10-8. Front view of #3731557.

Manifold #3731558

Outlet Size	Outlet Side	Year	Model	Engine	Horsepower	Notes
1.88	RH	1956	Passenger	265	225, 240 (aft. Feb. 1956)	Casting # in middle of "Rams Horn." Identical with #3731557 except generator bracket is dropped and heat tube boss is present for insertion of heat tube assembly, 3-bolt exhaust flange
			Corvette	265	210, 225, 245 (2nd Design)	

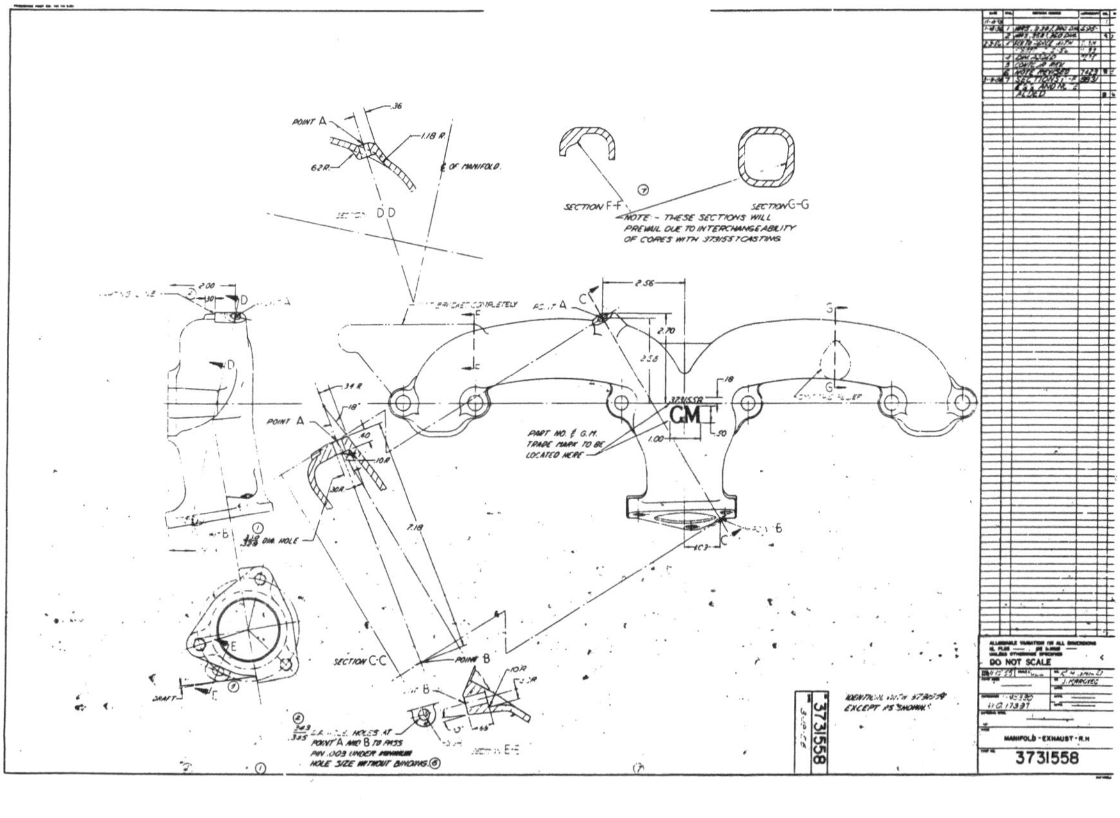

0023183

Fig. 10-9. Blueprint indicates that #3731558 is identical with #3731557 except as shown.

Manifold #3732793$^{\Delta}$

Outlet Size	Outlet Side	Year	Model	Engine	Horsepower	Notes
N/A	LH	1958	Passenger	348	250, 280, 315	$^{\Delta}$This manifold was also used in later years
		1959	Passenger	348	250, 280	

Manifold #3732794$^{\Delta}$

Outlet Size	Outlet Side	Year	Model	Engine	Horsepower	Notes
N/A	RH	1958	Passenger	348	250, 280, 315	$^{\Delta}$This manifold was also used in later years
		1959	Passenger	348	250, 280	

Manifold #3733975

Outlet Size	Outlet Side	Year	Model	Engine	Horsepower	Notes
2.016	LH	1957	Passenger	265	162 (Early)	Casting # on front of manifold face similar to 3731558. Has generator bracket
				283	185, 220 (Late)	
			Corvette	283	220, 245, 250, 270, 283	

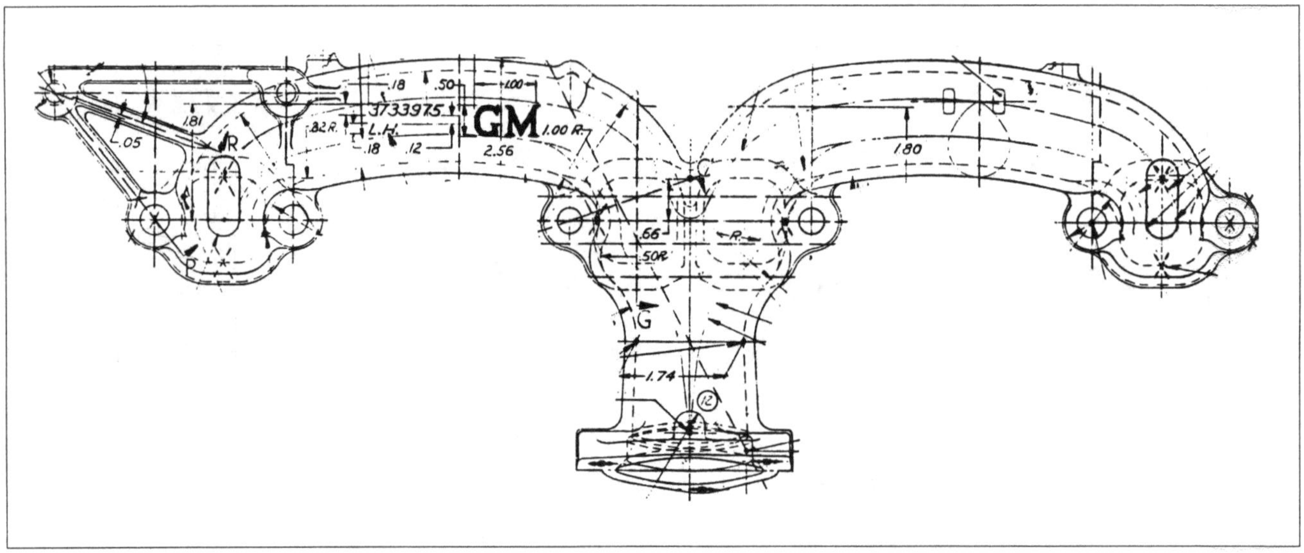

0023184

0023195

Fig. 10-10. Front view of #3733975.

Manifold #3733976(1)

Outlet Size	Outlet Side	Year	Model	Engine	Horsepower	Notes
1.96	RH	1957	Passenger	265	162 (Early)	Casting # on rear of manifold face. Heat tube boss present. No heat tube used on 250 or 283 HP engines
				283	185, 220 (Late)	
			Corvette	283	220, 245, 250, 270, 283	

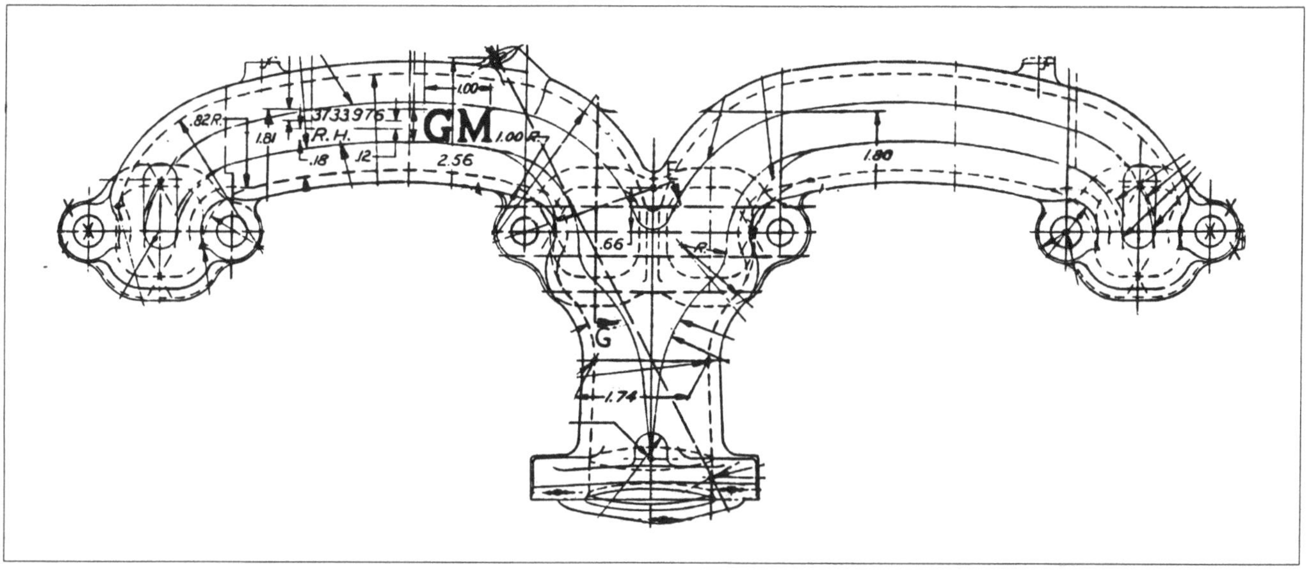

0023185

Fig. 10-11. Front view of #3733976.

Manifold #3733976(2)

Outlet Size	Outlet Side	Year	Model	Engine	Horsepower	Notes
2.016	RH	1957	Passenger	283	270 (2x4)	Manifold drawing released for production 5/23/56. Manifold manufactured from #3733976 casting, identical with #3733976 (1) casting except that this manifold outlet has been increased to a 2.40 diameter. The standard #3733976 manifold had a 1.96 outlet diameter

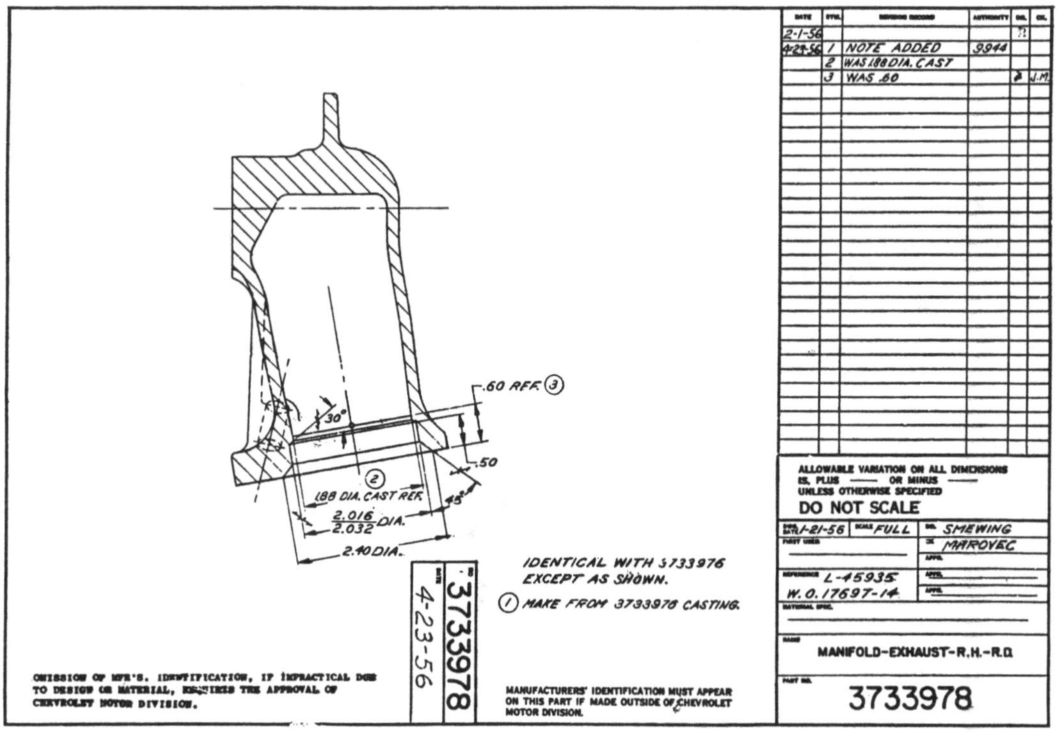

0023186

Fig. 10-12. Blueprint shows that #3733978 is identical with #3733976 except as shown. It also emphasizes the different machining process for this high performance application.

Manifold #3747038$^{\Delta}$

Outlet Size	Outlet Side	Year	Model	Engine	Horsepower	Notes
1.96	RH	1958	Passenger	283	185, 230, 250, 290	Manifold similar to #3733976. "Rams Horn" design, straight outlet, heat tube $^{\Delta}$This manifold was also used in later years
		1959	Passenger	283	185, 230, 250, 290 w/o A/C	

0023191

Fig. 10-13. Front view of #3747038.

Manifold #3749965$^{\Delta}$

Outlet Size	Outlet Side	Year	Model	Engine	Horsepower	Notes
2.026	LH	1958	Passenger	283	185, 230, 250, 290	Straight Outlet. "Rams Horn" Design
			Corvette	283	230, 245, 250, 270, 290	
		1959	Passenger	283	185, 230, 250, 290	
			Corvette	283	230, 245, 250, 270, 290	$^{\Delta}$This manifold was also used in later years

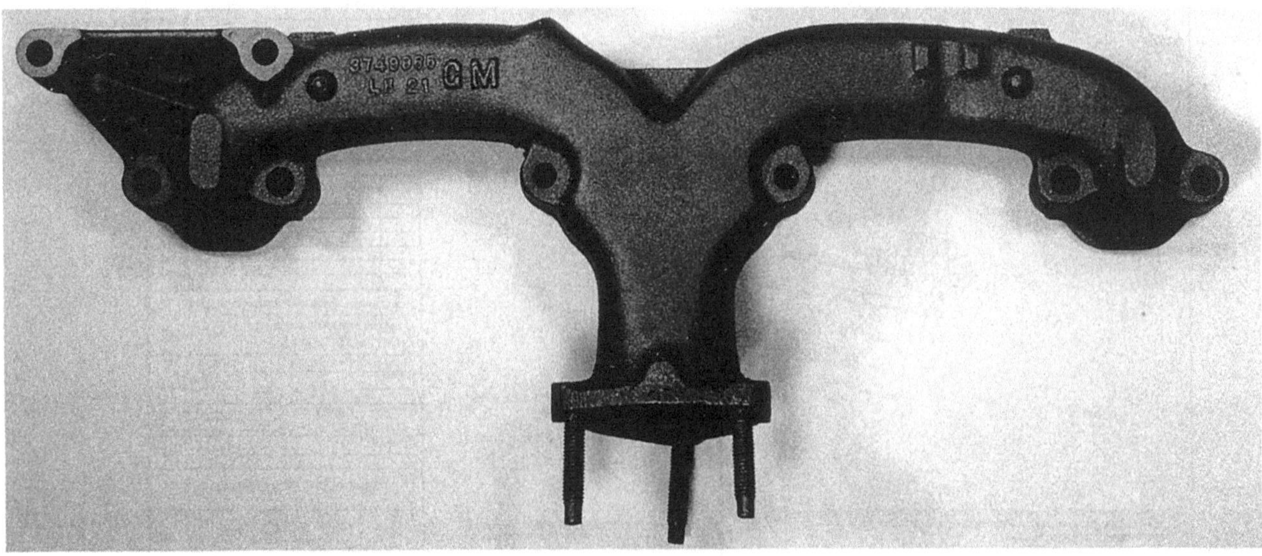

0023192

Fig. 10-14. Front view of #3749965.

Manifold #3750556^Δ

Outlet Size	Outlet Side	Year	Model	Engine	Horsepower	Notes
1.96	RH	1958	Corvette	283	230, 245, 250, 270, 290	Manifold identical with #3747042 except that generator mounting bracket is added. "Rams Horn" design, straight outlet, heat tube, A/C boss ^ΔThis manifold was also used in later years
		1959	Passenger	283	185, 230 with A/C	
		1959	Corvette	283	230, 245, 250, 270, 290	

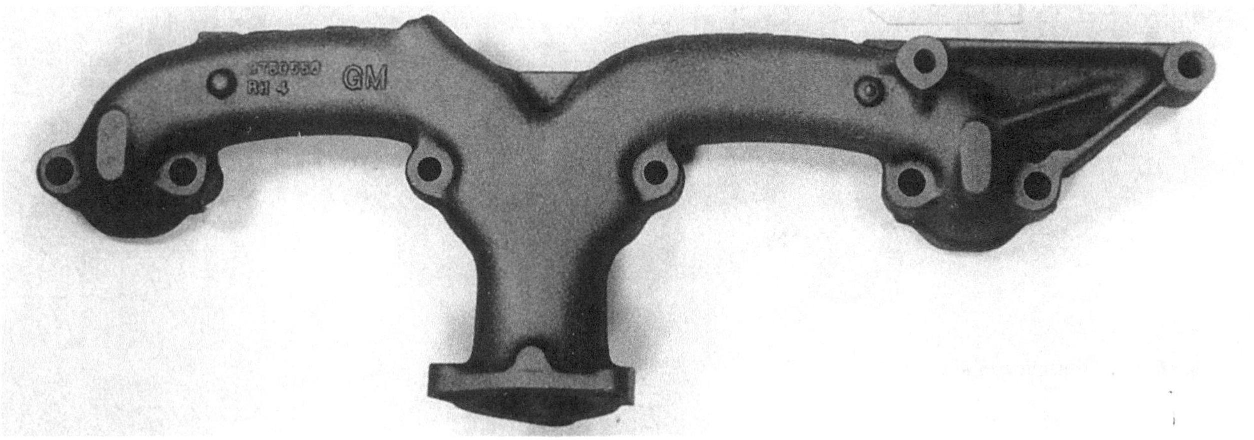

0023193

Fig. 10-15. Front view of #3750556.

Manifold #3767583^Δ

Outlet Size	Outlet Side	Year	Model	Engine	Horsepower	Notes
N/A	LH	1959	Passenger	348	305, 315, 320, 335	^ΔThis manifold was also used in later years

Manifold #3767584^Δ

Outlet Size	Outlet Side	Year	Model	Engine	Horsepower	Notes
N/A	RH	1959	Passenger	348	305, 315, 320, 335	^ΔThis manifold was also used in later years

Manifold #3836968

Outlet Size	Outlet Side	Year	Model	Engine	Horsepower	Notes
1.81	RH	1955	Corvette	265	195 (2nd Design, unverified)	Manifold identical to #3837069, except that generator boss has been omitted
		1956	Passenger	265	162, 170, 205	

0023194

Fig. 10-16. Front view of #3836968.

Manifold #3837069

Outlet Size	Outlet Side	Year	Model	Engine	Horsepower	Notes
N/A	LH	1955	Corvette	265	195 (2nd Design, unverified)	
		1956	Passenger	265	162, 170, 205	

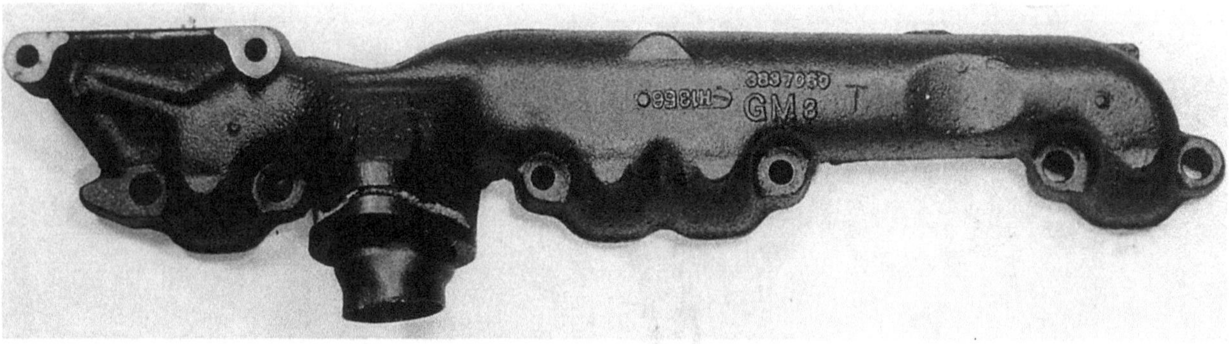

0023190

Fig. 10-17. Front view of #3837069.

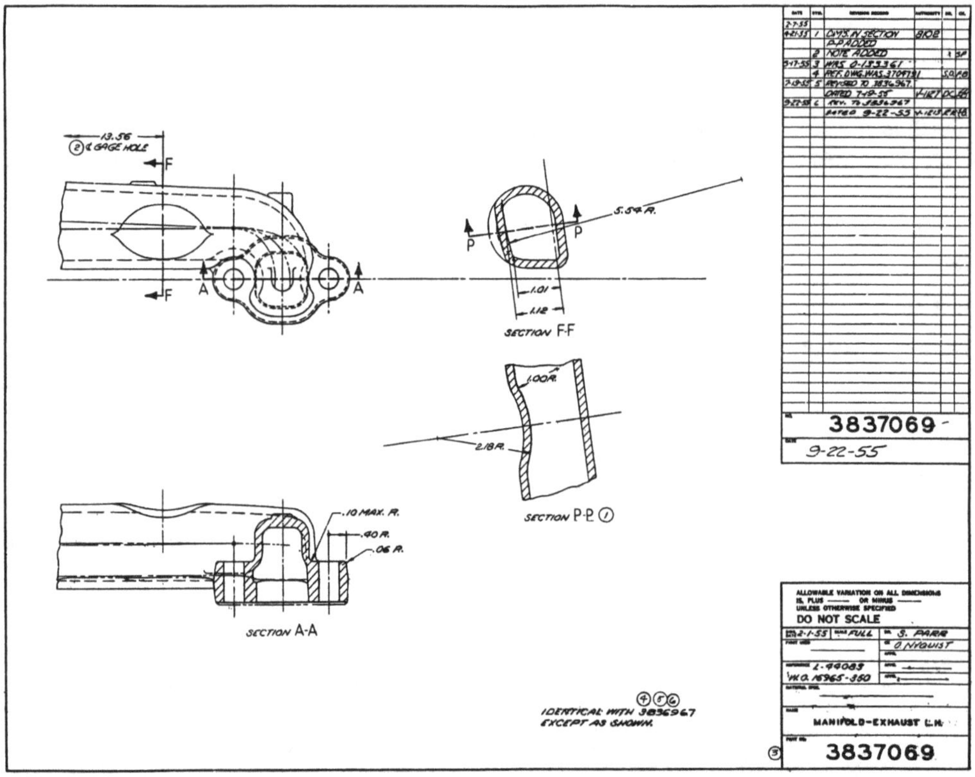

0023188

Fig. 10-18. Blueprint indicates that #3837069 is identical with #3836967 except as shown.

Chapter 11
Water Pump Identification

1. Introduction

There is great difficulty in assigning the absolute correct applications of water pumps installed on Chevrolet cars from 1955 through 1959. One reason lies simply in the great variety of water pump configurations used. A second reason is that water pumps with the same design were often produced concurrently by different manufacturers, but with different casting numbers. The last and most puzzling piece of the applications puzzle is due to water pump rebuilders who altered original design features to enable a manufacturer to use a water pump on additional applications. On top of all this, water pumps are an often-replaced part. The water pump on any particular engine is as likely as not to be a replacement part, so you can see how the problem of researching and validating original casting numbers to specific models and years is very difficult. It should be noted that original 1955–60 water pumps had a flat plate on the backside of the pump which was secured by six slotted pan-head screws,

There were two distinct water pump designs used on the cars covered by this book, the first from Flint, Michigan, and the second from Tonawanda, New York. From a restoration viewpoint, you should know that Flint engines were supplied with Flint water pumps and Tonawanda engines with Tonawanda pumps. The design differences between the two pumps are very easy to spot and can be a good indicator of a incorrectly restored engine.

The first difference is that Tonawanda water pumps have external ribs or ridges, while Flint water pumps do not. See Fig. 11-1. Also note that Tonawanda pumps have a cast "T" on them, and that on Tonawanda water pumps the casting date is visible when the pump is installed on the engine. On Flint pumps the casting date (if applicable) cannot be seen with the pump installed.

All cars covered by this book use a "short leg" water pump. In the following text and casting number break-

0023819

Fig. 11-1. *Tonawanda water pump (top) compared to Flint water pump (bottom). Note lack of ribs on Flint pump. On Tonawanda pump also note cast "T".*

0023821

Fig. 11-2. *Close-up of casting date on Tonawanda water pumps. Date reads E 20 60 (May 20, 1960).*

downs, please realize that this is a very reliable, but probably not perfect, chapter. Because of the complexity of this chapter, each specific engine family is listed separately and the verified casting numbers are listed chronologically.

1.1 Date Coding

Many of the early water pumps covered in this book do not carry a casting date. Please refer to the specific features given and the chart below to identify the pump you are searching for. Where dating of water pumps is known, it is noted in the application table. (Truck water pumps have dates and can be identified by the two reinforcement webs on the pump.)

Where casting date codes are present, they follow the same pattern as engine blocks, but some do not carry the year. The month code is always a letter, followed by a number signifying the day. The last number signifies the year of production.W-block water pumps (as well as big-block pumps beginning in 1970) used a two-digit year code.

Water Pump Month Codes (1st Letter)

A - January	E - May	I - September
B - February	F - June	J - October
C - March	G - July	K - November
D - April	H - August	L - December

Example: Date code B 18 9 (Flint small block)

- B = Month: February
- 18 = Casting date: 18th
- 9 = Calendar Year: 1959 (refer to casting number charts to confirm)

Example: Date code B 18 59 (Tonawanda small block and W-block)

- B = Month: February
- 18 = Casting date: 18th
- 59 = Calendar Year: 1959

Pump #3704911

Year	Application	Engine	Horsepower
1955*	Passenger	265	162, 180
	Corvette	265	195
1956**	Passenger	265	162, 170, 205, 225, 240
	Corvette	265	210, 225, 240
Note: The only difference between Tonawanda and Flint #3704911 pumps is the cast "T" on Tonawanda pumps.			
*No 1955 pumps have a boss. **Has flat boss on top of pump. No dates			

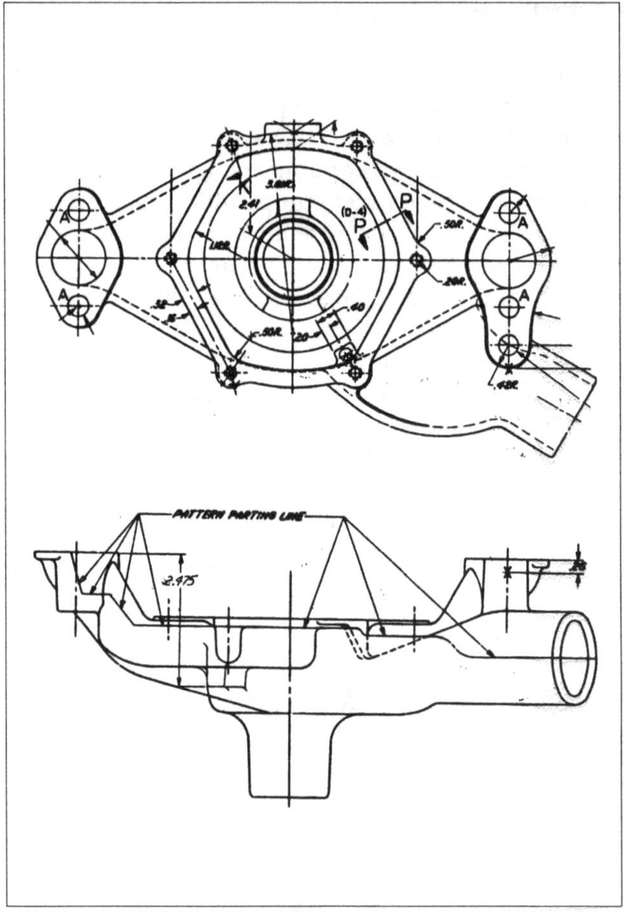

0023200

Fig. 11-3. Rear and top view of #3704911 water pump.

2. SMALL BLOCK WATER PUMPS

Small block Chevrolet engines used the "short leg" water pump on passenger cars through 1968, and on all Corvettes. Along with casting number changes through the years, there were also design changes due to the addition or deletion of accessory brackets. Note that a casting number water pump overlap has not been verified.

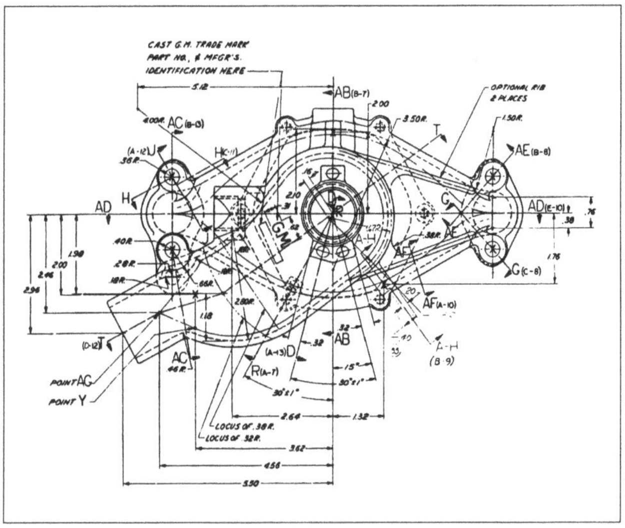

0023201

Fig. 11-4. Front view of #3704911 water pump.

Pump #3736493$^{\Delta}$

Year	Application	Engine	Horsepower
1957	Passenger	265	162 (w/flat boss on top of pump)
		283	185, 220, 245, 250, 270, 283
	Corvette*	283	220, 245, 250, 270, 283
1958	Passenger	283	185, 230, 250, 290
	Corvette*	283	230, 245, 250, 270, 290
1959	Passenger	283	185, 230, 250, 290
	Corvette*	283	230, 245, 250, 270, 290
This was the first Tonawanda water pump that had "ribs", and differed from Flint pumps in this way. Later pumps followed the same pattern.			
*Uses special Corvette front engine mounting bracket. $^{\Delta}$This pump was also used in 1960. No dates			

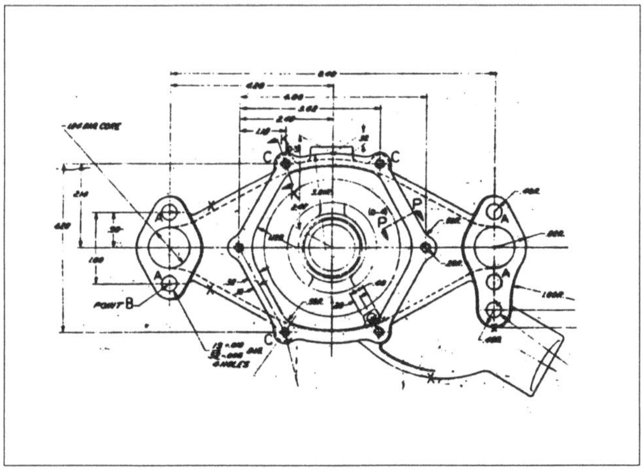

0022190

Fig. 11-5. Rear view of #3736493 water pump.

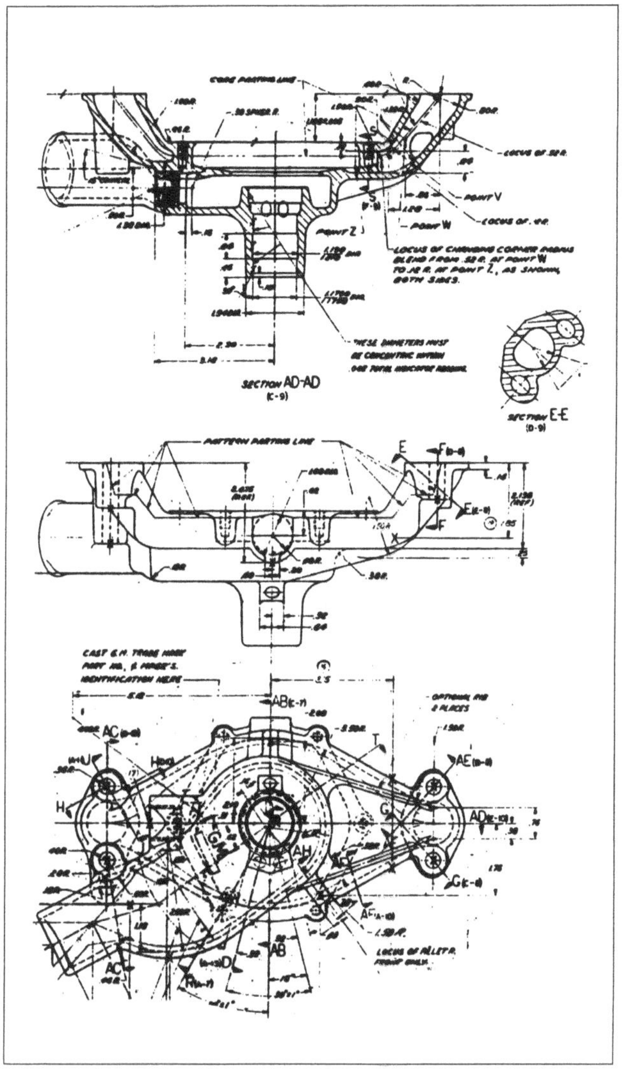

0022189

Fig. 11-6. Front and side view of #3736493 water pump.

3. 348/409 (W-BLOCK) WATER PUMPS

The 348/409 water pumps are basically all the same unit. In its first design in 1958, the 348 was initially built without a bypass hose to the intake manifold. Later in 1958, the water pump was drilled and tapped for use with a bypass hose. The #3755797 water pump was also used on the 1961 through early 1964 409 engines. In late 1964, the water pump casting number changed to #3850145 and continued through the 1965 model year. The 1963 Z11 427/430HP race engine also had a specific aluminum water pump. The actual changes to each water pump are being researched at this time, but the casting number breakdown is correct to date.

Pump #3732750

Year	Application	Engine	Horsepower
1958	Passenger	348	250, 280, 315 (Early) (w/o bypass)
All dated			

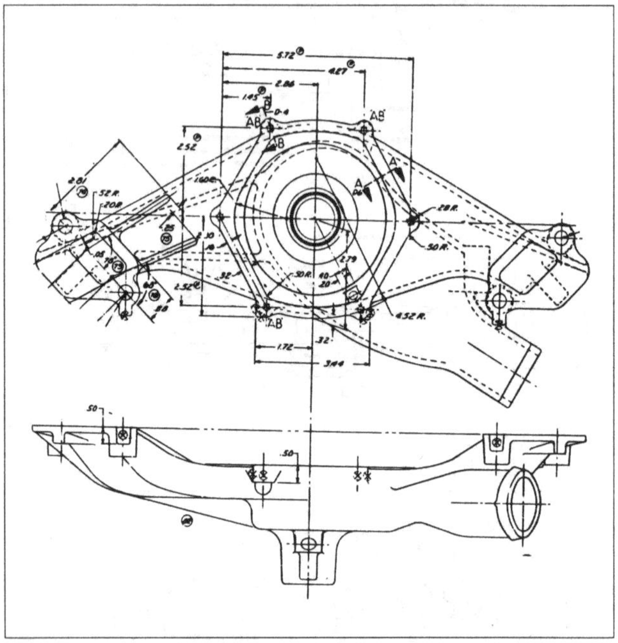

0023203

Fig. 11-7. Rear view of water pump #3732750.

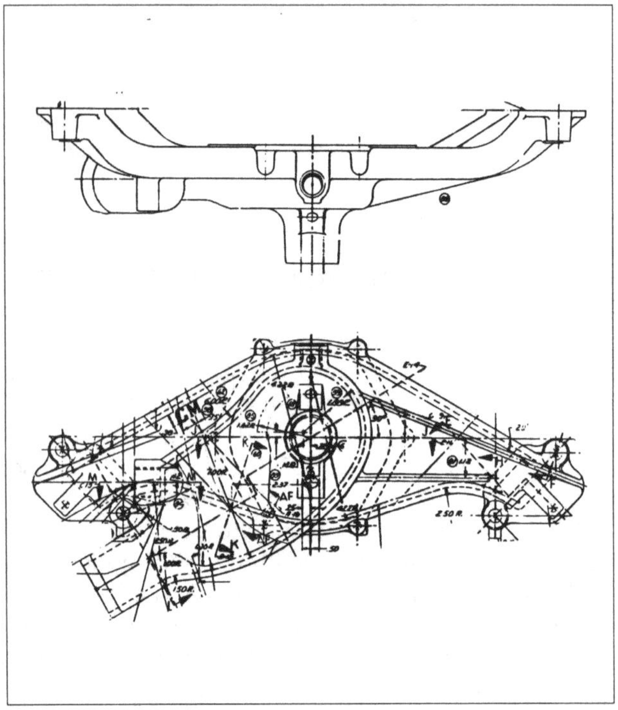

0023202

Fig. 11-8. Top and front view of #3732750 water pump.

Pump #3755797[Δ]

Year	Application	Engine	Horsepower
1958	Passenger	348	250, 280, 315 (Late) (w/bypass)
1959	Passenger	348	250, 280, 305, 315, 320, 335
ΔThis pump was also used in 1960–64. Some dated			

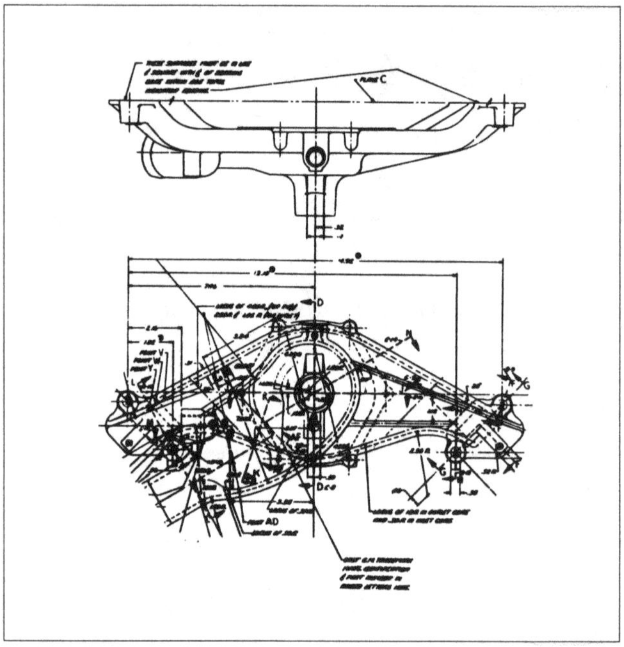

0022197

Fig. 11-9. Top and front view of #3755797 water pump.

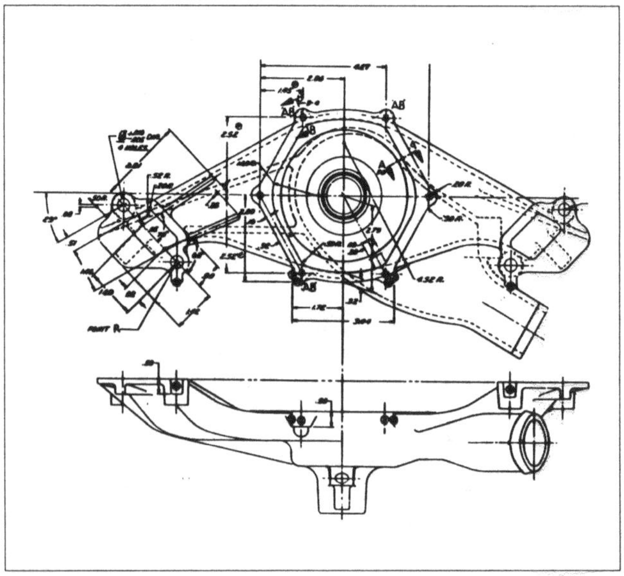

0022198

Fig. 11-10. Rear and side view of view of #3755797.

Chapter 12
Distributor Identification

1. Introduction

All Chevrolet distributors from 1955 through 1959 were manufactured by the Delco-Remy Division of General Motors in Anderson, Indiana. There were two plants involved in producing ignition components at Delco-Remy:

- Plant #10: All conventional (point-type) distributors and ignition coils
- Plant #6: All ignition amplifiers and capacitor discharge ignition systems

There are several different distributor component combinations that were used from 1955 through 1959. All distributors were of cast iron construction until 1962 when the die-cast aluminum 4- and 6-cylinder models were released. There were "Bowl" and "Non-Bowl" distributors produced in both aluminum and cast iron configurations. Early distributors had an external oiler tube for routine lubrication. There were also "Bowl" type cast iron units which had special two-piece housings with dual-point breakers inside the distributor.

0023211

Fig. 12-2. Typical V-8 distributor installation (1959).

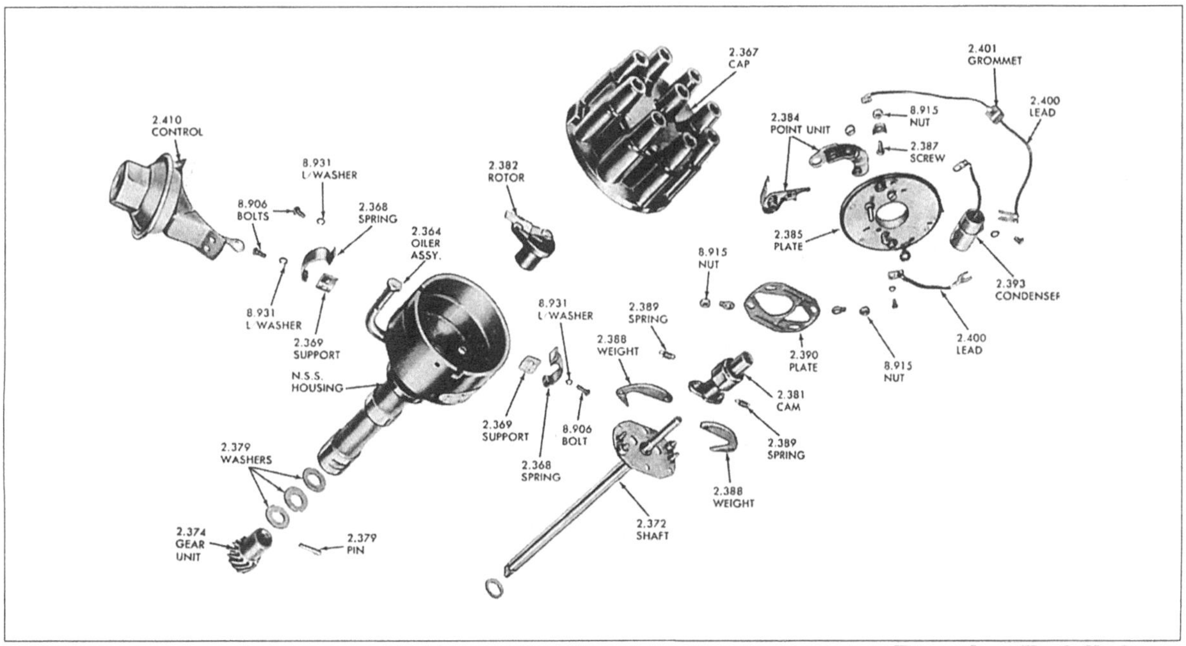

Fig. 12-1. Exploded view of 1955-56 8-Cylinder distributor.

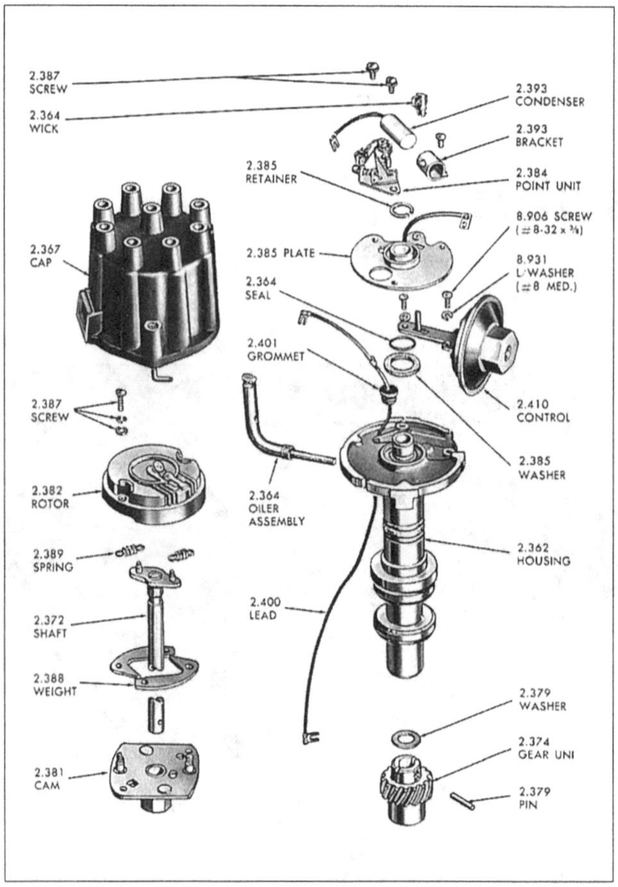

0023209

Fig. 12-3. *Exploded view of 1957–64 8-Cylinder ignition distributor.*

Due to the immense combinations that are possible, please see the distributor application list for your specific application.

1.1 Distributor Codes

All Delco-Remy distributors have a model number and a date code system either stamped or attached to the distributor. There are four basic locations in which this information can be found, which will vary from distributor to distributor.

On all 1955–56 distributors, the model number is found on an oval Delco-Remy tag, which is riveted to the outside of the distributor housing.

In the 1957 model year the identification process began to change. From 1957 through 1974 all cast iron non dual-point distributors used a small aluminum band, which wrapped around the top of the distributor. (See later Fig. 12-14.)

All 1957 through 1961 dual-point distributors used the oval Delco-Remy riveted tag. This band was imprinted with the model number and production date.

Fuel injection distributors from 1957 to mid-1958 used a Delco tag identical to other distributors. Starting in mid-1958, the fuel injection distributor was redesigned and was produced with a square tag which was held to the main distributor housing by four screws.

Late model aluminum distributor housings have the model number roll stamped right into the exterior of the housing with no attaching tag of any kind.

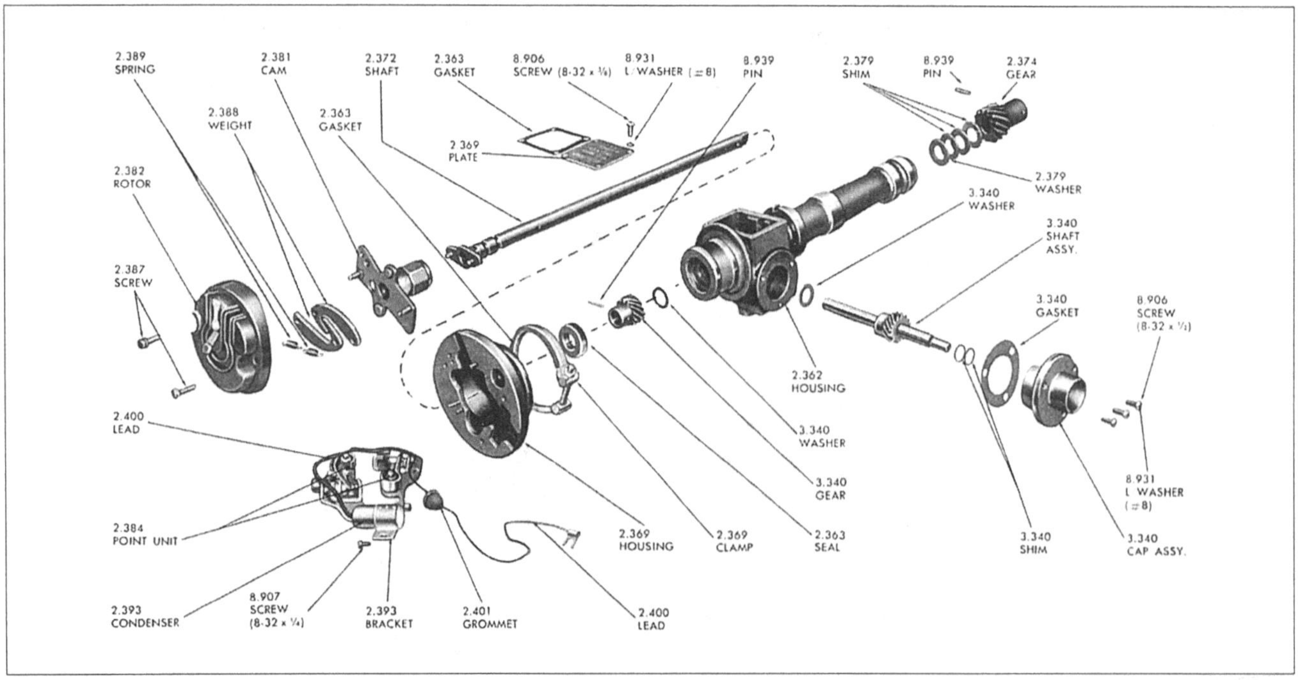

0023210

Fig. 12-4. *Exploded view of 1957-62 fuel injection ignition distributor.*

0022216

Fig. 12-5. ID number plate used on the external face of distributor housing, in this case #1110847. Date code reads 4-M-17 (1954, December, 17th day)

Date Code Deciphering

All Chevrolet distributors use the same date code style. The Julian code system is used as with many other Chevrolet parts. The actual build date is signified by a series of numbers and letters. Example: 5A28.

The date code is deciphered as follows: The first digit gives the calendar year of production. This is the last digit of the calendar year, 1955 in the example above. To determine the actual decade of manufacture, it is necessary to inspect the distributor for common features used during that time period. Please refer to the Distributor Application charts. The second letter indicates the month of production. See the table below for month codes. ("I" was not used because it is too easily confused with the number 1.) The final two digits indicate the day of the month of production (1 through 31). The code 5A28 therefore decodes as January 28, 1955.

Distributor Month Codes (2nd Letter)

A - January	E - May	J - September
B - February	F - June	K - October
C - March	G - July	L - November
D - April	H - August	M - December

Distributor Color Coding

Most distributors installed at a final engine assembly plant had a color code applied to the distributor housing. This was to enable engine assemblers to identify a distributor without reading the code number. In time, many of these paint marks wore off. Most Delco Remy blueprints call out these color codes as paint spots.

2. DISTRIBUTOR APPLICATIONS

The charts on the following pages list the distributor applications for 1955 through 1959. All distributors are in numerical order within each model listing. Each distributor is listed by model and engine application, and then further distinguished by housing type, point type and other features. Be sure to check the model years before and after your car to check for other uses. The abbreviations used in the charts are listed below.

Housing Type Designations

A: Aluminum housing distributor
AE: Aluminum external adjustment distributor
CB: Cast iron bowl distributor
CE: Cast iron external adjustment distributor
2: Two-piece housing

Point Type Designations

D: Dual-point distributor
S: Single point distributor

Letter Designations

BB: Ball bearing equipped distributor
CL: Cam lubricator mounted on breaker plate
CO: Copper standpipe oiler
EO: Engine oil lubrication distributor
FI: Fuel injection distributor
FT: Fuel injection distributor with tach drive
NV: No vacuum advance
PL: Permanent lubrication
SO: Standpipe oiler (standard)
TD: Tach drive/flexible cable drive
V: Vacuum advance

1955 Distributor Applications

Model	Distributor Number	Engine/HP/Application	Housing	Point	Notes
Passenger	1110847*	265/162, 180HP All	CB	S	SO/V
Corvette	1110855*	265/195HP All	CB	S	SO/V
Canada Passenger	1110847	265/162, 180HP All	CB	S	SO/V
*The primary difference between the #1110847 and the #1110855 was that most of the early '855 distributors did not have a vacuum advance boss but instead had centrifugal weights inside.					

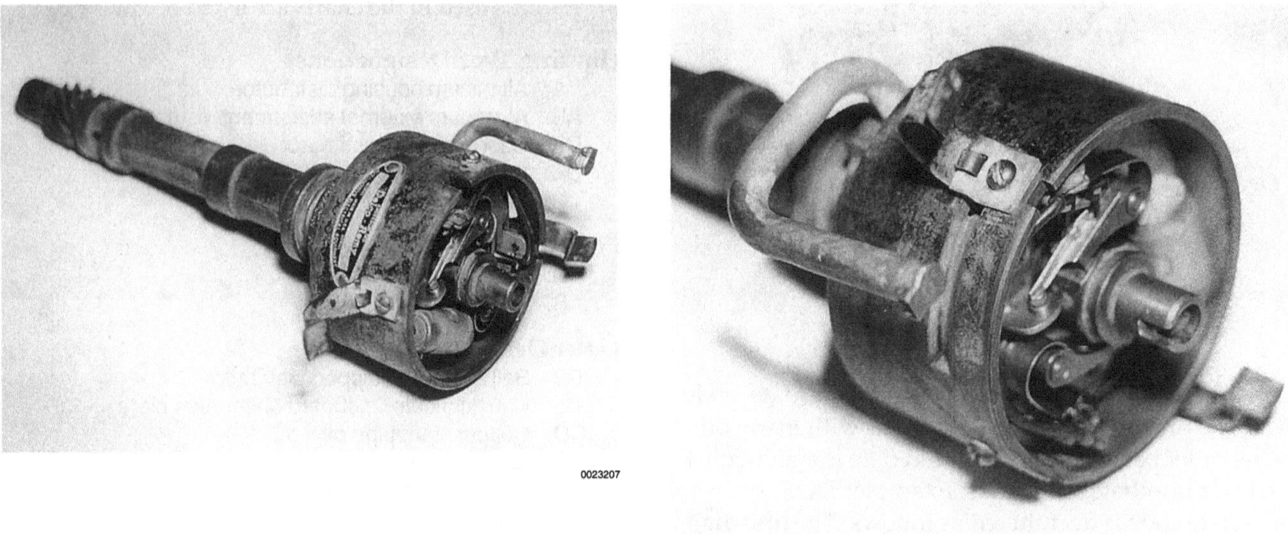

0023207 0023206

Fig. 12-6. Overall view of distributor #1110847. While the housing is correct for the above applications, the close-up of the distributor shows that a dual point breaker plate has been installed, which is incorrect. This is what can happen to older distributors. All original 1110847s have a single-point breaker system from Delco Remy. This is a perfect example of how using only the model number to identify a distributor can lead to a mistake.

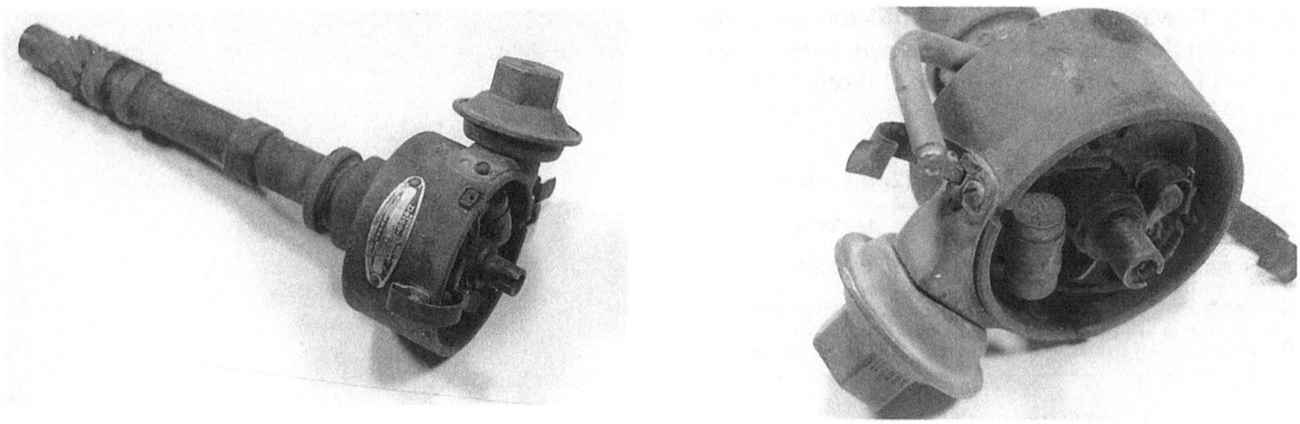

0023822/0023823

Fig. 12-7. Original, untouched early #1110847 distributor with correct early #1116085 vacuum advance. Note single point in distributor bowl.

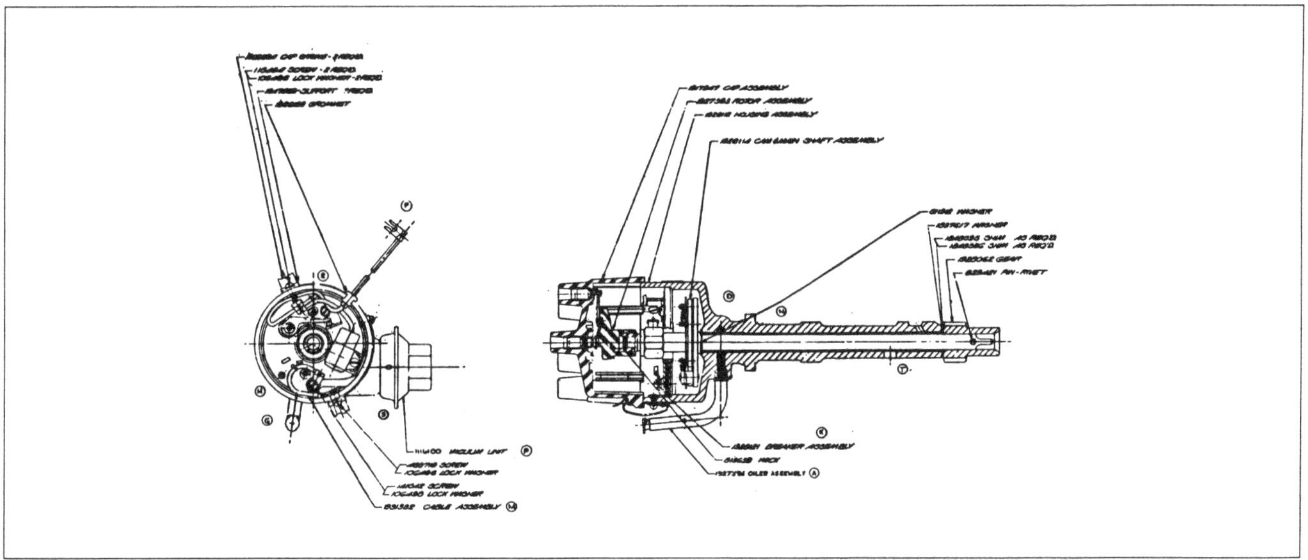

0023212

Fig. 12-8. Blueprint of #1110847 shows that original design of distributor was for single point breaker.

1956 Distributor Applications

Model	Distributor Number	Engine/HP/Application	Housing	Point	Notes
Passenger	1110847	265/162HP S/T	CB	S	SO/V
	1110866	265/162, 170HP A/T	CB	S	SO/V
	1110869	265/205HP All	B	S	SO/V
	1110872	265/225HP (2 X 4 Carb) early			
	1110879	265/225, 240HP (2 x 4 Carb) late	CB	D	NV/SO
Corvette	1110872	265/210, 225, 240HP*	CB	D	NV/SO
	1110879	265/210, 225, 240HP	CB	D	NV/SO
Canada Passenger	1110847	265/162, 205, 225HP All S/T	CB	S	SO/V
	1110866	265/162, 170, 205HP All A/T	CB	S	SO/V

*All early engines prior to May 11, 1956, probably received this distributor. Delco-Remy production records show that 2218 #1110872 distributors were shipped for production and four went to service in the 1956 calendar year.

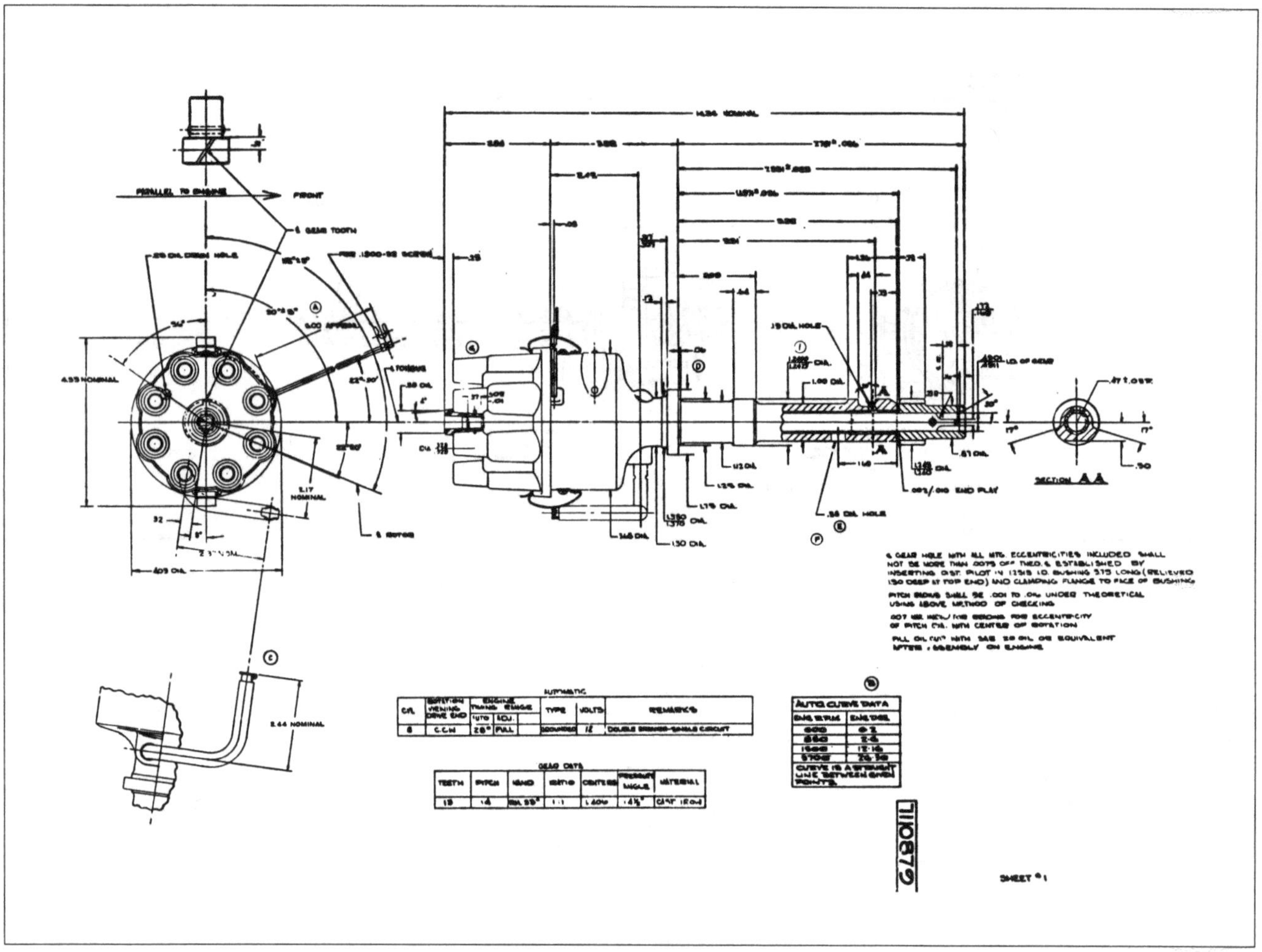

0023213

Fig. 12-9. A typical cast iron bowl distributor of which this particular #1110879 is a dual-point type.

1957 Distributor Applications

Model	Distributor Number	Engine/HP/Application	Housing	Point	Notes
Passenger	1110874	265/162HP, 283/185HP	CE	S	CL/SO/V
	1110889	283/250, 283 HP (before Jan. 1957)	CB/2	D	BB/EO/FI/NV
	1110890	283/220HP	CE	S	CL/SO/V
	1110891	283/245, 270HP (2 x 4 Carb)	CB	D	NV/SO
	1110905	283/250, 283 HP (aft. Jan. 1957)	CB/2	D	BB/EO/FI/NV/PL
	1110906	283/250HP (Late)	CB/2	S	BB/EO/FI/PL/V
	1110908	283/283 HP (Mid to Late) NASCAR	CB/2	D	BB/EO/FT/NV/PL/TD
Corvette	1110889	283/250, 283HP (Early) w/4360 FI unit	CB/2	D	BB/EO/FI/NV
	1110891	283/220, 245, 270HP	CB	D	NV/SO
	1110905	283/250, 283 HP (Mid to End), man. trans., w/4360, 4520, 4800, 4960 FI units; 283/250HP (Mid to Late), Powerglide	CB/2	D	BB/EO/FI/NV/PL
	1110906	283/250HP (Late), Powerglide, w/4520, 4800 FI units	CB/2	S	BB/EO/FI/PL/V
	1110908	283/283HP (Late), some w/4960 FI units; Mid to End RPO 579E	CB/2	D	BB/EO/FT/NV/PL/TD
Canada Passenger	1110874	265/162HP; 283/185HP	CE	S	CL/SO/V
	1110890	283/220HP All	CE	S	CL/SO/V

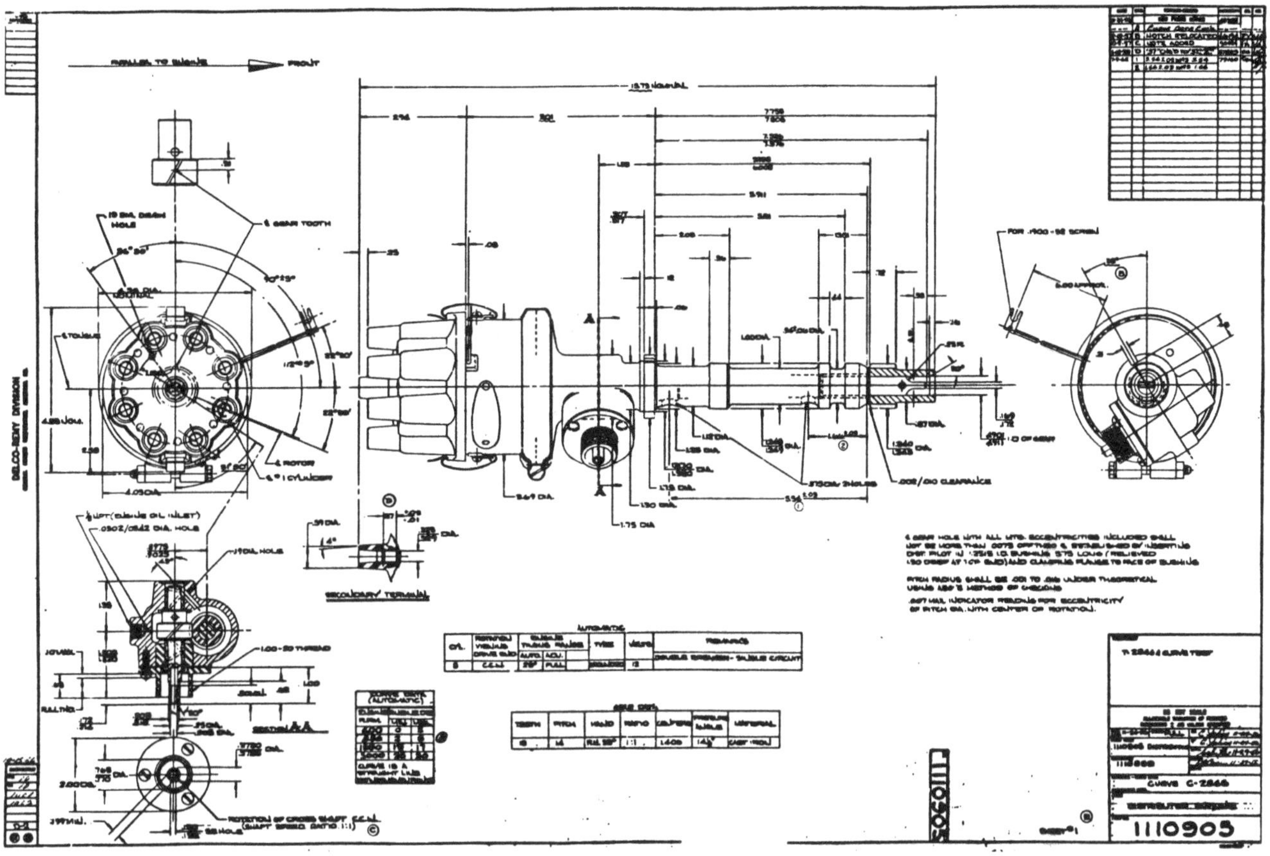

0023215

Fig. 12-10. Blueprint shows a typical two-piece cast iron bowl distributor of which this #1110905 is a dual-point type.

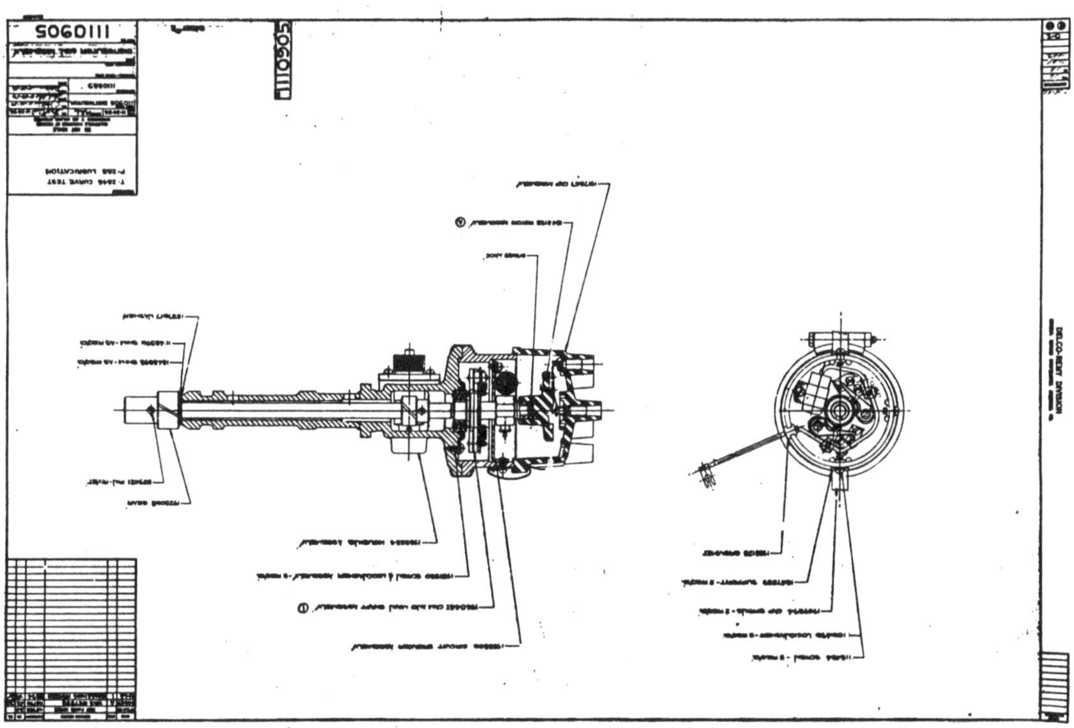

0023216

Fig. 12-11. Another view of #1110905. Note ball carrier (arrow) at top of distributor shaft.

0023204

Fig. 12-12. *A low HP 1958–61 distributor for fuel injection. Note single drive for fuel meter only. Tach was driven from generator. Also note hex type vacuum advance. Most "915" distributors are dated late 1957.*

1958 Distributer Applications

Model	Distributor Number	Engine/HP/Application	Housing	Point	Notes
Passenger	1110890	283/230HP All	CE	S	CL/SO/V
	1110907	348/250, 280, 315HP 1st Design	CE	S	SO/V
	1110915	283/290HP	CE/2	S	FI/SO/V
	1110920	283/185HP All	CE	S	CL/V
	1110927	348/250, 280, 315 2nd Design	CE	S	CL/SO/V
	1110930	348/250, 280, 315 3rd Design	CE	S	CO/V
Corvette	1110890	283/230HP All	CE	S	CL/SO/V
	1110891	283/245, 270HP All	CB	D	NV/SO
	1110906	283/250HP All (Early)	CB/2	S	BB/EO/FI/PL/V
	1110908	283/290 HP (Early) (Unverified)*	CB/2	D	BB/EO/FT/NV/PL/TD
	1110914	283/290 HP	CE/2	D	EO/FT/NV/TD
	1110915	283/250 HP All (Late)	CE/2	S	FI/SO/V
Canada Passenger	1110890	283/230HP All	CE	S	CL/S0/V
	1110920	283/185HP All	CE	S	CL/SO/V
	1110927	348/250, 280, 315 All	CE	S	CL/SO/V

*Delco-Remy records show that no #1110908 distributors were built for production for the 1958 calendar year.

1959 Distributor Applications

Model	Distributor Number	Engine/HP/Application	Housing	Point	Notes
Passenger	1110914	283/290HP All	CE/2	D	EO/FT/NV
	1110915	283/250HP All	CE/2	S	FI/SO/V
	1110919	348/305, 315, 320*, 335HP* w/Manual	CE	D	NV/SO
	1110946	283/230HP; 348/250HP	CE	S	CL/SO/V
	1110947	283/185HP All	CE	S	CL/SO/V
	1110948	348/280, 305, 315, 320*, 335HP* 348/305HP w/Powerglide (Late)	CE	S	CO/SO/V
Corvette	1110891	283/245, 270HP	CB	D	NV/SO
	1110914	283/290 HP	CE/2	D	EO/FT/NV/TD
	1110915	283/250HP All	CE/2	S	FI/SO/V
	1110946	283/230HP All	CE	S	CL/SO/V
Canada Passenger	1110946	283/230HP All	CE	S	CL/SO/V
	1110947	283/185HP All	CE	S	CL/SO/V
	1110948	348/280, 305, 315, 320*, 335HP*	CE	S	CL/SO/V
*Late Production					

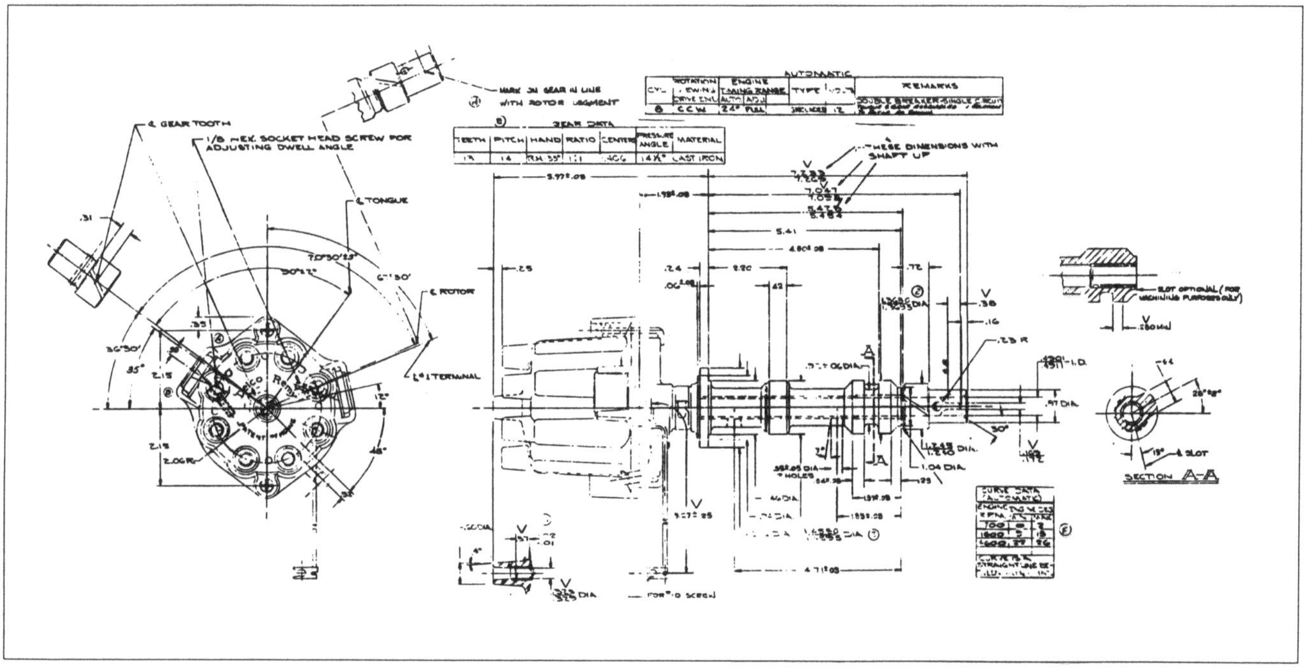

0023920

Fig. 12-13. Original Delco-Remy drawing shows the dimensions used to manufacture the #1110919 distributor.

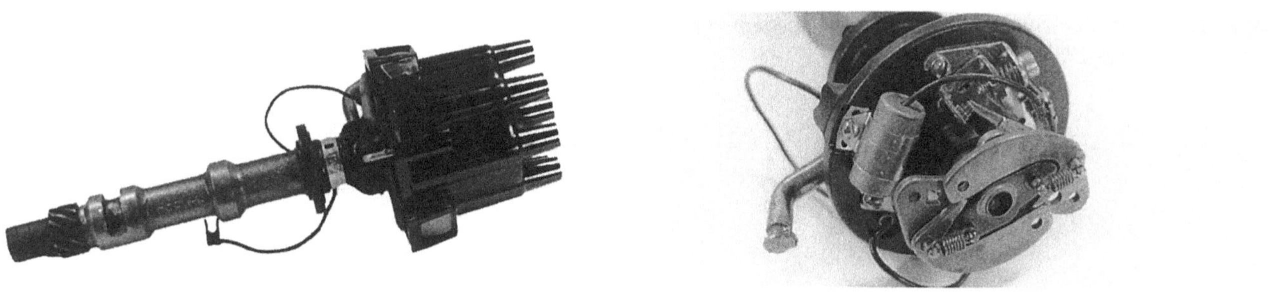

0022277 0022278

Fig. 12-14. Cast iron bowl external adjustment distributor #1110919. This particular model was used on all 348 engines (excluding the 250HP). It is unique in that it has dual windows in the distributor cap to set the points externally and in that it uses no vacuum advance.

3. DISTRIBUTOR VACUUM UNITS

Almost all distributors used a vacuum advance unit. Up until recently, all data pertaining to original vacuum unit applications had to be gleaned from Delco-Remy Parts Replacement Sheets, which only gave the current replacement vacuum unit. The following vacuum unit numbers were taken directly from the original Delco-Remy distributor blueprints.

Vacuum Unit Decoding

The vacuum unit usually has two sets of numbers stamped into the flat of the mounting bracket.

The first two-digits letter code signifies the original manufacturer for the vacuum unit.

The first three numbers usually refer to the last three numbers of the Delco- Remy part number. Occasionally, a vacuum unit will be stamped with a different number for reasons currently unknown. One example of this is the 1968861 unit, which is stamped "400."

The final two digits represent the number of crankshaft degrees of advance built into the vacuum unit. Typically the units are rated at 10, 15, or 20 degrees of advance.

Many vacuum units were used on a variety of distributors. There were often two or three units used on the same distributor over its usage period. This is reflected in the applications listed below.

Fig. 12-15. *Vacuum unit style used on 6-cylinders for the years 1955–57.*

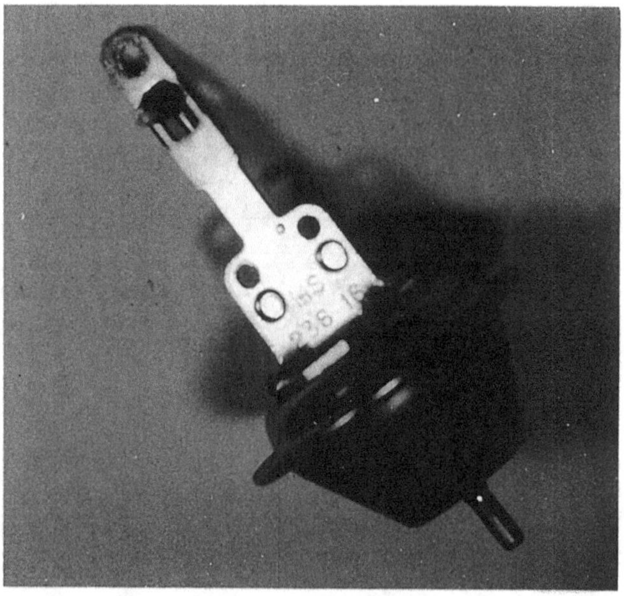

0022225

Fig. 12-16. *Typical vacuum unit style used from 1958-on on V-8 applications. Note letters and numbers stamped into flat portion of the advance arm. (Unit shown is #1116236, first used on 1964 models.)*

Distributor/Vacuum Unit Applications

Distributor	Vacuum Unit
1110847	1116085 early, 1116100 late
1110855	1116085/1116104 after 3/18/55
1110866	1116100
1110869	1116104
1110872	None
1110874	1116108
1110879	None
1110889	None
1110890	1116118
1110891	None
1110905	None
1110906	1116125
1110907	1116133
1110908	None
1110914	None
1110915	1116134
1110919	None
1110920	1116118
1110927	1116133
1110930	1116133
1110946	1116148
1110947	1116163
1110948	1116148

Chapter 13

Camshaft Identification

1. Introduction

The camshaft is the one part of the internal combustion engine which has the most bearing on how that engine will operate. The basic function of the camshaft is to control the timing, the length, the speed, and the height of the intake and exhaust valve openings inside the cylinder head. The camshaft in all Chevrolet engines is located within its own bearing chamber below the cylinder head face and above the oil pan rails. There have been some minor changes in rear camshaft bearing face design, but for the most part the camshaft has remained the same from 1955–75. It is important to verify which type of block, rear bearing face and camshaft bearing you need before you invest in a camshaft.

All 1955 and 1956 265 engines were produced with a grooved rear camshaft bearing. All 1957 265 and 283 engines were produced with the same type of "annular" groove behind the rear camshaft bearing. All small blocks produced after 1957 did not have a grooved rear cam bearing. Earlier grooved camshafts can be used in later model blocks, but not vice-versa. This same situation exists on the later big block Chevrolet engine as well. All 348 and 409 engines have the grooved camshaft rear journal.

Chevrolet always includes clearance ramps in their valve timing specifications for hydraulic camshafts. The clearance ramp is actually the portion of the camshaft which gradually takes up the clearance or lash of the valve train. It begins the acceleration of the lifter on the opening side and slows the lifter on the closing side until the valve is seated. Since this distance is quite a bit longer than the actual valve timing event, the actual valve timing is much milder than the theoretical timing specs and, consequently, is not the camshaft's actual valve timing. See Fig. 13-2.

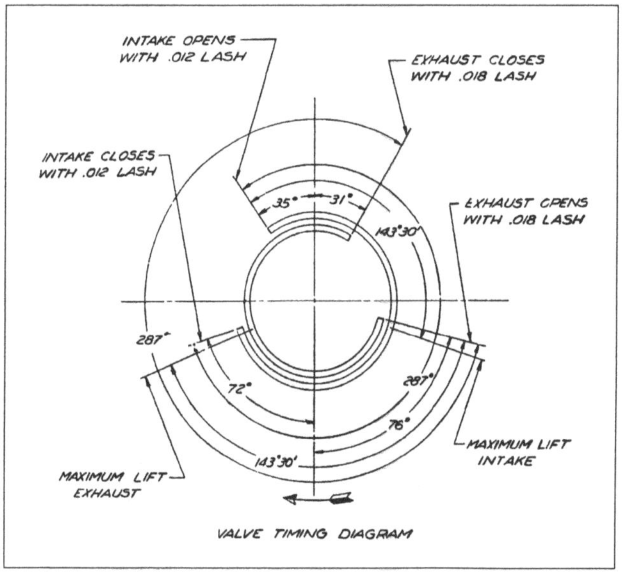

Fig. 13-2. Portion of blueprint of camshaft #3734078 illustrates how cam timing specifications are relative to opening and closing ramps on camshaft lobes.

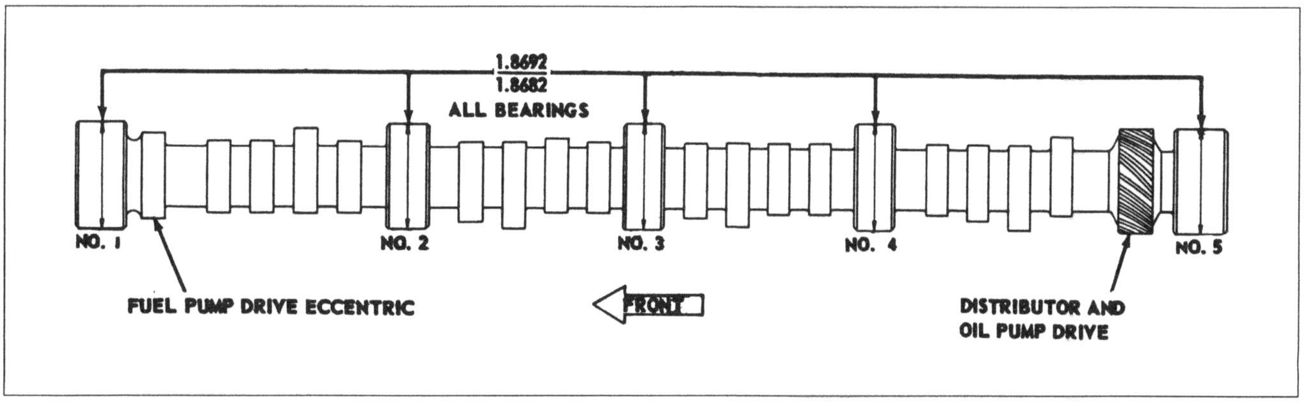

Fig. 13-1. Typical 8-cylinder camshaft.

2. Camshaft Identification Chart

All of the following cam specifications are listed at "0" lash setting. This is done to avoid confusion of comparing original Chevrolet camshaft figures and actual specifications. Also note that in the *Lifter* column, "H" stands for Hydraulic and "M" stands for mechanical. The column named *Casting Symbol* relates to the symbols cast into many of the camshafts. Fig. 13-3 shows the specifications for one of these symbols.

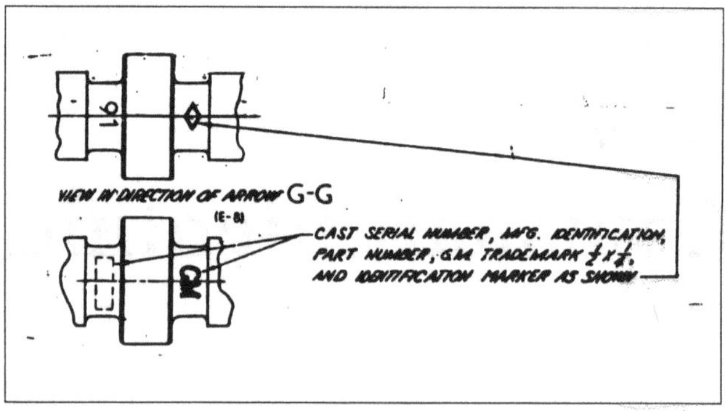

0022291

Fig. 13-3. Detail of blueprint for camshaft shows casting letters, casting symbol, and GM trademark information.

1955 Camshaft Identification

Engine	Horsepower	Lifter	Intake Lift	Exhaust Lift	Intake Duration	Exhaust Duration	Rocker Ratio	Part Number	Casting Number	Casting Symbol
265	162, 180 Powerglide	H	.334	.334	302	302	1.50	3704212	3703906	(2) Zeros
265	162, 180 Manual	M	.336	.343	246	246	1.50	3836700	3836686	None
265	195	M	.404	.413	264	266	1.50	3711354	3711355	(3) Zeros

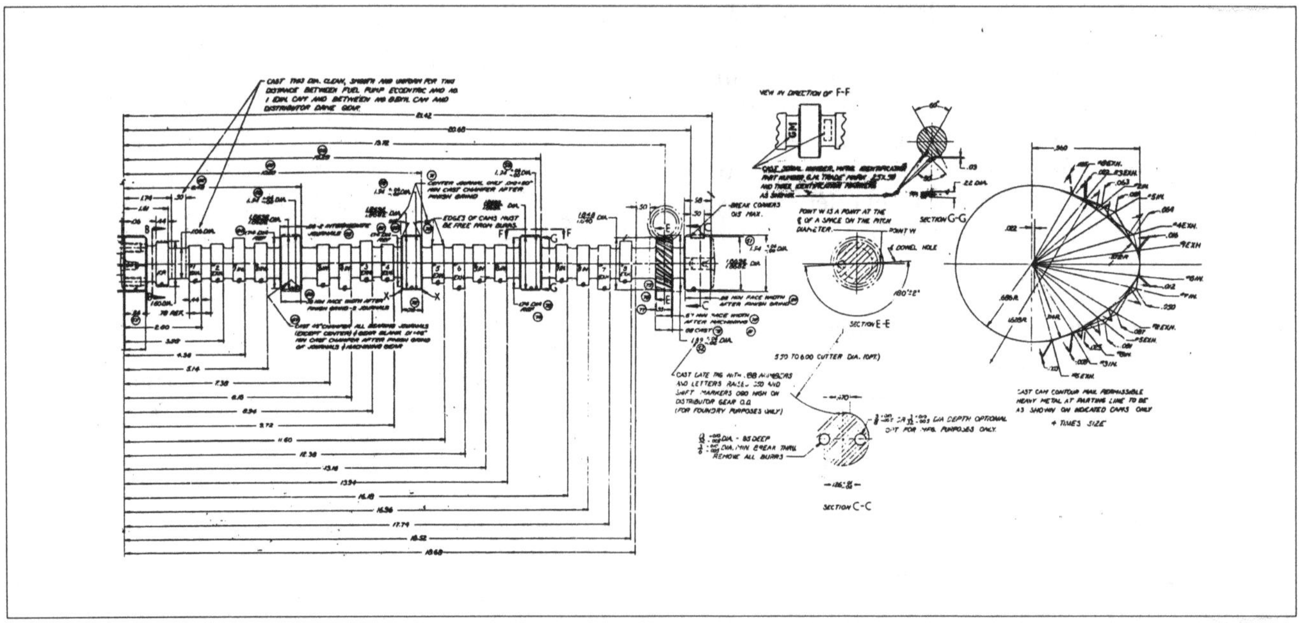

0023218

Fig. 13-4. Blueprint of camshaft #3711355.

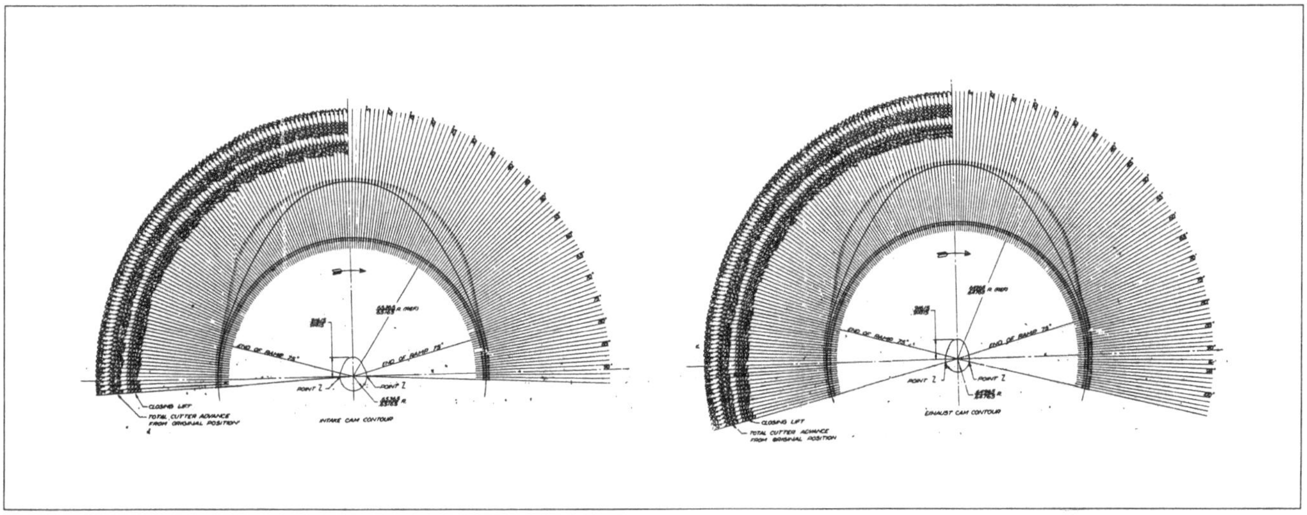

0023219

Fig. 13-5. Blueprint of camshaft #3734078 shows changes from #3711355.

1956 Camshaft Identification

Engine	Horsepower	Lifter	Intake Lift	Exhaust Lift	Intake Duration	Exhaust Duration	Rocker Ratio	Part Number	Casting Number	Casting Symbol
265	162, 205	H	.334	.334	302	302	1.50	3704212	3703906	(2) Zeros
265	170	H	.373	.373	270	270	1.50	3728779	3728284	Horizontal Rectangle
265	210, 225	M	.404	.413	264	266	1.50	3711354	3711355	(3) Zeros
265	240	M	.404	.413	287	287	1.50	3734077	3734078	(2) Squares

1957 Camshaft Identification

Engine	Horsepower	Lifter	Intake Lift	Exhaust Lift	Intake Duration	Exhaust Duration	Rocker Ratio	Part Number	Casting Number	Casting Symbol
265	162	H	.334	.334	302	302	1.50	3704212	3703906 or 3836862	(2) Zeros
283	185, 220, 245, 250	H	.398	.398	300	300	1.50	3733431	3732798	(3) Zeros
283	270, 283*	M	.394	.400	287	287	1.50	3736097	3736098	(2) Squares
*This is the introduction of the famous "Duntov" camshaft										

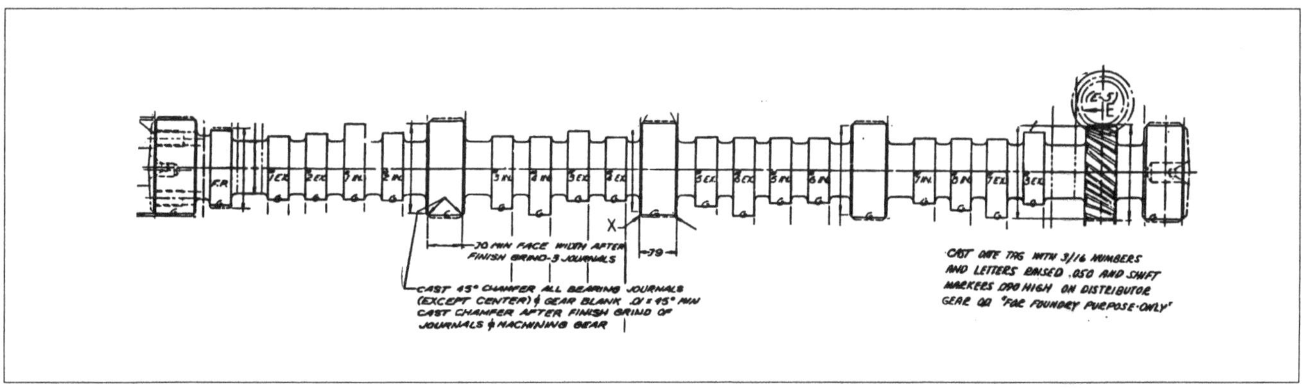

0023220

Fig. 13-6. Blueprint of "Duntov" camshaft #3736098.

1958 Camshaft Identification

Engine	Horsepower	Lifter	Intake Lift	Exhaust Lift	Intake Duration	Exhaust Duration	Rocker Ratio	Part Number	Casting Number	Casting Symbol
283	185, 230, 245, 250	H	.398	.398	300	300	1.50	3733431	3732798	(3) Zeros
283	270, 283, 290	M	.394	.400	287	287	1.50	3736097	3736098	(2) Squares
348	250, 280	H	.400	.412	266	274	1.75	3744901	3744430	Plus Sign (+)
348	315	M	.405	.412	287	287	1.75	3755946	3755947	Vertical rectangle on four sides

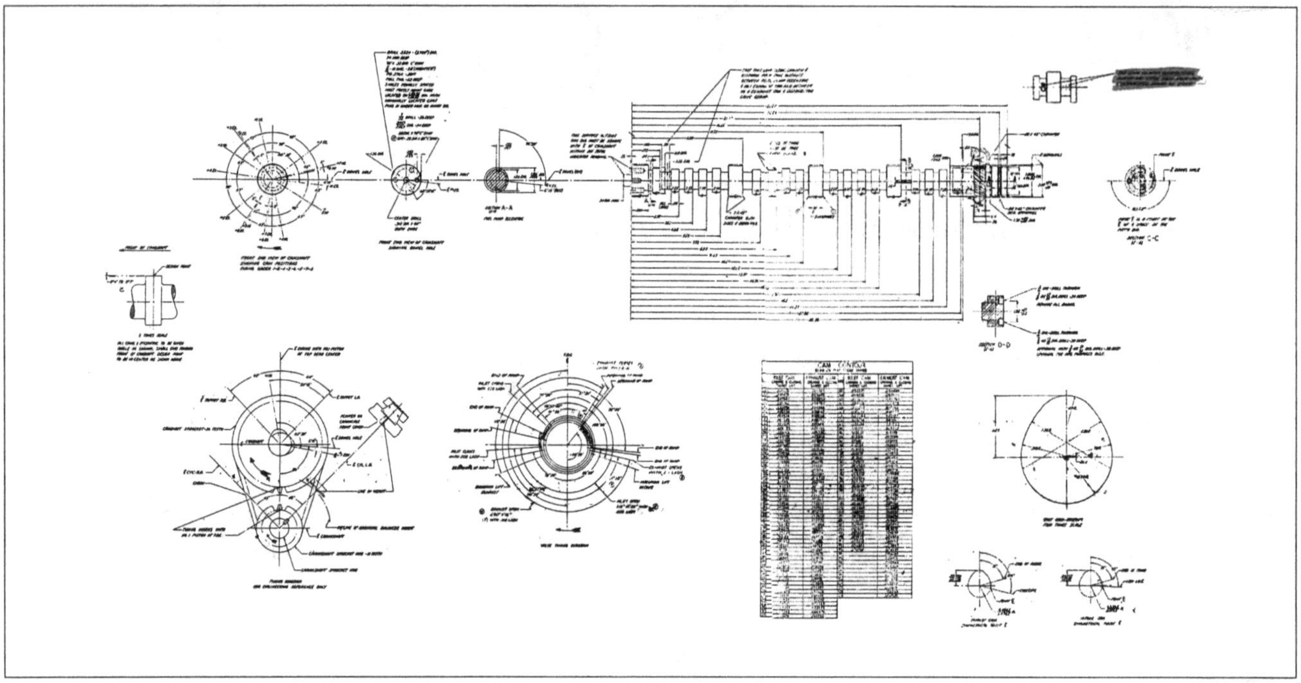

0023221

Fig. 13-7. Blueprint of camshaft #3755947. Note grooved rear journal as discussed in text.

1959 Camshaft Identification

Engine	Horsepower	Lifter	Intake Lift	Exhaust Lift	Intake Duration	Exhaust Duration	Rocker Ratio	Part Number	Casting Number	Casting Symbol
283	185, 230, 245, 250	H	.398	.398	300	300	1.50	3733431	3732798	(3) Zeros
283	270, 290	M	.394	.400	287	287	1.50	3736097	3736098	(2) Squares
348	250, 280	H	.400	.412	266	274	1.75	3744901	3744430	Plus Sign (+)
348	305	M	.407	.414	287	287	1.75	3764664	3764665	Horizontal rectangle on four sides
348	315, 320, 335	M	.405	.412	287	287	1.75	3755946	3755947	Vertical rectangle on four sides

CHEVROLET—CENTRAL OFFICE
DIVISION OF GENERAL MOTORS CORPORATION
DETROIT 2, MICHIGAN

TECHNICAL SERVICE BULLETIN
Service and Mechanical Department

SUBJECT: SERVICE SPECIFICATIONS
315 HP TURNPIKE CRUISER ENGINE
"348" 3 x 2 CARB. HI LIFT CAM

BULLETIN No. DR #362
SECTION VI

TO: ALL CHEVROLET DEALERS

June 12, 1958

Service carburetor and tune-up specifications for the 348 - 3 x 2 carburetor Hi-Lift camshaft equipped Turnpike Cruiser Engine are basically the same as for the standard camshaft "348" - 3 x 2 carburetor engine.

Complete specifications for the "348" - 3 x 2 standard camshaft engine are outlined in the May issue of the Service News.

The following items will apply only to the Hi Lift cam equipped Turnpike Cruiser Engine.

Valve Lash Adjustment *

Inlet	.012"
Exhaust	.018"

* Engine normalized.

Valve Timing

Inlet Opens	- 35° BTDC
Inlet Closes	- 72° ABDC
Exhaust Opens	- 76° BBDC
Exhaust Closes	- 31° ATDC

0023225

Fig. 13-8. *This Chevrolet Technical Service Bulletin gives specifications for 348/315HP valve lash adjustment and valve timing.*

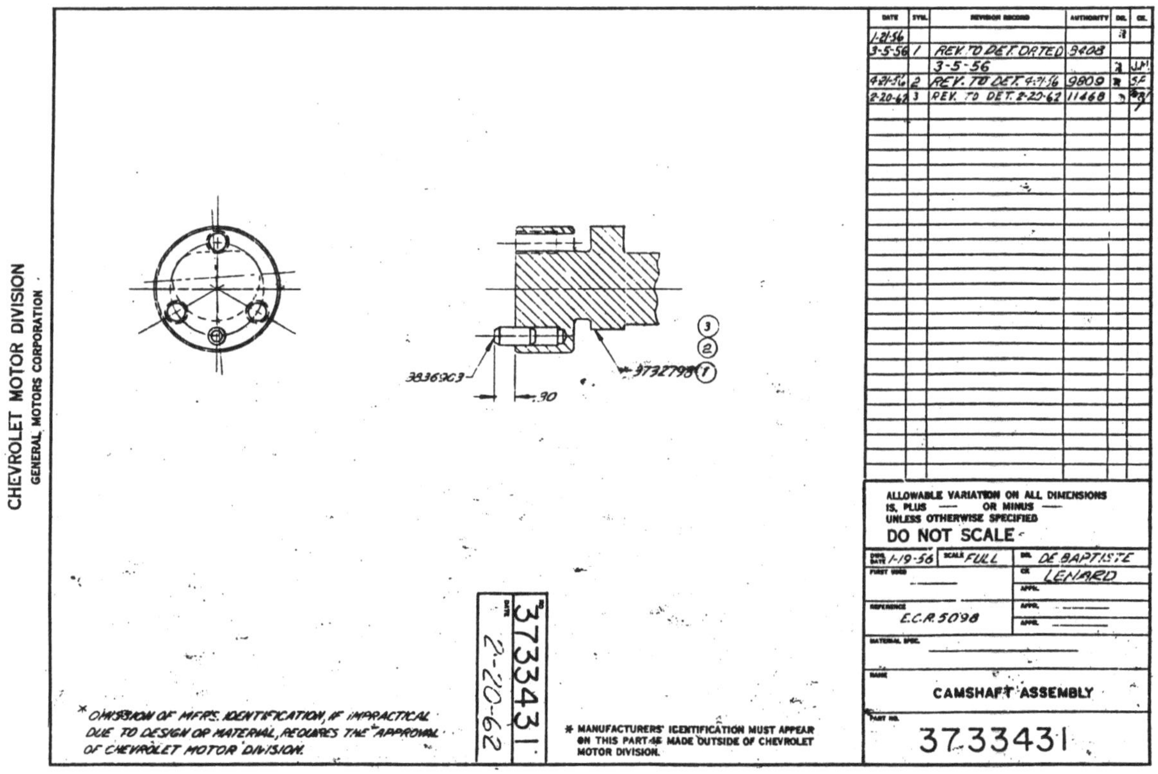

0023222

Fig. 13-9. *Blueprint of camshaft #3733431.*

Chapter 14
Generator Identification

1. Introduction

This chapter covers 1955 through 1959 generator model numbers. From 1955 to 1962, Chevrolet used 12-volt generators for most applications. Special applications and 6-volt generators are listed separately. From the 1963 model year on, alternators were used on most Chevrolet vehicles. (Corvairs used generators through the 1964 model year.)

Generator model numbers are located on a riveted tag attached to the generator housing. Black tags are 6-volt; red tags are 12-volt. Also on the tag above the "serial" is the date of manufacture of that generator.

The date code is deciphered as follows: The first digit gives the calendar year of production. This is the last digit of the calendar year. The following letter indicates the month of production. See the table below for month codes. The final two digits indicate the day of the month of production (1 through 31). For example, the code 6J22 decodes as September 22, 1956.

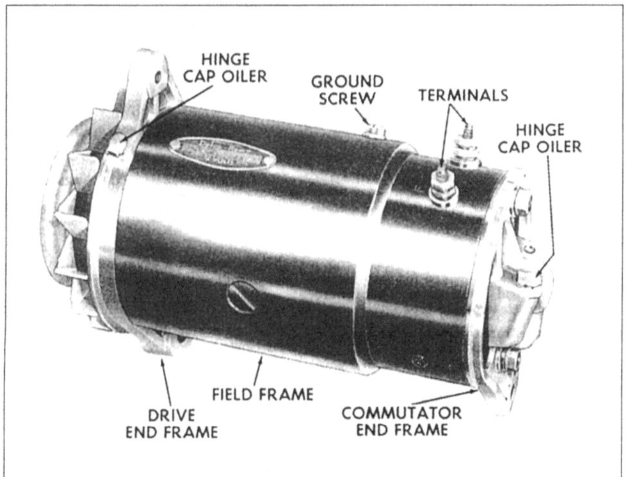

Fig. 14-1. *Overall view of typical D.C. generator. This generator was used on all cars from 1955 through 1962, except for Chevrolet passenger cars with air conditioning.*

Generator Month Codes (2nd Letter)

A - January	E - May	J - September
B - February	F - June	K - October
C - March	G - July	L - November
D - April	H - August	M - December

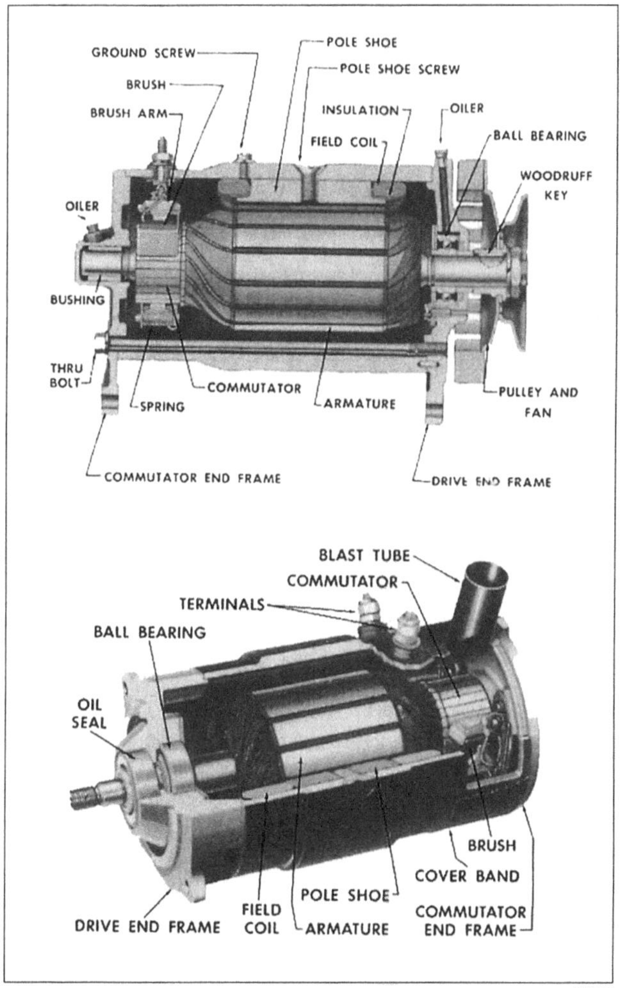

Fig. 14-2. *Cross-sectional view of typical 4-5/8" frame diameter generator (top). Bottom view shows typical 4-5/8" generator with provision for forced air cooling.*

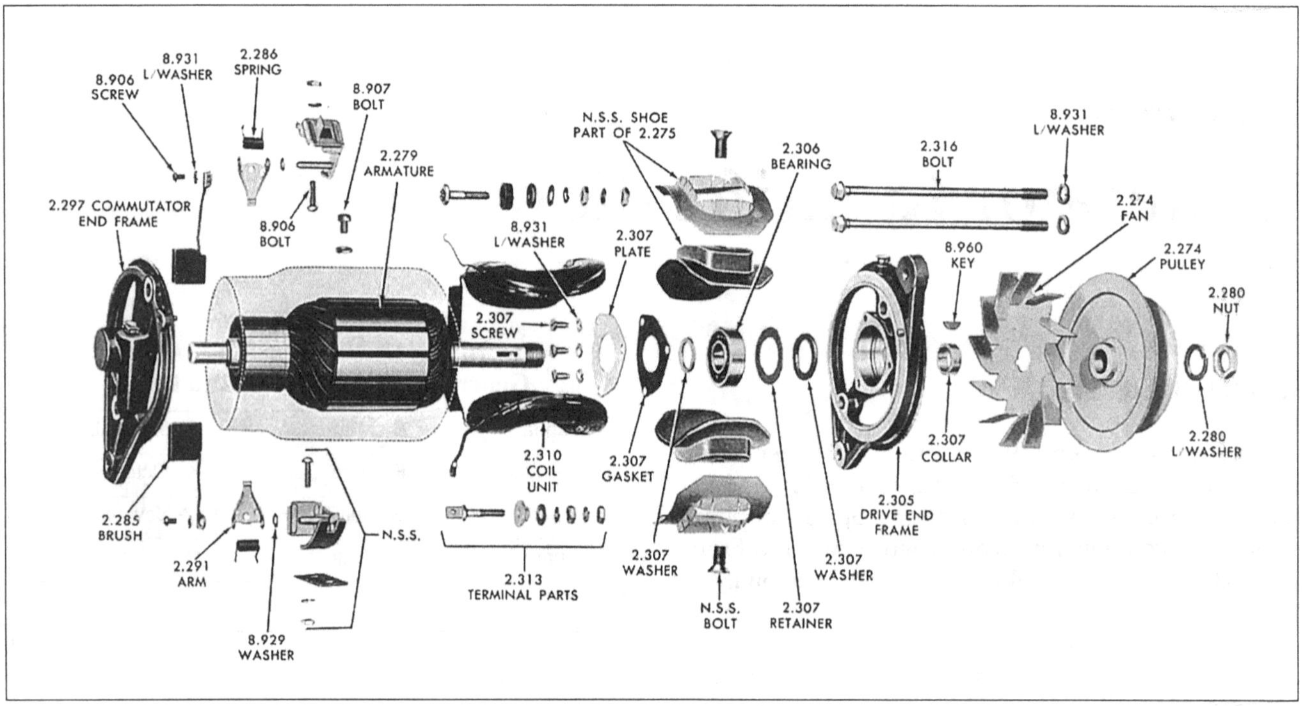

0023224

Fig. 14-3. Exploded view of typical 12-volt D.C. generator.

2. GENERATOR APPLICATIONS

1955 Generators

Model	Style	Engine	Type	No.	Notes
Passenger	150, 210, Bel Air	235 6-Cylinder, 265	25 Amp	1100310	Base Unit
			30 Amp	1102020	Optional, Power Steering
			30 Amp	1102014	Optional, A/C, State Police
			40 Amp	1106981	Optional, City Police, Taxi
			55 Amp	1117102	Optional, A/C, City Police, Taxi
			30 Amp	1105947	Optional, Taxi
Corvette			45 Amp	1102793	6-Cylinder All
			30 Amp	1102025	8-Cylinder All
Canada Passenger	150, 210, Bel Air	235 6-Cylinder, 265	30 Amp	1102014	Base Unit
				1102020	Optional, Power Steering

1956 Generators

Model	Style	Engine	Type	No.	Notes
Passenger	150, 210, Bel Air	235 6-Cylinder, 265	25 Amp	1100326	Base Unit, 6-Cylinder
			25 Amp	1100321	Base Unit, 8-Cylinder
			30 Amp	1102041	Optional, Power Steering, 8-Cylinder
			30 Amp	1102042	Optional, A/C, State Police
			30 Amp	1105947	Optional, Taxi
			40 Amp	1106981	Optional, City Police, Taxi
			50 Amp	1106985	State Police, School Bus
			50 Amp	1117102	Optional, A/C, City Police, Taxi
			30 Amp	1102816	6-Volt, Police, Taxi
			40 Amp	1105009	6-Volt, Police, Taxi
Corvette			30 Amp	1102043	8-Cylinder
Canada Passenger	150, 210, Bel Air Series 10, 12	235 6-Cylinder, 265	30 Amp	1102014	6-Cylinder exc. Power Steering
			30 Amp	1102041	Optional, Power Steering
			30 Amp	1102042	Base Unit, 8-Cylinder exc. Pwr Steering

1957 Generators

Model	Style	Engine	Type	No.	Notes
Passenger	150, 210, Bel Air	235 6-Cylinder, 265, 283	25 Amp	1100326	Base Unit, 6-Cylinder
			25 Amp	1100321	Base Unit, 8-Cylinder
			30 Amp	1102041	Optional Power Steering
			30 Amp	1102042	Special High Perf. Apps., State Police
			35 Amp	1102083	Optional, A/C, State Police
			35 Amp	1102084	Optional, A/C, Power Steering
			30 Amp	1105947	Taxi
			35 Amp	1105113	Optional, Taxi
			40 Amp	1106981	Optional, City Police, Taxi
			50 Amp	1106985	Optional, State Police, School Bus
			50 Amp	1117103	Optional, A/C, City Police, Taxi
			55 Amp	1117102	Optional, A/C, City Police, Taxi
			60 Amp	1117107	Optional, A/C, City Police, Taxi
			100 Amp	1117109	Optional, A/C, City Police, Taxi
			30 Amp	1102816	Special 6-volt, Police, Taxi
			40 Amp	1105009	6-Volt, Police, Taxi
			45 Amp	1105117	6-Volt, Police, Taxi
Corvette, NASCAR*			30 Amp	1102043	Std., Tach Drive
			30 Amp	1102059	Non-Tach Drive, 283 HP w Air Intake
Canada Passenger	150, 210, Bel Air Series 10, 12	235 6-Cylinder, 265	30 Amp	1102014	Std., 6-Cylinder exc. Power Steering
			30 Amp	1102041	Optional, Power Steering
			30 Amp	1102042	Std., 8-Cylinder exc. Power Steering

*In 1957, Chevrolet made a handful of 150 Sedan passenger cars, which were special built to run in the NASCAR series. The cars were sent to Southern Engineering Development Company in Atlanta, Georgia, where a variety of suspension modifications were made. These included different spindles, different rear end, and special added shock absorbers. These cars are commonly called "Black Widows."

1958 Generators

Model	Style	Engine	Type	No.	Notes
Passenger	1100, 1200, 1500, 1600, 1700, 1800	235, 283, 348	30 Amp	1102096	Base Unit, 6-Cylinder
			30 Amp	1102097	Base Unit, 8-Cylinder
			35 Amp	1102114	Optional, A/C, State Police
			35 Amp	1102115	Optional, A/C and Power Steering
			35 Amp	1105116	Base Unit, Taxi
			35 Amp	1105118	Optional, Power Steering, Taxi
	1100, 1200, 1500, 1600, 1700, 1800	235, 283, 348	45 Amp	1106985	Optional, City Police
			50 Amp	1106679	Optional
			50 Amp	1106680	Optional, Power Steering
			50 Amp	1117109	Optional, Delcotron, A/C, City Police, Taxi
			60 Amp	1117107	Optional, Delcotron, A/C, City Police, Taxi
			100 Amp	1117103	Optional, A/C, City Police, Taxi
		Special 6- and 12-volt Police, Taxi	30 Amp	1102816	6-volt
			40 Amp	1105009	6-volt
			45 Amp	1105117	12-volt
Corvette			30 Amp	1102043	Base unit, Tach Drive
			30 Amp	1102059	Non-Tach Drive, 290HP
Canada Passenger	1100, 1200, 1500, 1600, 1700, 1800	235, 283, 348	30 Amp	1102096	Base Unit, 6-Cylinder exc. Pwr Steering
			30 Amp	1102097	Base Unit, 8-Cylinder exc. Pwr Steering
			35 Amp	1102115	Power Steering
			100 Amp	1117103	Optional, A/C, City Police, Taxi
			50 Amp	1117109	Optional, A/C, City Police, Taxi
			60 Amp	1117107	Optional, A/C, City Police, Taxi

1959 Generators

Model	Style	Engine	Type	No.	Notes
Passenger	1100, 1200, 1500, 1600, 1700, 1800	235, 283, 348	30 Amp	1102096	Base Unit, 6-Cylinder
			30 Amp	1102097	Base Unit, 8-Cylinder
			35 Amp	1102114	Optional, A/C, State Police
			35 Amp	1102115	A/C, State Police, Power Steering
			35 Amp	1105116	Base Unit, Taxi
			35 Amp	1105118	Optional, Taxi, Power Steering
			40 Amp	1105123	Optional, Taxi
			40 Amp	1105124	Optional, Taxi, Power Steering
			35 Amp	1102174	Optional, Taxi, Ball Bearing C.E.
			45 Amp	1106985	Optional
			50 Amp	1106679	Optional
			50 Amp	1106680	Optional, Power Steering
		Optional, A/C, City Police, Taxi	50 Amp	1117109	
			60 Amp	1117107	
			60 Amp	1117070	Delcotron
			100 Amp	1117103	
		Special 6- and 12-volt Police, Taxi	30 Amp	1102816	6-Volt
			40 Amp	1105009	6-Volt
			45 Amp	1105117	12-Volt
Corvette			30 Amp	1102043	Base Unit, Tach Drive
			30 Amp	1102059	290 HP Engine, 1st Design, Non-Tach Drive
			35 Amp	1102173	290 HP Engine, 2nd Design, Non-Tach Drive
Canada-Passenger	1100, 1200, 1500, 1600, 1700, 1800	235, 283, 348	30 Amp	1102096	Base Unit, 6-Cylinder exc. Pwr Steering
			30 Amp	1102097	Base Unit, 8-Cylinder exc. Pwr Steering
			35 Amp	1102115	Optional, Power Steering
			50 Amp	1106985	City Service
		Optional, A/C, City Police, Taxi	50 Amp	1117109	Optional
			60 Amp	1117107	Optional
			100 Amp	1117103	Optional

Chapter 15
Transmission Identification

1. Introduction

This chapter covers all transmissions from 1955 through 1959. This introduction gives a brief overview of the transmissions, while the rest of the chapter is structured by model year to allow you to quickly and easily determine transmission applications. Under each year heading there is a quick-access section, transmission specifications with parts casting numbers, and stamping number decoding. At the end of this chapter are specific transmission casting number charts, which will allow you to access the individual casting numbers without reading through the entire text to extrapolate the information.

Casting Date Codes

Casting date codes can be found on almost all maincases, tailhousings, and sidecovers. Most casting dates are in an alphanumeric style, and usually follow the same pattern as blocks and cylinder heads. Many casting dates are difficult to read.

The first digit of a casting date code is usually a letter, to designate the month. The second digit will be a letter, designating the month. The third digit designates the day of the month, while the fourth (or last) digit designates the calendar year.

All dates on the transmission should be within three to four months of one another. If the transmission is original and untouched, all dates should precede the final assembly date code stamp. Note that parts are sometimes changed due to breakage or recalls, but this is not common. Always refer to the component casting charts at the back of this chapter to validate casting numbers and dates.

Assembly Date Code Stamping

All of the transmissions have an assembly date code stamped on the maincase. This stamping is different from the casting numbers of the individual parts that make up the entire transmission. Remember that any casting date codes on parts must always precede the transmission assembly date.

The location of the stamped code differs slightly from year to year and from application to application. This is very important to remember. For example, two similar Saginaw transmissions, one for a truck application and one for a car application, often have different date code stamping locations.

The date code typically identifies the plant where the transmission was assembled, the date of assembly, and sometimes application information. Note that the assembly date code will reflect the model year of stamping, not the calendar year. Some transmission plants did not begin to stamp the model year until 1967.

Transmission VIN Stamping

No transmissions covered by this book should have a VIN (vehicle identification number) stamped on them. Most transmissions originally installed in Chevrolet vehicles from the 1962 model year on should have a VIN. The VIN will be located on the top or side of the maincase. Specific information pertaining to this stamping is covered in the three later volumes of this book series.

1.1 3-Speed Transmissions

1955 Through 1959 Saginaw 3-Speed

The 3-speed transmission that Chevrolet used in 1955 was a Saginaw design transmission. This transmission is side-loaded with a side lever shift, and is found in all early 3-speed applications. Identifying features include a three-step countershaft cluster with the small step in the center, and a clutch-style synchronizer externally splined for the first and reverse shift gear. It is not easily distinguished from the 1964 and later Saginaw 3-speeds, but it is slightly smaller overall and has different gear helix angles. Externally, this transmission can be identified by the four-bolt sidecover and the elongated tailhousing. One of the main drawbacks of this transmission is that it was not fully synchronized. This led to a newly designed Saginaw transmission for 1966.

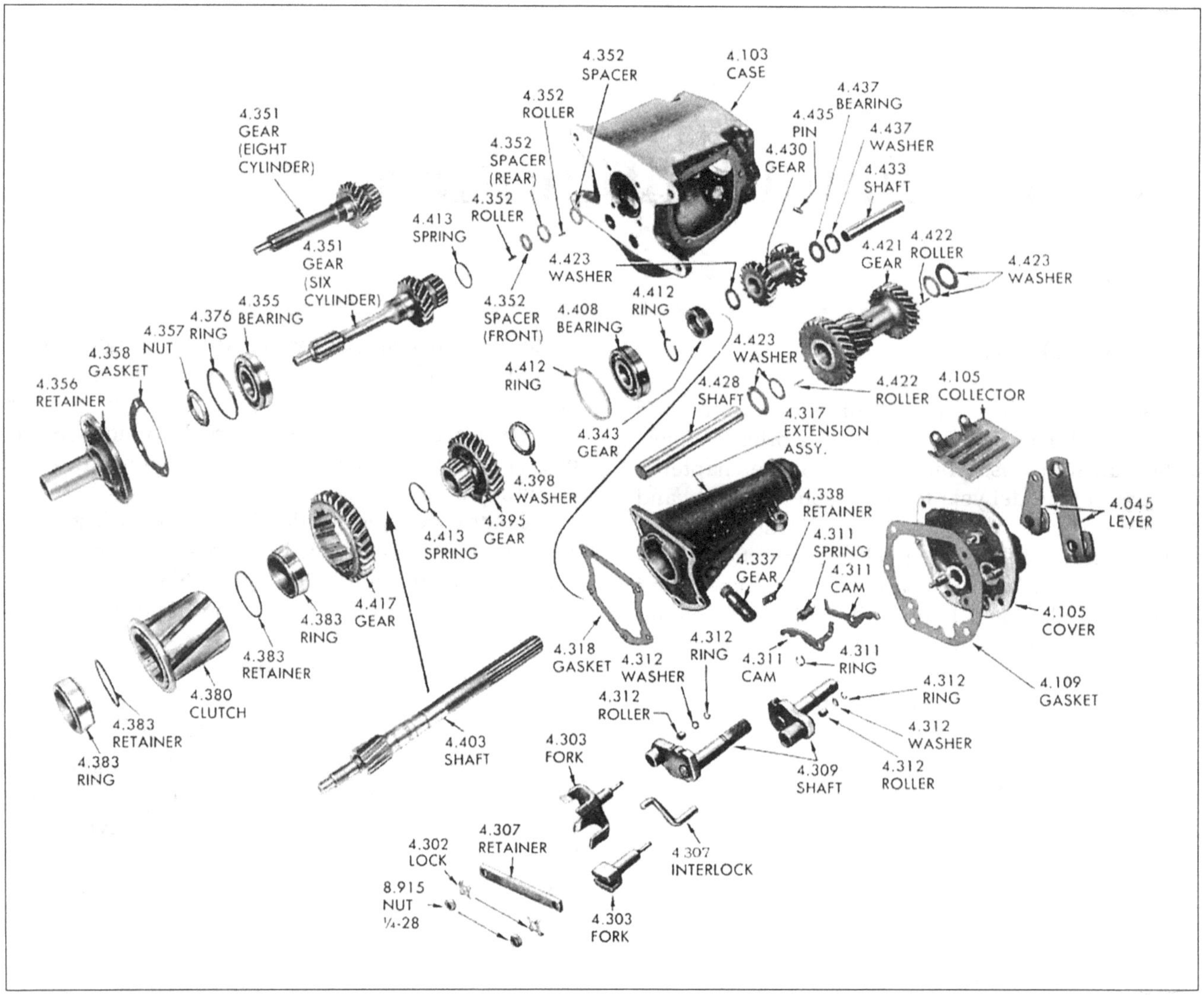

0022306

Fig. 15-1. 1955–65 Chevrolet Passenger car, Chevy II and Chevelle 3-speed Transmission exploded view (typical).

Saginaw Date Coding

All 1955–59 Saginaw 3-speeds have an assembly date located on the right side of the maincase at the flange where the tailhousing bolts to the maincase. This stamping is unlike the casting numbers which are raised off of the surface of the individual part. This stamping generally consists of an alpha code indicating the source of the transmission, and is then followed by several numbers to indicate the specific month and day the transmission was assembled. Saginaw 3-speeds were built in both Saginaw, Michigan, and Muncie, Indiana. A typical Saginaw assembly date stamp would be "S313," which indicates a Saginaw transmission produced on March 13. There is not a year identification in the assembly date code. You must refer to the casting dates of that particular case to discover the year of manufacture. Also remember that the casting date must always precede the assembly date.

0022308

Fig. 15-2. Stamped transmission build date S514 (Saginaw, May 14) from a #3743368 maincase with casting date E113 (May 11, 1963) (assembled 3 days later).

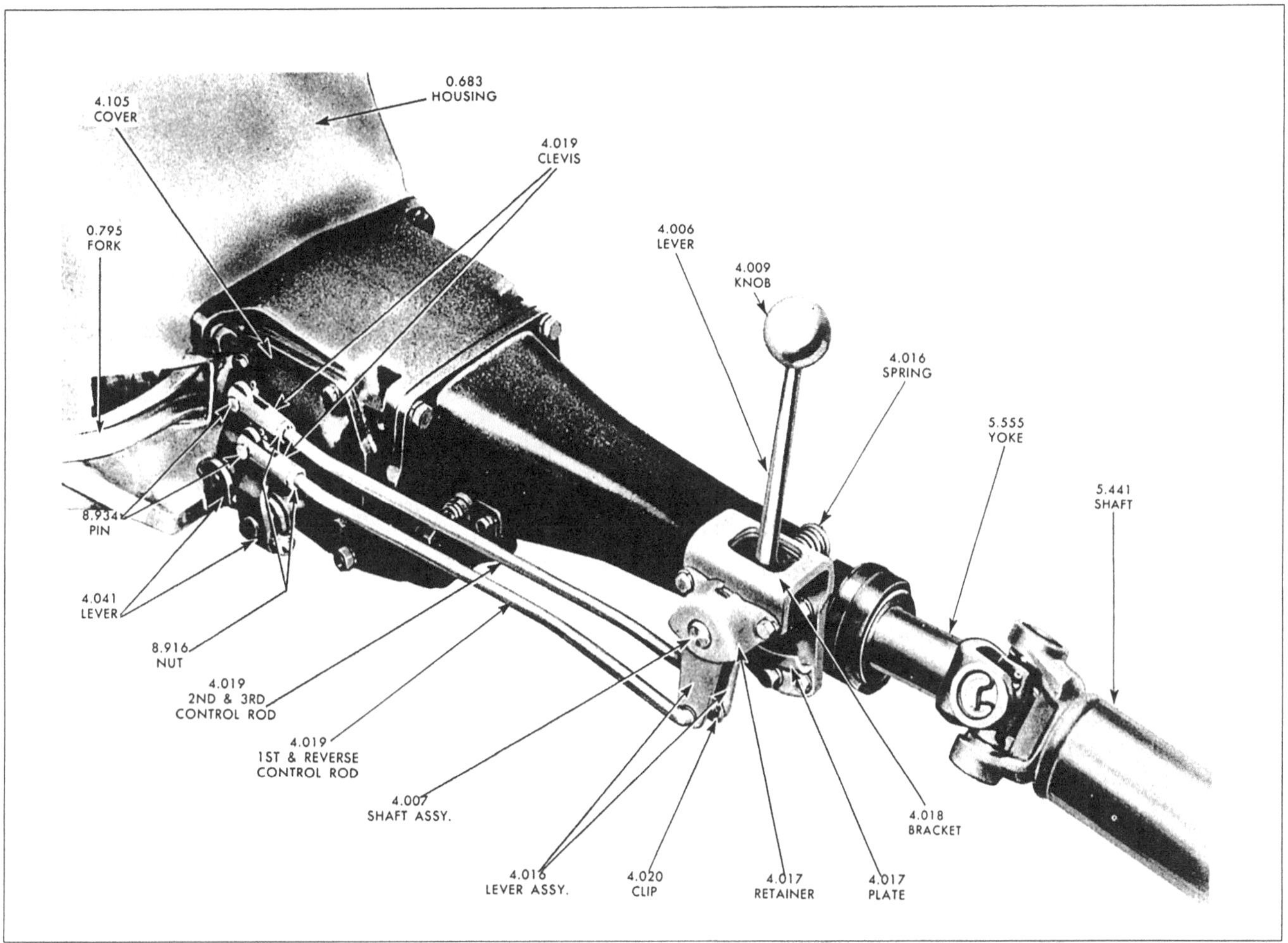

0022307

Fig. 15-3. 1957 Corvette Saginaw 3-speed transmission. Note how shifter mounts to transmission tailhousing.Sidecover is held by four bolts.

0022309

Fig. 15-4. Three-speed Saginaw maincase #3743368 dated E113 (from same transmission as previous photograph).

0022311

Fig. 15-5. 1955 Chevrolet Passenger overdrive transmission with the casting number on the tailhousing "R10K-1." "WG DIV" underneath indicates Warner Gear Division.

0022310

Fig. 15-6. *1969 3-speed (top) compared to 1955 Corvette 3-speed manual transmission (bottom) shows differences in design changes from early to late 3-speed.*

0022312

Fig. 15-8. *Two #3845122 maincases. One on the left has the extra holes (arrows) drilled into it for an overdrive transmission as discussed in text. The case on the right is a standard 3-speed maincase without the extra holes.*

Saginaw Maincase Identification

The 1955 3-speed transmission maincase is casting number #3845122. This casting number was used through the 1957 model year for both Passenger and Corvette applications. The 1955 case was revised without a casting number change during the 1955 model year. Venting was the apparent reason for a hole at the nine o'clock position on the rear face of the earlier case. Some #3845122 maincases have been found in early 1958 Corvette 3-speed applications.

The #3743368 maincase was used for most of the 1958 model year for all applications, and for some applications through the 1963 model year. This maincase was manufactured without a drain plug as an attempt to improve overall cost savings.

All maincases used during these years were manufactured out of cast iron. Also worth noting here is that beginning in the 1960 model year, all Chevrolet overdrive transmissions had their own specific casting number. Prior to 1960, the same maincase was used on both the standard 3-speed and the overdrive version. The only difference between the two cases is that the overdrive case has two holes drilled into the rear of the case that are used to tie the case into the intermediate case and solenoid area.

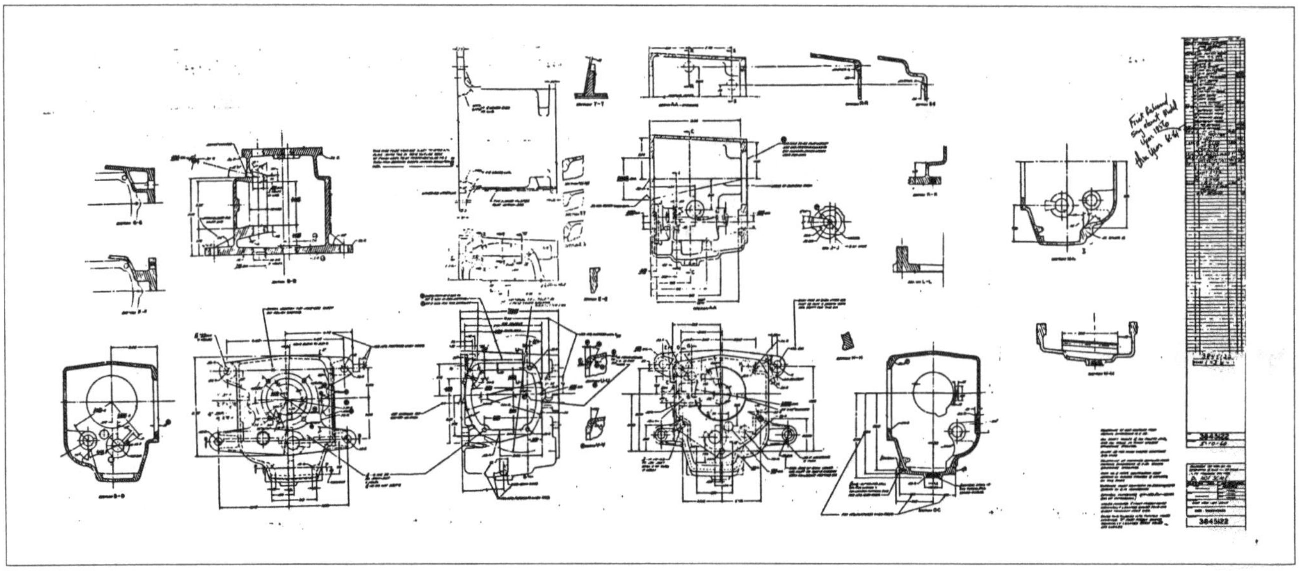

0023079

Fig. 15-7. *Blueprint of #3845122 maincase.*

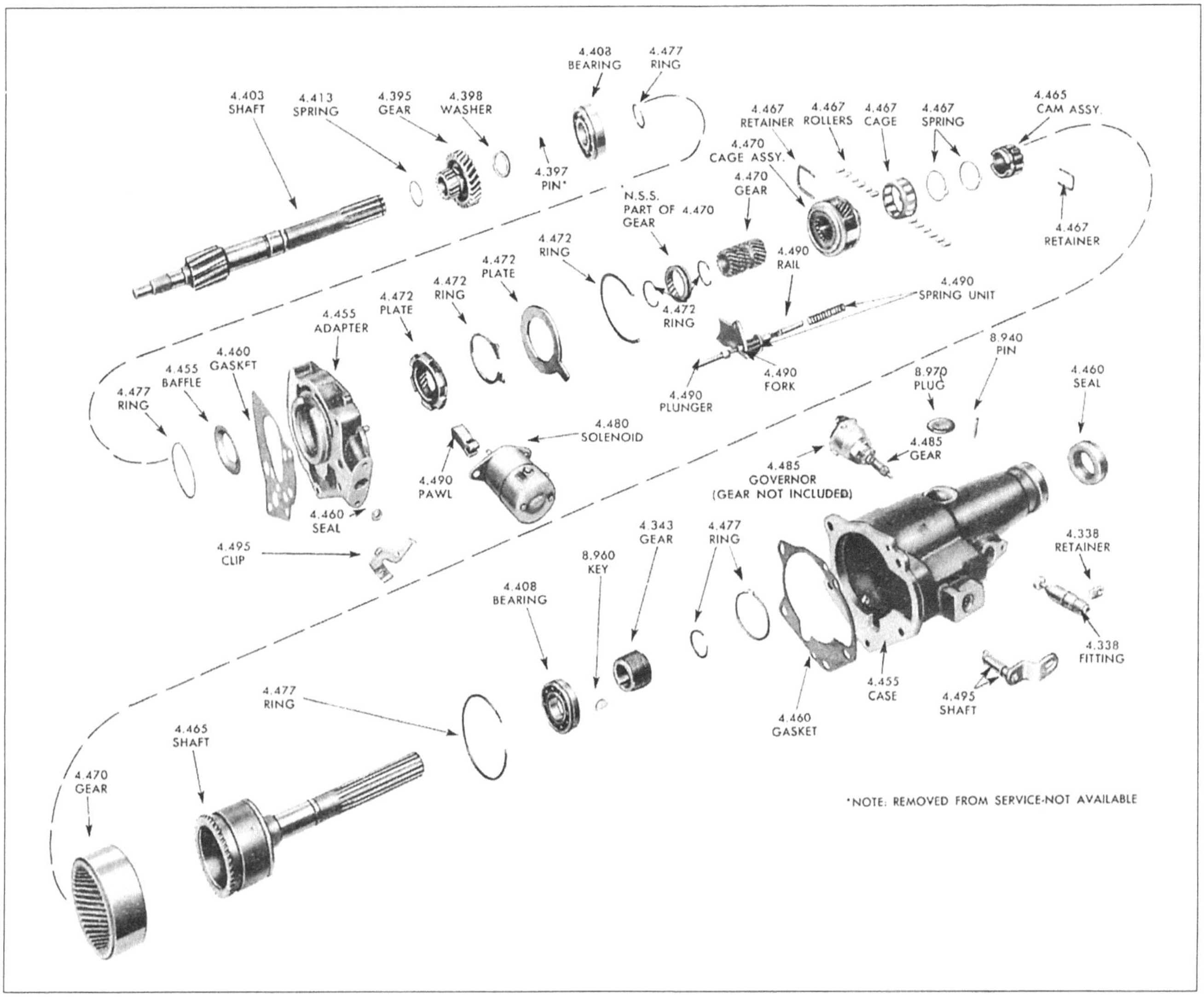

0022313

Fig. 15-9. Exploded view of 3-Speed Transmission with overdrive.

Saginaw Tailhousing Identification

There were several extensions or tailhousings used during the 1955–59 model years. The primary differences between each are tied to model usage. For example, all Chevrolet passenger car tailhousings do not have a mounting boss cast into the housing for the shifter assembly. In contrast, all Corvettes did have these shifter mounting bosses cast into the left rear of the housing. This difference was due to the Corvette floor-mounted shifter assembly, which was mounted directly to the tailhousing; passenger cars used a column-mounted shifter.

The 1955–59 passenger tailhousing casting number was #3707195. The 1955 and 1956 Corvette tailhousing was casting #3722946. This tailhousing appears rounded square in the forward section. Shifter mount provisions are present on the left rear part of the housing. Also, cast-in rear seal access cutouts appear on each side and no vent is present on the top forward center section. Some sources state that this housing was used into the early part of the 1957 model year.

The 1957–60 Corvette tailhousing carried the casting number #3737450. This housing was changed from the #3722946 with the addition of a vent that resembles the vent assembly on an early rear axle housing. A large machined area around the speedometer drive gear housing hole is also present.

Saginaw Sidecover Identification

There were four different sidecovers used during the 1955–59 model years. The differences in the grooved shafts that protrude through the sidecover are the best indicators as to whether a transmission is for a passenger car or Corvette. On Corvettes, the shaft grooves are

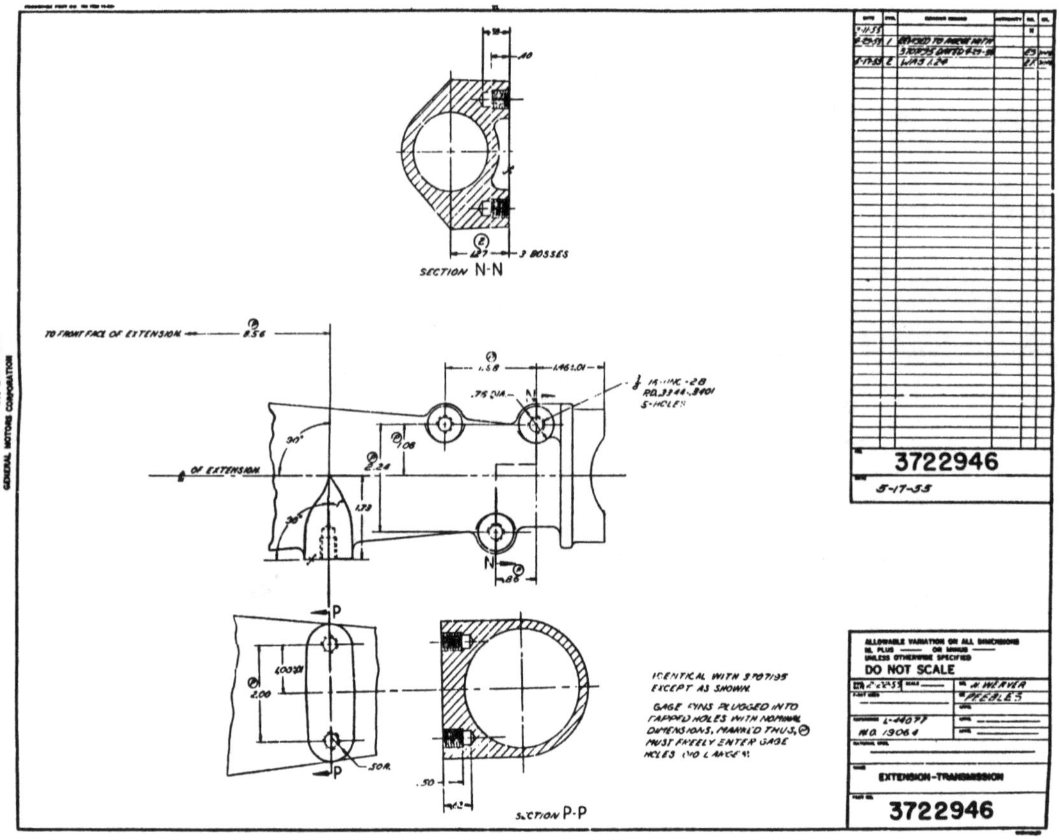

0022314

Fig. 15-10. *Blueprint of #3722946 tailhousing shows it is identical with #3707195 except as shown.*

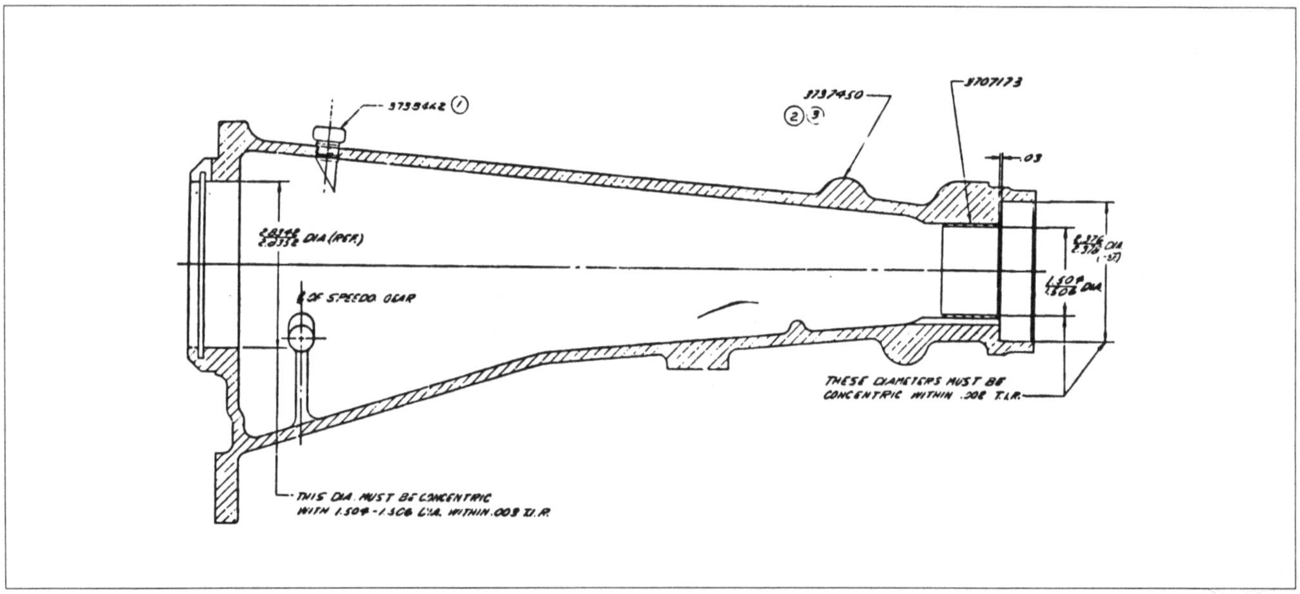

0023921

Fig. 15-11. *#3737450 tailhousing.*

0022318

Fig. 15-12. #3731911 sidecover from #3743368 maincase shown earlier.

on top with the shaft in the mounted position, which causes the shift levers to point upwards. On passenger cars, the levers point to the side or downward depending upon the particular car application.

During the 1955 model year there were first and second design sidecover casting numbers. Both designs were applicable to passenger cars and Corvettes. The first design casting number is #3845044. The second design casting number is #3845157. The change over date to the second design is still being researched.

In the 1956 model year the #3845157 sidecover was again used by both passenger cars and Corvettes. The 1957 model year brought two new casting numbers. #3741357 was used for passenger car, while #3731911 was used for Corvettes. This was maintained through the 1963 model year.

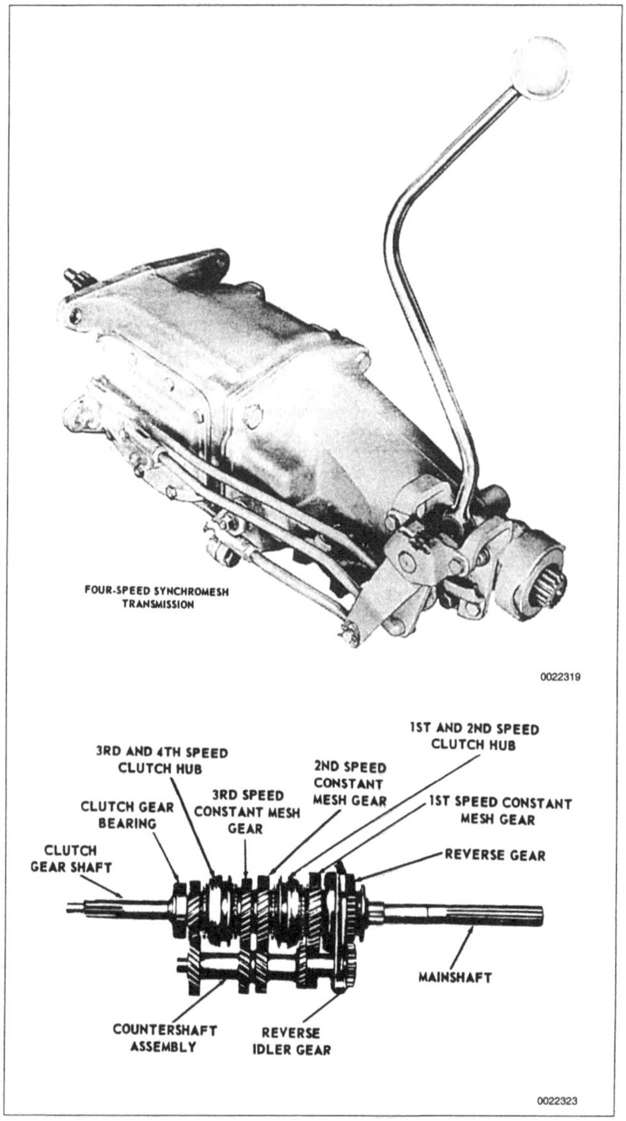

Fig. 15-13. Four-speed transmission and internal gear set schematic of a 4-speed transmission.

1.2 4-speed Transmissions

Borg-Warner 4-Speed Transmissions

The Borg-Warner T10 4-speed transmission began its six year production run around April 10, 1957. This is a side loaded transmission with the side-lever shift linkage derived from the Warner T85 three speed. It is synchronized in all forward gears. A spur sliding gear in the tailhousing engages the rear of a two-step reverse idler to provide reverse. This transmission used a Borg-Warner cast iron maincase, tailhousing, sidecover, and bearing retainer, with Borg-Warner casting numbers. The sidecover is retained to the maincase by nine bolts.

The T10 was used by several GM divisions which included Chevrolet Passenger cars (1958–63), Chevrolet Corvettes (1957–63), Pontiac (1960–64), and Oldsmobile (1962–63). It was also used from 1960–66 by the Ford Motor Company. As if this isn't confusing enough, many of the T10 parts are interchangeable and a majority of the complete transmissions left today are a mixed bag of parts. The T10 was not replaced by GM's "Muncie" 4-speed transmission until the latter part of the 1963 production year; however, Borg-Warner did introduce a "Super T10" in 1965 in American Motors cars.

The Borg-Warner T10 has six basic design variations that can be recognized over its twenty year production run. Only the 1st design is applicable to the 1955–59 model years covered in this book so all correct T10s will have the following listed features.

1st Design: 1957–59 model years. Mainshaft has a small diameter pilot (0.75), small diameter 3rd gear journal (1.37), and no thrust flange for 2nd gear. Mainshaft 3rd gear has a bushed hole. Reverse idler halves lock together with four lugs.

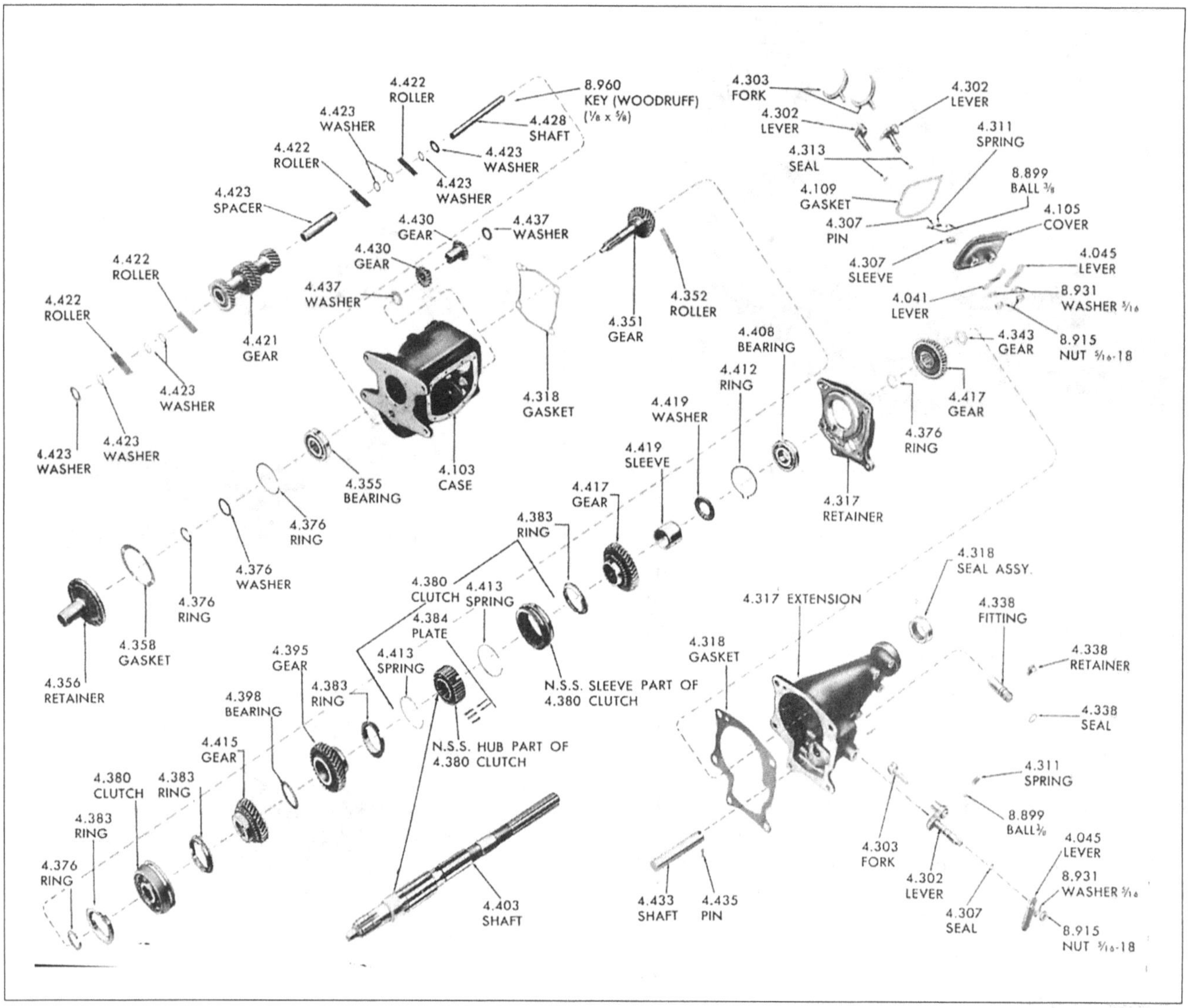

0022320

Fig. 15-14. 1957–63 Borg-Warner 4-speed transmission exploded view (typical).

Borg-Warner Maincase Identification

Two different T10 maincases were used in Chevrolet passenger cars and Corvettes from 1957–59. The T10-1 was the first maincase and was used from the start of T10 production in late 1957 until June of 1959. It is of cast iron construction.The T10-1B maincase was a second case design and was used from June of 1959 until January of 1961. It is also of cast iron construction. It is very similar to the earlier T10-1 case. The primary difference is the shape of the casting around the reverse idler gear area. Also, the bore diameter for the reverse idler gear set in the rear face of the case is 1.5", while the bore diameter in the T10-1 case is 1-23/64". The increased bore diameter in the T10-1B case was necessary to accommodate the 27-spline reverse idler gears.

0022324

Fig. 15-15. Borg-Warner T-10-1B maincase with T10-7A tail-housing, which is a late 1959 transmission assembly.

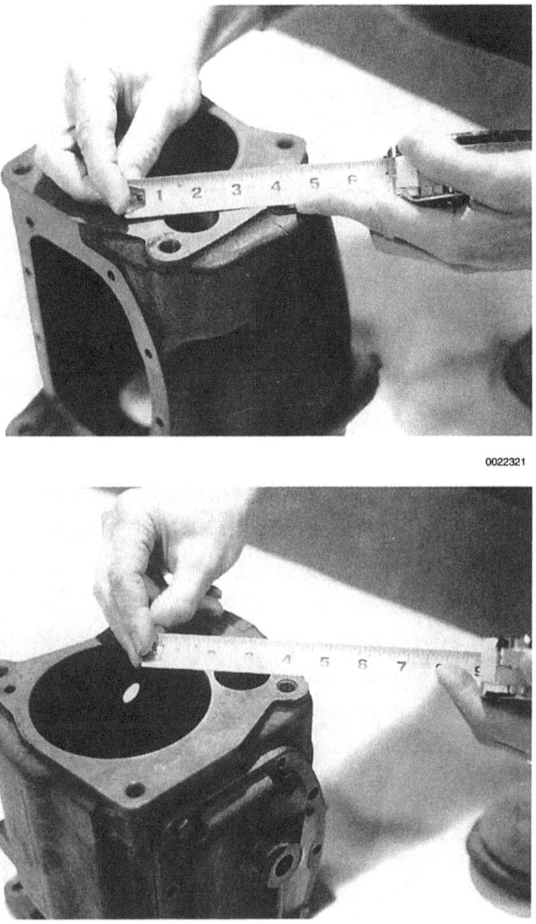

0022321

0022322

Fig. 15-16. ***Top:*** *T10-1 maincase with 1-23/64" bore for the reverse idler gear set.* ***Bottom:*** *T10-1B maincase with a 1-1/2" bore for the reverse idler gear set.*

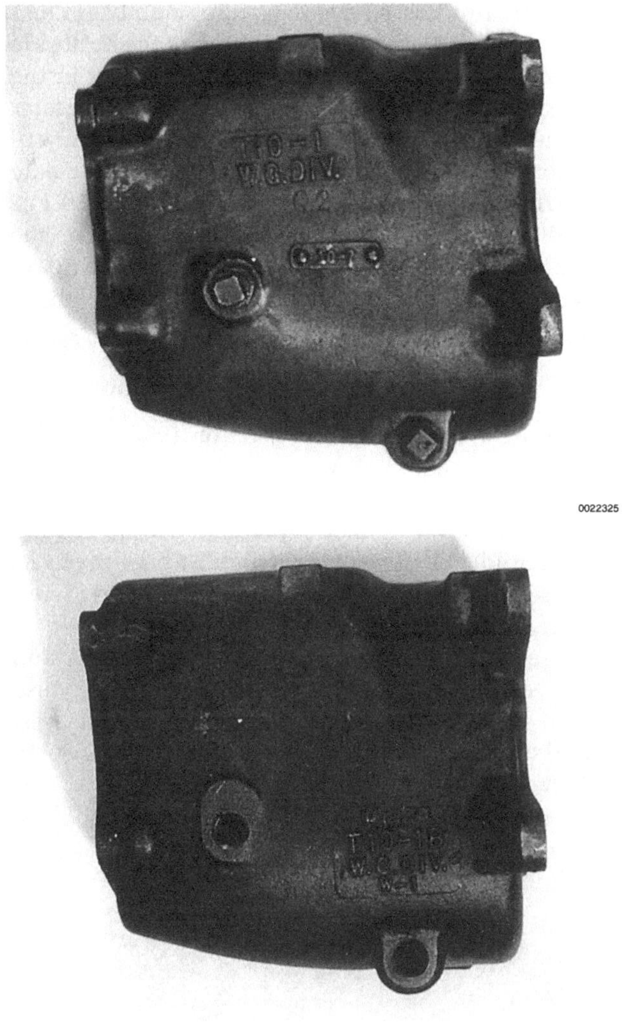

0022325

0022326

Fig. 15-18. ***Top:*** *T10-1 maincase. Note 10-7 casting date.* ***Bottom:*** *T10-1B late-model case as discussed in text.*

0022327

Fig. 15-17. *T10 maincase assembly code stamp "WM1872." This transmission was assembled on December 18th, 1957, second shift.*

0023080

Fig. 15-19. *T10 maincase assembly code stamp "WL1892". This transmission was assembled on November 18th, 1959, second shift.*

Both cast iron cases have the casting number (T10-1 or T10-1B) on the upper center portion of the right side of the case. T10-1B cases with the number cast in the lower front corner of the right side of the case are later style cases and are not correct for 1957–60 Chevrolet applications. The early cast iron cases carry a casting date on the right side of the maincase, just below the T10-1 or T10-1B designation. The month and the day of the month only are cast on a block in numerals. The calendar year was not included in the casting date on the early cast iron main cases.

Borg-Warner Sidecover Identification

There were two sidecovers used on 1957–59 T10 4-speed transmissions. All were cast of aluminum. Thei rst style was used from the beginning of production in 1957 through the 1958 model year and had the casting number of T10-148. This cover is simple to identify by its lack of reinforcing gussets cast around the bosses to support the shifter shafts on the outside of the sidecover.

The second style of sidecover is cast T10-148A and was used for the 1959 model year. This cover is also easy to identify in that the reinforcing gussets cast around the shifter shaft bosses extend all the way out to the bolt circle flange.

0022331

Fig. 15-20. Three typical sidecovers used in 1957–63 Chevrolet Passenger cars and Corvettes. T10-148 is on the left, T10-148A is in center, the T10-148B is on the right.

Borg-Warner Tailhousing Identification

There were two different tailhousings used in 1957–59 passenger cars and Corvettes. The T10-7 housing was used in 1957 Corvette applications only. T10-7A was used in 1958 in Corvette applications only, and in

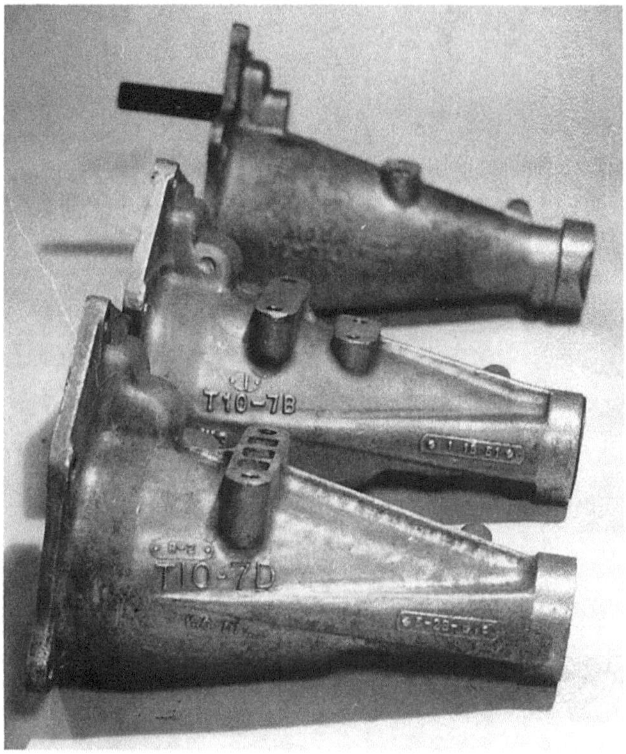

0022328

0022329

Fig. 15-21. Three Borg-Warner tailhousings: T10-7A on top, T10-7B in center, T10-7D on the bottom. Note differences in mounting pads as explained in text.

1959 for both passenger cars and Corvettes. These two housings are easy to recognize by their single small mounting boss underneath and by the three drilled and tapped shifter mounting bosses. Both of the aforementioned housings were cast in aluminum.

0022330

Fig. 15-22. Side view of tailhousings showing typical T10-7 and T10-7A (top) and T10-7B (bottom).

Borg-Warner Rear Bearing Retainer Plate Identification

Two rear bearing retainer plates are considered correct for 1957–59 T10 4-speeds. Both were cast in aluminum and carry a T10-107 casting number. The early (1957–60) retainer was used with the cast iron cases and is identified by two tapped holes along the lower edge to accept two cap screws retaining the tailhousing. The later retainer was used with the aluminum maincase (1961–63) and is identified by the absence of two tapped holes which allows all five tailhousing cap screws to thread into the maincase.

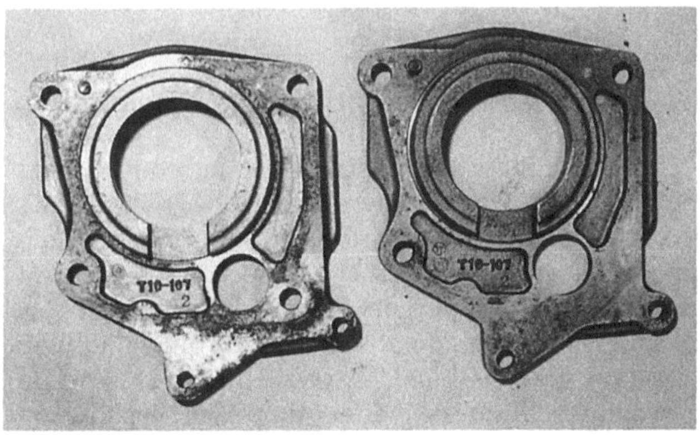

0022332

Fig. 15-23. Two Borg-Warner rear bearing retainer plates. The earlier style is on the left, the latter style is on the right. Note absence of the tapped hole on the later bearing retainer plate.

Borg-Warner Parts Identification

Borg-Warner main drive gear and countergear parts are easily identified when the transmission is apart. This is because Borg-Warner used a series of rings or circles on these parts to make identification easier at the assembly line. The following figures show the external differences between Borg-Warner parts to aid identification in the field.

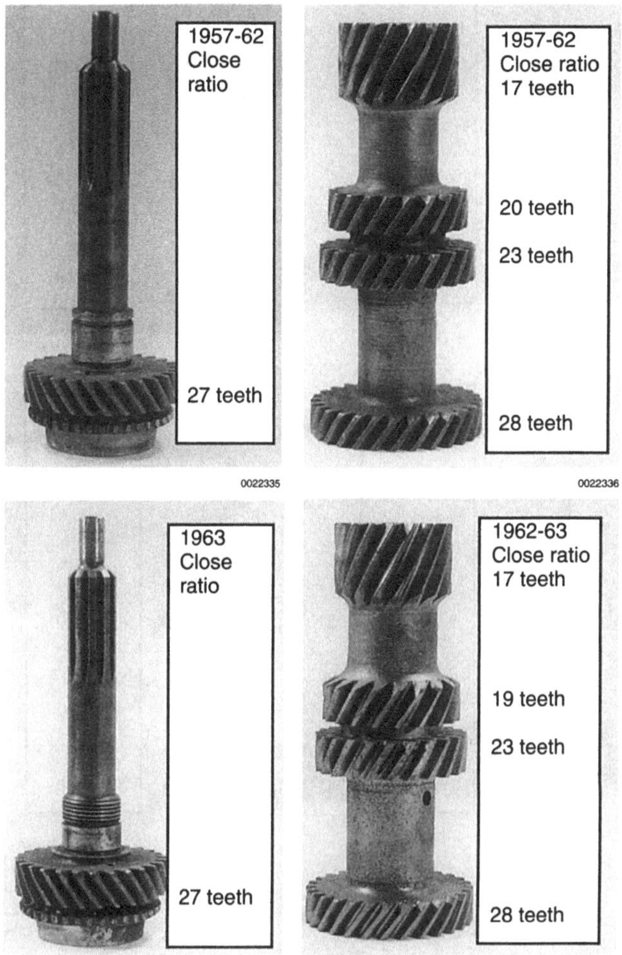

Fig. 15-24. Identification of Borg-Warner 4-speed close ratio main drive and counter gears.

1.3 Powerglide Automatic Transmissions

There were many design changes that were made to the 1955–59 Powerglide transmissions. These changes are discussed in detail underneath each model year heading in this chapter. What we intend to do here is to point out the major differences between passenger car and Corvette applications. This pertains to external differences only; the internal differences are discussed in each model year.

The Powerglide maincase, for all intents and purposes, is the same for both passenger cars and Corvettes. This is not the true for the tailhousings. The 1955–57 passenger car tailhousing is the same as the 1955 Corvette tailhousing since the 1955 Corvette floor shifter

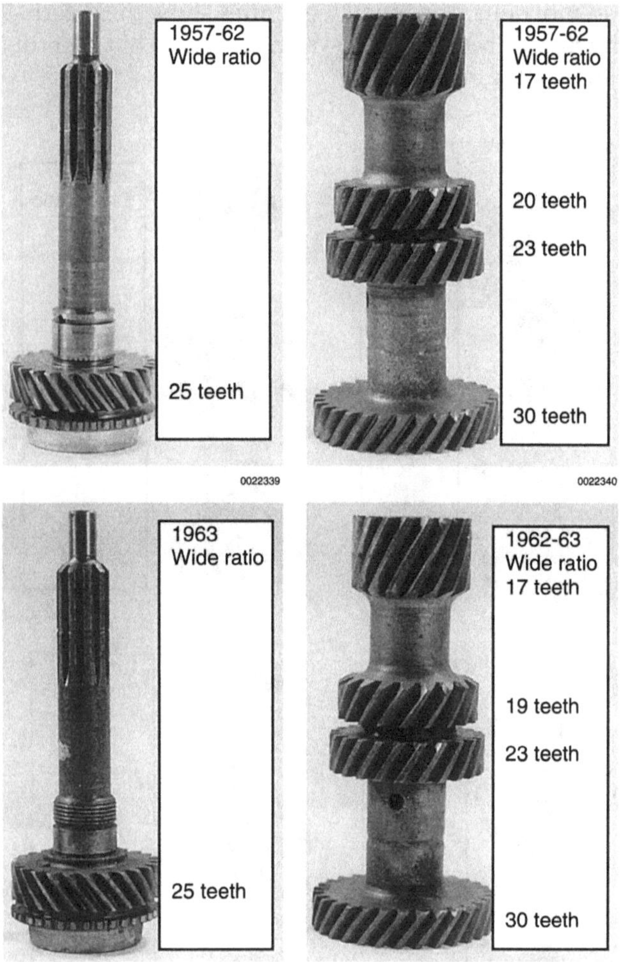

Fig. 15-25. *Identification of Borg-Warner 4-speed wide ratio main drive and counter gears.*

was mounted to the underbody and did not require shifter mounting bosses on the housing. The tailhousing for 1956–61 Corvette cast iron Powerglides has a special cast iron bracket bolted to it for transmission attachment to the Corvette's frame crossmember. The Corvette tailhousing also has three drilled and tapped bosses to accept the floor shifter. Chevrolet passenger car Powerglides all used a steering column mounted shifter and thus, did not require the mounting bosses.

There were two designs used on the Corvette tailhousing. The first design was used for the 1956–60 model years, the second design was used for the 1961 model year only. The major difference between these two designs is in the speedometer drive gear adapter fitting that attaches to the tailhousing. The 1956–60 fitting was 2-5/8" in length, while the 1961 measured 1-7/8" in length. Both housings will work on any 1956–61 Corvette, but for absolute correctness you should check for the correct length speedometer drive fitting. Both of these fittings were also used on various passenger car and truck powerglides, so you should be able to find them easily.

There were slight differences in sidecovers. On 1955–57 models with factory air conditioning the Powerglide sidecover had a plug in it for checking transmission fluid level. See Fig. 15-26.

Fig. 15-26. *Sidecover for 1955–57 Powerglides used on cars with factory air conditioning.*

1.4 Turboglide Automatic Transmissions

The Turboglide transmission was introduced after the beginning of the 1957 model year. It was Chevrolet's second automatic transmission, offered on most 283 engine applications. It was a two-speed, five-element geared-converter type that was modeled after the Buick Dynaflow transmission. It had three turbines and twin planetary gearsets plus a variable-pitch stator and a conventional torque converter pump. The transmission sent power to the driveshaft via turbine rotation through the torque converter pump's oil supply.

Although the transmission was very smooth when working properly, the complexity of the design proved too much for Chevrolet Service to handle. There were seemingly countless production changes and upgrades to this transmission until it was finally dropped in 1962. The Powerglide was the only automatic offered by Chevrolet from 1962 through 1964. In 1965, the new Turbohydramatic 400 was introduced in passenger cars with the 396 engine.

0022490

Fig. 15-27. Early Powerglide transmission with cast iron case.

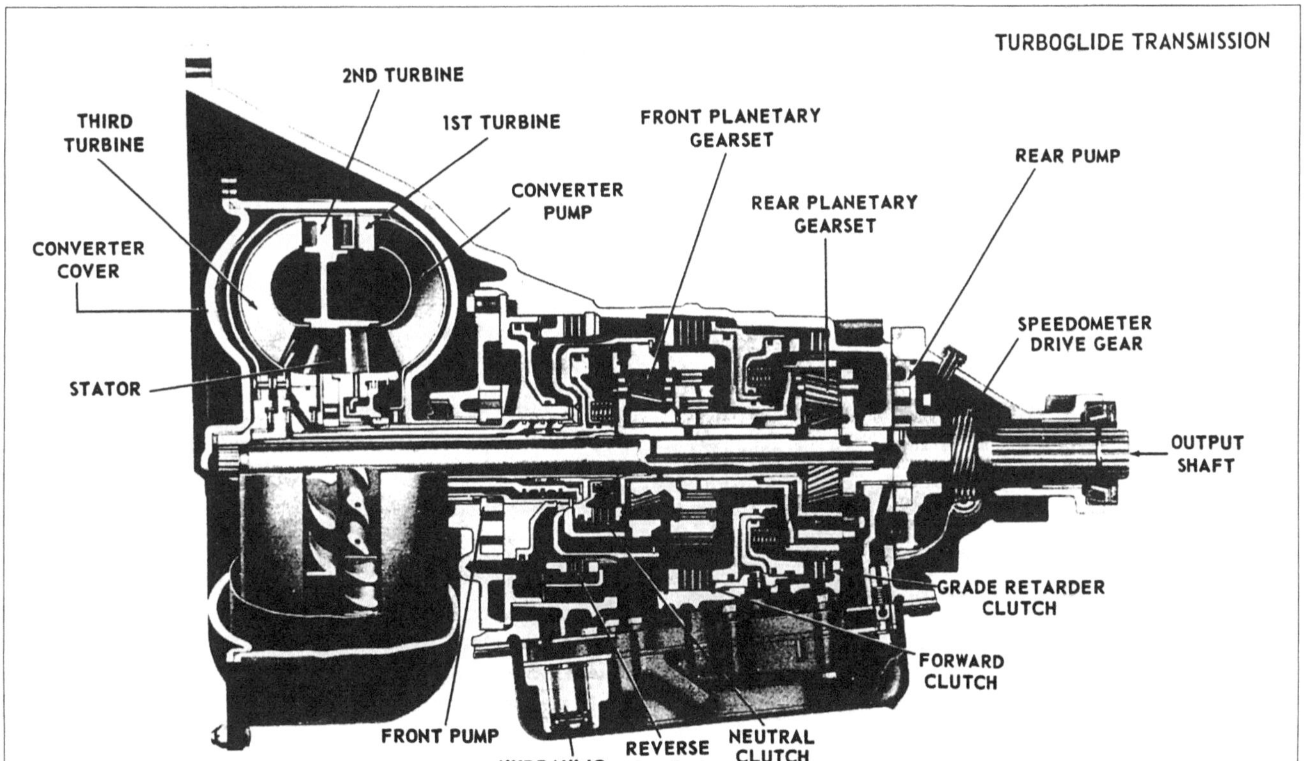

Fig. 15-28. Cutaway of Turboglide automatic transmission.

2. 1955 TRANSMISSIONS

1955 Transmission Applications

Transmission	Model and Engine
3-Speed Saginaw	Passenger 235, 265 Corvette 235, 265
3-Speed w/Overdrive	Passenger 235, 265
2-Speed Powerglide	Passenger 235, 265 Corvette 235, 265

2.1 Date Code

Assembly Date Code Location (Car)

Year	Transmission	Code Location
1955	3-Speed Saginaw	Rear face of transmission case, upper right hand corner.
	3-Speed Overdrive	Rear face of transmission case, upper right hand corner.
	Powerglide	Rear side of governor flange

3-Speed/Overdrive/Powerglide Example: S313

- S: Prefix = Saginaw 3-Speed
- 3: Month = March
- 13: Day = day 13

3-Speed Heavy Duty Warner Example: WB 1055 2

- W: Prefix = Warner H.D. 3-Speed
- B: Month = February
- 10: Day = day 10
- 55: Year = 1955
- 2: = 2nd Shift

1955 Transmission Letter Prefix Identification

Prefix	Plant	Transmission/Model
C	Cleveland	Powerglide
M	Muncie	3-Speed Passenger, Commercial
S	Saginaw	3-Speed Passenger, Corvette
T	Toledo	4-Speed Truck
W	Warner Gear	3-Speed H.D.Truck

2.2 Transmission Specifications

3-Speed Saginaw

Maincase		Cast Iron	
Tailhousing		Cast Iron	
Type		Synchromesh	
Gear Ratios		Passenger	Corvette
	1st:	2.94:1	2.20:1
	2nd:	1.68:1	1.31:1
	3rd:	Direct	Direct
	Reverse	2.94:1	2.20:1
Maincase No.	3845122 All		
Tailhousing No.	3707195 (Passenger) 3722946 (Corvette)		
Sidecover No.	3845044 (1st Design All) 3845157 (2nd Design All)		
Special Information: The tailhousing on this transmission is different from Passenger car models to the Corvette. The Corvette tailhousing has three tapped holes cast into the housing to accept the Corvette-only floor shifter. All Passenger models used the column shifter mechanism.			

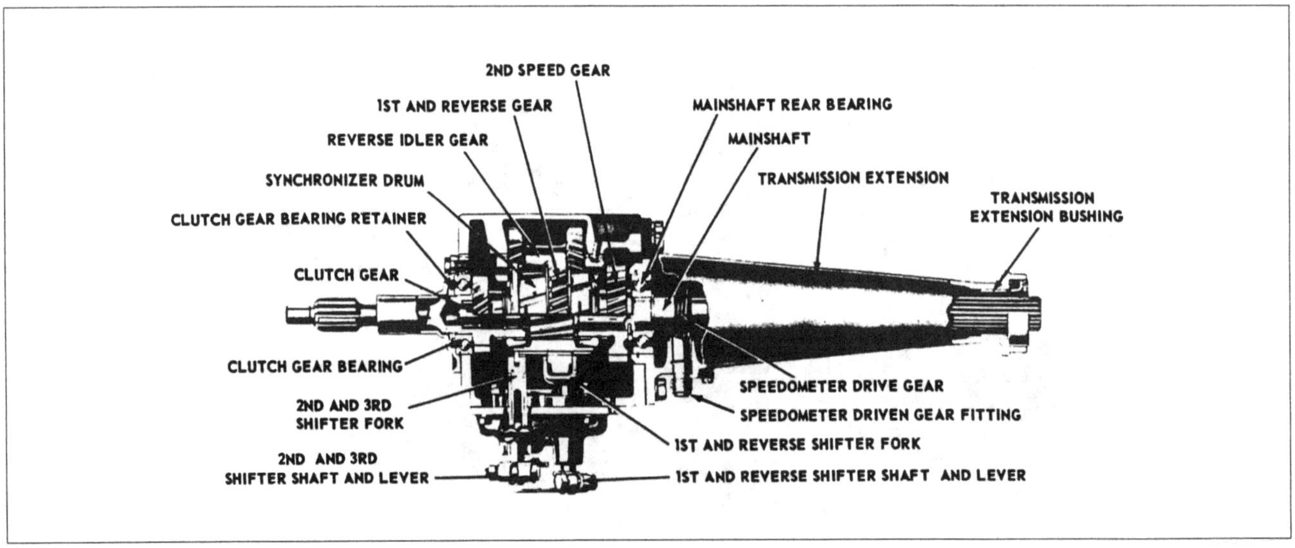

Fig. 15-29. Cutaway view of 1955 3-Speed transmission.

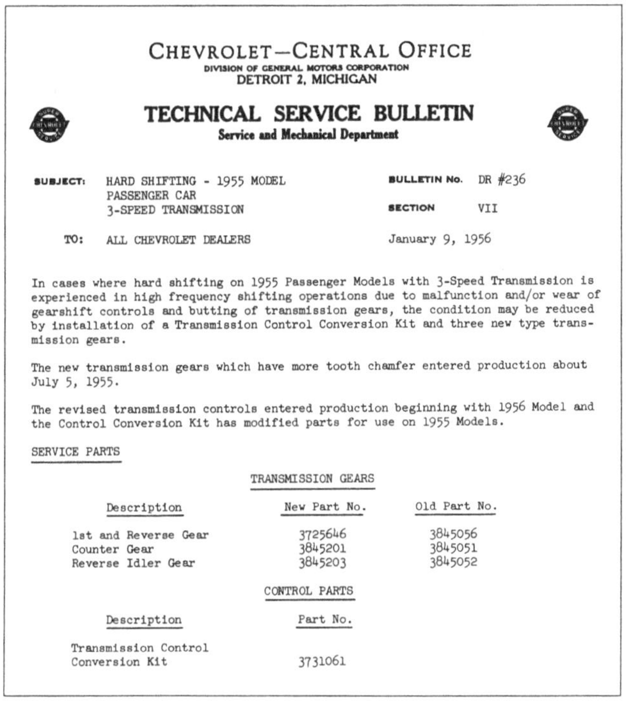

CHEVROLET—CENTRAL OFFICE
DIVISION OF GENERAL MOTORS CORPORATION
DETROIT 2, MICHIGAN

TECHNICAL SERVICE BULLETIN
Service and Mechanical Department

SUBJECT: HARD SHIFTING - 1955 MODEL PASSENGER CAR 3-SPEED TRANSMISSION

BULLETIN No. DR #236

SECTION VII

TO: ALL CHEVROLET DEALERS

January 9, 1956

In cases where hard shifting on 1955 Passenger Models with 3-Speed Transmission is experienced in high frequency shifting operations due to malfunction and/or wear of gearshift controls and butting of transmission gears, the condition may be reduced by installation of a Transmission Control Conversion Kit and three new type transmission gears.

The new transmission gears which have more tooth chamfer entered production about July 5, 1955.

The revised transmission controls entered production beginning with 1956 Model and the Control Conversion Kit has modified parts for use on 1955 Models.

SERVICE PARTS

TRANSMISSION GEARS

Description	New Part No.	Old Part No.
1st and Reverse Gear	3725646	3845056
Counter Gear	3845201	3845051
Reverse Idler Gear	3845203	3845052

CONTROL PARTS

Description	Part No.
Transmission Control Conversion Kit	3731061

0023230

Fig. 15-30. This TSB details a change to new transmission gears due to hard shifting that entered production about July 5, 1955.

3-Speed Overdrive Saginaw

Maincase	Cast Iron
Tailhousing	None
Type	3-Speed Synchromesh w/3-pinion planetary drive unit. The drive unit with its integral mainshaft replaces the mainshaft and tailhousing of the regular 3-Speed transmission.
Operation	Lockout switch manually controlled by "pull-type" cable located under instrument panel to the right of the steering column. Kickdown switch located on accelerator linkage. Pedal pressure controls overdrive operation.
Gear Ratios	Locked Out / Locked In 1st: 2.94:1 / 2.058:1 2nd: 1.68:1 / 1.176:1 3rd: Direct: / 0.700:1 Reverse: 2.94:1
Maincase No.	3845122
Sidecover No.	3845044 (1st Design All) 3845157 (2nd Design All)
Overdrive No.	R10K-1 W.G.DIV
Special Information: Maincase is identical with standard maincase except that an extra hole has been drilled in the rear of the maincase to accommodate the overdrive engagement rod.	

2-Speed Powerglide Transmission

Maincase	Cast Iron
Torque Converter Housing Material	Cast Iron
Tailhousing	Cast Iron
Type	Automatic Hydraulic torque converter with planetary gear system for reverse and low gear.
Gear Ratios	Drive: 1.82:1 Low: 1.82:1 Reverse: 1.82:1
Rear case No.	3708134
Torque Converter Housing Casting No.	1st Design 6-Cylinder: #3708446 2ndDesign 6-Cylinder: #3719240 8-Cylinder #3708188
Special Information: The only difference in the Passenger car and Corvette Powerglide transmission was the floor position of the shifting mechanism on the Corvette which constituted the change of the tailhousing with three tapped holes to accept the shifter. Only the Corvette had this tailhousing.	

3. 1956 TRANSMISSIONS

1956 Transmission Applications

Transmission	Model and Engine
3-Speed Saginaw (Standard)	Passenger 235, 265
3-Speed Saginaw (Close Ratio)	Passenger (5/9/56 Introduction), Corvette 265
3-Speed Overdrive Saginaw	Passenger 235, 265
2-Speed Powerglide	Passenger, Corvette 235, 265

Assembly Date Code Location (Car)

Year	Transmission	Code Location
1956	3-Speed (incl. Overdrive)	On rear face of transmission case in upper right hand corner.
	Powerglide	On rear side of governor flange.

3.1 Date Code

3-Speed Example: S 7 01

- S: Prefix = Saginaw 3-Speed
- 7: Month = July
- 01: Day = day 1

Powerglide Example: C 11 16

- C: Prefix = Cleveland Powerglide
- 11: Month = November
- 16: Day = day 16

1956 Transmission Letter Prefix Identification

Prefix	Plant	Transmission
C	Cleveland	Powerglide
M	Muncie	3-Speed
S	Saginaw	3-Speed, Overdrive

3.2 Transmission Specifications

3-Speed Saginaw

Maincase	Cast Iron
Tailhousing	Cast Iron
Type	Synchromesh
Gear Ratios	1st: 2.94:1 2nd: 1.68:1 3rd: Direct, Reverse: 2.94:1
Maincase No.	3845122
Tailhousing No.	3707195
Sidecover No.	3845157
Special Information: The #3707195 tailhousing has no shifter mount holes on its left rear side and there are cut outs present at the rear seal. The #3845122 maincase carried an under-designed rear reverse idler gear thrust washer (thin bronze disk).	

3-Speed (Close Ratio) Saginaw

Maincase	Cast Iron
Tailhousing	Cast Iron
Type	Synchromesh
Gear Ratios	1st: 2.20:1 2nd: 1.31:1 3rd: Direct Reverse: 2.20:1
Maincase Casting No.	3845122
Tailhousing Casting No.	3707195 (Passenger) 3722946 (Corvette)
Sidecover Casting No.	3845157 All
Special Information: The tailhousing on this transmission is different on Passenger models and Corvettes. The Corvette tailhousing has three tapped holes cast into the housing to accept the Corvette-only floor shifter. All Passenger models used the column shifter. The #3722946 tailhousing did not carry a metal vent assembly on its top, forward center section. No dates appear on these housings. There are cut outs present at the rear seal. The #3845122 main transmission housing carries a Flint single digit year date casting code. For the 1956 model year only a "6" appears for the year date. A higher capacity clutch gear bearing and mainshaft rear bearing provide greater durability, and a stronger snap ring is used for better retention of the synchronizer ring at high speeds. A neoprene "O" ring replaces the cork seal used on the shifter shaft for lower shifting friction.	

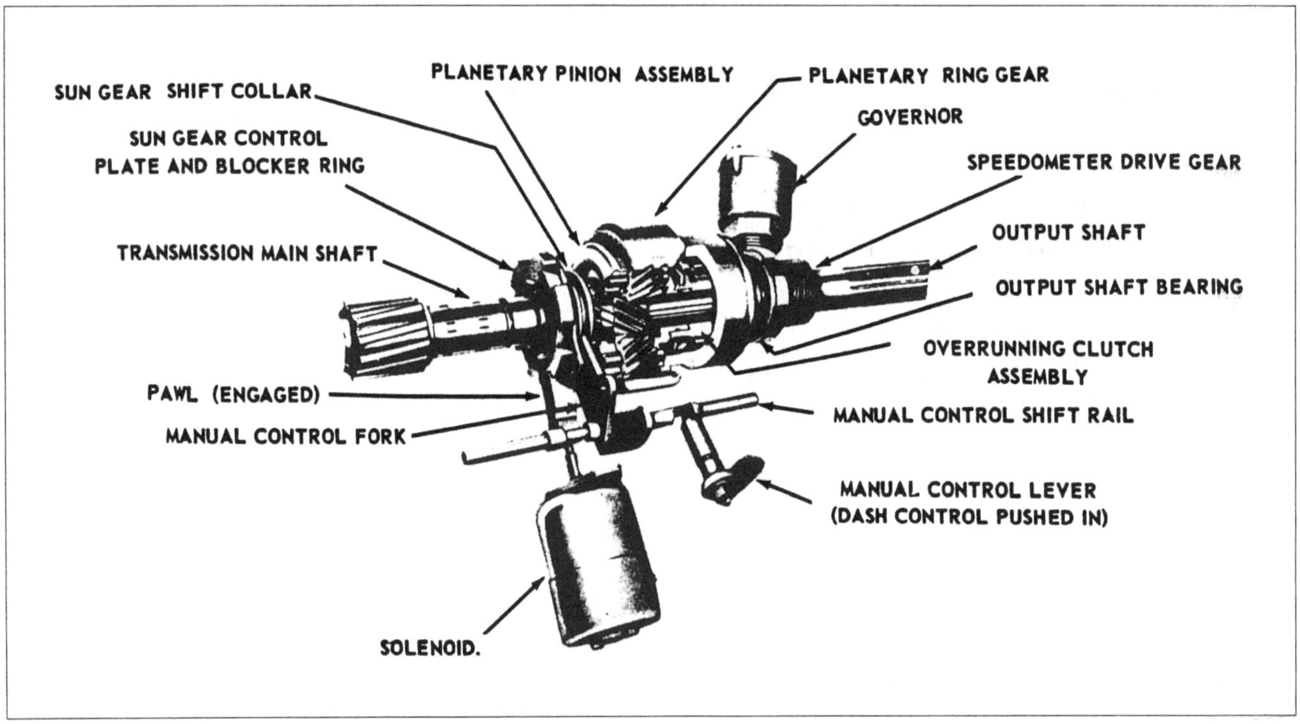

Fig. 15-31. 1956 3-Speed Overdrive assembly diagram.

0022363

Fig. 15-32. Typical Saginaw 3-speed transmission. Tapped holes (arrow) for shifter mounting on Corvette models only. Note four-bolt sidecover and elongated extension housing.

3-Speed Overdrive Saginaw

Maincase		Cast Iron	
Type		3-Speed Synchromesh with 3-pinion planetary drive unit. The drive unit with its integral mainshaft replaces the mainshaft and tailhousing of the regular 3-Speed transmission.	
Operation		Lockout switch manually controlled by "pull-type" cable located under instrument panel to the right of the steering column. Kickdown switch located on accelerator linkage. Pedal pressure controls overdrive operation.	
Gear Ratios		Locked Out	Locked In
	1st:	2.94:1	2.058:1
	2nd:	1.68:1	1.176:1
	3rd:	Direct	0.700:1
	Reverse:	2.94:1	
Maincase No.		3845122	
Sidecover No.		3845157	
Overdrive No.		R10K-1 W.G.DIV	
Special Information: Maincase is identical with standard maincase except that an extra hole has been drilled in the rear of the maincase to accommodate the overdrive engagement rod.			

2-Speed Powerglide

Maincase	Cast Iron
Torque Converter Housing	Cast Iron
Tailhousing	Cast Iron
Type	Automatic Hydraulic torque converter with planetary gear system for reverse and low gear.
Gear Ratios	Drive 1.82:1 Low 1.82:1 Reverse: 1.82:1
Rear Case No.	3708134
Torque Converter Housing No.	First Design 6-Cylinder: #3708446 Second Design 6-Cylinder: #3719240 8-Cylinder: #3708188
Special Information: The only difference between the Passenger and Corvette Powerglide transmissions was the floor position of the shifting mechanism on the Corvette, which meant a change of the tailhousing with three tapped holes to accept the shifter.	

4. 1957 TRANSMISSIONS

1957 Transmission Applications

Transmission	Model and Engine
3-Speed Saginaw	Passenger Car Only 235, 265, 283
3-Speed Saginaw Close Ratio	Passenger, Corvette 283
3-Speed Saginaw Overdrive	Passenger Car 235, 265, 283
2-Speed Powerglide	Passenger, Corvette 235, 265, 283
2-Speed Turboglide	Passenger Car 283
4-Speed Close Ratio (Borg-Warner*)	Corvette Only 283
* The 1957 Automobile Manufacturers Association specifications list the Borg-Warner 4-speed available as a heavy duty operation equipment option in the passenger car. This has never been verified through an original documented car.	

4.1 Date Code

Assembly Date Code Location (Car)

Year	Transmission	Code Location
1957	3-Speed	Rear face of transmission case in upper right hand corner. This includes the 3-Speed Overdrive transmission as well.
	4-Speed	Top of transmission case at left rear corner.
	Powerglide	On rear side of governor flange.
	Turboglide (early)	On rear face of case, on lower right corner.
	Turboglide (late)	Stamped on machined boss located on lower right rear face of case.

All transmission date coding is as follows: except for transmissions beginning with the prefix "W," one or more numerals designating the month using "1" for January, "2" for February, etc., "10" for October, "11" for November and "12" for December will be stamped immediately following the letter prefix.

Two numerals designating the production date of the month using "01" for the first day of the month, "02" for the second, etc., will follow the numeral or numerals designating the month.

3-Speed Example: S 7 01

- S: Prefix = Saginaw 3-Speed
- 7: Month = July
- 01: Day = day 1

Powerglide Example: C 11 16

- C: Prefix = Cleveland Powerglide
- 11: Month = November
- 16: Day = day 16

Warner Gear Date Codes

The letter and numeral or numerals following the source prefix "W" indicates the date the transmission was built. (A for January, B for February, etc., "1" for the first day of the month, "2" for the second date, etc.

Following the day designation, "7" or "57" indicates the year the transmission was built. Following the year numerals is a single numeral, either "1," "2," or "3;" "1" indicating 1st shift, "2" indicating 2nd shift, etc.

4-Speed Example: WC2871

- W: Prefix = Warner 4-Speed
- C: Month = March
- 28: Day = day 28
- 7: Year = 1957
- 1: Shift = 1st Shift

1957 Transmission Letter Prefix Identification

Prefix	Plant	Transmission
B	Toledo	Turboglide (Passenger)
C	Cleveland	Powerglide
M	Muncie	3-Speed (Passenger, Commercial) 4-Speed Truck (Late)
S	Saginaw	3-Speed (Passenger, Corvette)
T	Toledo	4-Speed Truck (Early)
W	Warner Gear	3-Speed H.D. (Truck)
W	Warner Gear	4-Speed (Corvette)

4.2 Transmission Specifications

3-Speed Saginaw (Standard Ratio)

Maincase	Cast Iron
Tailhousing	Cast Iron
Type	Synchromesh
Gear Ratios	1st: 2.94:1 2nd: 1.68:1 3rd: Direct Reverse: 2.94:1
Maincase No.	3845122
Tailhousing No.	3707195 (Passenger)
Sidecover No.	3731457 (Passenger)
Special Information: None	

3-Speed Saginaw (Close Ratio)

Maincase	Cast Iron
Tailhousing	Cast Iron
Type	Synchromesh
Gear Ratios	1st: 2.21:1 2nd: 1.32:1 3rd: Direct Reverse: 2.21:1
Maincase No.	3845122 All
Tailhousing No.	3707195 (Passenger) 3737450 (Corvette)
Sidecover No.	3731457 (Passenger Only) 3731911 (Corvette)
Special Information: This tailhousing transmission is different on Passenger and Corvette. The Corvette tailhousing has three tapped holes cast into the housing to accept the Corvette-only floor shifter. All Passenger models used the column shifter. Early 1957 #3737450 tailhousings do not have casting dated codes. Later tailhousings are dated in the same way as are the maincases. Very early 1957 Corvette 3-speed transmissions carried the #3722946 tailhousing, which was a non-vented, non-dated tailhousing. The #3730450 was initially vented, but not dated until mid-April of 1957 when dates were added to the left side of the casting.	

3-Speed w/Overdrive Saginaw

Maincase	Cast Iron		
Type	3-Speed Synchromesh with 3-pinion planetary drive unit. The drive unit with its integral mainshaft replaces the mainshaft and tailhousing of the regular 3-Speed transmission.		
Operation	Lockout switch manually controlled by "pull-type" cable located under instrument panel to the right of the steering column. Kickdown switch located on floor beneath accelerator pedal.		
Gear Ratios		Locked Out	Locked In
	1st::	2.94:1	2.058:1
	2nd:	1.68:1	1.176:1
	3rd:	Direct	0.700:1
	Reverse:	2.94:1	
Maincase No.	3845122		
Overdrive Unit Casting No.	R10K-1 W.G.DIV		
Sidecover No.	3731457		
Special Information: Maincase is identical with standard maincase except that an extra hole has been drilled in the rear of the maincase to accommodate the overdrive engagement rod.			

4-Speed Close Ratio

Maincase	Cast Iron
Tailhousing	Aluminum
Type	Synchromesh
Gear Ratios	1st: 2.21:1 2nd: 1.66:1 3rd: 1.31:1 4th: Direct , Reverse: 2.25:1
Maincase No.	T10-1
Tailhousing No.	T10-7
Sidecover No.	T10-148
Special Information	Became available in May 1957.

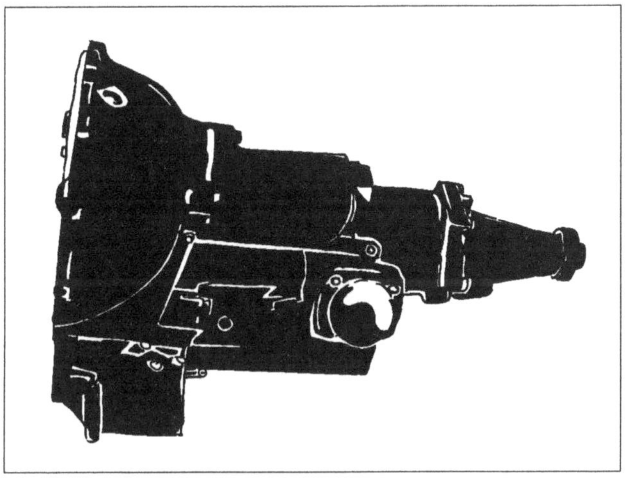

0022366

Fig. 15-33. 2-speed cast iron powerglide transmission.

2-Speed Powerglide

Maincase	Cast Iron
Torque Converter Housing	Cast Iron
Tailhousing	Cast Iron
Type	Hydraulic torque converter with planetary gear system for reverse and low gear.
Gear Ratios	Drive 1.82:1 Low 1.82:1 Reverse: 1.82:1
Maincase No.	3708134
Torque Converter Housing No.	First Design 6-Cylinder: #3708446 Second Design 6-Cylinder #3719240 8-Cylinder #3719243
Special Information: OnCorvette Powerglides the floor position of the shifting mechanism was different, which meant with three tapped holes on the tailhousing to accept the shifter.	

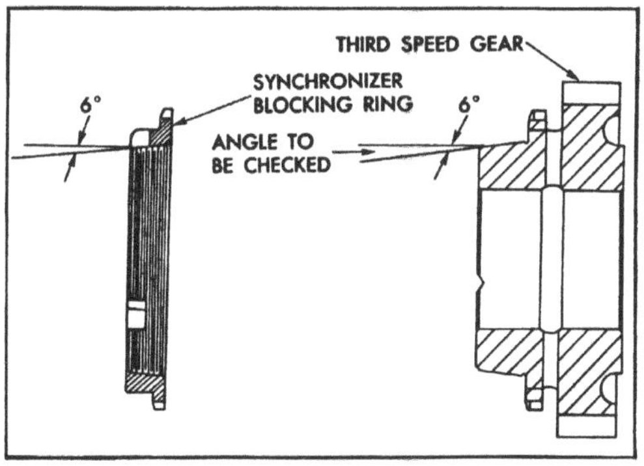

Fig. 3—Checking Third Speed Gear

Corvette 4-Speed Transmission —Harsh Shift Into Third Speed

Some 1957 and 1958 Corvette four-speed transmissions have been built incorporating a third speed gear with 7° cone angle rather than the specified 6°, as illustrated in Figure 3. This may cause a harsh shift into third speed due to the resultant improper engagement of the synchronizer blocking ring and third speed gear cone.

The suggested correction, if the harsh shift is encountered, is to replace the third speed gear assembly No. 3743452 and the synchronizer blocking ring No. 3709348.

The following outlines an angle checking procedure for field usage.

1. Coat I.D. of blocking ring lightly with a dye such as Prussian Blue.
2. Carefully install the blocking ring on the third gear cone to obtain an engagement impression.
3. If the Prussian Blue impression on the cone is all at the rear (or predominantly at the rear) the cone angle can be assumed to be 7° and should not be used. If the Prussian Blue is more or less evenly distributed on the cone surface, the angle is correct.

0023231

2-Speed Turboglide Transmission

Maincase	Cast Aluminum
Tailhousing	Cast Aluminum
Type	Three turbine hydraulic torque converter with first and second turbines driving output shaft through planetary gear sets. Planetary gear sets also provide reverse and hill retarder operation. Two position stator vanes provide extra multiplication.
Drive Gear Ratios	Drive Position Front Planetary Gear Set: 1.63:1 Rear Planetary Gear Set: 2.67:1 Hill Retarder Position Rear Planetary Gear Set: 2.67:1
Maincase No.	3727222
Tailhousing No.	3727210
Special Information	None

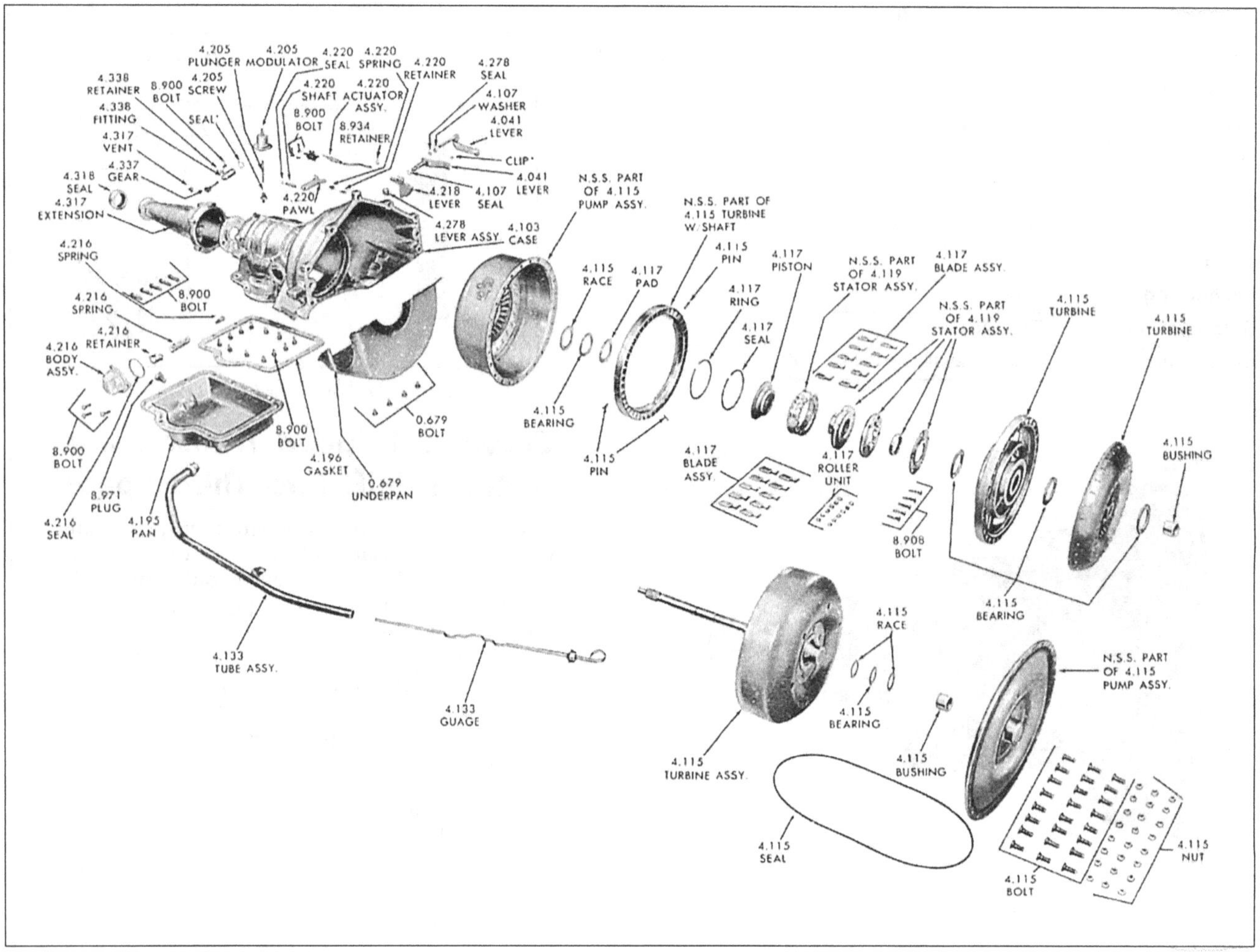

0023922

Fig. 15-34. Exploded view of 1957 Turboglide transmission housing and converter.

5. 1958 TRANSMISSIONS

1958 Transmission Applications

Transmission	Model and Engine
3-Speed Saginaw (Standard)	Passenger car, 235 Only
3-Speed Saginaw (Standard)	Passenger car, 283 Only
3-Speed Close Ratio Saginaw	Passenger/348 only, Corvette/Standard
3-Speed w/Overdrive Saginaw	Passenger car 235, 283
2-Speed Powerglide	Passenger car, Corvette 235, 283, 348
2-Speed Turboglide	Passenger car 283, 348
4-Speed Close Ratio	Corvette 283

5.1 Date Code

Assembly Date Code Location (Car)

Year	Transmission	Code Location
1958	3-Speed	On rear face of transmission case in upper right hand corner. This includes the 3-Speed Overdrive transmission as well.
	4-Speed	On top of transmission case at left rear corner.
	Powerglide	On rear side of governor flange.
	Turboglide	Stamped on machined boss located on lower right rear face of case.

All transmission date coding is as follows: except for transmissions beginning with the prefix "W," one or more numerals designating the month using "1" for January, "2" for February, etc., "10" for October, "11" for November and "12" for December will be stamped immediately following the letter prefix.

Two numerals designating the production date of the month using "01" for the first day of the month, "02" for the second, etc., will follow the numeral or numerals designating the month. The letter "D" or "N" following the date numerals would indicate the unit was built either by the day or night shift. This would pertain only to Powerglide or Turboglide transmissions.

3-Speed Example: S 7 01

- S: Prefix = Saginaw 3-Speed
- 7: Month = July
- 01: Day = day 1

Powerglide Example: C 11 16

- C: Prefix = Cleveland Powerglide
- 11: Month = November
- 16: Day = day 16
- D: Shift = Day Shift

Warner Gear Date Codes

The letter and numeral or numerals following the source prefix "W" indicates the date the transmission was built. (A for January, B for February, etc., "1" for the first day of the month, "2" for the second date, etc.

Following the day designation, "8" or "58" indicates the year the transmission was built. Following the year numerals is a single numeral, either "1," "2," or "3;" "1" indicating 1st shift, "2" indicating 2nd shift, etc.

4-Speed Example: WC2882

W: Prefix = Warner 4-Speed
C: Month = March
28: Day = day 28
8: Year = 1958
2: Shift = 2nd Shift

1958 Transmission Letter Prefix Identification

Prefix	Plant	Transmission
B*	Toledo	Turboglide(Passenger)
C*	Cleveland	Powerglide
M	Muncie	3-Speed (Passenger, Commercial) 4-Speed Truck
S	Saginaw	3-Speed (Passenger, Commercial) 3-Speed Corvette Close Ratio
W	Warner Gear	3-Speed H.D. Truck, 4-Speed Corvette
* The letter "D" or "N" following the date numerals would indicate the unit was built either by the day or night shift.		

5.2 Transmission Specifications

3-Speed Saginaw (Standard Ratio) (235 Engine)

Maincase	Cast Iron
Tailhousing	Cast Iron
Type	Synchromesh
Gear Ratios	1st: 2.94:1 2nd: 1.68:1 3rd: Direct Reverse: 2.94:1
Maincase No.	3743368
Tailhousing No.	3707195
Sidecover No.	3741357
Special Information	None

3-Speed Saginaw (Standard Ratio) (283 Engine)

Maincase	Cast Iron
Tailhousing	Cast Iron
Type	Synchromesh
Gear Ratios	1st: 2.47:1 2nd: 1.53:1 3rd: Direct Reverse: 2.80:1
Maincase No.	3743368
Tailhousing No.	3707195
Sidecover No.	3741357
Special Information	None

3-Speed Saginaw (Close Ratio)

Maincase	Cast Iron
Tailhousing	Cast Iron
Type	Synchromesh
Gear Ratios	1st: 2.21:1 2nd: 1.31:1 3rd: Direct Reverse: 2.21:1
Maincase No.	3743368 All
Tailhousing No.	3707195 Passenger 3737450 Corvette
Sidecover No.	3741357 Passenger 3731911 Corvette
Special Information: The tailhousing on this transmission is different on Passenger models and Corvettes. The Corvette tailhousing has three tapped holes cast into the housing to accept the Corvette-only floor shifter. All Passenger models used the column shifter. The #3737450 tailhousing lacks cut outs at the rear seal. The #3743368 maincase has reverse idler gear mounting webs spaced farther apart for use of the rear disk roller bearing to take the additional thrust.	

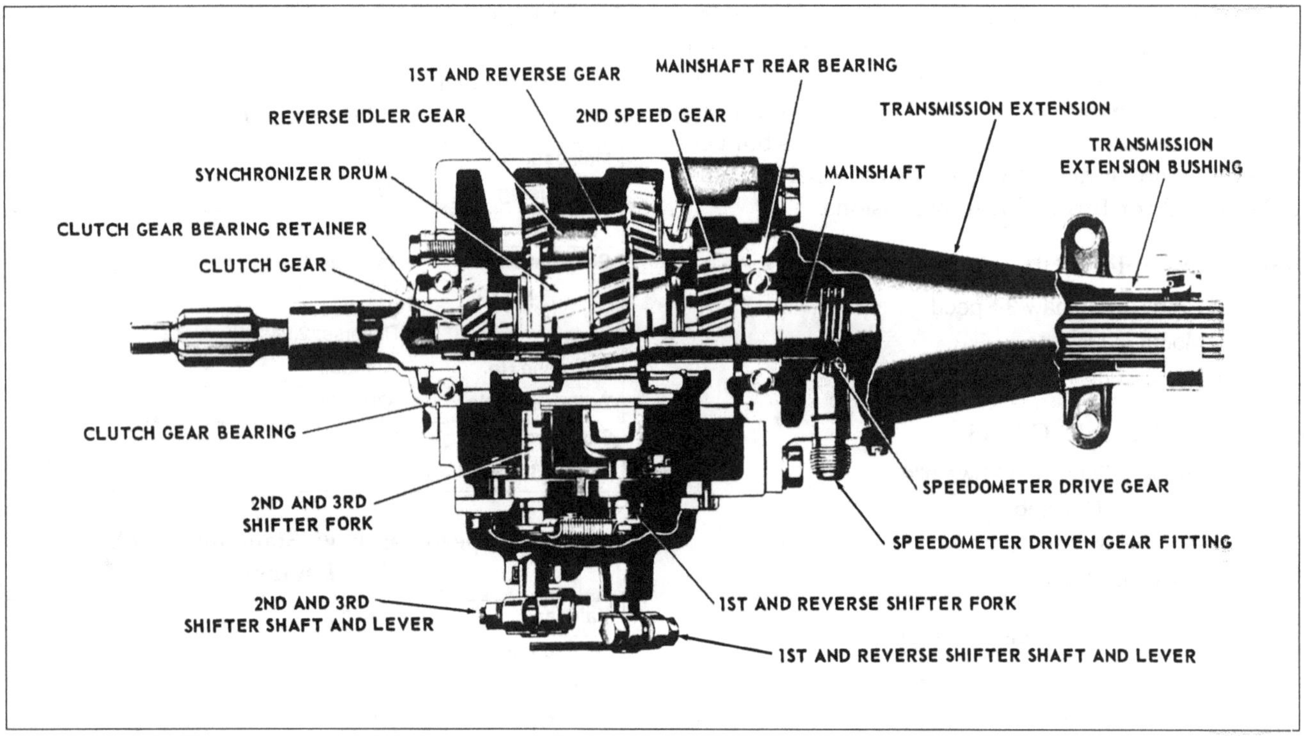

Fig. 15-35. Cutaway view of 1958 3-Speed transmission.

3-Speed Saginaw Overdrive

Maincase	Cast Iron		
Type	3-Speed Synchromesh with 3-pinion planetary drive unit. The drive unit with its integral mainshaft replaces the mainshaft and tailhousing of the regular 3-Speed transmission.		
Operation	Lockout switch manually controlled by "pull-type" cable located under instrument panel to the right of the steering column. Kickdown switch located on carburetor actuated by accelerator pedal.		
Gear Ratios		Locked Out	Locked In
	1st:	2.94:1	2.058:1
	2nd:	1.68:1	1.176:1
	3rd:	Direct	0.700:1
	Reverse:	2.94:1	
Overdrive Casting No.	Unknown		
Special Information:	None		

4-Speed Close Ratio Borg-Warner T10

Maincase	Cast Iron
Tailhousing	Aluminum
Type	Synchromesh
Gear Ratios	1st: 2.21:1 2nd: 1.32:1 3rd: Direct Reverse: 2.51:1
Maincase No.	T10-1
Tailhousing No.	T10-7A
Sidecover No.	T10-148
Special Information: There have been scattered reports of one or two 1958 Impalas with the 283/290HP engine being ordered very late in the year with a factory 4-Speed. This has yet to be verified as a factory documented occurrence.	

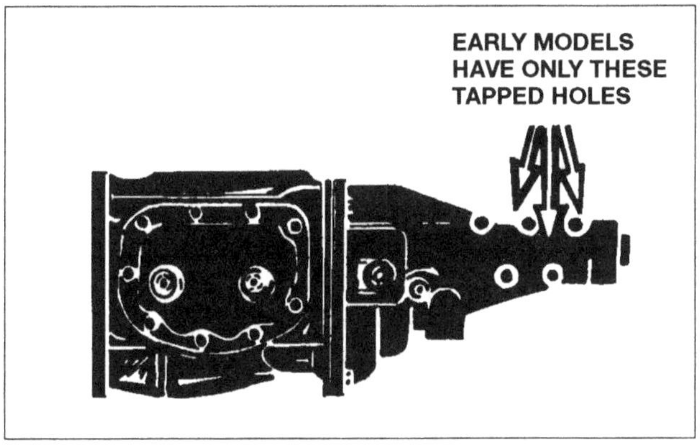

0022365

Fig. 15-36. Borg-Warner 4-speed transmission.

2-Speed Powerglide

Maincase	Cast Iron
Converter Housing	Cast Iron
Tailhousing	Cast Iron
Type	Hydraulic torque converter with planetary gear system for reverse and low gear.
Gear Ratios	Drive 1.82:1 Low 1.82:1 Reverse: 1.82:1
Maincase No.	Unknown
Converter No.	Unknown (6- and 8-cylinder)

Special Information: There were several changes to the 1958 Powerglide which were made during the model year. Two different low servo pistons were used. The low servo piston assembly used previous to serial No. C-1209D has the piston shaft pressed into the piston head. The piston head and shaft in the later design piston assembly are separate pieces permitting incorporation of a captive "cushion spring" beneath the piston head to reduce harshness of low band apply. With the servo cover removed, positive identification of piston construction can be made as the pin retaining the piston head will be visible on the cushion spring design. Also, a new design transmission reverse band link, pin and strut was incorporated into production to provide increased durability in the reverse band linkage. These new design parts entered production on transmission serial number C-108D. Also, as in past years, the Corvette powerglide transmission was only different from the Passenger car model in that the tailhousing was modified to accept the floor mounted shifter in the Corvette

2-Speed Turboglide Transmission

Maincase	Cast Aluminum
Tailhousing	Cast Aluminum
Type	Three turbine hydraulic torque converter with first and second turbines driving output shaft through planetary gear sets. Planetary gear sets also provide reverse and hill retarder operation. Two position stator vanes provide extra multiplication.
Drive Gear Ratios	Drive Position Front Planetary Gear Set 1.63:1 Rear Planetary Gear Set 2.67:1
	Hill Retarder Position Rear Planetary Gear Set 2.67:1
Maincase No.	3747393
Tailhousing No.	Unknown
Special Information	None

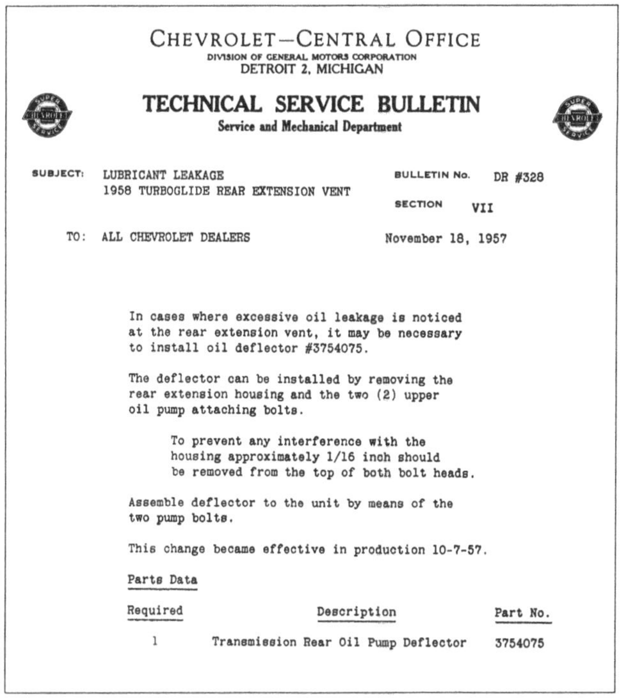

CHEVROLET—CENTRAL OFFICE
DIVISION OF GENERAL MOTORS CORPORATION
DETROIT 2, MICHIGAN

TECHNICAL SERVICE BULLETIN
Service and Mechanical Department

SUBJECT: LUBRICANT LEAKAGE
1958 TURBOGLIDE REAR EXTENSION VENT

BULLETIN No. DR #328
SECTION VII

TO: ALL CHEVROLET DEALERS

November 18, 1957

In cases where excessive oil leakage is noticed at the rear extension vent, it may be necessary to install oil deflector #3754075.

The deflector can be installed by removing the rear extension housing and the two (2) upper oil pump attaching bolts.

To prevent any interference with the housing approximately 1/16 inch should be removed from the top of both bolt heads.

Assemble deflector to the unit by means of the two pump bolts.

This change became effective in production 10-7-57.

Parts Data

Required	Description	Part No.
1	Transmission Rear Oil Pump Deflector	3754075

0023228

Fig. 15-37. The 1958 Turboglide has a short tailhousing with the speedometer gears located within 1/4" of the rear pump. This makes it possible for the drive gear to throw oil out of the transmission vent on top of the tailhousing. This TSB details that a new oil deflector at the rear tailhousing vent entered production on 10-7-57 (Transmission serial number B1007).

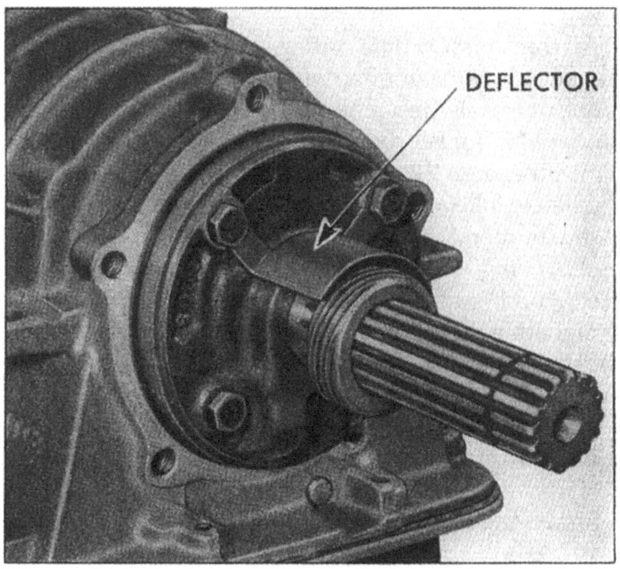

0023243

Fig. 15-38. Photo from Chevy Service News *Vol. 29 shows deflector described in TSB.*

6. 1959 TRANSMISSIONS

1959 Transmission Applications

Transmission	Model and Engine
3-Speed Saginaw (Low Performance)	Passenger 235
3-Speed Saginaw (Standard)	Passenger 283, 348
3-Speed Saginaw (Close Ratio)	Corvette 283
3-Speed Overdrive Saginaw	Passenger 235, 283
4-Speed Close Ratio Borg-Warner	Passenger 283/250, 290HP, 348 Corvette 283
2-Speed Powerglide	Passenger 235, 283, 348 Corvette 283
2-Speed Turboglide	Passenger 283, 348

6.1 Date Code

Assembly Date Code Location (Car)

Year	Transmission	Code Location
1959	3-Speed (incl. overdrive)	On rear face of transmission case in upper right hand corner.
	4-Speed	On top of transmission case at left rear corner.
	Powerglide	On rear side of governor flange.
	Turboglide	Stamped on machined boss located on lower right rear face of case.

All transmission date coding is as follows: Except for transmissions beginning with the prefix "W," one or more numerals designating the month using "1" for January, "2" for February, etc., "10" for October, "11" for November and "12" for December will be stamped immediately following the letter prefix.

Two numerals designating the production date of the month using "01" for the first day of the month, "02" for the second, etc., will follow the numeral or numerals designating the month. The letter "D" or "N" following the date numerals would indicate the unit was built either by the day or night shift.

This would pertain only to Powerglide or Turboglide transmissions.

3-Speed Example: S 7 01

- S: Prefix = Saginaw 3-Speed
- 7: Month = July
- 01: Day = day 1

Powerglide Example: C 11 16

- C: Prefix = Cleveland Powerglide
- 11: Month = November
- 16: Day = day 16
- D: Shift = Day Shift

Warner Gear Date Codes

The letter and numeral or numerals following the source prefix "W" indicates the date the transmission was built. (A for January, B for February, etc., "1" for the first day of the month, "2" for the second date, etc.

Following the day designation, "9" or "59" indicates the year the transmission was built. Following the year numerals is a single numeral, either "1," "2," or "3;" "1" indicating 1st shift, "2" indicating 2nd shift, etc.

4-Speed Example: WC2892

- W: Prefix = Warner 4-Speed
- C: Month = March
- 28: Day = day 28
- 9: Year = 1959
- 2: Shift = 2nd Shift

1959 Transmission Letter Prefix Identification

Prefix	Plant	Transmission
B*	Toledo	Turboglide
C*	Cleveland	Powerglide
M	Muncie	3-Speed (Commercial) 4-Speed Truck
S	Saginaw	3-Speed (Passenger, Commercial) 3-Speed Close Ratio (Corvette) 3-Speed Overdrive
W	Warner Gear	3-Speed H.D. Truck 4-Speed Corvette, Passenger
* The letter "D" or "N" following the date numerals would indicate the unit was built either by the day or night shift.		

6.2 Transmission Specifications

3-Speed Saginaw (Low Performance)

Maincase	Cast Iron
Tailhousing	Cast Iron
Type	Synchromesh
Gear Ratios	1st: 2.94:1 2nd: 1.68:1 3rd: Direct Reverse: 2.94:1
Maincase No.	3743368
Tailhousing No.	3707195
Sidecover No.	3741357
Special Information	None

3-Speed Saginaw

Maincase	Cast Iron
Tailhousing	Cast Iron
Type	Synchromesh
Gear Ratios	1st: 2.47:1 2nd: 1.53:1 3rd: Direct Reverse: 2.80:1
Maincase No.	3743368
Tailhousing No.	3707195
Sidecover No.	3741357
Special Information	None

3-Speed Saginaw (Close Ratio)

Maincase	Cast Iron
Tailhousing	Cast Iron
Type	Synchromesh
Gear Ratios	1st: 2.21:1 2nd: 1.32:1 3rd: Direct Reverse: 2.21:1
Maincase No.	3743368
Tailhousing No.	3737450
Sidecover No.	3731911
Special Information: The Corvette close ratio 3-Speed is identical to the Passenger car 3- Speed except for the gear ratio and gearshift location difference. The gear shift location dictates that the Corvette uses a different transmission tailhousing.	

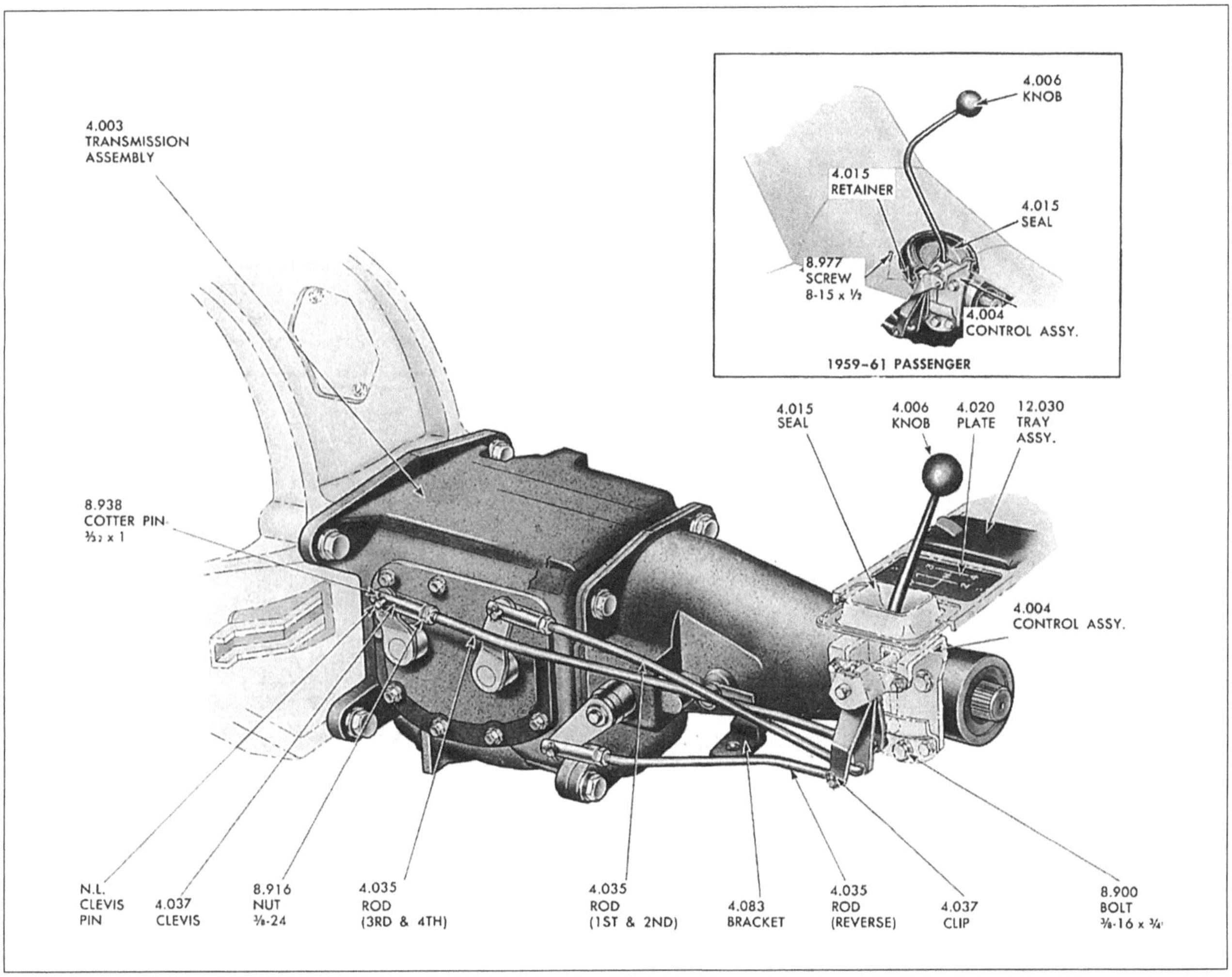

Fig. 15-39. Diagram of 1959–63 Corvette 4-Speed Transmission and controls (typical) with 1959–61 passenger 4-speed shifter in upper right hand corner.

3-Speed Overdrive Saginaw

Maincase	Cast Iron	
Type	3-Speed Synchromesh with 3-pinion planetary drive unit. The drive unit with its integral mainshaft replaces the mainshaft and tailhousing of the regular 3-Speed transmission.	
Operation	Lockout switch manually controlled by "pull-type" cable located under instrument panel to the right of the steering column. Kickdown switch located on carburetor actuated by accelerator pedal.	
Gear Ratios:	Locked Out	Locked In
1st:	2.94:1	2.058:1
2nd:	1.68:1	1.176:1
3rd:	Direct	0.700:1
Reverse:	2.94:1	
Overdrive No.	Unknown	
Special Information: None		

4-Speed Close Ratio Borg-Warner T10

Maincase	Cast Iron
Tailhousing	Aluminum
Type	Synchromesh
Gear Ratio	1st: 2.20:1 2nd: 1.66:1 3rd: 1.31:1 4th: Direct Reverse: 2.26:1
Maincase No.	T10-1 prior to 6/59 T10-B after 6/59
Tailhousing No.	T10-7A
Sidecover No.	T10 -148A
Special Information: Corvette 4-Speed is identical to the Passenger transmission except for the following: Reverse Inhibitor Positive manually controlled. Operation: Lift "T" handle allowing selector lever to enter reverse gate. Speedometer Gears Number of Teeth: Drive gear 8, Driven gear 21, Normal tooth pitch 30	

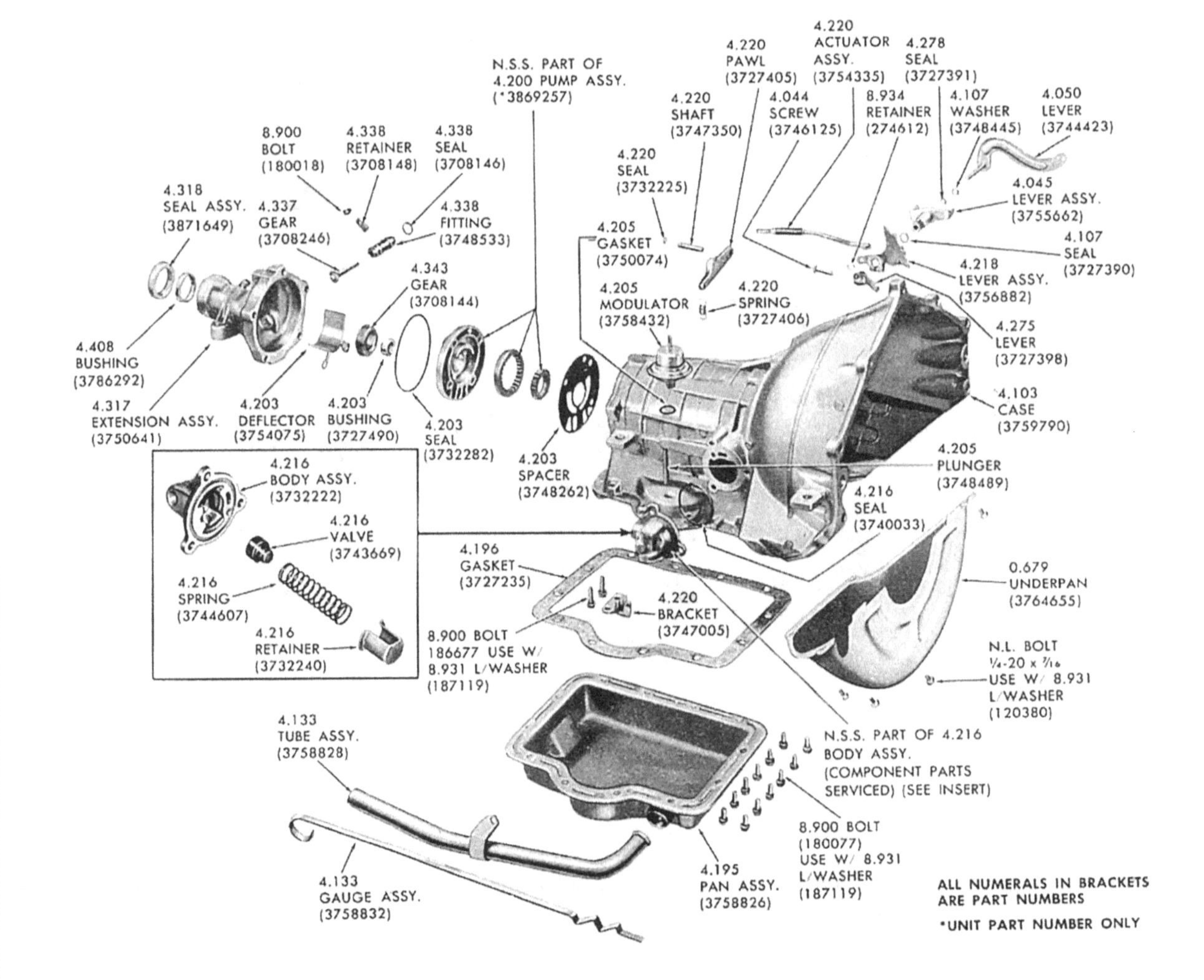

Fig. 15-40. 1959–61 Turboglide transmission housing exploded view (typical).

2 Speed Powerglide

Maincase	Cast Iron
Converter Housing	Cast Iron
Tailhousing	Cast Iron
Type	Hydraulic torque converter with planetary gear system for reverse and low gear.
Gear Ratio:	Maximum overall ratio 3.82:1 Low gear drive or low 3.82:1 to 1.82:1 Reverse 3.82:1 to 1.82:1
Maincase No.	Unknown
Converter No.	Unknown (both 18- and 33-bolt)
Special Information: There were several changes to the Powerglide during the 1959 model year. 1) Balance markings were used for the first time on engines and automatic transmissions to provide closer indexing of these components. 2) All automatic transmission flywheels had a "white" paint mark on the outer rim, on the transmission side, to indicate the heavy side. 3) All automatics had a stripe across the ends of both converter cover and housing to denote the "light" side of the transmission. These markings were to be aligned as closely as possible during the assembly of transmission to engine. 4) V-8 and L-6 flywheels for Powerglides were changed from three transmission attaching holes to six. The three holes were to permit more accurate indexing of the converter to flywheel, but the actual attachment remained three bolts. There are five configurations of 1959 Powerglides. See the following chart.	

1959 Powerglide Transmission Configurations

Application	Ident.	Notes
6-cyl. Passenger, Low Perf.	Blue Name Plate	Transmission housing peculiar to 6-cyl. model. Will not interchange with V-8.
8-cyl. Passenger, Standard	Blue Name Plate	18 converter housing to cover bolts. 6- and 8-cylinder transmissions differ in the size of the booster valves and sleeves and in the throttle valve spring.
Corvette	Blue Name Plate	33 converter housing to cover bolts. Tailhousing has three drilled and tapped bosses for shifter assembly. Longer output shaft. Special light weight governor. No oil cooler valve or piping for oil cooling.
Passenger 283/250HP Engine	Red Name Plate	33 converter housing to cover bolts. Corvette converter and governor.
Passenger 348/305HP Engine	White Name Plate	33 converter housing to cover bolts. Special 5400 RPM Governor. Special five-plate clutch assembly, identified by the number 054 stamped on the drum face. These plates are thinner than plates in other Powerglides and are identified as follows: Driven Plates: Number "6" stamped on 3 drive tangs. Drive Plates: One tooth removed every 120° around the inner diameter.

2-Speed Turboglide

Maincase	Cast Aluminum
Tailhousing	Cast Aluminum
Type	Triple turbine hydraulic torque converter with first turbine and second turbine driving output shaft through planetary gearsets. Third turbine drives output shaft directly. Planetary gear sets also provide reverse and grade retarder operation. Two position stator valves provide extra multiplication.
Drive Gear Ratios	Drive Position Front Planetary Gear Set 1.63:1 Rear Planetary Gear Set 2.67:1 Hill Retarder Position Rear Planetary Gear Set 2.67:1
Maincase No.	Unknown
Tailhousing No.	Unknown
Special Information	None

7. TRANSMISSION DATA CHARTS

Saginaw 3-Speed Component Casting Numbers

Year	Application	Maincase Casting #	Tailhousing Casting #	Sidecover Casting #	Front Bearing Retainer Casting #
1955	Passenger	3845122	3707195	3845044 1st 3845157 2nd	591620
	Corvette	3845122	3722946	3845044 1st 3845157 2nd	591620
1956	Passenger	3845122	3707195	3845157	591620
	Corvette	3845122	3722946	3845157	591620
1957	Passenger	3845122	3707195	3741357	591620
	Corvette	3845122	3737450	3731911	591620
1958	Passenger	3743368	3707195	3741357	3741458
	Corvette	3743368	3737450	3731911	3741458
1959	Passenger	3743368	3707195	3741357	3741458
	Corvette	3743368	3737450	3731911	3741458

Borg-Warner 4-Speed Transmission Component Casting Numbers (1957–59)

Year	Application	Maincase Casting #	Tailhousing Casting #	Sidecover Casting #	Rear Bearing Retainer Casting #
1957	Corvette	T10-1*	T10-7	T10-148	T10-107
1958	Corvette	T10-1*	T10-7A	T10-148	T10-107
1959	Passenger Corvette	T10-1* T10-1B* AFT. 5/59	T10-7A	T10-148A	T10-107
*Cast iron. Note: The T10-7B tailhousing was used on replacement transmissions and Oldsmobile/Buick applications because the mounting configuration allowed the transmission to be installed in the earlier applications.					

Powerglide Applications

Model	Year	Housing Material	Tailhousing Length (in.)	# of Output Shaft Splines	Special Information
Passenger	1955–57	Cast Iron	7-1/4 (Long)	16 (Coarse)	Column shift only
	1958–62	Cast Iron	5 (Short)	16 (Coarse)	
Corvette	1953–55	Cast Iron	5 (Short)	16 (Coarse)	Shifter bolts to floor
	1956–61	Cast Iron	7-1/4 (Long)	16 (Coarse)	Shifter bolts to tailhousing

Manual Transmission Dimensions*

Transmission	Front Of Input Shaft To Front Of Case (A)	Front Of Case To Mount Location (B)	Overall Length (C)	End Of Case To End Of Output Spline (D)	Mount Bolt Spacing	Spline Count (Input/Output Shaft)
Saginaw/Muncie 3-Speed	6-1/2	14	21-1/2	1/2	3-3/4	10/27
Saginaw 4-Speed	6-1/4	14	21-1/2	1/2	3-3/4	10/27
Muncie 4-Speed	6-1/2	14	21-1/2	1/2	3-3/4	M20/M21 1963-70; M22,1965-69: 10/27 M20/M21, 1971-74; M22,1970-74: 26/32
Borg-Warner T10 4-Speed (1957–63)	6-1/2	14	21-1/2	1/2	3-3/4	10/16
Borg-Warner Super T10 4-Speed (OEM Only) 1974–81 2nd Design	6-1/2	14	22-1/4	1/2	3-3/4	26/32
*Dimensions in inches; some converted from metric system						

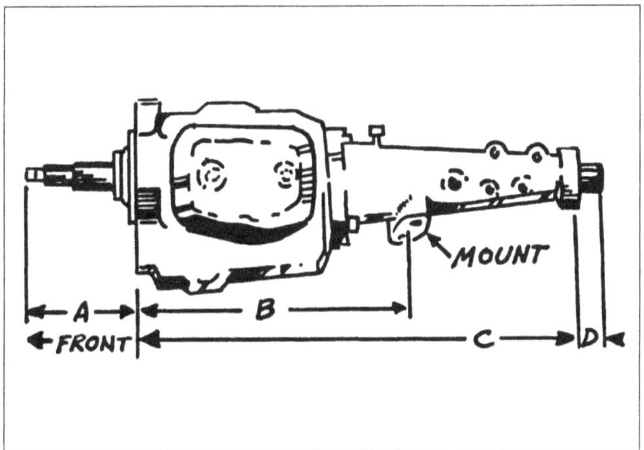

0022304

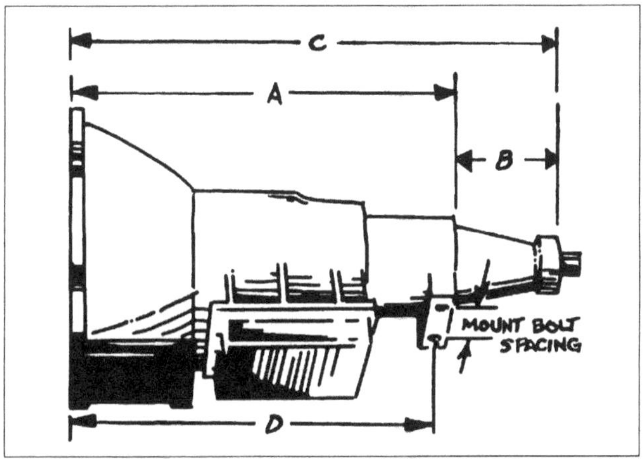

0022305

Automatic Transmission Dimensions***

Transmission	Case-to-Block Mounting Pattern	Case Length (A)	Tailshaft Length (B)	Overall Length (C)	Mount Location (D)	# Of Splines On Output Shaft	Mount Bolt Spacing
Powerglide (Cast Iron)	Chevrolet	22	5 or 7-1/4	27 or 29-1/4"	Varies	16	3-3/4
Powerglide (Aluminum)	Chevrolet	16	9 or 11-1/4	27-1/4"	21-1/4	27	3-3/4
TH-350*	Chevrolet B-O-P Composite	21-1/4	4 9-1/2 13-1/2	A+B	End Of Case minus 1-1/2	27	3-3/4
TH-400**	Chevrolet B-O-P	21-1/4	4 9-1/2 13-1/2	A+B	End Of Case minus 1-1/2	27/32	3-3/4 or 4-1/4

*Turbohydramatic 350 transmissions came with either a Chevrolet or BOP (Buick-Oldsmobile-Pontiac) bolt pattern. Some late model transmissions have a composite pattern which contains both Chevrolet and BOP bolt patterns
**Turbohydramatic 400 transmissions came in a variety of bolt patterns including Cadillac
***All dimensions in inches. Late model dimensions converted from the metric system

Chapter 16

Rear Axle/Differential Identification

1. Introduction

This chapter will focus on the different types of Chevrolet rear axle designs and differentials (together called the "rear end") used in the years from 1955 through 1959. There were numerous changes over that period. All rear end changes are grouped under two model headings: Passenger and Corvette.

Most rear ends covered here were built with a semi-floating "hotchkiss" design type rear axle, where a live rear axle is positioned by leaf springs. This rear axle has a front-loaded removable center section in which the ring and pinion can be easily switched without completely disassembling the rear axle. These axles do not use a rear inspection cover. I will cover the rear differentials in brief detail here to point out the specific differences that exist.

1.1 Passenger Rear Ends

1955 Through 1957 Passenger

The 1955 through 1957 rear end was a semi-floating "hotchkiss" drive type rear axle. It featured a pressed steel banjo of two-piece welded construction with the rear axle housing cover welded in place. The differential is a two-pinion type with a cast iron arma-steel housing. The rear end is mounted on multi-leaf semi-elliptic springs. The total leaf count ranges from four to six leafs, depending on model of car and optional load packages. The axle shafts were forged and hardened steel with the wheel drive flange forged integral with the axle shaft. The axle width is the same for all three years.

There were some changes to the axles and third member during the three year span. There were also positraction third members installed in some high

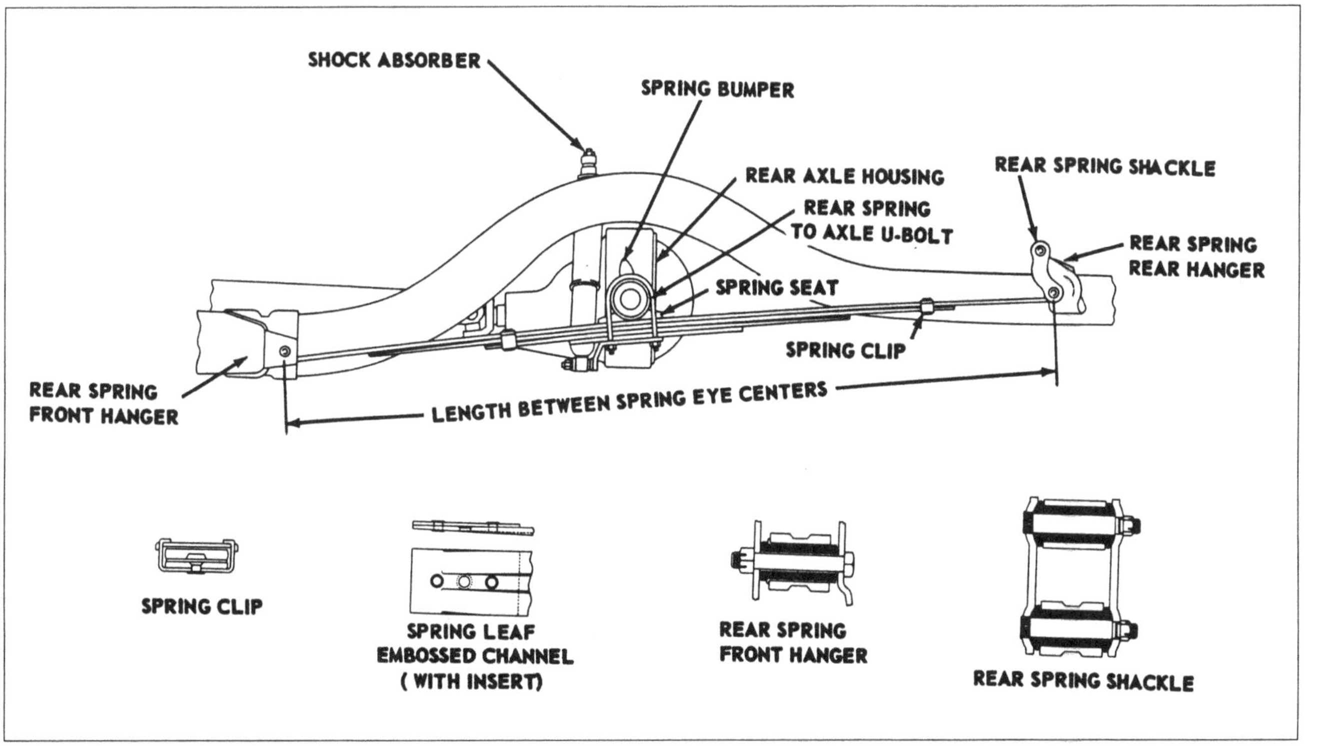

Fig. 16-1. 1955 Passenger rear end.

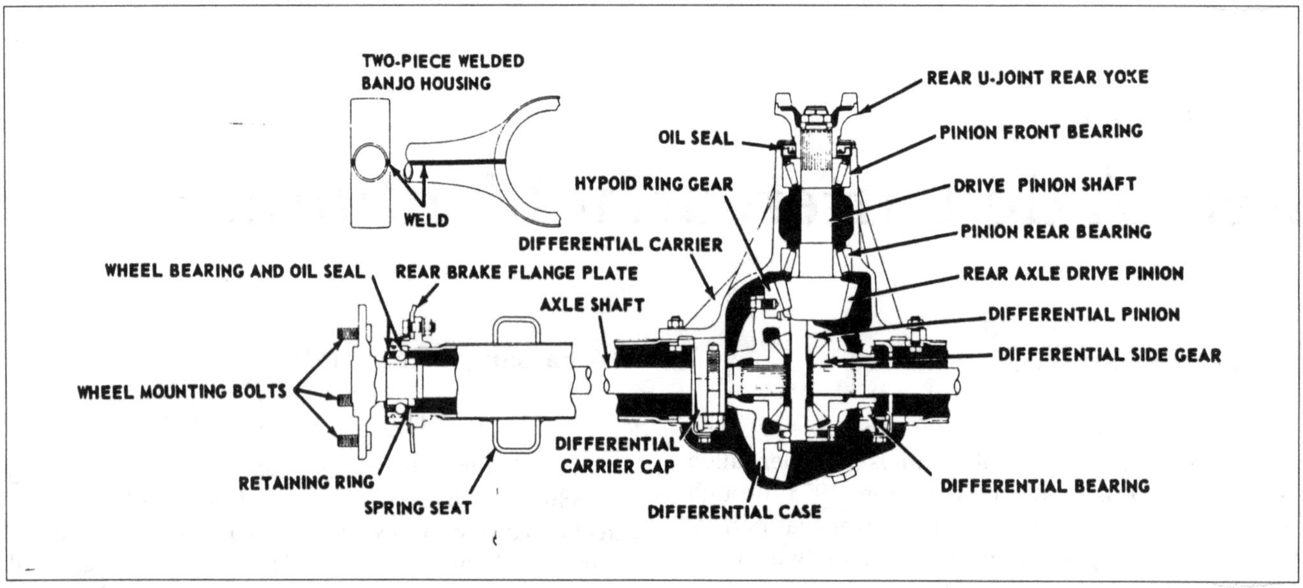

Fig. 16-2. Detail of 1955 Passenger car rear end.

performance models, mostly in Passenger cars and Corvettes after January 1957. Those third members had distinct lettering to signify a positraction housing. See 1955–57 Passenger Center Section Casting Numbers

The specifications for the 1955 through 1957 rear ends are as follows:

Passenger, 1955

Rear End Type	10 Bolt, dropout style
Ring Gear Diameter (in.)	8.20
Pinion Diameter (in.)	1.438
Pinion Splines	17
Axle Splines	17
Axle Spline Diameter	1.172
Overall Dimensions:	
Axle tube flange to axle tube flange	55"
Between centerlines of spring perches	46"
Axle shaft length	RH: 30-5/16" LH: 28-13/16"
Casting No.	RH: AAC-3714782 LH: DEE-3714781

Passenger, 1956

Rear End Type	10 Bolt, dropout style
Ring Gear Diameter (in.)	8.20
Pinion Diameter (in.)	1.438
Pinion Splines	17
Axle Splines	17
Axle Spline Diameter	1.172
Overall Dimensions:	
Axle tube flange to axle tube flange	55"
Between centerlines of spring perches	46"
Axle shaft length	RH: 30-5/16" LH: 28-13/16"
Casting No.	RH: AAC-3714782 LH: DEE-3714781

Passenger, 1957

Rear End Type	10 Bolt, dropout style
Ring Gear Diameter (in.)	8.20
Pinion Diameter (in.)	1.438
Pinion Splines	17
Axle Splines	17
Axle Spline Diameter	1.172
Overall Dimensions:	
Axle tube flange to axle tube flange	55"
Between centerlines of spring perches	46"
Axle shaft length	RH Open: 30-1/16" RH Posi: 30-3/16"
	LH Open: 28-9/16" LH Posi: 28-11/16"

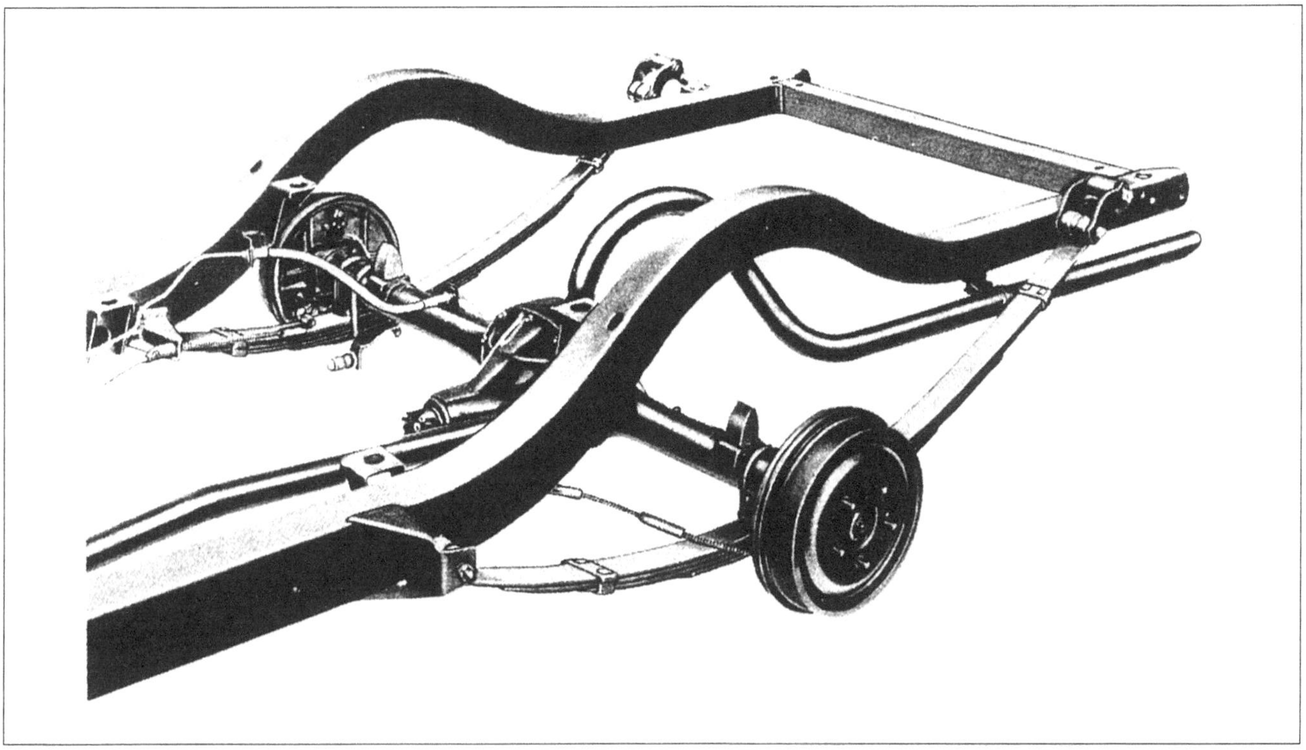

0023234

Fig. 16-3. 1956 Passenger car rear end.

1955–57 Passenger Center Section Casting Numbers

Model Year	Casting Number	Axle Type
1955	Unverified	Open axle only (Posi Unavailable)*
1956	3707306	Open axle (Posi unavailable)**
1957	3725899	Open axle
	3743833	Posi axle
*No casting date **1956 and 1957 axles have casting date		

Positraction Axles

The positraction option became available after December 1956. There were three specific early positraction cases. The first case is known as the "No X" case, which was cast in December 1956 and was built in January 1957 for standard production cars. This case will have a December casting date and no "X," which is present on later posi cases. The second case is known as the "X" case. This case was cast starting in the last of January through February of 1957, with build dates in February and March of that same year. This case has an "X" cast into the case near the letters GM but does not have the later "P" designation. After March 27, 1957, all factory posi cases have a "P" (designating positraction) cast into the carrier adjacent to casting number; the former "X" designation is now gone. Some 1957 model year posi "P" cases were also used as open (non-posi) rear ends. These specific "P" cases have an extra reinforcement rib inside the case that will not allow a positraction unit to be installed into the case. There have been three of these "P" cases discovered (dated December 56, March 57, & May 57) that have been verifiably used as non-posi rear axle assemblies. This "P" case was used through the 1964 model year in Passenger car and Corvette models.

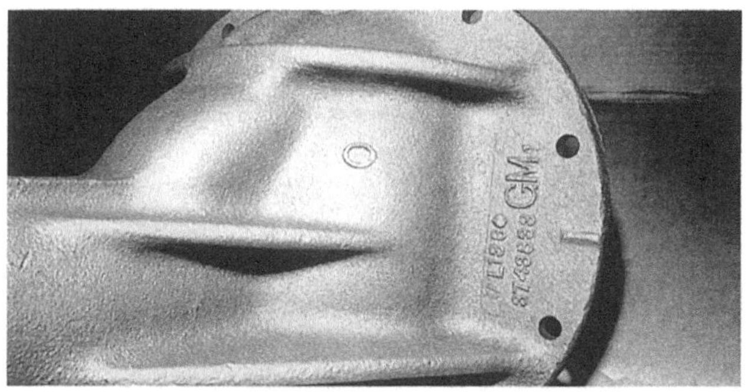

Fig. 16-4. First design positraction "No X" case. Note L136 casting date (December 13, 1956).

0023236

Fig. 16-5. Close-up of same first design positraction "No X" case.

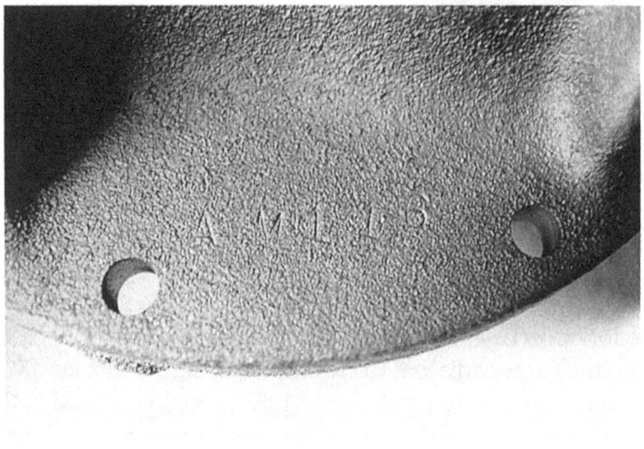

0023237

Fig. 16-6. Build date stamp of first design positraction "No X" case. Note AM 116 Passenger car date code (January 16, 1957).

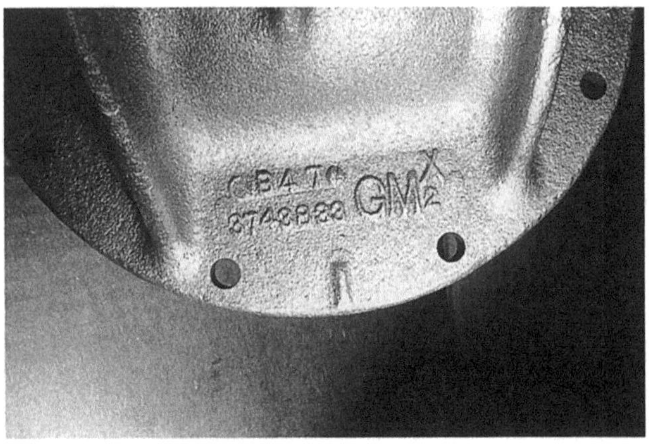

0023238

Fig. 16-7. Second design positraction "X" case. Note B47 casting date (February 4, 1957).

There are two types of "P" posi cases. One is regarded as the "thin P" case and the other the "thick P" case. The thin/thick designation refers to the size or thickness of the letter P on the case. The "thin P" was built in Detroit, Michigan, and used in all 1957–62 Corvettes and many 1958–64 Passenger cars. This type would also have a single-digit year date code. The "thick P" case was built in Buffalo, New York, and used in 1958–64 Passenger cars only and has a two-digit year date code.

Example for the 1959 Model Year:

Year Code (1959)	Case Type	Model Usage	Plant
9	Thin "P"	Passenger or Corvette	Detroit, MI
59	Thick "P"	Passenger	Buffalo, NY

0023239

Fig. 16-8. Third design positraction "thin P" case. Note single-digit D17 casting date (April 1, 1957).

1958–59 Passenger

This rear end was used from 1958 through 1964. It is a semi-floating four-link design which utilized coil springs with one upper control arm and two lower control arms. It featured a pressed steel banjo that was of two-piece welded construction with the rear axle housing cover welded in place. The differential was a two-pinion type with a cast arma-steel housing. The axle shafts were forged and hardened steel with the wheel drive flange forged integral with the axle shaft. The axle width is the same for all 1958–64 differentials. The differential third member and axles are the same for all 1955–58 Passenger cars and for the 1959–64 cars. The overall length of the differential is the same, but the 1955–57 rear end is leaf spring mounted where the 1958–64 differential is coil spring mounted.

1958 is the first year for the new four-link suspension under a passenger car. The upper control arm is totally different from 1959–64 designs in that the forward part of the arm has a two-position mounting to the frame crossmember. The rear position is mounted to a bracket

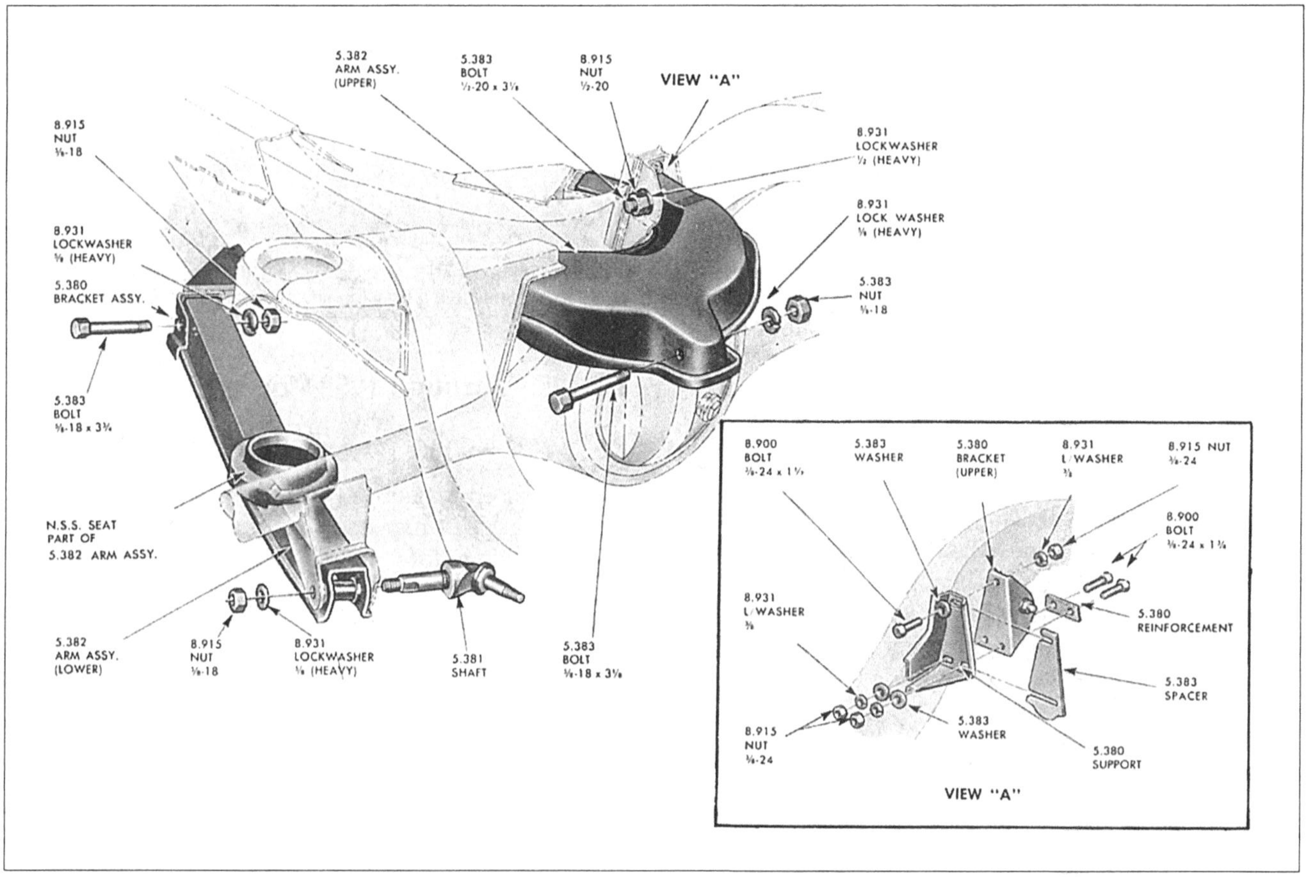

0023241

Fig. 16-9. 1958 Passenger rear suspension.

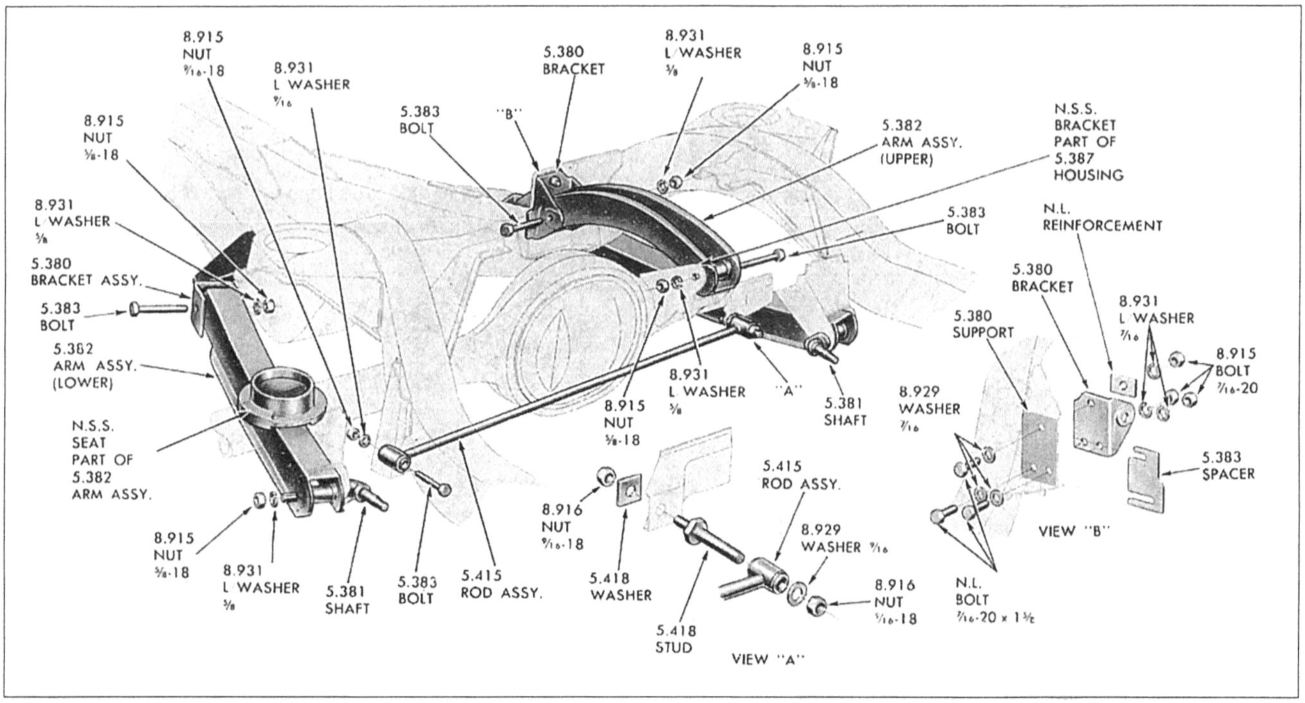

0023242

Fig. 16-10. 1959–64 Passenger rear end.

welded to the center section of the differential case. Also, the 1958 rear end does not have a lateral control bar.

The 1959 Passenger car differential had several major changes from the 1958 offering. The rear tread width was increased 1/2" and new wider brakes and wheels dictated a 1/2" widening of the rear axle. Consequently, the 1959 rear axle shafts were lengthened to account for this change. The upper control arm changed in several areas. The arm is pivot mounted at the front to the right frame side member and at the rear to the banjo area of the right axle housing tube. The 1958 double front mount upper control arm is now gone. A new lateral control bar or otherwise known as the rear axle tie rod has been added to control lateral movement of the axle. The lateral control bar is pivotally mounted at one end to the right axle housing tube and at the other end to the left frame side member. This design continued with a few minor changes through the 1964 model year on all Passenger cars. Although the 1958 and 1959–64 rear differentials are similar, many pieces will not interchange due to these design changes. The overall dimensions of the 1958–59 rear end are as follows:

Passenger, 1958

Rear End Type	10 Bolt, dropout style
Ring Gear Diameter (in.)	8.20
Pinion Diameter (in.)	1.438
Pinion Splines	17
Axle Splines	17
Axle Spline Diameter	1.172
Overall Dimensions:	
Axle tube flange to axle tube flange	55"
Outside control arm bracket around centerline of hole to opposite side outside control arm bracket hole	46-27/32"
Axle shaft length	RH Open: 30-1/16" RH Posi: 30-5/16"
	LH Open: 28-9/16" LH Posi: 28-13/16"

Passenger, 1959

Rear End Type	10 Bolt/Dropout style
Ring Gear Diameter (in.)	8.20
Pinion Diameter (in.)	1.438
Pinion Splines	17
Axle Splines	17
Axle Spline Diameter	1.172
Overall Dimensions:	
Axle tube flange to axle tube flange	55"
Outside control arm bracket around centerline of hole to opposite side outside control arm bracket hole	46-27/32"
Axle shaft length	RH: 30-1/2" LH: 29-1/2"

1958–59 Passenger Center Section Casting Numbers

Model Year	Casting Number	Axle Type
1958	3725899	Open axle (Has casting date)
	3743833	Posi axle*
1959	3725899	Open axle (Has casting date)
	3743833	Posi axle*
*See earlier text for "P" positraction case info. After May 1, 1958 all Posi rear axles have a Posi Identification tag attached to filler plug.		

1.2 1955 Through 1959 Corvette Rear End

1955 Corvette Rear End

This rear end was used from 1953 through the 1955 model year. This rear end was a semi-floating Hotchkiss drive type differential. It featured a pressed steel banjo that was of two-piece welded construction with a removable inspection cover. This axle center was much smaller than the passenger axle and the rear axles had a C-clip retention system similar to the late model 12-bolt axles. The axles in this differential are the same as the 1951–54 Passenger car axles. This axle has an exposed, unsupported driveshaft. The overall dimensions for the 1953–55 Corvette differential are as follows:

Corvette, 1955

Rear End Type	10 Bolt, C-Clip style
Ring Gear Diameter (in.)	8.20
Pinion Diameter (in.)	1.438
Pinion Splines	17
Axle Splines	17
Axle Spline Diameter	1.155
Overall Dimensions:	
Axle tube flange to axle tube flange	54-1/2"
Between centerlines of spring perches	47-5/8"
Axle shaft length	RH: 29-1/2", 2-3/4" pilot LH: 28 1/2", 2-3/4" pilot
Casting No.	RH: 3694756 LH: 3694755

1956–59 Corvette Rear End

This rear end was used from 1956 through 1962. This rear end was a semi-floating hotchkiss drive type differential. It featured a pressed steel banjo that was of two-piece welded construction with the rear axle cover welded in place. The differential was a two-pinion type with a cast arma-steel housing. The axle shafts were forged and hardened steel with the wheel drive flange forged integral with the axle shaft. The axle width is the same for all seven years that this year was produced. There were several changes to the third member and axle mounting brackets, but they are covered below. The rear end is mounted on semi-elliptic multi-leaf springs rated at 725 lbs. at ground level.

1956–58 Corvette Differential: All of these Corvette axles are the same and do not have the strut bar brackets welded onto the axle housing. All of these axles have a drain plug.

1959 Corvette Differential: All of these rear ends are identical with the earlier axles with the exception that radius rods have been added to each side of the rear axle. The radius rods mount to the axle on new axle brackets, which stand up between the U-bolt leaf spring mountings. The opposite end of the radius rod mounts to a bracket located on the side of the frame in front of the axle. These radius rods were added to provide greater vehicle stability and increased traction. Finally, no 1959–62 Corvette rear differentials have a drain plug. The overall dimensions of the 1956–62 Corvette and rear differential are listed below.

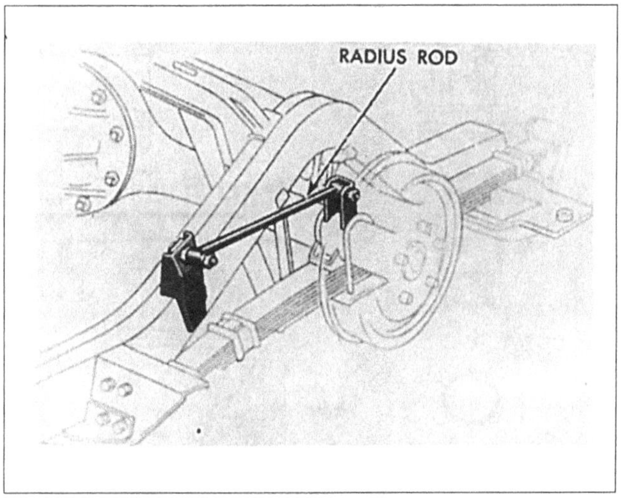

0022376

Fig. 16-11. *1959–62 Corvette rear end, with radius rod highlighted.*

Corvette, 1956

Rear End Type	10 Bolt, dropout style
Ring Gear Diameter (in.)	8.20
Pinion Diameter (in.)	1.438
Pinion Splines	17
Axle Splines	17
Axle Spline Diameter	1.172
Overall Dimensions:	
Axle tube flange to axle tube flange	55"
Between centerlines of spring perches	47-15/64"
Axle shaft length	RH: 30-5/16" LH: 28-13/16"
Casting No.	RH: AAC-3714782 LH: DEE-3714781

Corvette, 1957–58

Rear End Type	10 Bolt, dropout style
Ring Gear Diameter (in.)	8.20
Pinion Diameter (in.)	1.438
Pinion Splines	17
Axle Splines	17
Axle Spline Diameter	1.172
Overall Dimensions:	
Axle tube flange to axle tube flange	55"
Between centerlines of spring perches	47-15/64"
Axle shaft length	RH Open: 30-1/16" RH Posi: 30-5/16"
	LH Open: 28-9/16" LH Posi: 28-13/16"

Corvette, 1959

Rear End Type	10 Bolt, dropout style
Ring Gear Diameter (in.)	8.20
Pinion Diameter (in.)	1.438
Pinion Splines	17
Axle Splines	17
Axle Spline Diameter	1.172
Overall Dimensions:	
Axle tube flange to axle tube flange	55"
Between centerlines of spring perches	47-15/64"
Axle shaft length	RH: 30-5/16" LH: 28-13/16"

1955–59 Corvette Center Section Casting Numbers

Model Year	Casting Number	Axle Type
1955	3698950 (Pressed into case)	Open axle only (No casting date)
1956	3707306	Open axle (Posi unavailable*)
1957–59	3725899	Open axle
	3743833	Posi axle

*1956 and later axles have casting date. Special run of positraction axles using #3707306 case were built for factory sponsored Corvette race cars. These axles had "HT" stamped into axle center section to indicate "High Torque" posi rear axle. Positraction option became available after December 1956. See 1955–57 Passenger Center Section Casting Numbers for "P" positraction case info. After April 1, 1957 all factory posi cases will have a "P" cast into carrier adjacent to casting number. After May 1, 1958 all Posi rear axles have a Posi Identification tag attached to filler plug.

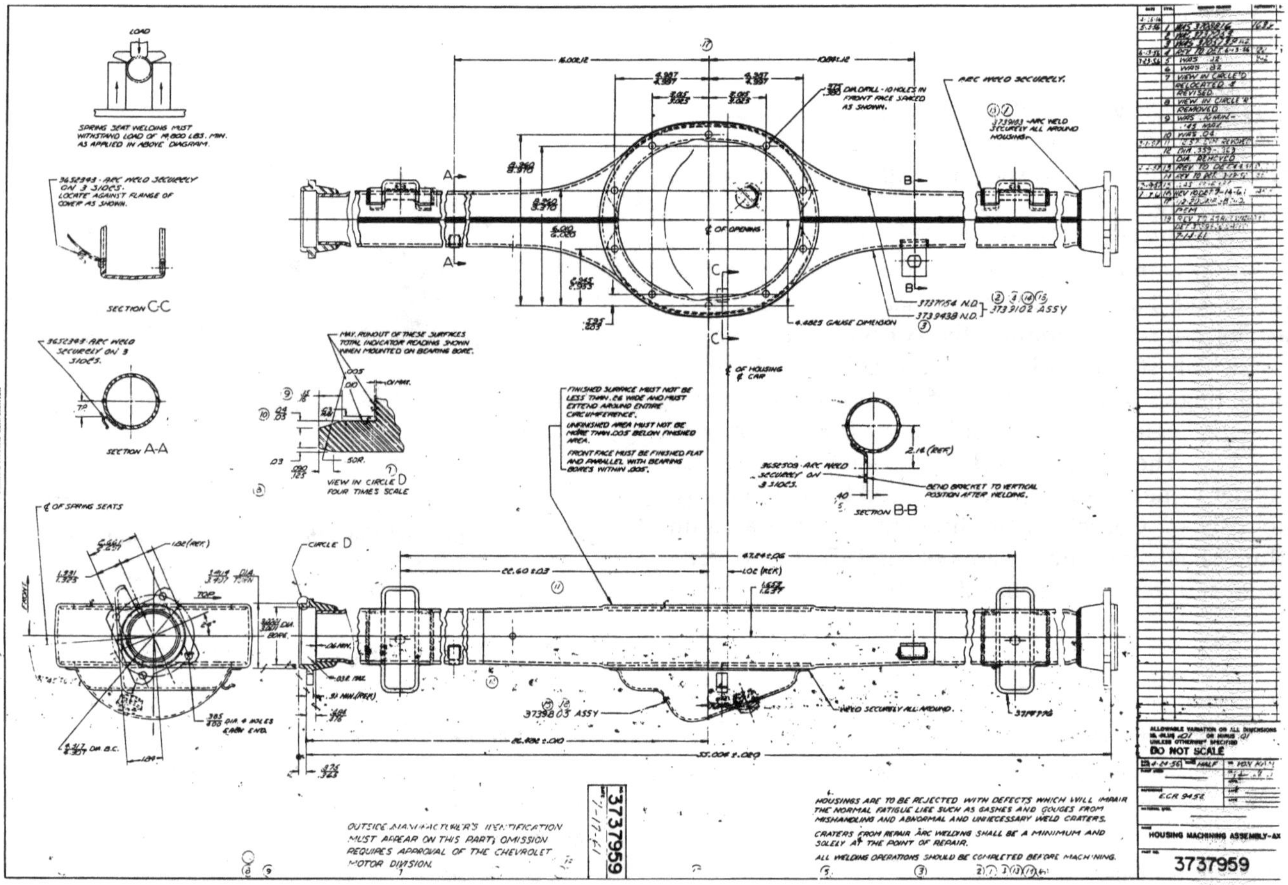

0022384

Fig. 16-12. Blueprint of 1959 Corvette rear axle housing machining assembly.

2. REAR AXLE IDENTIFICATION

The rear axle of a car has two separate date codes. The most commonly known code is the build date code. This code is usually stamped on the carrier of the axle assembly on earlier vehicles and Corvettes.On later vehicles, this code is stamped on the axle tube near the center section or carrier. This stamping designates the month/day axle assembly date, axle plant code, and model usage suffix code. See Fig. 16-13. Second, almost all rear axles after 1955 have a casting date on the carrier. It is always a smart idea to compare this casting date code to the build date code of the axle, always remembering that the carrier had to be manufactured prior to the final building of the axle.

Ring and Pinion Identification

The plant source for the differential pinion in the rear axle can be found by checking the pinion head. Fig. 16-14 shows the pinion heads for the rear axles manufactured at the plants covered by this book. Also see the end of this chapter for more information.

Positraction Unit Casting Numbers

There were two specific positraction designs used from 1957 through 1964. The positraction unit used from 1957–59 was the first design and is shown in Fig. 16-15. The second design was used from 1960–64 and can be identified from the first design primarily from internal changes to the unit.

There were two main differences between the designs:

1) The 1957–59 1st design used an eight piece clutch design (friction plates), while the 1960–64 2nd design used a 10 piece clutch design. The early production 1960 vehicles were equipped with a positraction similar to the 1957–59 design except for a change in the friction plates. The change consisted of the substitution of a Belleville or "dished" plate for each outboard plate. The later production 1960 vehicles were equipped with completely new differential assemblies incorporating a five plate positraction unit with two friction discs, two friction plates plus a Belleville plate. Also, the ramp angle on the pinion pins and case are 45° on the late 1960–64 unit, in contrast to the 30° design on the 1957–early

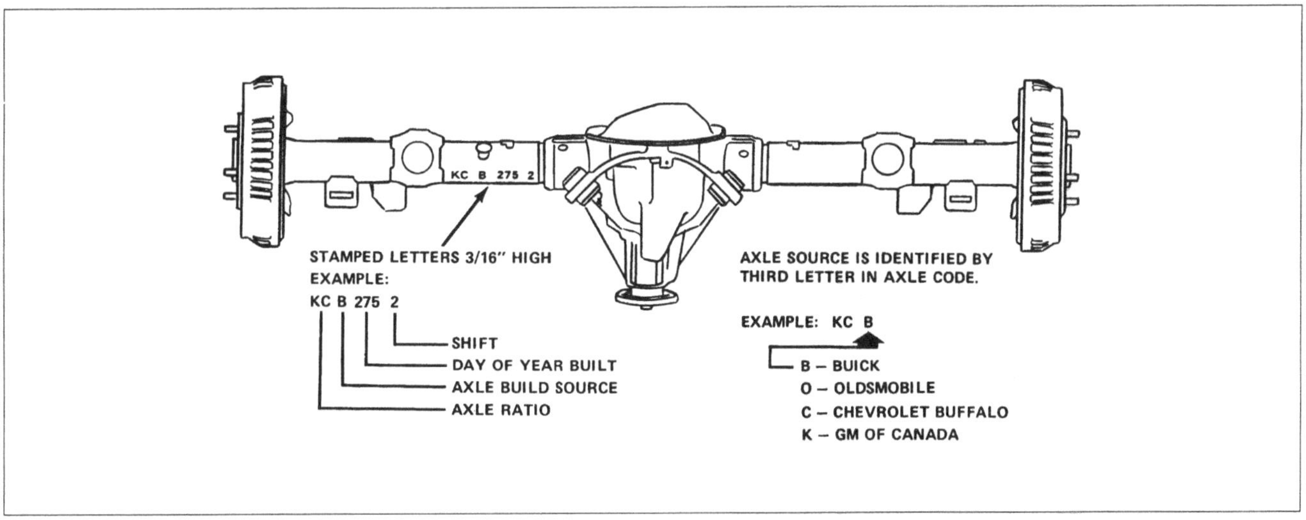

Fig. 16-13. Typical axle code location. Note that day of year built indicates 1971 and later coding.

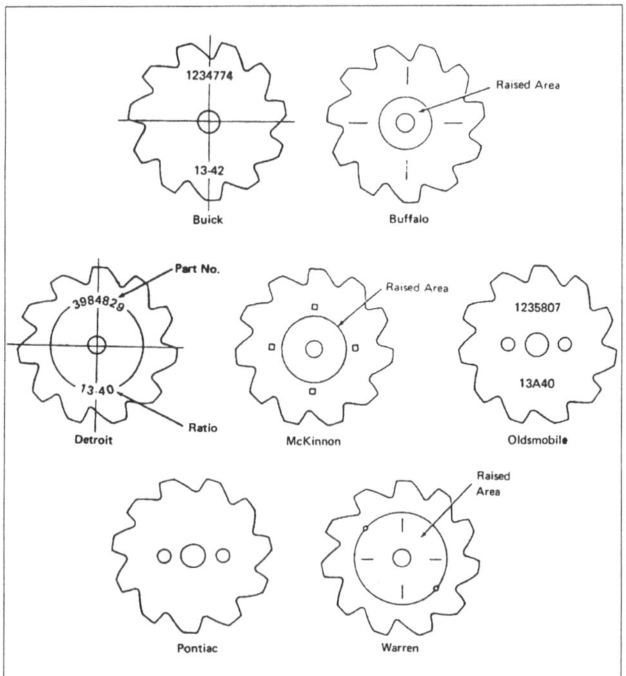

Fig. 16-14. Identification of differential pinion heads.

Fig. 16-15. Early 1957 positraction differential case. Note the almost rectangular openings in the unit.

1960 case. This ramp angle change prohibits the possibility of mistaken usage or interchangeability.

2) The 1957–59 1st design used eight 3/8-16 RH screws to connect the two halves together, while the 1960–64 2nd design used ten 3/8-24 LH screws with a special 1/2" washer to connect the two halves. This change was necessary due to the use of new cases and covers to accommodate the additional friction plates mentioned above.

The 1957–early 1960 unit was used by both Passenger cars and Corvette. The late 1960–64 unit was used by Passenger cars through 1964, while the Corvette only used the unit through the 1962 model year due to the introduction of the Corvette IRS suspension in 1963.

The following table lists casting numbers for positraction units. The notation "up" or "down" indicates that the positraction unit is applicable to gearing numerically higher or lower.

0022500

Fig. 16-16. Later 1957 3-series positraction unit. Note the round openings in the unit, the beveled ring gear flange and the 2 12 7 date code (January 12, 1957).

0022501

Fig. 16-17. Later 4-series positraction unit. Note the round openings in the unit and the thicker non-beveled ring gear flange.

Rear Axle Gear Ratios

Positraction Casting Numbers

Axle	Casting Number	Series	Gearing
10-bolt, dropout style, Passenger, Corvette	C-30743	3	3.08 to 3.70:1*
	C-30751	4	4.11:1 and up*
*There were several Chevrolet gearsets available through Chevrolet Service that had a thicker ring gear which allowed the use of the lower gear ratio ring and pinion without switching the carrier. These gearsets have been discontinued for several years.			

The gear tooth ratio of the ring and pinion, for example 10-41, is stamped on the pinion head or stem, and also on the ring gear. Dividing the ring gear tooth count (41) by the pinion tooth count (10) gives you the final rear axle ratio. The following are the more popular tooth combination counts.

Tooth Combinations	Ratio
16-41	2.56:1
15-41	2.73:1
14-43	3.07:1
13-40	3.08:1
13-43	3.31:1
12-37	3.08:1
12-41	3.42:1
11-37	3.36:1
11-39	3.55:1
11-41	3.73:1
10-41	4.10:1
9-37	4.11:1

All Chevy-built gearsets should incorporate a date code stamped into the ring gear, and the pinion head or stem. This date code will indicate the month and year (calendar) of gear manufacture. Example: 11-70 means November, 1970. Pontiac date codes their pinions, but Buick and Oldsmobile do not.

3. 1955 Rear Axles

All 1955 passenger car rear axles are stamped with an alpha-numeric code which identifies the build source, axle ratio, and date of manufacture.

The axle code is located on the front right or passenger side of the differential carrier at the same height as the axle tube. The axle code will read from left to right or bottom to top. The prefix or two-letter code designates the gear ratio and any other specific information about that rear differential. This code also refers to the manufacturer or source which built the rear end.

The numbers following the letter prefix designate the calendar month and day that axle was produced. From the 1955 through 1962 model years the calendar month was designated by a one-number code from January (1) through September (9). The October through December codes were designated as 10–12 respectively. Beginning with the 1963 model year, all month designations begin with a "0" so the January date code would show "01" instead of "1" as in previous years.

Month Code Designations

1 - January	7 - July
2 - February	8 - August
3 - March	9 - September
4 - April	10 - October
5 - May	11 - November
6 - June	12 - December

Plant Codes:

- B = Buffalo NY
- G = Detroit Gear & Axle

Example: AA-409

- AA = 3.70:1 Axle assembly for 3-speed passenger car built at Detroit Gear and Axle
- 4 = Month: April
- 09 = Day: 9th day

1955 Corvette Rear Axle Codes

Series	Ratio	Description	Code	Source
2934	3.55:1	Powerglide	AE	G
	3.55:1	3-Speed	AH*	G
	3.27:1	3-Speed	AD**	G
* Late production 3-speed **Unverified				

1955 Passenger Rear Axle Codes

Series	Ratio	Description	Code	Source
15-21-2400	3.70:1	3-Speed	AA	G
			BA	B
15-21-2400	3.55:1	Powerglide	AB	G
			BB	B
15-21-2400	4.11:1	3-Speed Overdrive	AC	G
			BC	B

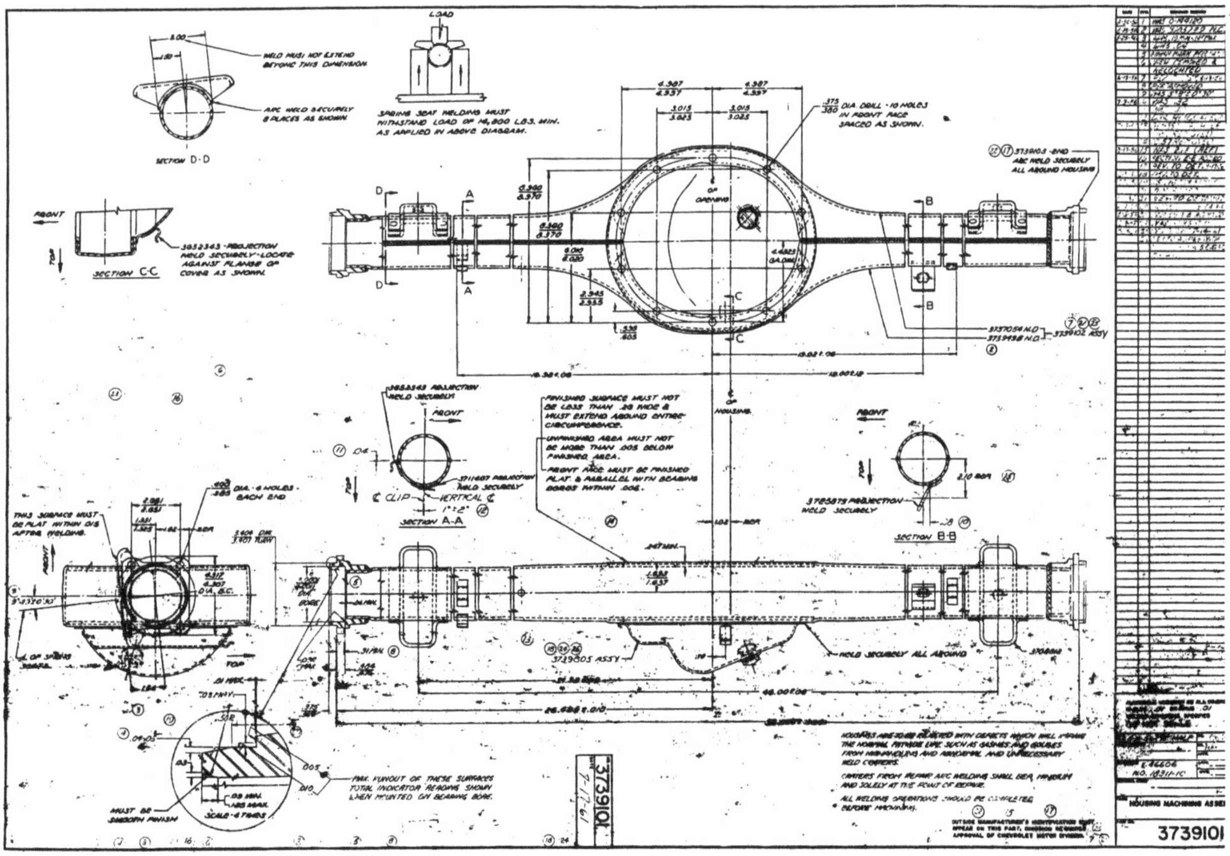

0023240

Fig. 16-18. Housing machining assembly blueprint for 1955–57 Passenger rear axle #3739101.

4. 1956 Rear Axles

All 1956 passenger car rear axles are stamped with an alpha-numeric code which identifies the build source, axle ratio, and date of manufacture.

The axle code is located on the front right or passenger side of the differential carrier at the same height as the axle tube. The axle code will read from left to right or bottom to top. The prefix or two-letter code designates the gear ratio and any other specific information about that rear differential. This code also refers to the manufacturer or source which built the rear end.

The numbers following the letter prefix designate the calendar month and day that axle was produced. From the 1955 through 1962 model years the calendar month was designated by a one-number code from January (1) through September (9). The October through December codes were designated as 10–12 respectively. Beginning with the 1963 model year, all month designations begin with a "0" so the January date code would show "01" instead of "1" as in previous years.

Month Code Designations

1 - January	7 - July
2 - February	8 - August
3 - March	9 - September
4 - April	10 - October
5 - May	11 - November
6 - June	12 - December

Plant Codes:

- B = Buffalo NY
- G = Detroit Gear & Axle

Example: AA-409

- AA = 3.70:1 Axle assembly for 3-speed passenger car built at Detroit Gear and Axle
- 4 = Month: April
- 09 = Day: 9th day

1956 Passenger Rear Axle Codes

Series	Ratio	Description	Code	Source
15-21-2400	3.70:1	3-speed	AA	G
			BA	B
15-21-2400	3.55:1	Powerglide	AB	G
			BB	B
15-21-2400	4.11:1	3-speed overdrive	AC	G
			BC	B

1956 Corvette Rear Axle Codes

Series	Ratio	Description	Code	Source
2934	3.55:1	Powerglide	AE*	G
	3.70:1	3-speed	AH	G
	3.27:1	3-speed	AD**	G
	3.70:1 Posi	3-speed	AN	G
	4.11:1	3-speed	AJ***	G

*Early Standard
**Early Optional RPO 471-A
***RPO 471-B

5. 1957 Rear Axles

All 1957 passenger car rear axles are stamped with an alpha-numeric code which identifies the build source, axle ratio, and date of manufacture.

The axle code is located on the front right or passenger side of the differential carrier at the same height as the axle tube. The axle code will read from left to right or bottom to top. The prefix or two-letter code designates the gear ratio and any other specific information about that rear differential. This code also refers to the manufacturer or source which built the rear end.

The numbers following the letter prefix designate the calendar month and day that axle was produced. From the 1955 through 1962 model years the calendar month was designated by a one-number code from January (1) through September (9). The October through December codes were designated as 10–12 respectively. Beginning with the 1963 model year, all month designations begin with a "0" so the January date code would show "01" instead of "1" as in previous years.

Month Code Designations:

1 - January	7 - July
2 - February	8 - August
3 - March	9 - September
4 - April	10 - October
5 - May	11 - November
6 - June	12 - December

Plant Codes:

- B = Buffalo NY
- G = Detroit Gear & Axle

Example: AA-409

- AA = 3.55:1 Axle assembly for 3-speed passenger car built at Detroit Gear and Axle
- 4 = Month: April
- 09 = Day: 9th day

1957 Passenger Rear Axle Codes

Series	Ratio	Description	Code	Source
15-21-2400	3.55:1	3-speed	AA	G
			BA	B
15-21-2400	3.36:1	Powerglide/Turbo glide	AB	G
			BB	B
15-21-2400	4.11:1	3-speed overdrive	AC	G
			BC	B
15-21-2400	3.55:1	3-speed Posi	AK	G
15-21-2400	4.11:1	3-speed Posi	AL	G
15-21-2400	3.36:1	Turboglide, Powerglide	AM	G
15-21-2400	3.55:1	LPO-1018-C	AW	G
			BW	B
15-21-2400	4.11:1	LPO-1018-B	AX	G
			BX	B
15-21-2400	3.36:1	LPO-1018-A	AY	G
			BY	B
15-2100	3.90:1	COPO-2081-T	AV	G

1957 Corvette Rear Axle Codes

Series	Ratio	Description	Code	Source
2934	3.36:1	Powerglide	AE	G
	3.70:1	Manual	AH	G
	3.70:1 Posi	Manual	AN	G
	4.11:1 Posi	Manual	AP	G
	4.56:1 Posi	Manual	AQ	G
	3.70:1 Posi	Manual	AS*	G
	4.11:1 Posi	Manual	AT*	G
	4.56:1 Posi	Manual	AU*	G
* These rear axles were part of number 684 option code released approximately 3/1/57 which included heavy duty brakes and suspensions.				

6. 1958 Rear Axles

All 1958 passenger car rear axles are stamped with an alpha-numeric code which identifies the build source, axle ratio, and date of manufacture.

The axle code is located on the front right or passenger side of the differential carrier at the same height as the axle tube. The axle code will read from left to right or bottom to top. The prefix or two-letter code designates the gear ratio and any other specific information about that rear differential. This code also refers to the manufacturer or source which built the rear end.

The numbers following the letter prefix designate the calendar month and day that axle was produced. From the 1955 through 1962 model years the calendar month was designated by a one-number code from January (1) through September (9). The October through December codes were designated as 10–12 respectively. Beginning with the 1963 model year, all month designations begin with a "0" so the January date code would show "01" instead of "1" as in previous years.

Month Code Designations:

1 - January	7 - July
2 - February	8 - August
3 - March	9 - September
4 - April	10 - October
5 - May	11 - November
6 - June	12 - December

Plant Codes:

- B = Buffalo NY
- G = Detroit Gear & Axle

Example: AA-409

- AA = 3.55:1 Axle assembly for 3-speed passenger car built at Detroit Gear and Axle
- 4 = Month: April
- 09 = Day: 9th day

1958 Passenger Rear Axle Codes

Series	Ratio	Description	Code	Source
1000	3.55:1	3-speed	AA	G
			BA	B
	3.36:1	Turboglide, Powerglide	AB	G
			BB	B
	4.11:1	3-speed Overdrive	AC	G
			BC	B
	3.55:1	3-speed Taxi	AG	G
			BG	B
	3.36:1	Turboglide, Powerglide Taxi	AD	G
			BD	B
	3.55:1 Posi	3-speed	AK	G
	4.11:1 Posi	3-speed overdrive	AL	G
	3.36:1 Posi	Turboglide, Powerglide	AM	G

1958 Corvette Rear Axle Codes

Series	Ratio	Description	Code	Source
867	3.36:1	Powerglide	AE	G
	3.70:1	Manual	AH	G
	3.70:1 Posi	Manual	AN	G
	4.11:1 Posi	Manual	AP	G
	4.56:1 Posi	Manual	AQ	G
	3.70:1 Posi	Manual	AS*	G
	4.11:1 Posi	Manual	AT*	G
	4.56:1 Posi	Manual	AU*	G
* These rear axles were part of number 684 option code released approximately 3/1/57, and included heavy duty brakes and suspensions.				

7. 1959 REAR AXLES

All 1959 passenger car rear axles are stamped with an alpha-numeric code which identifies the build source, axle ratio, and date of manufacture.

The axle code is located on the front right or passenger side of the differential carrier at the same height as the axle tube. The axle code will read from left to right or bottom to top. The prefix or two-letter code designates the gear ratio and any other specific information about that rear differential. This code also refers to the manufacturer or source which built the rear end.

The numbers following the letter prefix designate the calendar month and day that axle was produced. From the 1955 through 1962 model years the calendar month was designated by a one-number code from January (1) through September (9). The October through December codes were designated as 10–12 respectively. Beginning with the 1963 model year, all month designations begin with a "0" so the January date code would show "01" instead of "1" as in previous years.

Month Code Designations:

1 - January	7 - July
2 - February	8 - August
3 - March	9 - September
4 - April	10 - October
5 - May	11 - November
6 - June	12 - December

Plant Codes:

- B = Buffalo NY
- G = Detroit Gear & Axle

Example: AA-409

- AA = 3.55:1 Axle assembly for 3-speed passenger car built at Detroit Gear and Axle
- 4 = Month: April
- 09 = Day: 9th day

1959 Passenger Rear Axle Codes

Series	Ratio	Description	Code	Source
1000	3.55:1	3-speed	AA	G
			BA	B
	3.36:1	Turboglide, Powerglide	AB	G
			BB	B
	4.11:1	3-speed Overdrive	AC	G
			BC	B

1959 Passenger Rear Axle Codes (continued)

Series	Ratio	Description	Code	Source
1000 (cont'd)	3.36:1	Turboglide, Powerglide Taxi	AD	G
			BD	B
	3.55:1	3-speed Taxi	AG	G
			BG	B
	3.55:1 Posi	Manual	AK	G
			BK	B
	4.11:1 Posi	3-speed overdrive	AL	G
			BL	B
	3.36:1 Posi	Turboglide, Powerglide	AM	G
			BM	B
	348 3.08:1	Turboglide, Powerglide	AW	G
			BW	B
	348 3.08:1 Posi	Manual	AX	G
			BX	B
	3.55:1	Police car LPO 1108	FA	G
	3.08:1	Police car LPO 1108	FB	G
	3.36:1	Police car LPO 1108	FC	G
	3.70:1	3-speed overdrive	FE	G
			BE	B
	3.70:1 Posi	3-speed overdrive	FH	G
			BH	B

1959 Corvette Rear Axle Codes

Series	Ratio	Description	Code	Source
867	3.55:1	Powerglide	AE	G
	3.70:1	Manual	AH	G
	3.70:1 Posi	Manual	AN	G
	4.11:1 Posi	Manual	AP	G
	4.56:1 Posi	Manual	AQ	G
	3.70:1 Posi	Manual	AS*	G
	4.11:1 Posi	Manual	AT*	G
	4.56:1 Posi	Manual	AU*	G
	3.70:1	Manual, metallic brakes	FJ	G
	3.70:1 Posi	Manual, metallic brakes	FK	G
	4.11:1 Posi	Manual, metallic brakes	FL	G
	4.56:1 Posi	Manual, metallic brakes	FM	G

* Heavy duty brakes and suspension.

1955-59 Rear Axle Usage

Year	Model	Rear End Type	Ring Gear Dia.	Pinion Dia.	# of Pinion Splines	Read End Width	Spring Perch Width	Axle Length	Axle Splines	Gear Ratio	Casting No.
1955	Pass.	10-bolt (dropout)	8-13/64	1-7/16	17	55	46	L: 28-13/16 R: 30-5/16	17	3.55, 3.70, 4.11:1	Unknown (open)
	Corvette	10-bolt (C-clip)	8-13/64	1-7/16	17	54-1/2	47-5/8	L: 28-1/2 R: 29-1/2 2-3/4 pilot	17	3.27:1 3.55:1	3698960 (depressed)
1956	Pass.	10-bolt (dropout)	8-13/64	1-7/16	17	55	46	L: 28.13/16 R: 30-5/16	17	3.55, 3.70, 4.11:1	3707306 (open)
	Corvette	10-bolt (dropout)	8-13/64	1-7/16	17	55	47-1/4	L: 28-13/16 R: 30-5/16	17	3.27, 3.55, 3.70, 4.11:1	3707306 (open)
1957	Pass.	10-bolt (dropout)	8-13/64	1-7/16	17	55	46	L: 28-9/16 (open) 28-11/16 (posi) R: 30 (open) 30-1/64 (posi)	17	3.70, 4.56 (Hi- torque*) 3.36, 3.55, 3.70, 3.90, 4.11	3725899 (open) 3743833 (posi)**, after Dec. 1956
	Corvette	10-bolt (dropout)	8-13/64	1-7/16	17	55	47-1/4	L: 28-9/16 (open) 28-13/16 (posi) R: 30 (open) 30-5/16 (posi)	17	3.36, 3.70, 4.11, 4.56	3725899 (open) 3743833 (posi)**
1958	Pass.	10-bolt (dropout)	8-13/64	1-7/16	17			L: 28-9/16 (open) 28-13/16 (posi) R: 30 (open) 30-5/16 (posi)	17	3.36–4.11:1	3725899 (open) 3743833 (posi)***
	Corvette	10-bolt (dropout)	8-13/64	1-7/16	17	55	47-1/4	L: 28-9/16 (open) 28-13/16 (posi) R: 30 (open) 30-5/16 (posi)	17	3.36–4.56:1	3725899 (open) 3743833 (posi)***
1959	Pass.	10-bolt (dropout)	8-13/64	1-7/16	17	55	46-27/32	L: 29-1/2 R: 30-1/2	17	3.08–4.11:1	3725899 (open) 3743833 (posi)
	Corvette	10-bolt (dropout)	8-13/64	1-7/16	17	55	47-15/64	L: 28-13/16 R: 30-5/16	17	3.55–4.56:1	3725899 (open) 3743833 (posi, early) 3789812 (posi, late)

*Letters "HT" stamped into center section to indicate "High Torque" Posi rear axle, used only in factory sponsored race cars.
**After April 1, 1957, through the 1964 model year, all factory posi cases will have a "P" cast into the carrier, adjacent to the casting number.
***After May 1, 1958, all posi rear axles will have a posi ID tag attached to the fill plug.

Chapter 17
Wheel Identification

1. Introduction

Usually, what you look for in a wheel is only one thing: rim size. You can usually find the correct rim size for your car in your owner's manual, shop manual or other factory literature. This is a great start, but what you need to realize is that other factors affect wheel choice. For example, two wheels manufactured for different divisions may have the same rim size and bolt pattern but a different offset.

This chapter will focus on the cryptic coding found on almost all Chevrolet wheels. Most of the difficulty in identifying wheels relates to the decoding of the specific stampings. For this reason, Kelsey-Hayes was used as a source for this chapter. Kelsey-Hayes produced almost all of Chevrolet's production wheels, along with wheels for almost every other manufacturer.

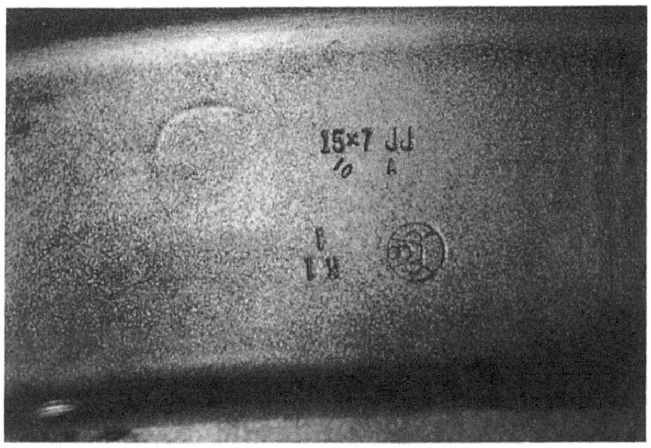

0022385

Fig. 17-1. *Inside of wheel (tire side) shows various interior wheel code stampings. See text for decoding. The logo stamping on the lower right is the logo for the Tire & Rim Association.*

1.1 Interior Wheel Stampings

All wheels should at least have stamped into them the size of the wheel and some type of manufacturer's trademark. On early wheels you will usually find the size stamping on the inside (tire side) of the rim. On later Chevrolet wheels you will also find a series of numbers stamped inside the wheel. Fig. 17-1 shows an example of several different stampings all in the same area.

Most obvious at the lower right of the photo is the Tire & Rim Association stamp indicating the wheel was made to their rim dimension specs. Immediately to the left of the Tire & Rim Assoc. logo is the code K-1-1 (upside down in the photo), stamped in a triangular pattern. The K-1-1 code is deciphered as follows:

- K: Kelsey-Hayes designation
- 1: Plant:
  - 1 = Romulus, MI
  - 2 = Windsor, ON, Canada
  - 3 = Philadelphia, PA
- 1: Last digit of year, in this case 1971

Note that there were three plants producing wheels for Kesley-Hayes during this period.

Of the group of numbers and letters above the K-1-1 code, the most obvious is the rim size, in this case "15x7 JJ." The letters JJ signify the type of rim contour of the wheel. Other rim contour designations that appear on Chevrolet wheels are K, J, JK and many others.

The number "10" stamped below the size signifies the actual day of the month this rim part was run. In the same manner, the letter "A" stamped below signifies that this rim part was built during the first production run of the year. In some cases, this letter designation coincided with the corresponding month of the year, i.e. A = first production run = January, but this was not always the case.

Note that the date code(s) on the inside (tire side) of the rim pertain only to the part or parts of the rim that were manufactured. The actual production date code for the rim as an assembled whole is found on the exterior of the wheel, near the valve stem. In many cases the dates on the inside and exterior will match, without any significance. Neither date has any reference to the other except that the exterior (assembled) date should never precede the inner (parts) date.

1.2 Exterior Wheel Stampings

Fig. 17-2 shows a typical Kelsey-Hayes exterior wheel stamping. These codes indicate the final assembly date of the whole wheel. Starting at the left and reading right, you first read the K-1-1 code. This is decoded exactly like the interior code given above. The next number to the right, "10," represents the month of wheel assembly, in this case the 10th month of the year, or October. It does not represent the actual day of the month as indicated on the inside of the rim. The stamped number on the opposite side of the valve stem hole, "4," represents the day of the month of the final wheel assembly. In this case the 4th day of the month. To the right of the "4" is the actual letter code of the wheel, which in this example is the letters "AG."

0022386

Fig. 17-2. Exterior of wheel shows various code stampings. See text for decoding. (Late model wheel shown.)

This letter coding did not begin until 1965 on passenger cars and not until June 1965 on Chevy IIs. In 1966, the codes were predominantly single letter codes, but in 1967 Chevrolet went to a two letter code system. The wheel codes were assigned by Chevrolet to each specific wheel, and the manufacturer was required to stamp the code onto that wheel. These codes were usually used on one specific vehicle in a particular model year, but in some cases could possibly be used on another model during that year or possibly the next model year. (In the example above, AG stands for a 1968 Corvette 15x7 Rally Wheel. This wheel was made on October 4, 1971, but was coded AG as a factory replacement.)

Fig. 17-3 shows the K-1-1 code again, stamped on the "spider," or center section of the wheel. This code is read the same as previous K-1-1 codes. The code can differ from the final assembly code stamped near the valve stem. Many Kelsey-Hayes wheels were built all in one day, but this would depend on plant scheduling, car sales, wheel demand, and so on.

0022387

Fig. 17-3. Additional exterior stamping is often found on "spider" section of wheel. (Late model wheel shown.)

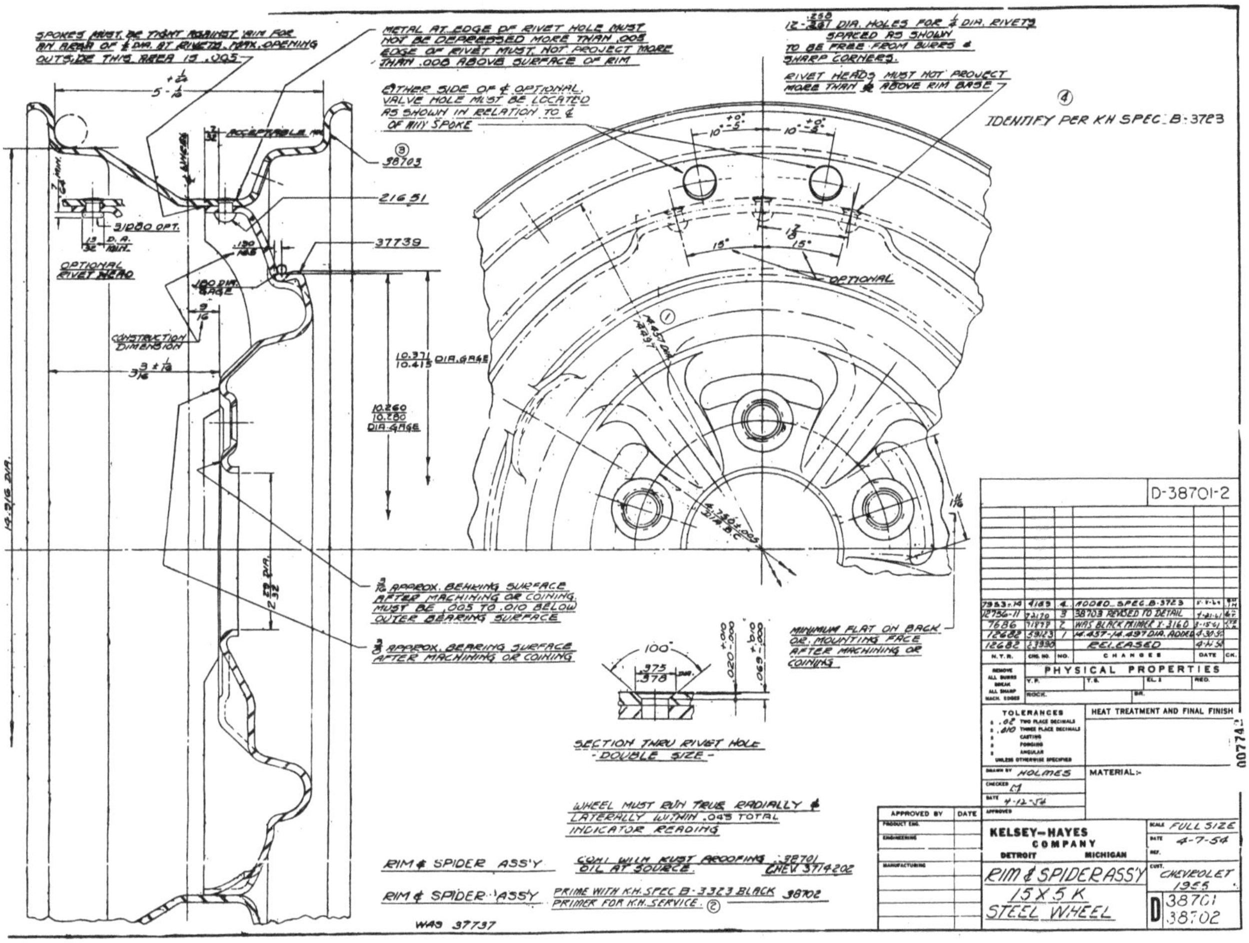

0023254

Fig. 17-4. 1955 Passenger/Corvette 15x5 K steel wheel.

2. 1955 THROUGH 1959 WHEEL APPLICATIONS

Included in the chart below are Chevrolet wheels produced from 1955 through 1959. The chart designates the specific model year, model usage, wheel size, wheel code, number of bolts, bolt center, center hole size, offset, type of construction, rim inside diameter, and wheel manufacturer. As stated previously, these wheels do not carry a wheel code but can be readily identified by the other specifications listed.

Wheel Table Codes

Wheel Construction	R: Riveted W: Welded
Wheel Manufacturers	KH: Kelsey-Hayes

NOTE—
If there are two types of construction listed, the second will always be the optional construction of that wheel.

1955 Through 1959 Wheel Applications

Year	Model	Size	Bolts	Bolt Center	Bolt Size	Center Hole	Offset	Const.	Rim I.D.	Mfg.
1955	Passenger	15x5 K	5	4-3/4	7/16	2-29/32	9/16	R	12.648	KH
	Corvette	15x5 K	5	4-3/4	7/16	2-29/32	9/16	R	12.648	KH
1956	Passenger	15x5 K	5	4-3/4	7/16	2-29/32	9/16	W	12.648	KH
	Corvette	15x5 K	5	4-3/4	7/16	2-29/32	9/16	W	12.648	KH
1957	Passenger	14x5 J	5	4-3/4	7/16	2.91	.56	W	12.328	KH
	Taxi, Police	15x5-1/2 K	5	4-3/4	7/16	2.786	.44	R	12.648	KH
	Corvette	15x5 K	5	4-3/4	7/16	2.91	.56	W	12.648	KH
		15x5-1/2 K*	5	4-3/4	7/16	2.786	.44	R	12.648	KH
1958	Passenger	14x5 J	5	4-3/4	7/16	2.91	.56	W	12.328	KH
	Taxi, Police	15x5-1/2 K	5	4-3/4	7/16	2.786	.44	R	12.648	KH
	Corvette	15x5 K	5	4-3/4	7/16	2.91	.56	W	12.648	KH
		15x5-1/2 K*	5	4-3/4	7/16	2.786	.44	R	12.648	KH
1959	Passenger	14x5 J	5	4-3/4	7/16	2.91	.56	W	12.328	KH
		14x5-1/2 J	5	4-3/4	7/16	2.91	.31	W	12.328	KH
	Taxi, Police	15x5-1/2 K	5	4-3/4	7/16	2.786	.44	R	12.648	KH
	Corvette	15x5 K	5	4-3/4	7/16	2.91	.56	W, R	12.648	KH
		15x5-1/2 K*	5	4-3/4	7/16	2.786	.44	R	12.648	KH

*H.D. brake option included this wheel.

Chapter 18

Rochester Fuel Injection

1. Introduction

Chevrolet became actively interested in the GM fuel injection system primarily for the Corvette sports car, in order to realize the full potential of the engine for high performance. GM had been aware of the theoretical advantages of fuel injection, but was also aware of the relatively high cost. Fuel injection had been used for many years on Diesel Engines and there were several types currently being manufactured in Europe and in this country for use on passenger cars. In 1957 General Motors decided to have a fuel injection system made by Rochester Products Division for the 1957 model year. The GM system promised maximum advantage, with a minimum of disadvantage, such as cost. As GM progressed in the application development of the GM system to the Chevrolet engine, it became obvious that they should extend its use to the regular passenger cars as well.

The first logical question for anyone to ask is, "Why did Chevrolet want Fuel Injection anyway?" Chevrolet had made tremendous advances in carburetion until they had a product which was the finest on the market and which provided amazing flexibility and dependability through the entire range of operation of the current high compression engines. However, there were a number of factors which limited the efficiency of a carbureted fuel system:

- Fuel Distribution: fuel/air mixture problems due to limited manifold design equality
- Air Flow: Manifold size limited due to operation range requirements
- Heat: Necessity for a "hot spot" in engine warm-up
- Height: Carburetor and air cleaner height were very low to clear the hood
- Horsepower: Low speed operation vs. high performance was a difficult problem to solve without going beyond carburetion.

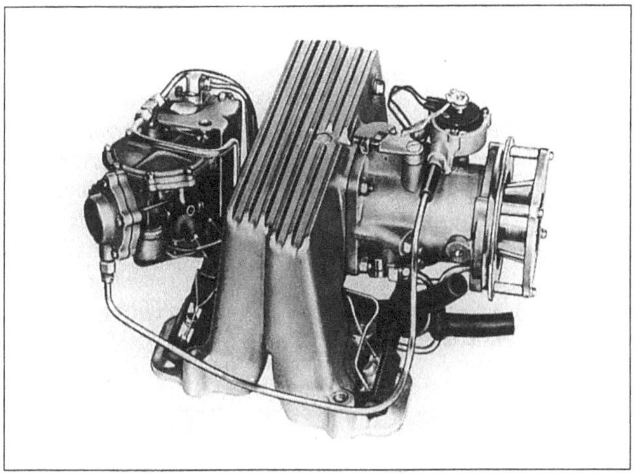

0022391

Fig. 18-1. 1957 Fuel injection unit.

Possible Advantages to Fuel Injection

- A better torque curve at low engine speeds which would help automatic transmission automobiles
- No cut-out because of sharp turns, steep grades, or quick stops
- Better starting and warm-up
- Stable slow idle
- No icing
- Improved fuel distribution
- Fewer unburned hydrocarbons during deceleration, since fuel can be shut off
- Fewer vapor troubles
- Use of a wider range of fuel elements

Possible Disadvantages to Fuel Injection

- Higher cost
- Poor vapor handling capacity
- Fuel economy
- Fuel filtration
- Maintenance of distribution accuracy
- Service

0022392

Fig. 18-2. *First production unit packed. Pictured from Rochester Products division are (left to right): E.A. Kehoe, Chief Engineer; E.F. DeTiere, Supervisor, Engineering Test; J. Matthews, Production Control Manager; H. Sutton, Production Foreman; H. Brandt, General Manager; H. Grassmick, Superintendent of Production (Fuel Injection); C. Brandon, Director of Production Control.*

0023257

Fig. 18-3. *Checking early fuel injection unit installed in car.*

Up until 1957 two types of fuel injection were considered and tested at the GM Tech Center and at Rochester, the "A" type, which was continuous flow injection and the "B" type, which was timed injection. The "A" system was developed at the GM Tech Center by the Engineering staff and the "B" by Diesel Equipment Division and the research staff. The "A" system was chosen for earliest release, primarily from a standpoint of simplicity and cost. From a Service standpoint we can be glad that the "A" system was chosen, since the "B" system, at least to those who are not familiar with it, looked like a plumber's nightmare.

The new fuel injection system built at Rochester for 1957 General Motors cars was the continuous flow type with the nozzle located directly outside each cylinder, spraying into the intake port. The nozzles are open orifices without spring control. The system called fuel injection is unique in several respects.

1.1 Basic Design

The Rochester Fuel Injection System has three basic components: the Air Meter, the Fuel Meter, and the Intake Manifold. The air meter supplies a control signal to the fuel meter in response to engine load (vacuum in the intake manifold is a measure of how much air is entering the engine). The fuel meter uses the vacuum control signal to regulate the fuel flow to the injection nozzles. The intake manifold provides the distribution system for the rammed air flow to the cylinders.

1.2 Rochester Fuel Injection Evolution (1957-59)

1957

The first Rochester fuel injection unit was #7014360. Very early units did not have the familiar black Rochester Products I.D. tag, and the unit number (serial) was stamped into the lower front of the plenum vertical face. Early plenums had the "Winters Snowflake" cast in the ribbed area of the plenum.

0023259

Fig. 18-4. *1957 #7014360 fuel injection unit, from the driver's side.*

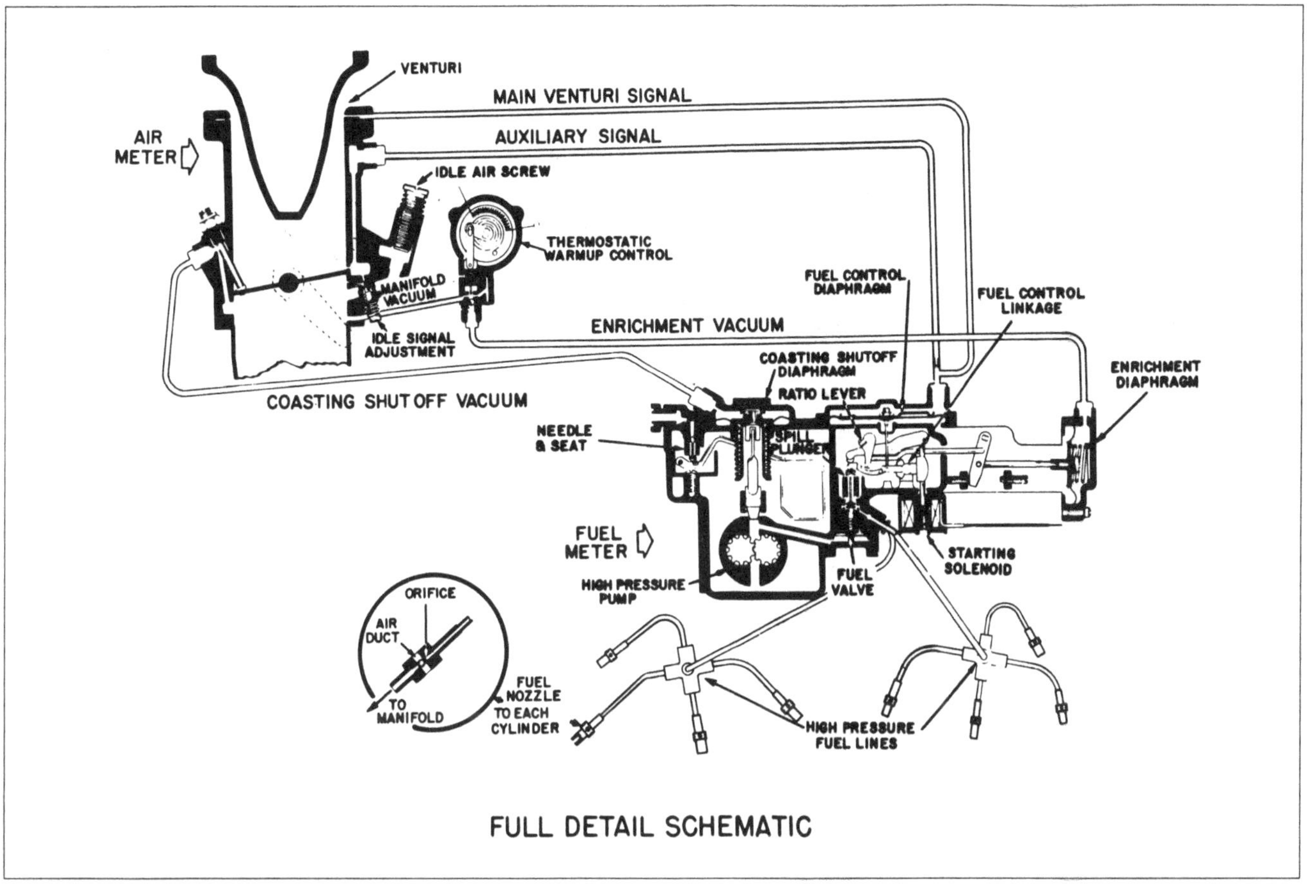

0022393

Fig. 18-5. *1957 Fuel Injection full detail schematic.*

0023260

Fig. 18-6. *1957 #7014360 unit passenger side view. Note the sand cast fuel meter and large main diaphragm cover. This unit is unrestored and rough.*

0023261

Fig. 18-7. *1957 #7014360 unit plenum top. Note the cast "snowflake" indicating Winters Foundry.*

0023262

Fig. 18-8. *1957 #7014360 air meter and choke detail. Note microswitch for cranking enrichment.*

0023263

Fig. 18-9. *1957 #7014360 front of air meter details.*

0023264

Fig. 18-10. *1957 #7014360 rear of air meter details.*

0023265

Fig. 18-11. *1957 #7014360 air meter flange stamping #7014361.*

0023266

Fig. 18-12. *1957 #7014360 Fuel meter stampings. #7014362 and 1523 (Serial number of components usually didn't match unit serial number).*

0023267

Fig. 18-13. *1957 #7014360 Sand cast fuel meter components.*

0023268

Fig. 18-14. *1957 #7014360 unit. Note the two tubes below air meter that attach to air cleaner base.*

Early #7014360 units used dual four-way fuel meter distributor or "spiders" to deliver fuel to the nozzles. Later #7014360 and subsequent units had a single right tube spider. This change took place around 2/1/57. It should be noted that the single spiders used through 1957 and on 1959 #7017300 and 7017300R units have lines individually attached by ferrules and nuts. Later spiders are soldered together beginning in 1958. Also, early #7014360 units had three designs changes for the fuel valve, gasket and strainer. There were many other changes in design to the #7014360 which cannot be covered here.

The next unit from Rochester for 1957 was the #7014520. It, as well as later #7014360 units, had the black I.D. tag on the plenum. Early #4520 units had a snowflake on top of the plenum. The #7014520 and subsequent units use a single type fuel meter spider. This unit was originally designated for passenger car use. This unit was similar to #7014360 with the following changes.

- The control diaphragm vent is relocated from the under side of the fuel meter cover to the outboard surface of the fuel bowl.
- Air for the nozzles is taken from a boss on the air meter casting, after the air has passed the venturi. The nozzle air pipes are redesigned to fit this arrangement.
- The cold enrichment system is completely redesigned, and now uses manifold vacuum as a signal boost rather than using the power enrichment system.
- New type nozzles containing an orifice plate and fuel strainer. This type of nozzle cannot be used on the #7014360 because of flow differences.

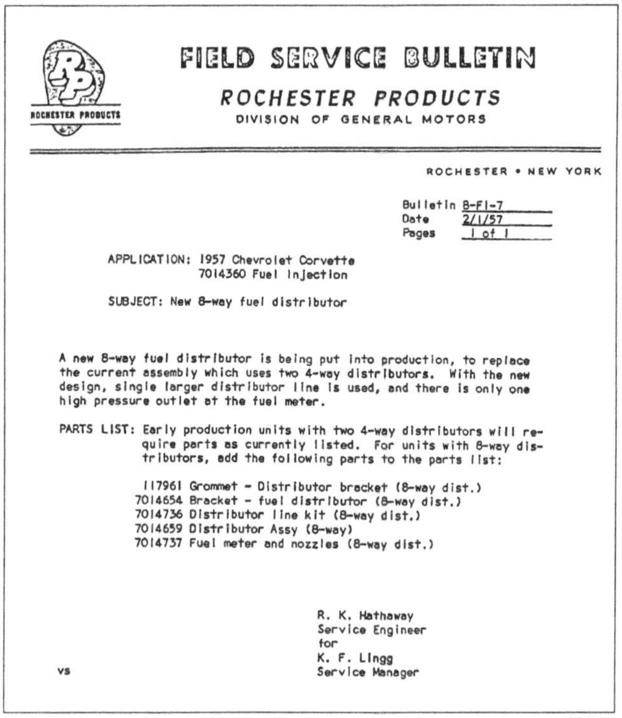

FIELD SERVICE BULLETIN

ROCHESTER PRODUCTS

DIVISION OF GENERAL MOTORS

ROCHESTER PRODUCTS

ROCHESTER • NEW YORK

Bulletin B-FI-7
Date 2/1/57
Pages 1 of 1

APPLICATION: 1957 Chevrolet Corvette
7014360 Fuel Injection

SUBJECT: New 8-way fuel distributor

A new 8-way fuel distributor is being put into production, to replace the current assembly which uses two 4-way distributors. With the new design, single larger distributor line is used, and there is only one high pressure outlet at the fuel meter.

PARTS LIST: Early production units with two 4-way distributors will require parts as currently listed. For units with 8-way distributors, add the following parts to the parts list:

117961 Grommet - Distributor bracket (8-way dist.)
7014654 Bracket - fuel distributor (8-way dist.)
7014736 Distributor line kit (8-way dist.)
7014659 Distributor Assy (8-way)
7014737 Fuel meter and nozzles (8-way dist.)

R. K. Hathaway
Service Engineer
for
K. F. Lingg
Service Manager

vs

0023269

Fig. 18-15. *Rochester Field Service Bulletin B-FI-7 dates the changeover to the new 8-way fuel distributor or "spider," along with a service parts list for earlier units.*

The third type of unit used in 1957 was #7014800. It was used in mid- to late-1957 and is a refinement of the #4520 design. The differences are as follows.

- The nozzles are longer, and extend into the air stream for better response. Nozzle classifications are the same as for #7014520.
- Cold enrichment uses two valves - one for power diaphragm vacuum, and another for signal boost vacuum. When the car is first started, enrichment is caused by a signal boost plus power enrichment; as the engine warms up, the signal boost valve closes, and only power enrichment is used. When normal operating temperature is reached, the power diaphragm vacuum valve opens and the system reverts to normal driving controls.

The fourth and final 1957 unit developed was the #7014960. It was used in late 1957 and usage spilled over into early 1958. The 1957 Rochester units used a microswitch and a solenoid (mounted on the fuel meter) to provide ample fuel during cranking. This was also used on 1959 units #7017300 and 300R. All 1957 units have a rough sand-cast fuel meter.

0023270

Fig. 18-16. #7014800 Rochester fuel injection unit.

1958

Early units were #7014960 and #7014800R from 1957. Many were used on passenger cars. #7014900 and #7014900R were released later and had many changes, the two most notable being a new die cast fuel meter with a newly designed spill valve assembly, and a "cranking signal" valve. The cranking signal valve used manifold vacuum to the fuel meter main diaphragm and thus eliminated the cranking enrichment solenoid and microswitch. It was fitted into the upper right front corner of the intake manifold. Another feature is the one-line signal system, which has a single vacuum line from the air meter to the fuel meter. The second line attached to the "T" is connected to a cranking signal valve.

0023271

Fig. 18-17. 1958 #7014900R unit. Driver's side view

0023272

Fig. 18-18. 1958 #7014900R unit. Passenger side top view.

0023273

Fig. 18-19. Tag on plenum of 1958 #7014900R unit. Too-large rivet heads are considered incorrect.

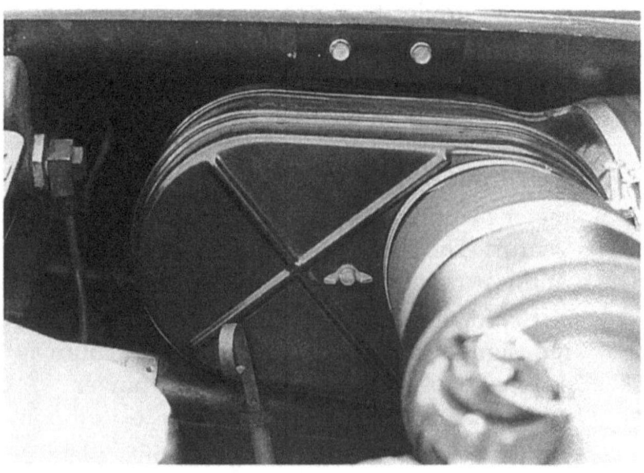

0023276

Fig. 18-20. Typical 1958–61 Corvette fuel injection air cleaner. 1962 is very similar with much smaller "x" on cover.

0023274

Fig. 18-21. *Air meter stamp of "901" on top of #7014900R mounting flange. Most air meters are stamped on rear vertical flange.*

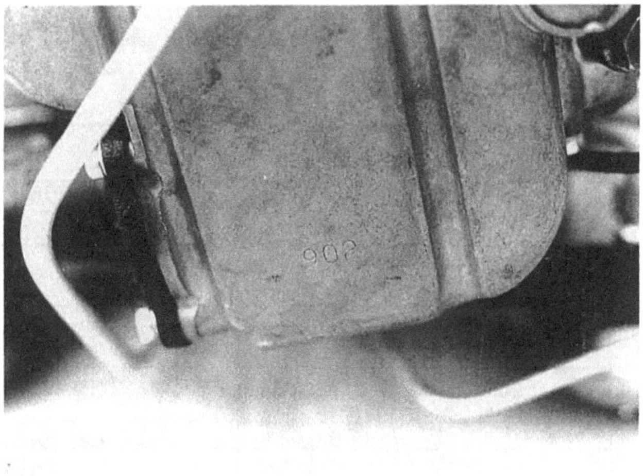

0023275

Fig. 18-22. *Fuel meter stamp of "902" on lower outside face of #7014900R fuel meter body.*

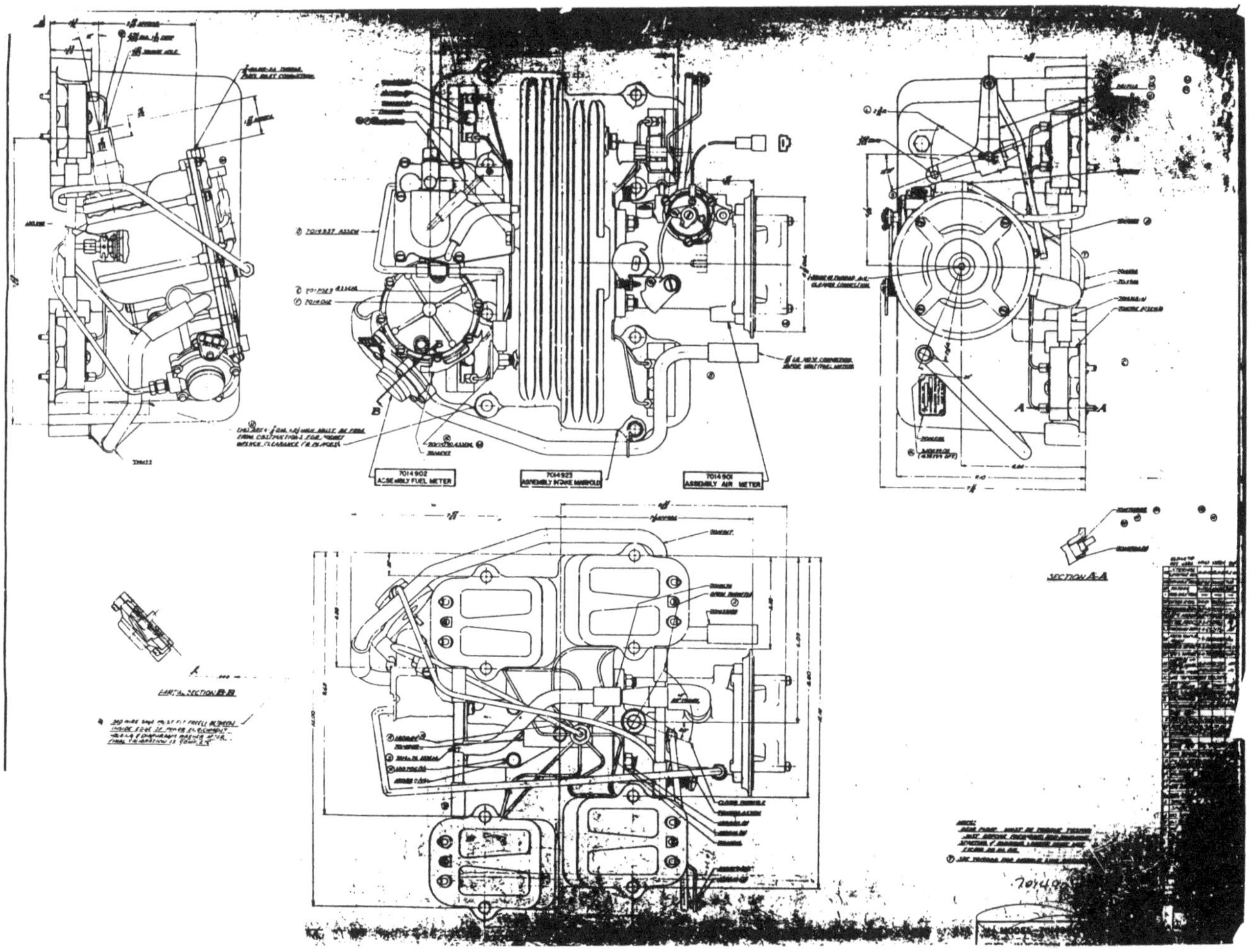

0023277

Fig. 18-23. *Blueprint of #7014900 unit.*

DISTRIBUTION	ROCHESTER PRODUCTS DIVISION GENERAL MOTORS CORPORATION ROCHESTER, NEW YORK					
CUSTOMER						
RELEASED MPH-8313#1 5-20-57	STOCK LIST					
CHECKED [illegible] 4-10-58	Revised & Retyped CN 20579 4-8-58	CN-21755 2-4-59 L-34,35	CN-20579#3 8-11-59 L-22,23	CN-22843 2-17-60 L-34,35	OBSOLETE CN-33140-1	NOT USED 6-27-67
TYPED 5-20-57 tw						

CHANGE NOTICE		QUANTITY	DRAWING OR SPEC. NO.	DWG.	NAME
	1	1	7014900	P	Fuel Injection System Complete
	2				
	3	1	7014923	[illegible]	Intake Manifold Assembly
	4	1	7014[illegible]		Ma[illegible]fold Intake
	5	4	7014[illegible]		S[illegible] - Air Meter
	6	1	7[illegible]		[illegible]tud - Accelerator and Throttle Lever L.D.
	7	1	[illegible]		Plug - 1/4 - 18 Pipe Threa[illegible]
	8	1	701[illegible]387	A	Tube - Hose Connection
	9				
	10	1	7014897	A	Coupling - Rubber
	11	1	7014902	D	Fuel Met[illegible] Assembly Complete
	12	2	1[illegible]706	A	Bolt - Fuel Meter
	13	1	120854	A	Bolt - Distributor Br[illegible]cket Retaining
	14	1	121797	A	Bolt-Fuel Meter
	15	4	120380	A	Lockwasher 1/4
	16	1	70[illegible]840	A	Bracket - Dist[illegible]butor
	17	1	12[illegible]92	A	Washer
	18	4	7014784	[illegible]	Gasket - No[illegible]le Holde[illegible]
	19	4	7014785	B	Nozzle Holder Assembly
	20	8	7014786	A	Sleeve - Nozzle
	21	4	70[illegible]826	A	Tube - Nozzle Hold[illegible]
	22	8	7014787	A	Gasket - Metering Nozzle
	23				
	24	4	7014367	A	Retainer - Nozzle Holder
	25	4	7014343	A	Screw - Nozzl [illegible]etaining
	26	4	121753	A	Lockwasher - External Tooth
	27	4	7014368	A	Hose - Nozzle Air Distr[illegible]butor
	28	1	7014016	A	Gasket - Air Meter
	29				
	30	1	7014901	D	Air Meter Assembly Complete
	31				
	32	4	120368	A	Nut - Air Meter Retaining
	33	4	120214	A	[illegible]ockwasher 5/16
	34	1	7017112	C	[illegible]ellcrank - Throttle Control
	35				
	36	1	148148	A	Retainer - Spring
	37	1	70170[illegible]	C	Throttle Drive Rod Assembly
	38				
	39	2	138479	A	Washer - External Tooth #10
	40	2	120614	A	Nut - #10 - 32
	41				
	42				
	43				
	44				
	45				
	46				
	47				

NAME FUEL INJECTION SYSTEM COMPLETE FOR 1958 V8 CHEVROLET — MODEL NO. 7014900 — SHEETS 2 — PAGE 1

FORM NO. 586 2R (REV.)

0023278

Fig. 18-24. Stock list for #7014900 unit (continued on next page).

ROCHESTER PRODUCTS DIVISION
GENERAL MOTORS CORPORATION
ROCHESTER, NEW YORK

DISTRIBUTION: CUSTOMER

STOCK LIST

RELEASED	CHECK	RETYPED
NPR-8313#1 5-20-57	R.L. 12-5-57	7-10-57 jal

CN-20302 1-7-58 Line 33	CN-21808 2-19-59 L-33	[illegible] 29 [illegible] 27-59 [illegible] 21	CN-23[illegible] [illegible] L-38, [illegible]	OBSOLETE CN-33880-1	NOT USED 6 27-[illegible]
revised CN-20177 12-4-57					

CHANGE NOTICE		QUANTITY	DRAWING OR SPEC. NO.	DWG SIZE	NAME
	1	1	7014946	A	Elbow - Idle Air Gallery
	2	1	701[illegible]394	B	Nozzle Air Distributor Assembly - Left
	3	1	7[illegible]	A	Gallery - Nozzle Air Distributor - Left
	4	1	70[illegible]669	A	Tube - Nozzle Air Distributor - Left
	5	1	701[illegible]676	B	Nozzle Air Distributor Assembly - Right
	6	1	701[illegible]670	A	Tube - Nozzle Air Distributor - Right
	7	1	7[illegible]679	A	Gallery - Nozzle Air Distributor - Right
	8				
	9				
	10	1	7014674	A	Hose - Nozzle Air Distributor - 1/2 Dia.
	11	1	7[illegible]947	A	Tube - Control Diaphragm Vent
	12	2	7[illegible]330	A	Hose - Air Cleaner 1 [illegible] Dia
	13	1	70[illegible]6[illegible]	A	Coupling - Rubber 3/[illegible]
	14				
	15	1	70[illegible]898	D	[illegible]ment Tube Assembly
	16	1	137396		[illegible] - Inverted Flared Tube 3/16
	17	1	7014899	A	C[illegible] Vent Tube
	18				
	19				
	20	1	70[illegible]526	A	Plate - Name
	21	2	220299	A	Screw - Drive (OPT [illegible]838599)
	22	1	7014[illegible]7	A	Shield - Fuel Meter
	23				
	24	1	701[illegible]090	A	Cranking Signal Valve Assembly
	25	1	70[illegible]96[illegible]	B	Body - Cranking Signal Valve
	26	1	701[illegible]	A	Screen - Flame Arrester
	27	1	[illegible]959	A	Cranking Signal Diaphragm Assembly
	28	1	[illegible]	A	Valve
	29	1	[illegible]	A	Diaphragm
	30				
	31				
	32	1	7014[illegible]	A	Tube - Hose Connection
	33	[illegible]	7017080	A	Spring - Cranking Signal Valve
	34	1	[illegible]	A	Cover - Diaphragm
	35				
	36	1	7017023	A	Cranking Valve Tube Assembly
	37	1	[illegible]4626	A	Ferrule
	38	1	7012002	A	Nut - Ferrule
	39	1	[illegible]014012	A	Coupling - Rubber
	40	1	701706[illegible]	C	Schematic - Nozzle Line
	41	1	70149[illegible]7	D	Idle Signal Tube Assembly
	42	1	[illegible]14626	A	Ferrule
	43	1	7012002	A	Nut - Ferrule
	44	1	701143[illegible]	A	Nut - Inverted Flared Tube
	45				
	46	1	7017046	B	Test Specification (3 sheets)
	47				

NAME FUEL INJECTION SYSTEM COMPLETE FOR 1958 CHEVROLET

MODEL NO. 7014900
SHEETS 2 PAGE 2

FORM NO. 886 8R (REV.)

0023279

Fig. 18-25. Stock list for #7014900 unit (continued from previous page).

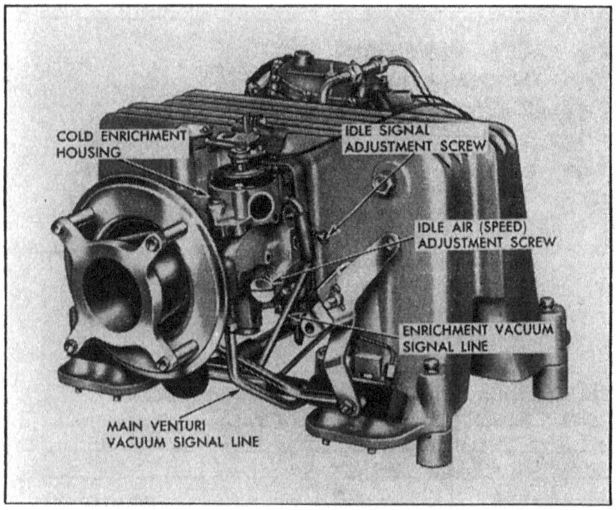

0023280

Fig. 18-26. *#7014900 Rochester fuel injection unit.*

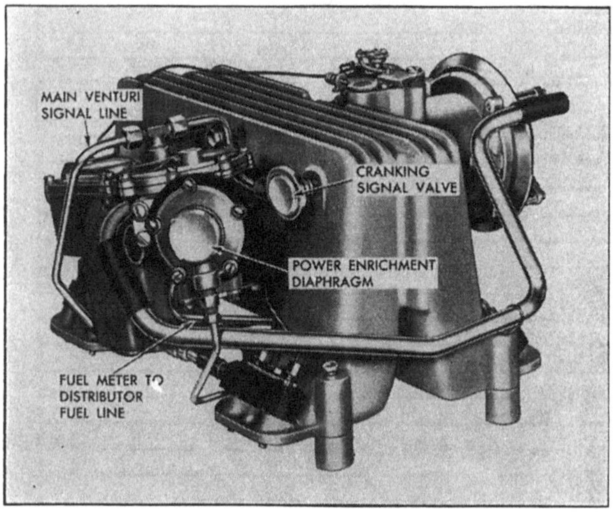

0023281

Fig. 18-27. *#7014900 Rochester fuel injection unit.*

0023283

Fig. 18-28. *Pen points to stamped number on 1959–61 #7017200 air meter mounting and flange.*

0023284

Fig. 18-29. *Close-up of 1959–61 #7017200 air meter stamping. Note that some early units carried seven digits on the component stamping. This one is #7017201.*

1959

Early 1959 usage were the #7014900 and #7014900R units. The #7014900 design eliminated the following external parts found on the #7014800 passenger car unit.

- Starting cut off switch
- Staring Solenoid
- Starting By-Pass Fuel Line
- Idle Vacuum Signal Tube
- Signal Boost Tube

The #7014900 units which have an "R" suffix on the identification plate are calibrated 6–8% higher on the power stop. These units were used on 290HP applications.

Also in 1959 two new units were released, the #7017200 and #7017250. The #7200 and #7250 are very similar to a #4900, and they may be very difficult to tell apart if the model plate is missing. Both of these units had a new fuel meter design that incorporated an internal "cast in" siphon breaker to stop the possibility of fuel flow from the reservoir into the engine cylinders. The siphon breaker can be found as a protrusion on the side of the fuel meter body closest to the intake manifold. These fuel meters were die cast, as were #4900 meters. This design was continued through 1965 with minor changes.

Also in 1959, some leftover #7014800 and #7014960 units were recalibrated by Rochester, plenum tags were changed to #7017300 or 7017300R, and the units were released for 1959 vehicle usage. These used 1957 fuel

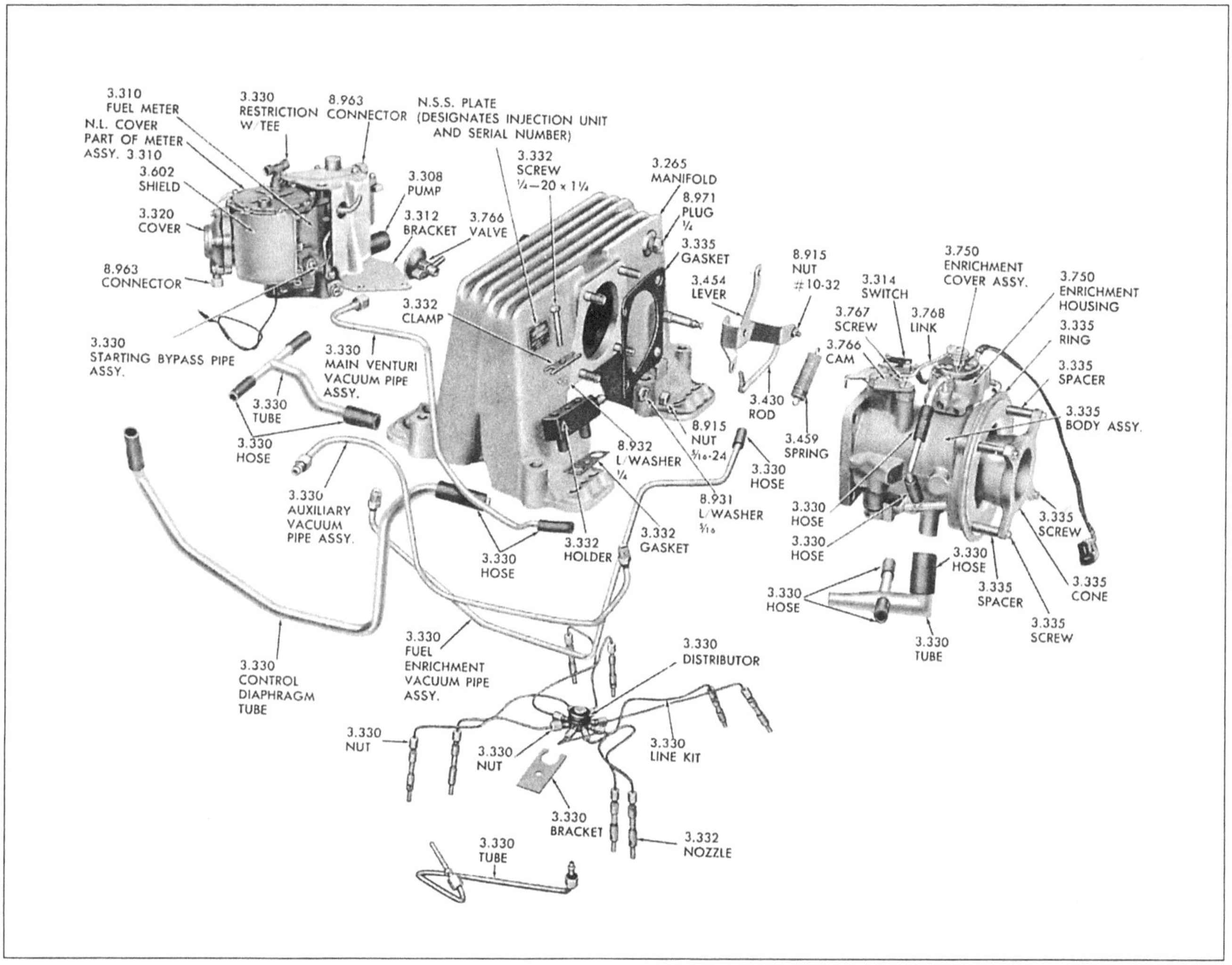

0022516

Fig. 18-30. Driver's side view of 1959–61 #7017200 unit.

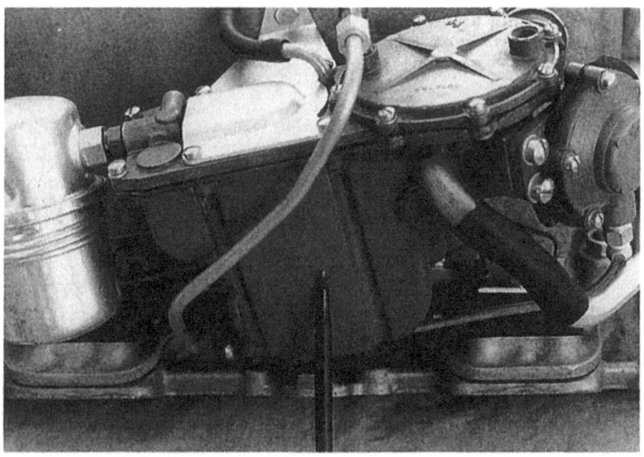

0023285

***Fig. 18-31.** Pen points to stamped number "202" on 1959–61 #7017200 fuel meter.*

meters, spiders, and cranking enrichment solenoids with a microswitch. On the #7017300 the signal line ends at the fuel meter in a simple elbow connection. These units did not have internal siphon breakers.

The intake manifold adapter has been redesigned for 1959, allowing easier distributor removal. The distributor pad is now 3/4" lower using a 3/4" spacer and gaskets to maintain the proper distributor height. Also, individual inlet manifold gaskets were used for the first time. An air cleaner adapter with the air cleaner element mounted on the radiator support was also changed for 1959.

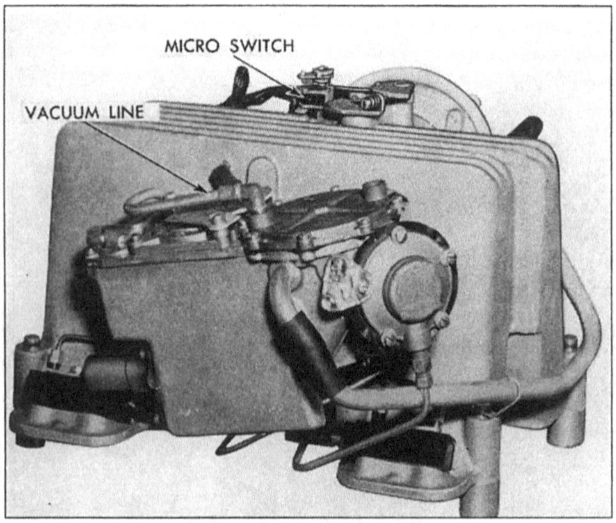

0023287

Fig. 18-32. *Note how #7017300 signal line ends at fuel meter in a simple elbow connection.*

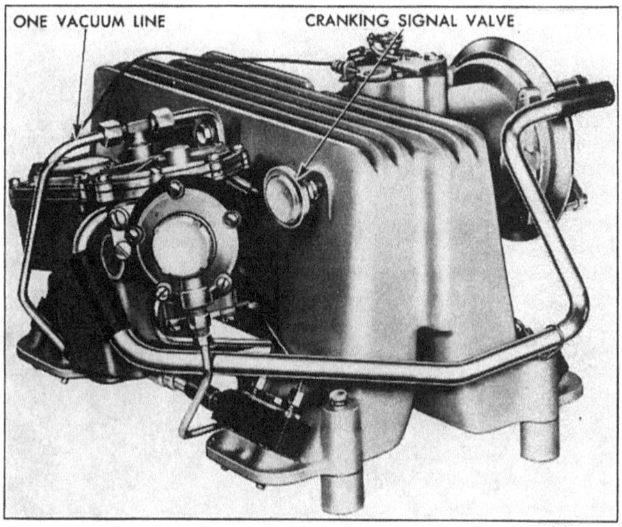

0023286

Fig. 18-33. *#7014900, #7014960, #7017200, and #7017250 units all look very similar, and are very difficult to tell apart if the I.D. plate is missing.*

2. IDENTIFICATION

Air meters and fuel meters were normally stamped with the last three digits of the unit number. Earlier units through the 1959 model year may have had all seven digits stamped on a part. For example, a 1958–59 #7014900 would have a 901 stamped on the air meter, and a 902 stamped on the fuel meter. The 1959 #7017200 fuel injection unit number has an air meter stamp of #7017201 with a fuel meter stamped 202. Most 1962 and all 1963–65 air and fuel meters were no longer stamped as described above. Some early 1962 fuel meters may have a 252 stamp.

1957–62 Fuel Injection Identification Chart

Model #	Two Vacuum Lines	Microswitch	Built-in Siphon Breaker	Two-Line System Without Cranking Signal Valve	Two-Line System With Cranking Signal Valve
7014360	Yes	Yes	No	Yes	No
7014520	Yes	Yes	No	Yes	No
7014800	Yes	Yes	No	Yes	No
7014900	No	No	No	No	Yes
7014960	Yes	Yes	No	Yes	No
7017200	Yes	No	Yes	No	Yes
7017250	Yes	No	Yes	No	Yes
7017300*	No	Yes	No	No	No
7017310	Yes	No	Yes	No	Yes
7017320	Yes	No	Yes	No	Yes
7017355**	Yes	No	Yes	No	Yes
7017360**	Yes	No	Yes	No	Yes

* 7017300 unit incorporates a one-line system without a cranking signal valve
** 7017355 and 7017360 units incorporated by-pass choke system

1963–65 Fuel Injection Identification Chart

Model	Microswitch	Two-Line System with Cranking Signal Valve	One-Line System without Cranking Signal, With Fuel Bypass Solenoid	Built-in Siphon Breaker
7017375*	No	Yes	No	Yes
7017380*	Yes	No	Yes	Yes
* Both of these units have the removable plenum cover				

Rochester Fuel Injection Identification Numbers

Year	Application	Engine/HP	Unit	Air Meter #	Fuel Meter #	Intake #
1957	Passenger	283/250, 283	7014520*	7014521	7014522	3741193
		283/283	7014360	7014361	7014362	3741193
		283/250, 283	7014800 (Late)***	7014801	7014802	3748947
			7014960 (Late)	7014801	7014962	3748947
	Corvette	283/250, 283	7014360 (Early)	7014361	7014362	3741193
			7014520 (Mid-year)	7014521	7014522	3741193
			7014800 (Late)**	7014801	7014802	3748947
			7014960 (Late)	7014801	7014962	3748947
1958	Passenger	283/250	7014800	7014801	7014802	3741193 or 3748947
			7014800R****	7014801	7014802	3748947
		283/290	7014900R*****	7014901	7014902	3748947
			7014960	7014801	7014962	3748947
	Corvette	283/250	7014800	7014801	7014802	3741193 or 3748947
			7014900	7014901	7014902	3748947
		283/290	7014800R	7014801	7014802	3748947
1959	Passenger	283/250	7014800	7014801	7014802	3741193 or 3748947
			7017200	7017201	7017202	3758932 or 3768233
			7017300R******	7017301	7014802, 7014962, 7017302	3758932 or 3768233
		283/290	7017250	7017251	7017252	3758932 or 3768233
	Corvette	283/250	7014900	7014901	7014902	3748947
			7017200	7017201	7017202	3758932 or 3768233
			7017300R	7017301	7014802, 7014962, 7017302	3758932 or 3768233
		283/290	7014900R	7014901	7014902	3748947
			7017250	7017251	7017252	3758932 or 3768233
			7017300	7017301	7014802, 7014962, 7017302	3758932 or 3768233

*Early March 1957 introduction
**Rochester Products Field Service Bulletin B-FI-13, Dated 5/15/57 states that 7014800 unit was to be used on Chevrolet Passenger cars only
***Early May 1957 introduction
****Unit manufactured from 7014520 units
*****Same as 4900 except calibrated richer
******Rebuilt 4800 and 4960 units using a single line Air Meter

NOTE—
I would like to especially thank Gary Hodges of RamJet, Inc., Salem, Oregon, for his help and photography in this chapter.

> *WARNING —*
> *• Automotive service and repair is serious business. You must be alert, use common sense, and exercise good judgement to prevent personal injury.*
> *• Before beginning any work on your vehicle, thoroughly read all the Cautions and Warnings listed near the front of this book.*
> *• Always read the complete procedure before you begin the work. Pay special attention to any Cautions and Warnings that accompany that procedure, or other information on a specific topic.*

Index

WARNING —

- *Automotive service and repair is serious business. You must be alert, use common sense, and exercise good judgement to prevent personal injury.*
- *Before beginning any work on your vehicle, thoroughly read all the Cautions and Warnings listed near the front of this book.*
- *Always read the complete procedure before you begin the work. Pay special attention to any Cautions and Warnings that accompany that procedure, or other information on a specific topic.*

Art Credits

Art Courtesy of AC Rochester

Chapter 18: 18-15, 18-23, 18-24, 18-25

Art Courtesy of M. Berry

Chapter 1: 1-35

Art Courtesy of Carter Federal-Mogul

Chapter 8: 8-2, 8-9, 8-10, 8-11

Art Courtesy of Delco-Remy Division

Chapter 12: 12-8, 12-9, 12-10, 12-11, 12-13

Chapter 14: 14-1, 14-2, 14-4

Art Courtesy of Pete Detiere

Chapter 18: 18-2, 18-3

Distributors Courtesy H. Edelstein

Chapter 12: 12-5, 12-6, 12-7, 12-14, 12-15, 12-16

Art Courtesy of Stan Edmunds

Chapter 15: 15-2, 15-6

Art Courtesy of General Motors Corporation

Chapter 1: 1-5, 1-6, 1-7, 1-8, 1-10, 1-11, 1-12, 1-13, 1-15, 1-16, 1-17, 1-18, 1-20, 1-21, 1-22, 1-23, 1-24, 1-26, 1-27, 1-28, 1-29, 1-30, 1-37

Chapter 2: 2-5

Chapter 3: 3-1, 3-3, 3-6, 3-8, 3-10, 3-12, 3-13, 3-14

Chapter 4: 4-1, 4-2, 4-3, and crankshaft dimensions

Chapter 5: 5-1, 5-4, 5-6, 5-8, 5-10, 5-11, 5-12, 5-13, 5-14, 5-18, 5-20, 5-21, 5-22, 5-23, 5-24, 5-25

Chapter 6: 6-1

Chapter 7: 7-1

Chapter 8: 8-12, 8-13, 8-14, 8-15, 8-16, 8-17

Chapter 9: 9-1, 9-2, 9-6, 9-7, 9-8, 9-9, 9-10, 9-12, 9-13, 9-14, 9-15, 9-16, 9-18, 9-19, 9-20

Chapter 10: 10-7, 10-8, 10-9, 10-10, 10-11, 10-12, 10-17

Chapter 11: 11-3, 11-4, 11-5, 11-6, 11-7, 11-8, 11-9, 11-10

Chapter 12: 12-1, 12-3, 12-4

Chapter 13: 13-1, 13-2, 13-3, 13-4, 13-5, 13-6, 13-7, 13-8, 13-9

Chapter 15: 15-1, 15-3, 15-7, 15-9, 15-10, 15-11, 15-13, 15-14, 15-28, 15-29, 15-30, 15-31, 15-34, 15-35, 15-38, 15-39, 15-40

Chapter 16: 16-1, 16-2, 16-3, 16-9, 16-10, 16-11, 16-12, 16-13, 16-14, 16-15, 16-18

Chapter 18: 18-1, 18-5, 18-26, 18-27, 18-30, 18-32, 18-33

Art Courtesy of John Harshe

Introduction: Photo of the author

Art Courtesy of Marty Hein

Chapter 1: 1-32, 1-33, 1-34, 1-40

Art Courtesy of Gary Hodges

Chapter 12: 12-12

Chapter 18: 18-4, 18-6, 18-7, 18-8, 18-9, 18-10, 18-11, 18-12, 18-13, 18-14, 18-17, 18-18, 18-19, 18-20, 18-21, 18-22, 18-28, 18-29, 18-31

Art Courtesy of Kelsey-Hayes

Chapter 17: 17-4

Art Courtesy of LGCA

Chapter 9: 9-18

Art Courtesy of Wayne Loron

Chapter 15: 15-15, 15-16, 15-17, 15-18, 15-19, 15-20, 15-21, 15-22, 15-23

Art Courtesy of Robert Odiorne

Chapter 1: 1-2 (1955 trim tag location)

Material Supplied Courtesy of Gary Pronesti

Chapter 1: 1-3, 1-4, 1-9, 1-14, 1-19, 1-25

Chapter 10: 10-1, 10-2, 10-6

Chapter 11: 11-1, 11-2

Chapter 15: 15-26

Art Courtesy of Allan Rea

Chapter 4: All crankshaft flange silhouettes

Chapter 5: All drawn casting symbols

Chapter 7: All pistons

Chapter 15: All transmission silhouettes, transmission dimension artwork

Art Courtesy of Darrel Shepherd

Chapter 8: 8-3, 8-4, 8-6

Chapter 16: 16-4, 16-5, 16-6, 16-7, 16-8

Chevrolet Clubs

1965–66 Full Size Chevrolet Club
336 Benbrook Road
Butler PA 16001
412-482-4554
Harold Foos, President

American Chevelle Enthusiasts Society
4636 Lebanon Pike, Suite 195
Nashville, TN 37076-1316
615-773-ACES
Chuck Hanson, Pres./Editor

Bow Tie Chevys
P.O. Box 60818
Orlando, FL 32860
408-880-1956
Denny Williams, Editor

Classic Chevy Club International
P.O. Box 607188
Orlando, FL 32860-7188
800-456-1957

COPO Connection
P.O. Box 1036
Lombard, IL 60148
708-620-1299
Edward J. Cunneen

Jersey Late Greats, Inc.
P.O. Box 1294
Hightstown NJ 08520
Verne Frantz, Jr., Pres.

Late Great Chevy Association
P.O. Box 607824
Orlando FL 32860
407-886-1963
Bob Snowden, Editor

National Corvette Restorers Society
6291 Day Road
Cincinnati OH 45252
513-385-8526
Gary Mortimer, Membership Chairman

National Impala Association
830 Third St.
Spearfish, SD
605-642-5864
Dennis Nansz, President

National Monte Carlo Association
P.O. Box 187
Independence, KY 41051
Ben Shipe, Editor

National Nostalgic Novas
P.O. Box 2344
York, PA 17405
717-252-4192
Wayne or Shirley Bushey

United States Camaro Club
P.O. Box 608167
Orlando FL 32860
407-880-1963
Ken Moorhead, Pres./Editor

Important Data For My Chevrolet:

VIN: ____________ Series: ____________

Model: ____________ Body Style ____________

Trim Tag:

1955–58

1959

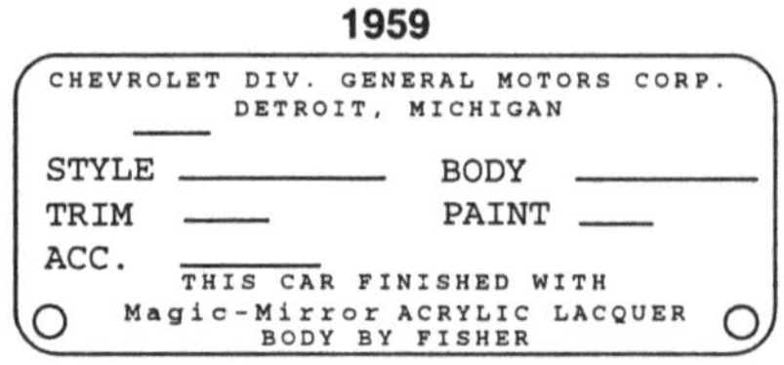

Engine code: ____________
Engine VIN stamp: ____________

Block Casting #: ____________
Block Casting Date: ____________
Main Bearing Cap: ❑ 2-bolt ❑ 4-bolt

Crank Casting #: ____________
Rod Journal: ____________
Main Journal: ____________

Head Casting #: ____________
Head Casting Date: ____________
Material: ❑ Cast Iron ❑ Aluminum

Carburetor Type: ____________
Stamping #: ____________
Date Code: ____________

Intake Casting #: ____________
Intake Casting Date: ____________

Camshaft #:

____

Exhaust LH RH
Casting #: ________/________
Casting Date: ________/________

Distributor: ____________
Date Code: ____________
Vacuum Unit: ____________

Alternator: ____________
Date Code: ____________

Water Pump #: ____________
Casting Date: ____________

Transmission Type: ____________
Build Date: ____________
Date Location: ____________
VIN Stamp #: ____________
Maincase #: ____________
Maincase Date: ____________
Extension #: ____________
Extension Date: ____________
Sidecover #: ____________
Sidecover Date: ____________

Rear Axle Type: ____________
Bolt: ❑ 10 ❑ 12
Axle Code: ____________
Build Date: ____________
Center Section #: ____________
Positraction #: ____________

Selected Books and Repair Information From Bentley Publishers

Motorsports

Alex Zanardi: My Sweetest Victory *Alex Zanardi and Gianluca Gasparini* ISBN 978-0-8376-1249-2

The Unfair Advantage *Mark Donohue and Paul van Valkenburgh* ISBN 978-0-8376-0069-7

Equations of Motion - Adventure, Risk and Innovation *William F. Milliken* ISBN 978-0-8376-1570-7

Engineering

Bosch Automotive Handbook *Robert Bosch GmbH* ISBN 978-0-8376-1732-9

Maximum Boost: Designing, Testing, and Installing Turbocharger Systems *Corky Bell* ISBN 978-0-8376-0160-1

Supercharged! Design, Testing and Installation of Supercharger Systems *Corky Bell* ISBN 978-0-8376-0168-7

Scientific Design of Exhaust and Intake Systems *Phillip H. Smith & John C. Morrison* ISBN 978-0-8376-0309-4

Physics for Gearheads *Randy Beikmann* ISBN 978-0-8376-1615-5

Audi

Audi A4 Service Manual: 2002-2008, 1.8L Turbo, 2.0L Turbo, 3.0L, 3.2L *Bentley Publishers* ISBN 978-0-8376-1574-5

Audi A4 Service Manual: 1996-2001, 1.8L Turbo, 2.8L *Bentley Publishers* ISBN 978-0-8376-1675-9

Audi TT Service Manual: 2000-2006, 1.8L turbo, 3.2 L *Bentley Publishers* ISBN 978-0-8376-1625-4

Audi A6 (C5 platform) Service Manual: 1998-2004 *Bentley Publishers* ISBN 978-0-8376-1670-4

BMW

Memoirs of a Hack Mechanic *Rob Siegel* ISBN 978-0-8376-1720-6

BMW 5 Series (E60, E61) Service Manual: 2004-2010 *Bentley Publishers* ISBN 978-0-8376-1689-6

BMW X3 (E83) Service Manual: 2004-2010 *Bentley Publishers* ISBN 978-0-8376-1731-2

BMW X5 (53) Service Manual: 2000-2006 *Bentley Publishers* ISBN 978-0-8376-1643-8

BMW 3 Series (E90, E91, E92, E93) Service Manual: 2006-2011 *Bentley Publishers* ISBN 978-0-8376-1723-7

BMW 3 Series (E46) Service Manual: 1999-2005 *Bentley Publishers* ISBN 978-0-8376-1657-5

BMW 3 Series (E36) Service Manual: 1992-1998 *Bentley Publishers* ISBN 978-0-8376-1709-1

BMW 3 Series (E30) Service Manual: 1984-1990 *Bentley Publishers* ISBN 978-0-8376-1647-6

BMW Z3 (E36/7) Service Manual: 1996-2002 *Bentley Publishers* ISBN 978-0-8376-1617-9

BMW 5 Series (E60, E61) Service Manual: 2004-2010 *Bentley Publishers* ISBN 978-0-8376-1689-6

BMW 5 Series (E39) Service Manual: 1997-2003 *Bentley Publishers* ISBN 978-0-8376-1672-8

BMW 7 Series (E38) Service Manual: 1995-2001 *Bentley Publishers* ISBN 978-0-8376-1618-6

Corvette

Corvette: America's Star-Spangled Sports Car *Karl Ludvigsen* ISBN 978-0-8376-1659-9

Corvette by the Numbers: The Essential Corvette Parts Reference 1955-1982 *Alan Covin* ISBN 978-0-8376-0228-2

Zora Arkus-Duntov: The Legend Behind Corvette *Jerry Burton* ISBN 978-08376-0858-7

Porsche

Porsche 911 (996) Service Manual: 1999-2005 *Bentley Publishers* ISBN 978-0-8376-1710-7

Porsche 911 (993) Service Manual: 1995-1998 *Bentley Publishers* ISBN 978-0-8376-1719-0

Porsche Boxster Service Manual: 1997-2004 *Bentley Publishers* ISBN 978-0-8376-1645-2

Porsche 911 Carrera Service Manual: 1984-1989 *Bentley Publishers* ISBN 978-0-8376-1696-4

Porsche 911 SC Service Manual: 1978-1983 *Bentley Publishers* ISBN 978-0-8376-1705-3

Porsche: Excellence Was Expected *Karl Ludvigsen* ISBN 978-0-8376-0235-6

Porsche — Origin of the Species *Karl Ludvigsen* ISBN 978-0-8376-1331-4

Volkswagen

Volkswagen Rabbit, GTI Service Manual: 2006-2009 *Bentley Publishers* ISBN 978-0-8376-1664-3

Volkswagen Jetta Service Manual: 2005-2010 *Bentley Publishers* ISBN 978-0-8376-1616-2

Volkswagen Jetta, Golf, GTI Service Manual: 1999-2005 *Bentley Publishers* ISBN 978-0-8376-1678-0

Volkswagen Jetta, Golf, GTI: 1993-1999, Cabrio: 1995-2002 Service Manual *Bentley Publishers* ISBN 978-0-8376-1660-5

Volkswagen GTI, Golf, Jetta Service Manual: 1985-1992 *Bentley Publishers* ISBN 978-0-8376-1637-7

Volkswagen Corrado Repair Manual: 1990-1994 *Bentley Publishers* ISBN 978-0-8376-1699-5

Volkswagen Passat, Passat Wagon Service Manual: 1998-2005 *Bentley Publishers* ISBN 978-0-8376-1669-8

MINI Repair Manuals

MINI Cooper Service Manual: 2007-2013 *Bentley Publishers* ISBN 978-0-8376-1730-5

MINI Cooper Service Manual: 2002-2006 *Bentley Publishers* ISBN 978-0-8376-1639-1

Mercedes-Benz

Mercedes-Benz C-Class (W202) Service Manual 1994-2000 *Bentley Publishers* ISBN 978-0-8376-1692-6

Mercedes Benz E-Class (W124) Owner's Bible: 1986-1995 *Bentley Publishers* ISBN 978-0-8376-0230-1

Mercedes-Benz Technical Companion *Staff of The Star and members of Mercedes-Benz Club of America* ISBN 978-0-8376-1033-7

BentleyPublishers®
Automotive Reference

Bentley Publishers has published service manuals and automobile books since 1950. For more information, please contact Bentley Publishers at 1734 Massachusetts Avenue, Cambridge, MA 02138 USA, or visit our web site at **BentleyPublishers.com**

Acknowledgments

General Motors

Patrick D. Moylan, General Motors Corporation, Service Technology Group, Coordinator, Copyright Licensing; Art Armstrong, CPC Group, Legal and Patent Liaison, Coordinator; Ms. Peg Holmes, Director of Public Affairs, Mid-Size Car Division Headquarters; Don Russ, GM Powertrain Group, Plant Manager, Tonawanda Engine Plant; Art Casper, GM Powertrain Group, Industrial Engineer, Tonawanda Engine Plant; Linda Deguire, Tonawanda Engine Plant Specifications; Ralph Kramer, Mark Broderick, Chevrolet Public Relations; Rick Johnson, GM Powertrain Group, Specifications, Flint Engine Plant; Bill Kornegay, Public Relations, Flint Engine Plant; Andy Herman, Joe Flaga, Joe Nazione Sr., Bob Kruszewski, Mid-Size Car Division Headquarters, Administrative Services; Ms. Sherrie Childers, Steve Gaut, Public Affairs, GM Powertrain Division; Robert Steele, Rocky Sparks, Delco Remy Division, General Motors Corporation; Ann James, CPC Group, Records Retention, Chevrolet Central Office; Tom Farqhar, Dick Gratz, Tom Allman, GM Tire & Wheel Systems, Milford Proving Grounds, Milford, Michigan; E.F. (Pete) DeTiere (retired), Rochester Products, Fuel Injection Engineer; Judy Middleton, Service Parts Coordinator, Delco Electronics Division; Reeve "Pug" Brown (retired), Paul W. Jones, Saginaw Division Final Drive & Forge; Ms. Louise Bellini, AC Rochester Division, Public Relations; Frank Sciabica (retired), AC Rochester Products, Fuel Injection Engineer; John Livecchi (retired), AC Rochester Division, Service Engineer; Delbert Greene, AC Rochester Division, Legal Department; Myra Moreland, Moreland Communications, New Venture Gear, Public Relations; Jim Lanzen, Chief Engineer, New Venture Gear; Larry Harrison, Coordinator Prototypes, Muncie Transmission Plant, New Venture Gear; Phil Evans, Matt Cookman, Materials, Muncie Transmission Plant, New Venture Gear; Cleo Powers (retired), Materials, Muncie Transmission Plant; John Barbier (retired), Inspection, Gear Sets, Muncie Transmission Plant; Jim Roof, Dan Ball, Inland Fisher Guide Division; Ron Bluhm, CPC Powertrain-Transmissions Group; Ernie Callard, Product Specialist, Performance Parts, GM Service Parts Operations; Robert D. Cheyne, Marketing Manager, Performance Parts, GM Service Parts Operations; Chevrolet Hobby Shop, Chevrolet Customer Assistance Center, Troy, MI; Warner Meier, Cadillac Motor Division

Business

Federal-Mogul Corp, Carter Automotive Co., Inc., Alan Somershoe, Marketing, Communications Manager, Gregory A. Bowles, Alan Klutho, Technical Services, Ms. Dorrie Younger, Public Relations; Kelsey-Hayes Wheel Corporation, Doug MacIntyre, Senior Technical Specialist, Libby-Owens-Ford, Dick Geltz, Harold Hamilton, Ken Mauer, Corporate Attorney; Motor Wheel Corporation, Ross Hill, Chief Engineer; Holley Replacement Parts Division, Brian Salvetti, Holley Custom Shop; Bob Kunz, Kunz Carburetors, St. Louis, MO; Gary Hodges, Ramjet, Inc., Salem, OR; Doug Marion, Simi Valley, CA, Argus Publishing Co., Former Editor of Super Chevy Magazine; Pollman Head Service, Mike Pollman, Sioux Falls, SD; Lamar Walden Automotive, Lamar Walden, Doraville, GA; Greg Mosier Engineering, Greg Mosier, Portland, IN; Car Connection, Cotton Tanner, West, TX; Classic Engines, Tom Luedike, Oshkosh, WI; Cliff's Classic Cars, Cliff Waldren, Portland, OR; CH Enterprises, Curt Harvey, Laguna Niguel, CA; Ellison Engines, Tom Ellison, Cincinnati, OH; Chirco Automotive, Sandy Chirco, Tucson, AZ; Borg-Warner Transmissions, Anderson, IN, Tom Brown, Sales & Service; Bill Mock, Bartlesville, OK; Huber Marine, Tom Huber, Franklin, TN; Detroit Public Library, National Automotive History Collection, Ronald Grantz, Automotive Curator, Inez Whitfield, Senior Clerk; National Hot Rod Association, Glendora, CA, Ms. Billie Petty, Danny Garcia, Dave Danish; OVC Industries, Dennis Mothershed, Ankeny, IA; Crash Enterprises, Eric Davidson, Kenosha, WI; Schwartz Photography, Tom Schwartz, Dayton, OH; John Harshe, Photographer, Dayton, OH; Color Techniques, Dayton, OH; Click Camera and Video, Dayton, OH; D & L Transmission, Larry Fischer, Huntington Station, NY; Cook Enterprises, Dennis Cook, Tipp City, OH; D & R Classic Automotive, Steve Druick, Naperville, IL; Jerry's Classic Cars & Parts, Jerry Huffman, Farmington, IL; National Corvette Restorers Society; ZL1 Organization, Ed Cunneen, Lombard, IL; Gary Kessinger Classic Auto Parts, Gary Kessinger, Beaver Dam, KY; NorVaJak Research, Jerry MacNeish, Randallstown, MD; Jasper Engines & Transmissions, John Spangler, Jasper, IN; Bob Van Landingham, Fuller Manufacturing, Falmouth, KY; Spradlin Brothers Welding, Jeff Spradlin, Mike Spradlin, Springfield, OH; O.E.M. Glass, Inc., Rick Peek, Bloomington, IL; Automotive Engine Rebuilders Association; Zimmer Gear, Earl Zimmer, Baton Rouge, LA; Corvette Repair, Kevin MacKay, Valley Stream, NY; Chevy II Only, Joe Grom, Jr., Taylorsville, KY; Auto Gear Company, Inc., Syracuse, NY; Frank Z Chevrolet, Parts Department, Brian House, Jeff Yeoman, Dayton, OH; Don Briggs Corvette Parts, Lighthouse Point, FL

Personal

Jody Anderson; John Krogh; Jeff Kirkpatrick; Greg Reimer; Jim McClear; Steve Carlson; Alan Kaplan; Dave Bartush; Tom Migut; Wayne O. Loren; Stan Edmunds; Paul Hendricksen; Doug Garrett; Dale Pearman; Mike Betz; Pete Vanish; Ken Nealy; Bill Glowaki; Warren Malkin Jr.; Tim Smith; Rick Calmes; Jim and Barb Farrelly; Ruth Quast; Rusty Symmes; Bravo Quikprint; Dave Lester; John Walsh; Bill Wilder; Michael Kowalchuk; Jeff Brost; Jim Napper; David Roberts; Donald Nickley; Steve Ewalt; Bob Elliott; Gary Jestice; Mike Del Duca; Cliff Ernst; Wayne Guinn, Edward Shockley

Special Assistance

Mary O'Connell, Typist; Carol Graham, Typist; Amber Harris, Typist; Jane Bond, Typist; Sharron Donnell, Typist; Bob and Gloria Luzier, Typist and Computer Support; Management Information Consultants, Darla K. Baker; Chuck Sumner, Proofreader; Jeff Delaney, Computer Specialist; Ben Pace, Computer Specialist

Clubs

United States Camaro Club, Ken Moorhead, Doug Moorhead; National Impala Association, Larry Rueppell, President, Technical Advisors: Bill Reid, Gaill Drumm, Jeffery Chase, Larry Neppl, Ronald Mroz, Barry Maurer; 1960–66 Full Size Chevy Club, Larry Neppl, Dick Washburn, and Roland Muchicko; National Monte Carlo Association, Charles Purcell, Ralph Wyatt; Jersey Late Greats, Inc., Verne Frantz, President, Mike Berry; National Writers Club, David Weinstein, Legal Counsel

Special Mention

Jeff Weyrauch, Bow Tie Matchmakers, Kenosha, WI; Bob Harris, Camaro Specialties, East Aurora, NY; Darrell Shepherd, 4-Speeds by Darrell, Vermillion, IL; Allan Rea, Graphic Artist, West Milton, OH; Bill Mock; Alan Kaplan; Chuck Hanson, National Dragster Advertising Sales Manager, Former Technical Editor of Car Craft Magazine; Curt Worden; Crash Enterprises, Eric Davidson, Kenosha, WI; Ed Hartnett 4-Speeds, Ed Hartnett, Lansdowne, PA; Hoss' Gear Shop, Keith Hoak, Mt. Pleasant, PA; Gary Hodges, Ramjet, Inc., Salem, OR; Al Maynard; Harvey Edelstein; Pat Boyd; Brian Futo; Tom Watt, Tom's Differentials, Paramount, CA; Alex Walordy, Alex Walordy Press, Westbury, NY; Gary Pronesti and Pete Sawatzki, technical assistance

CHEVROLET *by the numbers*™ 1955–59

The Essential Chevrolet Parts Reference

Summary of Changes Since the 1st Printing

Summary of changes for 2nd Printing

Page	Correction
25	Addition of 1955 Corvette Exterior-Interior trim combinations.
30	Addition of 1956 Corvette Exterior-Interior trim combinations colors.
34	Addition of 1957 Corvette Exterior-Interior trim combinations colors
37	5th paragraph, beginning 3rd sentence to read "Almost all..."
37	Fig. 2-2 caption, Bottom: "Typical 1957-1959 engine code stamping--here FI08C (January 8, 1957) for 1957 265/162 HP engine."
38	End of 1st sentence on to read "although some have been found on the right, such as the stamping in Fig. 2-2 bottom."
39	Fig. 2-4. 1957 through 1959 Engine Code Style T 04 14 DM to read "T 4 14 DM".
73	Head #3740997 Notes: change size of casting symbol so that vertical portion is narrower.
140	4th paragraph, end of last sentence to read "Fig. 12-14)."
141	Under 2. Distributor Applications, after Letter Designations, remove Color Code Designations list and Note.
148	Fig. 12-15. Caption to read "Vacuum unit style used on 6-cylinders for the years 1955–57.
148	Fig. 12-16. 1st sentence of caption to read "Typical vacuum unit style used from 1958-on on V-8 applications."
170	2nd full paragraph, delete last sentence, which begins "The Turboglide..."
170	Fig. 15-26, Caption: delete second sentence, which begins "Turboglide..."
175	Assembly Date Code Location (Car) table. Change Turboglide to "Tuboglide (early)" Add Transmission "Turboglide (late)", Code Location to read "Stamped on machined boss located on lower right rear face of case."
177	2-Speeed Turboglide Transmission table. Change Maincase to read "Cast Aluminum". Change Tailhousing to read "Cast Aluminum".
181	2-Speed Turboglide Transmission table. Change Maincase to read "Cast Aluminum". Change Tailhousing to read "Cast Aluminum". Change Maincase No. to read "3747393".
185	2-Speed Transmission table. Change Maincase to read "Cast Aluminum". Change Tailhousing to read "Cast Aluminum".
201	1957 Passenger Rear Axle Codes table. Change Description Powerglide Posi to read "Turboglide, Powerglide, Code AM".
203	Table title changed to "1955-59 Rear Axle Usage".

Summary of changes for 3rd Printing

Page	Correction
167	Fig. 15-17. Caption to read "T10 maincase assembly code stamp "WM1872." This transmission was assembled on December 18th, 1957, second shift."
167	Fig. 15-19. Caption to read "T10 maincase assembly code stamp "WL1892." This transmission was assembled on November 18th, 1959, second shift."

Summary of changes for 4th Printing

Page	Correction
14	1955-1958 Trim Tag Location table, 1955-56 with A/C, location, change "case" to "cases"
38	1955 Through 1959 Engine Development, first column, first paragraph, third sentence, change end to read "...two motor mount holes on each side of the block."
38	1955 Through 1959 Engine Development, first column, second paragraph, second sentence, change end to read "...the passenger side of the engine to the oil pan."
38	1955 Through 1959 Engine Development, first column, third paragraph, second sentence, change end to read "...the passenger side bypass breather tube and only two motor mounting holes on each side of the block."
52	Block #3737739, Notes, change beginning of third sentence to read "This block was the first small block to have three motor mount holes cast..."
59	265 Crankshaft, 1955 Through 1957, add Crankshaft Flange image
62	First column, second paragraph, second sentence, change end to read "...the head was cast."
64	Fig. 5-5 caption, change #3708523 to #3703523
90	Third table, 1957 pistons, replace image with correct image
92	Second table, replace image with correct image
98	Carter WCFB Carbueretors table, sixth column, Air Horn Casting, change "889, 6-" to "6-889" for Carb 2218 S and 2351 S
150	First paragraph, third sentence, change end to read "...many of the camshafts."
166	Second paragraph, delete "Borg-Warner T10-1B maincase with A T10-7A tailhousing, which is a late 1959 Transmission assembly."
184	4-Speed Close Ratio Borg-Warner T10 table, Maincase No., change to "T10-1 prior to 6/59 T10-1B after 6/59"
191	Positraction Axles, change end of paragraph, after "...the later "P" designation." to read "After March 27, 1957, all factory posi cases have a "P" (designating positraction) cast into the carrier adjacent to casting number; the former "X" designation is now gone. Some 1957 model year posi "P" cases were also used as open (non-posi) rear ends. These specific "P" cases have an extra reinforcement rib inside the case that will not allow a positraction unit to be installed into the case. There have been three of these "P" cases discovered (dated December 56, March 57, & May 57) that have been verifiably used as non-posi rear axle assemblies. This "P" case was used through the 1964 model year in Passenger car and Corvette models."
205	Fig. 17-1, change caption to read "Inside of wheel (tire side) shows various interior wheel code stampings. See text for decoding. The logo stamping on the lower right is the logo for the Tire & Rim Association."
251	1.1 Interior Wheel Stampings, second paragraph, change first two sentences to read "Most obvious at the lower right of the photo is the Tire & Rim Association stamp indicating the wheel was made to their rim dimension specs. Immediately to the left of the Tire & Rim Assoc. logo is the code K-1-1 (upside down in the photo), stamped in a triangular pattern. "

Summary of changes for 5th Printing

No changes.

BENTLEY PUBLISHERS™ | Automotive Reference™

1734 Massachusetts Avenue
Cambridge, MA 02138 USA
800-423-4595 / 617-547-4170

BentleyPublishers™.com

Please call or write us for information on other volumes in the **By the Numbers** series covering essential parts information for Chevrolet models from 1955 to 1975 and Corvette from 1955 to 1982. Ask for our free catalog of automotive books.

Reader Response Form

Are you having trouble identifying a part on your car? Is there a part on your car that you believe is original, but its casting number is not listed in this book? Are there codes that you don't understand? Are you interested in the national trim validation service mentioned in Chapter 1? If so, copy or print this form, fill it out, noting where your question or comment is, and mail it to the author at the address listed to the right. Help make this book the best reference it can be.

Send to:

Alan Colvin
3005 Barret Ave.
Plant City, FL 33566

Your Name: ______________________ Phone: ____________
Address: ______________________ Fax: ____________
______________________ E-Mail: ____________

VIN: ____________ Series: ____________
Model: ____________ Body Style: ____________

Trim Tag (fill in):

1955–58

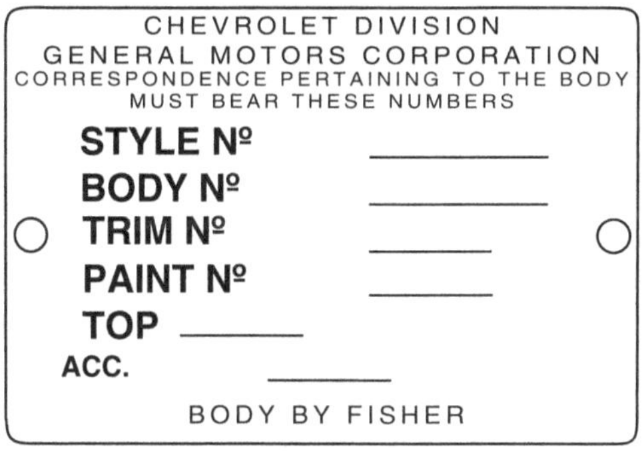

1959

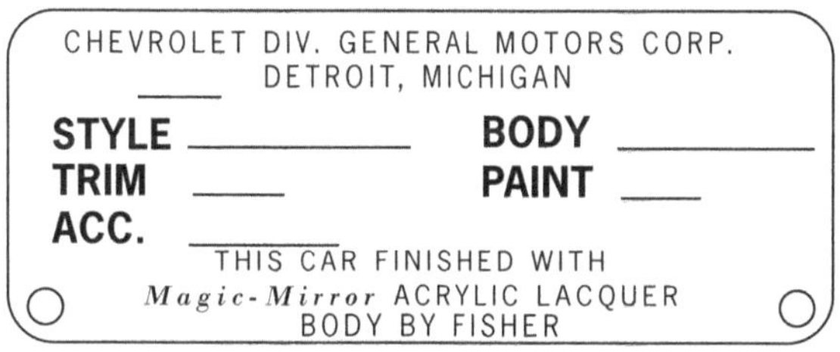

Trim Tag Position (be specific): ______________________

Engine code: ____________
Engine VIN stamp: ____________
Stamp: Gang Individual

Block Casting #: ____________
Block Casting Date: ____________
Main Bearing Cap: q 2-bolt q 4-bolt

Intake Casting #: ____________
Intake Casting Date: ____________

Head Casting #: ____________
Head Casting Date: ____________
Material: q Cast Iron q Aluminum
Symbol at end of head (if any): _____

Water Pump #: ____________
Casting Date: ____________

Crank Casting #: ____________

Exhaust LH RH
Casting #: ________/________
Casting Date: ________/________

Distributor: ____________
Date Code: ____________
Vacuum Unit: ____________

Alternator: ____________
Date Code: ____________

Carburetor Type: ____________
Stamping #: ____________
Date Code: ____________
Primary Metering #: ____________
Secondary Metering #: ____________

Camshaft #: ____________

Transmission Type: ____________
Build Date: ____________
Date Location: ____________
VIN Stamp #: ____________
Maincase #: ____________
Maincase Date: ____________
Extension #: ____________
Extension Date: ____________
Sidecover #: ____________
Sidecover Date: ____________
Front Bearing Retainer #: ________

Rear Axle Type: ____________
Bolt: q 10 q 12
Axle Code: ____________
Build Date: ____________
Center Section #: ____________
Positraction #: ____________
Length:
- Axle shaft (each) ________
- Between spring seat centers _____

List all special options that you believe the car was delivered with: ______________________

____

—Please Fill Form Out Completely—

About the Author

Since 1985, Alan has been a freelance automotive feature writer, with articles regularly appearing in national magazines such as *Corvette Fever, Super Chevy, Musclecar Review, Vette Vues, Corvette and Chevy Trader, Mustang Trader, High Performance Pontiac, Automotive Restorer, Pontiac Enthusiast, Old Cars Weekly, Chevy High Performance*, as well as CorvetteMagazine.com. He has also authored several Q & A columns in several publications. For many years, he also was President of Colvin Media Group, Inc., a group of freelance writers and graphic designers which specialized in advertising and catalog copy and design, copy writing and online catalog publications.

Born and raised near Falmouth, Kentucky, and a graduate of Pendleton County High School, Alan has been active in the old car hobby since 1975, when he purchased his first car, a 1957 Chevy. Later on, he owned a nationally known Chevrolet reproduction parts company that supplied many detailed reproduction parts to the old car hobby, one of which was the first stainless steel chambered exhaust system for Camaros. His involvement in this business has given him invaluable hands on experience in parts manufacturing in the restoration field.

He has also been heavily involved in various automotive club activities as a past or present member of the Society of Automotive Historians, the National Monte Carlo Owners Association, the United States Camaro Club, the American Chevelle Enthusiasts Society, the Worldwide Camaro Association, and the National Corvette Restorers Society. He served as a member of the Technical Advisory Board for the United States Camaro Club and the 1965 66 Full Size Chevy Club. He has also served as a senior judge and advisor to numerous other clubs and national automotive shows. In addition to being recognized as an expert in the automotive field, Alan is well respected as a freelance writer/author in the writers market and has shared his expertise with other writers in college workshops, several college classes and statewide writers conferences.

His greatest achievement to date has been the publishing of his landmark 4-book series *Chevrolet by the Numbers* which is the only authoritative reference for identifying the correct Chevrolet drivetrain parts for your vehicle. These books were the first books published outside of General Motors to carry a GM part number and have been sold worldwide through the General Motors parts system. His last book in the series, *Corvette by the Numbers*, was published in the spring of 2002. In 2000, he won a Gold and a Silver Medal for two articles submitted to the International Automotive Media (IAMA) Conference. He also won a Silver Medal for his *Corvette by the Numbers* book at the 2002 IAMA Conference. Most recently, he has become editor of *Corvette Fever*, one of the oldest, most successful and currently largest (verified circulation) Corvette magazines in the US.

Alan is married, has two children and lives near Tampa, Florida.

About The Front Cover

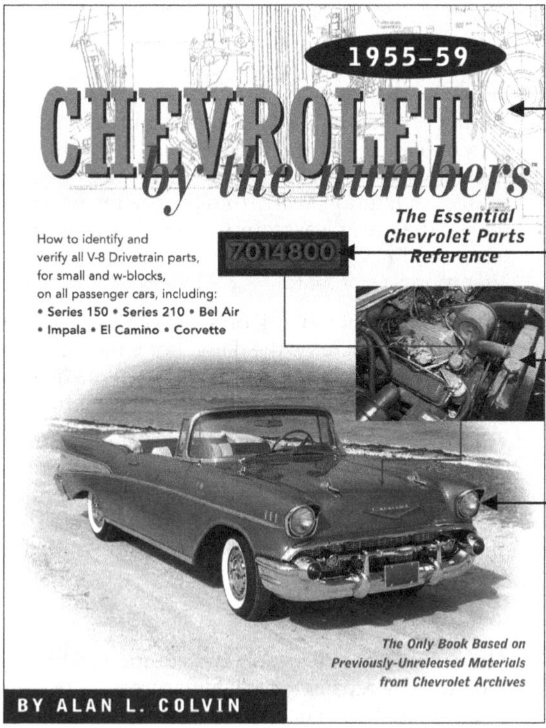

The cover illustrates the process of identifying a Rochester fuel injection unit: The ***original blueprint*** guided the manufacturing of the unit and its specific ***casting number***. This unit was then installed on a ***283/250 HP engine***, which was installed in a *1957 Bel Air*

Please read these Warnings and Cautions before proceeding with any work on your vehicle.

WARNING—

• Do not reuse self-locking nuts or any other fasteners that are fatigued or deformed in normal use. They are designed to be used only once, and become unreliable and may fail when used a second time. This includes, but is not limited to, bolts, washers, self-locking nuts, circlips and cotter pins that secure the subframe, control arms, stabilizer bar, ball joints and other suspension, steering and brake components. Always replace these fasteners with new parts.

• Never work under a lifted vehicle unless it is solidly supported on stands designed for the purpose. Do not support a vehicle on cinder blocks, hollow tiles, or other props that may crumble under continuous load. Do not work under a vehicle that is supported solely by a jack.

• If you are going to work under a vehicle on the ground, make sure that the ground is level. Block the wheels to keep the vehicle from rolling. Never work under the vehicle while the engine is running. Disconnect the battery ground strap to prevent others from starting the vehicle while you are under it.

• Never run the engine unless the work area is well ventilated. Carbon monoxide kills.

• Friction materials such as brake or clutch discs may contain asbestos fibers. Do not create dust by grinding, sanding, or by cleaning with compressed air. Avoid breathing asbestos fibers and asbestos dust. Breathing asbestos can cause serious diseases such as asbestosis or cancer, and may result in death.

• Greases, lubricants and other automotive chemicals contain toxic substances, many of which are absorbed directly through the skin. Read manufacturer's instructions and warnings carefully. Use hand and eye protection. Avoid direct skin contact.

• Tie long hair behind your head. Do not wear a necktie, a scarf, loose clothing, or a necklace when you work near machine tools or running engines. If your hair, clothing, or jewelry were to get caught in the machinery, severe injury could result.

• Disconnect the battery ground strap whenever you work on the fuel system or the electrical system. When you work around fuel, do not smoke or work near heaters or other fire hazards. Keep an approved fire extinguisher handy.

• Finger rings should be removed so that they cannot cause electrical shorts, get caught in running machinery, or be crushed by heavy parts.

• Keep sparks, lighted matches, and open flames away from the top of the battery. If hydrogen gas escaping from the cap vents is ignited, it will ignite gas trapped in the cells and cause the battery to explode.

• Catch draining fuel, oil, or brake fluid in suitable containers. Do not use food or beverage containers that might mislead someone into drinking from them. Store flammable fluids away from fire hazards. Wipe up spills at once, but do not store the oily rags, which can ignite and burn spontaneously.

• Always observe good workshop practices. Wear goggles when you operate machine tools or work with battery acid. Gloves or other protective clothing should be worn whenever the job requires it.

• Some aerosol tire inflators are highly flammable. Use extreme care when repairing a tire that may have been inflated using an aerosol tire inflator. Keep sparks, open flame or other sources of ignition away from the tire repair area. Inflate and deflate the tire at least four times before breaking the bead from the rim. Completely remove the tire from the rim before attempting any repair.

• Do not attempt to work on your vehicle if you do not feel well. You can increase the danger of injury to yourself and others if you are tired, upset or have taken medicine or any other substance that may impair you from being fully alert.

• Illuminate your work area adequately but safely. A fluorescent worklight is preferable to an incandescent worklight. Use a portable safety light for working inside or under the vehicle. Make sure the bulb is enclosed by a wire cage. The hot filament of an accidentally broken bulb can ignite spilled fuel or oil.

CAUTION—

• If you lack the skills, tools and equipment, or a suitable workshop for any repair or parts replacement procedure, we suggest you leave such work to an authorized Chevrolet dealer or other qualified shop. We especially urge you to consult an authorized Chevrolet dealer before beginning work on any vehicle that may still be covered wholly or in part by any of the extensive warranties issued by Chevrolet.

• Chevrolet is constantly improving its vehicles and sometimes these changes, both in parts and specifications, are made applicable to earlier models. Always check with your authorized Chevrolet dealer for the latest parts and service information.

• Before starting a job, make certain that you have all the necessary tools and parts on hand. Read all the instructions thoroughly, do not attempt shortcuts. Use tools appropriate to the work and use only replacement parts meeting Chevrolet specifications. Makeshift tools, parts, and procedures will not make good repairs.

• Use pneumatic and electric tools only to loosen threaded parts and fasteners. Never use these tools to tighten fasteners, especially on light alloy parts.

• Be mindful of the environment and ecology. Before you drain the crankcase, find out the proper way to dispose of the oil. Do not pour oil onto the ground, down a drain, or into a stream, pond, or lake. Consult local ordinances that govern the handling and disposal of chemicals and wastes.

• Do not quick-charge the battery (for boost starting) for longer than one minute, and do not exceed 15.0 volts at the battery with the boosting cables attached. Wait at least one minute before boosting the battery a second time.

Please read the Safety Notice and disclaimer on the Copyright page.